"If We Are Striking for Pennsylvania"

The Army of Northern Virginia and the
Army of the Potomac March to Gettysburg

Volume 2: June 22–30, 1863

SCOTT L. MINGUS Sr.
and ERIC J. WITTENBERG

Savas Beatie
California

Library of Congress Cataloging-in-Publication Data

Names: Mingus, Scott L., Sr., author. | Wittenberg, Eric J., 1961- author.
    Title: "If We are Striking for Pennsylvania": The Army of Northern Virginia and
    Army of the Potomac March to Gettysburg / Scott L. Mingus Sr., Eric J. Wittenberg.
  Description: First edition | El Dorado Hills: Savas Beatie, 2022 | Includes bibliographical references
    and index. Contents v. 1: June 3 - June 21, 1863. v. 2: June 22 - June 30, 1863 |
    Summary: "Scott L. Mingus Sr. and Eric J. Wittenberg, the authors of more
    than forty Civil War books, have once again teamed up to present a history of the
    opening moves of the Gettysburg Campaign in the two-volume study "If We Are Striking
    For Pennsylvania." This compelling study is one of the first to integrate the military,
    media, political, social, economic, and civilian perspectives with rank-and-file accounts
    from the soldiers of both armies as they inexorably march toward their destiny at Gettysburg.
    This first installment covers June 3-21, 1863, while the second, spanning June 22-30,
    completes the march and carries the armies to the eve of the Fighting." — Provided by publisher.
  Identifiers: LCCN 2022016968 | ISBN 9781611215847 (v. 1 alk. paper) | ISBN 9781611215854 (v. 1 ebk.)
    ISBN 9781611216110 (v. 2 alk. paper) | ISBN 9781611216127 (v. 2 ebk.)
  Subjects: LCSH: Gettysburg Campaign, 1863. | United States. Army of the Potomac. |
    Confederate States of America. Army. Department of Northern Virginia. | Soldiers–United
    States–Anecdotes. | Soldiers–Confederate States of America–Anecdotes. |
    United States–History–Civil War, 1861-1865–Regimental histories.
  Classification: LCC E475.51 .M558 2022 | DDC 973.7/349–dc23/eng/20220506
  LC record available at https://lccn.loc.gov/2022016968

First Edition, First Printing

SB

Savas Beatie
989 Governor Drive, Suite 102
El Dorado Hills, CA 95762
916-941-6896 / sales@savasbeatie.com / www.savasbeatie.com

All of our titles are available at special discount rates for bulk purchases in the United States. Contact us for information.

Proudly published, printed, and warehoused in the United States of America.

We respectfully dedicate this book to Ted Alexander and Ed Bearss,
two great Civil War historians and authors we lost in 2020.

Both were valued mentors, consultants, colleagues,
and, most of all, personal friends.

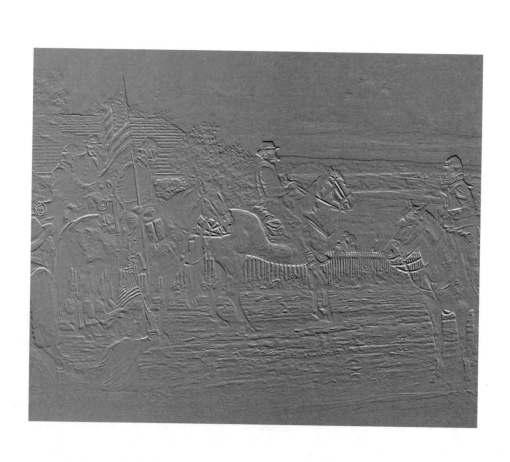

CONTENTS

LIST OF MAPS

LIST OF MAPS (continued)

Photos and illustrations have been placed
throughout the book for the convenience of the reader.

Abbreviations Used in the Notes

ACHS: Adams County Historical Society, Gettysburg, PA
ANV: Army of Northern Virginia
AOP: Army of the Potomac
BSF: Brandy Station Foundation, Brandy Station, VA
C&O: Chesapeake & Ohio
CCHS: Cumberland County Historical Society, Carlisle, PA
CV: Confederate Veteran
CWTI: Civil War Times Illustrated
FSNMP: Fredericksburg and Spotsylvania Military Park, Fredericksburg, VA
GNMP: Gettysburg National Military Park, Gettysburg, PA
HL: Huntington Library, San Marino, CA
HSOPRF: Historical Society of Oak Park and River Forest, IL
HSP: Historical Society of Pennsylvania, Philadelphia, PA
JCPL: Jasper County Public Library, Rensselaer, IN
JMSIUS: Journal of the Military Service Institution of the United States
KHS: Kittochtinny Historical Society, Chambersburg, PA
LCHS: Lancaster County Historical Society, Lancaster, PA
LOC: Library of Congress, Washington, DC
MDAH: Mississippi Department of Archives and History, Jackson, MS
MGRR: Manassas Gap Railroad
MHACV: Mennonite Historical Association of the Cumberland Valley, Chambersburg, PA
MOLLUS: Military Order of the Loyal Legion of the United States
NARA: National Archives and Records Administration, Washington, DC
NCSA: North Carolina State Archives, Raleigh, NC
NT: The National Tribune
NYSNG: New York State National Guard
OR: Official Records of the War of the Rebellion
PRR: Pennsylvania Railroad
SCV: Sons of Confederate Veterans
SHC-UNC: Southern Historical Collection, Wilson Library, Univ. of North Carolina, Chapel Hill
SHSP: Southern Historical Society Papers
UGA: Univ. of Georgia, Athens, GA
UM: Univ. of Michigan, Ann Arbor, MI
UNC: Univ. of North Carolina, Chapel Hill, NC
USAHEC: United States Army Heritage and Education Center, Carlisle, PA
UVA: Univ. of Virginia, Charlottesville, VA
VHS: Virginia Historical Society, Richmond, VA
VMI: Virginia Military Institute, Lexington, VA
VOTS: Valley of the Sun, a Civil War website of the Univ. of Virginia
YCHC: York County History Center, York, PA

INTRODUCTION

After the Army of Northern Virginia's dramatic victory at Chancellorsville in early May of 1863, Gen. Robert E. Lee met with the Confederate high command in Richmond to determine his next steps. Lee convinced President Jefferson Davis and most of his cabinet that moving his army into Maryland and Pennsylvania was the best course of action. The thrust would remove the war from Virginia during the summer growing season and hopefully force the enemy to withdraw forces from Mississippi threatening Vicksburg. A major victory north of the Mason-Dixon line might also induce France and Great Britain to recognize the Confederate States of America.

Lee's army remained around Fredericksburg, Virginia, preparing for the forthcoming invasion. On June 3, Maj. Gen. Lafayette McLaws's Division of Lt. Gen. James Longstreet's First Corps marched for Culpeper 35 miles northwest of Fredericksburg. Major General John B. Hood's Division of the same corps left the next day, as did the divisions of Maj. Gens. Robert Rodes and Jubal A. Early of Lt. Gen. Richard S. Ewell's Second Corps. Union balloonists spotted the departure of these three divisions and notified the Army of the Potomac's headquarters. Major General Joseph Hooker, the Potomac army's commander, ordered his men to prepare to follow. Hooker also sent the VI Corps across the Rappahannock River to test Lt. Gen. A. P. Hill's Third Corps positions. Several days of skirmishing followed.

Confederate cavalry, meanwhile, had been massing in Culpeper County. On June 5, Maj. Gen. J. E. B. Stuart, the commander of the Southern horsemen, held a noisy grand review of his troopers that drew the attention of Union cavalry operating in the area. The review featured mock charges and volleys fired by the horse artillery. Unable to attend that day, General Lee authorized a second grand review for June 8 so he could be there in person.

By nightfall on June 7, five of the Army of Northern Virginia's nine infantry divisions were in the Culpeper area while Hill's Third Corps remained in place around Fredericksburg. Stuart's cavalry paraded for General Lee the following day, unaware that more than 12,000 Union troopers and 3,000 infantry lay just across the Rappahannock with orders to "destroy or disperse the large concentration of Confederate cavalry" in Culpeper County.

The Union cavalry moved out about 5:00 a.m. on June 9. Brigadier General John Buford's 1st Cavalry Division splashed across Beverly's Ford on the Rappahannock and crashed into the Confederate cavalry on the south bank of the river, commencing a thirteen-hour battle. Several hours later Brig. Gen. David M. Gregg's 2nd Cavalry Division crossed at Kelly's Ford and advanced on Brandy Station, a depot of the Orange & Alexandria Railroad a few miles north of the town of Culpeper. An extended mounted combat at Fleetwood Hill swirled while the advance of Union Col. Alfred N. Duffié's 3rd Cavalry Division stalled near Stevensburg. Gregg broke off and withdrew after several hours of heavy fighting, leaving Buford and his troopers to fend for themselves. About 5:00 p.m. Buford received orders to break off and withdraw. His retreat ended the Battle of Brandy Station, the largest cavalry engagement fought on the North American continent. Brigadier General Alfred Pleasonton, the commander of the Union cavalry, failed to fulfill his objective of destroying or dispersing Stuart's horsemen. The mounted battle delayed the beginning of the next phase of the Confederate invasion by only one day.

Fears of an impending Confederate invasion began to reverberate through the North. Civilians grew increasingly anxious. Pennsylvania Governor Andrew G. Curtin called out the militia to defend the Keystone State. New York Governor Horatio Seymour also called out his state's militia and ordered it to Harrisburg, the capital of Pennsylvania, to reinforce militia gathering there. Major General Darius N. Couch, the former head of the Army of the Potomac's II Corps, was sent to Harrisburg to assume command of the newly created Department of the Susquehanna; Maj. Gen. William F. "Baldy" Smith volunteered to serve as Couch's deputy. The New York and Pennsylvania militiamen began constructing fortifications to defend Harrisburg. Meanwhile, as the Army of the Potomac slowly pursued Lee, another Union force under Maj. Gen. John A. Dix based on the peninsula between the York and James rivers in southeastern Virginia began moving slowly toward Richmond. Dix's goal was to threaten the Southern capital and thus draw forces away from Lee's army.

By June 13, Ewell's Second Corps was closing in on Winchester, where Maj. Gen. Robert H. Milroy commanded the 8,500-man Union detachment assigned to garrison the northern reaches of the Shenandoah Valley. Milroy, who had spent the winter and spring constructing extensive fortifications in and around Winchester and believed his command could defend them, disobeyed a direct order to evacuate to Harpers Ferry. Milroy's hubris would cost his troops dearly. In a brilliant three-day battle, troops from Ewell's corps overran the position and killed, wounded, and captured about one-half of Milroy's command. The remaining Yankees eventually made their way to either Harpers Ferry or Bloody Run, Pennsylvania. Ewell's performance at the Second Battle of Winchester suggested he was a worthy successor to the late Lt. Gen. Thomas J. "Stonewall" Jackson. Milroy, on the other hand, was banished to a backwater of the war, guarding railroads in middle Tennessee.

Rodes's Division, part of Ewell's corps, captured Martinsburg while a portion of the Confederate infantry headed toward the Potomac River crossings at Williamsport, Maryland. On June 15, part of Brig. Gen. Albert G. Jenkins's brigade of mounted infantry, which was escorting Ewell's troops on their advance, passed through Hagerstown, Maryland, and crossed the Mason-Dixon line. They were the first Confederates to enter Pennsylvania. On June 22, just north of the town of Greencastle, the 1st New York (Lincoln) Cavalry skirmished with Jenkins. Corporal William H. Rihl of Philadelphia, who was killed during that action and buried where he fell, was the first Union casualty north of the Mason-Dixon. Jenkins and his men occupied Chambersburg, 11 miles up the Valley Turnpike from Greencastle. Panic spread across the verdant countryside of the Keystone State.

Hill's Third Corps, meanwhile, had finally begun moving from its positions around Fredericksburg once it became obvious that the Army of the Potomac had abandoned the line of the Rappahannock to pursue the Army of Northern Virginia. The entirety of Lee's army was now on the march toward Pennsylvania. The lead elements of Ewell's infantry splashed across the Potomac River and entered Maryland on June 19.

Pleasonton's Union cavalry fought a series of sharp battles with Stuart's troopers in the Loudoun Valley of Virginia. The blue horsemen were doing their best to locate the Army of Northern Virginia in the Shenandoah Valley while Stuart shielded the infantry's advance. The competing cavalrymen clashed at Aldie on June 17, at Middleburg on June 19, and at Upperville on June 21. At the latter battle the Federal horse, reinforced by a brigade of V Corps infantry, drove the Southern cavalry from the field and behind the Blue Ridge. Upperville was the first time the Army of the Potomac's Cavalry Corps defeated Stuart and his vaunted troopers on the field of battle.

The next day Stuart received discretionary orders that would inaugurate one of the greatest controversies of the campaign. Lee authorized Stuart to leave two brigades to watch the South Mountain passes and guard lines of communication and supply while he took three other brigades and passed around the Army of the Potomac, crossed the Potomac, entered Maryland, and located and protected the flank of Ewell's marching infantry. Stuart could gather supplies along the way for the army's use.

As the respective armies marched, the politics of command reared its head on June when President Abraham Lincoln removed Joe Hooker from command and replaced him with V Corps commander George G. Meade. That evening a Confederate spy informed Lee of the change and warned him that the Union army was moving quickly in pursuit. Lee ordered his dispersed corps to coalesce at Cashtown or Gettysburg. Jeb Stuart and his cavalry, meanwhile, had not been in touch with the Virginia army in days.

MONDAY, JUNE 22, 1863

Terrifying rumors that "the Rebels are coming" had periodically circulated throughout Pennsylvania's south-central border counties since Jeb Stuart's October 1862 Chambersburg Raid. These unsettling reports proved untrue in every case, or the intruders consisted of a handful of cavalry raiders who just as quickly trotted back into Maryland after taking horses and supplies. Much to the chagrin of Keystone State residents, this day would be much different. A Confederate infantry division was about to step across the Mason-Dixon line for the first time in the war. The eventful day would also witness the first combat death of a Union soldier on Pennsylvania soil.

The sun was rising over Greencastle in southern Franklin County when Albert Jenkins's mounted infantrymen again made their appearance. This time, the Rebels announced they were the advance guard for Robert Rodes's Division of Richard Ewell's Second Corps. General Jenkins dispatched Capt. Joseph A. Wilson and Company I of the 14th Virginia Cavalry on a reconnaissance to Marion, a farming and railroad village six miles north of Greencastle. Once there, the Virginians seized David K. Appenzellar, a member of the 126th Pennsylvania returning home after his term of enlistment expired. Appenzellar planned to enroll in a local home guard company, but the Rebels appropriated his fine horse and questioned him about the number of troops defending Chambersburg. The new prisoner calmly repeated tales that General Couch was on his way from Harrisburg with 20,000 men. Captain Wilson's detachment took the unlucky Appenzellar with them, retired to their main force at Greencastle, and relayed the report to Jenkins. Not long after the Rebels rode off, Capt. William Boyd's 35-man company from the 1st

A Grand Army of the Republic Post
erected this monument to
Cpl. William R. Rihl in 1887.

Scott L. Mingus Sr.

New York Cavalry appeared in the trees on a nearby hill "and at once a scene of great excitement ensued," wrote an anxious resident named Charles Hartman.[1]

Wilson and his company were sent back to investigate. A pair of Boyd's Federals were inside a small blacksmith shop having the shoes on their horses tightened when the Virginians arrived. The Union troopers bolted outside and jumped on their mounts, but Wilson's men captured them before they could gallop away. Sergeant William D. Hall and several other troopers spotted the commotion, set their spurs, and attacked at a "swinging gallop." Wilson had orders to withdraw if confronted; within minutes he was back with the main body.[2]

With his men dismounted and their horses turned loose to graze with the rest of the brigade's steeds, Wilson moved troops men behind wooden fences at a sharp turn in the road leading to Greencastle and tore them down. Nearby, infantrymen from Rodes's Division deployed on high ground belonging to John Kissecker. Jenkins dismounted his men a quarter-mile beyond the infantry

---

1 *Greencastle Pilot*, July 28, 1863; Hoke, *Reminiscences*, 45. Some accounts suggest that Boyd had 43 men under his command.

2 Beach, *The First New York (Lincoln) Cavalry*, 248.

and formed a skirmish line in a wheat field belonging to William Fleming, in whose house he established his headquarters. As soon as the Federals came within range, the opposing skirmishers opened fire "and for a time the noise and clatter were lively." An errant bullet crashed through one of Fleming's windows, narrowly missing the head of one of his sisters peeking outside. The Yankees withdrew almost as soon as they arrived, but Jenkins was concerned they were trying to set a trap and did initiate a pursuit.[3]

Two of Boyd's troopers lay bleeding on the field; one of them would never rise again. The fighting killed 21-year-old Cpl. William H. Rihl, who was struck in the upper lip by a bullet that penetrated his head and splattered Fleming's fence with blood. The other trooper, Sgt. Milton Cafferty, was hit in the leg. Confederates carried him to Fleming's house, where the family tended his wounds.[4]

Jenkins's independent foraging raid had commenced on June 17 and spread throughout two counties before coming to an end in the brief but deadly firefight. "It would be difficult to estimate the value of property taken by this raid," concluded diarist Charles Hartman, "it coming in the season of the year when the farming interests required the use of the horses, followed a few days afterwards by Lee's vast army. Many croppers who had little else than their stock, were bankrupt."[5]

Jenkins's horsemen had done a good job scouring the countryside. In addition to demanding fresh bread and food, they routinely searched private residences and farms for hidden valuables. On some occasions they threatened to burn residences or other buildings if prompt cooperation was not forthcoming, and some destroyed property deeds and other important papers. Many of his men deliberately pastured their horses in wheatfields rather than those growing timothy

---

3 Hoke, *Reminiscences*, 45.

4 Charles Hartman, Diary, entry for June 22, 1863, Allison-Antrim Museum, Greencastle, PA. Charles Hartman was a local resident who kept a detailed diary of area activities during the war years. Rihl, a pre-war gardener, was the first Union soldier killed on Pennsylvania soil during the Gettysburg campaign. The Rebels buried him near where he fell, but the body was soon reinterred in the local Lutheran Cemetery. Twenty-one years later, the remains were returned to the death site in front of Fleming's house and reburied with great fanfare. A 21-foot-high granite shaft honors Rihl as a "humble but brave defender of the Union." Files of the Franklin County Historical Society.

5 Hartman diary, June 22, 1863 entry.

or clover, much to the consternation of the budget-minded farmers. Other Rebels pilfered threshed wheat from barns to feed their mounts.[6]

Excitement grew in Virginia as rumors about Jenkins's latest foray drifted southward. "While we are manifesting a tender regard for the subsistence of the burly Dutch farmers that inhabit the Valley of Pennsylvania, the brutes who are on their side are endeavoring to starve all the women and children in the Southern Confederacy," opined a Richmond newspaper. "This should not be our policy, had we the control of affairs, and it is very well for the broad-bottomed denizens of the Susquehanna that we have not." In hopes for what the future would bring, the editor fell back on a Biblical reference: "We should proclaim at once 'an eye for an eye, and a tooth for a tooth,' or rather, we should have half a dozen eyes for every eye, and half a dozen teeth for every tooth. This is the only way to bring the Yankees to their senses," he declared. "Let them take their own physic, and they will soon find how bitter it is. Let them see and feel what war is, and they will discover that it is not such an agreeable pastime as they are wont to consider it when contemplating it from a distance."[7]

"There are also rumours that our army is in Pennsylvania. So may it be!" declared Virginian Judith White McGuire, whose cousin John M. Brockenbrough led an infantry brigade in General Lee's advancing army. "We are harassed to death with their ruinous raids, and why should not the North feel it in its homes? Nothing but their personal suffering." McGuire made it clear that she did not want Yankee women and children to suffer, and would in no way condone Confederate soldiers following the example of their Northern counterparts by breaking into homes and stealing from the residents. "I want our warfare carried on in a more honourable way; but I do want our men and horses to be fed on the good things of Pennsylvania," she insisted. "I want the fine dairies, pantries, granaries, meadows, and orchards belonging to the rich farmers of Pennsylvania, to be laid open to our army; and I want it all paid for with our Confederate money, which will be good at some future day." The 50-year-old diarist also wanted to confiscate Pennsylvania horses for use with the Confederate cavalry and to haul Southern wagons, as payment in kind for the hundreds of thousands of animals the enemy had stolen, and "their fat cattle driven into Virginia to feed our army. It amuses me to think how the Dutch farmers' wives will be concealing the golden products of their

---

6 *Lancaster Daily Express*, July 8, 1863.

7 *Richmond Daily Dispatch*, June 22, 1863.

dairies," she added, "to say nothing of their apple-butter, peach-butter, and their wealth of apple-pies."[8]

* * *

While Jenkins's horse soldiers roamed southern Franklin County, Gen. Robert E. Lee was at his temporary headquarters near Berryville preparing to send the first of his infantry into Pennsylvania. "[I]f you are ready to move, you may do so," Lee informed Ewell in northern Maryland. "I think your best course will be toward the Susquehanna." Lee stipulated that "if Harrisburg comes within your means, capture it." Ewell's progress and direction, he added, "will of course depend upon the development of circumstances." He closed with a benediction by telling the corps commander that he was "trusting in the guidance of a merciful God, and invoking His protection for your corps." Ewell split his force by advancing Rodes's and Johnson's divisions through Chambersburg to Harrisburg. Early's Division would form a separate expeditionary force operating on Ewell's exposed right flank. Once in central Franklin County, Early's task was to march east through Gettysburg and on to York to "support the attack on Harrisburg by breaking the railroad between Baltimore and Harrisburg, and seizing the bridge over the Susquehanna at Wrightsville."[9]

With the Maryland roads cleared of Yankees thanks to Jenkins's northward thrust, Rodes prepared his infantry for another long day on the march. A nagging sense of uncertainty gripped many of the men. "Where we are going, or what is our General's intentions, I cannot even guess," declared the 2nd North Carolina's Capt. John C. Gorman in a letter to a friend. He continued:

> Since we left Virginia, all news is contraband; and we have not the slightest idea what is going on outside of our own department. . . . That we cannot remain long without fighting is evident. We are doubtless on the eve of the most decisive period of the war. The troops of our corps are in good condition, and as confident as when old Jackson infused us with his own ardor. Trusting in the justice of our cause, in the wisdom of our leaders, and the

8 McGuire, *Diary of a Southern Refugee*, 225.

9 *OR* 27, pt. 2, 316; pt. 3, 914; *SHSP*, 4:241-281. Early's field return on June 20 at Shepherdstown listed 487 officers and 5,124 men in his main column. After Second Winchester he had sent the 54th North Carolina (Avery's Brigade) and the 58th Virginia (Smith's Brigade) to escort prisoners from Milroy's force to Staunton. He also left Smith's 13th Virginia in Winchester to process captured supplies while the rest of the division headed for the Potomac.

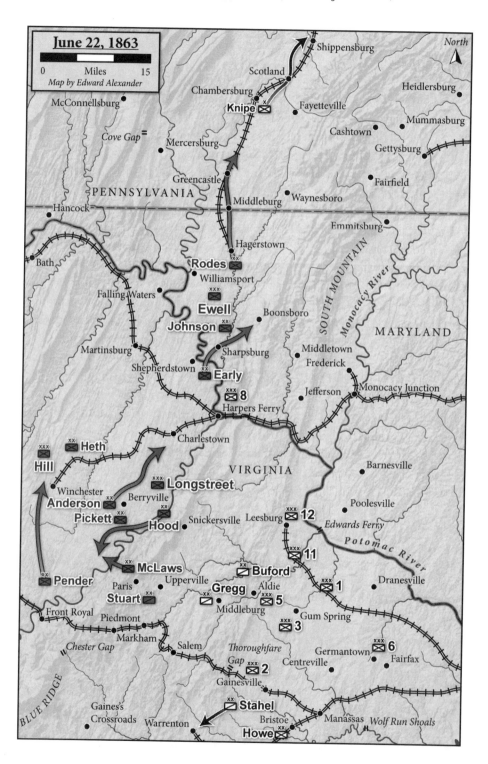

June 22, 1863

0 Miles 15

Map by Edward Alexander

help of the Omnipotent Being . . . we calmly await the issue, and whatever fate befalls us individually, we have an abiding faith that victory and triumph awards us in the end.[10]

Curious bystanders lined the roads as the long column of gray- and butternut-clad troops headed north. Dr. John F. Shaffner, a youthful surgeon of the 4th North Carolina in Stephen Ramseur's brigade, Rodes's Division, recounted the march in a letter to his future wife. "Our reception in Maryland was more cordial than last year, many people being really glad to see us. As we entered Hagerstown the men cheered, the ladies waved handkerchiefs, and showered bouquets upon our men," he boasted. "There are many good Southern people who really wish us success, some of whom have served months in Yankee bastilles, rather than take Lincoln's oath of allegiance. . . . The change of sentiment in Maryland can be accounted for easily. The abolition proclamation effected something—but the Yankee Conscription Bill much more," he continued. "These together have made many secesh sympathizers."[11]

Rodes's jubilant soldiers crossed the Mason-Dixon line and celebrated their arrival in Pennsylvania. "I hail it as the proudest day of my life—the day for which I have been looking so long, when Confederate infantry would invade this State," the 5th Alabama's Maj. Eugene Blackford proudly wrote to his father. "As we approached the line the band prepared to play, and just as the head of the column reached it, they struck up the 'bonnie blue flag' most cheerily." The 53rd North Carolina tramped through Middleburg about 11:00 a.m. and arrived in Greencastle at 1:30 p.m. "The people seemed downhearted and show their hatred to us by their grim looks and silence and I am willing to swear that no prayers will be offered for us poor ragged rebels in this town," concluded North Carolinian Louis Leon. "You may believe that the people was very near skerd to death but wee treated them with respect," Corporal J. F. Coghill of the 23rd North Carolina informed his parents.[12]

Many of the troops camped on the sprawling farm of retired reverend and schoolteacher Joseph S. Loose north of the Waynesboro Pike a mile east of

---

10 John C. Gorman to Dear Friend, June 22, 1863, NCSA, copy in GNMP.

11 J. F. Shaffner to "My Dearest Friend," (Caroline Fries), June 23, 1863, Fries-Shaffner Papers, SHC-UNC. The 24-year-old Dr. Shaffner became the surgeon of the 4th North Carolina in April after transferring from the 33rd North Carolina.

12 Eugene Blackford to his father, June 22, 1863, Lewis Leigh Collection, Box 33, USAHEC; *Charlotte Observer*, Nov. 16, 1892; Leon, *Diary of a Tar Heel*, 32; *Greencastle Pilot*, July 28, 1863; J. F. Coghill to Pappy, Ma and Mit, June 25, 1863, Chambersburg, PA, Jonathan Fuller Coghill Papers, SHC-UNC.

Greencastle. Foraging patrols combed the countryside. "We are taking all the horses & cattle that can be found, & have already got hundreds of horses & droves of beeves," gloated Samuel Pickens of the 5th Alabama. Rodes appointed Col. Edward Willis of the 12th Georgia as provost marshal and charged him with keeping order in Greencastle. Ably assisted by Capt. J. Thomas Carson and the regimental adjutant, Willis succeeded in his task. Local historian Jacob Hoke commented that the Rebels maintained "excellent order" during their stay.[13]

That "excellent order" did not apply to what befell local orchards and distilleries. "I had as many cherries as I could eat this evening," rejoiced Private Pickens. "There is a light colored cherry that is almost as large as our plums & very juicy: the finest I have ever seen." "Some of our boys foraging found some whisky hid in the woods," wrote a happy private in the 14th North Carolina named William A. Smith. "Our chaplain had a prayer service that night. Apparently some men are more susceptible to good influence of 'John and his corn,' as they had to crawl to the prayer service. It was ludicrous and to some, an amusing sight, to see with what eagerness they sought places in the congregation, crawling one over the other!"[14]

This was the first night in a free state for most of the enslaved or paid black servants and teamsters accompanying the Rebel division. At least one man took advantage of the situation. "Ben, the negro cook of Lieutenant [William A.] Liles, took French leave for the Yankees—never heard of him again," recalled Private Smith. "This is the only case of desertion in our company," he hastened to declare. The incursion was not all cherries and cheering. "Many of our boys have worn out our shoes and our feet in bad condition, bruised and bleeding, but they would keep up," continued the Tar Heel. "We often wonder if the Yankees would bear their hardships. General Rodes said, 'None but the best of soldiers would make such sacrifices. The love of Dixie, freedom and independence filled our hearts.'"[15]

David McConaughy, a Gettysburg lawyer and Union agent, had organized a group of wide-ranging civilian scouts for the approaching emergency. Some of them ventured south toward Greencastle and spotted the Confederate infantry. McConaughy wired General Couch the alarming news that 7,000 Rebels now

---

13 Hubbs, *Voices from Company D*, 179; Hoke, *Reminiscences*, 183; *Greencastle Pilot,* July 28, 1863. Loose's farm was north of today's Buchanan Trail and east of Grindstone Hill Road. An accidental fire in 1866 destroyed the barn that had sheltered several of Rodes's men. The land is still a working farm as of the date of this publication.

14 Hubbs, *Voices from Company D*, 179; Smith, *Anson Guards*, 200.

15 Smith, *Anson Guards*, 200.

occupied Greencastle. Throughout the region, efforts intensified to prepare for what now seemed inevitable—a Confederate thrust toward the interior of the state. Anxious residents who had not yet done so scrambled to evacuate or hide their valuables, property, and livestock. In Marion, Mennonite farmer Henry B. Hege hid the wheels of his farm wagon, and pretended to not know their whereabouts when pressed by Rebel inquiries. Hege had reason to be wary of the invaders because of the robbery and wanton murder of his neighbor Isaac Strite two days earlier. Other anxious farmers led their horses and cattle into the woods, ravines, and hills. Many would painfully discover that the Rebels were adept foragers and their hiding places inadequate. Farmers along the Monterey Pass on South Mountain began chopping down trees and blocking the gap as best they could.[16]

Chambersburg postmaster John W. Deal departed town and took the mailbags with him. Merchant Jacob Hoke watched as two companies of Col. Alexander K. McClure's home guards assembled in the square before marching out to join Brig. Gen. Joseph F. Knipe's New York militiamen on the outskirts of town. During the day, the out-of-state guardsmen "did a considerable amount of drilling with their artillery, and not a little boasting of what they would do in case the rebels came within reach of their guns," Hoke remembered. A woman wearing mourning attire sauntered into camp about 3:00 p.m., her black bonnet almost entirely hiding her face. She acted rather strangely, wandering about while repeatedly inquiring where a certain farmer lived that no one knew. Some of the Chambersburg volunteers believed she was a man in disguise and should be arrested as a spy. McClure scoffed at the notion and considered her to be nothing more than "some silly woman" who should be left alone. The mysterious stranger was last seen walking along the railroad south toward Greencastle. Hoke was not as convinced as McClure: "That this pretended woman was one of Gen. Jenkins' scouts, sent in advance to ascertain what preparations were inside for their reception, there can be no doubt."[17]

Soon after the stranger departed, Hoke heard a great commotion in the New York militia camp. Shortly after 5:00 p.m., officers dashed about the tents excitedly barking out commands. One of Boyd's patrolling cavalrymen had reported the proximity of Rebel infantry and cavalry. Captain Miller's artillery crews hastily abandoned their two howitzers and the entire command left in a hurry to march into town and board a waiting train. Tents, accoutrements, and other items of value

---

16 Henry B. Hege to Henry G. Hege, July 12, 1863, LMHS, in Lehman and Nolt, *Mennonites, Amish, and the American Civil War*, 134.

17 Hoke, *Reminiscences*, 40.

Jacob Hoke (seen here with his wife Margaretta) owned a retail store on the square in Chambersburg. He captured detailed observations of the campaign in his journal.

LOC

had been left behind in their wake. McClure ordered his home guardsmen to return to camp and haul the guns and caissons into town and put them on the train. Two panic-stricken Empire Staters suffered nervous spasms, one so badly that he could not continue with his comrades. Residents hid him in Emanuel Kuhn's house on East Market Street.[18]

Resident Solomon D. Swert thought little of the New York militia, "which came here during the war as upon a holiday excursion." He declared that their colonel, incensed when his horse fell into a cattle guard, "drew his pistol and shot him in the head" before stomping away on foot to the train station to join his regiment for the ride to Shippensburg. Swert mocked the cowardly conduct of the colonel and his "brave defenders," who had left their camp strewn with debris. A kindly citizen named Abram Metz, "in the goodness of his heart," according to Swert, "loaded a one-horse wagon full of pantaloons, blouses, blankets, buckets, camp kettles, pistols, etc., which he hauled after the panic-stricken party all the way to Shippensburg." After delivering the materiel, Metz headed back to Chambersburg, where he arrived just in time to encounter Rebel cavalrymen who appropriated his horse.[19]

Hoke had little good to say about any of the military authorities, including General Knipe. He argued that they were aware of the developing situation and had timely notice to leave, but had not followed through with actual orders to do so.

18 Ibid., 46. The stricken soldier remained hidden in Kuhn's house throughout the invasion.

19 Ibid., 184.

Hence, Hoke grumbled, there was "no occasion for their hasty flight." Before Jenkins's cavalry appeared, some Chambersburg residents had ventured out to the militia and carried back their tents and camp equipage, which they piled by the railroad tracks. "Among these were boxes of sardines and other delicacies, more suitable for a picnic than for the stern realities of the camp," marveled the disgusted merchant.[20]

With the militia steaming away toward Shippensburg, many citizens of Chambersburg worried that they had been left powerless to stop the oncoming Rebel infantry. "Guess there will be nothing to hinder them from coming now," Rachel Cormany despaired. "I do indeed feel like getting out of this place on that account but do not like to leave everything behind. I do really feel like leaving." "This afternoon affairs look a little blue," Amos Stouffer penned. "They are reported coming in strong force towards this place." "Our hopes are short lived," echoed another resident. "The troops have all been recalled to Shippensburg, the small battery is run out of town. Excitement is again intense in town. A meeting is held of prominent men, to face the enemy, if they should come and surrender the town on the best terms we can get," he continued. "Again there is a general stampede to leave town with valuables. The road to Shippensburg is again packed with fleeing citizens. There is not a Negro to be seen in town. At 11 o'clock, the streets are deserted. I did not go to bed till about one. All is quiet, but it is a sleepless town."[21]

Preparations continued in Gettysburg just in case the Confederates turned east across South Mountain. District commander Maj. Granville Haller, General Couch's aide-de-camp, dispatched the supply wagons of the First Troop, Philadelphia City Cavalry, to Hanover in southwestern York County. Haller sent local boys throughout Gettysburg to distribute handbills. "Citizens of Adams County: Your mountain, which, in the hands of a few determined patriots, would have been impassable, has been crossed by a handful of rebels, who have come to seize your stock, and bring upon you all the discomforts and horrors of an invasion," began the announcement. "Your committee of safety has appealed to you to organize into companies," it continued:

---

20 Ibid., 46.

21 Mohr, ed., *The Cormany Diaries*, 332-333; Stouffer diary, June 22, 1863 entry, "The Rebs Are Yet Thick About Us," 215; Heyser diary, June 22, 1863 entry.

bring what arms you have, and be ready for such an emergency as yesterday. You are tardy! I have been sent here by the major-general commanding the Department of the Susquehanna, to direct military operations. He is not unmindful of your situation, but trusts that every man will turn out and defend his fireside until the troops which he is (as it were) creating, are organized and ready to be sent to the frontier of his department. The South mountain is emphatically the key to the defense of your homes; it is now occupied by a small force of mounted rebel infantry. We must now organize without a moment's delay. Companies and squads will report at this place with such arms and ammunition as they can gather up for the purpose of repelling the invaders. Arms will be provided for such as have none. The mountain passes are comparatively easily defended with a small force, and all that is necessary for the protection of your homes and property, is your immediate action as suggested.[22]

"The report now is that a large force is in the mountains about eighteen miles away, and a call is made for a party of men to go out and cut down trees to obstruct the passages of the mountains," Sallie Broadhead told her diary. Her husband, Gettysburg Railroad employee Joseph Broadhead, was one of 50 men who volunteered to barricade the Chambersburg Pike. Shouldering axes and picks, they walked west until they reached the base of Rock Top, a high wooded peak. The men mistakenly assumed the Rebels were still miles away on the reverse side of South Mountain. To their horror, enemy horsemen appeared and fired a few long-range shots in their direction, scattering the woodcutters. About 70 Rebels leisurely followed the party to Cashtown, eight miles west of Gettysburg. The soldiers paused frequently to steal more horses and cattle before returning over the mountain pass into the Cumberland Valley after dark. Somehow, they missed a patrol of First City Troopers Haller had earlier dispatched to Cashtown.[23]

With the Confederates approaching, the crowds of refugees once more intensified. The Rev. Leonard M. Gardner, an Adams County native, was visiting Carlisle to participate in Dickinson College's commencement ceremonies. "The roads along the valley were crowded with horses, cattle, sheep and hogs. They were mixed up with long lines of wagons loaded with grain and many articles deemed of special value," wrote Gardner. "During the last week of June one steady procession

22 J. Howard Wert collection, ACHS.

23 Broadhead diary, June 22, 1863 entry. Rock Top rises 410 feet above Cashtown, or 1,210 feet above sea level, according to *The History of Cumberland and Adams Counties*. Cashtown featured "a fine church building, a well conducted hotel, a few good business houses and a number of comfortable private homes."

passed through Carlisle from early morning till late at night. It was amusing sometimes to see how in the general panic, the affrightened refugees sought to save their goods. The most useless and cumbersome things were taken," he marveled. "Amid the crowd I saw passing a one horse wagon filled with household goods and an old baby cradle perched on the top."[24]

Nettie Jane Blair, a young girl from New York who usually spent summers visiting her grandfather near Carlisle, was there that fateful June. "All the Negroes who had ever worked for grandfather had come down from the mountains with their belongings tied in bed quilts, gathering in the back yard," she recalled decades later. "They were literally fed and then piled into big Conestoga wagons drawn by mules. Another wagon was stacked with food and then the whole outfit including the stock started for Harrisburg." Nettie's grandfather and his two sons, James and Scott, headed the party. Several friends and neighbors, toting their most precious possessions, joined the procession. The column of refugees eventually crossed the Susquehanna River and found refuge in the Chester Valley, where they rented barns. They had nothing left to do but wait. Nettie's grandmother and two aunts remained behind, as did her Uncle Lank, a wounded Union soldier home on furlough.[25]

News of the large-scale invasion spread quickly. "Within the past two or three days the rebels have evidently augmented their force on this side of the State line," reported a *New York Times* correspondent working out of Hagerstown. "Their base seems to be at Williamsport, and from that point they sally forth in all directions taking all the horses, cattle and contrabands that come in their way. . . . It is the impression here that the enemy is endeavoring to get in the rear of Baltimore, and does not intend, at present, to advance a great way into the interior of Pennsylvania."[26]

Edward "Allegheny" Johnson's Second Corps division was still in Maryland when the head of Rodes's column poked into Pennsylvania. George Steuart's Brigade, with its large contingent of native Marylanders, camped near the old Sharpsburg battlefield. "This morning, after reading and praying in the woods," wrote Lt. Randolph McKim in his diary, "I saw a group of our men looking at some

---

24 Leonard Marsden Gardner, *Sunset Memories, 1861-1865* (Gettysburg, PA, 1941), 1-2.

25 Nettie Jane Blair, "Reminiscences of Nettie Jane Blair, August 1934," Miscellaneous Civil War Papers, CCHS.

26 *New York Times*, June 22, 1863.

Wartime image of Boteler's Ford, also known as Packhorse Ford. LOC

soldiers' graves, and, with their permission, read (the Bible) and prayed with them."[27]

Jubal Early's command, delayed by days of rain and high water, finally managed to cross the Potomac at Shepherdstown using Boteler's Ford. "The (water) was very high, and it was amusing to see the long lines of naked men fording it—their clothing and accoutrements slung to their guns, and carried above their heads, to keep them dry," noted Capt. William J. Seymour, the adjutant of the First Louisiana Brigade. "The water was very cold, and the men, as they entered it, would scream and shout most boisterously." The bands played "Maryland, My Maryland" when John Gordon's Brigade forded the river, recalled Sgt. Francis L. Hudgins of the 38th Georgia.[28]

Early's soldiers marched through Sharpsburg before going into camp on the Hagerstown Road three miles from Boonsboro. "I reckon I dont know where we are a going to nor how long we will stay in these diggings," admitted the 31st

27 McKim, *A Soldier's Recollections*, 160.

28 William and Isaac Seymour Papers, Schoff Civil War Papers, William L. Clements Library, University of Michigan, Ann Arbor, copy in GNMP; F. L. Hudgins, "With the 38th Georgia,"*CV*, vol. 26 (1918), 162.

Georgia's Cpl. Joseph H. Truett. "I think that we will go to Pensilvaney before [we] stop if the yankees dont stop us and I dont think they is many of them clost to us at this time.... This is Jacksons old army and it is hard to whip. Lawtons old brigade is all [in] yet it is holding out finely. We have got a good account of herself."[29]

Ewell assigned Col. William H. French's 17th Virginia Cavalry from Jenkins's Brigade to screen Early's advance. Many of these troopers had proven to be a bit rebellious and ill-disciplined, and more than a little free-willed. French's command, about 240 men strong, required Early's attention because it "was in such a state of inefficiency," a characteristic the irascible general associated with irregular or "wildcat" troops. Early encountered the 51-year-old French heading to the rear while claiming he was "very much fatigued" and needed rest. After shaming his old acquaintance into going forward with his regiment, Early decided to accompany it for several days himself to instill "some ideas of soldiering into the officers' heads."[30]

Early's men drew the attention of the enemy. "The rebel forces in and around Sharpsburg are exclusively employed collecting plunder in Pennsylvania and Maryland," reported Federal scouts. "A large train just passed the Shepherdstown Ford into Virginia, and also a large drove of beeves. This plunder is guarded from Shepherdstown by infantry, which, after a short absence, returns." Telegraph wires hummed with alarming news: Early was advancing northward.[31]

Concurrently, another large contingent of Rebels under Brig. Gen. John D. Imboden was operating in western Maryland. Imboden led his 3,300 cavalrymen to Cumberland with instructions to "sweep eastwardly down the Baltimore & Ohio Railroad and the Chesapeake and Ohio Canal, and destroy all the bridges, depots and canal boats and locks as far as Martinsburg," according to Jacob Hoke.[32]

Farther to the south, Maj. Gen. Richard H. Anderson's Division of the Third Corps marched from Berryville to James Roper's "Bullskin Farm" along the turnpike to Charles Town, West Virginia. Hood's First Corps division moved to Millwood in Clarke County, Virginia. The entirety of the Army of Northern

---

29 Gregory C. White, *A History of the 31st Georgia Volunteer Infantry* (Baltimore, 1997), 83, citing Joseph H. Truett letter, June 22, 1863, Georgia Department of Archives and History, Atlanta.

30 Jubal A. Early to Henry B. McClellan, Feb. 2, 1878, Manuscript M1324a6, LOC. Before the war, French represented Mercer County in the Virginia legislature.

31 *OR* 27, pt. 3, 162; pt. 2, 25-27. Scouts erroneously reported to Brig. Gen. Daniel Tyler, commanding at Harpers Ferry, that Early had 34 guns and 15,000 infantrymen.

32 Hoke, *Reminiscences*, 45.

Virginia was now headed toward Pennsylvania. The Keystone Staters were learning that the Rebel presence this time was no mere cavalry raid.[33]

*   *   *

Following the battle at Upperville, the cavalrymen of "Grumble" Jones and John Chambliss harassed the retreating Federal horse soldiers as far as Middleburg, skirmishing the entire way before breaking off and withdrawing to Rector's Cross Roads, west of Middleburg. Colonel Thomas T. Munford relocated his cavalry brigade to Bloomfield in response to a skirmish between Col. Thomas L. Rosser's 5th Virginia Cavalry and Col. Thomas C. Devin's brigade of Buford's division.[34]

The returning Confederate troopers had a clear view of the wreckage of battle in and around Upperville. Colonel Richard L. T. Beale of the 9th Virginia spotted a mass grave with a headboard indicating that six men from the 1st Maine rested there. "On the morning of the 22nd white men and negroes were engaged in burying the dead," recalled one of Maj. John S. Mosby's guerrillas years after the war. "One poor fellow lay in a fence corner his brains spattered over the rails, while another had one-half of his head carried away by a shell. Another looked as if calmly sleeping. . . . In one field, in front of Ayreshire, I counted 31 dead horses. The ground was torn up in great holes and furrows by shot and shell. The country," he concluded, "presented a scene of desolation."[35]

Jeb Stuart's favorite scout, Benjamin Franklin Stringfellow of the 4th Virginia, had been cut off from the cavalry when portions of the Army of the Potomac began marching. With Stringfellow unavailable, Stuart relied on his former favorite, Major Mosby, for intelligence reports. Mosby, who departed that day and was

---

33 *OR* 27, pt. 2, 613. The old turnpike running between Berryville to Charles Town, chartered in 1847, is today's U.S. 340 / Business 340. James Roper (1783–1867) was the wealthiest man in Jefferson County according to the 1860 Census. The elderly Union sympathizer owned several plots about four miles south of Charles Town running along the north fork of Bullskin Run. Roper's primary property, "River Farm," occupied 1,100 acres to the east along the Shenandoah River.

34 Beale, *History of the Ninth Virginia*, 77; Mohr, ed., *The Cormany Diaries*, 320; Neese, *Three Years in the Confederate Horse Artillery*, 184; Swank, *Sabres, Saddles, and Spurs*, 71.

35 Beale, *History of the Ninth Virginia*, 77; James J. Williamson, *Mosby's Rangers: A Record of the Operations of the Forty-Third Battalion Virginia Cavalry* (New York, 1896), 75.

nearly captured by a squad of the 5th New York Cavalry of Stahel's command, would not return until June 24.[36]

Recriminations against Stuart's performance during the fighting at Upperville began this day. "Our cavalry has done very badly," admitted Confederate horse artillerist Charles McVicar. "The Yanks have run them about as they pleased. General Stuart never sent any orders to General Jones at Union. He had to move according to the sound of the battle . . . to keep from getting cut off."[37]

A newspaper correspondent traveling with the First Corps wrote a stinging critique of Stuart's performance. Upperville "is considered quite discreditable to the Confederate cavalry, or rather to General Stuart," he declared in the *Savannah Republican*. The gray cavalier was driven "from the town and forced to seek shelter in Ashby's Gap, his officers discouraged and mortified, and his men bordering on a state of demoralization." He continued:

> Officers under Stuart declare that the effort to give him a large command and maintain him in his position is working great mischief to the cavalry service. Both officers and men have come to regard him as unequal to the duty of wielding and fighting so large a force as that now subject to his orders. . . . If some change not be made . . . the country need not expect much benefit from it in the future. . . . Indeed the cavalry service . . . has come to be regarded with contempt.

This sort of harsh criticism, coming on the heels of the charges made against Stuart after Brandy Station, angered the cavalry chief.[38]

While the Loudoun Valley fighting raged, Mosby scoured the area and studied the Potomac army's dispositions. He developed a plan and took it to Stuart on June 22. Stuart listened with interest and enthusiastically embraced Mosby's idea. In a note to Longstreet, Stuart proposed leaving two brigades to guard the mountain passes while he took three brigades into Maryland, passing through the scattered elements of the Army of the Potomac as they rode. Longstreet forwarded Stuart's note to Robert E. Lee.[39]

36 Mosby, *Stuart's Cavalry in the Gettysburg Campaign*, 77-81.

37 McVicar diary, June 21, 1863 entry, 15.

38 *Savannah Republican*, June 25, 1863.

39 Mosby, *Stuart's Cavalry in the Gettysburg Campaign*, 76-78; Clifford Dowdey, ed., *The War Time Papers of R. E. Lee* (Boston, 1961), 523.

Lee responded with an order written by his military secretary, Col. Charles C. Marshall:

General:

I have just received your note of 7.45 this morning to General Longstreet. I judge that the efforts of the enemy yesterday were to arrest our progress and ascertain our whereabouts. Perhaps he is satisfied. Do you know where he is and what he is doing? I fear he will steal a march on us, and get across the Potomac before we are aware. If you find that he is moving northward, and that two brigades can guard the Blue Ridge and take care of your rear, you can move with the other three into Maryland, and take position on General Ewell's right, place yourself in communication with him, guard his flank, keep him informed of the enemy's movements, and collect all supplies you can for the use of the army. One column of General Ewell's army will probably move toward the Susquehanna by the Emmitsburg route; another by Chambersburg. Accounts from him last night state that there was no force west of Frederick. A cavalry force (about 100) guarded the Monocacy bridge, which was barricaded. You will, of course, take charge of Jenkins' brigade, and give him necessary instructions. All supplies taken in Maryland must be authorized by staff officers for their respective departments—by no one else.

I will send you a general order on this subject, which I wish you to see is strictly complied with.[40]

After Marshall wrote the order, Lee directed him to repeat it. "I remember saying to the general that it could hardly be necessary to repeat the order, as General Stuart had had the matter fully explained to himself verbally and my letter had been very full and explicit," recalled Marshall in his postwar memoirs. "I had retained a copy of my letter in General Lee's confidential order book. General Lee said that he felt anxious about the matter and desired to guard against the possibility of error, and desired me to repeat it, which I did, and dispatched the second letter." The second set of letters mentioned by Marshall followed the next day.[41]

The military secretary also claimed that General Lee had met with General Stuart near Paris, at the mouth of Ashby's Gap. "General Lee explained to me that he had had a conversation with General Stuart . . . and that his own view was to

40 OR 27 pt. 3, 913.

41 Maurice, *An Aide-de-Camp of Lee*, 207.

leave some cavalry in Snicker's and Ashby's Gaps to watch the army of General Hooker, and to take the main body of the cavalry with General Stuart to accompany the army into Pennsylvania. It is much to be regretted," penned Marshall after the war, "that this course was not pursued." Stuart, continued Marshall, had also suggested to Lee that he should move his cavalry near Hooker and annoy him if he attempted to cross the Potomac, and when he found a good crossing, he could rejoin the army in good time. According to Lee, Longstreet had approved this plan.[42]

At 7:00 p.m., Longstreet received the order from Lee regarding Stuart's cavalry, and added his endorsement to it:

General:

General Lee has inclosed to me this letter for you, to be forwarded to you, provided you can be spared from my front, and provided I think that you can move across the Potomac without disclosing our plans. He speaks of your leaving, via Hopewell Gap, and passing by the rear of the enemy. If you can get through by that route, I think that you will be less likely to indicate what our plans are than if you should cross by passing to our rear. I forward the letter of instructions with these suggestions.

Please advise me of the condition of affairs before you leave, and order General Hampton—whom I suppose you will leave here in command—to report to me at Millwood, either by letter or in person, as may be most agreeable to him.

Most respectfully,

James Longstreet, Lieutenant-General.

N. B.— I think that your passage of the Potomac by our rear at the present moment will, in a measure, disclose our plans. You had better not leave us, therefore, unless you can take the proposed route in rear of the enemy.[43]

Longstreet next dashed off a quick note to Lee:

42 Ibid.

43 OR 27, pt. 3, 915.

General: Yours of 4 o'clock this afternoon is received. I have forwarded your letter to General Stuart, with the suggestion that he pass by the enemy's rear if he thinks that he may get through. We have nothing of the enemy to-day.[44]

These two brief orders set into motion one of the most enduring controversies of the Civil War.

Lee dispatched a message to Ewell informing him that Stuart and part of his command would be departing soon to rendezvous with him and his infantry. "I also directed General Stuart," continued Lee, "should the enemy have so far retired from his front to permit of the departure of a portion of the cavalry, to march with three brigades across the Potomac, and place himself on your right and in communication with you, to keep you advised of the movements of the enemy, and assist in collecting supplies for the army." Ewell was on notice to keep an eye out for Stuart's cavalry.[45]

Southern prisoners too seriously wounded to be moved were left in field hospitals near Upperville, and any remaining captives were sent to Fairfax Station on the Orange & Alexandria Railroad. "About one hundred rebel prisoners arrived," reported a Union soldier there, "among whom if we may be allowed to judge from appearance, were boys from the age of thirteen or fourteen years up to men of fifty-five or sixty, and all with one or two exceptions clad in different apparel, some having parts of stolen uniforms on and part citizen's clothing, others part confederate and part citizen and others again in rags which were so filthy that their dress would have readily passed for that of a Mongol Tartar."[46]

General Pleasonton interrogated a few prisoners and then met with his division commanders after the heavy combat of the previous day. For a change, he provided some detailed and accurate intelligence about the whereabouts of the enemy. "Ewell's corps went toward Winchester last Wednesday; Longstreet on Friday, and another corps (A. P. Hill's, I think) is to

44 Ibid.

45 Ibid., 914-915.

46 *Lancaster Daily Evening News*, June 30, 1863.

move with Longstreet into Maryland. Such is the information given by the negroes here. I have not been able to send to the top of the Blue Ridge. Stuart has the Gap covered with heavy Blakelys and 10-pounder Parrotts." The cavalry commander concluded: "I shall return to-morrow to Aldie. My command has been fighting almost constantly for four days, and must have a day or two to rest and shoe up and get things in order." In short, he intended to give up the ground his cavalry had fought so hard to gain, which in turn permitted the Army of Northern Virginia to resume its march without hindrance or prying eyes.[47]

Pleasonton ordered Col. John P. Taylor, now in command of Sir Percy Wyndham's brigade, to move his command up from Middleburg to cover the retreat of the rest of the Cavalry Corps, supported by Col. J. Irvin Gregg's brigade. Wounded men were evacuated to field hospitals near Aldie and Middleburg. Taylor deployed the 1st New Jersey to the right of the turnpike and his own 1st Pennsylvania on the left of the road. A skirmish line of the 1st Pennsylvania, the 1st Maryland, and eight companies of the 3rd Pennsylvania covered their front. The remaining four companies of the 3rd Pennsylvania supported a battery of horse artillery, which spent the day dueling with their Confederate counterparts of Chew's Battery. Although there was steady firing throughout the day, Taylor's brigade suffered only two casualties and several horses lost. By dark, the Northern pickets extended along a line centered at Dover while Pleasonton established his headquarters at Aldie.[48]

John Buford began pulling his division back about 6:00 a.m. He and his troopers passed through Middleburg and arrived near Aldie about noon, establishing their camp along the Snickersville Turnpike about a mile and a half west of the small hamlet. Stuart's scrappy troopers pursued him the entire way, skirmishing with the Union rearguard as they went. William Gamble's brigade stayed near Aldie to rest and draw rations, while Tom Devin's brigade was sent out to reconnoiter toward Snickersville. The constant crackling of picket fire meant that few in camp got much rest. "There has been considerable firing this afternoon . . . and we are in hourly expectation of being ordered out again," complained a trooper in the 8th New York. "We hope not, however, until our supply train comes

---

47 OR 27, pt. 1, 912-913.

48 Ibid., 969; William Brooke-Rawle, ed., *History of the Third Pennsylvania Cavalry, Sixtieth Regiment Pennsylvania Volunteers, in the American Civil War, 1861–1865* (Philadelphia, 1905), 252-253.

up, for our horses and selves are in need of provender, though the former have the advantage of us, as we are encamped in a large clover field."[49]

Devin's troopers advanced about two and a half miles beyond Gamble's camp, taking a position near Carter's Bridge over Goose Creek. They established their bivouac and threw out pickets. About noon, Rosser's 5th Virginia attacked Devin's outposts. The bugles blared "To Horse" and Devin's entire brigade mounted. A squadron of the 9th New York rode out to support the embattled picket line. The New Yorkers drove the Virginians to near Philomont until a determined countercharge sent them flying back in haste, with Rosser's men hot on their rear. The pursuit continued for about a mile until Lt. James Burrows, commanding the 9th New York's rearguard, shot and killed Maj. John Eells, who was leading the pursuit. Rosser withdrew once reinforcements arrived, but the Confederate cavalry, joined by Mosby's Rangers, continued probing Buford's positions throughout the day, at times charging his wagons east and west of Aldie. The skirmishing finally died out about midnight.[50]

Brigadier General James Barnes's V Corps division began withdrawing about 7:00 a.m. and reached its camps near Aldie about 4:00 p.m. Throughout the march, the foot soldiers watched and heard the harassing fire of the Confederate artillery and the skirmish fire of the mounted troops. "The cavalry followed closely and the enemy not far behind. Occasionally the proximity was annoying, and our cavalry massed to resist their charge . . . [and] were compelled to repeat the same maneuverings by the enemy's repetition of his hesitating tactics," recorded one Pennsylvanian. "Approaching Middleburg there was unmistakable evidence of massing for a determined effort, when our columns were opened, the roadway cleared, and a battery speedily unlimbered. With a little excellent practice the pursuing force rapidly disappeared," he concluded. The infantrymen spent the next few days resting.[51]

The hard fighting by the Cavalry Corps finally impressed their comrades in the infantry. "The achievements of our cavalry are the topic of much favorable comment among the men and officers of the army, particularly among the infantry

---

49 *The Rochester Daily Union & Advertiser*, June 29, 1863; George H. Chapman, Diary, entry for June 22, 1863, Archives, Indiana Historical Society Library, Indianapolis.

50 Newel Cheney, *History of the Ninth Regiment, New York Volunteer Cavalry, War of 1861 to 1865* (Jamestown, NY, 1901), 100; Hall, *History of the Sixth New York Cavalry*, 131; Cheney diary, June 22, 1863 entry; OR 27, pt. 2, 691.

51 OR 27, pt. 1, 616; Smith, *History of the 118th Pennsylvania*, 227-228; Swank, *Sabres, Saddles, and Spurs*, 71.

Brig. Gen. John T. Copeland commanded a brigade of Michigan cavalry in the Army of the Potomac during much of the early part of the Gettysburg Campaign.

USAHEC

who are fast getting in love with the cavalry," observed a correspondent for the *New York Times*, "there having been heretofore, plenty of room for an increase in affection between them."[52]

* * *

Julius Stahel and his cavalry division, meanwhile, scouted the upper Rappahannock region. Stahel's wagon train hindered his ability to move quickly; this frustrated Joe Hooker, who ordered the wagons to be returned. "The march was so rapid that the trains were left behind and a good portion of the time we were without forage or food," complained a trooper in the 6th Michigan. "The horses were fed but once on the trip." Stahel reached Warrenton and established his headquarters by noon on June 22. He directed his various regiments to scout the river. Brigadier General Joseph T. Copeland led his 5th and 6th Michigan and two companies of the 7th Michigan south, following the route of the Orange & Alexandria Railroad from Bealeton to Rappahannock Station. When they reached the latter, Copeland sent a squadron of the 5th Michigan splashing across the Rappahannock into Culpeper County. The brigadier expected Stahel to join him there the next day, at which time the entire division would cross. Instead, Stahel received orders to return to Fairfax Court House; Copeland was ordered to join him in Gainesville the next evening.[53]

---

52 *New York Times*, June 25, 1863.

53 OR 27, pt. 3, 255, 267, 269, 283; James H. Kidd, *Personal Recollections of a Cavalryman in Custer's Michigan Brigade* (Ionia, MI, 1908), 112; Boudrye, *Historic Records of the Fifth New York*, 62.

In Washington, Abraham Lincoln messaged Secretary of War Stanton about a recently dismissed cavalry officer. "Do you not remember the french officer, Col. Duffie, whom we saw at Gen. McDowell's Head Quarters near Fredericksburg, last May a year ago?" inquired the president. "I rem[em]ber he was then well spoken of. On the night of the 17th Inst. he was surrounded by Stuart's cavalry near Millersburg, and cut his way out with proportionate heavy loss to his then small command. Please see and hear him," he directed. "I think you have strong recommendations on file in his behalf."[54]

*   *   *

A black man from the Aldie area forwarded reliable information regarding Mosby's whereabouts to V Corps headquarters. The man overheard the partisan commander and Dr. Jesse Ewell discussing a meeting they were planning at Ewell's country chapel near Haymarket the next morning. This intelligence coup presented, as General Meade put it, "the prettiest chance in the world to dispose of Mr. Mosby." The V Corps commander issued orders to ambush the guerrilla leader.[55]

Captain William H. Brown of the 14th U.S. Infantry was tasked with the Mosby operation and received instructions to select 100 men and three officers, who would be joined by 33 troopers of the 17th Pennsylvania Cavalry. Brown intended to reach Ewell's Church before daylight, so it was still dark and raining when his column departed from near Aldie. The terrible weather delayed the march when the tramping feet and clopping hooves churned the unpaved road into a thick ribbon of mud. It did not help matters that the men were unfamiliar with the route. Captain Jonathan Hager was in command of the Union picket line that night when a messenger arrived about 2:00 a.m. No one had informed the pickets about the excursion because mission security was a high priority. "I passed them & found it was an expedition in search of Mosby the celebrated guerrilla Chieftain who had been infesting that region," wrote Hager in his diary. "I agreed with Brown to send him fifty men in case I heard firing & he went on."[56]

54 Basler, Pratt, and Dunlap, eds., *Collected Works of Abraham Lincoln*, 6:291-292.

55 *OR* 27, pt. 3, 255.

56 *OR* 27, pt. 1, 641-643; Jonathan Hager, Diary, entry for June 22, 1863, Albert and Shirley Small Special Collections Library, UVA.

The ever-present friction of war slowed the column to a crawl, and Captain Brown's men did not reach Ewell's Chapel until after daylight. It was poor ground for the ambush, so he divided his small command in an effort to launch a surprise assault to best advantage. Half of the horse soldiers and a few infantrymen took up a position behind the small church near the head of a lane leading to Dr. Ewell's house, "Dunblane." The rest waited behind a fence on the far side of the lane. A short time later, Brown received word from a lookout that a group of horsemen was approaching. The officer waited until the riders were within pistol range before ordering his command to open fire.[57]

To the surprise and dismay of the Federals, none of the weapons fired because the heavy rain had dampened their powder. The metallic snaps and shouting alerted Mosby and his rangers to the danger, and he immediately ordered them to charge, driving the handful of Keystone troopers back onto their infantry supports. The infantrymen, with dry ammunition and clear shots, returned fire, but hit little because Mosby had called a halt to any pursuit. His decision may well have saved his life, as it kept him and his men out of Brown's trap. Mosby's fast gallop in the opposite direction ended the failed effort. broke off and withdrew. This expedition resulted in a few casualties on both sides and angry recriminations at V Corps headquarters. Most importantly, the "Gray Ghost" lived to fight another day.[58]

* * *

"Thus far Hookers move has made but little difference to us," explained 20-year-old Cpl. Manley Stacey in a letter to his father, "but my opinion, is there will be an awful Battle Fought, here on Bull Run. Everyone seems to think the Decisive Battle will be Fought There." The men of Stacey's regiment, the 111th New York of Maj. Gen. Samuel Heintzelman's XXII Corps, had watched with some amusement as the men of the Army of the Potomac marched past their position at Centreville. Stacey was right—there would soon be "an awful Battle," but not along Bull Run; the fighting was destined for south-central Pennsylvania. He and his comrades had no way of knowing that within three days they would

---

57 OR 27, pt. 1, 641-643.

58 Ibid.; Timothy J. Reese, *Sykes' Regular Infantry Division, 1861–1864: A History of Regular United States Infantry Operations in the Civil War's Eastern Theater* (Jefferson, NC, 1990), 232-233; Virgil Carrington Jones, *Ranger Mosby* (Chapel Hill, 1944), 142-143.

Maj. Gen. Samuel P. Heintzelman commanded the XXII Corps in the Department of Washington.

LOC

belong to an entirely different corps and would take an active and bloody part in that "Decisive Battle" he had predicted in his letter home.[59]

Many soldiers in that heretofore luckless army were less certain that a major fight was imminent in the Centreville/Manassas region. Some openly doubted Hooker's fitness. "Our Division is here near Aldie and I don't think that the Comdg Genl knows where the main rebel army is," staff officer Capt. H. W. Freedley of Brig. Gen. Romeyn Ayres's division, V Corps, confided to a friend back home. "I am having quite exciting times hunting Mosby," he added, "who is picking up stragglers in every direction."[60]

Private Martin Haynes of the 2nd New Hampshire, part of Col. George Burling's brigade, Humphreys's division, III Corps, was camped near Gum Spring. "It is reported that several guerrillas picked up by our men are to be hanged," he recalled matter-of-factly years later. Haynes turned his attention to a vice circulating within his regiment: "The gambling craze broke out, and many 'sweatboards' were in full blast on the outskirts of the camp until Col. Bailey suppressed them."[61]

59 Manley Stacey to Dear Father, June 22, 1863, Camp Hayes, Centreville, VA, Historical Society of Oak Park and River Forest, IL.

60 H. W. Freedley to Dr. Joseph (Hiester?), June 22, 1863, Special Collections Department, William R. Perkins Library, Duke University, Durham, NC. Freedley, of the 3rd U.S. Infantry, had been a special inspector of Camp Butler and Alton Prison in Illinois in 1862. He would be badly wounded in the leg at Gettysburg.

61 Haynes, *A History of the Second Regiment*, 163.

The 141st Pennsylvania, another III Corps unit, spent the day along Broad Run resting and cleaning up. "Went over to the wagon train and changed my clothes, the first time I have had a chance to do so since we left Potomac Creek," remembered Maj. Israel P. Spaulding in his history of the regiment. "The next day the wagons were sent out to gather forage and Companies A and D of our Regiment were detailed as an escort," he continued. It was a bountiful outing. "Many of the officers went out with them taking their pack mules and attendants, and returned, the wagons loaded with forage for the horses, and the others bringing lambs, chickens, milk, butter, light bread, in short almost every variety of eatables they could lay hands on. More than one mess enjoyed the luxury that night of bread and milk for supper."[62]

The 33rd Massachusetts, an XI Corps outfit, was also in the area. "Here we watered and fed our teams, took a 'cold bite' (raw pork and tack) and proceeded for about four miles, arriving at a place that I shall call 'Zion's Hill,'" recalled Andrew Boies. "It yields a great quantity of 'Seceshism,' and I have had the opportunity of seeing it displayed among the women, as they would stand by the roadside, and as we passed by they would taunt us with the pleasant sound of 'Oh, the Yankee cowards are coming,' but we took it from whence it came. Here we halted, cooked our coffee, partook of some fresh beef, etc., and went on," he continued, "arriving at Leesburg late in the afternoon, and halted for the night."[63]

Writing from Thoroughfare Gap, General Gibbon described passing through the Brawner's Farm battlefield at Gainesville, the site of his first battle at the head of a brigade the previous August; it was during this fight that his command earned the moniker "Iron Brigade." "I never had had an opportunity of riding over the ground before, and could without difficulty trace the direction of my line by the broken cartridges and the bodies of the men which appear to have been simply covered with earth right where they fell. It will not be very long, however, before most of the traces of the battle will obliterated," he continued, "and I only wish all marks on the country could be wiped away as easily and as soon. For a long time yesterday we could hear guns up in the direction of Aldie and Middleburg, and were informed that Pleasonton was having a fight with the enemy's cavalry," he concluded with remarkable accuracy. "I think it probable Lee's main force is over in the Shenandoah Valley." Gibbon's II Corps division camped near the gap,

62 Craft, *History of the One Hundred Forty-first Regiment*, 109.

63 Boies, *Record of the Thirty-third Massachusetts*, 30.

resting there "very quietly and monotonously, undisturbed by anything of interest."[64]

Captain Charles Weygant recalled that six companies of the "Orange Blossoms" of the 124th New York were detailed for picket duty near Leesburg for three days. On "[t]his picket tour considerable foraging was done. Fresh beef, veal and poultry abounded," he penned. "Lieutenant J. O. Denniston, of Company G," he continued,

> who was decidedly the most accomplished forager and best liver in the regiment, managed somehow to get hold of a fat goose. Now Denniston was a good cook, as well as forager, and when at length he had succeeded in getting his goose roasted to his entire satisfaction, several of his brother officers who had been looking on from a distance, concluded to make him a social call—expecting, of course, to get an invitation to stay to dinner. We chatted and laughed, joked and told stories; the time slipped by, dinner hour passed, the goose got cold and so did Denniston, but not a word was said about dinner.[65]

Their ultimate destination, of course, would depend upon the movements of the Southern army. "You can hardly imagine what our poor loaded soldiers suffer on such marches," complained Maj. Rufus Dawes of the 6th Wisconsin. He did his best to explain the hard monotony of it all. "We camped Friday night at Deep Run. We marched at daylight Saturday and camped for the night near Bealton station. We marched Sunday morning and all day Sunday and all night, and until the middle of the afternoon to-day, when we reached this point, tired, sore, sleepy, hungry, dusty and dirty as pigs. I have had no wink of sleep for two nights. Our army," Dawes added presciently, "is in a great hurry for something."[66]

Some of the troops appreciated the beautiful vistas they encountered on the long, difficult marches. "If I were a free man," penned the 1st Minnesota's Isaac Taylor as he reconnoitered Thoroughfare Gap near Broad Run, "I should enjoy a whole day's ramble in this vicinity, but in these 'exciting times' a soldier does not venture very far from camp for fear that something may turn up that requires his presence."[67]

---

64 Gibbon, *Recollections*, 126.

65 Weygant, *History of the One Hundred and Twenty-Fourth Regiment*, 165.

66 Dawes, *Service with the Sixth Wisconsin*, 152.

67 Taylor, "Campaigning with the First Minnesota," 357.

"Leesburg was filled with rebel families, nearly every one of which was represented in the rebel army," surmised Pvt. Leonard G. Jordan of the 10th Maine Battalion, the headquarters guard for Sedgwick's VI Corps. "Yet the people were glad to dispose of bread, milk and so forth, for our 'green-backs.' The soldiers quartered in town would walk into the parlors at evening, where young ladies were gathered, and join in the conversation with the greatest freedom. Yet scarcely a case was reported in which there was otherwise disrespectful behavior, if this could be so called," continued the somewhat surprised private. "The ladies mildly avenged these acts by singing in the ears of passers-by various rebel airs, as 'The Bonnie Blue Flag' and 'Maryland, My Maryland.'"[68]

General-in-chief Halleck was busy in Washington reassigning troops and replying to messages. All the troops in Robert Schenck's VIII Corps east of Cumberland, Maryland, were put under the overall command of Hooker, who also gained partial control over Washington's defenses. The lack of certainty as to Lee's objectives frustrated the politicians in the capital as much as it did the officers in the field. Secretary of State William Seward lamented that the frequent movements of the cavalry of both armies thus far had been "unfruitful of important results. While due efforts have been made to prepare against surprise on our part," he added, "the enemy's plan of attack has not yet been satisfactorily ascertained."[69]

* * *

Thousands of recruits milled about Harrisburg while General Couch and commonwealth officials continued organizing the new Department of the Susquehanna. Most of the volunteers had little or no concept of proper military protocol. While developing an early admiration for Capt. Henry Landis's First Philadelphia Artillery, a member of the 22nd New York National Guard observed that "the battery did not unharness for two days. When it came to do so, the question arose, how was it to be done, particularly by worn out men, at a late hour on a dark night? The Gordian knot was cut by the order, 'Try all the buckles and unbuckle those that work easiest.'" Unfortunately, the harness was new and stiff, so each buckle presented a separate

---

68 Leonard G. Jordan, "History of the Tenth Me. Battalion," in John M. Gould, *History of the First-Tenth-Twenty-ninth Maine Regiment, in Service of the United States Army from May 3, 1861, to June 21, 1866* (Portland, ME, 1871), 352-353.

69 Baker, *The Works of William H. Seward*, 5:95.

challenge. The green Philadelphians finally gave up and tethered their horses after deciding to call for an instructor in the morning to show them how to put the harness together properly. The embarrassing failure amused the New Yorkers.[70]

The New York press was less than pleased with Harrisburg's residents. To the dismay of a reporter with the *New York Times*, not a soul cheered when Empire State regiments marched through town to their campsites, nor did anyone openly thank the militiamen for coming to protect their homes. "Such complete indifference, such extreme apathy, has seldom, if ever, been witnessed on any similar occasion," sniffed the correspondent. While some of the residents blatantly overcharged the militia for home-cooked meals, not every Harrisburg citizen was straining to make an extra buck. One woman managed to feed 125 soldiers in her home in just 12 hours. It was not enough to satisfy the *Times* reporter: "It would be a just retribution if the rebels should station themselves on a formidable eminence and throw a sufficient number of shells into this uncharitable city to wake the inhabitants to a sense of gratitude and liberality."[71]

The defenders of the "uncharitable city" included the 500 men of the 74th New York State National Guard. After a rousing send-off in Buffalo, they arrived in Harrisburg without guns or accouterments. The Federal government supplied them with used and substandard weaponry. "I drew from U.S. Quartermaster's Department uniforms for 450 men, together with camp equipage, and from U.S. Ordnance Department 450 Springfield rifled muskets, in very bad order; not one musket in order, having been used by nine-months Pennsylvania Volunteers," grumbled Col. Watson A. Fox. "The day was spent in issuing uniforms to the men and packing up their cast-off clothing, which was returned to Buffalo." At noon, Capt. Alexander Sloan arrived with a 40-man company of the Buffalo Cavalry. Colonel Fox learned soon thereafter from General Couch that it would be impossible for the government to provide horses for the newcomers. Instead of returning home as Couch ordered, Captain Sloan and his men volunteered to serve as infantry. When Couch agreed, Fox set about outfitting the company with rifles and cartridge boxes.[72]

"The war excitement continues unabated to-day, and troops are arriving incessantly," announced the *Harrisburg Evening Telegraph*. "The drum and fife is still

---

70 Wingate, *History of the Twenty-second Regiment*, 158, 160.

71 *New York Times*, June 24, 1863, dateline June 22.

72 OR 27, pt. 2, 271. A second company of the Buffalo Cavalry arrived on June 23 and similarly volunteered as infantry.

heard on the streets, and the pavements are thronged with men." Editor George Bergner praised the newly arrived 4th New York Artillery, deeming it "unsurpassed in point of efficiency and enthusiasm. It is probably one of the very best military organizations outside the regular army." The unit contained more than 500 foreign-born United States citizens, many of which had previous experience in European armies and "understood every prerequisite of discipline."[73]

In mid-afternoon at Camp Curtin, Col. Jacob G. Frick, a veteran of Fredericksburg and Chancellorsville, issued marching orders for his newly organized and equipped 27th Pennsylvania Volunteer Militia. Although Frick and several key officers had ample combat experience, many of his men were raw. They dutifully packed their knapsacks and struck tents to begin what many hoped would be a grand experience. They tramped through the streets of the capital and across the bridge to Camp Susquehanna at 4:30 p.m., not far from some of the earthen fortifications being built to defend Harrisburg. The boys were in high spirits, and soldiering was voted "a decided institution." The neophytes eagerly pitched tents and established a camp guard. "Lights were ordered out at 'taps,'" reported Lt. Francis W. Wallace, the editor of a Pottsville newspaper. "9 o'clock, and our first guard was unmarked by any episode more startling than the firing by one of the guard of his piece at 3 o'clock in the morning, at an imaginary rebel stealing upon him through the wheat of a neighboring field."[74]

While the militia continued their feverish preparations, another issue loomed in the capital city and the nearby Susquehanna and Cumberland valleys: the fear that a network of enemy agents was operating in the region. "Copperheadism is by no means extinct in Harrisburgh, much less at Chambersburgh and towns beyond," declared the *New York Times*. "Traitors are daily and hourly employed in gathering information and transmitting the same to the enemy. Farmers taking their horses and cattle to the mountains for safety are tracked by those despicable minions of treason who seize the first opportunity to let the rebels know where they can make a haul. The Copperheads utter their sentiments openly and boldly," he continued, "and almost invite the rebels to partake of their hospitality, and yet they are allowed to walk the streets and enjoy all the privileges of loyal citizens."[75]

Scarcely a week after his stunning defeat at Second Winchester, the 23rd New Jersey Militia's band serenaded General Milroy at 11:30 p.m. at the Jones House.

73 *Harrisburg Evening Telegraph*, June 22, 1863.

74 *Pottsville Miner's Journal*, Oct. 24, 1863.

75 *New York Times*, June 24, 1863, dateline June 22.

The mood at his Harrisburg hotel was festive and upbeat. Someone called for the general to give a speech, to which he ably responded. Darius Couch was present and also delivered a few remarks. The crowd gave three hearty cheers for Milroy, the Union, Couch, and several other well-known generals.[76]

Many Harrisburg residents went to bed that night feeling much better about the prospects of repelling any Confederate thrust toward the city. Others, lacking confidence in the militia and its leaders, quietly packed what they could while planning to take the northbound trains the next morning.

*   *   *

"This morning I find all sorts of trashy rumors in the papers, and actually heard a newsboy crying, 'Capture of Baltimore,'" explained the disgusted Salmon Chase to his daughter Kate. "So far as I heard anything authentic, I find no reason to believe that there are 2000 rebels this side of the Potomac from Cumberland down, including those who made the grand scare in Pennsylvania." Chase mentioned that one of "the most intelligent and candid correspondents I have seen" had visited the threatened areas before journeying to the nation's capital, where he told the treasury secretary that he thought Lee's army was moving toward the Kanawha River and intended to enter West Virginia, or perhaps through East Tennessee to join Gen. Braxton Bragg's forces. Chase did not believe either movement was probable. "In my judgment he is in the Shenandoah Valley or not far from it, and means to fight any part of Hooker's force he can find exposed and avail himself of any opportunities that may be offered to strike blows," he predicted. "My conviction is that he will not accomplish any great things; but, on the contrary, will find that he has made a false & disastrous move."[77]

---

76 *Harrisburg Evening Telegraph*, June 23, 1863. The Jones House stood at Second and Market streets on Market Square in Harrisburg. Abraham Lincoln had stopped there briefly on February 22, 1861, for dinner with Governor Curtin and other dignitaries while en route to his inauguration in Washington.

77 Niven, *The Salmon P. Chase Papers*, 4:68.

TUESDAY, JUNE 23, 1863

It was still dark when Lt. Hermann Schuricht and his men of Company D of the 14th Virginia Cavalry shook themselves awake in their camp near Mont Alto, Pennsylvania. They had a grueling ride ahead of them across South Mountain and into western Adams County.

"At dawn we moved on by roads to Caledonia Iron Works," wrote the German-born Schuricht, "catching only twenty-six horses and twenty-two mules, the great bulk having been moved on upon Mr. Use's [Hughes's] messages of warning." Alexander K. McClure's *Franklin Repository* mentioned that two fine riding horses belonging to Congressman Thaddeus Stevens, the owner of the ironworks, were among the mounts taken that morning. McClure believed the Rebels "had evidently been minutely informed of the whereabouts of Mr. Stevens' horses, as they described them and knew exactly where to go after them."

The Virginians forced Stevens's overseer John Sweeny to provide them with rations, which they ate quickly before departing about 2:00 p.m. They chased after the ironworks guards, who had taken most of the horses with them toward Gettysburg. After riding two miles they discovered felled trees blocking the turnpike just as it entered dense woods. Major Bryan, General Rodes's quartermaster who led the column, consulted with the officers and decided to press on. He sent Lieutenant Schuricht with nine men to clear the barricade. They cautiously approached on foot on both sides of the turnpike and encountered about 25 dismounted men waiting in ambush, but the enemy thought better of their opportunity and disappeared through the trees. Schuricht's detail cleared the blockages and Captain Moorman and the mounted Rebels galloped off to pursue the fleeing Yankees, who reorganized behind several mounted comrades. The

Republican Congressman Thaddeus Stevens of Lancaster, Pennsylvania, owned the Caledonia Iron Works.

LOC

enemy again fled before Moorman could deploy his men for an attack. The Rebels were pursuing when a bushwhacker squeezed a trigger and sent Pvt. Eli Amick tumbling off his horse with a mortal wound. Major Bryan ordered everyone to stop, return to the ironworks, and rejoin the regiment. "Having passed the buildings we were again fired upon from ambush," Schuricht related. "This section of Pennsylvania seems to be full of 'bushwhackers.'" His company met the rear guard, which was in charge of the captured horses, at Greenwood and instructed nearby citizens to feed his men and their animals.[1]

To the south, a patrol of 16 Rebels appeared without warning near Mercersburg, riding through the countryside to collect cattle, horses, and supplies. Seminarian Thomas Creigh had "just heard that Col. John McClelland had been taken prisoner by them and that the small force we had at Chambersburg has left that place. We are beginning to feel the horrors of this terrible war in other ways than have heretofore felt it," he admitted. "Persons passing through town flying with their horses from the enemy, groups of persons, men, women and children in all directions, discussing public affairs. Packed a trunk with records of church and sermons and private papers."[2]

Albert Jenkins's main force trotted once more toward Chambersburg. A pair of civilian riders galloped past "as fast as their horses could go," remembered Rachel Cormany. "One said—'those d—d buggers fired on us.' The other looked

1 Schuricht diary, entry for June 22, 1863, *Richmond Dispatch*, April 5, 1896; *Franklin* (PA) *Repository*, July 15, 1863.

2 Creigh diary, entry for June 23, 1863.

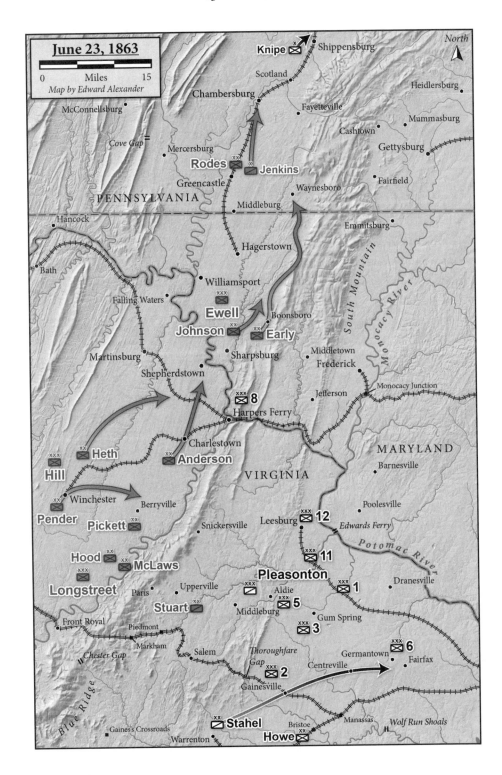

June 23, 1863

0 Miles 15

Map by Edward Alexander

North

Knipe

Shippensburg

Scotland

Heidlersburg

Chambersburg

Fayetteville

Mummasburg

McConnellsburg

Cashtown

Gettysburg

Cove Gap

Mercersburg

Rodes

Jenkins

Waynesboro

Fairfield

Greencastle

PENNSYLVANIA

Middleburg

Hancock

Emmitsburg

Hagerstown

Bath

Williamsport

Ewell

Boonsboro

South Mountain

Monocacy River

Falling Waters

Johnson

Early

Martinsburg

Sharpsburg

Middletown

Frederick

Shepherdstown

8

Jefferson

Monocacy Junction

Harpers Ferry

Charlestown

MARYLAND

Heth

Anderson

Barnesville

Hill

VIRGINIA

Pender

Winchester

Berryville

Poolesville

Leesburg

12

Edwards Ferry

Pickett

Snickersville

11

Potomac River

Hood

McLaws

Pleasonton

Dranesville

Longstreet

Paris

Upperville

1

Aldie

Stuart

5

Front Royal

Piedmont

Middleburg

Gum Spring

3

Markham

Salem

Thoroughfare Gap

Germantown

6

Centreville

Fairfax

Chester Gap

2

Gainesville

Blue Ridge

Gaines's Crossroads

Stahel

Bristoe

Manassas

Wolf Run Shoals

Warrenton

Howe

as pale as death; his mouth wide open—his hat lost—he was too badly frightened to speak." One of the riders sternly warned the people to go into their houses. "All at once I got so weak I could scarcely walk, but that was over in a few minutes & I could walk faster than before. The people were wonderfully frightened again, such a running." Within a short time Jenkins's mounted infantrymen were milling about in the crowded streets, their hands on the triggers of their muskets in case of trouble.[3]

"About nine or ten o'clock, Gen. Jenkins again entered our town," merchant Jacob Hoke recorded. "This time [he] came in slowly and confidently." A part of his force rode north toward Shippensburg while the rest of the Virginians remained in the town. Jenkins requisitioned large amounts of provisions and directed they be brought to the courthouse pavement. "Of course we had to respond to this order," admitted Hoke, "and like the citizens of Greencastle, who in response to a similar demand, were all of one mind and brought onions, so we all seemed to have been moved by one idea . . . that this was a good time to get rid of old bacon, and sides and jowls." The residents sprinkled in enough fresh bread to fulfill Jenkins's demands.[4]

Soldiers forced open J. Allison Eyster's locked warehouse and carried off more than $4,000 worth of food including large quantities of coffee, salt, beans, bacon, and crackers. They also broke into the nearby warehouse of Oaks & Linn and appropriated almost 300 barrels of flour belonging to miller Jacob Stouffer. Officers smashed the heads of 20 barrels of whiskey and unceremoniously dumped the contents onto the ground. The scene was repeated at Miller's drugstore by pouring a barrel of brandy into the gutter.[5]

According to Hoke, that afternoon "a raid of a most shameful and yet ludicrous character occurred." The Rebels had not yet discovered government supplies stored in a former freight forwarding warehouse, "and some of our people—mostly those who resided in the eastern part of the town, and had no scruples against taking anything from Uncle Sam they could, rather than have the rebels take them—made a raid upon these stores and in a short time cleaned out the whole stock." People carried large sides of bacon through the crowded streets or rolled barrels of crackers or beans. The throng soon became unruly with the

---

3 Cormany and Mohr, *The Cormany Diaries*, 333.

4 Hoke, *Reminiscences*, 46.

5 Ibid., 132-133. Jeb Stuart's cavaliers looted the same warehouse for military supplies during their October 1862 raid on Chambersburg.

jostling, shouting, and need for haste. The tension led to scolding and finally to kicking and fighting, even amongst the women.[6]

"The Rebs have been cutting up high," Rachel Cormany would write her cavalryman husband. "Sawed down telegraph poles, destroyed the Scotland bridge again, took possession of the warehouses & were dealing our flour by the barrel & molasses by the bucketful—They made people take them bread—meat—&c to eat—Some dumb fools carried them jellies & the like. Not a thing went from this place." Rumors spread that "from 7 to 15 thousand infantry are expected on tonight."[7]

The chaos and consternation spread throughout the lower Cumberland Valley as countless refugees streamed north. Amos Stouffer had left Chambersburg for Shippensburg on June 20. Now it was time for the businessman to move even farther away. "The excitement was very great," he admitted. "I went to Landis's and took my horses to the mountain below Newburg and staid there over night." A New York Herald correspondent wired his editor that 150 Rebel cavalrymen had ridden into Fayetteville, about six miles east of Chambersburg on the turnpike to Gettysburg. He reported that "a citizen mortally wounded one of the enemy as he came into Fayetteville."[8]

Rodes's Division was several miles behind Jenkins. Rodes ordered Brig. Gen. George Steuart to lead a multi-day expedition to McConnellsburg, a small town in Fulton County. To reach his distant objective, Steuart's force—the Third Brigade, an artillery battery, and Maj. Harry Gilmor's battalion of Maryland cavalry—would have to cross Tuscarora Mountain. The column, accompanied by Ewell's chief engineer Henry B. Richardson, left Sharpsburg, Maryland, at 5:00 a.m. It passed through Hagerstown about noon, "receiving there an enthusiastic reception from the ladies of the town," touted Steuart's aide Lt. Randolph McKim. "It was a proud day for the Maryland men, and they stepped out beautifully to the tap of the drum." After a 17-mile trek the soldiers camped at 3:00 p.m. some five miles north of Hagerstown near the state line.[9]

At Greencastle, Ewell's quartermaster Maj. John A. Harman demanded the town deliver 100 saddles and bridles and a dozen pistols to him by 2:00 p.m. A

---

6 Hoke, *Reminiscences*, 46.

7 Cormany and Mohr, *The Cormany Diaries*, 333-334.

8 Stouffer diary, entry for June 23, 1863; *Chicago Tribune*, June 27, 1863, quoting the *New York Herald*.

9 McKim, *A Soldier's Recollections*, 163.

second requisition signed by Maj. A. M. Mitchell listed onions, sauerkraut, potatoes, radishes, and other vegetables. Before the stunned civic leaders could recover, ordnance officer Maj. William Allen requisitioned "1,000 pounds of lead, 1,000 pounds of leather, 100 pistols, 12 boxes of tin, and 300 curry combs and brushes." The magnitude of the levy caused consternation and anxiety. "These demands were so heavy that the Council felt it impossible to fill them," declared resident William A. Reid. "The Rebels got a few saddles and bridles, and some vegetables, about town. They seized and carried away about $2,000 worth of leather from Mr. A[ndrew] Stiffel." The chief of Ewell's topographic engineers, Maj. Jedediah Hotchkiss, demanded two maps of Franklin County. "The people were much surprised to see us, but manifested no hostility—submitting to our rule," Hotchkiss later bragged.[10]

"Genl Lee is determined to carry on an aggressive war, and this is the only way that we can put a stop to hostilities, carry the war to them and let them taste its fruits," opined the 47th North Carolina's Lt. William Blount. "Let their homes be laid waste—Their lands destroyed—Their towns laid in ashes, and then they will be disposed to make terms of peace. Now is the golden opportunity! The enemy is weaker now than he has been in one year. Now is the time to strike. If we but act promptly our country can be saved, our independence achieved." Lee, he added, "is a general & you may expect to hear of brilliant achievements by his invincible army. We are all in fine spirits and confident of victory."[11]

The locals bemused the 2nd North Carolina Battalion's Lt. Col. Wharton Green. "Greencastle was our next halting place, for a day or two, where it seemed that all of the Pennsylvania Dutch for a hundred miles around about had come to look glum at our audacity in venturing so far in their midst," he sneered. Some of the onlookers were not so innocent, as they eagerly passed along information of military importance to Union authorities. "A lady who saw the rebels in Greencastle saw eight pieces of artillery on the Diamond, or public square of that place, and a large force of infantry," noted a reporter. "Another refugee counted seventeen pieces of artillery, and judged their force to be six thousand good men."[12]

---

10 *Greencastle* (PA) *Pilot*, July 28, 1863; Hotchkiss, *Make Me a Map*, 154.

11 William Blount to "My dear friend," June 23, 1863, Steed and Phipps Family Papers, #3960, SHC-UNC, copy at GNMP.

12 Green, *Recollections and Reflections*, 173; *Chicago Tribune*, June 27, 1863.

After establishing his campsite, 4th North Carolina surgeon Dr. John F. Shaffner wrote home to his friend and future wife Caroline Fries. "Our destination we know nothing of," he admitted, "but are willing to trust to the sagacity of our leader. Our men are in most excellent health and spirits, and when the hour of strife comes will make the enemy feel the effects of strong arms and a righteous cause."[13]

Many of Rodes's Rebels went foraging with varying degrees of success. The meager results garnered by Tom Trotter and Louis Leon of the 53rd North Carolina frustrated both men. Every time they went to a house to get food the residents either ignored their repeated knocking or closed the door in their faces. They finally managed to find two women who would listen to them. Their gracious manners convinced the ladies they were not wild animals or thieves. The residents gave them what they wanted but would not take pay for anything. Other citizens, fearful of the armed enemy soldiers, also freely gave them food and supplies. J. F. Coghill of the 23rd North Carolina wrote his father that the locals "you may believe was very near skerd but wee treated them with respect."[14]

Many Confederates visited a large spring near Greencastle that "breaks out of a rocky hill-side in half a dozen places near together & forms a good large branch," recalled Sam Pickens of the 5th Alabama. "The water is clear as crystal & cold as ice." The commissary staff passed out molasses "& also a small quantity of sundries, such as cigars, smoking & chewing tobacco, a few envelopes, a blank book & a cake of Maple Sugar, where were found, I suppose, in some captured sutler's establishment," he noted with satisfaction.[15]

While Jenkins's horsemen scoured the countryside, several bold citizens were secretly scouting their strengths and movements. John Whitmore, on whose farmland several infantry regiments camped just outside of Greencastle, "counted eighteen pieces of artillery, and estimated the column at thirty thousand," which was considerably more men than Ewell numbered on his muster rolls. When Whitmore's exaggerated report reached Harrisburg, hundreds of frightened residents packed their valuables and left town to seek safer environs.[16]

13 J. F. Shaffner to "My Dearest Friend," June 23, 1863, Fries-Shaffner Papers, SHC-UNC.

14 *Charlotte Observer*, Nov. 16, 1892; Leon, *Diary of a Tar Heel*, 32; J. F. Coghill to "Pappy, Ma and Mit," Jonathan Fuller Coghill Papers, SHC-UNC.

15 Hubbs, *Voices from Company D*, 179-180.

16 *New York Herald*, June 26, 1863. Whitmore owned much of the land immediately east and northeast of Greencastle.

News of Jenkins's return to Chambersburg alarmed the residents of Carlisle, who prepared to defend their town if the Rebels advanced in that direction. Most of the merchants had recently received their inventories back from storage in other cities, but the goods were still not back on most shelves. "To those not willingly blind, it was evident that it was no longer a mere raid . . . and the States of Maryland and Pennsylvania were indeed to be made into the battle-fields," declared S. K. Donivan. The 8th and 71st New York State Militia retreated from Shippensburg to Carlisle," continued the citizen, and Brig. Gen. Joseph Knipe "indicated that a stand would be made by our troops."

Knipe stationed the 8th New York on the Walnut Bottom Road and the 71st on the Valley Turnpike to guard the key southwestern approaches to Carlisle. Soldiers and citizens erected barricades across the two roads and began digging rifle pits on Rocky Ridge. Several townsmen organized themselves into a series of five informal militia companies. Members shouldering muskets included several senior citizens over 65, including the Rev. Francis J. Clerc of the local Episcopal Church and the Rev. Samuel Phillips, who pastored the German Reformed Church.[17]

*   *   *

While Carlisle residents prepared in case Jenkins came calling, Jubal Early's Division followed roads parallel and to the east of Rodes's earlier route toward southern Franklin County. Three of his four brigades marched north through Cavetown toward the state line, with the van tramping through Smithsburg at 9:00 a.m. via the Carlton Road. A reporter in Frederick mentioned that refugees arriving there claimed Early had "16 pieces of artillery, 2 regiments of cavalry, and 11 regiments of infantry, in all about 8,000 men." Trailing them was a train of 80 wagons, most of which were empty, at least until they reached the rich larders of Pennsylvania. After remaining in Smithsburg for almost two hours Early's soldiers "took up their line of march toward Mechanicsville, from which place they would probably take the road leading to Gettysburg."[18]

---

17 "The Invasion," *Carlisle American Volunteer*, July 9, 1863.

18 *Cleveland Plain Dealer*, June 25, 1863; *Chicago Tribune*, June 26, 1863. Union spies confirmed Early's passage and the troop count. According to Bartlett Malone of the 6th NC (Avery's Brigade), the division found a "good meney [sic] Secesh" in Smithsburg. *The Diary of Bartlett Y. Malone* (UNC, The James Sprunt Historical Publications, vol. 16, no. 2, 1919), 36. In Smithsburg, only four miles from decidedly Yankee-leaning Waynesboro, few espoused the

Ringgold was the next town on Early's route. "The nearer we get to the border the more grim the countenances of the people; the pall of death had stricken all these people and though bad enough looking by nature, fear had tortured them into the ugliest of creatures," concluded Robert D. Funkhouser of the 49th Virginia. Early's forces planned to rendezvous at Waynesboro, Pennsylvania.[19]

Brigadier General John B. Gordon's Georgia brigade, part of Early's command, took a parallel route through Leitersburg toward Waynesboro. The farmers "had put up long poles, upon the top of which was mounted an old cow's head with horns," according to the 26th Georgia's Pvt. George F. Agee. "This was for scare-crows, as they called them, to keep the hawks from the chickens. We boys would halloo and ask what had become of old Joe Hooker, and then answer their own question by saying he is on top of the pole. The women would get so red hot," he added, "you could see their eyes sparkle."[20]

Throngs of refugees crowded the country roads ahead of Gordon and Early, including scattered parties of Milroy's defeated force still retreating from Winchester. Anxious to return home, the beaten soldiers pushed their way through throngs of frightened citizens. Shortly before noon civilian scouts raced into Waynesboro with the alarming news that Rebel infantry was approaching. John Philips, the cashier of the First National Bank, hastily gathered up money and valuable documents. He headed east with his wife and son across Monterey Pass to Fairfield in neighboring Adams County. When Philips encountered the regional commander Maj. Granville Haller there, he informed him that 3,000 Rebels occupied Waynesboro.[21]

In the early afternoon General Early established his headquarters in the town hall and placed Waynesboro under martial law. A Confederate flag soon fluttered atop the building while military bands played in the square. Early stripped Chief Burgess Jacob R. Welsh and the town council of civil authority and transferred it to his provost marshal. He instructed former Union soldiers and "stay-at-homes" to canvass the town for bread and meat for his men. Women baked while guards enforced his demands. Some officers accosted Josiah F. Kurtz on the steps of the National Hotel and demanded the names and addresses of the wealthiest citizens.

Union cause. Residents of the two villages often quarreled over secession; see Stoner, *History of Franklin County*, 368. Mechanicsville is present-day Thurmont, Maryland.

19 Hale and Phillips, *History of the Forty-ninth Virginia*, 72.

20 *The Sunny South*, July 20, 1901.

21 Stoner, *History of Franklin County*, 381-382; 369-370; Haller, *Dismissal*, 68.

When Kurtz refused to comply, a Rebel drew a sword and severely gashed his hand. That was enough to send Kurtz out of town for Somerset almost 100 miles distant. Early ordered the bars closed and all whiskey destroyed. Several distillers had hidden or buried barrels of alcohol, but Rebel officers discovered most of the stashes and smashed in the barrelheads. A few drunken "Louisiana Tigers" from Hays's Brigade robbed citizens of clothing, money, watches, hats, and possessions.[22]

Late that afternoon Gordon's Georgians approached the Mason Dixon Line. The 31st Georgia's Gordon Bradwell recounted that a knock-kneed man of German descent in his company with a reputation for shirking battle was "a natural thief . . . a consummate coward and dodger; but when under the influence of spirits a very dangerous man. Some wag dubbed him 'Old Webfoot,' and the name was so appropriate as to stick." A few feet south of the state line sat a substantial residence, "evidently the home of well-to-do people." The German known as "Webfoot" fell out of the ranks of stragglers when he saw the home, entered it, and abruptly demanded food. "The folks treated his request with contempt, refusing to give him anything; whereupon he went through the dining room and pantry, taking the best of what he found. Not satisfied with this," continued Bradwell, "he examined the premises and found concealed in the basement under a quantity of hay a span of splendid dappled iron-gray horses, very suitable for artillery service. This he reported to our quartermaster, whose duty it was to impress horses for the army, and in a short while the horses were led out and inducted into the Confederate service."[23]

The Georgians reached Waynesboro before nightfall and joined in the fun. One officer admitted his part in relieving some "dreadfully frightened" locals of their footwear. "They expected they were to be the victims of the most atrocious barbarity. In Waynesboro, we made the people hand over what boots and shoes they had, also other articles that were needed for the comfort of the soldiers." "The first night we spent in Pennsylvania was between Ringgold and Waynesboro," Pvt. George Agee noted. "Here we drew two days of confederate grub, which was beef and bread." Some soldiers were billeted in area homes, but many slept in open fields and yards. Sixteen-year-old Lida Welsh, daughter of the deposed chief

---

22 Stoner, *History of Franklin County*, 369-378. This account draws upon Lida Welsh Bender's reminiscences, which appeared in the June 24, 1925, issue of *The Outlook*.

23 *Confederate Veteran*, vol. 30, no. 10 (Oct. 1922), 370.

burgess, heard hundreds of men "singing familiar old hymns" after chaplains led them in prayer.[24]

General Gordon wrote his wife that evening that the residents were "indifferent as to the result of the war" and would be delighted to see it end. He mailed Fanny a pair of size-four shoes, a gift from his ordnance officer, Lt. William D. Lyon. They were too large in his opinion, but she could exchange them. He had been unable to find the right size pair of gloves and had also failed in his quest to secure a piece of nice black silk in Maryland because Rodes's command had already swept the area. Gordon and his jubilant but foot-weary Georgians settled down for their first night on Pennsylvania soil.[25]

* * *

Major General J. E. B. Stuart repositioned his brigades. William "Grumble" Jones moved his brigade, along with Chew's battery, north to Snickersville, where it would remain on picket until June 29. Fitz Lee's Brigade, under Col. Thomas Munford, moved into the area to the south of Union in the direction of Middleburg. Stuart retained his remaining three brigades in the area between Rector's Crossroads and Ashby's Gap.[26]

In Berryville, Robert E. Lee's military secretary Col. Charles Marshall composed another order to Stuart to follow up on the one sent the previous day. It is important to quote the message in full:

General:

Your notes of 9 and 10.30 a.m. to-day have just been received. As regards the purchase of tobacco for your men, supposing that Confederate money will not be taken, I am willing for your commissaries or quartermasters to purchase this tobacco and let the men get it from them, but I can have nothing seized by the men.

24 *Mobile Advertiser & Register*, Aug. 9, 1863 (written by "an Alabamian in Lee's army," ascribed to Lt. William D. Lyon); *The Sunny South*, July 20, 1901; Bender, June 24, 1925, *The Outlook*.

25 John Gordon to Fanny Gordon, June 23, 1863, courtesy of Hargrett Rare Book & Manuscript Library, UGA.

26 OR 27, pt. 2, 751; Neese, *Three Years in the Confederate Horse Artillery*, 184; Swank, *Sabres, Saddles, and Spurs*, 71. Stuart's other three brigades were led by Wade Hampton (under Laurence Baker), John Chambliss, and Beverly Robertson.

If General Hooker's army remains inactive, you can leave two brigades to watch him, and withdraw with the three others, but should he not appear to be moving northward, I think you had better withdraw this side of the mountain to-morrow night, cross at Shepherdstown next day, and move over to Fredericktown.

You will, however, be able to judge whether you can pass around their army without hinderance, doing them all the damage you can, and cross the river east of the mountains. In either case, after crossing the river, you must move on and feel the right of Ewell's troops, collecting information, provisions, &c.

Give instructions to the commander of the brigades left behind, to watch the flank and rear of the army, and (in the event of the enemy leaving their front) retire from the mountains west of the Shenandoah, leaving sufficient pickets to guard the passes, and bringing everything clean along the Valley, closing upon the rear of the army.

As regards the movements of the two brigades of the enemy moving toward Warrenton, the commander of the brigades to be left in the mountains must do what he can to counteract them, but I think the sooner you cross into Maryland, after to-morrow, the better.

The movements of Ewell's corps are as stated in my former letter. Hill's first division will reach the Potomac to-day, and Longstreet will follow to-morrow.

Be watchful and circumspect in all your movements.[27]

Lee was giving Stuart absolute discretion to determine the route of his ride. That discretion would soon become the cornerstone of a controversy that rages to this day.

It rained heavily that night. Instead of sheltering in a house, Stuart camped under a tree. His adjutant, Maj. Henry B. McClellan, tried to dissuade Stuart from assuming his soggy bivouac. "No!" exclaimed Stuart. "My men are exposed to this rain, and I will not fare any better than they." Stuart reclined on his oilcloth and fell asleep despite the downpour.

Late that night a courier arrived from Lee carrying an envelope marked "confidential." McClellan opened and read orders from the commanding general. "The letter discussed at considerable length the plan of passing around the enemy's rear," he recalled. "It informed General Stuart that General Early would move upon York, Pa. and that it was desired to place his cavalry as speedily as possible with that, the advance division of Lee's right wing." Although this third letter has never been found, McClellan claimed he recalled its contents clearly:

27 OR 27, pt. 3, 923.

Pvt. Theodore S. Garnett of the 9th Virginia served capably on Jeb Stuart's staff as a clerk and courier. Stuart promoted him to lieutenant in January 1864.

LOC

The letter suggested that, as the roads leading northward from Shepherdstown and Williamsport were already encumbered by the infantry, the artillery, and the transportation of the army, the delay which would necessarily occur in passing by these would, perhaps, be greater than would ensue if General Stuart passed around the enemy's rear. The letter further informed him that, if he chose the latter route, General Early would receive instructions to look out for him; and York, Pa., was designated as the point in the vicinity of which he was to expect to hear from Early, and as the possible (if not probable) point of concentration of the army. The whole tenor of the letter gave evidence that the commanding general approved the proposed movement, and thought that it might be productive of the best results, while the responsibility of the decision was placed on General Stuart himself.

McClellan decided it was best to awaken the sleeping cavalier. Stuart read the orders, cautioned his adjutant about not opening and reading confidential dispatches, and went back to his waterlogged bed. The general was pleased: another ride around and behind enemy lines was in the offing. "Raiding was Stuart's hobby," observed his staff member Theodore S. Garnett, "and one which he rode with never failing persistence. What a glorious opportunity was now offered for the indulgence of his love!"[28]

"I . . . feel not unlike a tiger pausing before its spring, that spring will not be delayed much longer," Stuart had written his brother a few days earlier. His was a reference to Union cavalry commander Alfred Pleasonton and his active and

28 McClellan, *Life and Campaigns of Stuart*, 317-318; James Robbins Jewell, ed., "Theodore S. Garnett Recalls Cavalry Service with General Stuart, June 16-28, 1863," in *Gettysburg Magazine*, no. 20 (June 1999), 48.

diligent cavalry, which had delayed Stuart in his duties. Like a caged tiger, the gray cavalier was eager to escape.[29]

"This has been the most quiet day since the excitement began," Gettysburg resident Sarah Broadhead confided in her diary that night. "I expect news to-morrow, for it has been too quiet to last long."

After his foray to South Mountain, Maj. Granville Haller returned to his headquarters at Gettysburg's spacious Eagle Hotel. He sent a telegraph to York's committee of safety about the recent Rebel movements and authorized some recently arrived survivors of Milroy's 87th Pennsylvania to obstruct the roads in York County leading to Carlisle. Handbills distributed throughout the region announced an order from Maj. Gen. Darius Couch "directing that all horses, except those for cavalry or scouting purposes, and all cattle, be sent north or east of Harrisburg." Many citizens failed to comply with the directive, supposing that the Rebels were far off.[30]

The Rebel movement continued well into the night. Most Pennsylvanians slept blissfully unaware of the scope of the impending gray wave as elements of Jenkins's Brigade washed closer to Chambersburg. "During the night . . . a large body of rebel cavalry passed through the village on down towards Shippensburg," noted Dr. Charles T. McClay of Green Village, north of Chambersburg on the Carlisle turnpike. "Their arms and accoutrements seemed to be all muffled so as to make no noise."[31]

In Virginia earlier that day, A. P. Hill's Third Corps and James Longstreet's First Corps steadily drew closer to Maryland. Lafayette McLaws's Division,

29 Quoted in John W. Thomason, Jr., *Jeb Stuart* (New York, 1934), 412.

30 Broadhead diary, entry for June 23, 1863; Haller, *Dismissal*, 61. Major Haller had previously ordered the 50 or so members of the 87th Pennsylvania that had returned to Adams and York counties to reform in York under Lt. Col. James A. Stahle. See also John Gibson, *History of York County, Pennsylvania* (Chicago, 1886), 175.

31 Hoke, *Reminiscences*, 186.

part of the latter command, camped along the Shenandoah River in rural Clarke County. "Our Army is now a good deal scattered," wrote Lt. William L. Daniel of the 2nd South Carolina. "A part is said to be in Maryland, some in Pennsylvania, and a part in the Valley of Virginia. It is said that Harper's Ferry has been taken by Genl. Ewell who is a perfect Jackson. How true I don't know," admitted the lieutenant. "I don't doubt that Genl. Hooker is sorely puzzled by Genl. Lee who is one of the most consumate Generals of this age, in whom the troops have the strongest confidence."[32]

John B. Hood's Division of the same corps camped near Millwood, a quiet village 13 miles southeast of Winchester. Evander Law's Brigade spent a relaxing day there "on the estate of a wealthy gentleman," recorded the 4th Alabama's R. T. Coles. "There was a magnificent spring on the place, and a large deer park, which contained a herd of English fallow deer." In many places soldiers freely took whatever they fancied, sometimes offering Confederate scrip and often offering nothing. "A ragged, starving soldier in the ranks owes the world no apology for appropriating from the bounty of some one more fortunately situated, that which he needs to sustain his life and keep him fit to march and fight," reasoned Sgt. D. H. Hamilton of the 1st Texas.[33]

"There were many incidents on the route to amuse and depress one," recalled J. B. Johnson, the adjutant of the 5th Florida. "The men were fired by the sight of bare chimneys and ruined homes all through the valley. Just before crossing the Potomac, I met a lady, Miss Kate Seevers of Baltimore, Md., an enthusiastic rebel. She told me that the Marylanders were just waiting to flock to our army, they will join you by the thousands. We had one old man to join us and he had a fit and dropped out the first day," Johnson grumbled, and "that was all I saw of recruits in passing through Maryland."[34]

Tragedy struck as elements of one of Hill's divisions under Richard Anderson prepared to cross the Potomac at Shepherdstown. Pioneers of the 22nd Georgia pressed an old wooden ferry into service to convey Ambrose Wright's Brigade across the rain-swollen river just below the railroad bridge. Designed for 50

32 William L. Daniel, Letter, June 23, 1863, Clarke County, VA, www.soldierstudies.org. Lieutenant Daniel was killed at Gettysburg.

33 Coles, *R. T. Coles' History*, 101; D. H. Hamilton, *History of Company M: First Texas Volunteer Infantry, Hood's Brigade, Longstreet's Corps, Army of the Confederate States of America* (Waco, TX, 1962), 45.

34 Johnson, "A Limited Review," GNMP.

Maj. Gen. William Dorsey Pender
commanded an infantry division
in A. P. Hill's Third Corps.

LOC

passengers, the boat this night carried as many as 150 on each trip. The first round trip concluded without incident. Private William Judkins noticed on the second passage that the vessel was leaking significantly. On its third crossing it suddenly began sinking. The river was 30 feet deep, but somehow the boat only sank about three feet. Private William B. Gray, who had no idea how to swim, managed to grabbed a rope and survive. Thirteen others drowned, including three of the Norris clan from Warren County. Several soldiers clung desperately to those men who could swim, but the combined weight sank them. One soldier somehow swam ashore, replete with his knapsack on his back and his musket strapped around his shoulder, without getting his hair wet. When asked how he accomplished such a feat, he told his amazed comrades that he had been raised close to the Savannah River and knew how to swim. Lieutenant Charles McAfee's legs cramped in the chilly water, but comrades pulled him to the riverbank, where after much rubbing the cramping eased. Most of the bodies were recovered and buried, but the swift current carried some corpses downstream.[35]

Major General William Dorsey Pender, one of Hill's division commanders, wrote to his wife from Berryville. "[Lee] seemed yesterday in fine spirits," he began, "but said he was going to shoot us if we did not keep our men from straggling. They marched finely coming up here. I told him if he gave us authority to shoot those under us he might take the same privilege with us." He continued:

I think our prospects here are very fine. Gen. Lee has completely outgeneraled Hooker thus far and then our numbers are more equal than they have been. It is stated on all sides that Hooker has a small army and that very much demoralized. The General says he wants

35 Wm. Brock Judkins, "Memoirs," Robert L. Brake Collection, USAHEC.

to meet him as soon as possible and crush him and then if Vicksburg and Port Hudson do their part, our prospects for peace are very fine.

Gen. Ewell's Corps is in Md. and ours has started. I will move this evening or tomorrow morning, but will be three days before crossing. Our army is in splendid condition and everyone seems hopeful and cheerful. Cheer up my dear little girl and hope for good things ahead. Ewell captured 31 cannon and 4700 prisoners, but still Milroy claims a complete victory figuring it out that he lost only 300 men and no cannon or arms.[36]

"Order No. 72 of General Lee is being pretty generally carried out. To enforce it strictly, is impossible," wrote a war correspondent traveling with E. Porter Alexander's artillery battalion to the *Richmond Sentinel*. "The doctrine of not using or destroying some of the private property of an enemy while in his country, is a pure abstraction. You cannot possibly introduce an army for one hour into an enemy's country without damaging private property, and in a way often in which compensation cannot be made. . . . When I am hungry, I have a right to eat at an enemy's table, but I have no right afterward to turn round and break up his crockery." The distinction, he continued, "is too manifest to need further illustration; though, simple as it is, it seems not to be comprehended by some of our authorities."[37]

Rumors continued to spread in Europe that key political leaders watching the news of the invasion might soon recognize the legitimacy of the Confederate States of America.

The Paris correspondent of *The Times* of London opined that France's Emperor Napoleon III "would recognise the Confederacy tomorrow if England would join him." The Council of Ministries had met the previous Friday at the Palais des Tuileries to discuss the matter, and the reporter believed the French fully intended "to make fresh propositions to the English government." Other newspapers had earlier reported that Napoleon III had changed his mind on

---

36 Hassler, *One of Lee's Best Men*, 251. Ominously, Pender added that he might not be able to communicate with his wife over the coming summer. The outstanding division commander would be seriously wounded on July 2 and died sixteen days later.

37 "Advance into Pennsylvania," *Richmond Sentinel*, in Frank Moore, ed., *Rebellion Record: A Diary of American Events*, 7 vols. (New York, 1864), 7:324.

American affairs and would not get involved. The wild speculation continued for days.[38]

A loud and often boisterous crowd gathered in Preston, Lancastershire, on Tuesday evening to voice their support for the cause of Jefferson Davis and the Confederates. They passed resolutions urging the House of Commons to recognize the Confederacy and the British government to step in to stop the "disastrous war in America, which entailed so much suffering on the manufacturing districts of England." Opponents instead proposed that neutrality be maintained—a proposal that was rejected out of hand. The meeting grew increasingly raucous but somehow managed to avoid turning into a brawl.[39]

Several London papers advertised a newly arrived two-volume set titled "War Pictures from the South," by Colonel B. Estvan of the Confederate Army. The imported clothbound books published in New York included "eight portraits of the most distinguished Generals and Plans of Battles." No one was selling comparable treatments of Union topics.[40]

While Lee's Army of Northern Virginia steadily marched north, Joe Hooker's Army of the Potomac remained mostly in place guarding the roads leading to Washington while its road-weary troops caught up on much-needed rest. The exception was the cavalry, which continued its series of forays against Jeb Stuart's troopers east of the Blue Ridge Mountains.

A procession of ambulances conveyed more than 200 wounded soldiers from the various battles near the Blue Ridge "over the roughest of roads" toward Fairfax Court House for rail transport to hospitals in Washington. The vehicles passed by the U.S. Christian Commission's headquarters, with about four miles of bumpy corduroy roadway still ahead of them before they reached the train station. The injured men had not enjoyed any food or water since being loaded into the wagons, so the local commission agent rode to the station and had fires kindled and coffee boiled. According to field agent E. F. Williams, workers soon had "bread cut in

---

38 "The American War," *The Manchester Guardian* (Manchester, England), June 23, 1863.

39 *The Standard* (London), June 25, 1863.

40 Ibid., June 23, 1863.

Maj. Gen. Winfield Scott Hancock commanded the II Corps of the Army of the Potomac.

LOC

slices, buttered, and spread with jelly, water brought in, tin cups and sponges made ready." Volunteers spent several hours ministering to the unfortunates, who included Federals as well as Rebel prisoners.[41]

Much of George Meade's V Corps remained in a position to support the cavalry if needed, and June 23 proved uneventful for most his regiments. Several members of the 44th New York went sightseeing. "Not far from our camp at Aldie stood the country residence of President Monroe, then owned by Major Fairfax, who was absent in the Confederate Army," wrote Capt. Eugene A. Nash. "The original proprietor was present to the minds of many, but the present proprietor was absent from sight. Many of our soldiers visited the place and would have been much pleased to have met the proprietor. The country in this part of Virginia is productive and beautiful."[42]

Brigadier General John Caldwell's division of Maj. Gen. Winfield Scott Hancock's II Corps had been occupying Thoroughfare Gap since June 21. Corporal Thomas Meyer and the pioneers of the 148th Pennsylvania received orders to march "into the gap and for a long distance we cut every tree in reach into and across the road, while a brigade had taken position beyond to protect us in our

41 Rev. Edward P. Smith, *Incidents of the United States Christian Commission* (Philadelphia, 1871), 157.

42 Eugene Arus Nash, *A History of the Forty-fourth Regiment, New York Volunteer Infantry in the Civil War, 1861–1865* (New York, 1911), 137. John W. Fairfax purchased "Oak Hill" from the Monroe family in 1852. Mrs. Fairfax invited General Meade to visit the house during the V Corps's stay in the vicinity. The house is nine miles south of Leesburg in Loudoun County along today's U.S. 15. Fairfax served on the staff of James Longstreet as an inspector-general for the latter part of the war.

work. It was wonderful to see how these expert choppers kept the trees crashing in the road, and how cheerfully they worked, in the heat of the summer weather completely soaked with perspiration." Members of the detail cut down a cherry tree and began eating the ripe fruit while Meyer and others climbed a nearby tree. A provost officer rode up and pointed a revolver at the corporal: "Come down, or I will shoot you!" Meyer scoffed in reply: "Captain, we are your prisoners; no doubt you outrank General Hancock, by whose orders were detailed to do some work out here; we are the pioneers of the 148th Pennsylvania Volunteers." Meyer ordered the detachment to fall in. When their axes verified his story the provost captain relented: "I took you for stragglers; the devil take you." As he galloped away the pioneers "gave him a rebel yell, then finished our repast of cherries and returned to camp."[43]

"On the 23d, the supply wagons, from the train, came up to camp and the battery received a fresh supply of forage and rations," remembered Rhode Island artilleryman John Rhodes. "The visitor who, at this moment, would meet the warmest welcome was the post-courier. No mail had been received for the past two weeks and tidings from loved ones at home were greatly missed."[44]

Many soldiers, including the 120th New York's Lt. Edward Ketcham, focused their thoughts on home and loved ones. "I expect Milton [his hometown] is now dressed in its garments of purple and green, the dress it wears in June and among its green leaves and bright flowers, the young almost forget that, down here in Old Virginia, men are marching and fighting and dying and thinking of home and friends," wrote the "fighting Quaker" to his widowed mother. "But there are few that can think of the war without thinking of some friend tramping through the valleys and over the hills of old Virginia. Pshaw! we don't need pity; I am talking nonsense. It is only the young and strong at home, who feel that this fight needs their help, while circumstances they cannot control keep them away, that are deserving of pity!"[45]

Meanwhile, in the Centreville-Manassas region, word spread through Maj. Gen. John Reynolds's I Corps camps that they soon would be moving out. "Received orders to be ready to move. I hope we will not go," admitted Orderly Sgt. Frederick L. Reed of the 14th Vermont. "Nothing new in camp to-day only all

43 Muffly, *The Story of Our Regiment*, 457.

44 Rhodes, *The History of Battery B, First Regiment Rhode Island Light Artillery*, 192.

45 Duganne, *The Fighting Quakers*, 69-70. The 27-year-old Ketcham was killed at Gettysburg on July 2. His brother John of the 4th N.Y. Cavalry died in October in Richmond's Libby Prison.

are wondering where we are going. A. J. D. [his messmate] has gone to bed and I must go. I hope to have a good night's rest."[46]

The men of Brig. Gen. George Stannard's Vermont brigade guarding the approaches to Washington were nearing the end of their nine-month term of service. They had yet to see combat but now, supplied with ten days' rations, they readied themselves for a prolonged march. "And thus, the march that has been so long expected is yet to come. But will it be towards Richmond or Harrisburg?" queried Cpl. J. C. Williams of the 14th Vermont. "The next three weeks will tell. The time has now come when something must be done. The programme is for the present changed, and [I] hope it is to be the closing scenes of the war." Many others shared his hope that this would be the decisive campaign that ended the long and bloody war.[47]

*　　*　　*

While his cavalry rested, Brig. Gen. Alfred Pleasonton intensified his campaign to gain a promotion.

Hooker had endorsed Pleasonton's promotion on June 18 by citing his performances at Chancellorsville and Brandy Station. The promotion finally came through on June 22, and Pleasonton learned of it the next day. The cavalry leader also wanted to add Maj. Gen. Julius Stahel's cavalry division to his corps, but there was a major stumbling block. "With regard to General Stahel he ranks me & if put over me I shall retire," declared the xenophobic officer. In a letter to Republican Congressman John F. Farnsworth of Illinois, Pleasonton claimed that Stahel "has not shown himself a cavalryman & it is ruining cavalry to place it under him." He also claimed that "the guerrillas under Mosby are burning trains . . . & Stahel's force is watching empty air down about Washington," which was patently false. "I will not fight under the orders of a Dutchman," he confirmed. Pleasonton informed the congressman, "If the President prefers General Stahel, let him have all the cavalry, but concentrate it, or when the shock comes between the two armies he will painfully [realize] the truth of what I now tell him." Pleasonton also made a transparent plea to his political patron: "I am sadly in want of officers with the proper dash to command cavalry. . . . [your nephew] Captain [Elon J.] Farnsworth

46 John M. Currier, ed., *Memorial Exercises Held in Castleton, Vermont, in the Year 1885* (Albany, NY, 1885), 57.

47 Williams, *Life in Camp*, 131. The untried brigade would join the I Corps of the Army of the Potomac and would play a considerable role in repulsing Pickett's Charge at Gettysburg.

Representative John F. Farnsworth of Illinois was a political ally of President Lincoln. His nephew Elon was a newly minted brigadier in the Army of the Potomac's cavalry arm.

LOC

has done splendidly—I have serious thoughts of asking to have him made a Brigadier General, what say you?"[48]

The manipulating Pleasonton had the younger Farnsworth of the 8th Illinois Cavalry, who was also one of his staff officers, plead with his congressman uncle to have him promoted to brigadier general as part of his scheme to eliminate Stahel from the command equation. "At this time Stahel has four or five thousand cavalry in and around Washington just doing nothing at all," Elon told his uncle. "Now if you can get the cavalry consolidated and Stahel left out for Gods sake do it. . . . God hardly knows or can imagine the bitter feeling that exists among the officers of this cavalry towards Stahel and those who are trying to set him & other Dutchmen up."[49]

Pleasonton's troopers rested while their commander schemed. The men enjoyed some freedom of movement while in camp, but their company officers called rolls every two hours to ensure they did not stray from camp, where they could be snapped up by Mosby's guerrillas.[50]

* * *

While the Army of the Potomac continued what would mostly be a six-day rest in Virginia, Pennsylvanians scrambled to protect the

48 Pleasonton to John F. Farnsworth, June 23, 1863, Pleasonton Papers.

49 Elon J. Farnsworth to John F. Farnsworth, June 23, 1863, Pleasonton Papers.

50 *The Mount Carroll* (IL) *Mirror*, July 8, 1863.

commonwealth should the Rebels push into its interior. General Couch, a firm believer that this was no mere cavalry raid, ordered farmers in the threatened areas of southern Pennsylvania to move their livestock to safety. If this was not feasible, they were to hide their animals to afford as little aid to the enemy as possible. Private weapons and ammunition were also to be hidden so the Rebels could not confiscate and use them against Union troops. In some cases shotgun- and pistol-wielding civilians openly defied this order by patrolling their towns and guarding roads, public buildings, railroad depots, and bridges. Some 5,000 armed men from the counties bordering the Juniata River filled the mountain passes in the region, hastily erecting works to defend their central Pennsylvania towns. Couch derisively called these untrained civilians "an army of bushwhackers, commanded by ex-officers."[51]

Couch needed officers he could trust, so he appointed Capt. James S. Brisbin of the 6th U.S. Cavalry as chief of cavalry for the Department of the Susquehanna. Brisbin established his headquarters at the sprawling Camp Curtin training facility on the north side of town and began organizing the horse soldiers quartered in that vicinity. "He is said to be an accomplished and experienced officer," noted one reporter. Brisbin had his work cut out for him. Most of the assembled cavalrymen had little experience, especially in combat. Brisbin, an outspoken anti-slavery newspaperman before the war, had already suffered two wounds, the first at Bull Run early in the war and the second in 1862 at Beverly Ford. His cool conduct under fire during the latter fight earned him a brevet to major. No one doubted his willingness or ability to take on the Rebels.[52]

The previous day Governor Andrew Curtin of Pennsylvania had accepted the services of Maj. Gen. William B. Franklin, who had commanded a wing of two corps in the Army of the Potomac at Fredericksburg. The native of York would advise Curtin on military matters and serve as a consultant for the senior officers at the various posts protecting the capital city and environs. Franklin sternly warned his fellow Yorkers about the oncoming enemy: "His invasion will destroy your property, will degrade you and your country, and if allowed to proceed without strenuous resistance, will make you objects of contempt and scorn to your own country, and the remainder of the civilized world."

51 OR 27, pt. 2, 213.

52 "Chief of Cavalry," *Lancaster* (PA) *Inquirer*, June 23, 1863. Brisbin would be wounded again on July 26, 1863, in fighting at Greenbrier, VA, and again in 1864 at the battle of Mansfield, Louisiana.

Franklin toured the lines and met with some of the field officers. More than 12,000 militia now defended Harrisburg. Colonel James A. Beaver, the temporary commander of Camp Curtin, received high marks for his assistance to the new arrivals. "We were under many obligations for his kind attention to all our wants, and the gentlemanly and soldierly treatment received at his hands," declared Col. Watson A. Fox of the 74th New York State National Guard. The sudden influx of soldiers over the past week, however, threatened to overwhelm the infrastructure. Fox noted that each regimental commandant regulated his own campsite and established his own camp guard "without reference to any other regiment."[53]

"There are arrivals of troops daily, both from New York and Pennsylvania; and it is enough to make a Pennsylvanian blush for his State, to see the manner in which New York sends her men into the field," admitted John O. Beck from the 27th Pennsylvania Volunteer Militia's encampment at Bridgeport. "They are splendidly organized and are as fine a looking body of men as can be found. Our militia came here in 'rags and tags,' and, until they don Uncle Sam's uniforms, look but little like soldiers come to defend their own State."[54]

Many of the New Yorkers scorned their recently organized Pennsylvania counterparts. "Candor requires the statement that almost all the other Pennsylvania troops, and some of those from New York State, were of little value in the field," believed Cpl. George Wingate of the 22nd National Guard. "War is a trade, and hasty levies, undrilled and undisciplined, commanded by inexperienced officers, in whom they had no confidence, could not, except behind breastworks, be relied upon to efficiently oppose the largely superior force of Lee's veterans that were in their front." Wingate added, "The men composing the new regiments were plucky and confident—more so, perhaps, than more experienced troops would have been under the circumstances. But they were destitute of discipline, and without that confidence in each other which makes effective troops." The corporal believed he knew the cause:

The great difficulty, of course, was with their officers. The duties which a soldier has to perform in service are often extremely disagreeable, as well as dangerous. Yet, they must be done, and done without hesitation. The habit of command by the officer, and of obedience

53 Ibid., 271; Files of the YCHC. Beaver, who commanded the 148th Pennsylvania, had been wounded at Chancellorsville. He was assigned at his own request to recruiting duty at Camp Curtin while he recovered. He rejoined his regiment just before Gettysburg but was still too weak to assume command during the fighting.

54 *Pottsville* (PA) *Miner's Journal,* June 27, 1863.

by the soldier, which insures their being thus performed, cannot be acquired at once, and yet it is indispensable to a military organization. Where it has to be created, as in the case of hasty levies like those of Pennsylvania, the force, however patriotic, is of little military value when pitted against experienced troops.[55]

55 Wingate, *History of the Twenty-second Regiment*, 162-163.

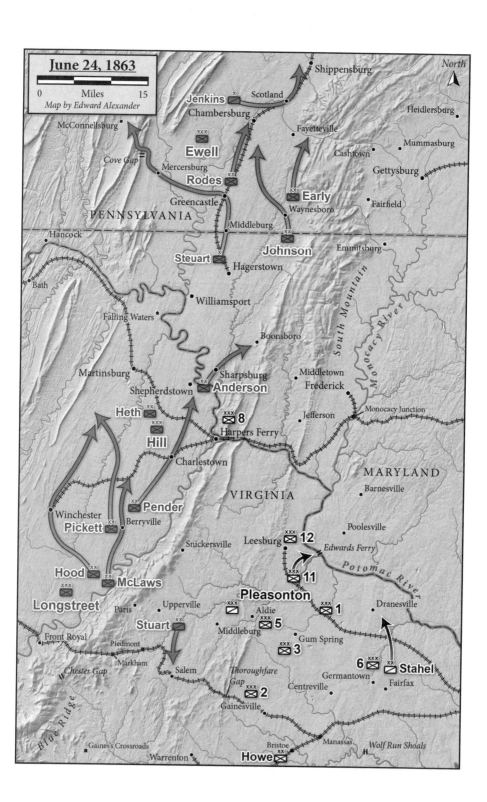

June 24, 1863

0   Miles   15

Map by Edward Alexander

North

Shippensburg

Heidlersburg

McConnellsburg

Scotland

Jenkins

Chambersburg

Fayetteville

Mummasburg

Cove Gap

Cashtown

Ewell

Mercersburg

Gettysburg

Rodes

Early

Fairfield

Greencastle

Waynesboro

PENNSYLVANIA

Middleburg

Hancock

Johnson

Emmitsburg

Steuart

Hagerstown

Bath

Williamsport

Falling Waters

Boonsboro

South Mountain

Monocacy River

Martinsburg

Sharpsburg

Middletown

Frederick

Shepherdstown

Anderson

Heth

Jefferson

Monocacy Junction

Hill

8

Harpers Ferry

Charlestown

MARYLAND

Barnesville

VIRGINIA

Winchester

Pender

Berryville

Poolesville

Pickett

Snickersville

Leesburg

12

Edwards Ferry

Potomac River

11

Hood

McLaws

Pleasonton

Dranesville

Longstreet

Paris

Upperville

1

Aldie

Stuart

5

Front Royal

Piedmont

Middleburg

Gum Spring

Markham

Salem

3

6

Stahel

Chester Gap

Thoroughfare Gap

Germantown

Fairfax

2

Centreville

Gaines's Crossroads

Gainesville

Bristoe

Manassas

Wolf Run Shoals

Blue Ridge

Warrenton

Howe

WEDNESDAY, JUNE 24, 1863

The first gleaming rays of the rising sun peeked over South Mountain into Pennsylvania's verdant Cumberland Valley and illuminated the campsites of Maj. Gen. Robert Rodes's Division near Greencastle. Drumbeats stirred the slumbering men and within minutes breakfast campfires crackled and strong black coffee boiled. Early in the morning the various regiments assembled and began marching northward. George "Maryland" Steuart's mixed brigade of North Carolinians, Virginians, and a small dusting of Marylanders marched alone toward McConnellsburg across Tuscarora Mountain in Fulton County while most of Rodes's troops headed for Chambersburg. "General Ewell passed through town, seated in a carriage, and closely examining a map," reported Greencastle newsman William A. Reid. "He appeared pale and delicate."[1]

The prescribed route guided the long twisting gray column through Marion and other Franklin County hamlets toward Chambersburg, 14 miles north of Greencastle. Major General Edward "Allegheny" Johnson's Division trailed Rodes. "As we would march through the towns the ladies would usually be at the up-stairs windows, waving their Union flags at us. We would laugh at them, but never disturb them," explained Pvt. John O. Casler of the 33rd Virginia, part of the old Stonewall Brigade. "One day there was a very red-headed one at a window, who was very insulting, when the boys got to calling her 'brick-top,' and such names," continued Casler. "She got so mad she fairly frothed at the mouth, and threatened

1 *Greencastle Pilot*, July 28, 1861. "Stuart" is Brig. Gen. George Steuart.

to fire into the ranks. We then tried to persuade her to don male attire and join the army and get satisfaction fighting us."[2]

Private I. J. Watkins of the 14th North Carolina also had a story to tell about a Northern woman. "Bennett Russell was our color sergeant. A brave, good soldier—but plain, homely (well if you must have it), 'ugly as home-made sin,'" admitted the Tar Heel. "A woman standing by the roadside, seeing our uniforms were worn, dirty and ragged, asked Bennett why we did not wear better clothes? Bennett replied, 'We always put on our old clothes in which to kill hogs.' He told her she was the finest-looking and purtiest 'gal' he 'had ever saw' and asked her for a kiss, which she indignantly refused. Bennett and this girl," continued the storyteller, "were two of the ugliest mortals the writer ever saw."[3]

"A great many [Rebels] came to our house for something to eat," Marion farmer Henry B. Hege grumbled to a kinsman. He continued:

> The roads got bad and they threw the fences down on both sides of the road and passed through the fields, so they had three roads along side each other. . . . They took all our corn, about twenty barrels, all our oats, about nine bushels, and nearly all our chickens. They also took mowing scythes and axes and all the salt they could find. Some of the rebels appear to be nice and clever men. Some of them would not harm any man or steal anything, but I tell you, the greatest portion of them were nothing but thieves and robbers and some murderers.

An angry Hege also noted the Rebels wore stolen clothes and hauled their loot in stolen wagons. "We have a good many neighbors that have no horses now. My father says his loss is $2,000 by this invasion of the rebels. They pastured all his hay, burned much of his fence, destroyed a great deal of his grain in the fields, and took 100 bushels of wheat out of the barn."[4]

While foraging for supplies, hungry Rebels marveled at the culinary skills of the farm wives. "Those people make the most delicious bread I ever tasted," a grateful infantryman opined. The women usually devoted one day each week entirely to baking, making all the bread they expected to need in the ensuing week. He believed the soldiers apparently "had reached every farmhouse just after baking

---

2 Casler, *Four Years in the Stonewall Brigade*, 170.

3 Smith, *The Anson Guards*, 200.

4 Henry B. Hege to Henry G. Hege, July 12, 1863, MHACV. Hege's father, also named Henry, was the neighbor of murdered farmer Isaac Strite.

Brig. Gen. Junius Daniel commanded a
brigade in Rodes's Division of
Ewell's Second Corps.

LOC

day." He sated his appetite on "such
oceans of bread I never laid eyes on
before. They supplied us with milk,
butter, and cheese in the most
extravagant abundance."[5]

"The valley was filled with Dutch
ovens," fondly remembered A. R.
Tomlinson of the 4th North Carolina
in Ramseur's Brigade. "The people were Dutch and there were cherries, apple
butter and vegetables galore. In every fence corner for miles we would find a cherry
tree. The command: 'Halt, Stack Arms. Cherry trees. Charge,' would be given." The
unusually relaxed march reminded another soldier of a summer picnic.[6]

Rodes's vanguard reached Chambersburg in the early afternoon. Henry W.
Thomas of Doles's Brigade recalled that "with bands at the head of the regiments
playing Dixie and other Southern airs, arms at the right-shoulder-shift, the boys
stepping out lively to the music, laughing and shouting to the gloomy-faced
citizens, 'Here's your played-out rebellion.' The Northern newspapers had been
trying to bolster up the faith of the Yankees in the success of their cause before this
by publishing that the rebellion was about played out, etc."[7]

The 53rd North Carolina's James E. Green studied the bystanders as his
regiment, part of Junius Daniel's Brigade, tramped into Chambersburg. "We
marched through Town the People looked on us very glum," he recounted. "They
had nothing to say to us only when we spoke to them. But they appeared very
liberel in feeding us, I think it was not out of good will but purely out of feare. For
they think we will treat as our Enemys do us in Eastern N.C. & other places, burn
them out &c." Another Tar Heel, Louis Leon, agreed with Green's assessment

5 *Mobile Advertiser & Register*, Aug. 9, 1863.

6 Tomlinson, "War Experiences of Major A.R. Tomlinson."

7 Thomas, *History of the Doles-Cook Brigade*, 7-8.

when he scribbled in his diary, "Not a smile greeted us as we marched through town." The brigade camped three miles outside of Chambersburg. General Daniel was concerned that Union militia might cause trouble and posted a strong picket.[8]

"Here we saw the old camps of the Pennsylvania 'Melish,' but the militia has fled and we took the town," a Georgian penned. "We marched through in perfect order; not a man allowed to leave his place in the ranks; our colors flying and our bands playing Southern airs. Chambersburg is a beautiful place." The stores had closed and locked their doors but women and men peered from almost every window on the main streets. "Yes, I say men, because they had on all the habiliments of the sterner sex," he mocked, "but they are not such [as] dwell South of the Potomac—or at least, I cannot yet think that there are any such in our land of heroes. Our boys would ask the strong healthy fellows why they were not in the army fighting for their flag and the glorious [Negro] that they love so much." Most of the women had sour expressions on their faces but they did find some Southern sympathizers in Chambersburg, as well as numerous Peace Democrats. "We found very few who wanted the war to go on; that whole country through which our army passed was completely conquered. When, at any time, our men went out from camp to get milk, butter, chickens, or anything they wanted to eat, the citizens would give it to us quickly, showing signs of great fear. Some of the citizens, he added, "had left their homes and gone farther North—for their health we presume."[9]

"We marched through Chambersburg and it is a very nice place but in thare I found a good meny disbanded soldiers from the Yankes army," observed J. F. Coghill of the 23rd North Carolina. "The militia here is going to fight us I suppose but wee will not stop for them I reckond wee will go to Harrisburg the capital of this state and thare wee will have to fight I guess but General Lee sais that he has got the Yankes just whare he wants them it has been a grand move in our army."[10]

Merchant Jacob Hoke watched long columns of infantry and artillery with immense trains of wagons and cattle stream through the streets north toward the Harrisburg Pike. About 10:00 a.m. he saw a carriage drawn by two horses stop in

8 James E. Green, Diary, entry for June 24, 1863, James E. Green Papers, SHC-UNC; *Charlotte Observer*, Nov. 16, 1892; Leon, *Diary of a Tar Heel*, 33.

9 "A Complete and Interesting Account of the Pennsylvania Campaign," *Augusta* (GA) *Chronicle*, Sept. 5, 1863.

10 J. F. Coghill to "Pappy, Ma and Mit," June 25, 1863, Jonathan Fuller Coghill Papers, SHC-UNC.

front of the Franklin Hotel. One of the occupants was "a thin, sallow-faced man with strongly marked Southern features and a head and physiognomy which clearly indicated culture, refinement and genius. When he came out of his carriage it was discovered that he had an artificial limb and used a crutch."

It was General Ewell. The newly elevated corps commander entered the hotel with his staff officers and established his headquarters in the front room. "A man of business," Ewell immediately went to work by ordering the seizure of the large public schoolhouse on King Street for use as a temporary hospital. He requisitioned the hotel owners to provide beds, which were taken to the school for his sick. Ewell also appointed a provost marshal and set up headquarters in the county courthouse. Within minutes a Confederate flag was flapping from its cupola. Chambersburg was an occupied town and would remain so for a week.

Some businessmen and civic leaders had fled at the news of the approach of the Rebels. Ewell summoned the remainder to a meeting in the bank's parlor. Hoke was among those who met with three staff officers. Ewell's men demanded:

5,000 Suits of Clothing, including Hats, Boots and Shoes, 100 good Saddles, 100 good Bridles, 5,000 Bushels of Grain (corn or oats), 10,000 lbs. Sole Leather, 10,000 lbs. Horse Shoes, 400 lbs. Horse Shoe Nails, Also, the use of printing office and two printers to report at once. All articles, except grain, will be delivered at the Court House Square, at 3 o'clock, P. M. to-day, and grain by 6 o'clock, P. M. to-day.

J. A. Harmon, Adj. and C. Q. M. 2nd Corps.

Two other requisitions soon followed:

By the command of Lieut. Gen. R. S. Ewell, the citizens of Chambersburg will furnish the following articles by 3 o'clock this afternoon: 6,000 lbs. Lead, 10,000 lbs. Harness Leather, 50 Boxes of Tin, 1,000 Curry Combs and Brushes, 2,000 lbs. Picket Rope, 400 Pistols, All the Caps and Powder in town. Also, all the Neat's Foot Oil.

By direction of Lieut. Gen. R. S. Ewell, the following are demanded: 50,000 lbs. Bread, 100 Sacks Salt, 30 Barrels Molasses, 500 Barrels Flour. 25 Barrels Vinegar, 25 Barrels Beans, 25 Barrels Dried Fruit, 25 Barrels Saurkraut, 25 Barrels Potatoes, 11,000 lbs. Coffee, 10,000 lbs. Sugar, 100,000 lbs. Hard Bread.

Ewell was far from finished. He prohibited the sale of intoxicating liquors unless one of his major generals stated otherwise in written orders. Anyone who had alcohol in their possession had to submit a list to the provost marshal or

THE REBEL FORAY IN PENNSYLVANIA—GENERAL VIEW OF CHAMBERSBURG.—Sketched by Mr. Davis.—[See Page 656.]

Rebel pickets guarding Chambersburg during Jeb Stuart's raid in October 1862. *Harper's Weekly*

nearest general so that guards could be placed to prevent the soldiers from accessing the liquor. Any violation would render the owners liable to the seizure of the beverages and other personal property. He cautioned the citizenry "to abstain from all acts of hostility, upon the penalty of being dealt with in a summary manner. A ready acquiescence to the demands of the military authorities will serve to lessen the rigors of war."

Confederate guards occupied John F. Croft's wholesale liquor store in one of the rooms of Franklin Hall to prevent looting. Officers, however, often at night, explained Hoke, called on Croft for "a gallon or two for hospital purposes. . . . Either the old and worn out plea of 'a little for the stomach's sake' was employed as a pretext, or else high living and Conococheague [Creek] water did not agree with them."[11]

Civic leaders were unable to meet Ewell's steep demands. Major Wells J. Hawks, the Second Corps's chief commissary officer, warned them, "It will not do for you to say that you can not furnish the articles we require." The result was squads of soldiers roaming the streets collecting the requested provisions. Robert Park of the 12th Alabama recalled General Lee's orders against misconduct and lawlessness. "We cannot afford to make war upon women and children and defenseless men," he reiterated. Misconduct, however, was rampant. "About two, the pillage of our stores began," wrote disgusted 67-year-old shopkeeper William Heyser. "Not a place escaped, never in the history of our boro was there such a scene." Armed soldiers forced storekeepers to "pack up the wagons with their goods, which is being sent to Richmond." Rebels queried bystanders about where

11 Hoke, *Reminiscences*, 47-48.

to find hidden goods. Within hours, Heyser observed, "all of our stores have been ransacked."[12]

Chambersburg's merchants were not the only victims. "The men went off by the scores to the neighboring houses & brought back a great many hens, & milk, butter, &c.," recounted the 5th Alabama's Cpl. Samuel Pickens. Some Confederates offered to pay for their purchases. "The people gave everything to the soldiers as they said our money would do them no good." Among the bounty was "a little apple butter, which was the first I ever saw & it was very nice." My son's mill and warehouse has suffered much from confiscation for which they gave him $800.00 in Confederate scrip," scoffed shopkeeper William Heyser. Topographer Jed Hotchkiss was thinking of his wife as he made the rounds in the occupied city. "I bought about $100 worth of calico, wool delaine, bleached cotton, hoops, gloves, thread, gingham, pins &c &c," he informed her by letter, "which I hope to get home in due time if we stop short of N.Y."[13]

Rumors spread through town that those living in the country were suffering more severely because the roving bands of Rebels could easily venture far from the watchful eyes of Ewell and his provost. "I hear my tenant farmer, Thos. Miller, was shot at while plowing his corn," noted Heyser. "I have felt much concern for him, but cannot get thru the line." "It is out of my power to give any estimate of the value of the property taken that day," admitted Hoke. "This much, however, can be said, that many persons who had toiled and economized for years to gain an honorable support, as well as lay up something for old age, were ruined financially, and although most of them started again in a smaller way, they never recovered from the losses of that day." Rachel Cormany, the Canadian native living in Chambersburg, predicted that "some of our merchants will be almost if not entirely ruined."[14]

Many Confederates, most of whom had never been north of the Mason-Dixon line, were predisposed to mock some of the Pennsylvanians. "Some of the border State, and most of the more southern rebels, have rather peculiar conceptions of the Pennsylvania Dutch," explained a local newsman. "Quite a number were astonished to find our people speaking English, as they supposed that the prevalent language was the German. At first when they attempted derisive remarks, they

12 Park, "The Twelfth Alabama Infantry," 245; Heyser diary, entry for June 24, 1863, 77.

13 Hubbs, *Voices from Company D*, 180; Jedediah Hotchkiss to Sara A. Hotchkiss, June 24, 1863, Augusta County, VA, Letters of the Hotchkiss Family, 1861-1865, VOTS.

14 Heyser, 78; Hoke, *Reminiscences*, 49, Cormany and Mohr, *The Cormany Diaries*, 334.

would imitate the broken English of the Germans; and judging from Ewell's demand for 25 bbls. of sourkraut at a season when it is unknown in any country, even the commanding officers must have considered our people as profoundly Dutch."[15]

The verdant abundance of the region impressed the Southern troops. "We are in the Cumberland Valley," marveled the 14th North Carolina's William A. Smith. "The rich, fertile land is covered with fine growing wheat, the finest ever. Our camp was in a wheat field. What a pity for the wagons, the artillery, the horses and ourselves to destroy it. It could not be avoided." Smith was surprised to find "several Southern sympathizers" there, as well as "some of Howard's corps we fought at Chancellorsville. They told us they did not stop running till they crossed the Rappahannock, and as their enlistment had expired they were now at home and were going to stay. They did not want to meet us again on the field of battle. One gentleman living here said he had three sons in the Confederate army."[16]

"To-day, for the first time, I stand upon Northern soil," marveled Sgt. William S. White of the 3rd Richmond Howitzers, part of Capt. Willis Dance's artillery battalion. "Now the people of Pennsylvania will have an opportunity to sip the sweets of war; let them drink deeply of the bitter cup, for we have well nigh drained it to the bottom." White had celebrated his 24th birthday by crossing into the Keystone State.[17]

General Rodes camped some of his division on Shirk's Hill, two miles south of Green Village on the Chambersburg Road. According to Dr. Charles T. McClay, the Rebels "planted a large number of cannon there. It was their intention to fortify this hill and wait the coming of the Union army. Rev. Wesley Howe, who at that time lived in the Village, had this from the officers, many of whom he knew when preaching in Virginia." Dr. McClay later watched the Rebels hold religious services "in Mr. John Immel's woods near the Village." It was filled, he admitted, with "[f]ine discourse, attentive congregation, and good singing."[18]

* * *

15 *Franklin Repository*, July 15, 1863.

16 Smith, *The Anson Guards*, 200-201.

17 William S. White, *A Diary of the War, or What I Saw of It* (Richmond, VA, 1883), 196-197.

18 Hoke, *Reminiscences*, 186.

Major General Jeb Stuart ordered the brigades of Fitz Lee, Wade Hampton, and John Chambliss to rendezvous at Salem, in northwestern Fauquier County, Virginia. Major John S. Mosby returned from his scouting expedition and reported his findings. "Stuart was anxiously waiting to hear what Hooker was doing," recounted the raider. "He must then have received General Lee's order of 5 p.m., of the 23d, to start the next day and put himself on Ewell's right on the Susquehanna. It gave him the choice of routes—through the Valley by Shepherdstown, or by Hooker's rear. The news I brought of the situation in Hooker's army determined him to take the latter route." Mosby reported that the Army of the Potomac was quiet, waiting to see what Lee's intentions were, and that there was no evidence of movement.[19]

Stuart was especially interested in the positions of the Army of the Potomac's various infantry corps. "They were so widely separated," explained Mosby, "that it was easy for a column of cavalry to pass between them. No corps was nearer than ten miles to another corps. On all the roads were wagon-trains hauling supplies. I pointed out to Stuart the opportunity to strike a damaging blow, and suggested to him to cross the Bull Run Mountains and pass through the middle of Hooker's army into Maryland. There was no force to oppose him at Seneca Ford about twenty miles above Washington—where I had recently crossed" the Potomac River.[20]

Mosby urged Stuart to use Hopewell Gap, which would enable the cavalier to ride between Hancock's II Corps at Thoroughfare Gap and Pleasonton's cavalry at Aldie. This route would avoid the heavily traveled Warrenton Turnpike by passing north of it. Stuart, however, preferred crossing at Glasscock's Gap on the other side of Hancock's position, a route that would have unexpected but significant consequences for his expedition.

"The contemplated enterprise, if it had not been defeated by a cause that Stuart could not control, was far less difficult, and involved far less hazard than the ride around McClellan on the Chickahominy," observed Mosby after the war. Mosby intended to take 20 to 30 of his men the following day and meet the head of Stuart's column 10 or 12 miles south of Aldie on the Little River Turnpike and lead the way toward Seneca Ford. Once his report was filed Mosby and his detachment spent

19 Mosby, *Stuart's Cavalry in the Gettysburg Campaign*, 91-92, 169. Salem is now named Marshall, after the influential Supreme Court Chief Justice John Marshall.

20 Ibid., 26.

the night of June 24 on the western side of the Bull Run Mountains getting ready for the morning's expedition.[21]

Stuart spent much of June 24 preparing operational orders for Brig. Gen. Beverly H. Robertson. Two brigades—Robertson's North Carolinians and William "Grumble" Jones's Virginians—would remain behind to guard the mountain passes. By virtue of seniority the 35-year-old Robertson, recently back with the Virginia army and still despised by Stuart, would command the two brigades. The orders Stuart left him were based on Mosby's recent intelligence report:

Hdqrs. Cav. Div., Army of Northern Virginia, June 24, 1863.
Brig. Gen. B. H. Robertson, Commanding Cavalry:

General:

Your own and General Jones' brigades will cover the front of Ashby's and Snicker's Gaps, yourself, as senior officer, being in command.

Your object will be to watch the enemy; deceive him as to our designs, and harass his rear if you find he is retiring. Be always on the alert; let nothing escape your observation, and miss no opportunity which offers to damage the enemy.

After the enemy has moved beyond your reach, leave sufficient pickets in the mountains, withdraw to the west side of the Shenandoah, place a strong and reliable picket to watch the enemy at Harper's Ferry, cross the Potomac, and follow the army, keeping on its right and rear.

As long as the enemy remains in your front in force, unless otherwise ordered by General R. E. Lee, Lieutenant-General Longstreet, or myself, hold the Gaps with a line of pickets reaching across the Shenandoah by Charlestown to the Potomac.

If, in the contingency mentioned, you withdraw, sweep the Valley clear of what pertains to the army, and cross the Potomac at the different points crossed by it.

You will instruct General Jones from time to time as the movements progress, or events may require, and report anything of importance to Lieutenant-General Longstreet, with whose position you will communicate by relays through Charlestown.

I send instructions for General Jones, which please read. Avail yourself of every means in your power to increase the efficiency of your command, and keep it up to the

---

21 "The part assigned to me was to cross the Bull Run at night with my small force by a bridle path, and uniting with Stuart near Gum Spring in Loudoun take command of his advance guard," explained Mosby. John S. Mosby, "General Stuart at Gettysburg," *Philadelphia Weekly Times*, Dec. 15, 1877; Mosby, *Stuart's Cavalry in the Gettysburg Campaign*, 174.

highest number possible. Particular attention will be paid to shoeing horses, and to marching off of the turnpike.

In case of an advance of the enemy, you will offer such resistance as will be justifiable to check him and discover his intentions and, if possible, you will prevent him from gaining possession of the Gaps.

In case of a move by the enemy upon Warrenton, you will counteract it as much as you can, compatible with previous instructions. You will have with the two brigades two batteries of horse artillery.

Very respectfully, your obedient servant,

J. E. B. Stuart,
Major-General, Commanding

[P.S.]—Do not change your present line of pickets until daylight to-morrow morning, unless compelled to do so.[22]

Jeb Stuart's orders were clear and unambiguous to everyone but Beverly Robertson.

Much remained to be done before a ride of that magnitude could begin. "Three days' rations were prepared, and, on the night of the 24th, the following brigades, Hampton's, Fitz Lee's, and W. H. F. Lee's, rendezvoused secretly near Salem Depot," Stuart would recount in his after-action report. "We had no wagons or vehicles excepting six pieces of artillery and caissons and ambulances. Robertson's and Jones' brigades, under command of the former, were left in observation of the enemy on the usual front, with full instructions as to following up the enemy in case of withdrawal, and rejoining our main army." Fitz Lee's Brigade had to ride from north of Snicker's Gap to the rendezvous point. Stuart was especially pleased to have his protégé and favorite subordinate back in command of his troopers. A bout of rheumatism had kept Fitz out of the saddle for weeks. "This brigade was now for the first time for a month under the command of its noble brigadier," reported Stuart, "who, riding under a painful attack of inflammatory rheumatism, nevertheless kept with his command until now."[23]

The Confederate horsemen camped in a field outside Salem uncertain about what the immediate future held in store for them. They kept their horses saddled so

---

22 OR 27, pt. 3, 927.

23 Ibid., pt. 2, 692. Inflammatory rheumatism is another name for rheumatoid arthritis.

that they would be ready to move on a moment's notice and spent the evening cooking three days' rations. It would be eight long days before they would have the luxury of unsaddling their mounts. "We were about to start on an expedition which for audacious boldness equaled if it did not exceed any of our dashing leader's exploits," Stuart's engineering officer Capt. William W. Blackford would pen years later with the benefit of hindsight.[24]

Stuart was going to take his three best brigades with him, along with his favorite subordinates, and leave Robertson and "Grumble" Jones behind. None of them had any way of knowing that their expedition would turn into one of the most virulent controversies of the entire Civil War.

*   *   *

The excitement in south-central Pennsylvania reached new heights at Shippensburg, Ewell's next objective, with the arrival of Albert Jenkins's Brigade.

"Our forces evacuated Shippensburg today at ten minutes past one o'clock," recorded a correspondent with the *New York Herald.* "The enemy charged into Shippensburg, and the telegraph operator and myself escaped out of the town on a hand car as the enemy was coming in. The enemy fired some volleys, but did no injury that we can hear of. There was a perfect stampede of the citizens of the town. The rebels brag that they will be in Carlisle tomorrow." Some of Jenkins's horsemen pursued fleeing blue troopers along the Pike Roade to Stoughstown, he continued. "We went to Newville, but had to leave that place at six o'clock, as a report came in that the rebels were on the State road, and our forces were below us." The Rebels halted about nine miles southwest of Carlisle at Palmstown, with some Union cavalry fronting them about a mile distant.[25]

Some of the five newly raised home guard companies in Carlisle manned barricaded streets while the rest tramped out of town to reinforce Rocky Ridge, where New York State Militia officers assigned them to freshly dug rifle pits. Pickets deployed a mile in advance to watch for any oncoming Rebels. "It was fully expected that a fight would take place either during the day or ensuing night,"

---

24 Donald A. Hopkins, *The Little Jeff: The Jeff Davis Legion Cavalry, Army of Northern Virginia* (Mechanicsburg, PA, 1999), 144; Swank, *Sabres, Saddles, and Spurs,* 71; Blackford, *War Years with Jeb Stuart,* 221.

25 *Chicago Tribune,* June 27, 1863, quoting the *New York Herald.*

according to S. K. Donivan. Captain William Boyd's detachment of the 1st New York Cavalry picketed the road to Shippensburg.[26]

The *Herald* reporter stopped at Grayson's Station on the Cumberland Valley Railroad about four miles east of Carlisle, which he noted was not secure, with Confederate pickets only two miles from the railroad depot. From there, the harried newsman wired a breathless dispatch to his editor:

> The rebels are taking the hats off people's heads, taking their watches and money, and a great deal of personal property. The rebels arrested Sheriff [J. Thompson] Rippey, of Cumberland county, but released him again. They took his hat away from him. At Newburg and Roxbury the people are in great alarm. In many instances the rebels are acting roughly to citizens, and doing much damage to the telegraph line, and scouring the country for plunder. They are mounting their infantry as fast as they can get their horses for them. There is a fair indication that we will have to skedaddle from here, perhaps to-night.[27]

Chambersburg refugee Amos Stouffer hid with his six horses in the heavily wooded mountains above Newburg. Cut off from reliable news, he occasionally heard rumors of Rebel movements and recorded them in his journal: "A fine day. The Rebs came to Shippensburg to day. They are in strong force—Cavalry, Infantry & Artillery—the whole under the command of Lee, Commander in Chief of the Rebel Army. This is no mere raid. It is a formidable invasion. Self at the mountain with a farmer by the name of Pie. Our forces at Harrisburg are under McClellan." Stouffer had no way of knowing the rumor was untrue; Darius Couch, not Little Mac, was in charge at Harrisburg.[28]

Rumors that George McClellan was in command refused to die. Matthew Hale Smith, a correspondent for the *Boston Journal* stationed in New York City who wrote under the penname "Burleigh," commented about Gov. Andrew Curtin's recent call for volunteers. "Burleigh" believed that if Lincoln issued an order that McClellan was to muster all the men he could gather and march at once to

---

26 Donivan, "The Invasion," *Carlisle American Volunteer,* July 9, 1863.

27 *Chicago Tribune,* June 27, 1863, quoting the *New York Herald.* Grayson's Station was near New Kingstown in Silver Spring Township. Skedaddle they did. The local telegrapher made good time on a hand-pumped conveyance. "The Shippensburg operator has just arrived at Newville, a distance of eleven miles from the former place," recorded another reporter. "He came the eleven miles on a hand car in fifty minutes."

28 Stouffer diary, entry for June 24, 1863.

Harrisburg to assume command there, 50,000 volunteers would be ready to follow him within just 12 hours. Mustered-out soldiers would return to the army by thousands, if only McClellan would lead them. "Other accounts corroborate this," he claimed. "But the malignant abolitionists who control the administration will heed no such wishes. They would sooner have our army defeated and see Pennsylvania laid waste by rebel invasion, than to owe victory to the hated McClellan." Warmed up, Burleigh continued. "They will never consent to restore him to command until their own practical safety is imminently endangered—until they think Washington can be saved in no other way," declared the correspondent. "Then the cowardly malignants would get down on their knees and crawl upon their bellies to him and implore him to save them again from merited destruction."[29]

Like Amos Stouffer and other anxious Cumberland Valley residents, the president of the United States wanted solid information about what was happening. "Have you any reports of the enemy moving into Pennsylvania? And if any, what?" a frustrated Abraham Lincoln wired General Couch. The need for reliable military intelligence was of paramount strategic importance. "Rebel cavalry are this side of Chambersburg," Couch replied at 9:30 a.m. "Scouts from Gettysburg report 7,000 at Greencastle. Deserters say A. P. Hill and Longstreet are across the Potomac; 40,000." Lincoln relayed Couch's alarming report to General Hooker early that afternoon.[30]

*   *   *

General Ewell's entire corps was now in Pennsylvania. Well to the southeast of Chambersburg, Jubal Early's infantry division advanced from Waynesboro north through Quincy and Mont Alto with bands playing and flags unfurled as it tramped along the Chambersburg-Gettysburg turnpike. The 31st Georgia's Cpl. Joseph H. Truett expressed his overall satisfaction with the campaign in a letter home: "We lived on the best that there was in the state and when we would get to a town we would press all of the sugar,

29 *New Hampshire Patriot & State Gazette*, June 24, 1863. Matthew Hale Smith was a Maine-born Unitarian minister and journalist in New York City who sent several letters to the *Boston Journal* during the war years.

30 Basler, Pratt, and Dunlap, *The Collected Works of Abraham Lincoln*, 6:293.

Brig. Gen. George P. Doles led a brigade in Rodes's Division of Ewell's Second Corps.

LOC

coffee, and whiskey and shoes that was in the towns. We took wagons, horses, beef cattle and every thing that we wanted to supply the army."[31]

General Early halted at Greenwood about eight miles east of Chambersburg in the afternoon shadows below Chestnut Ridge. His soldiers, like their counterparts in Rodes's Division, immediately began foraging. "Our quartermaster and commissary departments took every cow, sheep, horse, mule and wagon that they could lay their hands on, besides bacon and flour," declared the 61st Georgia's Pvt. G. W. Nichols. "Officers strictly prohibited foraging among the men in line—The cavalry and commissary department did this work. We boys, with guns, had more strict orders here than we ever had in our country; we just had to stay in line, and sometimes we almost suffered for water." According to Lt. Robert D. Funkhouser of the 49th Virginia, the locals were "frightened to death, trunks found hid in woods by men and they think that we were going to burn, plunder, rob and rape everything in our way."[32]

Early dispatched reconnaissance patrols east through the South Mountain gaps toward Gettysburg to determine whether there was any Union resistance in the area. "As I expected, the Rebels have, several times, been within two or three miles, but they have not yet reached here," Gettysburg resident Sallie Broadhead recorded in her diary. "The town is a little quieter than on yesterday. We are getting used to excitement, and many think that the enemy, having been so long in the vicinity

31 White, *This Most Bloody & Cruel Drama*, 84.

32 Nichols, *A Soldier's Story of His Regiment*, 115; Hale and Phillips, *History of the Forty-Ninth Virginia*, 73.

without visiting us, will not favor us with their presence. They have carried off many horses," she added. "Some, who had taken their stock away, returned, supposing the Rebels had left the neighborhood, and lost their teams."[33]

James W. Beck of the 44th Georgia, part of Brig. Gen. George Doles's Brigade, wrote a letter home. "We remained here until the morning of the 23rd (yesterday), and then started for Pennsylvania. We are now in the United States—the Yankees have been trying to whip us into the Union for two years and more, but have signally failed. We have whipped them and marched into the Union." The army, he continued, "is flushed with victory. We have marched over two hundred miles, and are in just as good condition to-day as when we left our camp on the Rappahannock."[34]

Like so many others, Ewell also took a few moments to write to his wife "Lizzie" that evening. "It is wonderful how well our hungry, foot sore, ragged men behave in this land of plenty—better than at home," scrawled the proud general. "The worst behaved men I have are the Marylanders who seem wild with the excitement of getting near home.—One of them just returned from a scout told me the ladies all send me word that if I go where they are they will give me no quarter in their delight at meeting me.—What a pity a Bachelor could not have such an offer." His wife had relatives in York, 55 miles east of Chambersburg. "It is like renewal of Mexican times to enter a captured town," he continued. "The people look as sour as vinegar, and I have no doubt would gladly send us all to kingdom come if they could. I don't know if we will go to York—yet—anyhow we will be tolerably close to it. I will let your relations off tolerably easy, on your account—probably not taking more than a few forks and spoons and trifles of that sort—No houseburning or anything of that sort."[35]

Most of A. P. Hill's Third Corps was much farther south of Ewell's three divisions and was just reaching the Potomac River. Dorsey Pender's Division, which trailed Richard Anderson's Division in the marching order, arrived at Shepherdstown and camped near Boteler's Ford. Once in camp the religious-minded Pender composed a long letter to his wife. "Tomorrow I do what

---

33 Broadhead diary, entry for June 24, 1863, GNMP.

34 William B. Styple, ed., *Writing & Fighting from the Army of Northern Virginia: A Collection of Confederate Soldier Correspondence* (Kearny, NJ, 2003), 237.

35 Ewell to "Lizzie," June 24, 1863, Chambersburg, PA, Richard S. Ewell Papers, LOC, copy at GNMP.

I know will cause you grief, and that is to cross the Potomac," he began. "The advance of our column," he continued,

> is at Chambersburg, Penna. tonight. May the Lord prosper this expedition and bring an early peace out of it. I feel that we are taking a very important step, but see no reason why we should not be successful. We have a large Army that is in splendid condition and spirit and the best Generals of the South. Our troops are sending [a] great deal of stock out of Penna. and Gen. Lee has issued [an] order which altho' [it] prevents plundering, as the same [time] makes arrangements for the bountiful supplying of our people.
>
> The inhabitants of this part of the country are very enthusiastic in our favor. We hear all sorts of reports of rebellions in Baltimore, etc. but how true they are of course [we] cannot know. One thing is certain, however, and that is that the General commanding the Federals is much scared and asking for reinforcements. No one seems to know where Hooker is, only [that] he is between us and Washington. I hope the conflict will soon come off, for I feel that the first battle is to settle the campaign, at least until they are able to get forces from the West.

"Hope and pray for the best," Pender concluded. "This is a momentous time but at the same time we are in better condition to meet it than we have ever been."[36]

"Crossed the Potomac at 7 a.m. Halted until our Division got cross. My horse fell in the river and hurt his knee," groused Adjutant A. L. Peel of the 19th Mississippi, part of Anderson's Division of Hill's Corps. "Passed through Sharpsburg at 1 p.m. through Cheatersville at 2 p.m. saw only two C.S. Flags. The women looked sour." "The portion of Maryland through which we passed was strongly 'Union' in sentiment," declared Quartermaster Sgt. Francis P. Fleming of the 2nd Florida. "We have a great many friends and sympathizers in Hagerstown. It was very gratifying to observe that in nearly every case the intelligent and higher class were our friends, while the lower class and the ignorant were unionists."[37]

A Georgian in the same division also described the army's morale as high. "The army is in fine spirits and confident of victory," he declared. "The men have stood the march better than expected, considering the oppressive heat and choking dust. Although General Lee has a large army, still success would be more certain if he

36 Hassler, *One of Lee's Best Men*, 252.

37 Peel diary, entry for June 24, 1863; Francis P. Fleming to brother, June 30, 1863, "Francis P. Fleming in the War for Southern Independence: Letters from the Front," *Florida Historical Quarterly*, vol. 28, 143. There is no such place as Cheatersville, Maryland. Peel was probably referring to Keedysville, Maryland, which is adjacent to Sharpsburg and the Antietam battlefield.

had a larger one." Many of the soldiers who had gone home on sick leave or to recuperate from combat wounds had not returned to the Army of Northern Virginia, he scoffed, and were "enjoying the ease and luxury of home, while their comrades have to fight their battles with diminished ranks. It is hoped that the enrolling officers will send the laggards back to their duty."[38]

Harry Heth's Division, which brought up the rear of Hill's Corps, was still in West Virginia. "Marched in rear of our div. today as rear guard," noted sharpshooter Robert T. Douglass of the 47th Virginia. "Went through Charlestown, that memorial spot where old John Brown was hung. We have now stopped about 2 ½ miles from Shepherdstown to bivouac for the night. Quite pleasant." He and his comrades looked forward to crossing the river into Maryland in the morning.[39]

Plenty of Confederates were already roaming the Old Line State. "Foraging parties are scouring the country in every direction, and seizing all the horses and cattle they can lay their hands upon," noted a reporter in Frederick. "Several thousand head of cattle have been gobbled up by the rebels in Washington county, and a great many have been driven across the river at Williamsport, to feed that portion of Lee's army which remains on the other side." The newspaperman added an ominous warning to his readers: "The rebel commanders have promised their soldiers that the moment they touch Pennsylvania soil all restraint upon them shall be removed, and they shall have unbridled license to plunder and devastate the country they pass through. The late movement of their cavalry into Pennsylvania, the rebels say, was intended merely as a feeler, but that this time Pennsylvania shall be taught the horrors of war in good earnest." One reason for the Confederates' cockiness was the perception of their likely foes: the hastily trained militia forces collected by Governor Curtin. "The rebels have a poor opinion of the troops assembled at Harrisburg," continued the paper, "characterizing them as unorganized, undisciplined men, who will oppose no serious barrier to their successful march through Pennsylvania."[40]

* * *

38 Styple, *Writing & Fighting from the Army of Northern Virginia*, 236.

39 Douglass diary, entry for June 24, 1863.

40 *Chicago Tribune*, June 26, 1863.

Maj. Gen. John A. Dix commanded the VII Corps in the Department of Washington and threatened Richmond from the east.

LOC

Down in the Shenandoah Valley, Lafayette McLaws's Division of Longstreet's First Corps arrived at Summit Point, West Virginia, and John Bell Hood's Division reached Bunker Hill. Concurrently George Pickett's Division, the third in Longstreet's Corps, marched from Berryville to Darkesville. During the afternoon Maj. Gen. Isaac Trimble caught up with Lee's headquarters near Berryville. The 61-year-old officer had spent the better part of a year recovering from a shattering leg injury suffered at Second Manassas. Now he was in search of a command and doing his best to rejoin the army. "You are tired and hungry," Lee told the supernumerary general after an exchange of pleasantries. "[I]f you will step down to the mess you may find some remains of a fine mutton which kind friends have sent us, and after eating come up and we will talk." It was only after he had dined that Trimble learned that he would not be restored to his former command. As tactfully as possible, Lee explained that he "had no time to wait for you, but you must go with us and help us conquer Pennsylvania."[41]

*   *   *

The movements by Maj Gen. John A. Dix's command in Virginia triggered an alarm in Richmond. Reports soon arrived that Union forces had landed on the James and York rivers. With most of the Confederate troops well north of the Potomac, Gov. John Letcher called for citizens to assemble at Capitol

41 Isaac R. Trimble, "The Battle and Campaign of Gettysburg," *SHSP*, vol. 26. Later in the day, Lee moved his headquarters north to near Martinsburg.

Square at 7:00 p.m. "There was also a meeting of the clerks of the departments, and it was agreed that at the sounding of the tocsin (alarm bell) they should assemble (day or night) with arms at their respective offices," war clerk John B. Jones wrote in his diary. "If some 30,000 of the enemy's troops make a dash at Richmond now, they may take it. But it will, of course, be defended with what means we have, to the last extremity."[42]

In Europe, meanwhile, newspapers craved any and all information they could get so they could inform their readers about the potentially war-changing developments as Lee moved northward. A newsman in Londonderry, Ireland, interviewed passengers from New York disembarking from the steamship *Jura* about the latest war news. Unfortunately, he concluded, "the intelligence by this arrival is entirely destitute of anything definite or important." Jeb Stuart had apparently been foiled in his attempt to make an incursion into Pennsylvania and General Lee, with a strong force of infantry, was last reported at Culpeper Courthouse in north-central Virginia. Lee had left a strong force at Fredericksburg and "made a movement with the design of destroying Hooker's army." The information, whatever it was worth, was more than a week old.[43]

Also on June 24, a pro-Confederate paper in Derby, England, lambasted a pro-Lincoln orator who had spoken recently in the local guild hall. The editor called the speaker "the weakest of the many weak agitators who urge the prosecution of the atrocious war in America." He castigated the "corrupt and incompetent government of Abraham Lincoln in carrying on the war which is desolating thousands of homes and making beggars of millions." As the newsman listened to the speaker, he was "irresistibly reminded of the bombastic boasts of Hooker —the famous general who never conquered anything but good taste and common sense." He finished his criticism by declaring that "nine-tenths of the people of Derby, aye of England too, believe that in denouncing the American war they denounce the most cruel, blood-thirsty, and useless struggle that has ever saturated soil with human blood, and hardened the sinful heart of man."[44]

42 Jones, *A Rebel War Clerk's Diary*, 1:359-360.

43 *The Freeman's Journal* (Dublin, Ireland), June 24, 1863.

44 "The Northern Champion," *The Derby Mercury* (Derby, England), June 24, 1863.

With Rebels running amok in Fulton and Franklin counties, some Northern newspapers castigated what appeared to be an abject lack of response to Governor Curtin's call for men to join the state militia. "I hardly like to say it, and still less do I like to believe it, but it is an incontestable fact, that the spirit of the people is not what it should be," declared an alarmed *New York Times* correspondent. "They do not come up to the crisis. Various reasons are assigned for this, but it seems to me that they are all superficial. . . . At the bottom there must be a want of heart in the cause. Excuses are plenty to those who are willing to hunt for them. But if a man is imbued with the true fire of patriotism, he wants no excuse. There are men enough here who are willing to go into the trenches and shoot their muskets off to save their property, but few who are willing to volunteer for the defence of their country. It is true," he questioned, "that Pennsylvania has given as many men as any State, to the cause of the Union; but has patriotism died out?"[45]

The *Times* reporter's opinion echoed what some leaders were thinking in Pennsylvania's border towns. In York, young Republican lawyer James Latimer lamented the lethargy among civic officials. "The latest intelligence we have here of the rebels is that they are at Shippensburg advancing towards Carlisle. There is little or no excitement here," he wrote in a letter to a family member. "We have mounted men out in the direction of Carlisle but no preparation for defence here." Latimer's emotions spilled through his pen. "There is the most extra-ordinary apathy with regard to this invasion," he grumbled. "If the information we have here is reliable we may have an attack on Harrisburg in a day or two, and yet nothing is being done here. We have sent one Company. I put my name down to another but it fell thro: If men won't go to the defense of their own State they don't deserve to be called patriots. I am ashamed of myself and my town."[46]

Some business and civic leaders in York and elsewhere did express strong concerns that the Rebels planned a major push toward the Susquehanna River. Authorities in several river towns accosted any person who seemed suspicious or out of place. "Numerous arrests have been made to-day on the south side of the river of parties suspected of being rebel spies and guerillas, but on the cases being

45 "The Spirit of the People," *New York Times*, June 26, 1863.

46 James W. Latimer to Bartow Latimer, June 18, 1863, York, PA, YCHC.

investigated, most of them proved to be refugees," observed a Harrisburg reporter. "The works on the opposite side of the river have been completed and guns are being mounted." Veterinary surgeon J. K. Martin found himself under arrest for uttering disloyal sentiments, and only received his discharge after he swore an oath of allegiance to the Federal government.[47]

"The opinion of Generals Franklin and Couch is that the rebels are now advancing with serious intent upon the State Capitol," reported a newsman in Harrisburg. "Their move is necessarily slow, as the cavalry march with the infantry. Every preparation has been made to give them a proper reception, and our soldiers are buoyant with the hopes of a speedy brush. The people are passive under the exciting intelligence."[48]

By June 24 the New York troops near Harrisburg had settled in at Fort Couch, situated in a hillside clover field on Hummel's Heights overlooking the Susquehanna. One of its new inhabitants, L. T. Hyde of the Brooklyn City Guard, took a few minutes to write home. "The camp begins to look more settled now," he began. "We have succeeded in flooring our tents comfortably. We can show no fancy appearance of Camp as it is on the summit of a very high hill about two hundred feet high above the Susquehanna. There is not a level spot in it, and every parade drill or sentry walk has to be with one foot much lower than the other. The Harrisburghers are a queer people," he concluded. "They walk around gaping at the fine looking New Yorkers. They don't seem inclined to do anything for their own defense, and manifest an apathy about it which the men of ours don't like at all."[49]

The 22nd National Guard's George Wingate also took a dim view of Harrisburg's citizens. "On June 24, the regiment was sworn in for thirty days. Although the roofs and spires of Harrisburg were in plain sight, there was but little desire to visit it. Its residents had not received the New Yorkers with the enthusiasm they had expected, and which they had received in Philadelphia. Besides," groused Wingate, "its storekeepers were unable to resist the temptation to make money out of their defenders, and put up their prices to 'all that the traffic would stand.' Fifteen cents for a cup of rye coffee, five cents for a glass of water, exorbitant charges for anything that the soldiers wanted, and an apparent general

---

47 *Chicago Tribune*, June 27, 1863.

48 Ibid.

49 L. T. Hyde, "Campaign of Brooklyn City Guard, June & July 1863: Memoranda & Extracts made by L T Hyde from his letters," Keith R. Keller Collection, USAHEC.

Maryland Heights was a key part of the Union defenses of Harpers Ferry, West Virginia. *LOC*

indifference as to which side would be the victors in the impending contest, soon put an end to any rush for the few passes that were issued."

From the hilltop fortifications along the York Road, Wingate noted that the stream of refugees, "steadily increasing, began to sweep by the camp of the Twenty-second, and in a short time every road leading to the bridge crossing to Harrisburg became blocked, by day and night, with fugitive farmers, driving their flocks and herds, and followed by wagons, piled high with their most precious household goods, showing that the enemy were rapidly approaching. Horses became such a drug in the market that several officers purchased them for from $10 to $15 each."[50]

While efforts continued to defend the river crossings fronting the capital, concerns grew in Maryland. Might the Confederates, as they had done in September 1862, threaten Harpers Ferry? "Orders received from General Hooker to evacuate the Maryland Heights," reported Charles Lynch of Robert Milroy's 18th Connecticut. Lynch's survivors had marched there following the debacle at

50 Wingate, *History of the Twenty-second Regiment of the National Guard*, 173.

Second Winchester on June 15. "All supplies and munitions that could be moved loaded on canal boats and taken to Washington by way of the Ohio & Chesapeake Canal. Great quantities of stores was left, salt beef, pork, beans, rice, coffee, and sugar. Some of it was gathered up by the people from Harper's Ferry." Confederate cavalry would later seize 15 abandoned canal boats and help themselves to the supplies before torching the vessels. The remnants of the shattered 18th Connecticut, 12th West Virginia, and 5th Maryland left the ferry to march to the District of Columbia. Like the rest of his former division of the VIII Corps, they would never again serve under the discredited General Milroy.[51]

The *New York Herald* continued to denigrate Milroy. "Why is he not brought to account by the War Department for the shameful loss of his post?" thundered its editor. "Why does not General Schenck place him under arrest and have him tried by court martial?"[52]

*   *   *

Many of the Union soldiers still in Virginia continued to question their destination and objectives. Part of Maj. Gen. Samuel Heintzelman's XXII Corps, a reserve unit organized in February 1863 from fresh recruits and several regiments of former prisoners of war, had been camping for several months near Centreville to guard the approaches to Washington City. "There is a thousand & one Rumors about where, we are going too, some say to the Peninsula, to join Hooker [and] everything else," wrote the 111th New York's Cpl. Manley Stacey. Tired of being jeered by Hooker's veterans as "fresh fish," Heintzelman's men itched for combat duty. Some of the older regiments, including Stacey's, had surrendered to Stonewall Jackson at Harpers Ferry the previous fall. They eagerly desired a chance to erase that stain and prove their moniker of "Harper's Ferry Cowards" unwarranted and undeserved. "When we move from here, it is good bye to White Gloves, then we will be Real Soldiers, not make believe," hoped Stacey. The corporal and his comrades would get their wish, for

---

51 Lynch, *Civil War Diary*, 24.

52 "How Milroy Was Surprised," *New York Herald*, June 24, 1863. Milroy spent the rest of the year and the first part of 1864 trying to justify his actions at Winchester and regain a field command. Lincoln eventually sent Milroy to Tennessee, where he was put in charge of troops defending the railroads against Nathan Bedford Forrest's Confederate horse soldiers.

George Willard's brigade was about to be transferred to the II Corps of the Army of the Potomac.[53]

Joe Hooker's army created significant consternation for the residents of northern Virginia, especially those deemed secessionists. "Nothing is going on along the lines worth mentioning except that the boys are prety well supplied with fresh meat," wrote an Indiana officer. "A certain man along the lines refused to take the oath of allegiance. The safe guard was taken from his property, and the boys told to help themselves."[54]

The raids on food supplies and wanton thievery strained relations between the local populace and the Union troops, as did suspicions within the ranks that some of the citizens were covertly aiding Confederate partisan rangers. "Rumors of deaths in the First corps from sunstroke are entirely unfounded, as are the exaggerated camp rumors of throat cutting by guerillas," declared a soldier named W. Young to the *New York Herald*. "Citizens are arrested and held in custody temporarily to prevent guerilla operations if possible."[55]

"The Regiment had four days of rest while in the vicinity of Thoroughfare [Gap]," recounted John Day Smith of the 19th Maine. "During this time the boys of the Regiment gathered and cooked green apples which afforded a change in the monotony of their diet. The apples of course were very small, but when cooked, they were very palatable. Other changes in diet also were noticeable," joked Smith, "to which changes the farmers in that locality unwillingly contributed." The Maine soldier also noted a command change when Brig. Gen. Alexander S. Webb was assigned to command the Philadelphia Brigade at Thoroughfare Gap. "He had been an officer of ability in the regular service, and his force of character and personal gallantry . . . contributed in no small measure to the renown of the Second Corps."[56]

At Centreville, Thomas Aldrich of Battery A, 1st Rhode Island, was sent with the wagons to hunt up forage and rations. The teamsters were upset because Rebel raiders had stolen a couple of their vehicles. "These men on the wagon trains were the worst lot I ever saw," griped Aldrich. "Even the mules seemed to know that there was trouble on foot, and appeared to be as excited as their drivers. After

53 Manley Stacey to Dear Father, June 24, 1863, Centreville, VA, HSOPRF.

54 Weist diary, entry for June 24, 1863.

55 *New York Herald*, June 25, 1863.

56 Smith, *The History of the Nineteenth Regiment of Maine Volunteer Infantry*, 57-58.

waiting a long while we at last succeeded in getting our load. The clerks were apparently as thoroughly frightened as the drivers, and, by their actions, expected every moment to be captured." The "trouble" proved to be a raid near Fairfax Station, where some Rebels dashed in and cut a few telegraph wires.[57]

"Aldie Gap again," the 11th U.S. Infantry's Dr. John Billings informed his wife. "We are still under our shelter tents just as we were dumped down three days ago—no news, no mail, nothing to eat but ham, hard bread and coffee—but the weather is pleasant, wood, water and grass are plentiful and there is no dust. The wicked rebellion still flourishes and J. Hooker, Esqr., is reported as being in good health and spirits. . . . We have no prospect of a move for a day or two, the Rebs show no disposition to attack, and J. Hooker, Esqr., is very comfortable where he is."[58]

"About midnight the bivouac of the 2nd Division was rudely disturbed by hideous outcries, followed by the noise of men rushing hither and thither amount frightened mules and horses," remembered Francis Walker, the II Corps's assistant adjutant general, after the war. "Headquarters turned out in dire alarm, and the soldiers, waked suddenly from the deep slumber that follows a painful march, seized their arms. The coolest believed that a band of guerillas hanging upon the flanks of the column had taken advantage of the darkness to dash among the sleeping troops. At last it turned out that all the fright sprang from a soldier being seized with a nightmare from which he waked screaming."[59]

* * *

Command changes rippled through the ranks of the Cavalry Corps as well when Col. John B. McIntosh returned to duty and assumed command of Brig. Gen. David M. Gregg's 1st Brigade.

Brigadier General John Buford's three mounted brigades began scouting the northern regions of Loudoun County in anticipation of the Army of the Potomac's advance to the Potomac River. William Gamble sent the 12th Illinois Cavalry to Leesburg, while most of Thomas Devin's small brigade reconnoitered that night through the small towns of Hamilton and Leesburg. The rest of the units

---

57 Aldrich, *The History of Battery A, First Regiment Rhode Island Light Artillery*, 188.

58 Garrison, *John Shaw Billings*, 57.

59 Francis A. Walker, *History of the Second Corps of the Army of the Potomac* (New York, 1886), 258.

Col. John McIntosh commanded the 1st Brigade, 2nd Division of the cavalry of the Army of the Potomac.

LOC

comprising the Cavalry Corps rested while Alfred Pleasonton waited to see whether his scheming and conniving would pay off.[60]

*　　*　　*

While the men in the Army of the Potomac were settling into their camps, Secretary of the Navy Gideon Welles was writing in his diary. "No definite or satisfactory information in regard to military movements. If it were clear that the Secretary of War and General-in-Chief knew and were directing military movements intelligently, it would be a relief," he continued,

> but they communicate nothing and really appear to have little or nothing to communicate. What at any time surprises us, surprises them. There is no cordiality between them and Hooker, not an identity of views and action, such as should exist between the general in command in the field and the Headquarters and Department, separated only a few miles. The consequence is an unhappy and painful anxiety and uncertainty, the more distressing to those of us who should know and are measurably responsible, because we ought to be acquainted with the facts. Were we not in that position, we should be more at ease.[61]

The Rebels were already in Pennsylvania in strength, and Welles believed Stanton and Halleck were dithering, and General Hooker was little more than a liability. His candid outlook reflected much of the North's attitude as Richard Ewell's soldiers enjoyed the bounties of the Cumberland Valley unimpeded.

60 *The Mount Carroll* (IL) *Mirror*, July 8, 1863; Brooke-Rawle, *History of the Third Pennsylvania Cavalry*, 253; Abner Frank diary, entry for June 24, 1863.

61 Welles, *Diary*, 1:342.

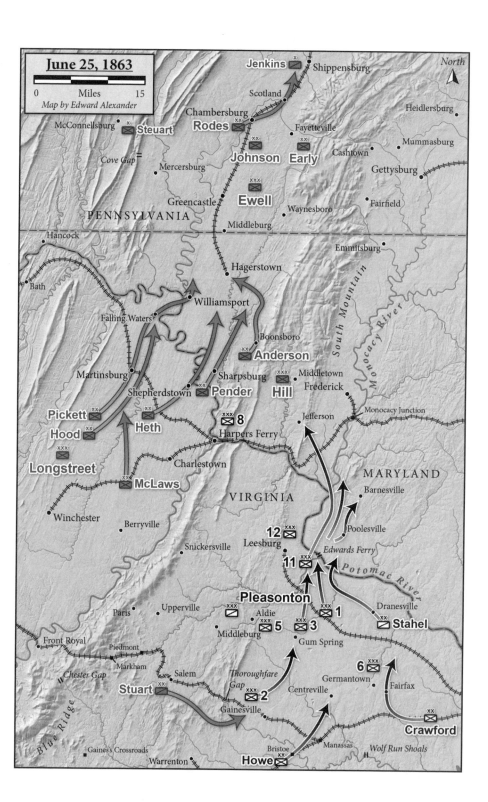

June 25, 1863

Map by Edward Alexander

0   Miles   15

North

Shippensburg

Jenkins

Scotland

Heidlersburg

Chambersburg   Fayetteville

McConnellsburg   Steuert   Rodes   Mummasburg

Cashtown

Cove Gap   Johnson   Early   Gettysburg

Mercersburg

Greencastle   Ewell   Fairfield

PENNSYLVANIA   Waynesboro

Middleburg   Fairfield

Hancock   Emmitsburg

Hagerstown

Bath   Williamsport

Falling Waters   Boonsboro

Martinsburg   Sharpsburg   Anderson   Middletown

Shepherdstown   Pender   Hill   Frederick

Monocacy Junction

Pickett   Heth   Jefferson

Hood   Harpers Ferry   **8**

Longstreet   Charlestown   MARYLAND

McLaws   Barnesville

Winchester   VIRGINIA

Berryville   Poolesville

Snickersville   **12**

Leesburg   *Edwards Ferry*

Paris   Upperville   **11**

Pleasonton   *Potomac River*

Aldie   **1**   Dranesville

Front Royal   Piedmont   Middleburg   **5**   **3**   **Stahel**

Markham   Salem   Gum Spring

Thoroughfare   **6**

Chester Gap   *Gap*   **2**   Germantown   Fairfax

Stuart   Centreville

Gainesville

Blue Ridge   **Crawford**

Gaines's Crossroads   Bristoe   Manassas   *Wolf Run Shoals*

Warrenton   **Howe**

Thursday, June 25, 1863

Dawn brought trouble for the beleaguered residents of McConnellsburg in Fulton County, Pennsylvania, where Brig. Gen. George Steuart's Confederate brigade had camped overnight. Previous Rebel parties had caused considerable trouble, unnerving the populace.

The Cove—the flat valley in which McConnellsburg lay—had already suffered considerably at Confederate hands. Brigadier General Albert Jenkins's mounted infantry had raided the merchants in McConnellsburg and Webster Mills and scoured the entire lower end of the county for horses and supplies. Officers with Steuart's command believed their soldiers were obeying General Lee's directive against pillaging. "The behavior of the men since we entered Pennsylvania had been most exemplary," claimed Steuart's mistaken aide-de-camp Lt. Randolph McKim. "At McConnellsburg there had been one breach of General Lee's orders, but that was the solitary exception." The 2nd Maryland's Maj. William W. Goldsborough thought the same: "These orders were strictly followed, much to the surprise of the inhabitants." They could not have been more wrong.[1]

The losses inflicted upon the local populace by Steuart's infantry were widespread and extensive, and at least one newspaper reporter believed the soldiers had offered Confederate money for the goods. "Mr. H. H. Dietrich, of Ayr township, lost heavily in this way," reported the *Fulton Democrat*. "The stores of Robinson and Patterson were stripped of their contents, and articles that were of

---

1 McKim, *A Soldier's Recollections*, 164; Goldsborough, *The Maryland Line*, 177.

Maj. Gen. Robert E. Rodes commanded a division in Ewell's Second Corps of the Army of Northern Virginia.

LOC

no use to the plunderers were destroyed wantonly. We can scarcely hear of a citizen who has not lost more or less in some shape." Some soldiers reportedly entered houses and stole private property. Five or six men stopped at the Unger house just as a large dinner was being served for a guest. The Rebels sat down at the table with the surprised family. In appreciation, the uninvited enemy guarded the house for the rest of their stay to prevent looting.[2]

While Steuart's soldiers rampaged at will in Fulton County, the remainder of Edward Johnson's and part of Robert Rodes's divisions remained camped near Chambersburg in neighboring Franklin County. Their foragers generally took what they wanted from the farmers and shopkeepers. "I did a fine job guarding a bed of onions just long enough to pull all I wanted for my own use, and I gave some to others who were not skillful in climbing palings as I was," boasted Pvt. John R. King of the 25th Virginia.[3]

During the previous night, with Jenkins's cavalry heading farther north from their camp at Shippensburg, General Rodes dispatched infantry to occupy that town. The men of Junius Daniel's Brigade were stirred by the long roll at midnight and marched at quick time through the night from Chambersburg. The Tar Heels began filing through town about 7:00 a.m. "The people of Shippensburg looked mad at us as usual in this country," remembered James E. Green of the 53rd North

---

2 *Reading Eagle*, September 11, 1927; *Fulton Democrat*, July 10, 1863; *Mercersburg* (PA) *Journal*, Jan. 16, 1903. William M. Patterson's store in the village of Webster Mills was particularly hard hit, with his shelves stripped almost bare, as was Robinson's store at Big Cove Tannery. Imboden established his headquarters in a tent along the turnpike between Charlestown and the gap.

3 Richard L. Armstrong, *25th Virginia Infantry and 9th Battalion Virginia Infantry* (Lynchburg, VA, 1990), 61.

Carolina. "This is a fine Country the fields all covered with the finest Wheat I ever saw. Clover, Herds grass, Oats, Corn &c &c. This is a thickly settled Country, and a bondance of little Towns . . . And the People Generly Ugly."[4]

Several of Rodes's soldiers, with a full day off from marching, used the opportunity to stroll around Chambersburg. "The citizens looked upon us with scorn and contempt, it is strictly a Union hole," grumbled Capt. William E. Ardrey of the 30th North Carolina. "After stopping at a place for a few days, the people would get over their fright when they had found out that we were not savages or demons as we had been represented to be," recollected one Georgian. The 12th Alabama's Robert Park breakfasted with a citizen who refused any payment, although Park assured him "Confederate money would soon take the place of greenbacks." Louis Leon's 53rd North Carolina served as Rodes's provost regiment for the day. "We were treated very cleverly by the ladies," recorded the Carolinian in his diary. "They thought at first we were going to burn their city, but when we told them that the strict order of Gen. Lee was to protect all private property they were very much relieved."[5]

"All quiet until about 9 o'clock when the locusts began to swarm again," bemoaned Chambersburg resident William Heyser. "On each side of the street they stop and make further requisitions. There isn't much left to take. All businessmen suffer." Rachel Cormany was as dismayed as she was appalled: "They must surely expect to set up stores or fill their empty ones judging from the loads they have been hauling away & they take every thing a body can think of."[6]

Merchant Jacob Hoke watched a seemingly endless parade of infantry, artillery, and long trains of wagons tramp, roll, and rumble past his store on the main street. "There were here and there along the line bands of excellent music," he admitted when describing the passing of the foot soldiers. "'Dixie' and 'My Maryland' were the favorite pieces played. These were followed by a train of artillery composed of cannon, caissons and forges; then a long train of heavily loaded wagons, filled with shot, shells and other ammunition. These wagons were each drawn by four or six horses or mules, and in passing through our streets they made that grinding noise

---

4 Green diary, entry for June 25, 1863, SHC-UNC.

5 William E. Ardrey diary, entry for June 25, 1863, in Taylor, "Ramseur's Brigade in the Gettysburg Campaign," 29; Park, "The Twelfth Alabama Infantry," 245; "A Complete and Interesting Account of the Pennsylvania Campaign," *Augusta* (GA) *Chronicle*, Sept. 5, 1863; *Charlotte Observer*, Nov. 16, 1892; Leon, *Diary of a Tar Heel*, 33.

6 Heyser diary, entry for June 25, 1863, 78.

which indicated immense weight of freightage." According to Hoke, the wagons were followed by the train of the reserve artillery and then a herd of 50-100 cattle. He could not help but notice that many of the wagons, horses, mules, and artillery pieces bore "U.S." markings.

The hodge-podge of clothing also caught Hoke's eye. "Their dress consisted of nearly every imaginable style and color, the butternut largely predominating," observed the surprised the merchant. "Some had blue blouses, which they had captured, or stripped from the Union dead. Hats, or the skeletons of what were once hats, surmounted their partly covered heads. Many were ragged, dirty and shoeless, affording unmistakable evidence that they sadly stood in need of having their wardrobes replenished. They were all, however, well armed and under perfect discipline." He continued studying the passing troops. "They seemed to move as one vast machine, and laughing, talking, singing or cheering," he marveled. There but little straggling—something that perhaps surprised the merchant given the free-booting appearance of the Rebels—but some of the men "did not hesitate to appropriate to themselves hats, boots, watches and pocket clocks."[7]

The passing Confederates, in turn, studied the gawking townsfolk. "The people in the towns seem to stir about as much as usual or more," wrote home Campbell Brown, General Ewell's stepson, "and behave pretty well except that now & then women turn their backs on us, or bring up a decided pout, which as they are naturally very much uglier & coarser than ours, doesn't improve them." He mailed home five dresses, five pounds of tea, some cloth, and other sundries that he purchased, paying $163.00 for them in Confederate currency, using "no threats for compulsion whatever."[8]

That morning, General Ewell moved his headquarters from the Franklin Hotel about one mile north to a small Mennonite church on the turnpike leading to Shippensburg. The church was just beyond newspaper editor Alexander K. McClure's sprawling farm, where Albert Jenkins's mounted infantrymrn had spent their first night in Pennsylvania. A Confederate colonel identified in the local paper as "R. H. Lee" presided over a court-martial for a quartet of soldiers accused of various disciplinary breaches. The officer doled out the steepest penalty to the 5th Alabama's Pvt. Patrick Herne, who had to forfeit his pay for three months, perform

---

7 Hoke, *Reminiscences*, 54-55.

8 G. C. Brown to "Dear Sister & Mother," June 25, 1863, Chambersburg, PA, Polk-Brown-Ewell Papers, SHC-UNC.

extra fatigue duty for two months, and was to be bucked two hours each day for seven days.[9]

The 1st Rockbridge Artillery camped about a mile west of Chambersburg. "This is a butifull Country through here," marveled Pvt. Joseph F. Shaner. "We can buy plenty of butter and apple butter through here." That evening the private went into Chambersburg, which he described as a "nice town," only to encounter his brother and a friend, Gardner Paxton. The trio dined together. "We are takeing all the horses in this state," Shaner added. "We got some very fine ones. We all so press all of the sugar coffee malassas and fish that we can get in the stores and they ishue them out to the men." The residents, added Shaner, are all "strong union people but they treat us very well." While the artillerymen enjoyed their repast their thoughts turned to the main reason they were in Pennsylvania. "I suppose that we will have a fight before long," he wrote later that night to his sisters. "They say that gen Hooker is comeing down on the other side of the mountain [South Mountain] and I dont recon that we can go much futher without fighting him."[10]

Like everyone else in the Virginia army, the specialists in the artillery and medical branches did their best to satisfy their needs. "Sometime during the day, two young men—officers connected with the artillery—came with a requisition for all the flannels and other woolen goods we had, suitable for making cartridges for cannon," complained Jacob Hoke. "Not long after the departure of these ordnance officers, two more from the Medical department came, demanding all the tea we had for their hospitals. Like the flannel, they got only what we did not think of sufficient value to hide away. During the day other officers also came for such articles as Castile soap, etc., for their own use."[11]

About 16 miles southwest of Chambersburg, Mercersburg seminarian Philip Schaff reported that between 50 and 80 independent guerilla cavalrymen occupied the town and stole "horses, cattle, sheep, store goods, negroes, and whatever else they can make use of, without ceremony, and in evident violation of Lee's proclamation read yesterday." These Marylanders and Virginians, he continued, appeared "brave, defiant, and bold." Their captain threatened to torch the town if

9 *The Franklin Repository*, July 15, 1863. The newspaper was wrong, for there was no Col. R. H. Lee in the Army of Northern Virginia.

10 Joseph F. Shaner to "Dear Sisters," Camp near Chambersburg, Pennsylvania, June 25, 1863. Courtesy of Paul T. Scott. Shaner, a native of East Lexington, Va., served in the Rockbridge Artillery from 1861 until the end of the war.

11 Hoke, *Reminiscences*, 54-55, 58-59.

anyone fired at his men. "They burned the barn of a farmer in the country who was reported to have fired a gun, and robbed his house of all valuables."[12]

The Keystone farmers fought back at times, including at the narrow Strasburg Pass on Blue Mountain that led west to Horse Valley. "Every nook and corner from Mercersburg to Newburg, along the entire mountain, was searched by the rebels and many horses were captured and taken away," recalled Christian H. Deck, who conceived a plan to protect his region's valuable animals. Deck and about 25 neighbors collected nearly125 horses and moved them onto Tuscarora Mountain near Keefer's Gap, where they pitched tents. Deck organized the farmers into an informal company armed with "their trusty guns and revolvers" and scheduled periodic discharges of the weapons to scare off intruders. A scout named Daniel Heckman narrowly escaped being shot when five angry Rebels took him for a Union bushwhacker and fired at him while he was carrying supplies from Deck's farm toward the mountain. The soldiers seized Deck and threatened to kill him if he did not reveal the man's identity. Several farmers heard Heckman's story, grabbed their guns, and doubled-quicked across the fields to intercept the Rebels, who departed before they arrived.[13]

While Ewell's Confederates enjoyed the bounties of Pennsylvania, Anderson's Division of Hill's Corps was still well to the south in Maryland. "We took up our march at 3 ½ a.m.," Adj. A. L. Peel of the 19th Mississippi recounted. "Passed through Boonsborough at 4 a.m. Saw a few secessionists. Crossed the Antietam River at 6 a.m. Came through Funckstown at 10 a.m. The ladies were all glad to see us. We halted at 12 [p.m.] near Haigerstown. Confederate money is of very little value here."[14]

Pender's Division, trailing Anderson, arrived at Shepherdstown. "We forded the Potomac, shouting and hurrahing as usual," recounted J. F. J. Caldwell of the 1st South Carolina. "This was not a spectacle fit for female eyes, for most of the men stripped off their nether clothing; but it was full of interest for a soldier, because they advanced in well-closed ranks, with active steps and hopeful of victory. The night of the 25th we spent in the rain, about eight miles from Hagerstown," he continued. "We heard very few words of encouragement now. Some Confederate flags were displayed on ladies' bosoms and there may have been

---

12 Schaff, "The Gettysburg Week," 24.

13 Hoke, *Reminiscences*, 186. Hoke noted that Daniel Heckman, "the scout they shot at, was afterwards killed by the explosion of a shell while he was attempting to take out its contents."

14 Peel diary, entry for June 25, 1863.

Brig. Gen. Joseph R. Davis, nephew of Confederate President Jefferson Davis, led a brigade in Heth's Division of Hill's Third Corps of the Army of Northern Virginia.

USAHEC

a few hung out of windows or balconies; but the welcome of words was charily extended to us, when at all, and the determination seemed, everywhere, to be to await the issue of our second invasion."[15]

Harry Heth's Division, the last of Hill's Corps, also waded the Potomac. "It was rather wide, but only about waist deep at the time," observed Cpl. Samuel W. Hankins of the 2nd Mississippi, part of Joseph Davis's Brigade. "The water, however, was swift. The river bed was very rough and slippery, so that wading was extremely difficult. Many got a ducking, to the great amusement of those who escaped. The wagons and those on horseback had to cross about a hundred yards below us," he added. "Some officer seated on his horse about midway the river was yelling at us to close up, when his horse stumbled and he went over the horse's head foremost into the water. An uproar by the soldiers followed his catastrophe. Our own brigade was the second to cross. Looking back after reaching the opposite side, we saw the army, miles in length, winding its way through the mountains like a huge snake down into the river. It was a grand sight."[16]

"Clear & warm. 5 AM marched 3 miles & waded the Potomac River hip deep," scrawled Gus Vairin, another member of the 2nd Mississippi, into his pocket journal. "Most of the men took off all their clothing carrying them & their arms & accoutrements on their shoulders and heads. It presented a lively scene. The current was swift & the rocky bottom made it hard on the feet. We crossed it 1 mile

15 Caldwell, *The History of the Brigade of South Carolinians*, 92.

16 Samuel W. Hankins, *Simple Story of a Soldier: Life and Service in the 2d Mississippi Infantry* (Tuscaloosa, AL, 2004), 46.

below Sheppardstown . . . This part of the country is much like the Shenandoah valley but the people especially the women I saw are very ugly."[17]

Later that day Heth's troops tramped through the Sharpsburg battlefield. "The low mounds which cover the bones of those who fell, the furrowed ground and scarred trees, all speak more plainly than words of that terrible conflict," penned Cpl. George W. Bynum of the 2nd Mississippi. "I saw the ground over which we charged on that memorable occasion and the very spot where I was wounded. Sad, sad thoughts are recalled by again reviewing the old battle-ground." The men marched on toward Hagerstown, which Gus Vairin thought was about eleven miles away. "[We made] 17 miles today. Went to the town to get boots but the stores were all closed."[18]

Pettigrew's Brigade crossed the Potomac at Boteler's Ford near Shepherdstown that morning. "On the north bank of the Potomac the disciplinarian, Pettigrew, delivered his strict commands against interfering with private rights and property, and right well were these commands obeyed," remembered Capt. John H. Thorp of the 47th North Carolina. "As we passed through Hagerstown, the eyes of our men were dazed by the fullness of an opulent city, but no one dared to loot it."[19]

"The whole of Gen. Lee's veteran army will have crossed the 'Rubicon' in a few hours," observed a newspaper correspondent with a historical bent traveling with the Confederates. "Great events, vital interests to our beloved sunny South, hang tremblingly in the balance. 'The wheeling sabre' of Ewell, like the sword which was suspended over Jerusalem, has already filled the hearts of our persecuting foe with dreadful apprehensions. Lee's victorious legions follow closely in his wake," he continued, "and God blessing us, they will be made to feel the bitter curse of war. They will be enabled to form some idea of what we have suffered, though they will not be visited with the fire grand, the vindictive cruelty, the warfare upon women, the desecration of churches, the demolition of grave yards—in a word, the heartless barbarity which distinguishes their own soldiery." The men expected to fight bloody battles to win the war, he added, "By these alone do we expect to accomplish the great object of our mission—the bringing about a

17 Vairin diary, entry for June 25, 1863.

18 Love, "Mississippi at Gettysburg," 28; Vairin diary, entry for June 25, 1863.

19 John H. Thorp, "Forty-seventh North Carolina," in Clark, *Histories of the Several Regiments and Battalions from North Carolina*, 3:88.

speedy peace. The army's in high hopes. God forbid that we should be disappointed."[20]

Around this time, a Northern newspaperman visited the marching Rebels and slipped away to Frederick, where he wired a report to his editor:

> Several thousand head of cattle have been gobbled by the rebels in Washington county, and a great many have been driven across the river at Williamsport, to feed that portion of Lee's army which remains on the other side. The rebel commanders have promised their soldiers that the moment they touch Pennsylvania soil all restraint upon them shall be removed, and they shall have unbridled license to plunder and devastate the country they pass through. . . . The rebels have a poor opinion of the troops assembled at Harrisburg, characterizing them as unorganized, undisciplined men, who will oppose no serious barrier to their successful march through Pennsylvania. They boast that they will be in Harrisburg by Sunday evening, whence they shall march on Philadelphia.[21]

Isaac Trimble, the combat general in search of a command, had finally reached the Army of Northern Virginia after several days on horseback. When he met General Lee at Hagerstown, Trimble suggested he send a brigade to seize Baltimore. Such an action would "rouse Maryland, and thus embarrass the enemy," he argued. The move was of special concern to Trimble because, although he was born in Virginia, he had spent most of his life in Maryland and the army associated him with the Old Line State. According to Trimble's postwar account, Lee considered the plan and even wrote to A. P. Hill to ask if he could spare a brigade for the raid. Trimble went on to claim Hill would later tell him that he had replied to Lee that he could not afford the loss of an entire brigade, and thus Lee shelved the scheme.[22]

Longstreet's Corps, meanwhile, marched northward through the Shenandoah Valley toward the Potomac River. McLaws's Division moved from Summit Point to Martinsburg, West Virginia. "On the fifth day of our march we passed through Winchester, with A. P. Hill marching parallel to us, some eight or ten miles to our right," penned Capt. Gus Dickert of the 3rd South Carolina. "Ewell had pushed on to the Potomac, and was turning Washington wild and frantic at the sight of the 'Rebels' so close to their capital. As we neared the border we could discover Union

---

20 Styple, *Writing & Fighting the Confederate War*, 154.

21 *Chicago Tribune*, June 25, 1863.

22 Trimble, "The Battle and Campaign of Gettysburg," *SHSP*, vol. 26.

sentiment taking the place of that of the South. Those who ever sympathized with us had to be very cautious and circumspect. Now and then we would see a window slowly raise in a house by the roadside, or on a hill in the distance, and the feeble flutter of a white handkerchief told of their Confederate proclivities."[23]

Hood's Division arrived at Falling Waters, a small West Virginia village on the Potomac, while Pickett's men and the Reserve Artillery crossed the river at Williamsport at 3:00 p.m. "The crossing was anything but pleasant, as the bottom was full of rock and a great crowd of men shoving and jostling you about the whole time you were in the river," remembered Lt. John T. James of the 11th Virginia. "But, like everything else, it had an end, and so after a great deal of labor we landed on the Maryland side. Across the Potomac and in the land of our enemy! How often had we looked forward and hoped for the long-expected time. Everything seemed to favor us," James added with confidence. "An army that had never been defeated, flushed by recent brilliant victories, and now by marching against its old antagonist—an antagonist we had met so often, and whipped as often as we had met."[24]

Pickett camped his division north of Williamsport. Major N. Claiborne Wilson noted in his diary that "little or no sympathy was shown us by the citizens of the town" before adding nonchalantly that before they went into camp, "we executed a Private from the 18th Va. Regt. for desertion." Morale was high, despite the occasional deserters. "As we advanced into Maryland, amid the green fields, the spirits of the troops began to gain new life," rejoiced Pvt. John H. Lewis of the 9th Virginia. "It began to look to them as if they were on the road to plenty, if not peace."[25]

*   *   *

The Confederate incursion into the counties of central Maryland and southern Pennsylvania deeply worried Gettysburg resident Sallie Broadhead. "Everyone is asking, 'Where is our army, that they let the enemy scour the country and do as they please?'" she penned in obvious distress. "It is reported that Lee's whole army is this side of the river, and marching on Harrisburg; also,

23 Dickert, *History of Kershaw's Brigade*, 229.

24 John T. James, "Storming Cemetary [sic] Hill," *Philadelphia Times*, Oct. 21, 1882.

25 N. C. Wilson, Diary, entry for June 25, 1863, Nathaniel Claiborne Wilson Papers, VMI; John H. Lewis, *Recollections from 1860 to 1865* (Washington, D.C., 1895), 66.

that a large force is coming on here, to destroy the railroad between there and Baltimore."[26]

"So many and various are the theories concerning the plans of General Lee in his recent operations in Virginia, Maryland and Pennsylvania, that it is almost idle to speculate concerning them," cautioned the *Gettysburg Star & Banner* before engaging in precisely that. "That he meditated a grand coup, cannot be doubted. It may have been, and may yet be his intention, to attack Baltimore and Washington. The expeditions sent into Maryland and Pennsylvania appear to have been intended chiefly to divert a part of our army, though plunder doubtless was one of the objects aimed at." Schoolteacher J. Howard Wert was also tired of the rampant speculation, as he wrote once it was all over. "[D]uring the whole invasion, even as now, there were a multitude of wise men in corner groceries, cigar stores and dram shops who knew it all," scoffed the educator. "They knew just what Lee's plans were and what our government ought to do. The trouble with this class of seers is that the result seldom corresponds with their very positive foreknowledge."[27]

Some citizens remained skeptical that Lee's true objective was Pennsylvania despite the heavy presence of infantry in two of the state's counties. Amos Stouffer, who was still hiding his horses in the mountains near Newburg, reported that "The rebs are scouring Franklin, Cumberland, York & Adams counties for horses and cattle. They have come no lower down than Shippensburg yet; think their object is to attack Baltimore."[28]

In Richmond, the *Daily Dispatch* urged the Confederate government to cultivate the Northern peace movement and vigorously prosecute the war. "Let us give them distinctly to understand that reconstruction is a thing not to be dreamed of; but, at the same time, let us not throw cold water upon their attempts to overthrow the Black Republican despotism at Washington." The editor believed the majority of Northern people "are heartily tired and sick of the war, but the military tyranny of the United States has hitherto rendered powerless their aspirations for peace. We should help them with a few more victories, and the balls and bayonets of our brave soldiers are the best reliance for bringing about this object."[29]

---

26 Broadhead diary, entry for June 25, 1863.

27 *Gettysburg Star & Banner*, June 25, 1863; J. Howard Wert account, ACHS.

28 Stouffer diary, entry for June 25, 1863.

29 *Richmond Daily Dispatch*, June 25, 1863.

*   *   *

While the Confederate infantry marched and pilfered, the cavalry set off on its great ride through the scattered corps of the Army of the Potomac. About 1:00 a.m., Jeb Stuart and his staff and escort mounted and rode from Rector's Crossroads in the direction of Upperville. "The next thing I remember, we were riding along the Upperville-Middleburg road with two or three brigades of cavalry following us," recalled Stuart's junior engineering officer Capt. Frank S. Robertson. The men remained as quiet as possible because Union troops still held the Bull Run Mountains and Winfield Hancock's II Corps occupied Thoroughfare Gap.[30]

"No one could ride along the lines of this splendid body of men and not be struck with the spirit which animated them," observed Capt. William W. Blackford, another of Stuart's engineering officers. "They knew they were starting on some bold enterprise, but their confidence in their leader was so unbounded that they were as gay and lively as it was possible for them to be." After jumping his horse over a stone fence just before reaching the arched stone bridge over Goose Creek, Stuart ordered a courier to turn the head of the column in a different direction. It was then that the cavalier's staff officers realized the troopers were not heading to the Shenandoah Valley, but toward the Army of the Potomac. "Little did we realize that this was the commencement of a march which lasted almost without halt for two weeks," recalled staffer Theodore S. Garnett.[31]

Stuart was surprised to find Hancock's infantry blocking his way. According to Mosby's intelligence report, the enemy infantry was still at Centreville, Union Mills, and Wolf Run Shoals. The cavalier general was surprised because Mosby was unable to alert him of the danger. "Stuart did not hear from me because Hooker's troops were marching on all roads between us," Mosby would later explain. "As the artillery firing had ceased in the morning, I concluded that he had gone back and I did the same." Mosby's decision not to try to locate Stuart deprived the cavalry leader of Mosby's latest intelligence reports.[32]

Stuart's advance drove a small detachment of pickets from the mouth of Glasscock's Gap and continued through the mountain pass to cut off any Union

---

30 Trout, *In the Saddle with Stuart*, 74; OR 27, pt. 2, 692.

31 Blackford, *War Years with Stuart*, 223; Cooke, *The Wearing of the Gray*, 230; Jewell, "Theodore Garnett Recalls," 48.

32 Mosby, *Stuart's Cavalry in the Gettysburg Campaign*, 177.

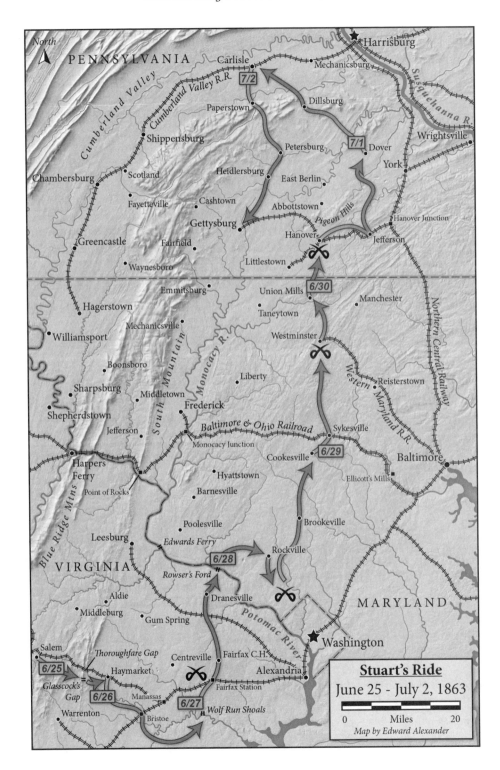

Stuart's Ride
June 25 - July 2, 1863
Map by Edward Alexander

troops lingering inside Thoroughfare Gap. They had no difficulty doing so and continued through the night toward Haymarket. The dawn found them near Buckland on the eastern slope of the Bull Run Mountains. "Across the plain, to our left, were the white tops of an immense wagon train, which, at the distance of two or three miles presented the appearance of a huge flock of sheep," Garnett recollected. "Here then, though, was the object of our silent march over the mountains. All that remained to be done was to 'charge the camp.'" The gray troopers aborted the idea when it was discovered that at least a division of Northern infantry guarded it.[33]

As Hancock's troops marched from Thoroughfare Gap and Gainesville toward Gum Springs, Confederate cavalrymen picked and prodded at the moving Unionists. "We had evidently finished our mission at the Gap," recounted Cpl. Thomas Meyer of the 148th Pennsylvania, part of Col. Edward Cross's brigade. "Artillery firing was heard a few miles out; all was now commotion. We packed up and moved out to Haymarket; we formed in battleline and waited for developments."[34]

At daylight "arrangements were made to repel attacks from the rear or flanks," commented Sgt. James A. Wright of the 1st Minnesota. "It was not exactly raining, but the air was surcharged with a descending moisture that saturated our clothing and obscured everything, at a distance of 200 to 300 yards." Desultory attacks occurred throughout the morning "by mounted men who attacked suddenly; galloping out of the shrouding fog and misty, firing a volley or two and riding away into the blending clouds of smoke and vapor; or behind a sheltering hill or grove, as soon as they met a return fire."[35]

Rebel horse artillery unlimbered and fired at the rear of the column shortly after the Minnesotans marched over the gap near Haymarket. The iron killed and wounded several soldiers and a shell fragment killed the horse of the 1st Minnesota's Col. William Colvill, who Lt. William Lochren remembered as being "well-plastered with a coating of dull red, Virginia mud." A trailing crowd of sutlers, surgeons, chaplains, and black servants "broke and rushed, in terror and disorder, from the vicinity of the rapidly bursting shells," throwing aside anything

---

33 *OR* 27, pt. 2, 692; Jewell, "Theodore Garnett Recalls," 48.

34 Muffly, *The Story of Our Regiment*, 458.

35 James A. Wright, "The Story of Company F, the First Regiment" (Minnesota Historical Society), 538, as cited by Hage, "The Battle of Gettysburg as Seen by Minnesota Soldiers," 247.

that might encumber their escape. The riflemen "shouted with glee" at the ludicrous scene.[36]

Corporal Meyer also mentioned the artillery fire. Stuart's cavalry "reached the slope of Bull Run Mountain, just below Thoroughfare Gap, and opened a brisk artillery fire on us, killing and wounding a number of our men," recalled the Pennsylvanian. "Our batteries rushed into position and opened a terrific fire in return and the Confederates were soon silenced; we withdrew . . . rapidly and continuously through steady rain and deep mud, twenty miles to Gum Springs, which we reached about midnight, and bivouacked in the mud, lying on our rubbers to await the coming of the morning." The shelling impressed Capt. David M. Earle of the 15th Massachusetts, II Corps, who admitted he "never saw such hard shelling before."[37]

The barrage also took Brig. Gen. William Harrow's brigade by surprise. "As the Regiment was proceeding quietly on its way, and when at Haymarket, from a lofty eminence to the right and rear came bursting shells into the midst of our Brigade and we lost one man in our Regiment, Israel D. Jones, of Company G, the first soldier in the Regiment killed by the enemy," chronicled the 19th Maine's John Day Smith. "In less than ten minutes from the time that Mr. Jones was chatting cheerfully with the man marching at his side, he was buried by the roadside and left to sleep his last sleep." The shelling also injured a private in regiment. "The attack was so unexpected," admitted Day, "that it created some confusion in our Division."[38]

General Stuart reported his side of the brief but deadly affair at Thoroughfare Gap in his after-action report. "Moving to the right with my brigades, we passed through Glasscock's Gap without serious difficulty and marched to Haymarket," he penned. "I had previously sent Major Mosby with some picked men to gain the vicinity of Dranesville, find where a crossing was practicable and bring intelligence to me near Gum Springs on June 25th. As we neared Haymarket we found that Hancock's Corps was enroute through Haymarket for Gum Springs, his infantry well distributed through his trains. I chose a good position and opened with the

36 William Lochren, "Narrative of the First Minnesota," in *Minnesota in the Civil and Indian Wars, 1861–1865* (Minneapolis, MN, 1890).

37 Muffly, *The Story of Our Regiment*, 458; Andrew E. Ford, *The Story of the Fifteenth Regiment Massachusetts Volunteer Infantry in the Civil War, 1861–1864* (Lancaster, MA, 1898), 258. The primary Union guns engaged in this skirmish were from Battery A, 4th U.S. Artillery and Battery B, 1st Rhode Island.

38 Smith, *The History of the Nineteenth Regiment of Maine Volunteer Infantry*, 58.

artillery on his passing column with effect, scattering men, wagons and horses in wild confusion; disabled one of the enemy's caissons, which he abandoned, and compelled him to advance in order of battle to compel us to desist. As Hancock had the right of way on my road, I sent Fitz Lee's Brigade to Gainesville to reconnoitre and devoted the remainder of the day to grazing our horses."[39]

Before withdrawing to Buckland in an effort to deceive the Federals as to his true intentions, Stuart dashed off a report concerning Hancock's movement to Robert E. Lee. "It is plain from General Lee's report that this messenger did not reach him, and unfortunately the dispatch was not duplicated," reported Stuart's staff officer Maj. Henry B. McClellan after the war. "Had it reached General Lee the movement of Hancock's corps would, of itself, have gone far to disclose to him the intentions of the enemy as to the place where a passage of the Potomac was about to be effective."[40]

The presence of Hancock's infantry made it impossible for Stuart to follow the route he had originally selected. He now had to choose between retracing his steps and crossing the Potomac at Shepherdstown, or continuing on and fulfilling the letter and spirit of Lee's orders. "To carry out my original design of passing west of Centreville, would have involved so much detention, on account of the presence of the enemy," Stuart explained, "that I determined to cross Bull Run lower down, and strike through Fairfax for the Potomac the next day. The sequel shows this to have been the only practicable course."[41]

Retracing his steps to cross the Potomac at either Shepherdstown or Williamsport would have required Stuart to push his horses over at least 60 miles of mountainous roads on a journey that would take at least two days. After crossing the Potomac he would have to ride another 60 miles to reach York, Pennsylvania, and would need to cross South Mountain while deep in enemy territory. "It should not therefore be wondered at if this consideration alone decided Stuart to persist in the movement already begun," observed Major McClellan, "especially when there was also the hope of damaging the enemy in his rear and thus delaying his movements. Moreover he had a right to expect that the information he had

39 OR 27, pt. 2, 692.

40 McClellan, *Life and Campaigns of Stuart*, 321. The message did reach the War Department in Richmond, where a clerk filed it away but did not pass it along to Lee, perhaps assuming the army commander had also received a copy. Lee moved his headquarters on June 25 to a site three miles north of Williamsport, Maryland.

41 OR 27, pt. 2, 693.

forwarded concerning the movement of Hancock's corps would cause [Beverly] Robertson and [William E.] Jones to be active on their front, and would put General Lee himself on the alert in the same direction."[42]

The timetable for Stuart's entire expedition was thrown off during its opening hours. He had no way of knowing that he would never get back on schedule.

The alarming events in Franklin and Fulton counties triggered a fresh spate of refugees, who crowded the hard-packed turnpike running through Carlisle to Harrisburg. Cumberland County residents received a scare when Albert Jenkins's mounted infantry slowly drove Capt. William Boyd's 1st New York Cavalry up the turnpike into Carlisle. Boyd reported that the Rebels had advanced that evening to within four miles of the town. "The information that the rebels were upon us, seriously affected the nerves of some of our citizens," admitted Cumberland County's deputy sheriff, Simpson K. Donavin. "Many of our prominent ones, and many not so prominent, concluded to leave town, and conveyances of all kinds were in great demand. Some unable to procure vehicles started on foot for Harrisburg and other points. The females, of course, were much alarmed and a scene of confusion and excitement ensued."

The commander of Carlisle's primary defensive force, Brig. Gen. Joseph Knipe, learned at 1:00 a.m. that the enemy was only two miles southwest of town. He considered it folly to offer resistance and ordered his two regiments of New York militiamen to withdraw north. Carlisle was now defenseless. "The residents of our town retired to bed on Thursday night under the full conviction that the rebels would occupy town before morning," wrote a resigned Donivan.[43]

When darkness fell the heavens opened and made the night miserable for men and horses alike. "That night was rainy and disagreeable, and we spent it without shelters or fires," complained Lt. George W. Beale of the 9th Virginia Cavalry. Unlike the men in the ranks who enjoyed few luxuries, Stuart and his staff passed a warm night inside a handsome mansion near Buckland, "where all slept under cover but Stuart." Per his usual practice, the general spread his blankets under a tree and slept in the rain—but not before enjoying a sumptuous dinner. "That supper is

42 McClellan, *Life and Campaigns of Stuart*, 322.

43 "The Invasion," *Carlisle American Volunteer*, July 9, 1863.

one of the pleasant memories the present writer has of the late war," recalled Capt. John Esten Cooke, Stuart's ordnance officer who made a name for himself as an author of some renown after the war. "How the companions laughed and devoured the viands of the hospitable host! How the beautiful girls of the family stood with mock submission, servant-wise, behind the chairs, and waited on the guests with their sweetest smiles, until that reversal of all the laws of the universe became a perfect comedy, and ended in an éclat of laughter! General and staff waited in turn on the waiters," Cooke concluded, "and when the tired troopers fell asleep on the floor of the portico, it is certain that a number of bright eyes shone in their dreams. Such is the occasional comedy that which lights up the tragedy of war."[44]

Instead of riding on, Stuart dawdled at Buckland Mills with his command for 10 hours waiting in vain for John Mosby to return. The guerrilla leader made a halfhearted attempt to reconnect with Stuart's column but never did make contact. The time lost at Buckland Mills—hours wasted for no good reason—knocked Stuart's schedule irretrievably off track. His sojourn at Buckland Mills was but one of several questionable tactical decisions Stuart would on his long ride to Pennsylvania.

The ongoing war in America, in particular the Confederate movements in the Eastern Theater and Ulysses S. Grant's investment of Vicksburg, continued to dominate the foreign news sections of European papers.

By June 25, speculation that French Emperor Napoleon III would announce his support for the Confederacy had waned. Two members of the British Parliament had visited the emperor at Fontainebleau, where they learned he was willing to intervene jointly with Great Britain to arrest the further progress of the American war. Napoleon reportedly "disavowed all unfriendly feeling towards the North, and solemnly declared that his only motive was to stop the horrible carnage in America, which was productive of no results, and never could restore the Union." A reporter in Liverpool postulated that if England decided not to cooperate with the French in this proposed diplomatic intervention, "France may

---

44 Cooke, *Wearing of the Gray*, 231. A viand is a delicious dish or food item.

join Spain on behalf of the Confederates, the effect of the war having pressed so heavily upon the Spanish trade at Cuba as almost to ruin it."[45]

Many international writers expressed open support for one side or the other. "The people of the North appear to have been seized by another panic as that produced last August and September, when the redoubtable Lee drove the Grand Army back to the Potomac," declared a pro-Confederate Canadian paper. "The accounts received are so conflicting and show such an ignorance of the real designs of the Confederate leaders, that it is almost impossible to arrive at a correct estimate of the magnitude of those dangers which the North seem always ready to apprehend whenever the fortune of war changes." After guessing as to possible Rebel goals, the editor concluded, "Thus far the Washington Government seem to be completely at a loss as to the whereabouts and the real designs of General Lee. The only fact of which we can be certain is that Stuart's bugles have once more been heard ringing our defiance in the valley of the Cumberland."

The editor was also at a loss when it came to understanding what was happening. The "bugles" belonged not to Stuart's troopers but to those who rode with Jenkins and Ewell. He was absolutely right, however, that senior Federal officials were uncertain about where Lee was heading.[46]

Thousands of terrified refugees, black and white, descended upon Harrisburg. "During the whole of last night and, up to the present time, long trains of wagons laden with goods and household furniture, have entered the city," reported one newspaperman. "The farmers are flocking in with their horses, and also any number of contrabands of all ages and sex. There are 600 contrabands between here and Carlisle, on the way. Many of our citizens are packing up their goods ready for shipment."[47]

"Large droves of horses are arriving from the border. Some of them would make excellent cavalry animals," concluded a *New York Herald* reporter. "A band of minstrels—Carncross & Dixey—fled from here at noon to-day. Their scare led them to flee towards Lancaster. They were advertised to stay all of this week." His

45 "Summary," *Liverpool Mercury* (Liverpool, England), June 25, 1863.

46 "The War in the States," *The Hamilton Spectator* (Hamilton, Ontario), June 25, 1863.

47 *Chicago Tribune*, June 26, 1863.

Maj. Gen. Darius N. Couch, the former commander of the II Corps, oversaw the newly formed Department of the Susquehanna with his headquarters in Harrisburg, Pennsylvania.

LOC

competitors "are flocking in from all quarters. None of them have any intelligence of a reliable character to report," continued the *Herald* reporter. "Major O. W. Sees, the attentive head of the telegraphic department here, has fitted up a complete set of rooms in the Capitol buildings for the use of correspondents. Newspaper [writers] have been restricted in the freedom heretofore given to their despatches. General Couch, though," he boasted, "has no complaints to make of the *Herald* corps." Officials contemplated declaring martial law to prevent able-bodied men from leaving the state capital. "The opinion of Gens. Franklin and Couch is, that the rebels are now advancing with serious intention on Harrisburg," concluded the *Herald* reporter. "Every preparation has been made to receive them. The politicians are leaving."[48]

General Couch and Governor Curtin faced the daunting task of energizing the populace to not only to join the militia, but to take other measures to resist the oncoming Rebels. "Strong, able bodied men are arriving here hourly from the border," observed the *Herald* writer. "They do not care about enlisting to defend their homes, but make quite a loud talk about what the authorities and government ought to do. . . . Parties of respectability have called upon the Governor and urged him to declare martial law." Another reporter reached the same conclusion. "Meanwhile, the apathy continues. The people are not awake," announced the *Chicago Tribune*. "I have no doubt that thousands will flock here when the town is

48 *New York Herald,* June 26, 1863. Philadelphia-based Carncross & Dixey's Minstrels typically performed in blackface. They were on a lengthy travelling tour when the Rebels threatened Harrisburg and frequently entertained Union troops at various camps in the region to remind them they were fighting to rescue blacks from slavery.

Brig. Gen. William F. "Baldy" Smith was in charge of the troops defending Harrisburg as part of the Department of the Susquehanna.

LOC

really invested, but at the present everybody is calm. Is it incredulity, or cowardice, or are they all Copperheads?"[49]

With the Rebels approaching Harrisburg, Couch realized he needed a more senior officer to command the troops south of the Susquehanna River. He dispatched Brig. Gen. William F. "Baldy" Smith to supersede Brig. Gen. William Hall. Smith, a 39-year-old native of Vermont, had led the Army of the Potomac's VI Corps during the disastrous battle of Fredericksburg. The stain of the loss dropped him out of favor with Lincoln and the war department; he lost his command and saw his rank reduced when the Senate failed to confirm his previous nomination to major general. On the credit side of the ledger, Smith had considerable combat experience against Lee's army and could be counted on to help instill confidence in the division of militia now under his command.

* * *

To the south, meanwhile, some of Baldy Smith's former colleagues in Joe Hooker's army were busy hustling northward. The I Corps marched from Guilford Station, Virginia, to Barnesville, Maryland. "After an all night's rainstorm, the Iron Brigade marched at 8 o'clock on Thursday morning, the 25th, crossed the Potomac at Edwards' Ferry on pontoons, and proceeding through Pool[e]sville, Maryland, bivouacked at dark at [B]arnesville near Sugar Loaf Mountain," recounted a soldier in the 24th Michigan. "A most beautiful sight was a large school of children at Poolsville, who gazed upon the soldiers as they marched by. One cannot imagine, without experience, the cheerful feeling such a sight induces among those who have not for months witnessed this feature of civilization. This reminder of home," he openly admitted, "brought tears to many an eye of those accustomed to hardships of the campaign."[50]

"Our foraging on the country now ceased," the 149th Pennsylvania's John Nesbit related after Stone's Brigade crossed at Edwards Ferry. "We began to realize that we were now on northern soil and would probably meet and fight Lee's army in Maryland or perhaps further north. We knew that the scene of action had been transferred from Virginia across the Potomac, but did not have any knowledge of the whereabouts of the Rebel army, or where we would come together."[51]

"Reports reached us that thousands of valorous militia were on their way to overwhelm the plundering invaders," observed Sgt. Thomas F. Walter of the 91st Pennsylvania about information he and his comrades got from their home state. "We had a pretty clear idea of what would happen [to] them if Lee's legions got a chance at them; and we wondered, too, whether the rebs would risk a fight with us, so far from their base. Most of us thought they would 'get up and git' when our army closed up with them." Few Pennsylvanians in the Army of the Potomac harbored illusions that Governor Curtin's motley collection of New York militiamen and the Keystone State's newly raised volunteers could defeat or even seriously delay the veteran Rebel army.[52]

For now, the focus was on getting Hooker's Army of the Potomac in a position to intercept the Army of Northern Virginia. "During some of those long June days we marched seventeen hours beneath the rays of a scorching sun," recounted the 91st Pennsylvania's Sergeant Walter. "The little fresh meat that we got seemed scarcely fit to eat, and this, with coffee and crackers, was our diet. The marching was terrible, but the men struggled along nobly."[53]

Brigadier General Gouverneur K. Warren, the Army of the Potomac's chief engineer, took some time to pen a letter to his new bride Emily in an effort to reassure her that she was safe in Baltimore. "We move at daybreak, and I expect hard, stirring times soon again; and we will give Lee something else to do besides robbing our people of cattle, and carrying colored people into slavery like any King of Dahomey," he jotted. "This army, that he takes such good care to go around and

50 Curtis, *History of the Twenty-fourth Michigan*, 150.

51 Nesbit, *General History of Company D, 149th Pennsylvania*, 13.

52 Thomas F. Walter, "The Personal Recollections and Experiences of an Obscure Soldier," in *Grand Army Scout and Soldiers' Mail*, vol. 3, no. 40 (Sept. 13, 1884), 1.

53 Ibid.

keep away from, will soon find him out, and God will certainly be on our side to stop his sinful career. Though we hope for Divine favor, we shall not fail to put our own shoulders to the wheel." Referring to Emily's hometown of Baltimore, he concluded, "It would take the enemy a long time to take the city, even if he could at all; and then our possession of the water communications prevent his investing it like we do at Vicksburg, and everything of value could be removed, even with Lee's army camped around it. But we are not going to let him get near Baltimore!"[54]

The III Corps left Gum Springs, crossed the Potomac at Edwards Ferry, and headed for the mouth of the Monocacy. "The field of hostilities was thus, for the second time, transferred to the free States," recalled Col. Regis de Trobriand, the French-born aristocrat, attorney, and writer who had a knack for combat. "The Antietam trial was to be made over again; but this time it was to be much more decisive."[55]

"Our march led us along large plantations, populated by negroes," remembered musician Frank Rauscher of the 114th Pennsylvania, "and when the band struck up they became wild with excitement and love of the music; and for miles they would keep along with us, dancing, jumping and yelling with delight. It seemed impossible for many of them to leave us. Probably it was the first time these dusky people had ever enjoyed the pleasure of hearing the music of a brass band, and the capers of these jubilant and mirthful colored followers were greatly enjoyed by the men of our regiment."[56]

Asa Bartlett of the 12th New Hampshire reported that Brig. Gen. Andrew A. Humphreys's division "marched with greater rapidity, if possible, than before. Space and time were now important factors in General Hooker's calculations, for the whole rebel army was on the north side of the Potomac before midnight of the 26th; and close following, as well as watching, on the part of the Union commander, had become a vital necessity, since upon his vigilance and activity, as well as ability, depended the future destiny of his country."[57]

The men made "an unprecedented forced march over the long tow-path to the mouth of the Monocacy," remembered Pvt. Thomas V. Cooper of the 26th Pennsylvania. "No man who participated in that march can ever forget the driving

54 Taylor, *Gouverneur Kemble Warren*, 116-117.

55 De Trobriand, *Four Years with the Army of the Potomac*, 478.

56 Rauscher, *Music on the March*, 79-80.

57 Bartlett, *History of the Twelfth Regiment, New Hampshire*, 116.

rain, the slippery and narrow pathway, with water to the right of us, water to the left of us, water above, water below—without opportunity to halt, or rest, or eat, or drink, until the late hours of night found us at our destination."[58]

The 17th Maine's Lt. Edwin Houghton remembered much the same thing. "It commenced to rain immediately after we crossed the Potomac, and continued to rain quite hard during our march along the tow-path and through the night. For the last fifteen miles of our march, staff officers were continually riding back to inform us that we had 'only two miles further' to march. At first," he continued, "the information was joyfully received, but it was soon an old story, and its reception was hailed with derisive shouts and jeers." The regiment finally halted at 11:00 p.m. after a march of nearly 30 miles. "The men being well-nigh exhausted and completely drenched," Houghton added, "but few tents were pitched, the majority preferring to sleep in the open air and the pouring rain."[59]

The XI Corps hoofed it from Edwards Ferry to Jefferson, Maryland, while the artillery reserve rumbled its way from Fairfax Court House to near Poolesville, Maryland. Levi W. Baker of Bigelow's 9th Massachusetts Battery found the march north exceedingly trying. "We break camp at 6 A.M.," he began,

> and march to Fairfax Court House, there to find everything in motion. While we were at Centreville we had 1,500 rounds of ammunition, which we turn in to the ammunition train here, and we are in light marching order. At 11 A.M., we wheel into column and start north. It was a hard march. Many of the batteries were like ours, having done garrison duty for some time, and were green in marching. The halts were frequent, and the gaps in the column also, and towards night the orders to 'close up' came faster and more emphatic. Many men had blistered feet and were giving out; some horses were showing signs of playing out; guns and caissons were separated by casualties; cannoneers were left behind. But we finally arrived in camp, near Edwards' Ferry, about 10 P.M., having covered about thirty-three miles. It was dark and muddy in camp, and we were too tired to get supper.[60]

* * *

58 Pennsylvania Gettysburg Battlefield Commission, *Pennsylvania at Gettysburg: Ceremonies of the Dedication of the Monuments Erected by the Commonwealth of Pennsylvania*, 2 vols. (Harrisburg, PA, 1904), 1:196.

59 Houghton, *The Campaigns of the Seventeenth Maine*, 77.

60 Levi W. Baker, *History of the Ninth Massachusetts Battery* (Framingham, MA, 1888), 53-54.

The lead elements of the Army of the Potomac were crossing the Potomac River on pontoon bridges at Edwards Ferry when General Pleasonton learned that his cavalry would serve as the army's rearguard and would cross only after the supply trains were safely over. Major General Julius Stahel's division, which was now attached to the army's left wing (commanded by Maj. John F. Reynolds), led the way.[61]

* * *

Persistent bad weather and long marches also exhausted the soldiers of Maj. Gen. George Meade's V Corps. The 11th U.S. Infantry's surgeon, Dr. John Billings, sent what must have been an alarming letter to his wife: "I have been playing sick a little since yesterday— a slight attack of fever I think, just enough to make me cross and blue. . . . I am getting demoralized and very much disgusted with the Army of the Potomac in every way." The doctor checked his watch and informed his wife that it was 6:00 p.m. "It is now raining and my disgust is increasing. . . . I have had a harder time on this march than I did at Chancellorsville. I hope and pray that a general engagement will occur before long—I think I had rather be killed at once than endure this a month longer."[62]

Meade received some much-needed reinforcements for his corps in the form of Brig. Gen. Samuel W. Crawford's division of the Pennsylvania Reserves. Crawford's command left the defenses of Washington and marched from Fairfax Station and Upton's Hill to Vienna, which it reached at 11:00 p.m. Crawford ordered his men to make camp just as a light rain began to fall. Another command, this one an untested Vermont brigade of more than 3,000 nine-month volunteers under Brig. Gen. George Stannard, departed the mouth of the Occoquan River to catch up with and attach itself to the I Corps. Meanwhile, Albion Howe's division of John Sedgwick's VI Corps moved from Bristoe Station to Centreville.[63]

Not all of the Federals were heading north. Captives from the Second Winchester debacle and the various recent cavalry engagements were being escorted in the opposite direction to Southern prisons. According to Joseph Waddell of Staunton, Virginia, a batch of prisoners was marched out that evening,

---

61 OR 27, pt. 3, 305 and 314-319.

62 Garrison, *John Shaw Billings: A Memoir*, 57-58.

63 Woodward, *Our Campaigns*, 261.

bound for Richmond. "These were captured in a recent fight near Aldie, Loudoun Co.," he penned in his journal. "The whole number was upwards of 600, but only 500 arrived, the remainder having been allowed by a very negligent guard to escape. Most of them belonged to a cavalry regiment from Rhode Island, and were very small, ill-looking men."[64]

* * *

Three days earlier on June 22, Secretary of the Treasury Salmon P. Chase had shared his theories with his daughter Kate about Lee's intentions. By June 25 the board game of war had come a bit more into focus.

"Matters are becoming more serious, though not at all alarming in this region," he assured her. "The situation as now understood indicates that Lee is about to try an invasion of Maryland & possibly of Pennsylvania. There is an opinion, not held, though, by many," he admitted, "that he may try to reach the Ohio at Pittsburgh or Wheeling. The days of six miles a day marches are over, however, and he will get no great distance, in any direction, without feeling Hooker strike him." The heavy combat at Brandy Station and Aldie were just samples of the sort of treatment Lee should expect, observed the secretary. "If God smiles on active and earnest work on the right side Lee will never take his army back to Richmond." Hooker, he continued, had told general-in-chief Halleck that a better officer was needed to command the garrison at Harpers Ferry. "Perhaps [Harpers Ferry] is in safe hands, already, but it is not thought best to risk it again as it was risked before. Where Hooker is this morning it wd. be hard to tell. He is, certainly, with his army and I suppose in motion. Where he will be tonight I cannot guess; but he will be where he thinks he can render most service & he will make no noise about it."

Chase, at least, had figured out that Maryland and Pennsylvania were Lee's likely object, but he was not yet aware that a large portion of the Army of Northern Virginia was already in Pennsylvania.[65]

* * *

64 Waddell diary, entry for June 25, 1863. The 1st Rhode Island Cavalry lost nearly 240 of its 280 men in the fighting on June 17 at Middleburg.

65 Nevin, *The Salmon P. Chase Papers*, 4:69.

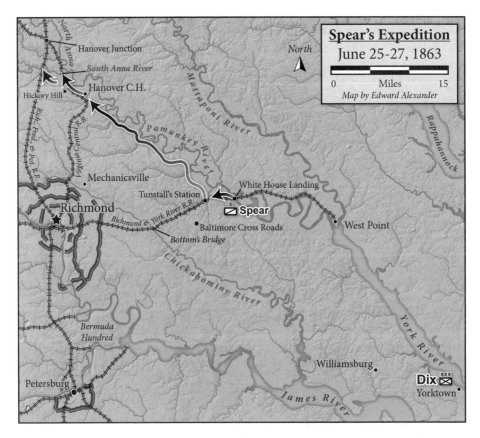

Eleven days earlier on June 14, while General Ewell's Second Corps was closing the trap on Milroy at Winchester, Halleck had ordered Maj. Gen. John A. Dix to take advantage of the golden opportunity in Virginia, courtesy of the nascent invasion. "Lee's army is in motion toward the Shenandoah Valley," Halleck advised Dix, who commanded a significant force on the peninsula created by the James and York rivers. "[A]ll your available force should be concentrated to threaten Richmond by seizing and destroying their railroad bridges over the South and North Anna Rivers, and do them all the damage possible. If you cannot accomplish this, you can at least occupy a large force of the enemy."[66]

This was sound strategy. It took Dix until June 24, however, to build up a force at Yorktown large enough to carry out Halleck's orders because of a lack of available river transports and pontoon bridges. It was not until June 25 that a cavalry force of just over 1,000 men, commanded by Col. Samuel P. Spear and comprised of the 11th Pennsylvania and detachments of the 12th Illinois and 2nd Massachusetts, arrived at White House Landing. Spears's troopers secured a beachhead for the expedition and set out to make their raid. White House was only some 20 miles east of Richmond on the Pamunkey River near where the Richmond & York River Railroad crossed it. Dix could strike directly toward Richmond from there, or move against the bridges and railroads north of the city. Spear had just over 1,000 horsemen.

Spear pushed his men forward three miles to Tunstall's Station on the Richmond & York, driving in about a dozen pickets of the 15th Virginia Cavalry and capturing one. The Union cavalry continued along the south bank of the Pamunkey toward Hanover Court House, where they arrived at 9:00 the following morning.[67]

"We have been startled by the account of Yankees approaching," declared 50-year-old Judith McGuire in her diary. "They have landed in considerable force at the White House, and are riding over the country to burn and destroy. They have burned the South Anna Bridge on the Central Railroad, and this evening were advancing on the bridge over the South Anna, on this railroad, which is but four miles above us." McGuire, who had moved to the capital with her husband and had found work in the Confederate commissary department, had reason to be alarmed. "We have a small force there, and a North Carolina regiment has gone up to-night to reinforce them. We are, of course, in considerable excitement. I am afraid they are ruining the Pamunky. Trusting in the Lord, who hath hitherto been our help, we are going very quietly to bed, though we believe they are very near us."[68]

---

67 Ibid., pt. 2, 795-799; pt. 3, 935; *History of the Eleventh Pennsylvania Volunteer Cavalry, Together with a Complete Roster of the Regiment and Regimental Officers* (Philadelphia, 1902), 76-78.

68 McGuire, *Diary of a Southern Refugee*, 223.

FRIDAY, JUNE 26, 1863

Dick Anderson's Third Corps division marched through Hagerstown in the early morning. "The people had very long faces," observed the 19th Mississippi's Adjutant A. L. Peel. One of them belonged to blacksmith Thomas McCamron, who together with scores of fellow residents stood by silently and watched the Rebels tramp fitfully through the streets. McCamron and several other pro-Union men counted the passing soldiers and artillery pieces. Two days later the blacksmith would ride out of town and deliver the information to the Federal army. "Officers and men in good condition say they are going to Philadelphia," he recorded. "Lots of Confederate money; carry it in flour barrels, and give $5 for cleaning a horse, $5 for two shoes on a horse, rather than fifty cents United States money."[1]

A correspondent estimated Anderson's strength at "7,000 to 10,000 infantry, cavalry, and artillery, accompanied by large wagon trains." Anderson, together with A. P. Hill, continued toward Greencastle, Pennsylvania, while the other two Third Corps divisions under Dorsey Pender and Harry Heth marched through Waynesboro toward Fayetteville. Shortly before 11:00 a.m. James M. Crow, Edmund D. Patterson, and H. Van Whitehead of the 9th Alabama asked a resident to show them the exact location of the Mason-Dixon line. Once there, the delighted trio stood with one foot in Maryland and the other in the Keystone State.

---

1 Peel diary, entry for June 26, 1863; Samuel P. Bates, *The Battle of Gettysburg* (Philadelphia, 1875), 262.

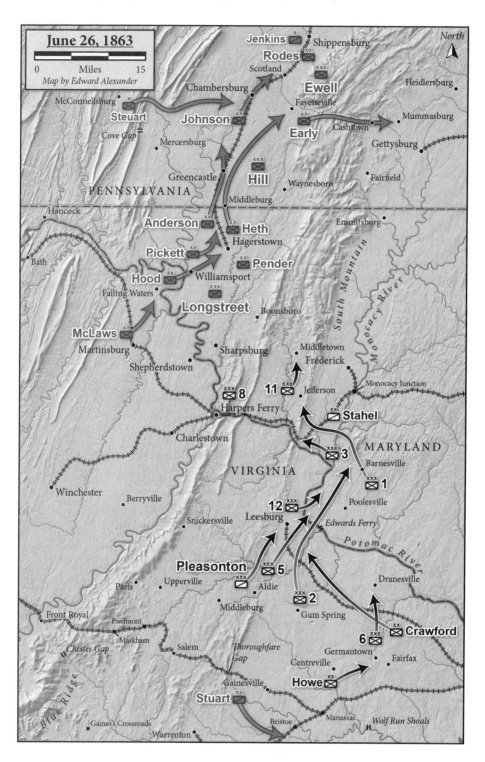

June 26, 1863

0 Miles 15

Map by Edward Alexander

Despite the drizzling rain they jubilantly drank a toast to the invasion, draining their canteens in celebration.[2]

A Georgian in Ambrose Wright's Brigade considered Pennsylvania's distinguishing features to be immense fields of grain ripened for the harvest, "nice large cherries, Dutch farmers, and ugly females." He lamented that "handsome females were much more scarce than Copperheads." Anderson camped his men two miles beyond Greencastle along the turnpike to Chambersburg. "We got into Pennsylvania at 8 a.m. at Little Richmond. We came 13 miles & camped," recalled Adjutant Peel. "It has rained all day. We issued whiskey to the men. Some of them are pillaging the country. We have a guard after them."[3]

Pender's Division was also battling the elements. "The march was resumed on the morning of the 26th, through rain and mud," noted the 1st South Carolina's Lt. J. F. J. Caldwell. "Fortunately, we had an excellent turnpike to travel. Provisions were abundant. Greenbacks purchased them at low rates, and in some places even Confederate money bought them more cheaply than we could do in Virginia. But money of every kind was so scarce," he admitted, "that we were compelled to rely for our extras on the charity of the citizens, or the lightness of our fingers. But there was not much thieving carried on. The people were so alarmed that they gave us many things with an alacrity not often witnessed by us south of the Potomac, and, in all probability, seldom experienced by the soldiers of their own army. A liquor ration was issued to us on the night of the 26th," he added, "the first we had had for months." Abner Perrin's Brigade was dogged by guerillas once it entered Pennsylvania. "Bushwhackers in abundance," reported the 1st South Carolina's Blackwood K. Benson in a letter home three days later. He and others heaved a sigh of relief when they reached their campsite in the Chambersburg area.[4]

Captain Robert W. Locke of the 42nd Mississippi, Joe Davis's Brigade, recounted the movements of Heth's Division in his diary. Bushwhackers wounded several men in the brigade during the march. Their passage through Waynesboro netted large numbers of horses. One of Locke's men named J. Carmichael

2 *Chicago Tribune*, June 27, 1863; John G. Barrett, ed. *Yankee Rebel: The Civil War Journal of Edmund DeWitt Patterson* (Chapel Hill, NC, 1966), 110; *Greencastle* (PA) *Pilot*, July 28, 1863. The correpondent's estimate was reliable, for Anderson's Division numbered 7,070 men with 16 pieces of artillery.

3 *Savannah Daily Republican*, Aug. 6, 1863; Peel diary, entry for June 26, 1863.

4 Caldwell, *The History of the Brigade of South Carolinians*, 93; Blackwood K. Benson to Berry G. Benson, July 29, 1863, Robert L. Brake Collection, USAHEC.

procured a nice filly. All in all "the citizens appear quite grim. Nearly all the doors shut they say we will be driven out before 4th July," scribbled the captain. "We hear the yanks have 200,000 militia + 100,000 regulars concentrated to head us off." Locke admitted that he and his comrades "may have bad times yet before we reach Washington City but still hope to get back to Dixie, but if the Yanks put all their strength the chance is slim but our trust is in God of battles & our own strong arms." The column camped in the rolling foothills near Fayetteville five miles east of Chambersburg near the turnpike to Gettysburg.[5]

* * *

Hood's Division, which formed the van of Longstreet's First Corps, crossed the Potomac at Williamsport. "We had to wade through. It had a very rough, rocky bottom. Water about four and a half to five feet deep, all got perfectly wet," complained the 15th Alabama's William Jordan. General Hood secured several barrels of good whiskey in Williamsport and had the surgeons issue a ration to each member of his division. It was the first such distribution in several months. About a third of the men in the 4th Texas "got pretty tight," admitted Pvt. John C. West. "Thirty minutes after the whiskey was issued, Hood's division presented the liveliest spectacle I ever saw," was how Capt. V. A. S. Parks of the 17th Georgia described the intoxication. "Good humor and wit ran high, and it was difficult even to hear one's self talk."[6]

Scores of drunken Confederates straggled far behind Hood's column. The 2nd Georgia's William R. Houghton confirmed that on "top of the hill in Maryland, were barrels of whisky with the heads out, from which each man was expected to take a gill, but those who had them filled their quart cups. About one third of our command, including some officers," he added, "failed to get to camp on Pennsylvania soil that night, and the red mud on their uniforms attested the tangle leg quality of the liquor." Most of the locals around Williamsport did not appreciate their Confederate visitors. "Some of the people here welcomed us with open arms, but by far the larger part looked rather blue, and would have preferred seeing the

---

5 Robert W. Locke Diary, entry for June 27, 1863, near Waynesboro, PA, "Soldier Studies," www.soldierstudies.com, accessed Dec. 16, 2020.

6 "Some War Sketches by Wm. Jordan, Company B, 15th Alabama Regiment," *Montgomery Advertiser*, Oct, 4, 1903; Coles, *R.T. Coles' History*, 102; West, *A Texan in Search of a Fight*, 91; "Letter from V.A.S.P.," June 28, 1863, *Savannah Daily Republican*, July 20, 1863.

blue coats rather than the gray," thought Sgt. John Dykes Taylor of the 48th Alabama, part of Evander Law's Brigade.[7]

The 4th Texas Infantry was approaching the Mason-Dixon line when Sgt. Val Giles dropped out of the column to await his friend, Capt. William "Howdy" Martin, so they could cross the border together. "Captain, I have fallen back for reinforcements," joked Giles when he spotted Martin. "I want you to help me capture the State of Pennsylvania." Martin laughed. "All right, Sonny. Show me the keystone and we'll smash her into smithereens." The pair linked arms and "invaded the United States." Giles and Martin waved their hats with glee and loudly introduced the Rebel yell to the locals.[8]

The good times lasted all day. The 2nd Georgia's Sgt. William R. Houghton estimated that a third of the men in Henry Benning's Brigade were too inebriated to make it to camp by nightfall. "We had breakfasted in Virginia, dined and wined in Maryland, and taken supper in Pennsylvania," observed Adjutant Coles. "It was reported by some that we had marched in four states that day, the fourth being in a state of intoxication."[9]

"About dusk we reached the Pennsylvania line and took supper in the United States," a delighted Private West boasted. "A brilliant and eventful day! Breakfast in Virginia, whiskey in Maryland, and supper in Pennsylvania." The industriousness of the farmers in the latter two states impressed him. "There was not a foot of surplus or waste territory. All had been made to answer the demands of the consumer." He deemed it the most thoroughly improved region he had ever set eyes upon. "Wheat, corn, clover, half a dozen varieties of grass, rye, barley—all in full growth and approaching maturity—met the eye at every turn, all enclosed in rock or strongly and closely built wooden fences. Apples, cherries, currants, pears, quinces, etc., in the utmost profusion, and bee hives ad infinitum." Huge barns were the most striking feature populating the landscape. Their size rivaled some of the largest buildings back home in the Lone Star State. "On the other hand," he added, "the dwellings, though neat and comfortable, were secreted in some nook or corner, as if there had been a close calculation that a horse or an ox being the larger animal, required a more spacious residence than a human being. I think the

---

7 Houghton, *Two Boys in the Civil War and After*, 85; *Montgomery Advertiser*, March 9, 1902.

8 Mary Lasswell, ed., *Rags and Hope: The Recollections of Val C. Giles, Four Years with Hood's Brigade, Fourth Texas Infantry, 1861–1865* (New York, 1961), 176-177.

9 Coles, *R.T. Coles' History*, 205.

class or position in society must depend somewhat on the size and elegance of the barn."[10]

"This really is the land of plentitude," marveled Lt. Sanford Branch of the 8th Georgia. "The whole country appears to be one broad field of grain. The people are all of Dutch descent," he scoffed, "and of course, are mean and cowardly." "We had left the war-wasted and battle-driven Old Dominion, and had come to the land of corn and wine, flowing with milk and honey," agreed the 4th Alabama's Pvt. W. C. Ward. "Everything indicated prosperity and abundance. It was a season of the year when the trees drooped with ripening cherries, and in every direction you could see these trees filled with them."[11]

Shortly before reaching Greencastle, an old lady standing alongside the road hailed a passing Confederate infantryman to inquire where he got his knapsack. The man's matter-of-fact reply was that he had taken it from a dead Yankee at Chancellorsville. The woman recognized a name written on the side of the pack: "That was my son," she quietly stated. The stunned Rebel halted to rummage through the knapsack. Within a few moments he had removed all of his possessions and handed the pack to the mourning woman, who "seemed to appreciate it very much."[12]

While camped at Greencastle that evening, Capt. Charles M. Blackford was "surrounded" by what he described as "enemies and black looks, Dutchmen and big barns. . . . So far as I have seen since crossing the Pennsylvania line, there is not much to indicate we are in the enemy's country. The people, of course, are not pleased to see us, but they are not demonstrative in their hatred or very shy in their treatment to us." He was surprised that "as no maltreatment is permitted, and no pillage of other than their stock, they are so favorably disposed toward us that they seem almost friendly."[13]

Staff officers erected General Hood's command tent near a fine farmhouse. Some of his soldiers chased and caught a few squawking chickens, an act that elicited a series of bitter complaints from the farm wife. "You would not complain if you could see how your soldiers have done over in Virginia," admonished Hood.

---

10 West, *A Texan in Search of a Fight*, 91.

11 Mauriel Phillips Joslyn, ed., *Charlotte's Boys: Civil War Letters of the Branch Family of Savannah* (Charlottesville, VA, 1996), 156-157; Coles, *From Huntsville to Appomattox*, 205.

12 *CV*, vol. 24, no. 2 (Feb. 1916).

13 Blackford, *Letters from Lee's Army*, 9.

"You cannot find a fowl or a hog in traveling fifty miles where your soldiers have been."[14]

Trailing Hood's soldiers came their comrades in Lafayette McLaws's Division, which had left Martinsburg, West Virginia, at 5:00 a.m. and tramped down (north) the Valley toward the crossing at Williamsport. McLaws informed his wife in a letter that "from Martinsburg to the river, eleven miles, the houses were all closed, the curtains drawn and the people either absent or invisible—showing an evident dislike to our cause." "The ford at Williamsport is a very good one the men crossing without difficulty," he added, confirming the tales told by other men of the division. "The wading across the Potomac was very deep and the men were very wet, and, as there was a quantity of whiskey in the city, a gill apiece was given to each man that wanted it, and in justice to my division," he joked, "I will assert that I never heard of anyone refusing it. The consequence was that the men were all in good humor, and as my division halted a considerable time, the men roamed over the village."[15]

McLaws was sitting on his horse near the Washington Bank when his aide-de-camp, Capt. Gazaway B. Lamar, rode up to notify him that the United States flag was being waved from its upper story. McLaws acted upon Lamar's concern that drunken soldiers might harm the flag-waving citizens and ordered the staffer to knock on the front door and insist that they withdraw the flag. Lamar did as instructed and returned to inform the division leader that a lady had answered, turned pale, and clasped her hands upon learning why he was there. She claimed those responsible must be young people displaying the flag without her knowledge. Lamar assured her no harm had been done, but the flag should be taken down to prevent trouble. The woman disappeared within the building and the flag was to see no more.[16]

After resting his men for a short time, McLaws put his four brigades back on the road leading north to Middleburg, Pennsylvania. Private Cully C. Cummings of the 17th Mississippi marched with Lt. Col. John C. Fiser at the head of William Barksdale's large Mississippi brigade. When the private spotted an old man supporting himself with a cane, the Mississippian asked the local to draw a line in the middle of the street to mark off Maryland from Pennsylvania. "He did so,"

14 *CV*, vol. 24, no. 2 (Feb. 1916).

15 McLaws and Oeffinger, *A Soldier's General*, 192; McLaws, "Gettysburg," *SHSP*, vol. 7.

16 McLaws, "Gettysburg," in *SHSP*, vol. 7.

Cummings recounted, "and with a running jump I bounded over into Pennsylvania."[17]

After reaching Greencastle, the 16th Georgia's Pvt. Eli Landers composed a brief letter to his mother. "This is the greatest wheat country in the world. I never saw the likes," he gushed. "This is a splendid country. Everything is plenty. The people has never felt the war in their country till now." His mind turned to the business at hand for William Wofford's Brigade. "We intend to let the Yankey Nation feel the sting of the War as our borders has ever since the war begun. The citizens . . . are almost scared to death. We intend to press all we can while we are in the Union. Us soldiers treats the people with respects when we want anything and we offer them our money for it and if they refuse it we just take it at our own price."[18]

Private William R. Stilwell of the 53rd Georgia in Paul Semmes's Brigade wrote that night to his wife Molly that he was in good health and spirits, although he admitted to being tired and footsore. "I guess you will be surprised to see that I am in Pennsylvania and still going farther," he explained. "We have stopped at twelve o'clock to rest two hours. I think old Abe is gone up this time. We are getting large quantities of stores of every kind. We passed through Hagerstown this morning, it is in Maryland. The ladies cheered us greatly but they can't fool me, they want to save their property." Stillwell believed the army was heading for Harrisburg—"that is the capital of this state," he informed her before acknowledging, "I do not know but one thing sure: we are now making the greatest movement of the war and will make Yankeedom howl and I hope to God, make them cry out, 'Peace, peace.'" The Georgia private was hopeful the expedition might bring the war to a close so he could come home. "Molly, I think this is the last year of the war, God grant it. I am no man for conquest. I had rather be with my wife and children than to be here and subdue the whole Yankee nation."[19]

George Pickett's Division, the rearguard of Longstreet's Corps, also crossed into the Keystone State. Brigade commander Richard B. Garnett received orders at 4:00 a.m. to march to Hagerstown, but was unable to get his command on the road until six hours later. A. P. Hill's Third Corps was already in the roadway and had to pass before the Virginians could follow. Because of the frustrating delay and

17 McLaws and Oeffinger, *A Soldier's General*, 192; C. C. Cummings, "Chancellorsville, May 2, 1863," *CV*, vol. 23, no. 9 (Sept. 1915), 406.

18 Elizabeth Whitley Roberson, ed., *Weep Not for Me, Dear Mother* (Gretna, LA, 1998), 161.

19 Stilwell, *The Stillwell Letters*, 180.

miserably wet weather, the quartermasters decided to distribute whiskey rations. "Every man in spirits, both good & bad," joked Maj. Nathaniel C. Wilson of the 28th Virginia. Once Hill's men cleared Hagerstown, Pickett's Virginians entered the community. "Hagerstown is about 7 miles from the river & about 5 from the Pa. line & contains between 4500 and 5000 inhabitants a large majority of whom are ultra unionist in sentiment," wrote Wilson in his journal. The division entered Pennsylvania at Middleburg, which failed to impress some of the Rebels. The First Corps's headquarters military court accompanied Pickett's command. One of the advocates, Lancelot M. Blackford, would soon write to his father, a judge in Lynchburg, and describe the village as "wretched." He said Middleburg, which "is situated immediately across Mason's & Dixon's line, [gives] but a poor idea of boasted Yankee civilization." His impression of Pennsylvania would change the farther north he marched.[20]

Sergeant Randolph Shotwell of the 8th Virginia, Garnett's Brigade, had a different experience. "Strange to say we met with a more marked exhibition of welcome at this Pennsylvania town than in any portion of Maryland," he wrote. "I saw fully a dozen miniature Confederate flags waving from windows, while all along the streets were ladies waving handkerchiefs and scarfs from the piazzas and upper windows." The unexpected reception dumbfounded him. "Can it be that these people are sincere? Or, are these demonstrations merely a part of Dutch cunning to placate the oft-pictured, wild, cantankerous, ravenous Reb of whom so many lies are told that simple people believe him a monster of cruelty? Possibly tho," he rationalized, "these are Democratic families that have been persecuted and harassed by their abolition neighbors until they really welcome the advent of our army as relief. Of course, we have little knowledge of the real feelings of the people." Dr. Charles Edward Lippitt, the surgeon of the 57th Virginia in Lewis Armistead's Brigade, mocked the thick guttural German accents of the locals in his diary: "The Dutch farmers say 'Take de horses take de cattle take eberyting put don't purn de parn don't purn de house & don't hurt de wife & leetle one.'"[21]

Robert E. Lee departed Williamsport and arrived in Hagerstown about noon to the applause of several locals. Later in the day he and James Longstreet crossed

20 Wilson diary, entry for June 26, 1863, VMI; L. M. Blackford to "Dear Father," June 28, 1863, Blackford Family Letters, Albert and Shirley Small Special Collections Library, UVA. Middleburg is now State Line, PA.

21 Shotwell and Hamilton, *The Papers of Randolph Abbott Shotwell*, 1:490-491; Charles Edward Lippitt Diary and Medical Record Book (#3157), SHC-UNC.

the Mason-Dixon line into Pennsylvania. The two generals camped for the night near the Bushtown Dunkard Church about midway between Middleburg and Greencastle.[22]

* * *

Irregular mounted forces operated on the fringes of Lee's army. "A terrible day," penned Mercersburg's Rev. Thomas Creigh. "The guerillas passing and repassing, one of the saddest of sights, several of our colored persons with them, to be sold into slavery, John Philkill and Findlay Cuff. The officer with a squad of men has just passed up the street making proclamation of something. I have just been to the door to inquire what it is. It is that they intend to search all houses for contrabands and fire arms," he continued, "and that wherever they discover either they will set fire to the house in which they may be found."[23]

The sight of blacks being dragged away disgusted Professor Philip Schaff. "On Friday this guerilla band came to town on a regular slave-hunt, which presented the worst spectacle I ever saw in this war," he lamented. "They proclaimed, first, that they would burn down every house which harbored a fugitive slave, and did not deliver him up within twenty minutes. And then commenced the search upon all the houses on which suspicion rested. It was a rainy afternoon. They succeeded in capturing several contrabands, among them a woman with two little children. A most pitiful sight," he concluded, "sufficient to settle the slavery question for every humane mind."[24]

* * *

The soldiers of Ewell's Corps, who had been resting near Chambersburg for a couple of days, headed for the Susquehanna River. Rodes's Division moved north toward Shippensburg while Johnson's Division trailed Rodes through Chambersburg. "Cannons, waggons & men have been passing since between 9 & 10 this morning," Rachel Cormany wrote in her journal at midday. "42 cannon & as many ammunition waggons have passed—so now there are 62 pieces of artillery between us & Harrisburg & between 30,000 & 40,000 men. O it seems dreadful to be thus thrown into the hands of the rebbels & to be thus excluded

---

22 Knight, *From Arlington to Appomattox,* 287.

23 Creigh diary, entry for June 25, 1863.

24 Schaff, "The Gettysburg Week," 24.

from all the rest of the world." Her mind wandered to her cavalryman husband. "I feel so very anxious about Mr. Cormany—& who knows when we will hear from any of our friends again," she wrote. "It is no use to try to get away from here now—we must take our chance with the rest."[25]

Widespread foraging continued as Ewell's men tramped through the Cumberland Valley. "We are delighted . . . to see that our troops begin to retaliate upon the Pennsylvanians, some of the outrages they have been perpetrating against us," thundered the *Richmond Daily Dispatch*. "We hope they will take deep and signal revenge for the injuries that have been inflicted upon us. Their armies with their approval, have stolen 500,000 negroes from the South, valued at $500,000,000, at the commencement of the war. They have no negroes to steal, but they have towns and manufactories to burn, and every one of these should be reduced to ashes." The editor continued by rationalizing,

> that property is property. There is no reason why one species of it should be exempt from the laws of war more than another. Were our troops to burn Harrisburg, the loss to the enemy would not counterbalance the loss we have sustained in the article of negroes alone. We say, then, make the whole Pennsylvania Valley an astonishment to future generations. They wage this kind of war because they hate us, individually and collectively—hate every man, woman, and child in the Southern Confederacy. The only way to stop it is to retaliate.[26]

Most Confederate commanders focused their retaliation on appropriating horses, mules, livestock, and supplies, which was in line with Lee's General Orders No. 72. "The rebs are in Newburg. Took about 100 head of cattle. They are every place you hear off in this part of the State, taking great many horses & cattle," wrote worried refugee Amos Stouffer. "Lee's whole army is in our valley—about 90,000 men. We do not know where Hooker is with our army. Some say on the Potomac by Williamsport, others at Baltimore."[27]

"We are in the dark as to Old Bob's plans, but are willing to go blindly wherever he directs," wrote the optimistic 2nd North Carolina's 19-year-old Lt. William Calder. Despite his youth, Calder commanded the sharpshooters of Ramseur's Brigade. "I trust & believe this campaign will do much towards ending

25 Cormany and Mohr, *The Cormany Diaries*, 336.

26 *Richmond Daily Dispatch*, June 26, 1863.

27 Stouffer diary, entry for June 26, 1863.

the war. The people up here are getting very much disgusted with the war since we came amongst them, and are willing to cry peace on almost any terms." Besides speculating on the destination, many Rebels compared their current surroundings to the familiarity of the home life they had left behind. According to Dr. Charles T. McClay, several of Rodes's passing officers in Green Village "were much interested in the Presbyterian churches of the valley, and made inquiries concerning church matters, and but little about politics or the war."[28]

"The people looked sullen," thought topographer Jed Hotchkiss. "Our cavalry is scouring the country for horses &c. The people are fearful of retribution from us." Eager for a dry place to rest, Hotchkiss and some of his fellow Confederates occupied several houses for the night. While he would claim no damage was done to them, he told a different story in a letter home. "We occupied a house night before last which the family had run away and left, we fared very well there and found many good things there," he informed his wife. "Once again, abandoned homes tended to be fair game for occupation and plunder." Before retiring for the night Hotchkiss made a few notes in his diary: "Gen. Lee wrote to Gen. Ewell that he thought the battle would come off near Fredericks City or Gettysburg."[29]

The increasing threat to the region convinced officials running the Cumberland Valley Railroad to suspend operations. "No cars came today," an unidentified girl in Carlisle recorded in her pocket diary. "All communication cut off—raining hard all day—scouts out all day." Albert Jenkins's mounted infantrymen, trotting at the front of Rodes's infantry, wreaked havoc on the vulnerable railroad by burning bridges, destroying rails, and severing telegraph lines. Union cavalry, which they occasionally spotted, usually withdrew without an engagement. A reporter noted one exception. "Captain Murray, with the Curtin troop, had a skirmish . . . at Stone Tavern, about five miles south of Carlisle," announced the *Chicago Tribune* two days later. "He checked the enemy, but lost seven men."[30]

Confederate commanders had to worry about enemy troops and occasional bushwhackers and, especially once they entered Pennsylvania, keeping their men in

28 William Calder to his mother, June 26, 1863, Robert L. Brake Collection, USAHEC; Hoke, *Reminiscences*, 186.

29 Hotchkiss, *Make Me A Map of the Valley*, 155; Jedediah Hotchkiss to Sara A. Hotchkiss, June 28, 1863, Augusta County, VA, Letters of the Hotchkiss Family, 1861–1865, VOTS.

30 "Young Girl's Pocket Diary," entry for June 26, 1863, transcribed by Frank Kline, CCHS; *Chicago Tribune*, June 28, 1863.

the ranks. Desertion was becoming more pervasive once over the state line. A handful of men who left the ranks were caught and punished, but many escaped and surrendered to Northern authorities. "Seven deserters came in below Mt. Union [in Huntingdon County]. They were handed over to the Provost Marshal of Harrisburg," announced a Chicago newsman. "Two other cavalrymen were taken near Chambersburg."[31]

Maryland Steuart's mixed infantry brigade had departed McConnellsburg after dawn and marched east through the gap on Tuscarora Mountain to Fort Loudon in northwestern Franklin County. From there the men tramped through Campbelltown (now St. Thomas), where according to Lt. Randolph McKim, Harry Gilmor's Maryland cavalrymen captured "sixty head of cattle, forty horses, some mules, and a few militia." The brigade halted just west of Chambersburg. An old man walked along with some of the Marylanders, recalled McKim. "They have been telling us you rebs were a ragged set, but you seem to have pretty good clothes," he declared, "and that you were badly armed . . . but you have good guns and what's funny to me, all of them have U. S. on them." Sgt. James Thomas in Company D of the 2nd Maryland Infantry would have agreed: "Our regiment was better clothed than most and all of our guns had been captured on battle fields."[32]

The rest of Ed Johnson's Division tramped through Chambersburg, following Col. Jesse Williams's splendid band of the 4th Louisiana Brigade. While the musicians played "Dixie" and "La Marseillaise," recalled a Georgia officer, "our redcross banners flaunted proudly over the dark columns of our gallant troops." The Rebels "passed in column after column, for hours," William Heyser recorded. "Next their batteries, army wagons, and ambulances, presenting a fearful sight. I have mixed feelings of indignation and humility. The passage of the army created a consternation among the people. Many feel all is lost, after seeing this show of power in the face of our inadequate defense."[33]

A persistent rain dogged Johnson's column north toward Shippensburg. "We had a very disagreeable march this morning to Shippensburg," the 5th Alabama's Cpl. Samuel Pickens noted in his diary. "It rained last night & nearly all to-day. The

31 *Chicago Tribune*, June 28, 1863.

32 McKim, *A Soldier's Recollections*, 165; Ross Kimmel, "Enlisted Uniforms of the Maryland Confederate Infantry: A Case Study, Part 1," in *Military Collector and Historian*, vol. 16, no.3 (Fall 1989), 106.

33 The Invasion of Pennsylvania—The Battle of Gettysburg—The Retreat to Hagerstown," *Macon Telegraph*, July 21, 1863; Heyser diary, entry for June 26, 1863.

One of the toll gates on the turnpike leading to Shippensburg, Pennsylvania. LOC

road was very wet & sloppy. S—bg is a place of considerable length, being built on each side of the road. It is a common looking place & is inhabited by common looking people—principally Dutch. I have not seen any nice, refined people since we have been in the State."[34]

The wet and miserable weather did not stop the men from appreciating the bountiful countryside. The famed Stonewall Brigade passed through "very flourishing country plenty of good wheat, plenty of the best meadows I ever saw in my life," marveled Pvt. John Garibaldi of the 27th Virginia. "The generality of the people haven't got more than eighty acres of land and they have it in the highest state of cultivation and living like princes."[35]

It was mid-afternoon when the head of Rodes's and Johnson's columns followed their bands into Shippensburg. Local druggist John Stumbaugh wrote a letter to his son a few weeks later with what he described as "a trembling hand. You never seen such scedadling of folks men women & children all fleeing beyond Harrisburg & thousands and thousands of Horses," he complained. The Rebels had "plundered all the stores . . . there was 5 different Sergeants in my shop [taking]

34 Hubbs, *Voices from Company D*, 180.

35 John Garibaldi Civil War Papers, VMI; John Garibaldi to Wife, July 19, 1863, Robert L. Brake Collection, USAHEC.

such drugs as would suit them and all the stores & shops in town & ware Houses, Mills. Suppose as near as can be sumbd up about 20 or 25 thousand dollars worth in this small place . . . the rebels took from me 100 to 1000 dollars worth of drugs."[36]

"The citizens, who turned out in large numbers to witness the passage of the invading army, were generally quiet," thought one Southern officer. "Occasionally you found a spirited girl, or a spunky person. But, if one fact was more remarkable than any other, it is this: That portion of Pennsylvania, which our army occupied, was completely subjugated, very few having the courage to raise their heads. Foraging thrived." The officer's report would appear in a Georgia newspaper more than three weeks later. "For a little Confederate note, and often for nothing, a soldier could get quantities of onions, apple butter, cow butter, ham, good Dutch loaves, cheese, and every delightful thing in the grand category of the productions of the great Cumberland Valley." The 53rd North Carolina's Louis Leon believed the citizens "looked mad at us as usual." Rodes camped near a spring south of town, with Johnson stopped on nearby Timber Hill. Ewell requisitioned supplies from the townspeople.[37]

"As soon as we would go into camp in the evening some of the soldiers would strike out into the country before they had time to put out a guard, and would come back loaded with grub," recalled Pvt. John O. Casler of the 33rd Virginia. The 12th Alabama's Robert Park noted the rains but managed "a nice bed of dry wheat straw at night, and slept soundly, undisturbed by dreams or alarms." Robert S. Bell of the 1st Rockbridge Artillery also found "a fine bed of straw," one he described as the "most comfortable bed we have had for some time—even better union lambs."[38]

*　*　*

Jubal Early's Division marched east from Greenwood on the macadamized turnpike through the South Mountain gaps into western Adams County. The Pennsylvanians along the way did "not impress one

36 John Stumbaugh to "My Dear Son," July 9, 1863, Shippensburg, PA, Harrisburg CWRT Collection, USAHEC. Stumbaugh believed "General Lee is a cunning dog."

37 *Macon Telegraph*, July 21, 1863; Wayne Wachsmuth, "June 1863: When History was Made," FCHS; Darrell L. Collins, *Major General Robert E. Rodes of the Army of Northern Virginia: A Biography* (El Dorado Hills, CA, 2008), 253.

38 Casler, *Four Years in the Stonewall Brigade*, 238, 246; Park, "The Twelfth Alabama Infantry," 245; "To Gettysburg & Back: The 1863 Diary of Robert Sherrard Bell," Old Court House Museum, Winchester, VA.

Col. Clement A. Evans commanded the 31st Georgia of Gordon's Brigade, Early's Division. He wrote extensively to his wife during the campaign.

LOC

favorably," Col. Clement Evans of the 31st Georgia informed his wife. They generally lived in "pretty good style," but most were uneducated and possessed little knowledge of the outside world. Evans was most surprised by the profane language employed by some of the women. Private Gordon Bradwell described these inhabitants as "rough and ignorant, living in little log shacks; but the men were not at home; they had business somewhere else at that time."[39]

Early paused at the Caledonia Furnace & Iron Works, which was owned by Congressman Thaddeus Stevens, the abolitionist Radical Republican who advocated "the most vindictive measures of confiscation and devastation" within the occupied South. Despite Lee's orders Early decided to lay waste to Stevens's facilities "on my own responsibility, as neither General Lee nor General Ewell knew I would encounter these works." The manager of the place, John Sweeny, argued in vain with Early not to destroy the forge, explaining it lost money and that Stevens only kept it operational to employ the region's poor. "Yankees did not do business that way," shot back the angry division commander, who ordered the 17th Virginia Cavalry to burn the furnace, rolling mill, and two forges, as well as Stevens's office, sawmill, and an attached storehouse. Early spared the houses and possessions of the workers, but appropriated large quantities of provisions for his command, including 4,000 pounds of bacon. Rebels also seized more than $10,000 in provisions and goods from company stores, along with large amounts of grain and corn in the grist mills and $4,000 in bar iron.[40]

---

39 *CV*, vol. 30, no. 10 (Oct. 1922), 370.

40 Early, *War Memoirs*, 255-256; *Chambersburg Repository*, July 15, 1863; Coddington, *The Gettysburg Campaign*, 166; *Gettysburg Times*, June 25, 1942.

Capt. Samuel Randall commanded the First Troop, Philadelphia Cavalry within the Department of the Susquehanna. He would go on to serve as the Speaker of the U.S. House of Representatives from 1876–1881.

LOC

The nearby mountains sheltered citizens bent on killing stray soldiers. "The bushwhackers occasionally fire on our stragglers, but this helps us to keep them in camp and in ranks," Colonel Evans informed his wife. Shortly after navigating the Cashtown Gap, scouts notified General Early that felled trees partially obstructed the turnpike leading to Gettysburg and that a Yankee force of unknown size defended the town some 10 miles to the east. The general decided to move John Gordon's Georgia brigade and Lt. Col. Elijah V. White's 35th Battalion, Virginia Cavalry along the pike to "skirmish with and amuse the enemy in front." Early intended to get men on the Yankee flank and rear and capture the entire force. About a mile and a half west of Cashtown, the balance of Early's Division and the 17th Virginia Cavalry turned left in the late morning onto an old country road running through Hilltown and Mummasburg.[41]

Waiting in Gettysburg were Col. William W. Jennings's hastily trained 26th Pennsylvania Volunteer Militia, along with two small companies of scouts comprised of Capt. Robert Bell's independent company of Adams County Cavalry and Capt. Samuel Randall's First Troop, Philadelphia City Cavalry. "At 10 a.m. with drums beating, sweethearts, relatives and friends waving us farewell, we proudly stepped out and passed through town," remembered 14-year-old militia drummer Henry Richards. Carried away with excitement, two townspeople joined the ranks; one was but a child who helped carry a bass drum for a mile before dropping out of the column, and the other was a civilian who stayed with Company A through the day. A reporter for the *Gettysburg Compiler* watching the soldiers parade through

41 Stephens, *Intrepid Warrior*, 218; Early, *War Memoirs*, 256; OR 27, pt. 2, 465.

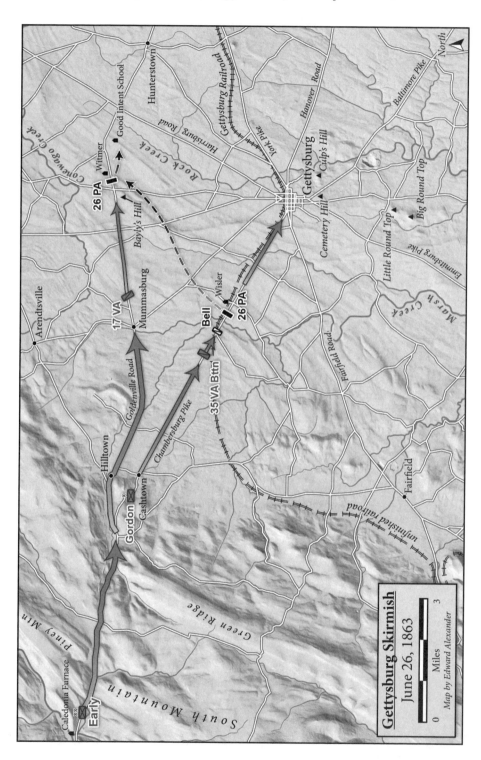

Gettysburg Skirmish
June 26, 1863

Miles

Map by Edward Alexander

town with flags flying was taken with the military spectacle: "All look like good fighting material, and will do their whole duty."[42]

Colonel Jennings selected his 40 "best" soldiers—veterans who claimed to know how to fire their rifles—and sent them beyond Marsh Creek to a small hill. An excited scout galloped in shouting that the enemy was "quite near." Jennings and Captain Bell ascended a nearby hill and spotted Rebel cavalry, infantry, and artillery less than a mile away. Fearing his men might soon be surrounded, Jennings concluded that the only route of escape was to get beyond the Mummasburg-Hunterstown Road before the Rebels cut their line of retreat. He ordered his infantry to withdraw and left his pickets and skirmishers near the shallow creek as a rearguard, fronted by some of Bell's cavalrymen.[43]

About 2:00 p.m. on what turned out to be a dismal, gray afternoon, 19-year-old Methodist preacher Lt. Harrison M. Strickler led 40 mounted troopers from Company E of Elijah White's 35th Battalion of cavalry toward the Yankee militia. Their "barbarian yells and smoking pistols" shocked Bell's inexperienced troopers, who without firing a shot wheeled their horses and scattered toward Gettysburg and Harrisburg. According to Jubal Early, they "fled across the fields at the first sight of White's advance party without waiting to see what was in the rear."[44]

"Lige" White's excited cavalrymen entered Gettysburg about 3:00 p.m. "with such horrid yells that it was enough to frighten us all to death," exclaimed Sallie Broadhead. Professor Michael Jacobs agreed, writing that the Rebels dashed through the town "yelling and shouting like so many savages from the wilds of the Rocky Mountains" and fired pistols into the air, "not caring whether they killed or maimed man, woman, or child." Lutheran minister Abraham Essick witnessed the charge down York Street: "They rode at the top of their speed and yelled like demons, their faces black with dirt and their hair streaming in the winds." Schoolgirl Tillie Pierce scrambled into her house, slammed the front door, and peered through her window shutters. "What a horrible sight!" she recalled. "There they were—human beings clad almost in rags, covered with dust, riding wildly, pell-mell down the hill toward our home shouting, yelling almost unearthly, cursing, brandishing their revolvers, and firing left and right." From their

42 Jacobs, *Notes on the Rebel Invasion*, 14; H. M. M. Richards, *Pennsylvania's Emergency Men at Gettysburg* (self-published, 1895), 9; *Gettysburg Compiler*, June 29, 1863.

43 Richards, *Pennsylvania's Emergency Men at Gettysburg*, 9-10.

44 Myers, *The Comanches*, 192; Jacobs, *Notes on the Rebel Invasion*, 14-15; Early, *War Memoirs*, 256-257.

Matilda "Tillie" Pierce, a school girl in Gettysburg, wrote extensively of her experiences during the campaign.

LOC

second-floor window, nine-year-old Gates Fahnestock and his three brothers enjoyed what they described as the "wild west show."[45]

"The Johnnies were entering Gettysburg," 17-year-old telegrapher Hugh D. Scott wired his counterparts in Hanover. "I will leave this place at once. This is my last message. A minute later I will have my instrument under my arm ready to drive down the turnpike to York, for I do not want to be captured." Scott cut his instrument loose, tossed it into the back of his open spring wagon, and rumbled off bound for York. Six Rebel cavalrymen chased after him, but their worn horses were unable to catch up.[46]

Confederates spotted two of Bell's cavalrymen, Pvts. William Lightner and George Washington Sandoe, on the Baltimore Pike and ordered them to surrender. Lightner spurred his horse over a fence and disappeared into the nearby fields. Sandoe, however, made a fatal mistake when he decided to fire before trying to escape. He might have made his getaway had his horse not balked at the same fence. One of the bullets during the ensuing brief flurry of return fire struck the 20-year-old. Sandoe had been a member of Bell's Cavalry for only three days when he died scarcely two miles from his house.[47]

---

45 Broadhead diary, entry for June 26, 1863; *Gettysburg Star and Banner*, June 28, 1863; Abraham Essick, *Franklin County Diary of Abraham Essick (1849–1864, 1883, 1888)*, UVA; *Gettysburg Compiler*, July 6, 1906, and June 29, 1863; Alleman, *At Gettysburg*, 18.

46 *Gettysburg Compiler*, Oct. 20, 1909.

47 *Gettysburg Compiler*, June 28, 1863.

Pvt. George Washington Sandoe of Bell's Independent Adams County Cavalry was killed on June 26—the first of thousands who would fall in the campaign.

Adams County Historical Society

Elizabeth Thorn was the acting caretaker of Evergreen Cemetery while her husband was away in the 138th Pennsylvania. The crackle of gunfire sent her rushing home. Rebels rode up to the graveyard gatehouse to demand bread, butter, and buttermilk. Catherine Masser, Elizabeth's mother, complied and the hungry soldiers dismounted to eat. Soon thereafter a mounted Southerner approached along the pike leading a saddled horse. "Oh, you have another one," said one of the Rebels. "Yes," he replied, "the —— shot at me, but he did not hit me, and I shot him and blowed him down like nothing, and here I got his horse and he lays down the pike." The man "blowed" down by the Rebel was George Washington Sandoe.[48]

White's jubilant troopers looted barns, stores, and chicken coops. Those who found liquor soon roamed the streets in "a half-horse, half wild-cat condition," recalled Capt. Frank Myers. Each "imagined himself to be the greatest hero of the war; in fact some were heard recounting to the horrified citizens of Gettysburg the immense execution they had done with the sabre in a hundred battles."[49]

"There had been [so] many rumours previous to that of the Rebels coming that the citizens of Gettysburg and the Neighbouring Town had partly prepared themselves for them by running off their Horses and Cattle and also shipping of[f] other valuables," wrote Kate Bushman after the war. "Nevertheless it found us somewhat alarmed when we saw a horde of drunken disorderly and dirty looking fellows for I cannot say Soldiers riding through our streets. We ourselves did not feel verry cheerfull when we heard a great noise and in looking out discovered the

48 Elizabeth Thorn account, GNMP.

49 Myers, *The Comanches*, 193. The *Gettysburg Compiler*, in its June 29, 1863, edition, verified that the Rebels purchased "a number of barrels of whiskey."

Rebels tearing down a Grocery that stood a short distance from our home. Well I can assure you," she concluded, "there was not much Dinner Eat[en] that day."[50]

It was drizzling rain when Gordon's Georgia infantry approached Gettysburg from the west along the Chambersburg Pike. The head of the 31st Georgia rose over "a little hill in the suburbs" when some of the men noticed "a fellow in his back yard waving his hat frantically and shouting at the top of his voice: 'Hurrah for Jeff Davis! Hurrah for Jeff Davis!'" Private Gordon Bradwell and his comrades "looked upon him as a sneak and a coward who wanted to curry favor with us, and they replied to him in language too inelegant to print, but among other things told him where to go and get a gun and fight." "Our military band took position on the principal corner and played 'Dixie' and many other selections; but none of the older citizens showed themselves," remembered Isaac Bradwell in an article decades later. "The younger set, however, of both sexes, considered it a holiday and turned out in force. They were anxious to know when we were going to burn the town. Crowds of these youngsters hung to us everywhere we went, asking this same question. Our only answer was that Southern soldiers didn't burn towns." The children, he continued, "seemed to think that was our only reason for coming, and they were anxious to see the fun begin. This question was perhaps answered a thousand times, but never seemed to satisfy the kids."[51]

The Georgians kept moving—even those with sore feet. "While passing through Gettysburg my dilapidated shoes gave completely out, and my feet, bruised, swollen and bleeding through tramping over the stone pike, were on the ground," recalled James J. M. Smith, a member of the 31st Georgia's color guard. "I could have taken a pair of shoes from a store, but General Lee had enjoined us to take nothing; we were not there to plunder, but to fight. There was no alternative but to keep up as best as I could."[52]

"We are not afraid, but it is exasperating that we are now under control of armed traitors," declared Sallie Myers. Professor Michael Jacobs observed Gordon's men with a wary eye and was unimpressed with what he saw. These Georgia Rebels were "exceedingly dirty, some rugged, some without shoes, and some surrounded by the skeleton of what was once an entire hat." Wet from the

50 Brian Matthew Jordan, "'Remembrance Will Cling to Us Through Life': Kate Bushman's Memoir of the Battle of Gettysburg," in *Adams County History*, vol. 20 (2014), 6.

51 Ibid.; Isaac G. Bradwell, "The Burning of Wrightsville, Pennsylvania," *CV*, no. 27 (1919), 300-301; Bradwell, *CV*, vol. 30, no. 10 (Oct. 1922), 371.

52 *The Sunny South*, Sept. 23, 1904.

rain and perspiring heavily after their long march, the Georgians filled the air with "filthy exhalations from their bodies" as they foraged through shoe, hat, and clothing stores. Ten-year-old Charles McCurdy was gazing enviously at Phillip "Petey" Winter's sweet shop when a big Rebel emerged with a hat full of candy and shared his booty with the boy.[53]

The sudden appearance surprised a few Federal soldiers. "Not being as well trained and practiced in running as the soldiers of Hooker's army, some few of them could not make the time required for their escape and were consequently captured," sneered a Georgian. Confederate guards escorted the captives a few blocks to Christ Lutheran Church, where they conversed with the citizens while seated on the steps. Several ladies felt sorry for them and arrived with dinners for the prisoners.[54]

Growing concerns about the actions of Southern sympathizers and potential saboteurs was on the minds of many. "The movements of the sympathizers here were closely watched while the rebels were among us, and we have heard of much that was said and done which we could not believe did it not come through reliable sources," recorded the *Star and Banner* on July 2. The paper continued:

There is no doubt that there were persons in this town (though their number is very few) who gave the rebels any information which they desired. It appears that they were informed of all the prominent Union men in the town, the positions they held and the very houses in which they lived. We know that rebel officers were entertained, and that certain women were desirous of procuring a feather from their hat or a button from their coat. We are proud to say, however, there are but few families in this town laying claim to respectability, that talked and acted in this way. Let them be discarded and shunned by their loyal neighbors. Have no intercourse with them in any shape or form. If we must tolerate such persons in our midst, they should at least be made to feel the contempt they are bringing upon themselves.[55]

*   *   *

Division commander Early accompanied the 17th Virginia Cavalry to Mummasburg, where a scout reported that a comparatively

53 Myers account, ACHS; Jacobs, *Notes on the Rebel Invasion*, 15-16; Charles McCurdy account, ACHS.

54 *Savannah Daily Republican*, Aug. 6, 1863; Henry Eyster Jacobs, *How an Eye Witness Watched the Great Battle* (undated, copy in ACHS).

55 *Gettysburg Star and Banner*, July 2, 1863.

small enemy force was occupying Gettysburg. He halted to await his slow-moving infantry slopping along muddy roads. Early dispatched a company of cavalry toward Gettysburg to reconnoiter, and it soon returned with a few captured militiamen who were straggling from their units. A courier arrived with news that the main Yankee force was hastily retreating through the fields between Mummasburg and Gettysburg. Early sent his cavalry in pursuit.[56]

Colonel William W. Jennings worried that the Rebels might be following him as he withdrew the main body of his barely trained and now retreating 26th Pennsylvania Volunteer Militia away from the Chambersburg Pike. A handful of Capt. Robert Bell's troopers led the way as the regiment hurried northward. Jennings intended to reach the Mummasburg-Hunterstown Road and circumnavigate Gettysburg by heading to a rendezvous point in Hanover. By this time straggling was a growing concern. The novice militiamen were loaded with knapsacks, blankets, and haversacks, and keeping pace in the mud, which in places was three to four inches deep, was a demand many could not fulfill.[57]

By the time Colonel Jennings's lead companies reached the Goldenville Road about four miles northeast of Gettysburg, the bulk of the regiment was strung out well behind them. The colonel halted his vanguard about 4:00 p.m. near the Henry Witmer farmhouse to allow time for the rest of his men to catch up. It was too late for some, who were scooped up by Colonel French's 17th Virginia Cavalry. French halted his troopers on Bayly's Hill, a low ridge running diagonally across the Mummasburg-Hunterstown and Goldenville roads. When a bugle sounded the advance, the Rebels charged and captured most of Jennings's rearmost company.[58]

Jennings watched in alarm as the howling Rebels swooped down Bayly's Hill toward his position at the Witmer house. Scattered rifle fire crackled from the brick farmhouse's western-facing windows, which were manned by several members of the militia. Jennings desperately tried to form his remaining men. Bugles sounded and drums beat as subordinate officers tried to rally the 26th Militia behind scrub-lined fences along a sunken farm lane. One of these new soldiers was future Pennsylvania governor Samuel Pennypacker, a private in Company F. "In the field, there was the greatest amount of confusion," he admitted. Most enlisted men did

---

56 Early, *War Memoirs*, 257.

57 Pennypacker, "Six Weeks in Uniform," 341; Richards, *Pennsylvania's Emergency Men at Gettysburg*, 9.

58 Pennypacker, "Six Weeks in Uniform," 341; Samuel W. Pennypacker, "The Twenty-Sixth Pennsylvania Militia," *Pennsylvania in American History* (Philadelphia, 1910), 391.

not even know their officers, who were "running around waving their swords, shouting and swearing, but no one dreamed of obeying them." Men became separated from their companies, and "each fellow did as he thought proper.... The commands from half crazy Captains and Lieutenants were often unintelligible, and perfectly contradictory."[59]

James H. Hodam of the 17th Virginia Cavalry would remember the scene as the terrified Yankee militia scattered. "Through lanes, over fields and fences we dashed after them leaving our infantry support far behind but the enemy could not sustain the unequal force long and soon the ground was strewn with guns and knapsacks, musical instruments, blankets, and clothing. On every side the blue coated fellows could be seen waving their white handkerchiefs in token of surrender." Hodam, a natural storyteller who kept meticulous notes of his service years, added, "All we did was to make them break their guns over a stump or fence and send them to the rear as prisoners." Some of the militiamen eventually realized that the shouted orders, drumbeats, and bugles were instructions to form into lines of battle. Colonel Jennings, who had taken up a position in the sunken farm lane, ordered his militia to fire a volley. The ragged line of flashes and smoke that erupted somehow managed to unhorse a few Rebel cavalrymen. For most or all of these Pennsylvanians, it was the first time that they ever discharged their weapons at the enemy.[60]

"Our pieces were in a bad condition," claimed militia private Frank Richards. "Half of them didn't go off at first firing, they being so wet." Henry Richards, who was sitting on his drum behind the line, could not help but notice the difference in action between the two bodies of troops, "both thoroughly brave," he noted, "but one also thoroughly disciplined by years of service, whilst the other was entirely undisciplined for lack of them." Young Richards believed the Rebels were losing more men than the militia, yet they "sat firm and steady on their horses, in straight and compact lines." By contrast the Pennsylvanians were "full of excitement, most of them yelling at the top of their voices." Several soldiers fired wildly without taking aim, while others were "so thoroughly worked up" they placed the powder on top of the Minié ball, rendering their Springfields useless. A few neglected to remove their ramrods and inadvertently sent them sailing at the Rebels.[61]

---

59 Pennypacker, "Six Weeks in Uniform," 342-343.

60 Hodam, "From Potomac to Susquehanna," 29; Pennypacker, *Pennsylvania at Gettysburg*, 786; Pennypacker, "Six Weeks in Uniform," 356.

61 Richards, *Pennsylvania's Emergency Men at Gettysburg*, 11.

"Some four or five hundred of the enemy managed to keep together with the Confederate charge upon them in some show of order," credited 17th Virginia trooper Hodam, who continued:

> The Pennsylvania Militia after crossing a deep ravine . . . halted behind a fence and fired a few shots at us. As the ground in our front was too rough and steep for horsemen, Companies D, E, and G were dismounted and charged them led by Colonel Tavenner. Major [Frederick F.] Smith with Companies A, B, and C deployed to the left to turn their flank but the enemy only waited long enough to divest themselves of knapsacks, haversacks, canteens, blankets, and everything that would impede their flight and away they went soon crossing a stream.

Colonel Jennings reformed his demoralized command almost half a mile farther east on higher ground near the Good Intent School. The fifteen or so isolated militiamen still in the farmhouse managed to get off a few final shots, but, "being very few in number, were obliged eventually to surrender." The entire fight lasted less than half an hour.[62]

The victorious Virginians discovered several beaten militiamen (described as "poor fellows") hiding in cherry trees. The troopers "pricked them with their sabres in that part of the body where a trooper generally half-soiled his trousers" before ordering them to climb down or be shot. Lieutenant Robert Gore's Company D captured nearly 100 terrified militia, a few bleeding from minor wounds. Sue King Black, who lived a short distance southwest of Good Intent School, saw students she knew from Gettysburg among the panicked militia. "One of the boys," she wrote, "hid under a bed where a Reb found him and asked if his mother knew he was out."[63]

* * *

A triumphant Jubal Early guided his mount to the courthouse in Gettysburg and openly chastised the militiamen captured earlier in the afternoon along Marsh Creek. "You boys ought to be home with your mothers and not out in the

---

62 Kesterson, *Campaigning with the 17th Virginia Cavalry*, 288, Richards, *Pennsylvania's Emergency Men at Gettysburg*, 11; Pennypacker, "26th Militia," 391. The stream is a tributary of Rock Creek.

63 Hodam manuscript; Kesterson, *Campaigning with the 17th Virginia Cavalry*, 288; Jim Slade and John Alexander, *Firestorm at Gettysburg: Civilian Voices June–November 1863* (Altglen, PA, 1998), 28.

fields where it is dangerous and you might get hurt," he admonished. Provosts locked the shamed captives in the courthouse. Early's disdain for the state militia remained evident years later when he wrote, "It was well that the regiment took to its heels so quickly, or some of its members might have been hurt, and all would have been captured."[64]

Early called for the mayor, but when he discovered he was absent met instead with town council president David Kendlehart. Early sat on his saddle while his horse gulped water from a sidewalk trough and scribbled a list of supplies to be delivered to his quartermaster: 60 barrels of flour, 7,000 pounds of bacon, 1,200 pounds of sugar, 60 pounds of coffee, 1,000 pounds of salt, 40 bushels of onions, 1,000 pairs of shoes, and 500 hats, all of which amounted to a value of some $6,000. If these could not be procured, the town could instead hand over $5,000 in hard currency. Kendlehart convened the council and returned to Early with a written response pleading poverty. What goods Gettysburg possessed, he explained, had already been removed to safety, but the Rebels were welcome to inspect the shops to see what they could find. Early ordered Gordon's soldiers to search the town but they discovered few items suitable for the commissary.[65]

About 5:00 p.m. Early ordered Elijah White to mount his cavalry battalion and follow the railroad east to find out what he could and snag more Yankees at the same time. He also posted sentinels to public buildings, stores, and even a few private dwellings to prevent looting. The biggest challenge was not from the enemy but from fellow Southern soldiers. Shortly after John Gordon first entered Gettysburg, a few Irishmen from Harry Hays's 1st Louisiana Brigade stacked arms and strolled along Baltimore Street to a bar on the southern outskirts of town. A brawl soon erupted. By the time the provosts arrived, drunken Tigers were "beating up the old citizens."[66]

While some of the Louisiana men threw fists and other Rebels guarded buildings, White's troopers passed the evening scouting and gathering horses and food. Jacob Brown, who lived east of Gettysburg, paid a steep price for his stubbornness. "I ain't goin' to move my horses," he insisted to a neighbor. "I'll just tell the Rebels I'm from Maryland and that they can examine the records and prove the truth of what I say." Some of White's Virginians took his three horses without

64 Early, *War Memoirs*, 258.

65 Vertical files, GNMP; *Adams County Sentinel*, June 27, 1863; *History of Cumberland and Adams Counties*, 153-158.

66 Early, *War Memoirs*, 257; Bradwell, "Burning of Wrightsville," *CV*, vol. 27 (1919), 300.

giving him a chance to plead his case."[67] The soldiers liked the appearance of the horses and believed they were fit for cavalry service. "No greater mistake was ever committed," admitted Capt. Frank Myers. In his opinion Southern cavalry horses—even played-out nags—could travel farther and better than those liberated from Pennsylvania stables. "Many a man bitterly repented of exchanging his poor old horse for a new one, even if he got a watch to boot," he rued. They also seized "every [horse]shoe and nail they could find."[68]

With darkness fast approaching Early did not have the time he needed to enforce his demands. "The day was cold and rainy and the roads were very muddy," he later recounted, "and as it was late when I reached the place, and desired to move upon York early next day, I had no opportunity of compelling a compliance with my demands on the town or ascertaining its resources, which, however, I think were very limited." Early put an end to the canvassing for supplies.[69]

Despite the cool temperatures and occasional drizzle, the regimental band of Colonel Evans's 31st Georgia broke out its instruments and began playing patriotic airs in the square that evening. Fifteen-year-old Albertus McCreary found the tooting and drumming "very exasperating" because he and every other resident else within earshot had to listen to it while trying to sleep. Several Georgians chopped down the municipal flagpole in the center of the Diamond (the local name for the town's center square). The discovery of 2,000 rations in a railcar was greeted with enthusiasm, and they were distributed to Gordon's Georgians. Other soldiers torched most of the rolling stock and then destroyed the covered railroad bridge spanning Rock Creek.[70]

Sallie Broadhead remained uneasy throughout the long night. "I was left entirely alone, surrounded by thousands of ugly, rude, hostile soldiers, from whom violence might be expected," she complained to her journal. "Even if the neighbors were at hand, it was not pleasant, and I feared my husband would be taken prisoner before he could return, or whilst trying to reach me." If Colonel Evans's account was accurate, Sally was safe, if justifiably concerned. "The town was kept very

67 *Springfield* (MA) *Republican*, June 29, 1863.

68 Myers, *The Comanches*, 194; OR 27, pt. 1, 923, 926.

69 *SHSP*, vol. 10 (1882), 540; *Macon Weekly Telegram*, July 16, 1863.

70 Albertus McCreary, "Gettysburg: A Boy's Experience of the Battle," *McClure's Magazine* (July 1909), 33:243-253; *Macon Weekly Telegram*, July 16, 1863; *Gettysburg Compiler*, April 24, 1907, and June 29, 1863; Thorn account, GNMP.

orderly & quiet," he insisted. "The citizens expected us to revel & riot all night, burning & destroying property. They were therefore very much surprised at the quiet of the town."[71]

As news of the arrival of Confederates in Gettysburg spread to neighboring York County, Quaker housewife Phoebe Angeline Smith took a few minutes to write to her sister. "[W]ell sister dear is thare such exciting times out thare," she scribbled. "[I]t appears that thoes suthern people are braking over and still drawing thare force onward to our country every day but we hope they will soon be checked."[72]

Thirty miles to the north, the remaining residents in Carlisle retired to bed that Thursday convinced the Rebels would occupy their town before dawn.[73]

*   *   *

Jeb Stuart and his three brigades of Confederate cavalry broke their bivouac early that morning and rode through Brentsville on their way to Wolf Run Shoals, a strongly fortified place on Occoquan Creek. Their horses were breaking down due to hard riding without grain. The opportunities to feed the mounts, however, were not good. "Had very poor grazing for horses, this being a miserably poor country & the armies having entirely consumed it," wrote a frustrated officer of the 3rd Virginia Cavalry. Fortunately, "no enemy disturbed our march and the only attack we made was upon some cherry trees which were along the road, bending beneath the rich, ripe fruit." The troopers bivouacked that night somewhere between Brentsville and Wolf Run Shoals.[74]

Beverly Robertson's and "Grumble" Jones's brigades spent June 26 holding Ashby's and Snicker's gaps to prevent Joe Hooker from interfering with the passage of the Army of Northern Virginia. Those positions would also allow them to counteract a potential movement on Warrenton by the Army of the Potomac. John D. Imboden, who commanded an independent brigade of cavalry that

71 Broadhead diary, entry for June 27, 1863; Stephens, *Intrepid Warrior*, 218.

72 Phoebe Angeline Smith to "Most Cherished Sister," June 26, 1863, Washington Township, York County, PA, courtesy of Elizabeth Valent.

73 "The Invasion," *Carlisle American Volunteer*, July 9, 1863.

74 OR 27, pt. 2, 693; Diary of Jesse R. Sparkman, entry for June 26, 1863, Archives, FSNMP, ("On our way down to Occoquon, very hard riding and a great many horses gave out."); Swank, *Saddles, Sabres and Spurs*, 72; Jewell, "Theodore Garnett Recalls," 48.

reported directly to Robert E. Lee, decided to cross the Mason-Dixon Line into Pennsylvania.[75]

"Lee's movements and invasion puzzle me more and more," Washington-based Count Adam Gurowski admitted to his diary. "The raid into Pennsylvania is the move of a desperate commander, almost of a madman, playing his whole fortune on one card. If Lee comes safe out of it, then doubtless he is the best general of our times, and we the best nincompoops that ever the sun looked upon and blushed for."[76]

Colonel Patrick Kelly's Irish Brigade, part of John Caldwell's division of Hancock's II Corps, marched at 10:00 a.m. Two hours later the veterans reached Sugar Loaf Mountain, about 10 miles south of Frederick. "At Sugar Loaf Mountain the three armies of the service met," observed Maj. St. Clair Mulholland. "Cavalry, artillery and infantry, coming seemingly from three different directions. The whole army began singing and shouting the 'Battle Cry of Freedom,' which resounded and filled the valley with music and was echoed from every mountain side—a grand tableau of War never to be forgotten." Shortly after noon the mixed brigade of Massachusetts, New York, and Pennsylvania troops reached the village of Urbana. The residents flew U.S. flags from the houses and gave "a cordial welcome and cheers for the Union Army."[77]

John Robinson's 2nd Division of John Reynolds's I Corps reached the Potomac in the late morning. Shortly after noon the 1st Minnesota ascended the heights on the Virginia side. "Troops and trains . . . massed down by the river, crossing and climbing the hills on the other shore," observed Sgt. James Wright. It would be several hours before the regiment's turn to cross arrived. With night fast approaching, guards ignited torches at either end of the pontoon bridges spanning the rain-swollen river. "The sun went down behind banks of clouds and it was scarcely dark before a thunderstorm broke over us and we were drenched with . . . ice cold water," Wright complained. "Peals of thunder shook the hills." Flashes of

75 Francis M. Imboden diary, entry for June 26, 1863, West Virginia State Archives, Charleston.

76 Gurowski, *Diary from November 12, 1862, to October 18, 1863*, 252.

77 Mulholland, *The Story of the 116th Regiment*, 128-129.

lightning allowed the sergeant to see large swaths of the marching column, "with heads bowed to the wind, moving slowly over the heaving pontoons across the storm-swept river."[78]

"Crossing into Maryland was like passing from a desert into a garden, from a land of desolation into a land of peace and plenty," observed a member of the 147th New York. "Save the fatigues of the long, toilsome marches it was a succession of delights." The 14th Vermont was a large, relatively new regiment that had not yet seen combat. "Camp near Harrington Station in a meadow. We marched very slow to-day; all are feeling good," noted the 14th's Sgt. Frederick Reed. "I am a little sore footed but I am bound to stand it. This is a nice country. We expect to see fighting to-morrow. It has been a good day to march."[79]

Dan Sickles's III Corps uncoiled itself early that morning to advance from its various campsites near the mouth of the Monocacy River north to Point of Rocks, Maryland. The long march provided some trying moments. A bugle sounded reveille at 5:00 a.m. in the camp of the 17th Maine. "We arose from pools of water," grumbled Lt. Edwin Houghton. "After wringing out our wet clothes we partook of a hasty breakfast, and were soon again en route." The men marched back to the mouth of the Monocacy and recrossed the same stone aqueduct they had traversed the previous day along a narrow footpath 60 feet above the water. Once several mounted officers crossed the aqueduct without difficulty the drovers began leading the pack mules over the span. Most of the horsemen forded the stream below the structure. "Several ludicrous incidents occurred in the crossing," Houghton recalled. "One or two officers' horses became unmanageable, and backed into the canal, and several pack animals, loaded with bedding and cooking utensils, after reaching the middle of the crossing, with characteristic stubbornness decided to go no further. The soldiers, whose path they were obstructing, would belabor them with their muskets, and not unfrequently 'Mr. Mule' and his entire load would be unceremoniously hustled into the canal."

Once everyone was across the aqueduct, the march continued through Licksville to a spot near Point of Rocks, where the regiment finally halted about 1:00 p.m. The "rainy day's march of twelve miles through a beautiful section of country, contrast[ed] favorably with the barren wastes of Virginia we had so recently left," observed Houghton. "On either side, wide fields of undulating grain,

78 Wright, "The Story of Company F," 552, as cited by Hage, "The Battle of Gettysburg as Seen by Minnesota Soldiers," 248-249.

79 Johnson, *History of Oswego County*, 87; Currier, *Memorial Exercises*, 57.

lovely scenery diversified by mountain and valley." Houghton found the farm houses to be "pleasant . . . resembling nearer our New England homes than any we had yet passed." The likeness, he added, "gladdened the heart of the soldier, reminding him of his own pleasant home and fireside." When the men approached Point of Rocks, they "were forcibly reminded of the beautiful village of Waterford, Maine; and in fact the scenery generally resembled that of some portions of our native State."[80]

"On this day we reached the Point of Rocks, and the most important discovery made was that the people were baking horrid pies, and cakes that were even worse," complained Frank Rauscher of Collis's Zouaves. "Our boys, however, eagerly snapped them up at high prices, as they were glad to make any kind of a chance from hardtack. They also bought plenty of onions, which were also sold on the gold premium principle."[81]

"Tomorrow I suppose we shall proceed to Harpers Ferry," predicted Chaplain Joseph Twichell of the 71st New York in a letter home. "What next you will learn in due time. Why we are here and what is before us is only the subject of surmise, but all agree that it means fight. God prosper us this time—at last—at last." Twichell noted that he finally had the chance to change his undergarments for the first time since the beginning of the march.[82]

Well behind the II Corps, George Sykes's V Corps rose early and marched from Aldie through the hilly Virginia countryside toward the Potomac. "There was a fine rain almost all day and the roads were very bad," remembered Cpl. John W. Dennett of the 3rd Massachusetts Independent Battery. He and his comrades trudged and rumbled their way through Carter's Mills and Leesburg before crossing the Potomac on the pontoons at Edwards Ferry.[83]

"Raining & roads muddy & of course hard & slippery marching," Sgt. Charles Bowen of the 12th U.S. Infantry noted in his diary. "We reached Leesburg at half past 11 A.M. & rested an hour then off again for Edwards ferry where we crossed the Potomac into Maryland & kept up the river to Poolesville. In all we march 24 miles & forded two streams. It rained nearly all day and was altogether the hardest

80 Houghton, *The Campaigns of the Seventeenth Maine*, 77-78. Licksville is now known as Tuscarora.

81 Rauscher, *Music on the March*, 80.

82 Messent and Courtney, *The Civil War Letters of Joseph Hopkins Twichell*, 245.

83 Parker and Carter, *Henry Wilson's Regiment*, 276.

march we have yet done. I saw two men lying dead side of the road just as they fell within a mile of camp."[84]

The historian of the 118th Pennsylvania of Col. William Tilton's brigade, James Barnes's V Corps division, recorded how his regiment marched "by the broad turnpike road through Leesburg" and crossed the Potomac "near the mouth of the now famous Goose Creek." It would not have been possible for the regiment to participate in a dress parade. . . . Wardrobes among the soldiers were so scanty that the clothing which was not upon their backs could easily have been disposed of in a pantaloon's pocket." He continued:

> The extra garments usually consisted of a pair of socks. Dress-coats did not average one to a dozen men. As the government did not furnish perambulating laundries for the convenience of the enlisted men, each man was forced to do his own washing. When the army halted near a suitable stream, the men disrobed and each washed his only shirt. When the march was resumed the dilapidated and tattered remnants of more prosperous days were tied to the bayonets, and flapped in the wind as the army moved on. An army with banners truly; not beautiful, but picturesque.[85]

Two brigades of Brig. Gen. Samuel Crawford's Pennsylvania Reserve Division, the newest additions to the V Corps, marched through Loudon County from Vienna to Goose Creek. "Through the day the rain was most violent and constant, rendering the roads almost knee-deep in mud," recalled Adjutant E. M. Woodward. The men were making forced marches, he continued, and "many of the wearied boys fell out, and did not get up with us until daylight the next morning. Rain, however," he added, "is preferable to dust."[86]

John Sedgwick's VI Corps departed its camps at Germantown and Centreville bound for Dranesville. "We wended our way over hill and dale at a rapid pace, we became much fatigued," complained the 15th New Jersey's Lucien A. Vorhees. "Many dropped out exhausted on the road. . . . [T]he country seemed to be in a state of cultivation, contrasting with the barren soil that we occupied for about 8 months. Cherries were abundant, and but few were left in the rear."[87]

---

84 Cassedy, *Dear Friends at Home*, 287.

85 *History of the 118th Pennsylvania*, 230-231.

86 Woodward, *Our Campaigns*, 261.

87 "Army Correspondence," *Flemington* (NJ) *Republican*, July 10, 1863.

Some of the marches involved more than rain, exhaustion, and stripping trees of cherries. According to Dr. George Stevens, the surgeon of the 77th New York of Tom Neill's brigade, Howe's division, the regiment was enjoying coffee before beginning the march when "some villain, belonging to the troops stationed at Centreville, set fire to the little Episcopal chapel that stood not far from us." The small structure "was the only building remaining in the little village which pretended to any appearance of modern architecture." Vandals follow an army "bent on nothing but destruction," wrote the disgusted medical man, and they "are among the unavoidable evils of war, and even the most severe discipline is insufficient to effectually arrest all mischief of the kind."[88]

Oliver Howard's XI Corps trekked from Jefferson, Maryland, toward Middletown a few miles west of Frederick. From there, the 154th New York of Col. Charles Coster's brigade took the lead heading west. "Started on about 11 A. M. Passed through Middletown and advanced into the Bolivar Pass, through the South Mountain range, wrote Maj. Lewis D. Warner in a letter to his local newspaper. "This Pass was supposed to be held by the Rebels, and great caution was used. The 154th formed the advance, and Companies C, H, and F, formed the advance guard. No Rebels were there, however, and I was directed to establish a line of pickets and hold the Pass."[89]

Back in Washington, the war department quietly made one command change that day that was later buried deep within most newspapers: "Col. Pierce has been assigned to the command of the troops at Bloody Run, General Milroy having been relieved." Milroy, the "Old Gray Eagle," would face a ten-month court of inquiry for the debacle earlier that month at Second Winchester.[90]

*   *   *

John Buford and his 1st Cavalry Division rode for Leesburg late in the afternoon and arrived there that evening. The troopers stood in the pouring rain holding the reins of their horses listening to an infantry band, whose members labored through what could only have been an unpleasant performance. David M. Gregg and his 2nd Cavalry Division endured a frustrating and exhausting

---

88 George T. Stevens, *Three Years in the Sixth Corps* (Albany, NY, 1866).

89 "Letter from Maj. Warner—the 154th," *Cattaraugus* (NY) *Freeman*, July 12, 1863.

90 *Chicago Tribune*, June 27, 1863. Milroy would eventually be exonerated and command Union troops in Tennessee in 1864.

day, their march delayed frequently by army wagons clogging the narrow roads. The troopers did not arrive near Leesburg until 1:00 a.m.[91]

That afternoon, Alfred Pleasonton heard reports from General Hancock that "a body of several thousand cavalry" had been spotted near Gainesville. The cavalryman ignored the idea that Jeb Stuart intended to pass through or around the Army of the Potomac and concluded instead he intended to strike some part of it. "My dispositions cover that," the cavalry leader assured Hooker's chief of staff Dan Butterfield shortly before 1:00 p.m. "I shall remain here [Leesburg] until the crossing is accomplished." Four hours later Pleasonton wrote to Butterfield once more. "Shall be over to see the General in a short time." Pleasonton did not yet know it, but his campaign to be rid of Julius Stahel was finally over. Hooker sent a note to Halleck about eight that evening asking that Stahel be relieved of command and his division assigned to the Army of the Potomac.[92]

*   *   *

Just a few miles north of Richmond, Col. Samuel Spear and his Union cavalry task force reached Hanover Court House about nine that morning. The blue-clad troopers seized a quartermaster's depot and attacked the 50-man detachment of the 44th North Carolina defending the Virginia Central Railroad bridge spanning the South Anna River. The surprised Tar Heels were reinforced and managed to hold out for about an hour until Spear slipped horsemen across the river below the bridge and attacked from both sides. "The enormous odds prevailed," admitted a defeated North Carolinian, "but only after a most desperate and hand-to-hand conflict with pistol, sabre, and bayonet, in which Confederates and Federals commingled."

Spear would report that nine of the Confederates were killed "and many so badly wounded I paroled them on the spot, by advice of my surgeon." The colonel also tried to attack the Richmond, Fredericksburg & Potomac Railroad bridge a little over two miles to the west, but a detachment of Confederate cavalry interjected itself and thwarted that attempt. All told, the fighting cost Spear three dead, 13 wounded, and one man missing, while the Southerners lost nine killed, 13 wounded, and 125 men captured. The Federals burned the Virginia Central bridge,

91 Gilpin diary, entry for June 26, 1863; Ball diary, entry for June 26, 1863.

92 *OR* 27, pt. 3, 333.

crossed the Pamunkey River, and ended the successful mounted expedition by riding back toward White House Landing.[93]

The cavalry raid had scored an unexpected coup. At Hanover Court House, "an old colored man" told Spear that a wounded Confederate officer was convalescing at a nearby plantation called "Hickory Hill." Spear dispatched Lt. David O. Tears and a detachment to investigate the report and they returned with a wounded brigadier general named William H. F. "Rooney" Lee—Robert E. Lee's second son who had been injured at Brandy Station. Rooney had been recuperating at the home of his father-in-law, Col. Williams C. Wickham of the 4th Virginia Cavalry.[94]

*   *   *

While the Army of the Potomac belatedly rushed northward to intercept Lee, anxious Pennsylvanians wondered, "Where's Hooker?" Few truly believed General Couch's hastily organized emergency men or the unpopular New York militia could stop a concerted Confederate effort to advance to the Susquehanna River, but that did not stop one major newspaper from arguing otherwise. "The rebels talk wildly about marching through Pennsylvania. Probably they will not try it," guessed a *New York Times* correspondent working out of Harrisburg. "Even now, without a single great battle, we believe that twenty thousand Pennsylvania militia, horse and foot, aided by an equal number of New Yorkers, could drive into Virginia all the rebels on this side of the Potomac by simply operating in the way we have suggested."[95]

At Harrisburg, Maj. Gen. William F. "Baldy" Smith assumed command of the forces stationed south of the Susquehanna. "Field works were built and positions on the Cumberland Valley Railroad and Pennsylvania Central [Railroad] were put in a defensive condition," Smith recalled after the war. "A force was sent to Marysville to save passes in the North [or Blue] Mountain to hold the Pennsylvania Central and North Central [rail]roads."[96]

Many observers believed Harrisburg, with fortifications and artillery crowning Hummel's Heights in Bridgeport and a broad river between there and the capital

---

93 OR 27, pt. 2, 795-799; pt. 3, 935; *History of the Eleventh Pennsylvania Volunteer Cavalry*, 76-78.

94 *History of the Eleventh Pennsylvania Volunteer Cavalry*, 77.

95 *New York Times*, June 26, 1863.

96 Schiller, *Autobiography of Major General William F. Smith*, 67.

city, was unassailable. "There is not much alarm among the residents, as that city cannot be taken, although great damage can be done in the Valley," penned a reporter with the *Chicago Tribune*. "[T]here are no rebels on the Upper Potomac this side of Harper's Ferry," he announced in error, "and everything in that vicinity is reported to be going on satisfactorily." Nevertheless, city officials prepared for a possible attack and the mayor closed all the saloons and bars. "A bleak, wet and dreary morning again brought us the usual influx of fugitives from the Cumberland valley," commented George Bergner's *Harrisburg Telegraph*. "Hundreds of horses are being driven over the bridges of the Susquehanna, followed by men, women, and children, the defenceless inhabitants of the Cumberland valley."[97]

"The stream of horses, cattle and terrified farmers became so great that it seemed as if a second Exodus was at hand," marveled the 22nd New York National Guard's George W. Wingate. "The fugitives talked as if a million of Lee's army was within gun-shot. The members of the regiment considered that they were cowards, and paid but little attention to their stories." Wingate was not so sure. "[T]hose reports really had a considerable foundation, and the general officers appreciated it, though the men did not," he continued. "Orders were issued to all the troops to be in readiness to move or attack at a moment's notice, and all commandants of forts were required to see that their guns were in position, and provided with ammunition. Whether they fully believed the reports or not, the men were skittish. That night," continued the New Yorker, "some spies, who had, for some inscrutable reason, concealed themselves in the camp of the Twenty-second, endeavored to escape under the cover of the night. They were detected, but safely ran the gauntlet of the fire of every sentry that could get a shot, while the regiment, aroused from its sleep by the firing, sprung at once to arms, expecting to be attacked."[98]

97 *Chicago Tribune*, June 27, 1863; *Harrisburg Evening Telegraph*, June 26, 1863.

98 Wingate, *History of the Twenty-Second Regiment of the National Guard*, 174-175.

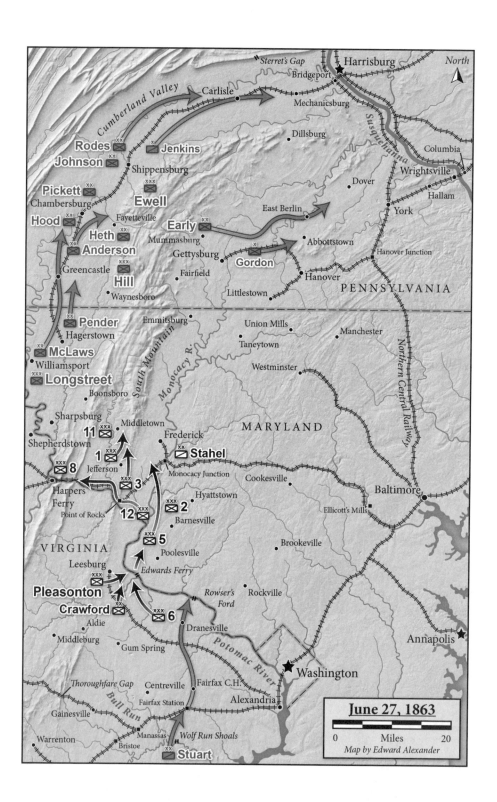

North

Sterret's Gap

Harrisburg

Bridgeport

Cumberland Valley

Carlisle

Mechanicsburg

Susquehanna

Dillsburg

Columbia

Rodes

Jenkins

Wrightsville

Johnson

Shippensburg

Dover

Hallam

Pickett

Ewell

York

Chambersburg

Fayetteville

East Berlin

Hood

Early

Abbottstown

Hanover Junction

Heth

Mummasburg

Anderson

Gettysburg

Gordon

Greencastle

Fairfield

Hanover

PENNSYLVANIA

Hill

Waynesboro

Littlestown

Emmitsburg

Union Mills

Manchester

Pender

Hagerstown

Taneytown

Northern Central Railway

McLaws

Williamsport

Westminster

Longstreet

Boonsboro

Sharpsburg

Middletown

MARYLAND

11

Frederick

Shepherdstown

1

Stahel

8 Jefferson

Monocacy Junction

Cookesville

Baltimore

3

Harpers
Ferry

Hyattstown

12

2

Point of Rocks

Barnesville

Ellicott's Mills

5

VIRGINIA

Poolesville

Brookeville

Leesburg

Edwards Ferry

Pleasonton

Rowser's
Ford

Rockville

Crawford

Annapolis

6

Aldie

Dranesville

Middleburg

Potomac River

Gum Spring

Washington

Thoroughfare Gap

Centreville

Fairfax C.H.

Bull Run

Fairfax Station

Alexandria

Gainesville

Warrenton

Manassas

Wolf Run Shoals

Bristoe

Stuart

June 27, 1863

0   Miles   20

Map by Edward Alexander

Saturday, June 27, 1863

June 27 was a watershed day in the unfolding campaign: Gen. Robert E. Lee arrived in Pennsylvania to join the corps of A. P. Hill and James Longstreet in and around Chambersburg. Richard Ewell's Corps, meanwhile, continued pressing toward the Susquehanna River in separate columns.

Early that cloudy morning Harry Heth's infantry division of Hill's Third Corps tramped through Chambersburg and camped east of town near Fayetteville. When reports circulated that Robert E. Lee was due to arrive at any moment, people lined the streets hoping to catch a glimpse of the legendary commander. Henry Bishop, Chambersburg's leading photographer, chatted with General Hill about the possibility of Lee stopping to pose for an image. Lee was in the midst of one of the war's most important campaigns, and as a result had no time for such trifles. Bishop tried to get his bulky camera equipment in position to capture an image as the general and his entourage passed through the town square about 9:00 a.m. but was unsuccessful.

"Gen. Lee, as he sat upon his horse in the public square of our town, looked every inch a soldier," observed storekeeper Jacob Hoke in one of the best word portraits of how the officer looked during operation. "He was at that time about fifty-two years of age, stout built, of medium height, hair strongly mixed with gray, and a rough gray beard. He wore the Confederate gray, with some ornamentation about the collar of his coat which designated his rank. His hat," added Hoke, "was a soft black without ornament other than the cord around the crown." General Lee rode along the turnpike east of town to George Messersmith's grove, where he established the headquarters from which he would direct the subsequent movements of his three corps.[1]

*   *   *

North of Chambersburg, hundreds of campfires flickered in the pre-dawn mists near Shippensburg as Albert Jenkins's men rose from their sleep and cooked breakfast. In the saddle by six, the long column of horsemen headed up the turnpike to Carlisle, determined to add another pearl to the string of Maryland and Pennsylvania towns they had occupied. The community of 5,700 people was an important railroad and manufacturing center, and also was home to the Carlisle Barracks, a U.S. Army post where Richard Ewell and several of his subordinates had trained in the antebellum cavalry and dragoons. Only 18 miles separated Carlisle from Harrisburg, meaning the Cumberland County seat could be used to stage an assault on the state capital. Numerous reports indicated Yankee militia defended the main roads, so Jenkins proceeded with caution. His advance skirmished occasionally with mounted enemy patrols. Once on the outskirts of Carlisle he deployed his force for a possible attack. Rifle pits protected the turnpike west of town and barricades blocked entry into its main streets. Jenkins ordered Capt. Wiley H. Griffin to unlimber a section of ten-pounder Parrott Rifles, and within minutes the artillery pieces were pointing ominously toward the town.[2]

When news arrived that the Rebels were within a few miles of town, recalled Sheriff Donavin, "it was very difficult to find anyone willing to believe the report. There had been too many 'scares,' and the people were absolutely exhausted with rumors and reports." Many thought this was the "cry of the wolf," and was simply untrue. Donavin recalled "the old town was more than usually quiet. Citizens met each other with a smile and talked about the 'big scare.' Scouts arrived and asserted positively that there was not a rebel nearer than Leesburg, three miles east of Shippensburg. There was a laugh all around, and the [New York] militia discussed the propriety of again going on duty." Thus "when it was definitely settled that the rebels were within a quarter of a mile of town," the people could scarcely believe it. A retreating detachment of Capt. William Boyd's 1st New York Cavalry stunned the residents by verifying the fact. "There was calmness amounting almost to

---

1 Hoke, *Reminiscences*, 59-61. Some local accounts place the date of Lee's arrival as June 26, but his order book states June 27. See Knight, *From Arlington to Appomattox*, 287.

2 Goldsborough, *The Maryland Line*, 285; Nye, *Here Come the Rebels*, 302-303.

indifference, and a resigned courage that was more than virtue prevailing everywhere."[3]

Though there may well have been "resigned courage," the news that the Rebels were closing in on Carlisle seriously affected the nerves of some of our citizens," admitted the *Carlisle American.* "Many of our prominent ones, and many not so prominent, concluded to leave town, and conveyances of all kinds were in great demand. Desperate for an avenue of escape despite the shortage of wagons and horses, some residents started on foot for Harrisburg and other points." Refugees from across Cumberland County hurrying through town increased the confusion and alarm. Most headed toward the Susquehanna River hoping to find safety on the East Shore in Harrisburg.[4]

Just before ten that morning, Jenkins's scouts spotted a handful of civilians emerging from Carlisle carrying a white flag. The civilian truce party informed Jenkins that no military force defended the town and no resistance would be made. The general ordered a small detachment to ride into Carlisle and ensure the veracity of the statements. The 14th Virginia Cavalry's Lt. Hermann Schuricht reported that his troopers "passed the obstructions and fortifications, and occupied the city at 10 o'clock." Wary of a trap, the main body of the 14th filed slowly into town from the west along the Walnut Bottom, Chambersburg, and Newville roads. A local newsman estimated the enemy at "four hundred in number, mounted infantry, and every many carried a gun in a position to use it on an instant with his hands on the hammer."[5]

Fifteen-year-old schoolboy James W. Sullivan described the riders as "big men, wearing broad-brimmed hats, and mounted on good horses," with "a picturesque air of confidence and readiness for action." It was market day, and the shoppers who were out and about scurried home. "The town looked as if the day were a Sunday," observed another youth named Edward C. Beetem. The long column passed along Main Street east to the junction of the Trindle Springs and Dillsburg roads, where a detachment filed to the north to the Carlisle Barracks along the

---

3 Donavin, "The Invasion," *Carlisle American Volunteer,* July 9, 1863.

4 Ibid.; "A Day of Quiet," *Carlisle Herald,* July 31, 1863.

5 Schuricht diary, entry for June 27, 1863, *Richmond Daily Dispatch;* Donavin, "The Invasion." S. K. Donavin and others placed the Confederate arrival at 11:00 a.m. The truce party included Assistant Burgess Robert Allison and William M. Penrose, a prominent attorney who had served as colonel of the 6th Pennsylvania Reserves earlier in the war. Declining health brought about by exposure to the elements had forced him to return home.

turnpike leading to Harrisburg. Others continued to the eastern outskirts where they established a picket line; the remainder returned to the town square.[6]

Jenkins summoned the borough authorities. When Chief Burgess Andrew Ziegler and several councilmen arrived, the general demanded the delivery of 1,500 rations to the market house within one hour. Ziegler and other leaders canvassed Carlisle and insisted that each family furnish a share. "The request had to be complied with," wrote Sheriff Donavin, "and was done with alacrity, as Jenkins had threatened that on failure to furnish [it], his men would help themselves. In less than an hour, the stalls of the market house were filled will all kinds of eatables, and considerable hungry secessionists were filling themselves with good food." After dining to their heart's content many soldiers rode around town sightseeing while others emptied John Noble's corn crib to feed their hungry horses.[7]

Late that afternoon the lively strains of "Dixie" announced the arrival of Rodes's Division. "The inhabitants were expecting us," a soldier in the 44th Georgia informed his hometown paper. "We marched with colors streaming and bands playing. The citizens seemed anxious to get a glimpse of us as we went to our respective camps." Sheriff Donavin was unimpressed. The infantrymen "presented a sorry appearance. Many were barefooted, others hatless, numbers of them ragged, and all dirty." Nevertheless, "they exhibited a cheerfulness which was indicative of great spirit and endurance. They had marched twenty miles on that day, yet none of them appeared to be fagged or tired. They went along shouting, laughing, and singing 'Dixie' and other camp airs. A few by their manner showed insolence."[8]

Teenager James K. Sullivan disagreed with Donavin's description of the uninvited visitors. "Where were those 'ragged uniforms?' those 'half-starved stragglers?'" he queried. "The passing uniforms undergoing our inspection were if not new, newish; there was no showing of torn coats and badly frayed trousers. A party of students on a walking tour would look little better at the end of the season." The longer he studied the Rebels the madder he became:

---

6 Sullivan, *Boyhood Memories*, 13; Charles Gilbert Beetem, *Experiences of a West Ward Boy* (Carlisle, PA, 1963), 1.

7 Donavin, "The Invasion."

8 "A Complete and Interesting Account of the Pennsylvania Campaign," *Augusta* (GA) *Chronicle*, Sept. 5, 1863; Donavin, "The Invasion." Rodes arrived via Walnut Bottom Road and then took South Pitt Street to Main Street before turning north and proceeding to the Carlisle Barracks.

Knapsacks and haversacks, the whole personal kit, was in order; arms were at every man's command . . . my first impression of a fit, well-fed, well-conditioned army. . . . Everything was moving along with the regularity of a well organized parade. By the time I got back home any notion I had of seeing an army foretelling defeat by signs of impoverishment and exhaustion was dislodged from my mind. We had been fed on lies.[9]

Within an hour after the division's arrival Confederate officers were thronging the hotels and riding around town. "The most of them were gentlemen in manners, evidently educated, and carefully guarded against any expression calculated to evince the real bitterness which they felt for our people," observed Donavin. "Occasionally one was to be heard who laid aside his restraint and was unmeasured in his abuse of Northern people, their manners customs and habits." Many of them boasted about the "certain capture" of Hooker's army and the subsequent fall of Baltimore and even Washington. Some "expressed the greatest contempt for the Militia, asserting that they would pass through an ocean of them, and nothing would afford them a finer opportunity of replenishing their wardrobe than to meet an army of them."[10]

"Carlisle was a lovely place and its people not half as sullen as they are farther down the Valley, the German element not being as strong & the humanizing influences of schools &c have made a better population," recalled topographer Jed Hotchkiss. "We found them in quite a state of alarm, expecting us to burn pillage & destroy as they have done, but when they saw the conduct of our army they seemed surprised." The 1st North Carolina's Lewis Leon agreed with Hotchkiss. "The city is certainly a beautiful place." The Tar Heel and his comrades were "treated very good by the ladies" who worried the Rebels would destroy their fair city, "but when we told them the strict orders of General Lee they were rejoiced."[11]

Colonel Edward O'Neal's Alabamans filed through town and bivouacked to the east after establishing a strong picket line. George Doles camped his brigade on the grounds of Dickinson College on the west side of Carlisle. The venerable school was preparing for commencement exercises when its president, the grave old Dr. Herman M. Johnson, received word that the Rebels were coming. "Two

9 Sullivan, *Boyhood Memories*, 17-19.

10 Donavin, "The Invasion."

11 Hotchkiss, *Make Me A Map of the Valley*, 155; Jedediah Hotchkiss to Sara A. Hotchkiss, June 28, 1863, Augusta County, VA, Letters of the Hotchkiss Family, 1861-1865, VOTS; *Charlotte Observer*, Nov. 16, 1892.

Old West is a landmark on the campus of Dickinson College in Carlisle, Pa. LOC

days of the examination had already passed," sneered a soldier in the 44th Georgia. "But how perplexing to the seniors to think that they would not be permitted to deliver their addresses! Oh, cruel Confederates. Why molest these peaceable debonair gentlemen?" The Rev. Leonard M. Gardner was in town for the planned graduation ceremony. "The public excitement was intense; the college exercises were abandoned," wrote the disappointed religious leader after the war. "No forces were there to offer resistance and before the slow steady march of the great invading army everyone fled or submitted." Gardner collected his belongings and slipped away as well on a walk of 14 miles to his father's house in York Springs in northeastern Adams County.[12]

12 *Augusta* (GA) *Chronicle*, Sept. 5, 1863; Gardner, *Sunset Memories*, 2. Dickinson College received its charter in 1783, six days after the Treaty of Paris ended the Revolutionary War. Benjamin Rush, a signer of the Declaration of Independence, founded the school and recommended that it be named for fellow founding father John Dickinson and his wife Mary. At the time, it was the westernmost college in the new United States of America. Notable graduates included future president James Buchanan and Roger Taney, later to be the chief justice of the Supreme Court.

The campsite of Doles's Georgians impressed the local young men. "The pictures these troops presented on the campus, with their tents, stacked rifles, and baggage, as one which attracted us boys as much as any circus come to town," recalled Edward Beteem. The boys gradually lost their fear of the Rebels and began conversing with them, "but as these troops were from Georgia, and as their expressions and the accent given their words were strange to us, we never gleaned any important information."[13]

The brigades of Junius Daniel, Alfred Iverson, and Stephen Ramseur, along with General Ewell, quartered at Carlisle Barracks. The irony of the situation could not have been lost on the new corps commander, who knew it well from his younger days. After he graduated from West Point in 1840, Ewell received training for the 1st Dragoons there before heading off for the Indian Territory. Many of the men fanned out to search the stables for grain and other supplies, but Union troopers had already removed most of whatever was usable. Other than muskets, holsters, tents, and a small amount of subsistence stores the Rebels later discovered, there was little gleaned from the barracks. Ewell requisitioned a vast array of provisions from the townspeople—25,000 pounds of bacon, 100 sacks of salt, 1,500 barrels of flour, 25 barrels of potatoes, 25 barrels of molasses, 5,000 pounds of coffee, 3,000 pounds of sugar, 25 barrels of dried fruit, and vast quantities of quinine, chloroform, and other medicines.[14]

With Carlisle secure, Ewell dispatched Jenkins and his mounted infantry, along with Chief Engineer H. B. Richardson, to reconnoiter Union positions on the West Shore opposite Harrisburg. Jenkins advanced his brigade toward Mechanicsburg and went into camp about five miles from the town. "Our pickets were attacked several times," reported Lt. Hermann Schuricht.[15]

Edward Johnson's Division, meanwhile, halted its march about four miles west of Carlisle on the Line farm. "We passed through Chambersburg and Green Village and on to Shippensburg, through which we pressed to Stoughstown, seven miles farther, and camped at Big Spring near Springfield," recalled Lt. Randolph McKim of "Maryland" Steuart's staff. "At Springfield I bought seven copies of the

13 Beetem, *Experiences of a West Ward Boy*, 3.

14 "Entrance of Ewell's Army," and "The Requisitions," *Carlisle Herald*, July 31, 1863; OR 27, pt. 2, 551; "The Original Requisition Upon the Authorities of the Borough of Carlisle, Pa., during the Confederate Raid June 27, 1863," *The Evening Sentinel*, June 21, 1863.

15 Sullivan, *Boyhood Memories*, 13; Schuricht diary, entry for June 27, 1863, *Richmond Dispatch*, April 5, 1896.

New Testament for distribution among the men. The surprise of the storekeeper when an officer of the terrible Rebel Army desired to purchase copies of the New Testament may be imagined," joked the religiously inclined staff officer. "Perhaps he thought if the rebels would read the Good Book, they might repent of their wicked Rebellion."[16]

Lieutenant Thomas F. Boatwright of the 44th Virginia, John M. Jones's Brigade, took the opportunity to shop for gifts to send home to his wife. Boatwright purchased two dresses for her, as well as a pair of shoes. His men bought "whiskey, and candy, sigars, nuts of different kinds." Foraging patrols scoured the verdant countryside for additional supplies, horses, cattle, and livestock. Nettie Blair, a New York girl caught up in the invasion while visiting her grandfather in Pennsylvania, claimed the Rebels also searched the houses for any hidden blacks.[17]

*   *   *

Jubal Early's Division arose about 6:00 a.m. after what its commander described as a "most uncomfortable and dreary" night. Most of his men had slept on "the naked ground . . . their covering the sky above them" because they had left their tents at Greenwood. They headed farther east toward York County. The 9th Louisiana of Harry Hays's Brigade broke camp just north of Gettysburg along the Mummasburg Road but left one of its members, an extremely ill private named John Shackleford, behind in a barn on the David Schriver farm. Dr. John W. C. O'Neal, a Virginia-born physician living in Gettysburg, arrived to tend to the dying soldier. During the march east "many of the men were drunk and caused me much trouble to make them keep up with the column," complained Adjutant William Seymour.[18]

16 McKim, *A Soldier's Recollections*, 166. Native Americans had camped at Big Spring for generations, as did U.S. troops on their way to Ohio during the War of 1812.

17 Thomas Boatwright to his wife, June 27, 1863, Thomas Frederick Boatwright Papers, SHC-UNC. Boatwright would be killed the following May at Spotsylvania. Blair, *Reminiscences of Nettie Jane Blair*, 6-7, CCHS.

18 Early, "The Invasion of Pennsylvania," 232; Seymour account, GNMP. Professor Michael Jacobs of Pennsylvania College kept detailed notes on the local weather: "The entire period of the invasion is remarkable for being one of clouds, and, for that season of the year, of low temperature. From June 15th until July 22nd, 1863, there was not an entirely clear day. On the

Early's tail units left their camps near Gettysburg, Mummasburg, and Hunterstown about eight that morning. "The bird has flown," scribbled a reporter with the *New York Herald* when he learned of the Rebels' departure. Three daring Union scouts from Cole's Maryland Cavalry dashed into Gettysburg at 9:30 a.m. Their sudden arrival surprised two of Ewell's couriers, both of whom were quickly captured. One was a chaplain and both were seeking General Early. "Considering all things we were well treated," admitted resident Alice Powers, "but when Saturday noon found the Rebels gone every citizen felt satisfied to have them depart."[19]

Early sent Elijah White's 35th Battalion, Virginia Cavalry, on to Hanover and Gordon's Georgians and Capt. William Tanner's Courtney Virginia artillery through New Oxford and Abbottstown toward York. The remaining three infantry brigades, the 17th Virginia Cavalry, and a trio of Hilary Jones's batteries moved through Hampden and East Berlin. White's cavaliers took every horse and mule within sight before raiding Hanover's stores. The cavalrymen ripped down telegraph wires and burned three bridges along the tracks to Hanover Junction, nine miles northeast of Hanover. Many of the locals mystified the raiders by making strange gestures and repeatedly declaring "peace, peace" while waving paper certificates. The Rebels eventually learned that fast-talking swindlers from New York had duped these Pennsylvanians by selling them worthless membership cards, secret signs, and passwords to the Knights of the Golden Circle, a secret pro-Confederate organization that had almost no presence inside the Keystone State.[20]

"We gave the old dutch in Penn. fits," bragged Pvt. Joseph Trundle, one of White's Marylanders. "Our army left a mark everywhere it went. Horses, cattle, sheep, hogs, chickens, spring houses suffered alike. They cried peace, peace most beautifully everywhere we went." In some cases, when told the horses had been sent away, cavalrymen forced the farmers to pay the net value of the missing steeds.[21]

---

evening of June 25th at 8 p.m. a rain began. . . . This rain continued at intervals until Saturday June 27th, at 7:00 a.m., the perception being in inches 1.280."

19 Jacobs, *Notes on the Rebel Invasion*, 19; *Gettysburg Compiler*, June 29, 1863, and June 24, 1903.

20 Wert account, June 25, 1913, GNMP.

21 Joseph H. Trundle, *Gettysburg Described in Two Letters from a Maryland Confederate* (Rockville, MD, 1959), 211-212.

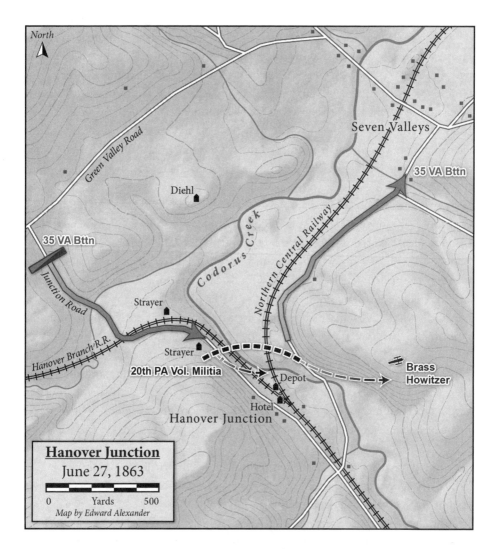

North

Seven Valleys

35 VA Bttn

Green Valley Road

Diehl

35 VA Bttn

Codorus Creek

Northern Central Railway

Junction Road

Strayer

Strayer

20th PA Vol. Militia

Depot

Brass Howitzer

Hanover Branch R.R.

Hotel

Hanover Junction

Hanover Junction
June 27, 1863

0   Yards   500

Map by Edward Alexander

White's battalion reached Hanover Junction about 2:00 p.m. and promptly (and quite easily) chased off three companies of the inexperienced 20th Pennsylvania Volunteer Militia. The stunned Philadelphians and Lt. Col. William H. Sickles fled to nearby hilltop fortifications and watched helplessly as the Rebels rode about the junction.

Inside the station house, meanwhile, the dutiful telegrapher tapped out a message warning the authorities that Rebels were destroying the railroad. The news triggered a flurry of messages between Federal commanders in the region. Officials in Baltimore relayed the telegram to the war department in Washington before noting that while the size of the enemy was unknown, it was believed to be only a small cavalry force.[22]

White's Confederates lifted iron rails, destroyed switches, severed telegraph lines, and burned valuable rolling stock, a turntable, and a nearby bridge. After an hour the cavaliers withdrew to raid area farms. After finding and destroying a large stockpile of homemade whiskey at the Fishel farm near the village of Seven Valleys they rode through Jefferson to their assigned campsite near Spring Forge. On the way they paused at Jefferson Station and burned a privately owned railcar full of tanbark.[23]

* * *

Earlier that morning as White's horsemen approached Hanover, John Gordon's Georgians marched four abreast along the turnpike through eastern Adams County. The old pike, constructed in 1819, featured a pulverized stone surface, meaning the soldiers did not have to worry about the mud that comprised the roads and farm lanes on either side. The exchange was more dust. Before long the fine powder covered men and horses alike and turned the bareheaded soldiers into gray-headed ghouls. They were, recollected Gordon, "the most forbidding looking set of men doubtless."[24]

The dusty march did not prevent the men from marveling at the "most beautiful and highly cultivated country. Everything that science could furnish had been applied to a soil already fertile," exclaimed one infantryman. "The houses were neat and well built. Everything was in the most perfect order, and everything that man or beast could want abounded in the greatest plenty." The inhabitants of this fertile land were primarily German, and most of them were "intensely afraid," continued the narrator. Except in the management of their sprawling farms, continued the soldier, they were "the most ignorant people. It seemed as they felt that the Northern people deserved severe treatment at our hands, and expected, as a matter of course, to get their share of it." The locals, he added, did have one redeeming value: As other soldiers in a host of regiments, brigades, and divisions

---

22 *OR* 27: Pt. 3, 360.

23 Gladfelter, *The Flowering of the Codorus Palatinate*, 260; Myers, *The Comanches*, 194. Spring Forge is now known as Spring Grove.

24 *Atlanta Journal*, Sept. 16, 1888.

noted in their diaries and letters home, the Pennsylvania Dutch made the world's best bread.[25]

After Gordon paused for a midday rest at Abbottstown, a leading York industrialist named Arthur Briggs Farquhar arrived on the turnpike and demanded to see the general. The 24-year-old businessman was acting on his own accord to spare the women and children of York, he explained (not to mention his own burgeoning agricultural implement business). Gordon demanded that the town's defenders retreat and allow him to march unimpeded through town the next day. Farquhar raced his buggy back to York to relay Gordon's demands to the Committee of Safety while Gordon resumed his leisurely eastward march to the hamlet of Farmers in York County. Farquhar and other leading citizens met Gordon later that afternoon to resolve the terms by which York would accede to Confederate occupancy. The delegation returned home at midnight to inform anxious residents that the next morning, a Sunday, the Rebels would march into town unmolested.[26]

While Gordon dictated terms to Farquhar, Jubal Early's northern column marched on muddy back roads through Hunterstown, New Chester, and Hampton before finally halting a little over three miles past East Berlin. After he oversaw the placement of his brigades for the night (his division was without camp equipage or baggage wagons), Early sought shelter for his staff and himself. He directed Col. William H. French's 17th Virginia Cavalry to turn their horses out into a cornfield bordering a road. Early, meanwhile, turned his own mount toward a large barn in the distance. The approaching Confederate officer frightened the farmer, who could not (or would not) speak English. The inability to communicate frustrated Early, who eventually gave up the idea of quartering there and rode on into Big Mount, where he found "a decent looking" brick house with a good-sized front porch.

A recently widowed Germanic woman named Elizabeth Zinn nervously walked to her gate as the group of mounted Rebels drew near. "Are you goin' to destroy us, are you goin' to take all that we've got?" she exclaimed in broken English. "No madam, and to give you the best protection possible, I will stay with

25 *Mobile Advertiser & Register*, Aug. 9, 1863.

26 A. B. Farquhar and Samuel Crowther, *The First Million, The Hardest: An Autobiography of A. B. Farquhar* (New York, 1922), 69-73. For many more accounts of the Confederate occupation, see Scott L. Mingus, Sr. and James McClure, *Civil War Stories from York County, Pa.* (York, PA, 2020).

you, with my staff, and no one shall trouble you," Early reassured her. He directed his aides to guard the property and announced that her porch would do for sleeping. With his quarters secured, Early and his escort rode southeast four miles to Farmers to give Gordon final instructions on entering York the next day. The division commander returned to Big Mount about 9:00 p.m. to discover that his staff had already eaten supper. Mrs. Zinn, however, had saved a plentiful meal for him that included various meats, several vegetable dishes, coffee, and cold milk. With her mind now at ease the widow talked incessantly. She also prepared a good clean bed for the general, who enjoyed an excellent night's sleep.[27]

All except one of Early's soldiers fared well that evening. "Our men are living finely, applejack, fresh butter and milk, chickens and most everything else," rejoiced Capt. Robert D. Funkhouser of the 49th Virginia of William "Extra Billy" Smith's Virginia brigade. "The Louisianans," observed Funkhouser, "particularly pay no regard in foraging and supply themselves on all occasions." According to his service records, Pvt. Charles Brown of the 8th Louisiana "straggled on the march from Gettysburg to York and [was] supposed to have been killed by the citizens of Pennsylvania." Longstanding local tradition in York County suggests that Private Brown was attempting to obtain a horse when its irate owner murdered the German immigrant, dug a hole, and buried him in an unmarked grave near the village of Big Mount.[28]

*   *   *

Well to the west of the brigades of Early and Gordon, the divisions of William Dorsey Pender and Richard Anderson, both of Hill's Third Corps, passed through Chambersburg and marched east to Fayetteville and Greenwood. They finally went into camp within supporting distance of Harry Heth's men. Private Robert T. Douglass of the 47th Virginia, part of Col. John

---

27 Gibson, *History of York County*, 686.

28 Laura Virginia Hale and Stanley S. Phillips, *History of the Forty-Ninth Virginia Infantry, C. S. A., Extra Billy Smith's Boys* (Lanham, MD, 1981), 72. See also Andrew B. Booth, *Records of Louisiana Confederate Soldiers and Louisiana Confederate Commands*, 3 vols. (Baton Rouge, LA, 1984), 1:141-142; Brown's service records are at Tulane University. Research by Mark Snell and Scott Mingus has narrowed the location of Brown's grave to two possible locations: one near the intersection of Canal and Big Mount roads, and the other near Canal and Lake roads. For more details, see Scott L. Mingus, *Marauders & Murderers: Civil War Mysteries of York County, Pa.* (York, PA, 2022), 25-31.

Brockenbrough's Brigade, thought little of the "hard looking crowd in this country, mostly dutch."[29]

Lieutenant J. F. J. Caldwell of the 1st South Carolina, part of Samuel McGowan's Brigade, recounted Pender's morning march toward Chambersburg. "There was a good deal of discussion as to when we crossed the Pennsylvania line, but once certainly across, there was great rejoicing," wrote Caldwell in a well-received history of his brigade. "This was, we felt, our really first invasion of Federal soil; for we regarded Maryland as Southern, and allowed ourselves to believe that she only needed our army well established in her borders to become Confederate. But the land of Penn was quite another thing," he continued. "We were now in a beautiful country. In every direction yellow fields of grain extended themselves; on every farm were droves of the largest fattest cattle; gardens thronged with inviting vegetables; orchards gave promise of a bounteous fruit-field, and already extended to us an earnest in the most delicious cherries; full dairies, flocks of sheep, and poultry were almost monotonously frequent."[30]

Corporal Edmund D. Patterson, an Ohio-born soldier in the 9th Alabama, Cadmus Wilcox's Brigade, found the ladies in Chambersburg to be "very spiteful." They "make faces, sing Rally round the flag, wave their little banners, etc. . . . I think if they had a hole burned out in their town about the size and extent of which the Yankees burned in Florence or Athens, Alabama, these patriotic females would not be quite so saucy." Patterson would get his wish a bit more than a year later when Confederates torched much of Chambersburg.[31]

"Marched at 5 a.m. our Regt in rear of the Division. Genl Longstreet passed us," recorded Adjutant Albert L. Peel of the 19th Mississippi, part of Carnot Posey's Brigade of Anderson's Division. "Passed through Chambersville [Chambersburg] at 1 p.m. The people looked mad. Passed Genls Lee & Longstreet. They looked splendidly as they stood on the road side. The two greatest living generals," declared the Magnolia State staff officer to his diary. "Our men have been pillaging a great deal & have acted shamefully. I disapprove of it because it demoralises our army, not that I sympathize with the people."[32]

---

29 Hoke, *Historical Reminiscences*, 62; Douglass diary, entry for June 27, 1863.

30 Caldwell, *The History of the Brigade of South Carolinians*, 93-94.

31 Patterson, *Yankee Rebel*, 111. For a detailed account of Brig. Gen. John McCausland's July 1864 burning of Chambersburg, see Scott L. Mingus, Sr. and Cooper H. Wingert, *Targeted Tracks: The Cumberland Valley Railroad in the Civil War* (El Dorado Hills, CA, 2019).

32 Peel diary, entry for June 27, 1863.

Many civilians and some Confederates later accused Robert E. Lee of casting a blind eye to the extensive plundering. The brigadiers and colonels, claimed the 3rd South Carolina's Tally Simpson, did not attempt to enforce the commander's general orders, and "Lee himself seemed to disregard entirely the soldiers open acts of disobedience." Simpson, a member of Joseph Kershaw's command, described one example in which Lee witnessed 30 to 40 soldiers stealing poultry from an old lady's farm. The owner launched into a venomous tirade against the thieves, to no effect. According to the South Carolinian, she spotted Lee and asked to speak to him. The general, "without turning the direction of his head, politely raised his hand to his hat and said, 'Good morning madam,' and then went on his way. It caused a great deal of amusement as the old lady, panting with anger, was compelled to witness the departure of her last favorite pullet and the old family gobbler. Thus you can see that even our Commander-in-Chief sanctioned their marauding expeditions."[33]

"Some of the boys have gone off foraging, in other words gone off to try and see if they can buy or steal something," joked Sgt. J. E. Whitehorn after the 12th Virginia of William Mahone's Brigade set up camp at Fayetteville. "We are having a regular feast," he recalled, "the boys are constantly coming in with apple butter, milk, light bread, hams, chickens, etc." Whitehorn continued:

> In reply to my questions as to how they obtained these articles, their invariable reply is I bought it. I don't dispute the point with them but I draw my own conclusions about the matter. We have not been paid off for a long while, and I don't suppose twenty five dollars could be raised in the entire company, yet the men have brought in at least $100.00 worth of provisions.[34]

The steady progression of Confederate soldiers, wagons, guns, and horsemen drew the interest of nearly everyone. "The Rebel troops commence their forward movement and continue without interruption until dark," observed Chambersburg

---

33 Simpson and Everson, *Far, Far from Home*, 262. Simpson's claim does not have the ring of truth. The woman would not have recognized Lee and the general would not have been on foot. Further, it would have been out of character for him to have rudely ignored a woman's pleas under such circumstances—especially having issued a specific order against pillaging. Although Simpson may well have witnessed such a scene, the officer in question almost certainly was not Lee.

34 J. E. Whitehorn, and Fletcher L. Elmore, Jr., ed., *Diary of J. E. Whitehorn, 1st Sergt. Co. F, 12th Va., A. P. Hill's 3rd Corps, A. N. Va.* (Louisville, KY, 1995), 24-25.

banker William Heyser. "We estimate by actual count nearly 35,000 men, officers and all, 165 pieces ordinance. I notice many of the gun carriages had the U.S. mark upon them, having been captured from our army." The observant man of finance caught what would be his first and only firsthand look at the Southern army commander, and produced one of the best descriptions of the general in the field. "About 11 o'clock Gen. Lee passed with his staff. He is fine looking man, medium size, stoutly built, has the face of a good liver, grey beard, and mustache, poorly dressed for an officer of his grade. He wore a felt hat, black, and a heavy overcoat with large cape. His horse appeared to be rather an indifferent one, for a man who reputedly is fond of fine stock." Heyser next turned his attention to the rest of the soldiers and the civilian onlookers:

> Many of the officers were fine looking men, and rode fine horses. During their passage, I noticed their ever watchfulness on every side. The citizens were crowded along the sidewalks and doors, observing their passage; the rest, inside, behind drawn blinds, watched unobtrusively. There were many remarks and exclamations, but all in a subdued tone of voice or whisper. Occasionally a German would stop me and complain in his native tongue, as if I could help this situation, or was responsible for it. Lee offered to place a guard for the protection of the town, but the sheriff could not be found.[35]

Hill's men were tramping through town when Lee, from his roadside headquarters in Messersmith's Woods, issued General Orders No. 73. "The Commanding General has observed with marked satisfaction the conduct of the troops on the march, and confidently anticipates results commensurate with the high spirit they have manifested. No troops could have displayed greater fortitude, or better performed their arduous marches of the past ten days," began Lee. The directive continued:

> Their conduct in other respects has, with few exceptions, been in keeping with their character as soldiers, and entitles them to approbation and praise. There have, however, been instances of forgetfulness on the part of some, that they have in keeping the yet unsullied reputation of this army, and that the duties exacted of us by civilization and Christianity and not less obligatory in the country of the enemy than in our own.
>
> The Commanding General considers that no greater disgrace could befall the army, and through it, our whole people, than the perpetuation of the barbarous outrages upon the

---

35 Heyser, 79-80.

unarmed and defenseless, and the wanton destruction of private property, that have marked the course of the enemy in our own country. Such proceedings not only degrade the perpetrators and all connected with them, but are subversive of the discipline and efficiency of the army, and destructive of the ends of our present movement. It must be remembered that we make war only upon armed men, and that we cannot take vengeance for the wrongs our people have suffered without lowering ourselves in the eyes of all whose abhorrence has been excited by the atrocities of our enemies, and offending against Him to whom vengeance belongeth, without whose favor and support our efforts must all prove in vain.

The Commanding General, therefore, earnestly exhorts the troops to abstain, with most scrupulous care, from unnecessary or wanton injury to private property, and he enjoins upon all officers to arrest and bring to summary punishment all who shall in any way offend against orders on this subject.[36]

On the same day Lee issued orders restraining his men from pillaging, down in Virginia, the fiery editor of the *Richmond Dispatch* was openly advocating retaliation for the wanton destruction inflicted by the Federals on parts of the South. "The Yankees knowing the enormity of their own offences dread a righteous judgment, and hence their terror at the bare announcement that General Lee had taken up the line of march towards their country," he reported. "While he moves, the fires of our Southern homes and manufactories are illuminating our Southern skies. They may well tremble at every report of the ravages of the robbers and murderers they have sent amongst us. Yet General Lee is both deliberate and determined," he concluded, "and in the measures it may be in his power to take he will have in view alike a just retaliation and the safety and welfare of his army. We may confidently expect this from a man of his well attested wisdom and sagacity."[37]

* * *

TWO of the Army of Northern Virginia's three corps were now in proximity to Lee and Chambersburg. The city was a good place from which to direct the next stage of the Pennsylvania operations, which would be crucial to the army's success.

---

36 OR 27, pt. 3, 942-943.

37 *Richmond Daily Dispatch*, June 27, 1863.

That afternoon, Lee met with Isaac Trimble, the major general without portfolio. According to Trimble's postwar account, the pair talked inside Lee's tent, where the army commander unfolded a map of the area between South Mountain to Gettysburg. "As a civil engineer you may know more about it than any of us," he began. Trimble knew the area well from his antebellum days as a railroad construction engineer, and counseled Lee that almost every square mile contained good positions for battle or skillful maneuvering. "Our army is in good spirits, not over fatigued, and can be concentrated on any one point in twenty-four hours or less," Lee is said to have responded. "I have not yet heard that the enemy have crossed the Potomac and am waiting to hear from General Stuart. When they hear where we are," continued Trimble, "they will make forced marches to interpose their forces between us and Baltimore and Philadelphia. They will come up, probably through Frederick; broken down with hunger and hard marching, strung out on a long line and much demoralized, when they come into Pennsylvania." It was Lee's plan, reported Trimble, to "throw an overwhelming force on their advance, crush it, follow up the success, drive one corps back on another, and by successive repulses and surprises before they can concentrate, create a panic and virtually destroy the army." Lee next asked for Trimble's opinion: the supernumerary general thought the plan ought to be successful because of the troops' high spirits. Trimble claimed Lee told him that "Ewell's forces are by this time in Harrisburg; if not, go and join him, and help take the place."[38]

* * *

The men in Lafayette McLaws's Division of Longstreet's First Corps rose at dawn near Williamsport, Maryland, tramped through Hagerstown and Middleburg, and reached the state line. "In passing through Pennsylvania," related Capt. D. Augustus Dickert of the 3rd South Carolina, Kershaw's Brigade, "many curious characters were found among the quaint old Quaker settlers, who viewed the army of Lee not with 'fear' or 'trembling,' but more in wonder and Christian abhorrence." When the head of the column came to the line dividing Pennsylvania and Maryland, a delegation of "those rigorously righteous old Quakers" stepped into the middle of the road and commanded, in the name of God, "So far thou

---

38 Trimble, "The Battle and Campaign of Gettysburg," *SHSP*, vol. 26 (1898), 120-121. Trimble's account, which he wrote and published in 1898, almost 30 years after Lee's death, almost certainly inflates his own contributions and must be read with skepticism.

canst go, but no farther." Satisfied they had performed their duty according to their faith and abhorrence of war and bloodshed, "they returned to their homes perfectly satisfied."[39]

The encounter with the pious Quakers behind them, McLaws's soldiers passed on through Greencastle. "On the 27th, General Longstreet's Corps went through. His was the largest and most destructive set of men," claimed newspaperman William A. Reid of the *Greencastle Pilot*. "Their whole route was marked by destruction. To General McLaws was reserved the honor of cutting down the Union Pole, which had been left standing by all preceding forces."[40]

The 3rd South Carolina's Tally Simpson marveled at the sweeping vistas. "Pennsylvania is one of the prettiest countries through which I have ever passed. The scenery is beautiful, and the soil is exceedingly fertile," he wrote before recording another scene that seems to have taken him by surprise: "I saw very few negroes, the most of the labor being performed by the whites." While the local fare was good, the Palmetto State soldier wished they served hot heavy biscuits. Their bread, he concluded, "was too light." He also had little good to say about their horses or their women, the former being "too fat" and the latter "the ugliest women I ever saw. The horses are tremendous, almost as large as elephants," he exclaimed, "but they are so bony and clumsy that they can't stand as much as our smallest mules. The women are what you would call the flat-headed dutch . . . the gals are ugly, broad-mouthed specimens of humanity. But they are always neat and clean and very industrious," he admitted. "In my trip through the country I don't believe I saw a single pretty woman, and it was remarked by several."[41]

Henry Benning's command of John B. Hood's Division "marched through fields of wheat & corn tearing down fences & not respecting scarsly any thing," recalled the 15th Georgia's Thomas L. Ware. He and his comrades robbed "bee gums & poultry yards. We were gathering up all the horses & beeves in the country. People all very much frightened along the road."[42]

L. M. Blackford was the clerk of Longstreet's military court. He deemed the 27th of June "a fine day for marching. Nor rain, but cloudy and cool for the season." The soldiers reached Chambersburg at noon after a short trek of 12 miles.

39 Dickert, *History of Kershaw's Brigade*, 230.

40 *Greencastle* (PA) *Pilot*, July 28, 1863.

41 Everson and Simpson, *Far, Far from Home*, 263.

42 Mark Nesbitt, ed., *35 Days to Gettysburg: The Campaign Diaries of Two American Enemies* (Mechanicsburg, PA, 1992), 122-123, 129.

Like so many others, Blackford felt compelled to marvel in writing at the lush scenery and productivity of the Cumberland Valley. "[T]he fields are much smaller, the houses more frequent & handsomer (generally of stone or brick) and the barns bigger and more complete than any I have ever seen. Many are of stone and brick, and have glass window sashes," he informed his father in a letter the following day. The clerk firmly believed that the most inferior Pennsylvania barn was superior to the best barns in eastern Virginia. "One I saw, on the premises of a Mr., or Judge [Alexander K.] McClure, this side of Chambersburg, which was not only of very large size, but really elegant: painted snow-white, with ornamented eaves, pendants. The house and whole property of this individual however are beautiful and complete beyond description."[43]

"The rebels poured in already. They just marched through," wrote diarist Rachel Cormany. "Such a hard looking set I never saw. All day since 7 oclock they have been going through. Between 30 & 40 pieces of cannon—& an almost endless trail of waggons." The native Canadian and wife of a lieutenant in the 16th Pennsylvania Cavalry recorded her thoughts while the men tramped past. The Confederates were "such a rough dirty ragged rowdyish set one does not see often." She also noticed Generals Lee and Longstreet as they rode past. To her, it seemed as though "the whole south had broke loose & are coming into Pa. It makes me feel too badly to see so many men & cannon going through knowing that they have come to kill our men." Some of the soldiers carried chickens or buckets of honey; many were poorly clad and were barefoot. Some snatched the hats from the onlookers and gave them their old ones in exchange. The sight enraged Rachel: "I did wish I dared spit on their old flag."[44]

One of Rachel's neighbors described as a "stout Dutch girl" zealously waved a small U.S. flag in the faces of the passing men. A member of Parker's Virginia battery with "quite a reputation as a wag," Lt. Col. E. Porter Alexander recalled, "stopped square in front of her, stared at her a moment, then gave a sort of jump & shouted 'Boo.' A roar of laughter & cheers went up along the line, under which the young lady retreated to the porch."[45]

The forever nameless "stout Dutch girl" was not the only one with a visible American flag. "When we were passing through Chambersburg, all the ladies had pinned to their dresses the Union flag, and as the [slaves] passed, these same

43 L. M. Blackford to Dear Father, June 28, 1863.

44 Mohr, *The Cormany Diaries*, 336-337.

45 Alexander, *Fighting for the Confederacy*, 228-229.

broad-mouthed abolition dutch gals would stop them and entreat them to slip into a back street, desert their masters, and remain with them," reported South Carolinian Tally Simpson. The thought of Pennsylvanians attempting to persuade his slave to desert infuriated Simpson. "If I could have heard one of them persuading Lewis, I would have felt like jerking the very hide off of her back with a Confederate cow skin, woman or not."[46]

"The people here have quite a chagrined and subdued look as we march through these towns and villages," reported the observant John C. West of the 4th Texas. "A lady encouraged some little girls to sing the 'Red, White and Blue' as we passed through Chambersburg. She remarked as I passed, 'Thank God, you will never come back alive.' I replied, 'No, as we intend to go to Cincinnati by way of New York.'"[47]

A sergeant with 48th Alabama named John Dykes Taylor recalled the memorable march through the town many years after the war for one of the state's newspapers: "[W]e found the sidewalks, the doors, the windows and in many instances the housetops along the streets which we passed crowded almost to suffocation with the beauty and the fashion of the place, all decked out in their best attired and many adorned with U. S. flags, who had gathered to see the 'rebs' pass, and not a few were the cutting and witty remarks from both the people and the soldiers."[48]

Banker William Heyser later set eyes on A. P. Hill, whom he described as "a tall red-headed man, not over thirty-five." Heyser insinuated that Hill and Longstreet were riding in proximity, though this is doubtful. What is not in question is that he considered Hill's men to be "a far less respectable lot, and constantly shouting, singing, and hooting at females who showed themselves at doors or windows. They were loud in their denunciation of the Union, and insulting to citizens on the sidewalks, shouting, 'Boys, this is Pennsylvania. We should destroy her as they did in Virginia, dam the Union. Harrisburg will be ours, Hurrah for the Southern Confederacy, and Jeff Davis.' Every brigade as it passed sent a file of soldiers around to examine the stores and places of business, requiring them to open up. This," he added in disgust, "continued all day."[49]

46 Everson and Simpson, *Far, Far from Home*, 263-264.

47 West, *A Texan in Search of a Fight*, 81-82.

48 *Montgomery Advertiser*, March 9, 1902.

49 Heyser, 79-80.

"The springs and milk houses or dairies were also a noted feature of the country," Texan John C. West wrote to his brother. "But the most singular phenomenon which impressed me was the scarcity of visible inhabitants, in this apparently densely populated region. Women and children were seen peeping about but as shy as partridges, but in the towns and villages men, women and children thronged by hundreds." West believed that two full brigades of able-bodied men under 30 years of age could have been raised just in Chambersburg. "We were, of course, coldly received everywhere," he added. Some soldiers of the 4th Alabama, tired of poor-quality beef, appropriated several white fat Chester pigs that soon became spareribs and boiled hog's head. The soldiers stuffed their haversacks with the meat and freshly baked wheat bread and marched on.[50]

Hundreds of other Rebels, meanwhile, strolled along the streets. "The stores were all closed when we entered the place, but many of them were opened by threats of violent entrance by armed force if it was not done quickly," recalled L. M. Blackford. "When opened, guards in most instances—not all—were posted at the door and but a limited number allowed to enter at a time. When we did get in we bought what few things we could find that we wanted with C. S. money." He secured some needed things for his mess and picked up a handsome black felt hat and cloth for military shirts for himself. "To send home I could only get a few dozen spools sewing cotton, superior quality, No's. 16, 40, & 24 and some buttons. These are for home and Sister Sue. The stock of dry goods I got at was very meagre. Shoes, gloves, pins, etc. unattainable. I shall keep the interests of the 'home department' constantly before me, however." All of his men procured new hats for themselves.[51]

"Robberies are now common on the street, particularly where they are unguarded," claimed William Heyser. "Dechart's hat store was cleaned out today, not a single item left in stock. They opened up my son, William's store today, and started to help themselves." There was nothing anyone could do but stand by and watch and complain to the commanding officers, who "refer to the same treatment our soldiers gave the Confederacy in Virginia." He finally found a Col. "Greene" that listened to his pleas and had the men removed and the door shut. That was not all. "While the troops were passing today," continued Heyser, "I was sitting by my door, the victim of many insulting remarks. One even attempted to take my hat. He

50 West, *A Texan in Search of a Fight*, 92; Coles, *R.T. Coles' History*, 205.

51 L. M. Blackford to Dear Father, June 28, 1863.

withdrew when I offered to resist, as I would have struck him. Were it not for the rigid discipline they were under, I shudder to think what our lot would have been. There are exceptions, many of the Rebels are gentlemen, and act as such," he added. "Mostly, those from Florida, Texas, and Louisiana, generally speaking, are a band of cutthroats."[52]

Tally Simpson agreed that "most of the soldiers harbor a terrific spirit of revenge and steal and pillage in the most sinful manner. They take poultry, hogs, vegetables, fruit, honey, and any and every thing they can lay their hands upon. Last night Wofford's Brig. of this div. stole so much that they could not carry what rations they drew from the commissary." He added, "Everything in the shape of vegetables, from a cow pea up to a cabbage head, was pressed without the least ceremony, and all animal flesh from a featherless fowl to full grown sheep and hogs were killed and devoured without the least compunction of conscience."[53]

"One evening after we had gone to bivouac a soldier run a chicken under General Hood's chair and catch it and the General appeared perfectly unconscious of the act, so intent was he on examining a map, while sitting in the yard of a Pennsylvania citizen," related Alabamian R. T. Coles. Hood was not the only person in Pennsylvania seemingly in a mindless daze. South Carolinian Captain Dickert thought the people "to be in a state of lethargy, and to take little interest in the contest one way or the other."[54]

* * *

George Pickett's Division trailed Longstreet's main column and crossed the Mason-Dixon line south of Greencastle. "The heavens were dark and gloomy, but our hearts were glad as we now stepped forward for the first time upon the soil of the foe, never stopping until we pitched camp in the very midst of the Philistines at Chambersburg," Lt. John T. James of the 11th Virginia gleefully informed his father in a letter home.[55]

"The country from the Md. line to Chambersburg is rather rugged & the soil not half so fine as that portion of Maryland we passed over on yesterday," observed

52 Heyser, 79-80. It is possible that Heyser's "Col. Greene" was Francis M. Greene, acting colonel of the 11th Mississippi, Davis's Brigade, Heth's Division, Hill's Corps.

53 Everson and Simpson, *Far, Far from Home*, 261.

54 Coles, *R.T. Coles' History*, 102; Dickert, *History of Kershaw's Brigade*, 230.

55 *Philadelphia Times*, Oct. 21, 1882.

Maj. N. C. Wilson of the 28th Virginia, part of Richard Garnett's Brigade. "There is a great quantity of the limestone & it is too near the surface. The country immediately around Chambersburg is as pretty & well cultivated as any country we have traveled through. All the farms are on a small scale, but are finely cultivated. Private dwellings are all neat & conveniently built, but no elegance of style whatever."[56]

Details of soldiers destroyed the Cumberland Valley Railroad along their line of march. "That they did this work thoroughly was patent to all who had opportunity of viewing the dismantled shops and ruined roadbed between Chambersburg and Hagerstown," attested Waynesboro historian Benjamin M. Nead. "It was a scene of desolation; the shops and depot buildings could not have been shattered worse by an earthquake. The track was torn up for miles, and, to make destruction certain, pyres of cross ties were erected at intervals along the line, across which the iron rails were laid, and, when the fire was applied, the rails, heated, bent double by their own weight, and were thus rendered wholly useless."[57]

"The Cumberland Valley in Pennsylvania was entered, a magnificent land, the counterpart of the lovely valley of Virginia, the sight bringing homesickness to the heart of not a few Virginia boys," teenaged Pvt. David E. Johnston of the 7th Virginia recounted. "Nothing was seen indicating that these people knew that a terrible war had been raging for two years, only a few miles away. At Greencastle was noted among the people defiance and vindictive men; while not speaking out," he added, "their looks indicated that deep down in their bosoms was rancor and the wish that all the rebel hosts were dead and corralled by the devil."[58]

Young Dolly Harris created quite a stir when the Virginians tramped through Greencastle. The 17-year-old daughter of a local cabinetmaker "rushed to the street in front of the leader of the southern band, waved the stars and stripes in his face and roundly denounced the troopers as traitors to their country, cutthroats, and plunderers." "Why the bravest woman I ever saw was a Pennsylvania girl who defied Pickett's whole division as we marched through the little town called Greencastle," recounted an amused Col. William R. Aylett of the 53rd Virginia. "She had a United States flag as an apron which she defiantly waved up and down as our columns passed by her and dared us to take it from her." General Pickett,

56 Wilson diary, entry for June 27, 1863.

57 Benjamin Mathias Nead, *Waynesboro: The History of a Settlement* (Harrisburg, PA, 1900), 227.

58 David E. Johnston, *The Story of a Confederate Boy in the Civil War* (Portland, OR, 1914), 195.

recorded a newspaperman, "saluted her and the boys all along the line gave her one of the old rebel yells."[59]

Pickett's road-weary soldiers shuffled into Chambersburg later in the day. The 1st Virginia's Charles T. Loehr believed the town "had the appearance of a deserted village on a wet Sunday." All of the liquor had been placed in the courthouse under guard. "The few people we saw had no great friendship to bestow on us, but the farmers outside the town took things more pleasantly, and we got along agreeably with them." Pickett detailed the 28th Virginia as the provost regiment to maintain order in Chambersburg. Major Wilson deemed the town "an abolition den with very few sympathizers for the Southern cause." "Some ladies appeared and volunteered to deliver a sharp, spicy address, which was responded to by the band of our regiment, with 'Dixie,'" recalled the 7th Virginia's Pvt. David E. Johnston. "The boys sang 'Dixie' and 'Bonnie Blue Flag,' laughed and cheered lustily, then marched on a few miles on the York road and went into camp."[60]

Nighttime brought another round of foraging. "We are sitting by a fine rail fire," penned William Berkeley of the 8th Virginia. "It seems to do the men good to burn Yankee rails as they have not left a fence in our part of the country. In spite of orders, they step out at night and help themselves to milk, butter, poultry, and vegetables."[61]

The concentration of Maj. Gen. John Dix's large Federal force in Virginia continued to spread alarm throughout the corridors of Richmond. "I learn, however, that there are some 25,000 or 30,000 of the enemy at Yorktown," scribbled Confederate war department clerk John B. Jones in his diary. "[I]f we can get together 12,000 fighting men, in the next twenty-four hours, to man the fortifications, there will not be much use for the militia and the clerks of the departments, more than as an internal police force. But," added Jones in a

59 *Greencastle* (PA) *Public Opinion*, Feb. 23, 1906; *Auburn* (NY) *Semi-Weekly Journal*, Feb. 23, 1906; *Chicago Daily Inter Ocean*, July 19, 1887. The latter paper erroneously identified the plucky girl as Miss Sadie Smith.

60 Loehr, *War History of the Old First Virginia*, 35-36; Wilson diary, entry for June 27, 1863; Johnston, *The Story of a Confederate Boy*, 196.

61 William N. Berkeley to his wife, June 27-28, 1863, as cited in Wiley, *The Life of Johnny Reb*, 47.

demonstration of his doubt of the outcome, "I am not quite sure we can get that number."[62]

Imboden's cavalrymen conducted "a destructive raid" through the lower part of Fulton County. "They paid no respect to any kind of property; and what they could not carry away with them, they destroyed," fumed one resident. "These bands of plunderers are more to be feared along the borders than the regular rebel army."[63]

While Lee's main body camped around Chambersburg, Rebel partisans were on the move in southern Franklin County. "This morning the guerilla band which was encamped up the pike took their departure through town toward Greencastle taking with them about a dozen colored persons, mostly contrabands, women and children; a large flock of sheep and horses and barouche," reported the Rev. Thomas Creigh. "Sad that we can make no resistance and that the Government has sent us no help. Here we are as in a port or a prison, beleaguered on all hands and can receive no reliable intelligence in regard to the movements of our army. Reports we have in abundance, but they are so vague, and so conflicting that we can repose no confidence in them."[64]

"Early in the morning the guerilla band returned from their camping-ground, and, drove their booty, horses, cattle, about five hundred sheep, and two wagons full of store goods, with twenty-one negroes, through town and towards Greencastle or Hagerstown. It was a sight as sad and mournful as the slave-hunt of yesterday," lamented seminarian Dr. Philip Schaff. "They claimed all these negroes as Virginia slaves, but I was positively assured that two or three were born and raised in this neighborhood. One, Sam Brooks, split many a cord of wood for me. There were among them women and young children, sitting with sad countenances on the stolen store-boxes. I asked one of the riders guarding the wagons: 'Do you not feel bad and mean in such an occupation?' He boldly replied that 'he felt very comfortable. They were only reclaiming their property which we had stolen and harbored.'" Schaff believed the guerillas to be "far worse than the regular army,

62 Jones, *A Confederate War Clerk's Diary*, 1:362.

63 *Chicago Tribune*, June 28, 1863.

64 Creigh diary, entry for June 27, 1863.

who behaved in an orderly and decent way, considering their mission." One of the guerillas said to him, 'We are independent, and come and go where and when we please.'"[65]

* * *

In northern Virginia, meanwhile, far to southeast of Lee's main force, Jeb Stuart and his three brigades of veteran cavalrymen were again in the saddle early in the morning. "Having ascertained that on the night previous the enemy had disappeared entirely from Wolf Run Shoals, a strongly fortified position on the Occoquan, I marched to that point, and thence directly for Fairfax Station," reported Stuart, "sending General Fitz Lee to the right, to cross by Burke's Station and effect a junction at Fairfax Court-House, or farther on, according to circumstances."[66]

Several of Stuart's staff officers searched for a blacksmith to re-shoe their horses. They found one near Fairfax Station and in the process also discovered Union cavalry. Fitz Lee's troopers were resting and feeding their mounts near the depot when the advance guard of about 20 Rebels, who had left to scout in the direction of Fairfax Court House, began firing in the woods not far from the main body. "One after another of the advance guard emerged from the woods, halting occasionally to fire back," recalled staffer Theodore Garnett, "at what we could not tell; but it sounded unpleasantly to say the least of it." The eruption of fire was their second "unpleasant" surprise in just two days—yet another threat that had to be dealt with.[67]

Stuart and his staff and escort were resting with their horses unbridled, "not dreaming of an enemy nearer than the Court-House, some two miles distant, nothing between us but some fifteen or twenty men, and these retreating toward us," remembered Garnett. When they reported that the staff officers who had gone in search of the blacksmith had probably been captured, Stuart doubted the news. "Oh! They are too intelligent to be caught," he replied dismissively. When the bulk of the Confederate column reached the outskirts of town, "The First North Carolina Cavalry, of Hampton's brigade, was seen coming over the hill near the

65 Schaff, "The Gettysburg Week," 24-25.

66 OR 27, pt. 2, 693.

67 Jewell, "Theodore Garnett Recalls," 48.

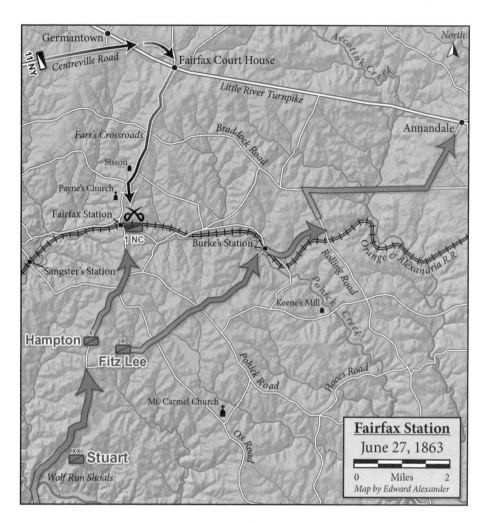

Fairfax Station
June 27, 1863

0   Miles   2
Map by Edward Alexander

station . . . General Stuart sent word to General Hampton to bring it up on a gallop." The fight was on.[68]

"In a few minutes, Hampton came galloping up, and close behind him Major [John H.] Whitaker, leading the First North Carolina Cavalry. Stuart pointed to the woods and told Hampton to push ahead, as his horse was unbridled, and see what the firing meant," recalled a North Carolina trooper. The Tar Heels thundered off into the woods at a gallop. "Presently a blue-coat was seen galloping off ahead of us and we raised a yell which must have made the retreating vidette shake to his very

68 Ibid.; Cooke, *Wearing of the Gray*, 231.

spurs," recalled a North Carolinian. "On we dashed, more in the spirit of a fox chase than a cavalry charge."

The Tar Heels spotted a squadron of the 11th New York Cavalry, also known as "Scott's Nine Hundred," in a woodlot about one hundred yards away. The New Yorkers were "in beautiful order, sabers flashing and unforms glittering in the bright sunlight, under the full headway of a gallant and well-ordered charge." The New Yorkers, who were part of the cavalry forces assigned to Maj. Gen. Julius Stahel's division, were on their way to Centreville on a reconnaissance mission when they ran into Stuart's column. The Empire State men did not realize that they had found Stuart's main body, convinced instead the Southerners in their front were Mosby's guerrillas on a horse rustling expedition. A rude surprise awaited them.[69]

Lt. George A. Dagwell of the 11th New York reported to Maj. S. Pierre Remington, the Federal commander, that they would be gobbled up if they did not get to the rear.

"What?" queried a stunned Remington.

Dagwell replied, "Turn back, turn the other way and run, there is a whole rebel brigade under the hill!"

Remington would have none of it. "Front into line—march!" he shouted."That settled it, the gallant old boy had blood in his eye, and was always in for a fight whenever and wherever the opportunity presented itself, and say d—n the conditions," remembered Lieutenant Dagwell. "I shall always believe the major thought at this point of the fight that we were still fighting Mosby."[70]

On they came, looking determined to ride through the advancing Confederates. Major Remington foolishly ordered his men to draw their sabers and charge the enemy. "With a mighty yell that had been pent up for five or six minutes, and which seemed an hour, we went for them: down our side and up their side of the ravine, but they did not wait for us," recalled a New York lieutenant. An Irish private named Malone set his spurs and took off after one of the Rebels. "Surrender, ye divil, or I'll shoot the top ave the ave ye!" he hollered, brandishing his sword. The charge, noted a local newspaper, was made "with so much

---

69 Thomas West Smith, *The Story of a Cavalry Regiment: "Scott's 900," Eleventh New York Cavalry from the St. Lawrence River to the Gulf of Mexico, 1861–1865* (New York, 1897), 77-78.

70 Ibid., 81. A comrade later described Remington as "a brave, dashing soldier, and a loyal comrade all through our term of service." Major Remington was the father of Frederic Remington, the famous sculptor of the Old West.

Maj. S. Pierre Remington commanded the 11th New York Cavalry in Stahel's division during the Gettysburg Campaign.

The Story of a Cavalry Regiment

impetuosity that half of the Confederates were captured before recovering from their surprise."[71]

"Major Remington charged upon the enemy with drawn sabers, and succeeded in capturing about one-half of the enemy," reported Col. James B. Swain, commander of the 11th New York Cavalry. "Before, however, he could succeed in rallying his small force, the rebels recovered their presence of mind, and Companies B and C were forced to cut their way through, abandoning prisoners and all." Within minutes each man was doing his best to slash and ride his way to freedom.[72]

"Our squadron in advance, which was commanded by one of our most gallant officers, had just reached the Court House when they were attacked with drawn sabers by a squadron of Federal cavalry mounted on magnificent gray horses, which chased them from the Court House, driving them pell-mell back upon the main body," recounted a Southern officer.[73]

"The suddenness and impetuosity of this charge was the occasion of serious disorder in the ranks of the leading squadron of the First North Carolina," concluded a New Yorker. "They were close upon us before the command to draw sabers was given, but seeing our numbers increasing as the column closed up, they

71 Ibid., 79; *Alexandria Gazette*, June 30, 1863.

72 *OR* 27, pt. 1, 1037.

73 Smith, *The Story of a Cavalry Regiment*, 84.

halted and delivered a volley, which mortally wounded Major Whitaker, who was trying to rally his men." The Yankee volley also cut down a few of Whitaker's men.[74]

The loss of their commander briefly demoralized the Tar Heels, prompting Wade Hampton to cry out, "Stand fast!" and the next squadron to "Come ahead!" The New Yorkers veered off their course and headed for the woods as if they intended to attack Hampton's rear. The South Carolinian spotted this move and sent a squadron to pounce upon them from the flank while he pressed from the front. "This movement virtually surrounded the Federals, and as soon as they saw their predicament, they broke and fled incontinently. The most exciting chase then took place," added Garnett, "and when the men were recalled there was not a foe to be seen or heard of, save some thirty or forty prisoners and a few dead and wounded."[75]

Major Remington's horse was shot in the breast in two places during the melee. Captain Alexander G. Campbell, commander of Company B, was last seen charging the Confederates after killing an enemy officer with his revolver. Lieutenant Augustus B. Hazleton, also of Company B, was twice fired at but safely led part of his command out of the chaos. Sergeant Henry O. Morris escaped being wounded and managed to shoot the officer who assaulted Remington. Lieutenant Dagwell, who had wisely suggested to Remington that they turn tail and gallop away, charged at the head of about ten men. Remington and 18 of his men escaped. Others straggled in over the next several days. [later you write none escaped?] "We found the rebs, and here are all that are left of us," reported Remington to his senior officer. The Confederates killed, wounded, or captured "the greater portion, among them several officers; also horses, arms and equipments," Stuart later reported. "The First North Carolina Cavalry lost its major in the first onset—Major Whitaker—an officer of distinction and great value to us." After the sharp and unexpected fight, Stuart had in hand 82 of the New Yorkers, which meant that he now had prisoners of war to contend with.[76]

"I think that without exception the most gallant charge, and the most desperate resistance that we ever met from the Federal cavalry, was at Fairfax, June [27] 1863 when Stuart made a raid around the Union army just before the battle of

74 *Washington Evening Star*, June 29, 1863; Jewell, "Theodore Garnett Recalls," 48-49.

75 Jewell, "Theodore Garnett Recalls," 49.

76 *Daily National Intelligencer*, June 29, 1863; McClellan, *Life and Campaigns of Stuart*, 323; Smith, *The Story of a Cavalry Regiment*, 83, 86; OR 27, pt. 2, 693.

Gettysburg," recalled a Confederate officer. "The Federals, though outnumbered ten to one, fought until every man of them was ridden down, shot down, or cut down; none escaped. We ever afterwards spoke of this affair as the 'charge of the Gray Devils.'" "Had we known that we were attacking the advance of Gen. J.E.B. Stuart's division of cavalry and artillery," admitted one of the Federals, "it is doubtful if even the dashing major would have ordered a charge."[77]

The New Yorkers indeed suffered frightful losses in their foolhardy charge and as one Confederate correctly noted, none of them escaped unscathed. Of the approximately 100 men who went into battle, four were killed, one officer and 20 men were seriously wounded and captured, and 57 others, including three officers, were taken prisoner. All 57 had their mounts shot out from under them or otherwise lost them, and many were badly injured when Southern horses trampled them. Colonel Swain of the 11th New York praised Remington's valor. "He went out supposing that he was to go and recover and return Government property, in charge of a guard," noted Swain. "He found himself and his handful of men precipitated upon a regiment of rebel cavalry. Whatever valor, coolness, and determination could perform was accomplished by Major Remington and his command." Swain concluded, "I am agreeably surprised to see even the remnant he brings into camp." However gallant his actions, Major Remington's courage cost his command dearly; it also further delayed Stuart's advance by half a day.[78]

Stuart interrogated his prisoners before paroling them. He asked one man how many troopers had made the charge. The prisoner told him that there was only a single squadron. "But where are the rest?" asked an incredulous Stuart. "Are you not the advance of Pleasonton?" The prisoner claimed he knew nothing of Federal Cavalry Corps commander Alfred Pleasonton or his command. "And you charged my command with eighty-two men? Give me five hundred such men and I will charge through the Army of the Potomac with them," declared Stuart in response. He had no way of knowing that just such a scene would play out three days later.[79]

The Confederate troopers continued riding to Fairfax Court House, where Stuart received a message from Fitz Lee at Annandale. While advancing on Annandale Lee had captured a sutler's train and its small cavalry escort. A local businessman names Moses Sweitzer, described as an army purveyor, was also

---

77 Smith, *The Story of a Cavalry Regiment*, 84, 85.

78 OR 27, pt. 1, 1037-1038; Smith, *The Story of a Cavalry Regiment*, 86.

79 Smith, *The Story of a Cavalry Regiment*, 88-89.

riding with the train, along with a few sutlers. Fitz's men pounced on the train and helped themselves to all sorts of treats.[80]

Fitz Lee's and Stuart's inspection of Fairfax Court House and its environs revealed ample evidence of recent Union occupation, "but the information was conclusive that the enemy had left this front entirely, the mobilized army having the day previous moved over toward Leesburg, while the locals had retired to the fortifications near Washington." Although Stuart had not heard back from Mosby, all indications were that he would be able to pass in the rear of the Army of the Potomac. Since General Hooker had earlier made his headquarters at Fairfax Court House, plenty of supplies and other surprises were to be had there. Stuart halted his column for a few hours to rest and refresh men and horses and enjoy the abandoned Federal supplies.[81]

While his men enjoyed the respite and the bounty, Stuart sent a galloper to Robert E. Lee with this intelligence and cabled a duplicate to the war department in Richmond. "I took possession of Fairfax C. H. this morning at nine o-clock, together with a large quantity of stores," he wrote. "The main body of Hooker's army has gone toward Leesburg, except the garrison of Alexandria and Washington, which has retreated within the fortifications." Although the message reached Richmond, the courier never reached Lee, meaning the Southern army commander never received this critical intelligence.[82]

After a rest of several hours the column mounted up and headed for Dranesville. The cavalrymen arrived late in the afternoon to find the campfires of Maj. Gen. John Sedgwick's VI Corps burning west of town. Chambliss's Brigade prepared for a fight, but the enemy was gone. They captured several of Sedgwick's stragglers, however, who indicated that the blue-clad infantry had moved out that morning for the Potomac River fords.[83]

Stuart now faced a difficult choice: Where should he try to cross the Potomac? Fortunately, he found that Rowser's Ford below Leesburg had been accidentally left unguarded by troopers of Col. Charles Russell Lowell's 2nd Massachusetts Cavalry. It was the only unprotected ford along the river west of Georgetown. Stuart ordered Hampton's Brigade to seize the crossing.

80 *Alexandria Gazette*, June 29, 1863.

81 Matthews, "Pelham-Breathed Battery."

82 Jones, *A Confederate War Clerk's Diary*, 1:366.

83 Beale, *History of the Ninth Virginia Cavalry*, 78; OR 27, pt. 2, 693.

Captain Richard B. Kennon of Stuart's staff examined the ford. "The Potomac was about a mile wide, the water deep, and the current strong," recalled Kennon. "I made the plunge in early night. The horse swam magnificently. When tired I would get off on a boulder, holding the bridle to let him rest. I reached the Maryland side. The night was calm, but no moon. However, as soon as the breathing of [the horse] came back to normal I sprang into the saddle and we took the plunge to return." A shadowy figure emerged from the woods when Kennon returned to the Virginia side. He could not make out who it was in the darkness. The man placed his hand on Kennon's bridle and the captain dismounted to a bear hug from Stuart himself, who declared, "God be praised. I never expected to see you again."

Kennon saluted. "Where did you come from General?"

"I have been here all the time," responded the cavalry chief. "Can we make it?"

Kennon informed him of the current and the other disadvantages of crossing at Rowser's Ford, but Stuart was determined to at least try it. "The ford was wide and deep and might well have daunted a less determined man than our indomitable General, for the water swept over the pommels of our saddles," recalled engineering officer Capt. William W. Blackford.[84]

"The spectacle was an impressive one as we forded the river," recalled a trooper of the 13th Virginia Cavalry who rode with Chambliss. "The moon was shining beautifully, and a solemn silence seemed to pervade the troops, unbroken save by the splash of the horses' feet in the water as we passed from Virginia's soil." The 3rd Virginia Cavalry was the first to cross in the perfect darkness. "You could hardly see your horse's ears," recalled a horse artillerist. "Each man as he rode past the battery was given a shell or cartridge to carry over. They did not relish the idea of handling the ammunition and growled very much at this duty imposed on them. This had to be done, as the water reached the backs of an ordinary size horse, and of course was over the limber chest and caissons," he continued. "Gen. Stuart knew that if his ammunition got wet his artillery would be useless and would hamper his movements very much. His artillery was his right arm and saved him from defeat on many a battle field."[85]

Once on the other side, the shell-bearers deposited their precious cargo on the shore, leaving it to be reloaded into the caissons. "The guns and caissons, although

84 Kennon to his daughter, quoted in Trout, *They Followed the Plume*, 190; Blackford, *War Years with Jeb Stuart*, 223.

85 "The Thirteenth Regiment of Virginia Cavalry in Gen. J.E.B. Stuart's Raid into Pennsylvania," *The Southern Bivouac*, no. 1 (1883), 205; Matthews, "Pelham-Breathed Battery."

entirely submerged during the nearly whole crossing, were safely dragged through the river and up the steep and slippery bank, and by three o'clock on the morning of the 28th, the rear-guard had crossed and the whole command was established upon Maryland soil," recalled a delighted Maj. Henry B. McClellan. "No more difficult achievement was accomplished by the cavalry during the war."[86]

While Stuart made his way through northern Virginia and on to Rowser's Ford, Beverly Robertson and "Grumble" Jones remained in position at Ashby's and Snicker's gaps even though the Army of the Potomac had already moved north in Maryland.

* * *

Brigadier General John D. Imboden and the 2,100 men of his Northwestern Brigade splashed across the Potomac River, marched across the narrow neck of Maryland, and entered the Little Cove, a narrow 11-mile gap that extended north to Cove Gap. The men of his 62nd Virginia Mounted Infantry captured many horses that day.[87]

The soldiers of Joe Hooker's Army of the Potomac, meanwhile, marched steadily north to reach Pennsylvania and interdict Lee's roving Confederates.

While at Middleburg, Maj. Gen. Henry Slocum received a letter from Hooker directing him to hold his XII Corps in readiness to march at a moment's notice to Williamsport. Hooker intended to place the troops then at Harpers Ferry under his command and throw that force and the XII Corps on Lee's line of communication. Hooker assured Slocum that he would concentrate the other corps within supporting distance. General-in-Chief Henry Halleck and the war department thwarted this plan in mid-morning by denying the release of the forces on Maryland Heights. Hooker repeated his request: "Ten thousand men are at Harper's Ferry, in condition to take the field. At that point they are of no earthly account. All public property could be secured to-night, and the troops marched where they could be of

---

86 McClellan, *Life and Campaigns of Stuart*, 323-324.

87 Francis Imboden, Diary, entry for June 27, 1863.

service." Halleck once again refused the request. Slocum would not receive the additional troops.

"Had the request of General Hooker to use the 10,000 men at Harper's Ferry been granted, that force and our corps would on the 28th of June have been on the line of Lee's communication, with ample time to entrench," Slocum later complained. "That we would have been able to hold our position till General Hooker could have brought all the other corps to our assistance, I feel very confident." It was not to be. The Army of the Potomac continued its course northward while Lee maintained an uninterrupted supply and logistics route back into Virginia.[88]

Furious with the denial, Hooker sat at his desk at his headquarters at Sandy Hook and penned a letter of resignation to Halleck. "My original instructions require me to cover Harper's Ferry and Washington. I have now imposed upon me, in addition, an enemy in my front of more than my number. I beg to be understood, respectfully, but firmly, that I am unable to comply with this condition with the means at my disposal, and earnestly request that I may at once be relieved from the position I occupy." Halleck dutifully responded at 8:00 p.m., seven hours after the time stamp on Hooker's letter. "Your application to be relieved from your present command is received. As you were appointed to this command by the President, I have no power to relieve you. Your dispatch has been duly referred for Executive action." Secretary of War Edwin Stanton handed a copy of the letter to an ashen-faced Lincoln and asked, "What shall be done?" Lincoln instructed him to accept the resignation. Secretary of the Treasury Salmon P. Chase, one of Hooker's friends and supporters, started to protest the decision but Lincoln cut him off: "The acceptance of an army resignation is not a matter for your department." The issue was settled. Lincoln would convene a meeting in the morning to inform the rest of his cabinet.[89]

The war department wanted a more experienced combat general at Harpers Ferry and thus relieved Brig. Gen. Daniel Tyler—who was largely an administrator—and replaced him with Maj. Gen. William H. French. The latter had commanded a division of the II Corps at Antietam, Fredericksburg, and Chancellorsville. "The merits and services of the new commander were made the topic of discussion in the tents of officers and soldiers during the night," wrote one

---

88 *Final Report on the Battlefield of Gettysburg*, 2 vols. (Albany, NY, 1900), 1:258.

89 OR 27, pt. 1, 60; Michael Burlingame, *Abraham Lincoln: A Life*, 2 vols. (Baltimore, 2008), 2:503.

Lt. Col. Rufus R. Dawes, who led the
6th Wisconsin of the Iron Brigade,
I Corps, Army of the Potomac, who went on
to pen one of the war's best memoirs.

LOC

of French's subordinates to the *Philadelphia Press*. "'Here's to Gen. French,' was toasted by every jovial coterie. 'Long may he prosper,' was the prayer of all." Work crews began felling or burning the trees on Maryland Heights to render them useless as cover in the event of an attack.[90]

Reports that the Rebels were fortifying the passes on South Mountain, the scene of bitter fighting during the 1862 Maryland campaign, resulted in part of the I Corps being dispatched to the scene. During the morning the 121st Pennsylvania halted for a rest break near Middletown, within eight miles of Boonsboro. "At this time all kinds of rumors were running through the army about the doings of the rebels in Pennsylvania, one of which was that Harrisburg had been taken; and the excitement on the part of the men appeared to affect the desire to move on and get within striking distance as soon as possible," recalled a soldier. "It was quite common to see the sore-footed and shoeless men marching over the stones barefooted, and submitting without complaining while climbing the stony mountain roads, trudging away, contented that at least they were after the 'rebs.'"[91]

The Iron Brigade reached Middletown in mid-afternoon. "Our marches, except to-day, have been long and toilsome," recalled Lt. Col. Rufus Dawes of the 6th Wisconsin. "What do you think of trudging along all day in a soaking rain, getting as wet as a drowned rat, taking supper on hardtack and salt pork, and then wrapping up in a wet woolen blanket and lying down for a sleep, but waked up

90 "Maryland Heights," *Philadelphia Press*, June 29, 1863, dateline June 27.

91 Survivors Association, *History of the 121st Regiment Pennsylvania Volunteers: "An Account from the Ranks"* (Philadelphia, 1906), 49.

during the night three or four times to receive and attend to orders and finally turning out at three o'clock in the morning to get the regiment ready to march?" he asked in his memoirs. "Well—that is soldiering, and it is a great deal more comfortable soldiering, than to march through suffocating clouds of dust under a hot sun. In the dust, men are dogged and silent. In the rain they are often even hilarious and jolly."[92]

Artillery commander Charles S. Wainwright was among the soldiers who marched through Pleasant Valley that Saturday. It had been a refreshing day, with fine cool weather and a broad smooth improved road—a welcome change from the heavily rutted, narrow roads previously encountered. Wainwright and his comrades relished the peaceful pastoral scenery, which in the artillerist's opinion was unequaled in all his travels. Clover, oats, corn, and wheat were thriving and the farmers appeared to be ready to enjoy a bumper harvest. What caught his attention even more than the lush fields of crops and the tidy, freshly painted farmhouses and immense barns were the bountiful orchards. "Cherry trees as big as oaks line the road a good ways," he marveled, "so that half the corps have been eating cherries all day, and stand a very good show for an attack of stomach ache tonight."[93]

One of Wainwright's subordinates, New York artilleryman Lt. George Breck, penned a letter to the *Rochester Union*. "The contrast between the two sections of country, Virginia and Maryland, was immediately perceptible. The former had presented to us a wasted, desolated look, an abandoned, unhomelike appearance, the houses . . . unworthy of the name, and almost everything told of the ravages of war," he explained. "The latter presented thrift, plenty, beautiful homes, cultivated farms, fields of waving grain fast ripening for the sickle, and everything denoted peace and abundance. The lines of fences running along fields and road in Maryland, added much to the contrast—poor Virginia having been completely stripped of these old land marks, wherever the army has been quartered." To Breck, "the soldiers seem fully sensible of the difference between a loyal and disloyal State."[94]

* * *

---

92 Dawes, *Service with the Sixth Wisconsin*, 156-157.

93 Allen Nevins, ed., *A Diary of Battle: The Personal Journals of Col. Charles S. Wainwright, 1861–1865* (New York, 1998), 225.

94 George Breck, *Rochester* (NY) *Union and Advertiser*, July 3, 1863.

Winfield Hancock's II Corps tramped through Poolesville, Maryland. The men of Col. George Willard's brigade, newly transferred from the XXII Corps, had spent months in camp at Centreville, so the long trek took its toll. "We marched, until 9 PM, when we halted for the night," recalled the 111th New York's Manley Stacey. "I never have been so Completely exhausted in my life, as I was then, it seemed as if I could not drag one foot, before the other. They marched us cruelly, so fast, that the Capt, said he did not expect, to have half, of his men, when they Halted. We should not have gone quite as far, but the General [Alexander Hays] was Signaled, to march his men as far as possible."[95]

The weather remained hot and sultry with sporadic rain showers. "Our clothing was wet and spattered and smeared with mahogany colored mud," recalled the 1st Minnesota's Sgt. James Wright. "The moisture, the sand, and the sharp stones of the road, which the wheels of the artillery and the trains had broken up badly, had been very destructive to shoe leather. Men who had left the Rappahannock twelve days before, with new shoes on their feet, were now practically bare-footed; and there were quite a number with feet so badly bruised or blistered that they walked like foundered horses." Each soldier, he continued, "carried a rifle which, with bayonet &c. weighed about 11 pounds. Also 100 rounds of ammunition, knapsack, haversack, canteen, coffee pot and whatever cooking utensils he had; his blanket, tent cloth, rubber [sheet], all extra clothing and whatever else he might have—writing paper, envelopes, keepsakes or a book." The equipage totaled 40 pounds, quite a lot for hard marching.[96]

The II Corps finally stopped near Barnesville, a small Maryland town nestled at the foot of Sugarloaf Mountain that offered commanding views of the distant Catoctin Mountain and the Blue Ridge ranges. It was a scenic and well-watered place for a military campsite, and for many of the veterans it provided pleasant memories. "It was noon before the battery was ordered to hitch up, and, after breaking camp, resumed the march," wrote John Rhodes of Battery B, 1st Rhode Island. After leaving Edward's Ferry, the artillerymen rolled through some familiar country, passing through Poolesville and taking the road to Barnesville before halting and bivouacking at 7:00 p.m. "Sixteen months had made but few changes in the features of the spot, or of its surroundings," Rhodes recalled. "The old fields,

95 Manley Stacey to Dear Father, June 28, 1863, Monocacy Junction, MD, HSOPRF.

96 Wright, "The Story of Company F," 552, as cited by Hage, "The Battle of Gettysburg as Seen by Minnesota Soldiers," 247.

the scenes of many thorough drills, the adjacent hills and those near the river (the Potomac), from whose summit skillful gunnery was occasionally displayed, the prostrated forest, exposing an uninterrupted view of the 'Sugar Loaf' lifting its head to the skies in the wild pomp of mountain majesty, all remained essentially as they appeared when we first pitched our tents in Secessia." The gunner's thoughts darkened when he realized that many of his comrades who had marched with him in 1862 would never again answer a roll call.[97]

Despite the natural beauty, the grueling pace of the northward march prostrated hundreds of men, including dozens of officers. "I am still in command of the brigade," Col. George H. Ward of the 15th Massachusetts penned that evening in Poolesville. "General Gibbon has returned, but General Harrow is sick and rides in an ambulance. I expect it will be my turn next, as I feel very much like it now. All are surprised to see how well I stand it. I have not had my leg off for three days, neither has it been dressed." (Ward had lost a leg after the battle of Ball's Bluff in October 1861.) Ward's thoughts turned to the invasion. "I have always said the war was too far off for the North to fully realize its magnitude. The time has now come for action. The vigorous and earnest prosecution of the war is inevitable, and the quiet slumber of the people of the North will get most shockingly disturbed." Ward enclosed a cloverleaf, which he he had just picked from a nearby field. "We have not seen the worst of this rebellion yet, and I almost shudder at the thought of what we are to pass through before the struggle is over, but I still trust and believe that things will come out well. . . . One thing is certain," he closed, "our men will fight much better with their faces turned homeward."[98]

*   *   *

The III Corps marched from Point of Rocks, Maryland, to Middletown. The 63rd Pennsylvania started about 8:00 a.m. and passed through Jefferson with colors unfurled and its band playing patriotic airs. After spending so much time in Confederate territory, the warm reception brought joy to the soldiers. Most houses had Old Glory flying and the women greeting the passing column with "approving smiles and words of welcome," recalled the regimental historian with pride. "A thousand handkerchiefs waved from windows and house tops, and

97 Rhodes, *History of Battery B, First Rhode Island Artillery*, 196.

98 Ford, *Story of the Fifteenth Massachusetts Infantry*, 259-260. Colonel Ward was killed at Gettysburg.

on every side from loyal citizens, old and young, we received assurances of sympathy, welcome, and good will. Such enthusiasm and demonstrations of patriotism were indeed gratifying to men who had been so long in an unfriendly country and surrounded by the bitterest foes. The soldiers cheered the old flag and the ladies vociferously, and enjoyed the occasion to the fullest extent." Confederates had passed through the area a few days previously, "and the citizens hailed our coming with unmistakable pleasure."[99]

While marching his III Corps division through Maryland, Brig. Gen. David B. Birney always halted his men until the band could take position at the most prominent intersection. Only once it was thus ensconced would the column march past. The tramping men, recalled musician Frank Rauscher, "kept precise step, and besides making an imposing appearance before the inhabitants, it prevented the men from straggling, as they became imbued with the pride of making a soldierly display. After the men had passed, of course, the band had to make haste and get to its place in the line of march."[100]

"We were again in line, on the morning of the twenty-seventh, and marched to near Jefferson Village, where we halted a short time for dinner," recounted Lt. Edwin Houghton of the 17th Maine. The regiment then passed through Jefferson in column by company, with colors unfurled and bands playing. "Here we witnessed the first expression of Union sentiment that had gladdened our eyes since we joined the Army of the Potomac," he rejoiced. The flags, cheers, and proffered food gladdened the foot soldiers. "One man, as he marched along with as proud and light a step as if on review and just from camp, remarked that 'he forgot that he had a knapsack on.' . . . We marched about twelve miles through a pleasant country . . . It was cloudy during the day, which rendered the march more comfortable."[101]

Some soldiers later complained that the Marylanders' hospitality often came with a price. "The only thing I received was a cup of sour milk from a woman who stood by the middle of the road with a pail full of that commodity," recalled Sgt. J. D. Bloodgood of the 141st Pennsylvania, "giving each one a cup full as long as it lasted, and, I said, though it was skimmed, it did taste wonderfully good. In nearly

99 Gilbert A. Hays, *Under the Red Patch; Story of the Sixty-Third Regiment, Pennsylvania Volunteers, 1861–1864* (Pittsburgh, 1908), 190.

100 Rauscher, *Music on the March*, 80.

101 Houghton, *Campaigns of the Seventeenth Maine*, 78.

every place we passed through stands were erected where we could buy weak lemonade for ten cents a glass, pies, cakes, bread, etc., at corresponding rates."[102]

Colonel Regis de Trobriand took a few minutes to write home that evening. "We are going to start off again at any moment, because we are following the enemy, and it is rumored that we have captured some of their wagons, and if this is true, and Lee's forces are in front of us, we are going to cut off their line of retreat and in that way force them to fall back to join battle with us," he penned. "If we have a second edition of Antietam, I hope that this time, we will throw their army into the river and we won't let them withdraw to their liking to Virginia."[103]

*　*　*

Charles E. Sprague of the 44th New York Infantry recalled the march of George Meade's V Corps from Edwards Ferry toward Frederick, Maryland. "Cherries were now ripe and we ate all we could hold. I have no doubt the acid fruit did us good on the whole, though some of us got badly doubled up," he wrote to his loved ones back home. "We felt in good spirits too; we knew we were going to fight, but somehow we felt that was going to be a different affair from the buckling against their fortifications which we had tried so many times. We talked it over and concluded that the fight was going to be something like Antietam."[104]

Dr. John Billings of 11th U.S. Infantry, another V Corps regiment, disagreed that there would be another fight on the scale of Antietam. He was glad, too, because he believed the Army of the Potomac would lose. "10 a.m. We have now halted at the base of Sugar Loaf Mountain in the woods and the men are making some coffee," he wrote in a letter home. "I suppose we are going somewhere near Frederick. I feel somewhat better today than yesterday although I am quite weak but I hope we shall have two or three days' rest now for I don't think J. Hooker will attack immediately—if he does he will surely get thrashed. Nobody here seems to think that Lee contemplates anything more than a grand raid, and do not believe

102 "Personal Reminiscences of the War, Rev. J. D. Bloodgood, Ph. B," in *Northern Christian Advocate* (Syracuse, NY), July 18, 1889.

103 Styple, *Our Noble Blood*, 112.

104 "Fourth of July, '63, As It Dawned for a Soldier at Gettysburg," *Canton* (OH) *Repository*, July 3, 1886.

that he has the remotest intention of approaching Washington or even of having a battle if he can help it."[105]

The prosperous region captivated many Union soldiers just as it had their counterparts. "The troops were in a section wholly unacquainted with great bodies of armed men," a Pennsylvania officer marveled. "Thickly peopled, highly cultivated, alternating between wood, meadow and field, it rolled in easy undulations, and from its gently rising knolls one scene of rich grandeur appeared as the other faded from view. . . . Men, maidens, matrons and children gazed in wonderment as the column hurried through their villages, and gathered around the bivouacs eager listeners to the soldiers' stories of war."[106]

Meade halted the V Corps for the night at Ballinger's Creek near Frederick. A frequent and favorite topic among the men was the performance of their commander. Many berated "Old Four Eyes" when he was too far off to hear them. They complained that he was too harsh on the officers when they disregarded orders for the perceived benefit and comfort of their men, sometimes to the point of death by firing squad, claimed one.[107]

"In the evening a brigade of cavalry came over the mountain into Burkettsville," observed a member of the 153rd Pennsylvania. "They were the drunkenest brigade that I ever saw. Officers and privates were alike. I saw two privates trying to keep an officer on the saddle, I also saw officers trying to keep a private in the saddle. Some of them had to lay over till the next day, before they were able to follow up their command. I was informed that they had struck a distillery, but I think the distillery must have struck them."[108]

*   *   *

Well to the south, John Sedgwick's VI Corps left Dranesville and crossed the Potomac at Edwards Ferry before camping near Poolesville. Henry Slocum's XII Corps departed its camps near the mouth of the Monocacy River and marched past Point of Rocks to Knoxville, a small Maryland village in Frederick County. John Buford's cavalry division rode from Leesburg, Virginia, via

105 Garrison, *John Shaw Billings*, 58.

106 *History of the 118th Pennsylvania*, 231.

107 Ibid.

108 Keifer and Mack, *History of the 153rd Pennsylvania*, 206.

Edwards Ferry to near Jefferson, Maryland, while Irvin Gregg's mounted division marched from Leesburg via Edwards Ferry toward Frederick. The artillery reserve rolled from Poolesville to Frederick, which Julius Stahel's mounted division also reached.

"I have seen a Baltimore paper today for the first time for 3 days that I have seen any paper," reported VI Corps brigade commander Col. Charles Brewer. "It reports Lee crossing the Potomac with his whole Army if this is true and we don't annihilate him this time, I shall believe we never can whip him. We expect a fight within a day or two," continued the infantry leader, "but do not know whether we shall get into it or not but it will be something unusual if a fight comes off and the sixth Corps does not have a hand in it."[109]

The 23rd Pennsylvania, known popularly as "Birney's Zouaves" for its early war commander and colorful attire, marched with John Sedgwick's VI Corps to White's Ford near Leesburg. The men camped on the farm of Lt. Col. Elijah "Lige" White, who that day was busy leading his 35th Battalion, Virginia Cavalry through the southwestern part of Pennsylvania's York County. White's partisans had captured most of Company B of the 23rd Pennsylvania near the ford the previous year. White had treated his captives well and they now returned the favor. According one of the Zouaves, "On their return from rebel prisons the members of the company spoke so highly of the treatment accorded them by White and his command that nothing was disturbed on his place. Here the regiment was given rations, and quite a supply was left at White's home for use of his family, he then being absent with Lee's army." What the thoughtful Pennsylvanians did not know was that White's wife and child had moved deeper into Virginia to escape the war.[110]

Sergeant Levi W. Baker served in Bigelow's 9th Massachusetts Battery in the army's Reserve Artillery. "We take our line of march through Poolsville, over the northerly side of Sugar Loaf Mountain, a rough road, and passed the wreck of many an ambulance and baggage wagon," narrated the prewar wheelwright. "We passed through Frederick City, finding at the doors buckets of water for the thirsty ones, and camped about one mile beyond, at 9 P.M. Our ambulance broke down on the mountain and they had to stay there all night, arriving in camp at 10 o'clock Sunday morning." Once there, the men turned in their knapsacks and reduced their

---

109 Blight, *When This Cruel War is Over*, 238.

110 *History of the Twenty-third Pennsylvania Infantry*, 93.

baggage to a single change of underclothing, an overcoat, a blanket, and a shelter tent.[111]

*   *   *

The Federal cavalry began crossing the Potomac River that morning, and by the end of the day the entire Cavalry Corps was in Maryland. By the time the tail crossed, elements of Stahel's division were already moving into Pennsylvania. Victor Comte, a French-Canadian serving in a Michigan cavalry regiment, wrote his wife that "the roads we're following would lead us right straight to Detroit. But, as the Rebels will not go so far we'll stop when we meet them. I think it will be in Pennsylvania."[112]

*   *   *

Confidence remained high in Harrisburg that the Rebels would never cross the Susquehanna River because the water level "is rapidly rising and all the fords will be impassable," predicted one Chicago newspaper reporter. "Gen. [William F. "Baldy"] Smith, commanding the troops on the opposite side of the river, considers his position impregnable. There is not as much excitement here now as there was when the rebels entered Hagerstown. The great fear is that the railroad and other bridges across the river will be destroyed."[113]

Many locals believed the defenses at Bridgeport would be sufficient. "The entrenchments across the river from the town are extensive and admirably situated," announced a member of the Blue Reserves from Camp Taylor below Harrisburg. "They command all the approaches, and others are now in the process of erection." Despite pelting rain and high wind from a northeaster, he and his fellow Philadelphia militiamen busily wielded spades and pickaxes to further fortify their position. It was tiring and thankless work. "We will, however, have the satisfaction of knowing that we have at least tried to do our duty in defending our

111 Baker, *History of the Ninth Massachusetts Battery*, 55.

112 Victor Comte to his wife, June 28, 1863, Victor E. Comte Papers, Michigan Historical Collections, Bentley Historical Library, UM.

113 *Chicago Tribune*, June 28, 1863.

State, instead of sitting idly at home indulging in dreams of ease and indolence, waiting for our neighbors to do our duty for us."[114]

When a report reached the 22nd New York National Guard that the enemy was only four miles out, Cpl. George Wingate refused to believe it. Companies C and G were manning the picket line some five miles from the main camp, and they had not been driven in. The Rebels were near enough, and closer than anyone wanted, but they were not a mere handful of miles away. Still, supply officers distributed 40 cartridges to each man and the entire regiment, minus the pickets, began digging rifle-pits to command the York Road, a possible route of enemy approach. By 2:00 p.m. they had constructed a respectable entrenchment. Their diligent actions more than annoyed the Copperhead farmer on whose land they camped. According to Wingate, the farmer loudly declared "that he did not believe there were any rebels in the State and that the whole affair was an election dodge of Andy Curtin." Some vengeful New Yorkers deliberately dug a large rifle pit across his garden "as a practical demonstration to him that the situation had not been exaggerated by the patriotic Governor of his State."

Later that afternoon officers distributed new axes and sent the men out to fell a large grove of hickory trees screening the road from the guns of the fort. "The men had by this time become impressed with the fact that the resemblance between digging a rifle-pit on a hot day and a laborer's work in excavating a sewer was very close, and they were glad to exchange it for chopping, which was more like fun," recalled Wingate. Not to be outdone by his men, Col. Lloyd Aspinwall shouldered an axe with zeal. The work was more dangerous than some anticipated because not all the blades were properly fastened to the handles. Occasionally one flew off, making "proximity to the working parties quite exciting."

When only four neighbors, two of them black, volunteered to assist in the labor, Aspinwall sent out details to impress any able-bodied civilian who could be found. With the quartet of volunteers as examples, Aspinwall soon had his men engaged in inter-company rivalries. The big hickories crashing down in all directions led some correspondents across the river to telegraph news of "heavy firing at Harrisburg."

The work finally stopped at 7:00 p.m., "with blistered hands and muscles aching from the unaccustomed labor," wrote a weary New Yorker. The result, once back in camp, was a regiment of men "plunged in a dreamless slumber, although

114 "The Blue Reserves," *Philadelphia Press*, June 29, 1863, dateline June 27.

General Dix's Union expeditionary force came ashore in northern Virginia at
White House Landing on the south side of the Pamunkey River. LOC

sleeping in their clothes and on their arms, so as to be able to respond in an instant,
if called upon. No alarm, however, broke the stillness of the night."[115]

* * *

Far to the southeast on the Virginia Peninsula east of Richmond, Col. Samuel
Spear and his mounted column finally reached White House Landing
that morning. The troopers handed off their prisoner, Rooney Lee, to a
detachment of the 118th New York Infantry. The wounded Lee, recalled one of the
New Yorkers, was "a full-bearded, fine resolute looking officer, but not inclined to
conversation." He would be held as a prisoner of war at Fortress Monroe until
March 1864.[116]

115 Wingate, *History of the Twenty-second Regiment*, 175-176.

116 John L. Cunningham, *Three Years with the Adirondack Regiment: 118th Volunteer Infantry*
(Norward, MA, 1920), 70.

By the time Spear and his troopers made it back to White House Landing, Maj. Gen. John A. Dix had accumulated a sizeable force of infantry there. Some had marched up from Yorktown on the Peninsula. "[As] the roads were heavy with mud and the clothing and equipment damp," recalled a member of the 127th New York, "the march was very trying." Some units were carried up the Pamunkey River on transports; that waterway was "at times so narrow that our steamer often touched the bordering tree branches on each side, and so crooked that steamers ahead of ours seemed going in a contrary direction." More than 18,000 Union soldiers were now camped around White House Landing. By that time the house had been destroyed.[117]

Dix's movements triggered outright panic in Richmond. Secretary of War James A. Seddon declared that the enemy force at White House Landing "will probably advance for a real attack on this city." That afternoon, President Jefferson Davis, Governor John Letcher, and Mayor Joseph Mayo issued proclamations calling the citizens to take up arms to defend the capital. Every militia unit was called up, issued arms, and taught some rudimentary drills.[118]

117 Ibid; Franklin McGrath, *History of the 127th New York Volunteers* (New York, 1898), 56-57; OR 27, pt. 3, 938.

118 OR 27, pt. 3, 945, 948, 956-957, 969.

SUNDAY, JUNE 28, 1863

The enthusiastic if road-weary infantrymen of the Army of Northern Virginia celebrated their first Sabbath in the Keystone State on this last Sunday of the month.

"Here we are away up in Central Pennsylvania, how strange it seems!" exclaimed the 5th Alabama's Maj. Eugene Blackford in a letter to his mother. "I can scarcely realize that a rebel army has actually left poor old Virginia for a season at least and is now living upon the substance of its enemies." Blackford found comfort in the fact that the Old Dominion was "almost entirely free from the Yankees, long may she so remain." Like so many others in their letters home or in messages to their diaries, he commented on the immense barns and the bounty of the land. The Dutch he found quite quaint: "All drink 'lager' and eat 'sauer- krout' from one year's end to the other."[1]

For the tens of thousands of soldiers in A. P. Hill's and James Longstreet's corps camped in the fields outside Chambersburg, the cloudy and warm day offered the promise of some much-needed rest. For the citizens of south-central Pennsylvania, however, the day brought high anxiety and more financial losses. The manner in which the Virginia army helped itself to whatever it could use or take did not sit at all well with everyone within its ranks. "Our army treats sitisens tremedious bad," complained the 13th South Carolina's Marcus M. Willis in a creatively written letter home to his father. "[I]t is scandleous goin to their dwelling

1 Eugene Blackford to his mother, Chambersburg, Pa., June 28, 1863, GNMP.

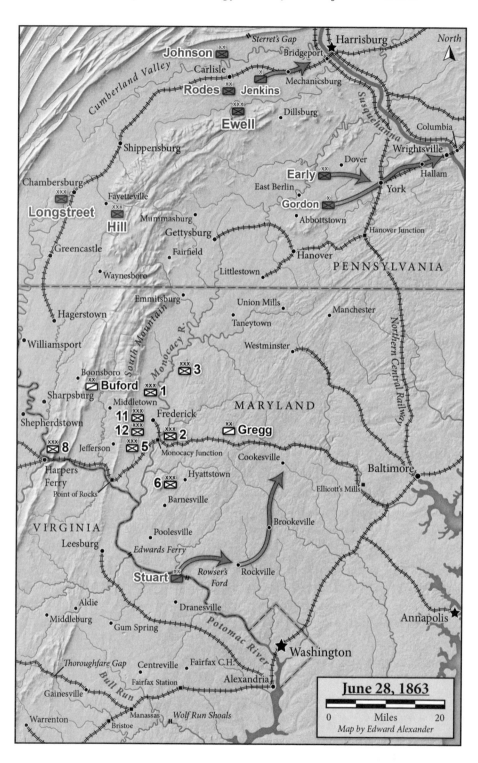

June 28, 1863

0   Miles   20

Map by Edward Alexander

houses taking privet propperty watches money milk butter chickens anything they can put hands on."[2]

Dorsey Pender camped his division west of Chambersburg near Fayetteville. His men spent the day resting after marching 157 miles in just twelve days. The regular letter-writing general let his wife know that the men had "generally behaved well" until crossing the Mason-Dixon line, but that they were engaging in plundering the countryside. "I am tired of invasions," he continued,

> for altho' they have made us suffer all that people can suffer, I cannot get my resentment to that point to make me feel indifferent to what you see here. But for the demoralizing effect plundering would have on our troops, they would feel war in all its horrors. I never saw people so badly scared. We have only to wish for a thing and it is done. I have made up my mind to enjoy no hospitality or kindness from any of them.
>
> Everything seems to be going on finely. We might get to Phila. without a fight, I believe, if we should choose to go. Gen. Lee intimates to no one what he is up to, and we can only surmise. I hope we may be in Harrisburg in three days. What a fine commentary upon their 90 days [militia units] crushing out, if we should march to the Capital of one of their largest states without a blow. It seems to be the impression that Hooker will not leave Washington, but [will] leave the states to take care of themselves.
>
> We are in Adams Co., having marched through Franklin. If we do not succeed in accomplishing a great deal all of us will be surprised. Our men seem to be in the spirit and feel confident. They laugh at the idea of meeting the militia.

"I wish we could meet Hooker and have the matter settled at once," he concluded. It was the last letter Dorsey Pender would send home.[3]

Unlike General Pender, Dr. Spencer G. Welch, the regimental surgeon for the 13th South Carolina of Abner Perrin's Brigade, enjoyed the invasion north of the Mason-Dixon Line. The very idea of it "buoyed me up all the time" he admitted in a letter home to his wife. "The people seem frightened almost out of their senses. They are nearly all agricultural people and have everything in abundance that administers to comfort. . . . Such wheat I never dreamed of, and so much of it! I noticed yesterday that scarcely a horse or cow was to be seen. The free negroes are all gone, as well as thousands of the white people." Welch's black servant "Wilson"

2 Marcus M. Willis to Father, June 28, 1863, Vertical File V7-SC13, GNMP.

3 Hassler, *One of Lee's Best Men*, 253-254. Pender was mortally wounded on July 2 at Gettysburg and died on July 18, 1863.

made it clear that "he 'don't like Pennsylvania at all,' because he 'sees no black folks' . . . I must say that I have enjoyed this tramp."[4]

It was easy to be "buoyed" at the expense of others in wartime. Chambersburg merchant Jacob Hoke returned home after attending church to the sound of a ringing axe in his ears. Several soldiers were busy chopping through the doors to reach his private cellar. Once inside, an officer jotted down the contents in a blank book. He left a small contingent of soldiers behind to protect the premises. That evening, however, the guards ransacked the cellar and carried off cans of fruit and other valuable private property. "Hats, boots, watches and pocket books were taken, but never in the presence of an officer," Hoke elaborated. "The Rev. Dr. B. S. Schneck was caught on the outskirts of the town, and his pocket book containing about fifty dollars and a valuable gold watch were taken from him. The watch had been presented to him by a friend while in Europe a few years previously. Rev. Father Cullom of the Catholic church was also robbed of his boots and pocket book. It is said that when he returned to town he used some language neither complimentary to the rebels nor in harmony with the sanctity of his profession."[5]

Chambersburg diarist Rachel Cormany complained of Georgia troops who "took the hats & boots off the men—Took hat off Preacher Farney. Took $50 off Dr. Sneck & his gold watch valued very highly—took the coats off some, totally stripped one young fellow not far from town." Several Rebels broke into Franklin Hall, the home of the Odd Fellows. They ripped or cut most of the lodge's regalia and vandalized locked desks and drawers.[6]

The plundering was more extensive in the surrounding farmland. "Our commissaries & quartermasters are gathering horses, beef cattle from the people in great numbers," recalled the 2nd Mississippi's Gus Vairin. "Some of our men forage after chickens, eggs, butter, vegetables, apple butter, Honey &c, in a few cases doubtless get what they should not, but at worst nothing to compare with the brutality the enemy used in our part of the country." The Magnolia State soldier was of two minds on the matter. "It is bad policy & contrary to orders for our men to disturb private citizens in any manner & any citizen is to be furnished with a guard if desired. Besides this foraging business is very demoralizing to soldiers."[7]

---

4 Welch, *A Confederate Surgeon's Letters to His Wife*, 57-58.

5 Hoke, *Reminiscences*, 52, 63.

6 Mohr, *The Cormany Diaries*, 337-338; *Chambersburg Spirit & Times*, July 15, 1863.

7 Vairin diary, entry for June 28, 1863.

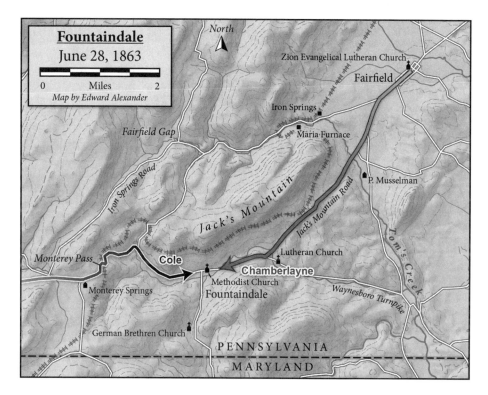

Foraging could also be deadly. Early that morning, several members of Crenshaw's Virginia battery scoured the countryside southeast of Chambersburg for livestock and supplies. They paused at Zion Evangelical Lutheran Church in Fairfield, where Lt. John H. Chamberlayne held the stunned congregants at pistol point while his men unhitched their horses in the yard. The officer passed out receipts, declaring the bills would be paid once the Confederate States and the United States made peace.

After hearing that Confederate cavalrymen were impressing livestock, a 25-man detail of the 1st Maryland Cavalry Battalion, Potomac Home Brigade, under the command of Lt. William A. Horner was sent to investigate. It did not take long before the Federals spotted Lieutenant Chamberlayne and his men with 20 stolen horses in their possession. Chamberlayne realized the game was up and ordered his men to ride off and save themselves. The lieutenant, meanwhile, spurred his own horse and charged at the Yankees—alone. Horner and his troopers easily captured Chamberlayne, killed one of his men, and wounded another. The same group of Marylanders also captured a Confederate officer carrying dispatches from Gen. Robert E. Lee to General Ewell later that day. The paperwork would eventually wind its way up the Union chain of command and prove to be important intelligence that helped clarify a bit more of the unfolding puzzle.[8]

Plundering continued on a grand scale. "Hogs, sheep, and Poultries stand a poor chance about here for their lives. We are living off the fat of the land," bragged James B. Clifton, a surgeon in Brig. Gen. Paul J. Semmes's Georgia brigade. Thomas L. Ware of the 15th Georgia in Henry Benning's Brigade mentioned that the Confederates "burnt all the fences around the corn fields, & [took] wagons & horses in the wheat & corn field." A trio of soldiers in the 3rd Arkansas conspired to steal the honey from a beehive on a German farm by distracting the woman of the house so they could grab the sweet golden syrup and run. The men paused at the spring house to snatch crocks of milk and butter before leaving.[9]

A garden full of fresh vegetables beckoned men belonging to Maj. Gen. Lafayette McLaws's Division. The field was so close to the general's headquarters, however, that they felt obliged to ask for permission rather than risk a raid under his watchful eye. Would the general negotiate with the farmer to obtain some of the vegetables?, asked one or more of the men. Probably to the surprise of many, McLaws agreed.

The general made his way over and visited the lady who owned the property to inquire whether she would sell some, or all, of the produce. He only had Confederate money, he continued, but if she preferred he could give her a receipt for what his men took. The unnamed woman replied that from what she had heard about how Federal troops treated Southerners, the Rebels had a right to take anything without asking. McLaws dodged the comment by telling her that General Lee had forbidden his men to plunder. The woman granted McLaws permission for his men to take what they wanted. At his request, she went into her garden and gave the vegetables away. McLaws relayed this incident to his wife in a letter,

---

8 John Hampden Chamberlayne, *Ham Chamberlayne, Virginian: Letters and Papers of an Artillery Officer in the War for Southern Independence, 1861–1865* (Richmond, 1932), 191-192; Timothy H. Smith, "Northern Town Lot Histories of Fairfield, Pennsylvania," *Adams County History*, no. 19 (2013), 36-37; Armour C. Newcomer, *Cole's Cavalry, or, Three Years in the Saddle in the Shenandoah Valley* (Baltimore, 1895), 52. The 1st Maryland Cavalry Battalion, Potomac Home Brigade, was known as Cole's Cavalry after its commander, Col. Henry Cole.

9 Calvin L. Collier, *They'll Do To Tie To!: The Story of the Third Regiment, Arkansas Infantry, C. S. A.* (Little Rock, 1959), 128; J. B. Clifton, Diary, entry for June 28, 1863, North Carolina Historical Commission, as cited in Wiley, *The Life of Johnny Reb*, 47; Mark Nesbitt, ed., *35 Days to Gettysburg: The Campaign Diaries of Two American Enemies* (Mechanicsburg, PA, 1992), 122-123, 129.

adding that the people of Chambersburg were "decidedly hostile," and most women excelled "in being vulgar."[10]

Many soldiers in the Confederate ranks also discussed the Pennsylvania women. The 16th Georgia's Pvt. Eli Landers of Wofford's Georgia brigade "saw a heap of pretty Yankey girls but somehow I can't help but hate them." Other soldiers were far more condescending. "The portion of Pennsylvania through which we have passed is settled by a class of low Dutch," judged Pvt. Francis P. Fleming of the 2nd Florida of Perry's Florida Brigade. "I have scarcely seen a refined and highly intelligent person since I have been in the State." William Stilwell of the 53rd Georgia, Semmes's Brigade, echoed Fleming. "The people here are mostly dutch. It hurts them very bad to see the rebel occupying their country. We don't destroy anything, but what we need to eat and wear, such things as vegetables and chickens, honey, has to get eaten. An old dutch woman got after me today for getting onions from her garden," he continued. The woman "gave me fits, but I made her no reply, but yes'em."[11]

The men of George Pickett's Division thought Chambersburg "had the appearance of a deserted village on a wet Sunday." According to the 1st Virginia's Charles T. Loehr, "All the liquor had been placed in the court-house, and was under guard. The few people we saw had no great friendship to bestow on us, but the farmers outside the town took things more pleasantly, and we got along agreeably with them."[12]

"Many of the people of Pennsylvania seemed to think that we would eat them," wrote John H. Lewis, a surprised private with the 9th Virginia. The private and two other men in his company received permission to get cherries and approached a house where a woman was busy baking. Lewis politely asked for the fruit and was chatting with the lady when her husband arrived and joined the conversation. He told Lewis that as fast as his wife could bake, soldiers would line up and buy the bread. Their supply of flour was gone and the last of the bread was in the oven. When asked why he didn't sell it to them, the farmer intimated that he was afraid to refuse the soldiers. The Virginian assured him there was no danger in keeping the last of the bread for his family. "With his consent I went up the cherry

10 John C. Oeffinger, ed., *A Soldier's General: The Civil War Letters of Major General Lafayette McLaws* (Chapel Hill, NC, 2002), 194.

11 Landers and Roberson, *Weep Not for Me, Dear Mother*, 130; Francis P. Fleming to His Brother, Robert L. Brake Collection, USAHEC; Stilwell, *The Stilwell Letters*, 181-182.

12 Loehr, *War History of the Old First Virginia*, 35-36.

tree, and while there had the satisfaction of hearing the lady refuse the next buyer, and she was surprised at the gentlemanly manner in which he took the refusal."[13]

Colonel William S. Christian of the 55th Virginia, part of Brockenbrough's Brigade, intended to take revenge against the locals because of atrocities the Yankees had committed in the South. The 33-year-old had a change of heart and admitted as much in a letter to his wife Helen penned from his camp near Greenwood. When he got among these people, he explained, he "could not find it in my heart to molest them. They looked so dreadfully scared and talked so humble, that I have invariably endeavored to protect their property, and have prevented soldiers from taking chickens, even in the main road." Christian "sent out today to get a good horse; I have no scruples about that, as they have taken mine." Capturing blacks and sending them south was too much for him. "We took a lot of negroes yesterday. I was offered my choice, but as I could not get them back home I would not take them. In fact, my humanity revolted at taking the poor devils away from their homes."[14]

A widow named Ellen McLellan worried that all the plundering would leave little food for the residents. The bold woman finagled an interview with Robert E. Lee to discuss the matter. She marveled at Lee's campsite, where "[e]verything was in most perfect order; even the horses were picketed so as to do no injury to the trees in the grove where their tents were pitched." She informed the general that "starvation would soon be at hand upon many families, unless he gave us aid." This pronouncement appeared to startle Lee, who pointed to the surrounding rich fields of grain and rebutted, "such destitution seemed impossible in such a rich and beautiful grain growing country." He finally relented and agreed to have a miller estimate the amount of grain required for the populace. When the widow asked him for his autograph, Lee responded, "Do you want the autograph of a rebel?" Ellen replied, "General Lee, I am a true Union woman, and yet I ask for bread and your autograph." Lee acquiesced. She later claimed he "assured me the war was a

---

13 Lewis, *Recollections*, 67. Tally Simpson, a South Carolinian in McLaws's Division, agreed. "This whole country is frightened almost to death. They won't take our money, but for fear that our boys will kill them, they give away what they can spare." Everson and Simpson, *Far, Far from Home*, 251.

14 William S. Christian to My Own Darling Wife, June 28, 1863, in "Advance into Pennsylvania" in Moore, *Rebellion Record*, 7:325. Christian's wife Helen never received the letter, which was found on the battlefield after the fighting. He was captured at Falling Waters on July 14 and imprisoned at Johnson's Island in Ohio. The twice-wounded officer was exchanged in 1864 and served until the final weeks of the war. He composed a long poem, titled "The Past," that described in rhyme his life and his love for his wife and family.

cruel thing, and that he only desired that they would let him go home and eat his bread there in peace. All this time I was impressed with the strength and sadness of the man."[15]

At least one young Pennsylvanian tried to join the Confederates. "A six or seven year old boy came into our office at 11 o'clock at night inquiring for the Provost Marshal," recalled Maj. N. C. Wilson of the 28th Virginia, Garnett's Brigade. "Says he is badly treated at home (his mother being dead & his father absent for the past three years, he knows not exactly where) and desires to join us. We offer to send him back to his home, but he refuses to go & asks permission to stay with us for the night. Sleeps with the surgeon on the floor."[16]

*　*　*

Similar scenes played out in Carlisle. "An immense rebel army has marched through our midst," complained a local editor, "wasting our substance, devastating our fields, robbing our granaries and warehouses, searching our dwellings, and visiting on us many other calamities of war." Private William A. Smith of the 14th North Carolina mentioned, "These people are amazed at Lee's audacity in invading Pennsylvania and, knowing the great inferiority of our numbers to the enemy's, the rank and file think so too; for all our Southern soldiers are accustomed to think and act for ourselves—individualistic—which is one of the reasons we fight so well."[17]

Some Confederates had varied experiences in Carlisle. The 12th Alabama's Capt. Robert Park and some fellow officers breakfasted at the home of a Pennsylvanian named Lee, whose daughters waited upon the tables. The girls served "hot rolls and waffles, butter and honey. Fried chicken also graced the table, and, I need not say, everything was hugely enjoyed." Later, Park visited the local Episcopal church "and, after the close of the service, was passing some well dressed ladies, to whom I lifted my hat, when one of them spoke to me kindly and inquired what State I was from, and upon reply told me that their minister was from Florence, Alabama. She spoke very gently and without a word of abuse, or reproof, or remonstrance." Park's mood soured shortly after he went alone to the National

15 Hoke, *Reminiscences*, 63-64.

16 Wilson diary, entry for June 28, 1863, VMI. The fate of the lad, and his identity, remain unknown.

17 *Carlisle Herald*, July 10, 1863; Smith, *Anson Guards*, 201.

A rare wartime photo of market day on Hanover Street in Carlisle, Pennsylvania. LOC

Hotel for dinner. "Found an unfriendly and scowling crowd of rough looking men in the office, but I walked up to the desk and registered and called for dinner," he griped. "I was late and the dinner was quite a poor one, and was rather ungraciously served by a plump, Dutchy looking young waitress."[18]

Many soldiers attended religious services in their camps. "Bro. [Beverly T.] Lacy preaches to three North Carolina Brigades in the forenoon," announced Dr. Alexander D. Betts, a Methodist Episcopal chaplain with the 30th North Carolina of Ramseur's Brigade. "I preach in the afternoon and baptize five by pouring. . .

18 Park, "The Twelfth Alabama Infantry," 244.

Bro. Brooks and I baptise four each, in a pool near by. Pleasant day, but not much spirituality among the soldiers."[19]

Not far from Carlisle's churches, an empty wooden flagpole stood in the town square. Several Confederate officers thought it was time for a symbolic change of control. "It was resolved that the Stars and Stripes, which had been cut down from the flagpole, should be replaced by the Stars and Bars," boasted the 2nd North Carolina's Lt. Col. Wharton J. Green, also a member of Ramseur's command. "The pole was replaced with the young flag floating at the masthead." Another Confederate flag was soon fluttering above the Carlisle Barracks, where Generals Rodes, Trimble, Daniel, Ewell, and other officers turned out to make morale-boosting speeches.[20]

Ewell installed Maj. Rufus W. Wharton of the 1st Battalion, North Carolina Sharpshooters, as the provost marshal of Carlisle. Wharton's task was not easy because hundreds of Confederates wandered the streets, most of them bent on some sort of mischief. He later complained that the only thing he received for governing the captured town and trying to keep order for two days was "one glass of beer."[21]

Captain James I. Harris of the 30th North Carolina toured Carlisle that evening. He was seated near a water pump when a few locals started maneuvering the handle. He offered his services and was soon bantering with them. To Harris's dismay, they deemed Southern women as "contemptible." The sharp remark took him by surprise. As he wrote after the war, "I felt the blood tingling in my ears and rushing in my face like a whirlpool, and I feared almost to trust myself to speak." Harris took a moment to comport himself before replying. "Our ladies are not contemptible," he began gently. "They have to act in self defense; it is your soldiery that is both cowardly and contemptible." Soon thereafter, a truce having been called, Harris headed back to Carlisle Barracks, but not before stopping for dinner at a house where the elderly resident chattered non-stop. "She was all talk," he groused. "If I had such a wife, I should divide the day into several parts and

19 Rev. A. D. Betts, *Experience of a Confederate Chaplain, 1861–1864* (privately printed, SC, 1904), 38. Virginia native Beverly T. Lacy was the Presbyterian chaplain for the Second Corps. Reverend Henry E. Brooks was chaplain of the 2nd North Carolina Battalion in Daniel's Brigade.

20 Green, *Recollections and Reflections*, 174; Hotchkiss, *Make Me a Map*, 155.

21 "Col. R. W. Wharton's History, 1st Battalion Sharpshooters," *Charlotte Observer*, July 21, 1895.

prohibit her from coming in my presence oftener than once or twice per day at farthest."[22]

Major General Edward Johnson's Division camped just outside Carlisle. A local reporter chastised the invaders: "The foraging parties were in reality marauders, and destroyed what they could not make use of." He also claimed that despite Lee's strict orders that anyone who molested a woman would be executed, "We hear of one case where the person of a Miss Lephart, of Frankford township [northwest of Carlisle], was outraged by one of the scoundrels." The reporter did not define the term "outraged."[23]

That same day, General Ewell sent a scouting party eight miles north from Carlisle toward Sterrett's Gap. The steep pass on the Blue Mountain range near the Cumberland-Perry county line led to the sprawling Duncannon Iron Works and the Pennsylvania Railroad's vital bridge over the Susquehanna River at Rockville. The riders, possibly Capt. Frank Bond and his 60-man Company A of the 1st Maryland Cavalry, approached the pass via Carlisle Springs, a famous summer resort. The proprietor there lied that 50,000 Union men defended the gap. The Confederates dismissed the report out of hand and continued riding a mile north to the Joseph Miller farm. They made it halfway up the pass before the captain learned the roads were impassable. "The Perry county people," recalled a local, "have the gaps in the mountain blockaded with felled trees and 'defended' by themselves, with shot guns, old muskets, etc." The Rebel riders, whoever they were, had just made history without knowing it. Sterrett's Gap marked the northernmost point in Pennsylvania the Confederates reached during the Gettysburg campaign.[24]

* * *

West of Mechanicsburg that morning, Brig. Gen. Albert G. Jenkins's vanguard chased off Capt. Frank Murray's Curtin Guards, a home guard cavalry company from Harrisburg. Church bells clanged from a steeple in

---

22 Taylor, "Ramseur's Brigade in the Gettysburg Campaign," 31.

23 "Johnson's Division," *Carlisle Herald*, July 31, 1863.

24 "Tablet Unveiled at Spot Where Rebels Turned," *Carlisle Sentinel*, Oct. 26, 1929. Captains Joel F. Fredericks and Jacob Fenstemaker of the Old Perry Militia led the local home guardsmen, who had barricaded the Cumberland County side of the mountain. Companies B and I of the 12th New York State National Guard also defended the gap during portions of the campaign.

nearby Shiremanstown to warn a nearby detachment of the 11th New York National Guard that Rebels were approaching. Jenkins met with Murray under a flag of truce in Trindle Springs. He sent two riders under another flag of truce into Mechanicsburg to summon Chief Burgess George Hummel to hear his demands, and reinforced his point by unlimbering two artillery pieces just outside town. After Hummel surrendered the place and agreed to supply 1,500 rations within 90 minutes, Jenkins rode into Mechanicsburg. He entered the Railroad House Hotel along the Cumberland Valley Railroad, sat, propped his feet on a table, and ordered a pitcher of water. He also calmly asked the proprietor to bring him the local newspapers so he could look for reports concerning the disposition of the enemy troops guarding Harrisburg, eight miles away across the Susquehanna River.

After collecting necessary food and supplies, Jenkins proceeded east on Trindle Springs Road. He dispatched Maj. James H. Nounnan and part of the 16th Virginia Cavalry south into York County to scour that region for fresh horses. The detail rode through Dillsburg down to Dover before turning around and returning to Carlisle the following day with their booty. They raided a few country stores along the way. For some reason Nounnan and his men did not ride the few miles farther south to York to connect with Jubal Early's outriders, or, if they did, no records of such a meeting remain.[25]

Jenkins sent Lt. Col. Vincent A. Witcher and the 34th Battalion, Virginia Cavalry and Capt. Thomas E. Jackson's Kanawha Battery north on Hogestown Road. Reaching Salem Church about noon, Witcher encountered a heavy line of Union militia a mile to the east in an orchard on Sporting Hill. He unlimbered two guns near the church and prepared to attack Brig. Gen. Joseph Knipe's 8th and 71st New York State National Guard and Capt. Spencer Miller's Philadelphia battery, which had retreated earlier in the week from Chambersburg; the Yankees had, all told, about 1,000 men. "It was no humbug this time," a New Yorker recalled. "The rebels were shelling the woods as they advanced." Miller's battery, posted on the Samuel Eberly farm near the crest of Sporting Hill, replied to Jackson's fire for about half an hour. Worried that Jenkins's column to his south on the parallel Trindle Springs Road could flank him, Knipe wisely withdrew. His men "retreated as fast as they could walk" to Fort Washington at Bridgeport.[26]

25 For details, see Scott L. Mingus, Sr., "Jenkins' Cavalry Raid Through Northwestern York County," *Gettysburg Magazine*, no. 44, (Jan. 2010), 41-52.

26 Henry Wittemore, *History of the Seventy-first Regiment, N.G.N.Y., 1861–1901* (New York, 1886), 76; James Boggs Beale, Diary, entry for June 28, 1863, HSP.

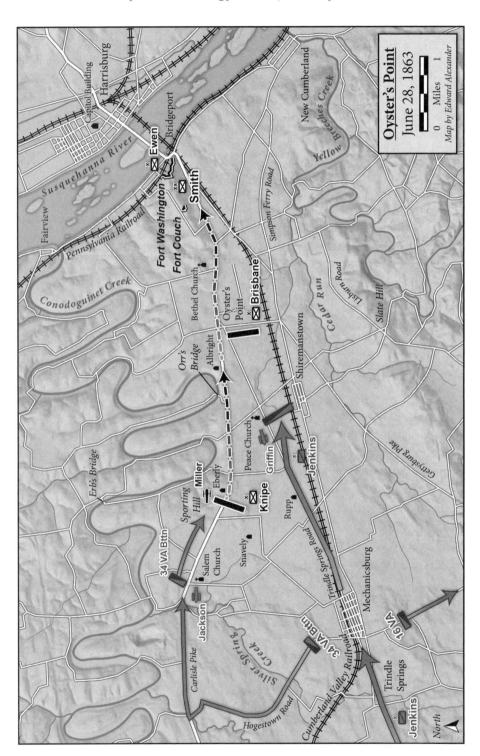

Oyster's Point
June 28, 1863

0   Miles   1
Map by Edward Alexander

Witcher pursued the Yankees to the Samuel Albright farm on the Carlisle Pike, not far from Oyster's Point where Trindle Springs Road meets the pike. There he once more unlimbered two of Jackson's guns. Meanwhile, Jenkins and the main force raided farms along Trindle Springs Road and paused at Die Friedens Kirche, or the Peace Church. About 2:00 p.m. the general deployed his men on the surrounding hilltop and unlimbered four guns of Griffin's Baltimore battery. Peering to the east through his field glasses, Jenkins noticed Federals—elements of the 28th, 30th, and 33rd Pennsylvania Volunteer Militia and Miller's battery—near Oyster's Point. Lieutenant Colonel Witcher sent skirmishers from the 34th Battalion, Virginia Cavalry, to confront Col. William Brisbane's Pennsylvania Emergency Militia. The sparring continued for two hours, with neither side gaining an upper hand, before petering out about 4:00 p.m. Jenkins withdrew a mile west on Trindle Springs Road to the Rupp farm outside of Mechanicsburg, while Witcher bivouacked near Orr's Bridge. Jenkins called his main subordinates to a meeting that evening inside the stone farmhouse to plan how best to attack the Federals on the morrow.[27]

* * *

That same Sunday, Richard Ewell's third infantry division under Jubal Early prepared to march into York.

After breaking camp near Farmers Post Office at 5:00 a.m., John Gordon's Georgia brigade headed east on the Gettysburg Turnpike. As the vanguard approached York, the U.S. Army General Hospital's chief surgeon, Maj. Henry Palmer, wired Maj. Gen. Darius Couch: "This city was formally surrendered to General Gordon's command of rebel forces last evening—9 miles toward Gettysburg. They are 4,000 to 6,000 strong, and sent a force last evening to destroy bridge at Glen Rock. All the forces left last evening for Columbia, taking most of the Government stores." Palmer, formerly the chief surgeon of the Iron Brigade, added, "The rebels will occupy the town today; they will not destroy private property."[28]

27 For a detailed examination of the skirmishing on the West Shore, see Cooper H. Wingert, *The Confederate Approach on Harrisburg: The Gettysburg Campaign's Northernmost Reaches* (Charleston, SC, 2012), 95-105.

28 OR 27, pt. 3, 389. After the war, Palmer helped establish Milwaukee's largest hospital. He also was a co-founder of the American Medical Association.

Brig. Gen. John B. Gordon commanded a brigade of Georgians in Early's Division of Richard Ewell's Second Corps, Army of Northern Virginia.

LOC

Mary Fisher, the wife of a prominent York judge, was not as worried as some. "Inasmuch as we were utterly without means of defense," she reasoned, "there was not much danger of opposition." Bells rang to call residents to worship and scores of residents in their Sunday best strolled along the sidewalks. An excited rider dashed into town to shout that the Rebels were at Bott's Tollgate just to the west! Within minutes a handful of Confederate cavalrymen trotted into York and halted in Centre Square. The nurses at the army hospital were debating how best to save their flag when some of the staff simply lowered the banner. Mary Ruggles volunteered to take it home. The other women folded the flag around her waist and stuffed it in the folds of her petticoat. Mary calmly walked six blocks to her home near the Codorus Creek and hid it there safely.[29]

Gordon's six regiments entered York on three parallel streets. The 31st Georgia's Capt. William Henry "Tip" Harrison recalled, "The citizens of York, who witnessed the entry of the first Confederate regiment, will probably remember a small squad of cavalry, followed by one of infantry of perhaps sixty, stationing a sentinel at each cross street in the town. . . . A lady was heard to say, 'I am ashamed of York, to quietly surrender to forty or fifty nasty, dirty rebels, when there are hundreds of able-bodied men here to fight them.'" An amused Harrison aimed his thumb behind him and assured her there were "several thousand just behind."[30]

29 Mary C. Fisher typescript, YCHC. Mary "Mammy" Ruggles lived on Washington Street with her daughter and son-in-law. Company C of the 17th Virginia Cavalry fronted Gordon's advance to York.

30 *Columbia Spy*, Jan. 16, 1886.

Resident Cassandra Small spotted "the first ones to appear—an immense number with shovels, spades, pickaxes, hoes and all sorts of tools—carried them like guns. One lady told us she thought that she would see first officers on prancing horses with handsome uniforms, but when she saw these frightful creatures, she raised her hands and exclaimed: 'Oh, my Heavenly Father, protect us; they are coming to dig our graves.'" Elderly attorney John L. Evans implored town leaders to take down the massive 18' x 35' American flag flying over the square: "Is it possible to have lived to this day to see the flag torn down and trampled in the dirt?" Committee member Latimer Small replied defiantly, "Let them take the flag, and I will replace it."[31]

"York was much larger than Gettysburg," the 31st Georgia's Pvt. I. Gordon Bradwell observed. In fact, the place impressed him. Its inhabitants, he continued,

> did not shut themselves up in their houses through fear of us, but were so anxious to see us and converse with us that we had some difficulty in forcing our way through the city. . . . The people of York were the most refined and intelligent folk we met in the State and reminded us of our friends at home, both in manners and personal appearance. They did not seem to be a bit reserved, and if we had not known where we were, we might, from their conduct, have supposed ourselves in Dixie.[32]

Gordon could not help but notice the stark contrast between his decrepit infantry and the churchgoers clad in their Sunday best. His men, horses, and wagons were begrimed from "head to foot with the impalpable gray powder" of long days of marching. It was "no wonder that many of York's inhabitants were terror-stricken as they looked upon us," he penned after the war. "Barefooted men mounted double upon huge horses with shaggy manes and long fetlocks" speckled the column.[33]

Anxious to reassure the restless crowd, Gordon halted his horse and delivered a brief speech. "Ladies and gentlemen of York," he began. "It is doubtless a painful sight to you to see a hostile army in your midst." The brigadier reminded the crowd that Southerners were accustomed to seeing such sights but the Confederate soldiers "have entered your state in no spirit of retaliation. We are here simply to

---

31 Cassandra Small to Lissie Latimer, July 20, 1863; Fisher typescript, YCHC; Gibson, *History of York County*, 436.

32 I. G. Bradwell, "Crossing the Potomac," *CV*, vol. 30, no. 10 (Oct. 1922) 371.

33 Gordon, *Reminiscences*, 142.

fight the armies which are invading our soil and destroying our houses. The men who are before you in dusty gray uniforms, barefooted many of them and ragged, are gentlemen and the sons of gentlemen. . . . I beg to assure you that no private property will be disturbed, and if one woman in this city is insulted by one of these soldiers, I promise you the head of such a man." He added, "They have just read in the *Philadelphia Inquirer* of this morning of the destruction, by order of Federal commanders, of the town of Buford, South Carolina, and of Darien, Georgia. Some of these men were citizens of Darien, and naturally feel some indignation at the destruction of their homes, but as I have already stated, there is in their hearts no spirit of retaliation, and they fight only the men with arms in their hands."[34]

As they marched through York, Gordon's soldiers paid close attention to the ladies lining the sidewalks and balconies. Ordnance officer William Lyon claimed that he never encountered a single female who appeared delicate and refined during the entire time he was in Pennsylvania. Even the well-dressed ones in York and other towns "showed unmistakable signs of lowness and vulgarity." Residents felt about the same way regarding the dirty, foul-smelling Southern troops marching through their streets. In some cases bareheaded Confederates lifted hats from the heads of bystanders, including 17-year-old David Landis. Some terrified inhabitants withdrew into their homes, shutters and curtains drawn tight. A handful of Copperheads waved handkerchiefs from two leading hotels and some residences. A few Rebels carried knapsacks confiscated from the 87th Pennsylvania after Milroy's debacle at Winchester, causing anxious family members to wonder about loved ones in that regiment.[35]

Private George F. Agee of the 26th Georgia Infantry recalled how a "gentleman stepped up to me and asked what troops we were. I told him we were Stonewall Jackson's foot cavalry." Another Georgian named James J. M. Smith, a member of the the 31st Georgia, was marching without shoes. In York, he recalled, "an old lady came out to the sidewalk and gave me a pair of coarse woolen socks

34 *Atlanta Journal*, Sept. 16, 1888. According to resident Cassandra Small, a few minutes later Gordon stopped his horse in front of her porch and again made short address: "Ladies, I have a word to say. I suppose you think me a pretty rough looking man, but when I am shaved and dressed, my wife considers me a very good-looking fellow. I want to say to you we have not come among you to pursue the same warfare your men did in our country. You need not have any fear of us, whilst we are in your midst. You are just as safe as though we were a thousand miles away. That is all I have to say." Gordon politely bowed, wheeled his horse, and rode away. Cassandra Small to Lissie Latimer, July 8, 1863.

35 *Mobile Advertiser & Register*, Aug. 9, 1863; James Latimer to Bartow Latimer, July 8, 1863.

with some kind of words—bless her. There were many soldiers in the same pitiable plight."[36]

Gordon later claimed he was riding along the main street when a young girl slipped out of the crowd and handed him a bouquet of red roses. Much to his surprise, he discovered a handwritten note hidden inside claiming that only militia defended the crucial bridge leading to Lancaster County. With flags flying and bands playing, his brigade marched away from York toward Wrightsville while the general and his staff remained behind to await Jubal Early's arrival. About noon, Early and Col. I. E. Avery's North Carolina brigade entered York from the north and took quarters at the fairgrounds and army hospital. Early met with Gordon and repeated earlier instructions for him to proceed to the Susquehanna and secure the bridge.[37]

As Gordon rode east to rejoin his command, Early established headquarters in the sheriff's office inside the courthouse. He soon laid York under tribute. Commissary officer Capt. William Thornton requisitioned 165 barrels of flour or 28,000 pounds of baked bread, 3,500 pounds of sugar, 1,650 pounds of coffee, 300 gallons of molasses, 1,200 pounds of salt, and 32,000 pounds of fresh beef or 21,000 pounds of bacon or pork. All were to be delivered to the market house on Main Street at 4:00 p.m. Early's chief quartermaster, Maj. Charles E. Snodgrass, demanded 2,000 pairs of shoes or boots, 1,000 pairs of socks, 1,000 felt hats, and $100,000 in greenbacks. In response, Chief Burgess David Small informed Early that the banks had already sent off their assets and the town could not raise that amount of money. Authorities went door to door soliciting cash. Attorney James Latimer "very foolishly gave them one hundred dollars." Says who? Major Snodgrass eventually wrote a receipt for $28,610—well below Early's goal of $100,000. "I was satisfied that they had made an honest effort to raise the amount called for," Early later wrote. "The people of York were wise in 'accepting the situation.'"[38]

---

36 *The Sunny South*, July 20, 1901, and Sept. 23, 1904.

37 Gordon, *Reminiscences*, 143; OR 27, pt. 2, 466; Early, *War Memoirs*, 259; Stiles, *Four Years under Marse Robert*, 210-212. Early's main column marched east from Weigelstown and then south on what is now N. George Street from Emigsville to reach York.

38 Prowell, *History of York County*, 1: 410; "General Early's Report of the Gettysburg Campaign," *SHSP*, 10:540; Jubal A. Early, "The Invasion of Pennsylvania, by the Confederate States Army, in June 1863," *The Historical Magazine and Notes and Queries*, vol. 1, series 3 (1872-73), 233.

Telegraph wires buzzed with the news that Confederates occupied York. In Harrisburg, the vice-president of the Pennsylvania Railroad, Col. Thomas A. Scott, wired the news to fellow railroader J. H. Black. He instructed Black to send all engines and trains of the PRR subsidary Northern Central Railway over the Wrightsville bridge. "The rebels must not get a footing on this side of the Susquehanna," he wrote. "Can you keep them off? I hope every man will place as musket to his shoulder, and never surrender the town."[39]

The Rebels indeed sought a foothold on the eastern bank of the rain-swollen river. Early, who knew the state militia was "utterly inefficient" and could never defend the bridge against veteran troops, decided to seize it instead of following Ewell's original orders to burn it. About 2:00 p.m., after a lunch break just east of York, Gordon's Georgians marched east through Hallam, a sleepy village along the turnpike to Wrightsville. Private I. G. Bradwell thought they were heading toward Philadelphia. Knowing that the estate of former President James Buchanan lay just across the Susquehanna, Bradwell was "eager to visit the old gentleman in his home and shake hands with him." Between 4:30 and 5:00 p.m., the Rebels arrived outside of Wrightsville. Gordon halted just out of sight of the enemy and ascended a ridge to observe the horseshoe-shaped Yankee defenses surrounding the town. Small flags waved along freshly dug entrenchments. Several different Yankee units were in sight but, to his relief there was no artillery.[40]

The 1,500 defenders tasked with holding the place comprised a mishmash force, with Col. Jacob G. Frick's 27th Pennsylvania Volunteer Militia, remnants of the widely scattered 20th and 26th Pennsylvania Volunteer Militia, convalescent veteran soldiers and their guard detachment from the York army hospital, Capt. Robert Bell's Adams County Cavalry, the First Troop of Philadelphia City Cavalry, and others who had assembled there under General Couch's aide, Maj. Granville Haller. The troops included more than four dozen soldiers of the 87th Pennsylvania who had returned home to York County after escaping Milroy's debacle at Carter's Woods. An armed, non-uniformed company of 53 local black home guardsmen also manned the entrenchments.

Shortly after 5:30 p.m., Gordon initiated a double-envelopment movement to cut off the route to the bridge. Captain William Tanner's Courtney (Virginia) Artillery opened fire, decapitating one of the black defenders. The 31st Georgia's Col. Clement A. Evans later informed his wife that the Pennsylvanians were

---

39 OR 27, pt. 3, 367; *History of Franklin County, Pennsylvania* (Chicago, 1887), 425.

40 Bradwell, "Burning of Wrightsville," *CV* (1919), 27:300; Gordon, *Reminiscences*, 143-144.

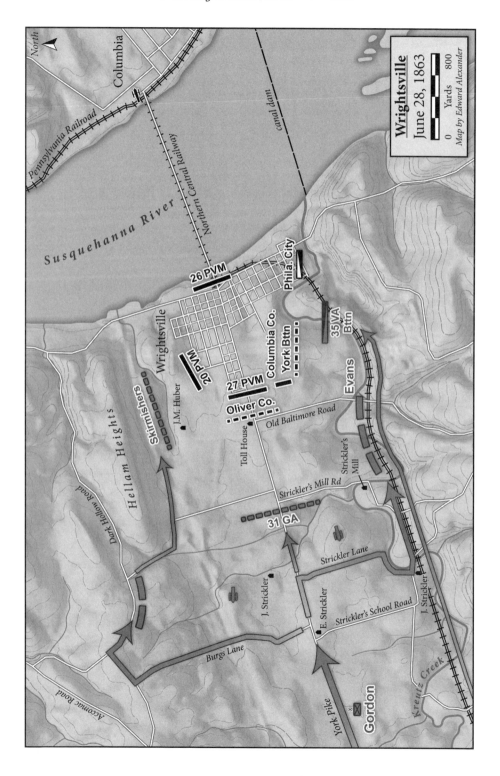

Col. Jacob G. Frick commanded the 27th Pennsylvania Volunteer Militia of the Department of the Susquehanna.

LOC

sheltered inside "rudely constructed" trenches. "Not knowing their strength, we cautiously advanced upon them from two directions, dividing the Brigade," he explained. "I was sent along the railroad in command of a portion of the Brigade to attack their flank."[41]

Colonel Frick had written a pass the previous day in anticipation of this moment: "Robert Crane and E. K. Smith have permission to go upon the bridge with a party of carpenters, and bridge builders, there to await the orders of Colonel Frick in writing or in person. Guards will pass them." Frick ordered Crane, a railroad executive, to prepare to demolish the fourth span from the Wrightsville end 800 feet from the riverbank. The carpenters sawed the arches and heavy timber preparatory to using gunpowder to blast the bridge. After most of Frick's men safely retreated across the river to Columbia about 7:30 p.m., the ensuing explosions merely knocked chunks of the roof and sidewalls into the cloudy evening sky and failed to destroy the bridge section. The sturdy decking remained intact.[42]

A frantic Frick ordered the bridge to be burned. A few volunteers had previously rolled barrels of coal oil and kerosene from a small Columbia refinery onto the old mile-and-quarter-long viaduct. More now dragged the fuel and some boards and wood shavings to the fourth span on the Wrightsville side, where they knocked in the barrelheads and soaked the kindling and the bridge's oaken floor.

41 Stephens, *Intrepid Warrior*, 221. For more on the skirmish of Wrightsville, see Mingus, *Flames Beyond Gettysburg.*

42 *Pottsville Miners' Journal*, Oct. 24, 1863; John E. Spicer, *The Columbia Civil War Centennial* (Lancaster, PA, 1976), 37.

Civilian John Q. Denney and three companions tossed torches onto the combustibles just as the first Confederates arrived at the bridgehead. "With great energy my men labored to save the bridge," Gordon later lamented. "I called on the citizens of Wrightsville for buckets and pails, but none were to be found." The fire cut off those Union troops still on the western bank of the Susquehanna. Twenty infantrymen and Lt. Col. William H. Sickles of the 20th Militia surrendered, while Captain Bell's Adams County Cavalry, arriving from the south after a scouting expedition, braved the artillery fire and managed to escape at the gallop, minus two men who had been unhorsed.[43]

Jubal Early rode toward Wrightsville with a sinking heart as he spotted a column of dense, oily black smoke rising in the distance. By the time he arrived the bridge was an inferno. "I regretted this very much," he explained, for he had planned to enter Lancaster County, sever the Pennsylvania Railroad, and mount his men on the hundreds of horses he expected to capture. Once that had been accomplished, the general intended to march on the undefended rear of Harrisburg while Ewell advanced against that city from the front. "This scheme, in which I think I could have been successful, was, however, thwarted by the destruction of the bridge, as there was no other means of crossing the river."[44]

After Early departed for York, Gordon focused his attention on saving the town from destruction because wind-blown embers from the burning bridge had caught several riverfront businesses on fire. "Buckets and tubs and pails and pans innumerable came from their hiding-places, until it seemed that, had the whole of Lee's army been present," he wrote, "I could have armed them with these implements to fight the rapidly spreading flames. My men labored as earnestly and bravely to save the town as they did to save the bridge." Early's soldiers formed a bucket brigade to transfer water from the river and a nearby canal to the men fighting the fires.[45]

Across the river in Columbia, meanwhile, thousands of fascinated spectators including Frick's and Haller's militiamen watched the fire. A reporter penned, "A vast sheet of flame, at one time half a mile in length, crept slowly from Wrightsville to Columbia, illuminating the waters of the Susquehanna for miles each way, and lighting everything up as clear as gaslight illuminates a room. The crackling noise

---

43 Bridge files, Columbia (PA) Historic Preservation Society; Gordon, *Reminiscences*, 147-148; *York* (PA) *Gazette*, June 30, 1863; OR 27, pt. 2, 999.

44 Early, *Autobiographical Sketch*, 260-261.

45 Gordon, *Reminiscences*, 148.

produced by the burning bridge, and the shouts and confusion of the people, all made up such a scene such as is seldom witnessed." A Philadelphian described the scene as "magnificent." Some of the bridge's sturdy arches remained intact even when their timbers were all in flames, reflecting on the dark water and giving the appearance of "a fiery skeleton bridge." Burning timbers floated downstream "like infernal ferry boats of the regions pictured by Dante."[46]

Gordon encountered a Wrightsville woman he later hailed as "the heroine of the Susquehanna." Chief Burgess James McGee's daughter, newlywed Mary Jane Rewalt, invited the Georgian and his staff to come to her father's house for breakfast in the morning as a way of thanking the Confederates for saving Wrightsville from further destruction. "She would take no excuse, not even the nervous condition in which the excitement of the previous hours had left her," Gordon observed.[47]

*   *   *

That same night some 65 miles to the west in Chambersburg, a civilian-clothed scout arrived in Longstreet's camp with bombshell intelligence. Tennessee-born Henry Thomas Harrison delivered a brief report to "Old Pete." Harrison, began the general,

> told me he had been to Washington and had spent his gold freely, drinking in the saloons and getting upon confidential terms with army officers. In that way he had formed a pretty good idea of the movements of the Federal army and the preparations to give us battle. The moment he heard Hooker had started across the Potomac he set out to find me. He fell in with the Federal army before reaching Frederick—his plan being to walk at night and stop during the day in the neighborhood of the troops. He said there were three corps near Frederick when he passed there, one to the left and one to the right, but he did not succeed in getting the position of the other.

Longstreet had an aide usher Harrison to General Lee's headquarters to immediately share the news.[48]

---

46 *New York Herald*, June 30, 1863; *Philadelphia Inquirer*, June 30, 1863.

47 Gordon, *Reminiscences*, 148.

48 James Longstreet, "Lee's Invasion of Pennsylvania," *The Century Magazine*, vol. 33, no. 4 (Feb. 1887), 624. For more on Harrison, see James O. Hall, "A Modern Hunt for a Fabled

* * *

John D. Imboden's cavalry brigade made its way up Little Cove with the Tuscarora Mountains on the west side of the valley and Cove Heights to the east. The vanguard reached Cove Gap that afternoon and made camp. Pickets atop Tuscarora Mountain spotted Union cavalry in and around the town of McConnellsburg. Colonel George W. Imboden of the 18th Virginia Cavalry, the general's younger brother, ordered a squadron from his regiment to ride six miles across the mountains to investigate.

The Virginians arrived in McConnellsburg to find that most of the Union soldiers had left save for a handful of men of Company G of the 12th Pennsylvania Cavalry—refugees from Milroy's command. "We went up on the mountain with 12 men and met the Rebel advance and had a pretty brisk skirmish with them, finding they were too many for us," recounted Sgt. John Black of the 12th Pennsylvania. "We fell back slowly, firing all the while. Sorry to say, we had three men wounded in a fray."[49]

A local newspaper recalled Imboden's arrival. "A . . . company of Imboden's cavalry dashed into town. There was no force present except for a few of our pickets, who retired on the approach of the rebels," reported the *Fulton Democrat*, though not until July 10. "They did not dismount. The captain of the gang rode up to our office and inquired where we were to be found. Someone pointed out where we were standing. He rode up, and put some questions with regard to the force in town, the reported arrest of Milroy, etc., to all of which we refused to give him any reply."[50]

Although the journalists provided no useful information when they eventually published the account, such was not the case with some of the 11 Federals from Company L of the 12th Pennsylvania Cavalry captured on the east side of Cove Mountain. A crowd of cheering Virginians greeted the prisoners when they arrived at Cove Gap. More good news came when they reported that a strong force of

---

Agent: The Spy Harrison," in *CWTI*, vol. 24, no. 10 (1986), 18-25. Longstreet deemed Harrison "an active, intelligent, enterprising scout." His chief of staff Moxley Sorrel described Harrison in his memoirs as "altogether an extraordinary character." Sorrel, *Recollections*, 156.

49 John H. Black, "'Powder, Lead and Cold Steel': Campaigning in the Lower Shenandoah Valley with the Twelfth Pennsylvania Cavalry—The Civil War Letters of John H. Black," *Magazine of the Jefferson County Historical Society*, 25 (1959), 58.

50 "McConnellsburg Taken," *Fulton Democrat*, July 10, 1863.

Union soldiers—remnants of Milroy's Winchester command—could be found at Bloody Run (modern-day Everett), about 20 miles to the west.[51]

Imboden's horsemen raided the merchants in McConnellsburg and Webster Mills and scoured the entire lower end of the county for horses and supplies. "Mr. H. H. Dietrich, of Ayr township, lost heavily in this way," noted the *Fulton Democrat*. "The stores of Robinson and Patterson were stripped of their contents, and articles that were of no use to the plunderers were destroyed wantonly. We can scarcely hear of a citizen who has not lost more or less in some shape." Some soldiers entered houses and took private property. Five or six stopped at the Unger house just as a large dinner was being served for a visiting guest. The Rebels sat at the table with the surprised family to partake. To show their appreciation for the home-cooked meal, they guarded the house for the rest of their stay.[52]

* * *

South of the border, meanwhile, roving Rebel raiders created havoc for Union railroads and communication lines. The Baltimore & Ohio ceased running its trains farther west than Harpers Ferry. Railroad president John Garrett diverted a vast amount of freight and locomotives to Baltimore for safekeeping.[53]

Once north of the Potomac River, Jeb Stuart's troopers seized possession of the C&O Canal, which paralleled the river and constituted one of the major lines of supply for the Army of the Potomac. Colonel Williams C. Wickham of the 4th Virginia Cavalry, Fitz Lee's Brigade, commanded the Confederate rear guard. His men captured several canal boats, some containing troops and contraband blacks. "One, a splendidly rigged craft, with the stars and stripes flying profusely over it, and freighted with a live cargo, in the shape of Yankee officers and officials, was anchored and taken in, to their great surprise and mortification," recalled one of

---

51 Imboden diary, entry for June 28, 1863; Steve French, *Imboden's Brigade in the Gettysburg Campaign* (El Dorado Hills, CA, 2013), 45-46.

52 *Reading Eagle*, September 11, 1927; *Fulton Democrat*, July 10, 1863; *Mercersburg* (PA) *Journal*, Jan. 16, 1903. William M. Patterson's store in the village of Webster Mills was particularly hard hit, with his shelves stripped almost bare, as was Robinson's store at Big Cove Tannery. Imboden established his headquarters in a tent along the turnpike between Charles Town and the gap.

53 Scharf, *History of Western Maryland*, 1:272.

Col. Williams C. Wickham commanded the 4th Virginia Cavalry in Fitz Lee's Brigade of Stuart's cavalry division.

LOC

Wade Hampton's jubilant South Carolina troopers. "The others were richly laden."[54]

Stuart developed a scheme to put the canal out of commission while saving the valuable boats. "I propose to turn all of them crosswise in the canal and then cut the sluice gate to the river," he explained. "That will tear out such a big opening that it will leave them high and dry for sixty to ninety days." They did just that, stranding the canal boats. "We took the mules, 24 in number, on with us," recalled Pvt. Rufus Peck of the 2nd Virginia Cavalry. "We helped the women and children from the boats and took their furniture out, as we didn't want to destroy private property. It was hard to do then, with them all crying like they did, but such is war." Stuart interrogated the prisoners and ascertained that the Army of the Potomac had been at Poolesville the day before and was now in motion toward Frederick. He also learned some stunning news: Maj. Gen. George G. Meade had replaced Hooker as commander of the Union army.[55]

Stuart was already well behind schedule, and now the river crossing, combined with the capture of the canal, further exhausted his men and their animals. Captain William W. Blackford, Stuart's engineering officer, had brought two horses with him on the expedition—his favorite mare Magic, and a stallion named Manassas.

54 D. B. Rea, *Sketches of Hampton's Cavalry, Embracing the Principal Exploits of the Cavalry in the Campaigns of 1862 and 1863* (Columbia, SC, 1864), 114. The Confederates narrowly missed capturing $20,000 in cash, which had been sent to Washington for safekeeping a day earlier. *Alexandria Gazette*, June 30, 1863.

55 Robert J. Driver, Jr., *1st Virginia Cavalry* (Lynchburg, VA, 1991), 63; Rufus H. Peck, *Reminiscences of a Confederate Soldier of Co. C, 2nd Va. Cavalry* (privately published, Fincastle, VA, 1913), 32; OR 27, pt. 2, 694.

"Not a mouthful of grain had I been able to beg, borrow, or steal for my horses," he lamented, "and where I could not find it, there was apt to be none to be found." Magic was becoming so gaunt that Blackford was afraid to ride her; instead, he led the mount behind Manassas. "The necessity for stopping to graze the horses on this march had delayed us a great deal, both in the time it took and the weakening of the animals from such light diet." Stuart knew his command was in a weakened condition and that his horses needed rest. Despite the impact on his schedule, he called a halt to give the men and animals time to recuperate.[56]

The men enjoyed their respite that morning. "Had an excellent feed for horses and men," remembered an officer in the 3rd Virginia Cavalry. The troopers scattered in the fields, unsaddled their horses, and turned them out to graze. "It was refreshing to watch the canal boats come gliding innocently and unexpectedly into these sleepy Rebs," recalled Capt. Frank Robertson of Stuart's staff. "I was lying only a few steps from the canal when one packet, well loaded with Yankee officers and many ladies, came trotting in," he continued. "The astonishment, if nothing more, of the passengers when they saw hundreds of rebs filling the landscape was intensely interesting. They stared blankly at us as they passed on to where we had a committee at work giving paroles and burning freight boats. We were in no condition to accept prisoners, so the passengers proceeded joyously to Washington, the gorgeously uniformed officers with paroles in their pockets." The other boats, including two loaded with whiskey, were burned.[57]

Stuart established his headquarters in a nearby home, where several ladies prepared a sumptuous breakfast for the general and his staff. "The sun was rising and everybody was preparing to move off," recalled Theodore Garnett. "The ladies expressed an earnest desire to see our command, so they walked with me to the gate and I pointed out about two brigades in the meadow below the house, which could scarcely be seen through the thick fog. But soon the mist cleared away and they looked long and eagerly at the first Confederate troops they had ever seen, expressing their great astonishment at which seemed to them, such an immense multitude."[58]

"I realized the importance of joining our army in Pennsylvania, and resumed the march northward early on the 28th," wrote Stuart after the campaign had ended. He sent Hampton to Rockville via Darnestown while the remaining two

---

56 Blackford, *War Years with Jeb Stuart*, 223-224.

57 Trout, *In the Saddle with Stuart*, 74.

58 Jewell, "Theodore Garnett Recalls," 50.

brigades took the direct route to Rockville. Along the way, Hampton occasionally encountered small parties of the enemy which, with several wagons and teams, he captured. The efficient South Carolinian reached Rockville in advance of the main body. Chambliss's brigade, led by the 9th Virginia Cavalry, had a running fight with the 2nd New York Cavalry, but "a dashing charge made by one squadron of the Ninth Virginia cleared the road effectively," according to Garnett. "I remember seeing several prisoners pass me going to the rear with bloody heads, showing that the saber had been at work." The fresher horses of the New Yorkers outpaced the tired Confederate mounts, preventing the Southerners from taking many prisoners during the clash.[59]

In Rockville, Hampton encountered what he believed to be a large force of the enemy. When he reported this to Stuart, the cavalier ordered up Chambliss's Brigade to reinforce Hampton. "It was past noon when Stuart entered Rockville," recalled Maj. Henry B. McClellan, but the enemy had already disappeared, retreating toward Great Falls. The Confederates speedily took possession of the important town, which was on the direct wagon road from Washington to the Army of the Potomac. In short, Stuart lay directly astride the Union army's lines of communication with the war department. His troopers enjoyed tearing down miles of telegraph lines, rendering it temporarily inoperable.[60]

Not long after seizing possession of the town, the Confederate troopers stumbled upon an unexpected and stunning sight: a massive Union wagon train eight miles long. Quartermaster officer Capt. Henry Page commanded the snake-like train approaching Rockville from the direction of Washington, which had only half a dozen or so cavalry escorts for support. The teamsters were largely unarmed. The train consisted of 140 new wagons and mule teams. Most of the vehicles carried at least one bale of hay and one bag of high-quality grain. As this ponderous column of supplies bound for the Army of the Potomac approached Rockville, a local clergyman galloped to the head of the train to report the advance of a large force of Confederate cavalry that had captured another train of 28 wagons, and that enemy troops occupied the town.[61]

Panic gripped the unarmed teamsters when they spotted the oncoming Rebel horsemen. With only a few options open to them and none of them good, the

59 Robert J. Driver, Jr., *5th Virginia Cavalry* (Lynchburg, VA, 1997), 57; Jewell, "Theodore Garnett Recalls," 50; *OR* 27, pt. 2, 694.

60 McClellan, *Life and Campaigns of Stuart*, 324; *OR* 27, pt. 2, 694.

61 *Alexandria Gazette*, June 29, 1863; *Washington Evening Star*, June 29, 1863.

teamsters up front tried to turn their wagons to effect an escape. "Seeing the necessity of prompt action if we captured this train," recalled clerk William J. Campbell of Col. Richard Beale's 9th Virginia Cavalry, "we sent a man back to Col. Beale . . . for a squadron to charge the train, but before the squadron reached us Gen. Stuart arrived and asked for volunteers to join us in the charge we had offered to lead, and several promptly volunteered." Captain John Esten Cooke watched Stuart's face flush at the thought of capturing such a glittering prize; the general shouted "to a squadron to follow him, and the main column to push on, he went at a swift gallop on the track of the fleeing wagons." Stuart sent Chambliss's men in hot pursuit with orders to push ahead at the gallop and not draw rein until they had overhauled the leading wagon. "A circus was on that I have never seen paralleled," recalled Captain Robertson.[62]

The Confederate troopers dug their spurs and surged forward. Union quartermaster Henry Page was riding in the middle of the train when the enemy charged his command. Knowing there was no way to protect his charge, the captain jumped his horse over a fence and dashed into the woods, dodging a hail of bullets as he abandoned his wagon train and teamsters. Page would eventually make his way to safety in Washington, having lost both his wagons and his dignity.[63]

Lieutenant Thomas Lee and a handful of troopers from the 2nd South Carolina Cavalry of Hampton's Brigade led the chase. "After them we flew, popping away with our pistols at such drivers as did not pull up, but the more we popped the faster those in front plied the whip," recalled Captain Blackford, "finally, coming to a sharp turn in the road, one upset and a dozen or two others piled up on top of it, until you could see nothing but the long ears and kicking legs of the mules sticking above bags of oats emptied from the wagons upon them." This pileup forced the rest of the column to halt and ended the pursuit. "In several places I saw as many as four wagons, with their teams, gully with poor mules stretched upon the ground between the wagons, struggling in vain against their heavy burden and strong harness that held them, sufferers, in their places," recalled Lieutenant Beale, whose squadron had played a major role in the pursuit.[64]

Stuart burst into laughter when he spotted this absurd spectacle, turned to a fellow officer, and exclaimed, "Did you ever see anything like that in all your life!"

62 William J. Campbell, "Stuart's Great Ride Around the Enemy," *CV*, vol. 9 (1901), 222.

63 Ibid.; *Washington Evening Star*, June 29, 1863.

64 Blackford, *War Years with Jeb Stuart*, 224; George W. Beale, "A Soldier's Account of the Gettysburg Campaign," *SHSP*, 11 (July 1883), 321.

The most distant wagon was just three or four miles from the outskirts of Washington. "The dome of the capital was distinctly visible from the spot at which this wagon was halted," wrote Garnett. "When we neared the end [of the train] we were in sight of the steeples of Georgetown," recounted William J. Campbell of the 9th Virginia Cavalry.[65]

Some of the panicked Union teamsters tried to cut their teams loose in a desperate effort to escape, while others set their wagons ablaze to prevent them from being taken by Stuart's men. "Not one [wagon] escaped, though many were upset or broken, so as to require their being burned," Stuart would later report. "More than one hundred and twenty-five best United States model wagons and splendid teams with gay caparisons were secured and driven off. The mules and harness of the broken wagons were also secured."[66]

As the Southern cavalrymen happily discovered, most of the wagons contained oats intended for the animals of the Army of the Potomac. "Here was a godsend for our poor horses," remembered a relieved Blackford. "It did one's heart good to see the way the poor brutes got on the outside of those oats." The rest of the wagons were carrying bread, hardtack, bottles of whiskey, sugar, hams, knives, forks, and other useful items. "The bacon and crackers, as well as the whiskey, proved to our jaded and hungry troopers most acceptable.," explained Colonel Beale of the 9th Virginia.[67]

The fodder-filled wagons allowed Stuart to fulfill part of Lee's orders, which included gathering supplies for the use of the army. The serendipitous meeting with the wagon train boosted the morale of the Southern troopers, but the wagons also created logistical problems. Stuart was well behind schedule and the cumbersome train would only serve to further slow him down. Mules, notoriously stubborn and with minds of their own, offered little in the way of cooperation. Stuart's column was now moving at the rate of the slowest wagons.

Stuart, meanwhile, turned his attention to the Federal capital. The pursuit of the wagons meant that Fitz Lee's Brigade would not reach the defenses of Washington until darkness set in, allowing the city's defenders plenty of opportunities to defend the road leading into it. "I firmly believe we could have

65 Cooke, *Wearing of the Gray*, 238, Jewell, "Theodore Garnett Recalls," 50; Trout, *In the Saddle with Stuart*, 50.

66 OR 27, pt. 2, 694.

67 Blackford, *War Years with Jeb Stuart*, 80; Beale, *History of the Ninth Virginia Cavalry*, 80.

captured Washington that day," was Captain Robertson's optimistic but completely mistaken opinion.[68]

Determined to at least investigate the opportunity, Stuart and Garnett rode along the length of the train until they stopped in front of a farmhouse to ask how far they were from Georgetown. "Six miles," responded the frightened farmer. Garnett remembered watching Stuart closely. "As the General rode away, I noticed the expression of his countenance. He was evidently balancing in his mind the chances in favor of our entering Washington City, and he was trying to make up his mind to give up the attempt," concluded the staffer.[69]

Stuart soon did so. "To attack at night with cavalry, particularly, unless certain of surprise, would have been extremely hazardous; to wait till morning, would have lost much time from my march to join General Lee, without the probability of compensating results," was how he explained his decision. "I therefore determined, after getting the wagons under way, to proceed directly north, so as to cut the Baltimore & Ohio Railroad (now becoming the enemy's main war artery) that night. I found myself now encumbered by about 400 prisoners, many of whom were officers. I paroled nearly all at Brookeville that night, and the remainder next day at Cooksville. Among the number, were Major [James C.] Duane and Captain [Nathaniel] Michler, Engineers, U. S. Army."[70]

The Confederate cavalry's proximity to Washington set off recriminations about the loss of the wagon train and triggered panic in the capital. That night a few of Chambliss's stragglers were captured seven miles from Georgetown. The prisoners reported that Stuart's column was en route to attack the Baltimore & Ohio Railroad. This intelligence, combined with the loss of the wagons, meant "Washington has been in a state of great alarm today, although there has been very little manifestations other than usual upon the streets," reported a newspaper correspondent. "Little knots of men are to be seen everywhere eagerly discussing 'the impending crisis.' No story is too incredulous to find plenty [who] will credit it all. The public, as a general thing, however, know very little of the real condition of affairs."[71]

---

68 Trout, *In the Saddle with Stuart*, 76.

69 Jewell, "Theodore Garnett Recalls," 50.

70 *OR* 27, pt. 2, 694.

71 *Brooklyn Daily Eagle*, June 29, 1863.

The Union high command tried to mount a credible pursuit of Stuart but lacked sufficient force to tangle with three full brigades of Confederate cavalry. Only 300 troopers of Col. Charles Russell Lowell's 2nd Massachusetts Cavalry rode out to pursue the enemy. "You may laugh and think it preposterous for one Battalion, three hundred strong, chasing three Brigades of the renowned cavalry, twelve thousand in number," exaggerated one of the Massachusetts men, "yet such is the fact, and we followed them up so close that at times our advance guard was not more than three quarters of a mile from the rebel column. We arrived at Rockville at 10 p.m. and saw a number of army wagons yet burning, having been set on fire by the rebels." The Bay Staters could do little other than follow at a safe distance and helplessly watch as the enemy rode away.[72]

As soon as Stuart left Rockville the problems with escorting the cumbersome wagon train became obvious to all. "We had scarcely set out from Rockville before many of us began to regret our capture," admitted one Virginian, "foreseeing that the train would impede our movements, and be very difficult to guard in passing through the enemy's country."[73]

As the wagons bumped and rolled along, Stuart's troopers fanned out across the Maryland countryside, "pouncing with special vim upon the fat animals owned by the Quakers about Sandy Spring," observed a Washington newspaper. "Some of them skirted as near Washington as Silver Spring, on the Seventh Street road, but left again in considerable haste." The reporter speculated that numerous Maryland citizens had joined the Confederate column, "swelling their numbers considerably and making themselves useful as guides from their knowledge of the country and the locality of good stock."[74]

The Confederate column arrived at Brookeville at 6:00 p.m. before continuing on to Cookesville, where the advance encountered and scattered a small party of the enemy and took a few prisoners. "Having heard that part of the enemy were ahead, sent forward two Regiments to surprise & capture them," recorded an officer of the 3rd Virginia Cavalry, "but they had themselves captured one of Gen. Lee's couriers & learning of our proximity, fled." Stuart paroled these prisoners in a time-consuming process that Major McClellan described as "a useless task; for the Federal authorities refused to acknowledge the parole, and returned officers and

---

72 "Letter from the Californians in the Massachusetts Contingent," *Alta California*, Aug. 2, 1863.

73 Beale, *History of the Ninth Virginia Cavalry*, 80.

74 *Washington Evening Star*, June 29, 1863.

Maj. Gen. Arnold Elzey was grievously wounded in the head early in the war at Gaines Mill. He recovered enough to command the defenses of Richmond during the Gettysburg Campaign.

LOC

men immediately to duty." Stuart also paroled his remaining prisoners, including Duane, Michler, and sutlers captured by Fitz Lee at Annandale. The Rebel horsemen bivouacked for a few hours of much-needed rest after what had been a long and exhausting day.[75]

*   *   *

While Stuart was riding his column hard and capturing wagons, the brigades of Brig. Gens. Beverly H. Robertson and William E. "Grumble" Jones remained mostly inactive holding Ashby's and Snicker's gaps—an odd waste of horseflesh given that the Army of the Potomac was in Maryland. These brigades should also have been in Maryland by this time carrying out Stuart's orders, but Robertson dillydallied and did not move from his assignment.

Farther south in Virginia, meanwhile, Maj. Gen. D. H. Hill arrived from Petersburg to direct operations in Richmond in case Maj. Gen. John A. Dix decided to move his command into position and assault the vulnerable Confederate capital. Hill's arrival proved uncomfortable because it created a command problem. Major General Arnold Elzey was the nominal commander of the sprawling Richmond defenses, and he and Hill were the same rank. It took a couple of days and the involvement of President Jefferson Davis to sort out this

---

75 *Alexandria Gazette*, June 30, 1863.

thorny problem or rank before Hill was put in charge of the troops defending the capital.[76]

Major General G. W. C. "Custis" Lee, Robert E. Lee's oldest son serving in Richmond as an advisor to President Davis, oversaw the arming of militia companies to defend the capital. "These, with the militia in the streets (armed by the government today), amounted to several thousand efficient men for the batteries and for guard duty. They are to rendezvous, with blankets, provisions, etc., upon the sounding of the tocsin," recorded war department bureaucrat John B. Jones. "I learn that 8000 men in the hospitals within convenient reach of the city, including those in the city, can be available for defense in an emergency. They cannot march, but they can fight. These, with Hill's division," concluded Jones, "will make over 20,000 men; an ample force to cope with the enemy on the Peninsula." The weather was thankfully cool, he continued, "else the civilians could not have stood several hours exercise so well. A little practice will habituate them by degrees to the harness of war. No one doubts that they will fight, when the time for blows arrives. Gen. [Micah] Jenkins has just arrived, with his brigade, from the south side of the James River."[77]

"There have been great efforts to made to get the citizens of Richmond to organize for local defence, but with very indifferent success," complained Robert Garlick Hill Kean, another war department employee, in his diary. "The clerks in the department have organized, also the operatives in all the shops, marking an aggregate of over two thousand men, half of whom have served in the army." Kean went on to note that Governor John Letcher and Mayor Joseph Mayo had made strident appeals to the populace, "but I believe they have not got out over five or six companies—about 300." The small turnout frustrated Letcher, who ordered the militia to turn out the next day or be treated as deserters. "The occasion of all this is the information received from the lower James that the enemy have concentrated 25,000 men at Williamsburg and [that General] Dix has taken command. Five thousand landed on Friday at [White House Landing], and two regiments of cavalry went up and burned the bridge over the South Anna, of the [Virginia] Central railroad."[78]

---

76 OR 27, pt. 3, 945, 948, 956-957.

77 Jones, *A Confederate War Clerk's Diary*, 1:362.

78 Edward Younger, ed., *Inside the Confederate Government: The Diary of Robert Garlick Hill Keen, Head of the Bureau of War* (New York, 1957), 76-77.

Col. James Hardie of the War Department delivered the message to General Hooker relieving him of command.

LOC

James Cornell Biddle, a 28-year-old native of Philadelphia, had only recently joined the staff of V Corps commander George G. Meade. On June 28 he witnessed a slice of history when he watched Col. James A. Hardie, an assistant adjutant general on Secretary of War Stanton's staff, rein in his mount in Frederick. Hardie, Biddle explained in a letter to his wife that same day, rode in "with some mysterious communication for General Meade." It was not yet dawn, but the momentous hour had arrived. Hardie carried a message from President Lincoln ordering Meade to assume command of the Army of the Potomac. Hooker was gone, and Lincoln believed the Pennsylvanian would "fight well on his own dunghill" if placed in command of the army.[79]

Hardie wasted no time after making the arduous trip to V Corps headquarters. He awakened Meade at 3:00 a.m., telling the sleepy general that he had come "to give [him] trouble." Meade initially believed "that it was either to relieve or arrest me, and promptly replied to him, that my conscience was clear."[80] Hardie handed him the order:

Headquarters of the Army, Washington, D. C., June 27, 1863.
Major General G. G. Meade,
Army of the Potomac

79 James C. Biddle to his wife, June 28, 1863, James Cornell Biddle Letters, HSP.

80 Meade, *Life and Letters*, 2:11-12.

General:

You will receive with this the order of the President placing you in command of the Army of the Potomac. Considering the circumstances, no one ever received a more important command; and I cannot doubt that you will fully justify the confidence which the Government has reposed in you.

You will not be hampered by any minute instructions from these headquarters. Your army is free to act as you may deem proper under the circumstances as they arise. You will, however, keep in view the important fact that the Army of the Potomac is the covering army of Washington, as well as the army of operation against the invading forces of the rebels. You will therefore manoeuvre and fight in such a manner as to cover the Capital and also Baltimore, as far as circumstances will admit. Should General Lee move upon either of these places, it is expected that you will either anticipate him or arrive with him, so as to give him battle.

All forces within the sphere of your operations will be held subject to your orders. Harper's Ferry and its garrison are under your direct orders.

You are authorized to remove from command and send from your army any officer or other person you may deem proper; and to appoint to command as you may deem expedient.

In fine, General, you are intrusted with all the power and authority which the President, the Secretary of War, or the General-in-Chief can confer on you, and you may rely on our full support.

You will keep me fully informed of all your movements and the positions of your own troops and those of the enemy, so far as known.

I shall always be ready to advise and assist you to the utmost of my ability.

Very respectfully,

Your obedient servant,

H. W. Halleck,
General-in-Chief.[81]

A careful reading of these orders makes it clear that control of the garrison at Harpers Ferry was not really the issue with Hooker. Rather, it was the means used to achieve his removal. George Gordon Meade had neither sought nor wanted army command. Dutiful soldier that he was, he obeyed the order that he ostensibly

81 Ibid., 2:3-4.

regretted receiving for the rest of his life. As Meade would write to his wife Margaretta, "Ah Dearest you know how reluctant we both have been to see me placed in this position, and it appears to be God's will for some good purpose . . . as a soldier I had nothing to do but accept & exert my utmost abilities to command success. This so help me God I will do."[82] As an officer in the V Corps would later note, "We must place ourselves in Gen. Meade's position in order to realize the self-sacrifice and the noble character displayed by him in assuming the supreme command."[83]

Joe Hooker, of course, was still with the army when Hardie arrived. Hooker had heard of his arrival and prepared himself for the inevitable. He was decked out in his full uniform when Meade and Hardie called upon him at daybreak. "It was a bitter moment to all, for Hooker had construed favorably the delay in responding to his tender of resignation, and could not wholly mask the revulsion of feeling," recalled a staff officer. Hooker's chief of staff, Daniel Butterfield, was called in to join them, and "the four officers set themselves earnestly to work to do the state some service by honestly transferring the command and all that could help to make it available for good." When Meade expressed dismay about the scattered disposition of the far-flung elements of the Army of the Potomac, "Hooker retorted with feeling." Meade thought he might bring the entire army together and review it to determine its condition, but Butterfield correctly pointed out that a review was impractical given the circumstances. Instead, the disparate columns would remain on the move. Meade also favored leaving the Harpers Ferry garrison intact to provide military access to and from the Cumberland Valley. Hooker and Butterfield both protested, arguing that a small enemy force could easily cut communications and prevent the re-supply of the garrison. They prevailed upon Meade, who wisely ordered the garrison to abandon the place.[84]

Understandably, things got a bit heated during this meeting. "Hooker's chagrin and Meade's overstrung nerves," recalled Charles F. Benjamin, "made the lengthy but indispensable conference rather trying to the whole party." Still, Meade's insistence that Hooker be considered a guest at headquarters while he was still with the army helped, as did his request that Butterfield—a firm Hooker man—remain

---

82 Meade to his wife, June 29, 1863, Meade Papers.

83 "Sickles at Gettysburg. His Claim Sharply Controverted by a Pennsylvania Comrade," *National Tribune*, Nov. 4, 1886.

84 Meade, *Life and Letters*, 2:355, 362; OR 27, pt. 1, 21.

in place as his chief of staff.[85] Still, Meade would later claim, "I received from [Hooker] . . . no intimation of any plan, or any views that he may have had up to that moment."

When the conference ended, Meade emerged with a grave look on his face. Captain George Meade, a member of his father's staff, was waiting for him. With "a familiar twinkle of the eye, denoting the anticipation of surprise at information to be imparted," recalled the son, the elder Meade announced, "Well, George, I am in command of the Army of the Potomac."[86]

It was still before dawn when Meade woke Brig. Gen. Gouverneur K. Warren, the army's chief engineer. "Get up! I'm in command of the Army of the Potomac," Meade declared. "I want you to be my chief of staff." To Meade's disappointment Warren demurred, suggesting that Meade should retain Butterfield in that position.[87]

News of Hooker's relief spread quickly. When word reached I Corps commander John F. Reynolds, the Pennsylvanian "dressed himself with scrupulous care and, handsomely attended, rode to headquarters to pay his respects to the new commander," observed a staff officer. Meade, he continued,

who looked like a wagon-master in the marching clothes he had hurriedly slipped on when awakened in his tent, understood the motive of the act, and after the exchange of salutations all around, he took Reynolds by the arm, and, leading him aside, told him how surprising, imperative, and unwelcome were the orders he had received; how much he would have preferred the choice to have fallen on Reynolds; how anxious he had been to see Reynolds and tell him these things, and how helpless he should hold himself to be did he not feel that Reynolds would give him the earnest support that he would have given to Reynolds in a like situation.[88]

Fortunately, Meade had nothing to worry about when it came to Reynolds' support. The latter expressed that "the command had fallen where it belonged, that he was glad that such a weight of responsibility had not come upon him, and that

85 Charles F. Benjamin, "Hooker's Appointment and Removal," *Battles and Leaders*, 3:239; *Report of the Joint Committee on the Conduct of the War, at the Second Session, Thirty-Eighth Congress*, 3 vols. (Washington, D.C., 1865), 1:355.

86 Meade, *Life and Letters*, 1-2.

87 William B. Styple, ed., *Generals in Bronze: Interviewing the Commanders of the Civil War* (Kearny, NJ, 2005), 87.

88 Benjamin, "Hooker's Appointment and Removal," 3:243.

George G. Meade, Jr. served on his father's staff with the rank of captain. He was just 19 during the Gettysburg Campaign.

USAHEC

Meade might count upon the best support he could give him." Meade explained to Reynolds "all that he had learned from Hooker and Butterfield concerning the movements and positions of the two armies, and hastily concerted with him a plan of cooperation which resulted in the fighting of the battle of Gettysburg upon ground selected by Reynolds." Satisfied that the army's senior subordinate would support him, General Meade set about the important business awaiting him.[89]

"I never saw such universal satisfaction, everyone is delighted," reported young Captain Meade to his mother. "Reynolds, Slocum & Sedgwick have all given in and behaved very well. . . . I think Papa will receive all the assistance the other Corps commanders can give him." The younger George was correct. Morale within the officer corps of the Army of the Potomac—which had been depressed since the defeat at Chancellorsville—rose with those men who had been dissatisfied with

---

89 Ibid. For the most part, Reynolds and Meade enjoyed a warm working relationship. As with any friendship, rough patches arose from time to time. On Dec. 30, 1862, after Reynolds and Meade's wife saw one another at a social event in Philadelphia, Meade told Margaretta, "I am not surprised Reynolds did not indulge in any complimentary remarks about me because in the first place he is a man who never says or does such things, and in the second place, we had a few little rubs during the latter part of our association. . . . I think he is in some measure responsible for my not being supported [at the battle of Fredericksburg] as he was commanding the corps & had authority to order up other troops and it was his business [to see] that I was properly supported, and the advantage I had gained secured by promptly advancing reinforcements." Meade to Margaretta Meade, Dec. 30, 1862, Meade Papers. Meade and Reynolds moved past their respective difficulties and ended up working together well for the short remainder of Reynolds's life.

Hooker's performance as army commander. As far as morale, the timing could not have been better.[90]

Charles C. Coffin, a correspondent for the *Boston Journal* traveling with the Army of the Potomac, spotted Meade in thought. His demeanor impressed the reporter. "There was no elation, but on the contrary he seemed weighed down with a sense of the responsibility resting on him," thought Coffin. "He stood silent and thoughtful by himself."[91] George Meade's tenure in command of the Army of the Potomac began under difficult circumstances, and he harbored few illusions about the challenges awaiting him in this new and unwanted role.

The decision to replace Hooker with Meade had not yet been communicated to all of Lincoln's cabinet members. According to Secretary of the Navy Gideon Welles, the president convened the cabinet at 10:00 a.m. and drew from his pocket Hooker's letter of resignation. According to Welles, "The President said he had, for several days as the conflict became imminent, observed in Hooker the same failings that were witnessed in McClellan after the Battle of Antietam—a want of alacrity to obey, and a greedy call for more troops which could not, and ought not to be taken from other points. He would, said the President, strip Washington bare, had demanded the force at Harper's Ferry, which Halleck said could not be complied with; he was opposed to abandoning our position at Harper's Ferry. Hooker," continued Welles, "had taken umbrage at the refusal, or at all events had thought it best to give up the command."

The officials debated Meade, Sedgwick, and Couch as possible successors. In Welles's opinion, however, the discussion was just to make it appear that everyone had been consulted because Halleck had already issued the orders to replace Hooker with Meade. "We were consulted after the fact," Welles grumbled even though he was glad for the change. If Welles had the power he would have relieved Hooker immediately after Chancellorsville. "Of Meade I know very little," Welles confided to his diary. "He is not great. His brother officers speak well of him, but he is considered rather a 'smooth bore' than a rifle."[92]

Reaction to the change in command was generally positive within the Army of the Potomac, though often muted. The V Corps's Dr. John S. Billings visited both General Headquarters and Alfred Pleasonton's headquarters. He saw an "immense

---

90 George G. Meade, Jr., to Margaretta Meade, July 1, 1863, Meade Papers; Stephen W. Sears, *Lincoln's Lieutenants: The High Command of the Army of the Potomac* (Boston, 2017), 543.

91 Charles Carleton Coffin, *The Boys of '61 or Four Years of Fighting* (Boston, 1896), 283.

92 Welles, *Diary*, 1:348-349.

number of officers—the general feeling seems to be utter apathy and indifference. I saw no man with a smile on his face and heard no one say that he was glad of Meade's appointment, although there is approval of Hooker's removal."

Most of these men were hardened veterans by the summer of 1863, their responses tempered by the knowledge of what was yet to come. "The news came on Sunday morning when listening to the very unusual sound of the church bells coming over the fields from Frederick town," remembered the Irish Brigade's Maj. St. Clair Mulholland. A soldier in Mulholland's 118th Pennsylvania opined, "General Sykes, an officer of splendid reputation, high soldierly attainments and superior military education, by virtue of his seniority, became General Meade's successor.

There were some mild comments among the rank and file, in homely phrase, as to the propriety of 'swapping horses in crossing a stream,' but it had no material effect on the morale or temper of the army. The soldiers were occasionally demonstrative when attempts were made to arouse enthusiasm, but matters were generally viewed more stolidly than in the earlier days of the war."[93]

"Meade was but little known at this time in the army," explained the adjutant of the 3rd Wisconsin, Edwin E. Bryant, "but since Chancellorsville there was small faith in Hooker's infallibility; and we could only hope the best of Meade, and hope he would faithfully be supported by the generals of the corps and divisions as faithfully as the men of the ranks were sure to do all that was required of them." Captain Daniel S. Root of the 3rd Michigan commented along the same lines: "The feeling in the army is one of indifference. The men have learned to place less dependence on their generals than in McClellan's time and they know that the men and not the general decide the battles. All they ask is to face the foe. Meade is comparatively unknown but if he wins the impending battle will be a made man."[94]

Brigadier General John Gibbon was marching that day when an officer announced, "Well, Hooker is relieved from the command of the army." The news

93 Garrison, *John Shaw Billings: A Memoir*, 59; Mulholland, *The Story of the 116th Regiment*, 129; *History of the 118th Pennsylvania Volunteers*, 231. Andrew Ford of the 15th Massachusetts noted the following about the change in command: "Quiet, with little self-assertion, scholarly, courageous, but never reckless, he seemed by nature more adapted to the retirement of academic life than to the turmoil of campaigns. He was entirely unknown to the great body of the soldiers. This promotion was accepted by them without protest, but without enthusiasm." Ford, *The Story of the Fifteenth Regiment Massachusetts Volunteer Infantry*, 260.

94 Edwin E. Bryant, *History of the Third Regiment of Wisconsin Veteran Volunteer Infantry, 1861–65* (Madison, WI, 1891), 177; Soper, *The Glorious Old Third*, 251.

stunned Gibbon. "Who is in command?" he asked. The hardened II Corps officer heaved a sigh of relief when he heard it was Meade. "Although anticipating, somewhat, that a change would be made, the order, at that particular time took me by surprise," he later admitted. "I should have regarded it as hazardous but for the total loss of confidence in Gen. Hooker, a feeling I believed, shared by the vast bulk of the army."

Once the II Corps halted for the day, Hancock and Gibbon rode on to see George Meade. "He appears very anxious, but said with a laugh when I first saw him, that he intended to have me shot, I suppose for speaking of him as commander of this army!" joked Gibbon after the war. The change in command restored Gibbon's confidence, and he informed his wife that the men "believe we shall whip these fellows." While the two II Corps generals were at army headquarters Pleasonton appeared to ask Meade about the disposition of the mounted arm, to which Meade curtly answered, "I can give you no detailed instructions but simply want you to protect well the front and flanks of this army with your Cavalry."[95]

Not everyone felt satisfaction or indifference. "The necessity for making a change of commanders of the army at this juncture was deplorable," groused Capt. Eugene A. Nash of the 44th New York. "The affairs of the country had become such as to cause widespread anxiety among the people. A great battle was imminent, the enemy was confident and aggressive, and a misstep now might mean defeat for the army and dire disaster for the country." "The army was startled by the news that General Meade had succeeded General Hooker in command of the army," recalled Lt. Camille Baquet of the 1st New Jersey Infantry of Brig. Gen. Horatio G. Wright's VI Corps. "The change was then commented upon unfavorably by the men as 'spite work' of General Halleck, and no doubt there was a grain of truth in their reasoning."[96]

June 28 was a day of multiple command changes, albeit none of the magnitude that tossed Meade to the top of the army. A few days earlier at Thoroughfare Gap, General Gibbon had ordered the arrest of Brig. Gen. Joshua T. Owen, the long-time leader of the often-unruly Philadelphia Brigade. "The vacancy so created was filled by the appointment of Gen. Alex. S. Webb, a most accomplished officer, who had been serving on staff duty and with the artillery, but who was destined to

---

95 Gibbon, *Recollections*, 128-29.

96 Nash, *A History of the Forty-Fourth Regiment*, 138; Baquet, *History of the First Brigade*, 91.

become an efficient commander. Old 'Paddy' Owen went back to Philadelphia," was how a member of the 1st Minnesota explained the affair.[97]

*   *   *

General Meade's first day in command saw the bulk of his army still marching northward through central Maryland. The I Corps headed to Frederick. Early in the morning, the 143rd Pennsylvania paused at Middletown and dispatched guards. The women and girls of a nearby church had to pass through the picket line to return home from Sunday School. When one of the guards, Charley Wilson, denied the ladies safe passage they were much alarmed and began to cry. Wilson replied that they indeed could pass, but only at the price of a kiss. The ladies obliged and soon returned home. Later in the morning two other women approached the regiment and informed the soldiers that if any had letters that needed to be mailed, they would stamp them at their expense and ensure they were posted. A large supply of letters (mostly unstamped) was gathered and the volunteers followed through with their offer to mail them.[98]

Unlike their previous grueling treks that often had stretched until dark, Hancock's II Corps leisurely tramped just 15 miles from Barnesville to Monocacy Junction, a B&O Railroad intersection three miles southeast of Frederick. "This has been the easiest days march that I have ever had," remembered Manley Stacey of the 111th New York. "Genl Hayes [Alexander Hays] had command & rested us often, we have just taken it slow & easy arriving here at 4 PM, we have Pitched our Tents on the Bank, of the River, & tonight have had a good wash. . . . This is a Beautiful sunday evening, I would give a great deal, to go to Church tonight, it has seemed but little like sunday, to us today."[99]

Private Robert Laird Stewart of the 140th Pennsylvania, V Corps, remembered being ordered to use only broken fence rails for firewood because they were in Maryland and no longer in Virginia. It sounded good until the men when into camp without any woods nearby. The soldiers promptly ignored the directive and began breaking up rails to fuel their fires to boil their coffee. "The portion of Maryland into which we were so unceremoniously conducted was rich and singularly

---

97 *History of the First Regiment Minnesota Volunteer Infantry, 1861–1864* (Stillwater, MN, 1916), 317.

98   *New York Times*, June 29, 1913.

99   Manley Stacey to Dear Father, June 28, 1863, HSOPRF.

Maj. Gen. Daniel E. Sickles, who commanded the III Corps in the Army of the Potomac, would play a controversial role in the upcoming battle.

LOC

beautiful," recalled Stewart. "This was especially true of the country in the vicinity of Frederick and the South Mountain."[100]

Like rumors earlier in the campaign concerning a possible third battle at Manassas, many believed the next large battle would take place on another former field over which they had already fought. Lieutenant Colonel Franklin Sawyer realized the 8th Ohio camped at Monocacy Bridge "on the same ground precisely that we occupied on the night of September 13th of the year before. Antietam was apparent in our minds, and its repetition quite probable."[101]

The III Corps welcomed the return of its erstwhile commander, Maj. Gen. Daniel E. Sickles, who had been absent since May 29—ostensibly because of injuries suffered at Chancellorsville. Sickles had returned to New York City to visit his wife and daughter. With a battle looming, the political general pronounced himself fit to return to duty. David B. Birney, a Sickles confidant, had been acting as corps commander, but now resumed the leadership of his division.[102]

Sickles's corps was marching from Middletown toward Frederick, recalled the 114th Pennsylvania's Frank Rauscher, when a "kind-hearted old man brought us a

100 Stewart, *History of the One Hundred and Fortieth Regiment*, 87.

101 Sawyer, *A Military History of the 8th Regiment Ohio Vol. Inf'y.*, 122.

102 James A. Hessler, *Sickles at Gettysburg: The Controversial Civil War General Who Committed Murder, Abandoned Little Round Top, and Declared Himself the Hero of Gettysburg* (El Dorado Hills, CA, 2009), 71. Sickles was not the only high-ranking officer to return to the Army of the Potomac that day. Brigadier General Samuel W. Crawford rejoined the army at the head of his Pennsylvania Reserves, which finally caught up with the V Corps just outside of Frederick. Woodward, *Our Campaigns*, 262.

quantity of tobacco; another, thinking we needed something to keep us in good spirits, bought us a flask of whisky, saying, 'You boys must want something like this to keep the wind up.'" Likely not a man in the ranks offered a word in disagreement.[103]

If the march toward Frederick was good, the city itself proved spectacular. Edwin Houghton of 17th Maine, part of Col P. Régis de Trobriand's brigade, was more than happy to leave enemy Virginia for the reception awaiting them in Maryland. "We passed through Fairview, and arrived at Frederick City at about three o'clock, p.m., where we again adopted the column by company, with bands and drum corps playing and colors flying," recalled the handsome and full-bearded first lieutenant of Company H. "Frederick is a beautiful city, and was, judging from our reception, thoroughly Union in sentiment. From nearly every house the stars and stripes floated in the breeze, and the windows, housetops, and door-ways were lined with ladies in their holiday attire, waving their handkerchiefs and American flags." Houghton and his comrades marched nearly a mile through the city enjoying cheers, claps, and shouts of encouragement with every step. "Nothing since our military career commenced equaled the enthusiasm we witnessed here," he reminisced just a year after the war ended. "The day, the occasion, and the reception we received, will forever be cherished in the memory of the soldiers of the Third Army Corps."[104]

Colonel de Trobriand, the French aristocrat who commanded a brigade in Birney's division, rode into Frederick with the rest of his brigade. The foreign officer took note of a pretty young girl of 10 to 12 years of age who left a group of children on the front porch to stand in the middle of the street. Her mother had handed her a large bouquet of flowers before pointing toward the colonel. The little girl advanced toward him holding the flowers in her arms. When de Trobriand leaned forward to receive the gift, the smiling little girl exclaimed, "Good luck to you, general!" He thanked her with words, but "I would have liked to have embraced the little messenger with her happy wishes," he recalled. Alas, "the march could not halt for so small an affair." When the little girl rejoined her family, de Trobriand blew her a kiss. The embarrassed little girl nodded, and blushing, hid her face in her mother's bosom. "Well!" de Trobriand told himself, "that little girl ought to bring me good fortune." The response of the local citizenry, as his soldiers

---

103 Rauscher, *Music on the March*, 80-81.

104 Houghton, *Campaigns of the Seventeenth Maine*, 79-80.

Col. Philippe Régis Dénis de Keredern de Trobriand, a native of France, led the 3rd Brigade of the 1st Division, III Corps, Army of the Potomac.

LOC

noted in their letters home, boosted the spirits of the Union men as they passed through Frederick and headed toward Pennsylvania.[105]

Once the III Corps went into camp near Walkersville, de Trobriand penned a quick letter home. "We learned on the road that Hooker was relieved of his command of the army," explained the frustrated officer. "The movement is more than inopportune, but it is in the way that things are done in Washington. General Meade is appointed his successor. Why, and at which title? is what everyone is asking to himself."[106]

John Sedgwick's VI Corps, meanwhile, departed its camps near Poolesville and trekked to Hyattstown. In their haste to cover ground the soldiers often left the roads, much to the chagrin of local landowners. "By Sunday morning," admitted Lucien A. Vorhees of the 15th New Jersey, part of Alfred T. A. Torbert's brigade, "we were again tramping down grain, over fields, and through by roads, marking our trail in unavoidable destruction of property."[107]

Like Hancock's II Corps, Oliver Howard's XI Corps moved from Middletown to near Frederick, while Henry Slocum's XII Corps arrived in Frederick after having marched from its previous encampment near Knoxville. A member of the 137th New York in George S. Greene's brigade recalled taking the pike for Frederick before camping "in a nice oak grove, one and a half miles from the city. The inhabitants treated us with respect, furnishing us with bread, butter, &c., at reasonable rates." Marching without a defined objective took a toll, both physically

105 de Trobriand, *Four Years with the Army of the Potomac*, 479-480.

106 Styple, *Our Noble Blood*, 113.

107 "Army Correspondence," *Flemington* (NJ) *Republican*, July 10, 1863.

and emotionally. "We are as ignorant of our destination as though we lived in another world," complained the 20th Connecticut's Cpl. Horatio D. Chapman. "I asked our captain for some information, but apparently he is as ignorant in regard to the matter as I am."[108]

Lieutenant Delevan Bates of the 121st New York, Joseph Bartlett's brigade, found this leg of the march especially difficult. He and his comrades moved "in quick time, the long line splashed through the dust, which rose in clouds, and where it touched the skin it burned like particles of molten brass. The hard yellow glare of the burning sunbeams seemed to eat into one's brain, and the temptation was strong to lie down in the cool recesses of some one of the copses of timber through which we passed, and abandon all else to bodily comfort." Men fell onto the road or straggled out of the column to stagger "into the shade of the trees, and was left as we hurried on. Along the road under our feet articles of clothing, haversacks, blankets, and even guns and cartridge boxes were thickly strewn, but no canteens. Those tin receptacles of lukewarm water are the last thing a soldier throws away."[109]

The ovations and cheering were helpful, but the long marches exacted a steep toll on the men. Hundreds of soldiers dropped out along the way because of fatigue, sunstroke, illness, or other maladies. Many others were far removed from fighting condition. The 93rd New York's Lt. Robert S. Robertson informed his parents, "This is the hardest marching on record since the war began and we are completely used up. The sides of my feet are covered with large blisters and the soles are so sore, I can scarcely bear my weight . . . and cannot get my boots on at all, my feet are swelled to such a size. . . . 54 miles in two days would be an extraordinary march on the best roads, but in the mud it was more than any army did before."[110]

Farther north in Gettysburg, meanwhile, Sarah Broadhead noted that "a large body of our cavalry [the 5th and 6th Michigan] began to pass through town, and we were all busy feeding them as they passed along." It was about ten o'clock, and to the diarist, "It seemed . . . that the long line would never get through. I hope they may catch the Rebels and give them a sound thrashing. Some say we may look for a

108 "Letter from the 137th," *Onondaga Standard* (Syracuse, NY), July 25, 1863; Horatio D. Chapman, Diary, entry for June 28, 1863, in *Civil War Diary of a Forty-niner* (self-published, 1929), 19-20.

109 "The March to Gettysburg," *Otsego* (NY) *Republican*, January 20, 1894.

110 R. S. Robertson to his parents, June 28, 1863, transcription at FSNMP.

battle here in a few days, and others say it will be fought near Harrisburg. There is no telling where it will be."[111]

* * *

Alfred Pleasonton's scheming and conniving finally paid dividends. Major General Julius Stahel was relieved of command of the cavalry division assigned to the defenses of Washington and received orders to report to Darius Couch in Harrisburg. Stahel's former command was transferred to the Army of the Potomac's Cavalry Corps, redesignated as the 3rd Cavalry Division, and assigned to Brig. Gen. Judson Kilpatrick. In this way, Pleasonton removed his rival for the top slot of the Cavalry Corps and placed one of his favorite officers in command of the division.[112]

Pleasonton wasn't finished. "I shall require three brigadier generals, able competent men, capable of commanding cavalry," he wrote army headquarters. "I urgently recommend the following named officers for promotion & appointment as brigadiers for these commands. Cavalry must have able commanders with dash & spirit or it will inevitably fail. The officers I mention have proven themselves by their brilliant & distinguished conduct at *Beverly Ford . . . Aldie . . .* and at Middleburg & Upperville . . . to be suitable selections for cavalry commander [emphasis in original]." His recommendations were two staff officers, Capts. Elon J. Farnsworth and George A. Custer, and the commander of the 2nd U.S. Cavalry, Capt. Wesley Merritt. Pleasonton wanted Custer to lead the Michigan Cavalry Brigade of Kilpatrick's division, Farnsworth to command Kilpatrick's 2nd Brigade, and Merritt the Reserve Brigade. Pleasonton also selected Capt. John C. Tidball to command his horse artillery and Col. John B. McIntosh to replace Col. John P. Taylor at the head of Gregg's 1st Brigade. Finally, he asked for a second brigade of horse artillery.[113]

"On Sunday, June 28, we mounted early, and, under a summer Sabbath morning sun, shining alike upon lands at peace and at war, upon kneeling worshippers and mounted troopers, rode up the eastern slope of the Catoctin Range. From the summit a magnificent prospect met our view," recalled Maj. John

---

111 Broadhead diary, entry for June 28, 1863.

112 *OR* 27, pt. 1, 915 and pt. 3, 373-376.

113 Pleasonton to Seth Williams, June 28, 1863, RG 393, Part 1, Entry 3986, "Two or More Name File," 1861–1865, NARA.

L. Beveridge, the commander of the 8th Illinois Cavalry. Beveridge likened the panoramic sight to the view Moses and Aaron witnessed of Canaan from Mt. Pisgah after forty years of wandering through the desert. Buford's tired troopers were happy to be back on friendly soil. They also knew that what would likely be one of the most important fights of the war awaited them as they went about preparing for the challenge.[114]

John Harvey of the 9th New York Cavalry captured (and inexplicably released) a Rebel spy. Trooper Charles Whitney, also of the 9th New York, recaptured the spy the next day and took the man to Buford's headquarters in the Catoctin Valley near Frederick. The cavalry commander was just then grappling with the news that three of his young captains—Wesley Merritt, Elon J. Farnsworth, and George A. Custer—had been promoted several grades to brigadier general, jumping past many officers senior to themselves.[115]

The spy, a man named Will Talbot, was placed before Buford for a drumhead court-martial. On the way to Buford's headquarters, Talbot attempted to talk his way out of his predicament by spinning an impressive yarn about the large family he supported. Buford's provost marshal, Lt. John Mix, smiled when he heard the tale and pointed out a lone tree to the man. When Talbot acknowledged seeing it, Mix blandly predicted the Rebel sympathizer would be hanging from one of its branches within five minutes. When the papers he was carrying betrayed his intentions, Talbot admitted being a member of Elijah V. White's 35th Battalion of Virginia Cavalry scouting for General Lee. Buford promptly pronounced the spy guilty, turned to Mix, and announced, "I guess you had best hang him." Buford also ordered that Talbot's body be left dangling for three days as a message to other potential spies. Talbot was hanged from the same tree Mix had pointed out on the way to Buford's headquarters.[116]

Several townspeople viewed the hanging as barbaric and complained to Buford about the execution. Instead of summarily killing him, they inquired, why didn't he send the spy back to Washington for further interrogation? Perhaps Buford was exhausted, or maybe he was bitter about the promotion of the three "boy generals"

114 John L. Beveridge, "The First Gun at Gettysburg," *War Papers, MOLLUS, Illinois Commandery*, vol. 2 (Chicago, 1894), 87-88.

115 Merritt, Farnsworth, and Custer quickly became known as the three "boy generals." Cheney, *History of the Ninth Regiment*, 132.

116 Thomas J. Smith, "Two Spies Instead of One," *National Tribune*, May 1, 1884; John Kelly, "The Spy at Frederick, Maryland," *National Tribune*, Feb. 9, 1888.

after his own difficulties in obtaining a field command. Whatever the reason, Buford flashed some of his sarcastic humor and informed the citizens that "the man was a spy and he was afraid to send him to Washington because he knew that the authorities would make [the spy] a brigadier general." Buford was a no-nonsense military man who had little tolerance for civilians or spies. Most of the Army of the Potomac passed the corpse on its march north into Pennsylvania. The gruesome sight left quite an impression on them.[117]

"I have always believed that if Talbot had got to Gen. Lee's headquarters with the information he had of our army," concluded Charles Whitney of the 9th New York, the man who captured the spy the second time, "there never would have been a Battle of Gettysburg. Lee would have cut off our trains and gone to Baltimore." Buford would encounter Whitney in Gettysburg on the morning of July 1, where the trooper asked for permission to find a carbine and join the growing fight west of town. According to Whitney, Buford told him to fall back because "I had done my country more service by capturing the spy than if I killed a whole brigade of rebels."[118]

Before he was relieved, Hooker had ordered "that the cavalry be sent well in advance of Frederick in the direction of Gettysburg and Emmitsburg and see what they can learn of the movements of the enemy."[119] In response, General Pleasonton ordered David M. Gregg's 2nd Division to guard the army's right flank and Judson Kilpatrick's 3rd Division to cover its center. Buford was directed to move from Middletown, Maryland, by way of Emmitsburg to Gettysburg, with orders to cover the army's left flank, and "hold Gettysburg at all hazards until supports arrive."[120]

---

117 Moyer, *History of the Seventeenth Regiment*, 58; J. McGardner, "Fighting Them Over." "[O]n June 27 in Frederick City, Maryland. Buford stopped there long enough to hang a rebel spy or two." John Kelly of Company F, 2nd U.S. Cavalry, recalled that Buford's comment about not sending the spy back to Washington was, "Well, if we send him a prisoner up to Washington, it's ten to one that he will be back inside of a month with a commission in his pocket." "The Spy at Frederick, Maryland." For more on the issue of Buford's treatment of spies during the Gettysburg campaign, see Eric J. Wittenberg, "And Everything is Lovely and the Goose Hangs High: John Buford and the Hanging of Confederate Spies during the Gettysburg Campaign," *Gettysburg Magazine*, no. 18 (Jan. 1998), 5-14.

118 Thomas J. Smith, "Two Spies Instead of One."

119 Joseph Hooker to Maj. Gen. E. D. Townsend, Sept. 28, 1875, Civil War Collection, Musselman Library, Gettysburg College, Gettysburg, PA.

120 Walter Kempster, "The Cavalry at Gettysburg," MOLLUS, Wisconsin Commandery, read October 1, 1913, 399.

Before they moved out, Buford's men spent a quiet day near Middletown reshoeing their mounts and refitting. Citizens reported that the Confederate army had crossed the Potomac at Williamsport and was in strong force. One man claimed to have counted nearly 100 pieces of artillery. Late that day word reached Buford's camp that Hooker had asked to be relieved of command of the army, and Pennsylvanian George G. Meade, the commander of the V Corps, had replaced him. The response throughout the army was mixed; Buford's response is not recorded.[121]

Pleasonton also directed David M. Gregg to send two of his three brigades and a battery of horse artillery to scout in the direction of Ellicott's Mills near Baltimore; a brigade of Confederate cavalry was reported to have crossed the Potomac at Seneca Mills, supposedly making for the Baltimore & Ohio Railroad between Seneca Mills and Baltimore. Gregg's orders were to prevent this force from damaging the railroad and its accompanying telegraph lines. He was also to detach a regiment to guard supplies at Edwards Ferry to cover the withdrawal of all public property at that point.[122]

* * *

Outside of Philadelphia in Norristown, several leading businessmen decided to close their factories "until the Rebels are driven from the State." They raised $10,000 to pay the volunteers their lost wages for the entire period of their absence. Five hundred men responded to the call and planned to leave for Harrisburg the following morning.[123]

During the morning, a Pennsylvania militia regiment passed by the camps of the New York guardsmen at Bridgeport, across the Susquehanna from Harrisburg. The Rebels, reported the Keystone men, were only three miles away. "Matters assumed quite a serious aspect," admitted the 22nd New York National Guard's George Wingate. "At noon the Twenty-second assembled in front of the colonel's tent for religious service, feeling rather more disposed to be pious than usual, for none knew what might occur before another day was passed." The services never took place. "The men were in their positions," continued Wingate,

121 OR 27, pt. 1, 926; Henry Norton, *Deeds of Daring: or History of the Eighth New York Volunteer Cavalry* (Chenango, NY, 1889), 68; Hall, *History of the Sixth New York Cavalry*, 132.

122 OR 27, pt. 3, 376-377.

123 *Chicago Tribune*, June 29, 1863.

their prayer-books distributed, the chaplain had risen, and was on the point of announcing his text, when the colonel dashed up at full gallop, with the order, "Go back to your company streets and strike tents at once." The men rushed back to their quarters and preparations for breaking up camp went on in the greatest possible haste, in the midst of which the chaplain disappeared, never to be seen by the regiment until its return. . . . In a few minutes the regimental camp was struck, and shelter-tents and more cartridges were distributed. Knapsacks were packed, and the men marched away little thinking, as they took leave of the pleasant spot, where their nice new tents were being loaded in wagons pressed for the occasion, of the length of time that would elapse before their heads would get under their (or any other) shelter again.[124]

Theodore D. Rand of the Landis Artillery was not too far from Wingate's 22nd New York, though he and his comrades were able to enjoy Sunday service. "At half past ten we had Divine service read by our first lieutenant, a remarkably fine officer, and one unusually respected by the men. The service was very impressive, and I believe will not soon be forgotten by those who participated in it," thought Rand. Once finished, the men examined their ammunition and enjoyed a meal.

They were still eating when they were ordered to their guns, "an advance of the rebels being expected." Knipe's New York State Militia, continued the artillerist, "came pouring into the fort with reports of the near approach of the rebels. In an incredibly short time all the guns were manned and all the infantry drawn up in line of battle behind the parapet—a fine sight.

The rebels were but three or four miles off. We could hear their firing distinctly." Rand watched while a heavy force armed with axes levelled the trees within close range. The clang of the axes mixed with the crash of the falling trees, recalled Rand, "made a sad music, for a beautiful landscape was being shorn of its greatest ornament and these seemed like its moan."[125]

*   *   *

In Virginia, meanwhile, Maj. Gen. John A. Dix continued developing a plan for a movement against Richmond. The plan would not be completed and ready to implement until July 1. Until then, his soldiers remained idle.[126]

124 Wingate, *History of the Twenty-second Regiment*, 177.

125 Ibid.

126 *OR* 27, pt. 3, 439-440.

Dix's delay irritated the authorities in Washington, whose primary focus remained centered on Lee. "A large portion of the Rebel army is unquestionably on this side the Potomac," Secretary Welles confided in his journal. "The main body is, I think, in the Cumberland Valley, pressing on toward Harrisburg, but a small force has advanced toward Washington. The War Department is wholly unprepared for an irruption here, and J. E. B. Stuart might have dashed into the city to-day with impunity. In the mean time," continued the frustrated navy secretary, "Philadelphians and the Pennsylvanians are inert and inactive, indisposed to volunteer to defend even their own capital." Welles attributed part of their lethargy to what he called "the incompetency of General Halleck to concentrate effort, acquire intelligence, or inspire confidence."

Governor Andrew Curtin of Pennsylvania, described by Welles as "excitable," did not escape the wrath of the secretary's pen. Curtin, he recorded, "is easily alarmed and calls aloud for help on the remotest prospect of danger. He is very vigilant—almost too vigilant for calm consideration and wise conclusion, or to have a commanding influence." The governor, concluded Welles, was "not only anxious but susceptible, impressible, scary."[127]

127 Welles, *Diary*, 1:350-351.

MONDAY, JUNE 29, 1863

After the fighting at Oyster Point in Camp Hill the day before, Brig. Gen. Albert G. Jenkins' Virginia cavalrymen pulled back to their artillery position near Peace Church, where they spent the night. They intended to advance again the next day.

Colonel William Brisbane's Pennsylvania emergency militiamen spent a restless night near Oyster's Point. Though they knew the Confederates would likely return in the morning, the lack of food was foremost on the minds of the nearby men of Company I of the 71st New York National Guard. Shortly after daybreak several Empire State men fanned out from their campsite looking for something to eat. Southern artillerists from Capt. Wiley Griffin's 3-inch rifles of the Baltimore Artillery at the Peace Church opened fire. A few errant shells reached Bethel Church (near present-day 21st Street in Camp Hill) and drilled holes in the walls and roofs of several buildings. Shells also struck the tollgate and nearby trees, but failed to explode.

After a lull that lasted most of the morning, Jackson's Kanawha Battery unlimbered at the Albright farm on Carlisle Road about noon and began shelling the area around Limekiln Lane and Oyster's Woods. Colonel Brisbane thought the shelling portended a major fight and sent a courier galloping back to the fortifications on Bridgeport Heights to request reinforcements. About 1:00 p.m. he deployed his three regiments in a wheatfield with Miller's Philadelphia guns in support while Lt. Col. John Elwell and 150 men from the 8th, 23rd, and 56th New York State National Guard regiments rushed to his aid. After a fitful artillery fire that lasted a couple hours, Lt. Col. Vincent A. Witcher advanced his dismounted Virginia skirmishers to hold the Federals' attention while Albert Jenkins's mounted

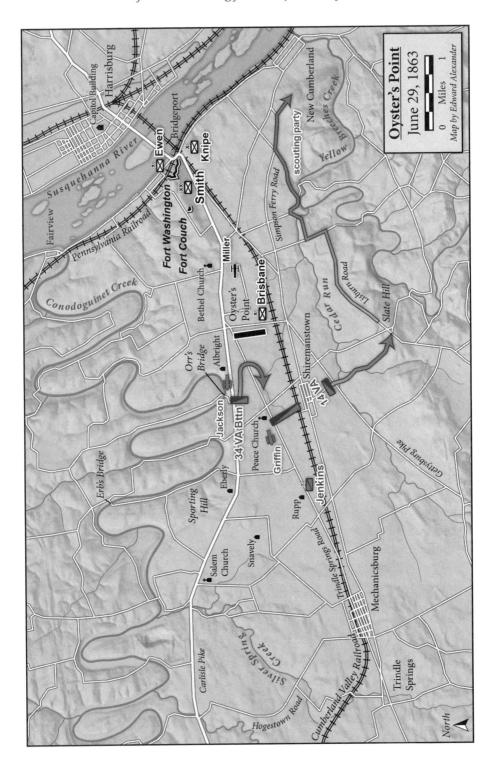

Oyster's Point
June 29, 1863

0   Miles   1
Map by Edward Alexander

infantry reconnoitered the main defenses of Harrisburg. Witcher sent several horsemen and a limbered cannon galloping east on the turnpike toward Oyster's Point, where the blue-clad militiamen fired from behind a barricade of logs and felled trees. The Rebels halted briefly and left the cannon beside the pike. One man was shot from his saddle fell into the tall grass. The Southerners temporarily abandoned the gun and disappeared down Trindle Springs Road. Some of the New Yorkers retrieved the wounded soldier and carried him to a barn that was doubling as an aid station for the 71st New York. Once his wounds were bandaged, stewards carried the stricken Rebel to a nearby house, where doctors amputated one of his legs.[1]

Despite being "nearly exhausted by constant and exciting service," the 14th Virginia Cavalry's Lt. Hermann Schuricht received orders that morning to take his company and report to General Jenkins as his escort for the day. Jenkins and three army engineers—Maj. John J. Graham Clarke, Capt. Henry B. Richardson, and Capt. Samuel R. Johnston—accompanied Lieutenant Schuricht's 60 horsemen south through Shiremanstown to Slate Hill. The officers used that "dominant hill" to study Harrisburg and the fortifications on Bridgeport Heights through their field glasses. Some of Jenkins's men continued riding east on Lisburn Road to another hill for a second look. Encouraged by what they saw, the engineers reported their findings to General Ewell at the Carlisle Barracks. Ewell, in turn, ordered Maj. Gen. Robert Rodes to prepare his division to capture Harrisburg the following day. The news excited Rodes, who declared that his men were full of enthusiasm and confident of success.[2]

* * *

Shortly after 3:00 p.m. a courier reined in at Ewell's headquarters carrying an order from General Lee: Ewell was to withdraw his command from Carlisle to Chambersburg. The news of the reversal disappointed Ewell, who had his heart set on seizing Harrisburg. Within a short time a galloper thundered his way to Edward Johnson's headquarters to tell him of the change of plans and that he was to march his infantry division to move on Chambersburg

---

1 For details, see Wingert, *The Confederate Approach on Harrisburg*, 111-115.

2 Schuricht diary, entry for June 29, 1863, *Richmond Dispatch*, April 5, 1896; OR 27, pt. 2, 235-236, 552. Clarke was detached from Longstreet's staff and Johnston from Lee's staff.

without delay, taking his wagons and artillery with him. Rodes and his division would follow at a later hour.[3]

"We had been up since reveille, ready to resume the day's march to Harrisburg, which we hoped to reach that day," recalled one of Johnson's staff officers. The morning passed without orders, and the men began to get restless. Noon ticked by, as did the early afternoon hours. Finally, he continued, "an aide was observed to dash up to brigade headquarters and in a few minutes came the welcome 'Fall in!' We were surprised to see the head of the column upon reaching the turnpike to file abruptly to the left instead of right, and we found ourselves retracing our steps of the 27th. Our disappointment and chagrin were extreme."[4]

Not long after Johnson's infantrymen began tramping toward Chambersburg, a second order reached Ewell changing the concentration point to Cashtown or Gettysburg. Ewell sent the order on to Johnson. Because it was late in the day, Ewell allowed Rodes to rest his men that night and begin his march early the next morning. Rumors flew that they would be moving south to fight a big battle. The men departed their bivouacs at the Carlisle Barracks and formed in the streets, some sleeping that night on the sidewalks.

Meanwhile, Capt. Elliot Johnson, one of General Ewell's aides, guided his horse into York to locate his superior's third division under Jubal Early. Once he had a copy of Lee's orders to concentrate the army, Early ordered a local printer to produce a broadside explaining his recent actions. "To the citizens of York," it began,

> I have abstained from burning the railroad buildings and car shops in your town, because, after examination, I am satisfied the safety of the town would be endangered; and, acting in the spirit of humanity, which has ever characterized my Government and its military authorities, I do not design to involve the innocent in the same punishment with the guilty. Had I applied the torch without regard to consequences, I would have pursued a course that would have been vindicated as an act of retaliation for the many authorized acts of barbarity perpetrated by your own army upon our soil. But we do not war upon women and children, and I trust the treatment you have met with at the hands of my soldiers will

---

3 Ibid., pt. 3, 943-944. Ewell had his cartographer, Jedediah Hotchkiss, prepare a map of Adams County, Pennsylvania. After dark, he roused Hotchkiss from his sleep and summoned him to headquarters, where he peppered him with questions According to Hotchkiss, Ewell was "quite testy and hard to please . . . [and] had everyone flying around." Hotchkiss, *Make Me a Map*, 156.

4 Goldsborough, *The Maryland Line*, 127-130.

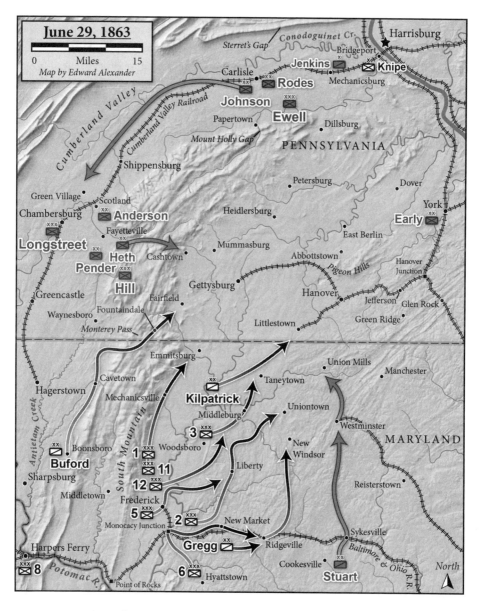

open your eyes to the monstrous iniquity of the war waged by your government upon the people of the Confederate states, and that you will make an effort to shake off the revolting tyranny under which it is apparent to you all you are yourselves undergoing.[5]

5 Early, *War Memoirs*, 263.

Early's foragers and quartermasters scoured the countryside for mules and horses, often with considerable success. Artilleryman Maj. Robert Stiles was less than enthusiastic about the impressed animals, which were mostly "great, clumsy, flabby Percherons or Conestogas" requiring more than twice the feed as the compact, hard-muscled, and smaller Virginia horses. Despite their immense size, many of these plow horses could not stand the hardship and exposure of a military campaign and would eventually prove unreliable in combat.[6]

* * *

While Dorsey Pender's and Richard Anderson's Third Corps divisions remained camped at Fayetteville, Harry Heth marched his division from Fayetteville east across South Mountain into Adams County before halting near Cashtown. The sweeping vista impressed the 47th Virginia's Robert T. Douglass, who scribbled in his diary, "We are camped at the foot of the mountains and can see a good part of Pa."[7]

Chambersburg dentist Jacob L. Suesserott visited General Lee's headquarters to convince the army leader to issue orders to return a blind mare owned by Col. D. O. Gehr. Suesserott needed the animal to plow his corn because he had taken his horses to safety. Lee agreed and asked an aide to prepare the paperwork. The astute dentist studied Lee's features and left a fascinating and often overlooked account of a general under stress just days before the beginning of the battle of Gettysburg. "[N]ever since have I seen so much emotion depicted on a human countenance," he later wrote. "With his hand at times clutching his hair and with contracted brow, he would walk with rapid strides for a few rods and then, as if he bethought himself of his actions, with a sudden jerk he would produce an entire change in his features and demeanor and cast an enquiring gaze on me only to be followed in a moment by the same contortions of face and agitation of person."[8]

Except for foragers, the soldiers of James Longstreet's First Corps were largely inactive. The 4th Alabama "materially reduced the supply of apple butter and light bread of our Pennsylvania Dutch hosts," bragged adjutant Robert T. Coles. Sergeant William R. Houghton of the 2nd Georgia was up in a large cherry-laden

---

6 Stiles, *Four Years under Marse Robert*, 200-201.

7 Douglass diary, entry for June 29, 1863.

8 Hoke, *Reminiscences*, 66.

tree helping himself to the luscious fruit when two women emerged from a nearby house talking and gesticulating in his direction. The Georgian could not understand a word because they spoke only in German. He didn't know if he "was getting curses or blessings, but the probabilities were strongly against the latter."[9]

The 4th Texas's John West took the opportunity to write a letter to his distant family. "We are now between the Blue Ridge and the Alleghany; the entire landscape covered with the most magnificent farms, orchards and gardens, for miles along the road," he explained. The "elegant residences and barns" impressed the Texan, who declared them "positively more tastily built than two-thirds of the houses in Waco, and as fine as the dwelling houses anywhere. I have not seen a barn in the last three days that was not more substantially and carefully build [sic] and fitted out than any house I have ever seen in the country in Texas." The wheat crop was "splendid; just ready to cut," he continued. "The apple trees are loaded and the cherries delicious. I enclose two varieties of cherry seed, and will endeavor to bring some if I ever get back."

Putting pleasantries aside, West turned his thoughts to the impending conflict. "My impression is, that we will have a desperate battle in a few days, but I cannot tell, as a soldier who minds his own business knows less than an outsider," he explained. "I would not have missed this campaign for $500.00. I believe that if successful it will do a great deal towards bringing about a peace or our recognition by foreign powers." He had a $50.00 bounty and $30.00 in pay due in a week. Because of the possibility of a battle, he would "not draw it, but will leave it in the hands of somebody so that you can get it, as I do not wish a Yankee to make anything by rifling my pockets on the battlefield."[10]

Weeks into the campaign, good shoes were at a premium. The 2nd Georgia's Sergeant Houghton admitted to wearing out "three pairs in a month. The leather had been hurriedly tanned and the shoes came to pieces." That circumstance seemed universal among Ewell's men. A member of the U.S. Christian Commission studied John Gordon's Georgians in York and found "Their shoes, as a general thing, were poor; some of the men were entirely barefooted."[11]

---

9 Coles, R.T. *Coles's History*, 103; Houghton, *Two Boys in the Civil War*, 671.

10 West, *A Texan in Search of a Fight*, 81-82.

11 *Columbus* (GA) *Daily Enquirer*, March 29, 1903; Houghton, *Two Boys in the Civil War*, 671; J. H. Douglas, "Report of the Operations of the Sanitary Commission during and after the Battles at Gettysburg," in *Documents of the U. S. Sanitary Commission*, 2 vols. (U.S. Sanitary Commission, 1866), 2:78.

According to John H. Worsham of the 21st Virginia, shoes were not the only thing wearing out. Clothing, he lamented, "was in a sad plight. . . . Hundreds had no shoes, thousands were as ragged as they could be, some with the bottom of their pants in long frazzles, others with their knees out, others out at their elbows, and their hair sticking through holes in their hats." Some of the soldiers had patched their clothing as best as they could, "one man having the seat of his pants patched with bright red, his knees patched with black; another with a piece of gray or brown blanket; in fact, with anything one could get," he continued. When the regiment passed a group of females standing along the road, a girl asked her mother how the officers differed from the privates. That was easy, replied the mother: the officers wore pants that had been patched, and the privates did not.[12]

"Bud," a soldier in the 2nd South Carolina, was impressed with just about everything in Pennsylvania except for the fairer sex. "We passed through the prettiest country that I ever saw in my life," he closed in a letter to his sister. "It has [some] of the finest land in the world and some of the ugliest women that I ever saw."[13]

*   *   *

Brigadier General John D. Imboden's command continued terrorizing western Franklin County. "Imboden's brigade encamped between here and the Gap. Infantry, artillery, and cavalry. They came from Western Virginia, Cumberland, and Hancock. They clean out all the surrounding farm-houses," complained Mercersburg seminarian Dr. Phillip Schaff. "They have discovered most of the hiding places of the horses in the mountains, and secured to-day at least three hundred horses."[14]

Captain Abram Jones and a detachment of 31 troopers of the 1st New York (Lincoln) Cavalry arrived at McConnellsburg about 8:30 a.m. and halted in front of a popular tavern called the Fulton House. About 50 local home guards under Capt. B. Mortimer Morrow joined them there. The newcomers, observed one eyewitness, were patriotic but "a motley crowd and not enlisting under any proclamation. They have just assembled to defend their homes but wish to do no

---

12 Worsham, *One of Jackson's Foot Cavalry*, 175.

13 "Bud" to his sister, July 18, 1863, Michael Musick Collection, USAHEC.

14 Schaff, "The Gettysburg Week," 25.

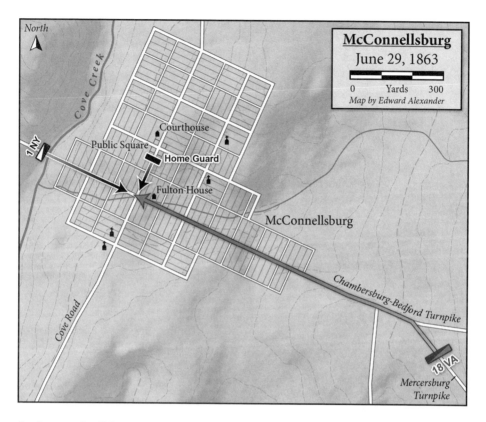

further service." Jones was leaning out an upstairs window to call down to Morrow when he spotted one of his scouts galloping toward him. "What's the matter, sergeant?" called out Jones. The man yelled back that no less than 200 Confederate cavalrymen were coming down off the mountain and heading toward town. Jones trotted downstairs and exited the tavern. "Get on your horses and get to your places," he ordered in a calm, clear voice. "I'll fight them." With that, the Union troopers swung into their saddles, formed up, and drew their sabers. Jones guided his command back toward Bloody Run. The militia rode out as well but turned right onto Cove Road, moved another block, halted in the square in front of the county courthouse, and waited there while the cavalry led the way.[15]

15 J. H. Greathead, "The Skirmish at McConnellsburg—A Reminiscence of the War," *Fulton Democrat*, Sept. 21, 1894; Beach, *The First New York (Lincoln) Cavalry*, 259-260; John H. Nelson, *Confusion and Courage: The Civil War in Fulton County, Pa., June 1863* (McConnellsburg, PA, 1996), 19.

Capt. Abram Jones commanded a detachment of the 1st New York Cavalry in the skirmish at McConnellsburg, Pa.

Ken Turner

When the head of the Confederate cavalry column spotted the Federals, their sabers glinting in the sunlight, Capt. William D. Ervin of the 18th Virginia Cavalry of Imboden's Brigade cried out, "Charge, charge, charge the damned Yankees!" The Rebels spurred their horses and started surging forward. Private Lantz G. Potts, riding near the front, spotted the Yankee militia off to the right squarely on their flank. "Flankers on the right of us!" he screamed, which prompted Captain Ervin to order "Right about!"[16]

The fleeing Confederates dumped their plunder from their saddles as they tried to escape what looked to be a closing trap. "But when the clear voice of Captain Jones rang out, 'Charge!' the order had not to be repeated; led by that gallant officer, his men, with one wild whoop, that sent terror into the hearts of their cowardly foe, sabre in hand, sprang forward to the work," wrote an observer. He continued:

> Had the rebel lines been braced with iron, they never could have stood that shock; they broke and fled, and, amid the waving of handkerchiefs and the cheers of the citizens, the New Yorkers dashed after their flying foe. The sharp ring of the carbine, the clang of the sabers, and the shouts of the pursuers created a scene at once so wild, so exciting, and so full of interest that I doubt whether it has been equaled during the war. The rebels were overtaken at the edge of the town; our cavalry dashed in amongst them, and a regular

16 Lantz G. Potts, "Recollections of the Civil War," *Randolph Enterprise*, Dec. 15, 1921.

hand-to-hand fight ensued; for a few moments, the crack of the revolvers and the rattle of the sabres were incessant.[17]

The New Yorkers captured Captain Ervin, but Potts and a couple of others tried to free him. When Potts called out, "Captain, do you want us to run or fight?" Ervin replied, "Form and fight!" A short-lived hand-to-hand mêlée whirled in the streets. Potts parried a blow from one Yankee, but another staggered him with a blow to the shoulder that nearly cut his collarbone in two. "Now, damn you, will you surrender?" demanded the Northerner. Stunned and in terrible pain, Potts had little choice but to capitulate.[18]

The small fight was over almost as quickly as it began. Jones's ambush had worked brilliantly. The New Yorkers and the militia punished Imboden's men at the cost of just one man slightly wounded (and a uniform jacket riddled with bullet holes). Two Virginians lay dead, several were seriously wounded, and 32 out of 55 of them, including Captain Ervin, had been captured. Once the two dead Rebels were buried on the side of the road, Jones and his victorious little band rode off to rejoin the rest of Milroy's refugees at Bloody Run. The local citizenry of McConnellsburg cheered the victors loudly and enthusiastically as they clattered down the streets. As a reward for their enthusiastic support, Jones ordered the remaining plunder taken from the saddles of the Virginians be left for the townsfolk to divide amongst themselves.[19]

* * *

Jeb Stuart and his horse soldiers had been in the saddle for five full days, and both troopers and mounts were approaching the limits of their endurance. The combination of the detour, the skirmish at Fairfax Station, and the capture of the wagons had thrown their schedule out the window.

Their intent to reach Hanover, Pennsylvania, by the morning of June 28 was already a full day behind them. Despite their fatigue, Stuart had his command on the move at 1:00 a.m. The general was so exhausted he fell asleep in the saddle. Tottering from side to side, he presented a comical appearance. Many of his men

17 "Exploit in McConnellsburg," in Moore, *The Rebellion Record,* 7:327.

18 Potts, "Recollections of the Civil War."

19 Stevenson, *"Boots and Saddles,"* 207; "Exploit at McConnellsburg," 327-328. The two Confederate casualties are still buried by the roadside.

followed suit and also rode along while sound asleep. "I remember that laughable specter of Major McClellan, sitting grave, erect, and motionless on his horse in front of a country store by the roadside, to which the animal had made his way and halted," recalled Capt. John Esten Cooke. "The Major seemed to be waiting—for somebody, or something—meanwhile he was snoring." Many fatigued troopers leaned too far to one side and dropped from the saddle, only to be rudely awakened when their bodies hit the ground.[20]

Fitzhugh Lee's Brigade reached the Baltimore & Ohio Railroad soon after daylight. "Much time was consumed in tearing up the track at Hood's Mill, destroying the bridge at Sykesville and the telegraph lines," recalled one of Capt. James Breathed's gunners. This lengthy process delayed the advance of the Confederate column and set Stuart's schedule back even further. Although the destruction of the railroad, bridge, and telegraph line had taken some time, Stuart later explained that "this work was effectually accomplished, and the last means of communication between General Meade and Washington was destroyed." "The effect of the raid," confirmed the *Daily Constitutional Union*, "is to interrupt communication with the Army of the Potomac." Stuart, however, overestimated the extent of the destruction. "The damage done to the road at the two points named can be repaired in two or three hours, and if nothing further is done the travel will not be interrupted," declared a Washington newspaper the next day.[21]

Stuart also established measures to intercept trains on the B&O. By this time he was aware that Hooker had been relieved of command of the Army of the Potomac and expected the deposed general to return to Washington via the railroad. Stuart intended to capture Hooker, but when word reached the Federal authorities that Stuart's command was lying in wait, the train reversed course. The Rebels remained in possession of the railroad nearly all that day and spent the night there.[22]

In addition to Hooker's removal, Stuart also learned that the Union army was moving north through Frederick. "It was important for me to reach our column [main army] with as little delay as possible, to acquaint the commanding general with the nature of the enemy's movements, as well as to place with his column my

---

20 Cooke, *The Wearing of the Gray*, 239.

21 Matthews, "Pelham-Breathed Battery"; OR 27, pt. 2, 695; McClellan, *Life and Campaigns of Stuart*, 326; *Daily Constitutional Union*, June 30, 1863.

22 Swank, *Saddles, Sabres, and Spurs*, 73.

Maj. Napoleon B. Knight (seen here on his horse), led two companies of the 1st Delaware Cavalry stationed at Westminster, Md. LOC

cavalry force," explained Stuart after the fact in his campaign report. At 10:30 a.m., the cavalrymen were in the saddle again and heading for Westminster.[23]

Westminster marked the terminus of the Western Maryland Railroad, an important supply line for Union troops operating in this area. Lieutenant Pulaski Bowman's detachment of the 150th New York had been guarding the railroad spur for several weeks. On June 27, Maj. Gen. Robert C. Schenck had ordered the inexperienced Maj. Napoleon B. Knight and companies C and D of the 1st Delaware Cavalry (about 94 officers and men) to march to Westminster to perform outpost and picket duty.[24]

The Delaware horsemen, almost all of whom were inexperienced, arrived in Westminster without fanfare about 11:00 a.m. on June 28. The town was quiet, which was to be expected on a Sunday morning. Knight and his men rode so silently through the streets that for some time many of the locals were not aware the Delaware cavalrymen were in their midst. Captain Charles Corbit, the commander

23 OR 27, pt. 2, 695.

24 Ibid., 201; A. H. Huber, "The Real Facts About the Fight at Westminster, Maryland, June 29, 1863," RG 1810.035, Box 390195, Public Archives of Delaware, Dover, DE.

of Company C, was a tall, strong, and natural-born leader. He would soon find himself in tactical command of the detachment of four officers and 89 enlisted men.[25]

Their presence did not go unnoticed for long. "The entry of the troops occasioned considerable excitement for though but little news was permitted to be furnished, it was known that the Government anticipated a Confederate advance in the direction of Baltimore," remembered one witness, "and with Longstreet and Hill on the principal thoroughfare 25 miles northwest and Ewell 40 miles east the sending of a few hundred cavalrymen to Westminster intensified the nervous alarm." Major Knight and Captain Corbit camped their troopers on high ground on the northern edge of town in an area known as "The Commons," adjacent to the campus of today's McDaniel College. This high ground, which had been used as a picnic area for decades before the war, commanded not only the town but also the main route through Westminster. It was also an integral part of the Pipe Creek line, a potential defensive position chosen by the Army of the Potomac's engineers. Major Knight could see his outpost on the far end of the town without having to lift his field glasses.[26]

Blue-clad troopers picketed the roads leading into the town as part of the effort to hold the crucial railhead. The Delawareans were confident they had established a sufficient early warning network. Lieutenant Bowman's 150th New York infantry detachment guarded the railroad depot. Bowman advised the recently arrived Knight that there was no enemy at Gettysburg or Hanover. When local citizens confirmed these reports, Knight passed the intelligence along to General Schenck and settled down for the evening. He fully expected to spend a quiet night in the hospitable town.[27]

Many of the 1st Delaware's horses had been "rendered almost unfit for service by marching over the stony road without shoes." When there was no sign of the Confederates on the morning of June 29, Major Knight ordered the mounts shod.

---

25 Frederic Shriver Klein, ed., *Just South of Gettysburg: Carroll County, Maryland in the Civil War* (Westminster, MD, 1963), 43.

26 A. H. Huber, "Account of the 1st Del. Cavalry at Westminster, MD, 1863," Governor's Correspondence, RG 1801, Box 55510, Delaware Public Archives, Dover. Today, The Commons is known as College Hill. The campus of McDaniel College, formerly known as Western Maryland College, was built in 1866 and occupies a significant portion of this prominent piece of high ground. Western Maryland College was the first co-educational college south of the Mason-Dixon line.

27 *OR* 27, pt. 2, 201-202.

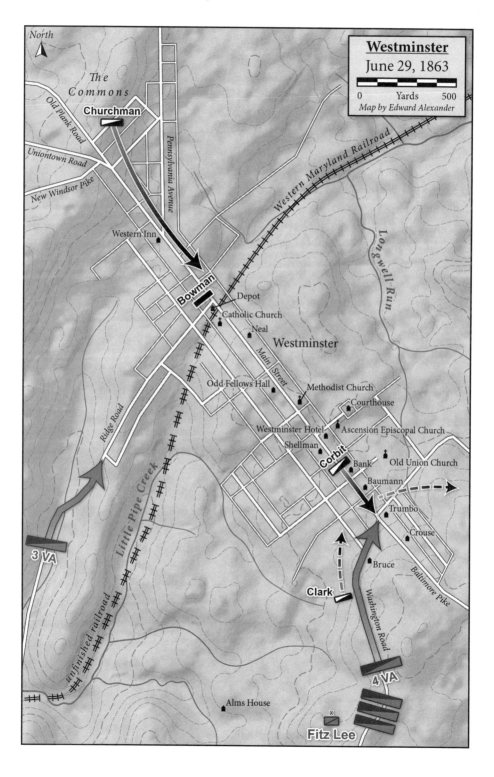

North

The
Commons

Churchman

Old Plank Road

Uniontown Road

New Windsor Pike

Pennsylvania Avenue

Western Inn

Bowman

Depot

Catholic Church

Neal

Western Maryland Railroad

Longwell Run

Westminster

Westminster
June 29, 1863

0   Yards   500
Map by Edward Alexander

Main Street

Odd Fellows Hall

Methodist Church

Courthouse

Westminster Hotel

Ascension Episcopal Church

Shellman

Corbit

Bank

Old Union Church

Ridge Road

Baumann

Trumbo

Crouse

Little Pipe Creek

Bruce

Baltimore Pike

3 VA

unfinished railroad

Clark

Washington Road

4 VA

Alms House

Fitz Lee

The battalion's blacksmiths ordered up their wagons and went to work, a laborious process that consumed most of the day.

Stuart intended to pass through Westminster on his way to Pennsylvania. He had no precise idea of the whereabouts of the main body of Lee's army and seems not to have appreciated the danger facing him in Maryland. Reports of the enemy moving north through Frederick made advising Lee of the news that much more imperative. Stuart, however, was unaware that Major Knight and his intrepid little band of cavalrymen were squarely astride his proposed line of advance. The head of Stuart's column followed a ridge road and approached Westminster between 4:00 and 5:00 p.m.[28]

The bright and clear early morning had given way to rising temperatures as the sun climbed higher into the sky. The presence of the men from the 1st Delaware Cavalry did little to disrupt the local citizens, who did their best to go about their normal affairs. Nor did the presence of Westminster's civilians deter Major Knight, who spent a pleasant afternoon refreshing himself in the tavern of the Westminster Hotel on Main Street. By the time Stuart's Confederates arrived, the major was so intoxicated that he was unable to take the field. His troopers had spent a restful day tending to their horses and writing letters—a welcome respite that was about to end in a way few imagined.[29]

Five Delawareans were having their horses shod in Michael Baumann's blacksmith shop on the east end of town "a stone's throw from the point on Main Street where it was intersected by the Washington road" when the small advance guard of Fitz Lee's column pounced on them. The assault captured all five men together with their mounts, a small but important victory that, along with the earlier loss of the pickets, deprived the 1st Delaware Cavalry of its early warning system. Major Knight's lackadaisical deployments were about to cost his command dearly.[30]

Luckily for the Union troopers, a young lawyer from Westminster named Isaac E. Pearson spurred his well-lathered horse into town to report Stuart's approach along the Washington Road. When Captain Corbit heard this news, he called out "to horse!" and formed his small squadron of about 70 troopers, which had been depleted by the deployment of picket posts on the roads surrounding Westminster

28 Ibid., 202.

29 Klein, *Just South of Gettysburg*, 44; James H. Wilson, *Captain Charles Corbit's Charge at Westminster with a Squadron of the First Delaware Cavalry, June 29, 1863* (Wilmington, DE, 1913), 16.

30 Huber, "Account," 5.

Capt. Charles Corbit led a stirring charge of the 1st Delaware Cavalry on the streets of Westminster.

USAHEC

and by the poor condition of its horses. Corbit formed his men on East Main Street, and the green Delawareans moved out toward the intersection of East Main Street and Pennsylvania Avenue to find Stuart's horsemen. The Delawareans rose in their stirrups, waved their sabers, and hollered for the curious civilians to clear the street, prompting those who had not yet hidden to scramble indoors. Corbit dispatched Lt. D. W. C. Clark and an advance guard of 12 men to feel for the enemy and ascertain his position. After advancing a short distance out the Washington Road, Clark and his men turned and galloped back with the news that a large force of Confederate horsemen was in their immediate front. The lieutenant escaped with a hole in his hat and an arm wound to prove it.[31]

Corbit paused at the tavern long enough to report the news to Major Knight and ask for orders. Knight promptly instructed Corbit to move at once against the enemy. Knight, apparently afraid of being captured and treated as a deserter as a consequence of his very brief service for the Confederacy in 1861, declined to leave the tavern or assume tactical command of the fight, leaving Corbit in command by default.[32]

Trotting to the front, the intrepid captain and his little band of inexperienced horsemen spotted the head of Stuart's column approaching the town. "Draw sabers!" cried Corbit. With his bugler sounding the charge and the encouraging cheers of some of the local women ringing in their ears, Corbit led his troopers

31 Mary J. Shellman, Diary, entry for June 29, 1863, in Klein, *Just South of Gettysburg*, 48; *Baltimore American*, July 3, 1863.

32 Shellman diary, entry for June 29, 1863.

forward into the astonished vanguard of what proved to be Stuart's 4,000 horsemen. The Delawareans demonstrated "an almost suicidal bravery" in launching their charge, remembered one witness. The attack slammed into the massed gray cavalry at the intersection of the Washington Road and East Main Street. The two roads intersected at a sharp angle which, together with the stout rail fencing on all sides, created a natural bottleneck. The sudden attack prompted a member of the Delaware battalion to claim that the charge "was more heroic than Cardigan's Six Hundred at Balaclava." In addition to the Delaware soldiers, Stuart's men also had to deal with the town's civilians. According to a sergeant riding with the 2nd Virginia Cavalry, the citizens "disputed our entrance by firing into our ranks from windows and behind houses."[33]

The shock of the audacious charge drove Fitz Lee's troopers back in confusion and forced them to reform under difficult circumstances. The Southerners rallied and countercharged with the 4th Virginia Cavalry in the lead. "Gen'l Fitz Lee came galloping to the head of our regiment and led us in a charge," recalled a member of the 2nd Virginia Cavalry. Fitz Lee sent the 3rd Virginia on a flanking maneuver, but the route was a long one and the skirmish ended before the Virginians could take further part in the "short, sharp, and decisive" fight. Corbit's stubborn and vastly outnumbered horsemen obstinately repulsed two or three charges in the narrow roadway, but the weight of Southern numbers finally told. According to Gen. James H. Wilson, "A pistol shot killed [Corbit's] horse while it was throwing up its head under pressure of the rein and thus fortunately covering its rider behind." Corbit struggled free from the dead animal and, with his pistol in hand, stood to face his enemy. Rebels swept in and captured the gallant captain while he was standing astride his dead charger.[34]

Lee's devastating countercharge gobbled up most of Corbit's Company C. "Our boys were crowded out of the Baltimore Pike by an overwhelming force, some escaping . . . and some being taken prisoners," recalled Lt. William W. Lobdell, the 1st Delaware's adjutant. The Confederates forced Lobdell into a barnyard on the western edge of town at the intersection of Main Street and

---

33 Letter of Eugene W. LaMotte, Feb. 10, 1864, in Klein, *Just South of Gettysburg*, 56; OR 27, pt. 2, 202; Huber, "Account," 5; Benjamin J. Haden, *Reminiscences of J.E.B. Stuart's Cavalry* (Charlottesville, VA, 1912), 63. The reference to Lord Cardigan is, of course, to the charge of the Light Brigade at the battle of Balaklava in the Crimean War.

34 Robert J. Driver, Jr., and Harold E. Howard, *2nd Virginia Cavalry* (Lynchburg, VA, 1995), 90; Swank, *Saddles, Sabres, and Spurs*, 71; Huber, "The Real Facts"; Wilson, *Captain Charles Corbit's Charge*, 17.

Pennsylvania Avenue. The adjutant escaped by running and jumping his thoroughbred to safety down the Baltimore Pike. Once clear of the town's confines, he hightailed it to the safety of Reisterstown. Lieutenant William J. Reedy had two horses shot from under him and only escaped from Lee's troopers by mounting the animal of a comrade who had been shot dead by his side. A pistol ball passed through the rim of Lt. D. W. C. Clark's hat, and his arm was badly bruised by the side stroke of a Virginia saber.[35]

Lieutenant Caleb Churchman and his men of Company D were deployed on the north end of town. They pitched into the fray once they spotted Company C's plight. These Delawareans also fought desperately in a hand-to-hand mêlée that raged through the streets of Westminster. Two of them were killed during this fighting. A member of the 4th Virginia's Company K recalled that the Yankees "fought like Turks, killing a good number of our best men, but strange to say our company, which was in front, lost none. Companies C and D, which came to our relief, lost several good officers and some men."[36]

Lieutenant St. Pierre Gibson, a member of the 4th Virginia's Company D (Little Fork Rangers) of Culpeper County, Virginia, could usually be found at the head of his company when it went into battle. "Give me some crackers, boys, I'll do your fighting for you," he quipped as the Rangers formed to charge. "Lieutenant Gibson, too proud and too brave to yield an inch, maintains his position alone," recounted a civilian who watched the Virginian's duel in the streets. "In an instant, scores of foes were around him, and pistols blazed in his face; but his enemies awed by his stern and defiant courage, for a few moments dared not approach within striking distance of his terrible sword-arm." Alas, the officer's reckless bravery caught up with him in the streets of Westminster. A Delaware sergeant rode straight at Gibson, "a pistol flash, and a bluecoat rolled in the dust dead; another flash, and the gallant Southerner also fell shot through the brain." Gibson toppled from his horse in front of an undertaker's office; his horse somehow made it back to Fitz Lee's camp.[37]

Lieutenant John W. Murray of Company C, 4th Virginia Cavalry, also rode at the head of his charging troopers. When he and his men came together with Lieutenant Churchman's Company D, Murray lifted his sword arm and began

35 Ibid., 27-28; *Baltimore American*, June 30 and July 3, 1863.

36 Woodford B. Hackley, *The Little Fork Rangers: A Sketch of Company D Fourth Virginia Cavalry* (Richmond, 1927), 100.

37 Ibid., 100; Account of I. Everett Pearson, in Klein, *Just South of Gettysburg*, 69.

slashing his saber right and left. "Alas, for the noble brave!" recalled Everett Pearson of Westminster, who watched the fighting raging in the streets. "Just as the first flush of victory had crowned his gallantry he too fell." One of Stuart's staff officers believed that Gibson and Murray were "among the best" officers of the 4th Virginia and would be sorely missed. "Gallant and meritorious, they were noble sacrifices to the cause," lamented Stuart.[38]

Joe Stallard, another trooper with Gibson's Little Fork Rangers, was chasing a Yankee horseman when the Northerner abandoned his horse and took refuge in a nearby home. The owner of the house refused to turn his new guest over to the Confederates, but when Stallard threatened to burn down the place he reluctantly complied. Few of the men of the 1st Delaware Cavalry escaped the dragnet cast by Fitz Lee's Virginians.[39]

"The enemy having been so heavily re-enforced, drove the two companies back to the main pike, the men of my command fighting all the time with the greatest bravery and determination, and contending hotly for every inch of ground," was how Major Knight explained the debacle. The rookies had indeed fought well in the face of overwhelming odds. "I cannot close this report without calling your attention to the bravery and intrepidity of the officers and men of my command, whose efficiency and determination of purpose has saved us from utter annihilation." Whatever credit the 1st Delaware Cavalry deserved that day went to Capt. Charles Corbit, whose courage and willingness to assume command briefly halted Stuart's advance. Stuart's adjutant Maj. Henry B. McClellan, who described the resistance of the 1st Delaware Cavalry as "brief but stubborn," was less charitable regarding Major Knight's decision-making, which he called "more gallant than judicious."[40]

Soon after the skirmish Knight learned of the Confederate flanking column on Ridge Road advancing on his rear. The news prompted him to fall back via the Reisterstown Road. Knight ordered Lieutenant Churchman and the survivors of his company to cover the retreat. Churchman's company still had plenty of fight left and contested every step. The skirmishing was so brisk the company lost all but seven of its men and Churchman joined Corbit as a prisoner of war. Knight and his handful of survivors fell back to Reisterstown while elements of Lee's brigade followed. Once there, Knight ordered a lieutenant with the 1st Connecticut Cavalry

---

38 Pearson account, 69; McClellan, *Life and Campaigns of Stuart*, 326; OR 27, pt. 2, 202.

39 Hackley, *Little Fork Rangers*, 100.

40 OR 27, pt. 2, 202; McClellan, *Life and Campaigns of Stuart*, 326.

to hold the pursuers in check while Knight rallied his little force on the south side of town. Knight also directed Lieutenant Reedy, who was now in command of the shattered remnant of Company C, to push on, corral, and turn back seven or eight fugitives who were about a mile in advance. Reedy tried but could not rally the panicked greenhorns, who fled to safety in Baltimore with the lieutenant accompanying them. "The fugitives were pursued a long distance on the Baltimore road, and I afterward heard created great panic in the city, impressing the authorities that we were just on at their heels," crowed Jeb Stuart in his after-action report.[41]

Major Knight, whose entourage had been whittled down to Adjutant Lobdell, another lieutenant, and two enlisted men, halted his retreat about one mile from the town. Knight was determined to return to Reisterstown, which they would then occupy. The major was making his dispositions to confront another attack when a courier spurred up with a dispatch from General Schenck. The 1st Delaware was to return to Baltimore forthwith. Knight and his survivors willingly complied with the order, leaving behind 67 men killed, wounded, and missing, including Corbit and Churchman. The 1st Delaware also lost a wagon laden with hospital supplies, camp and garrison equipment, and the regimental books and papers. The Confederates also captured Lt. Pulaski Bowman and his detachment of the 150th New York Infantry, all of whom they took along when they departed.[42]

The balance of Jeb Stuart's command passed slowly through the streets of Westminster. "Some of the regiments marched by in silence, others sang familiar ballads as they marched along," recalled a local watching the spectacle. "A few riotously disposed shrieked, whistled and cheered. The flags were nearly all folded, the bugles made no sound, the orders were few and short, and there was an immediate lack of that pomp and pageantry which all expected to see in an army." The hard truth soon set in: "It was very evident that the men meant 'business' and not play."[43]

A handful of Southern troopers foraged in town and, to the disgust of the merchants, paid for their prizes with Confederate money. "The men got hats, boots, shoes & such things as they needed," observed one of Fitz Lee's officers. Stuart's troopers fanned out and generously helped themselves to whatever bounty they could find. Fitch's dry goods store was completely gutted. Bowen & Gehr,

41 OR 27, pt. 2, 202, 695.

42 Ibid., 202, 695.

43 Hering account, in Klein, *Just South of Gettysburg*, 64-65.

commission merchants at the depot, suffered heavily, as did Meixell & Orndorf, which lost about $700 in flour and feed.[44]

When some of Stuart's men spotted the Federal flag flying above the cupola of the county courthouse, they ascended the steps and happily tore the banner down. Thirteen local ladies had sewn the oversized flag and had signed their names on its stars, so the loss was particularly devastating for the Westminster civilians. Other troopers destroyed railroad property to deny this critical resource to the advancing Union infantry.[45]

Stuart triumphantly entered the town in the wake of his weary horsemen, who had been riding and fighting for days. "Here, for the first time since leaving Rector's Cross-Roads, we obtained a full supply of forage, but the delay and difficulty of procuring it kept many of the men up all night," Stuart admitted in his campaign report. "Several flags and one piece of artillery without a carriage were captured here. The latter was spiked and left behind." The cavalrymen welcomed the respite offered by a comfortable campsite a few miles north of Westminster. According to local legend, Stuart was riding along his column on East Main Street when a saucy little girl named Mary Shellman announced that the Southern cavalry chief was a "Johnny Red Coat." Stuart is said to have stopped his horse and informed the little lady that punishment would be summarily meted out for her brash display of loyalty to the Union: a kiss. Motioning for her to approach, the cavalier leaned over and scooped her up. "The kiss delivered, the general moved on," the legend concluded, with Stuart leaving in his wake a slightly embarrassed and thoroughly charmed Maryland girl.[46]

Having meted out Mary's punishment, Stuart's first order of business in Westminster was a call for his commanders to assemble. On the east side of the old City Hotel, Stuart, Fitz Lee, John Chambliss, and Wade Hampton huddled to decide their next course of action. Once the council of war concluded, Stuart took tea at the home of John C. Frysee, a Southern-sympathizing cashier with the Westminster Bank, enjoying "all the honors" his cheerful host could bestow. The cavalry general, recalled a citizen who got a good look at the cavalry chieftain, "seemed to have a heavy load of care on his mind, and whilst at tea it was noticed

44 Swank, *Saddles, Sabres, and Spurs*, 73; *Baltimore American*, July 2, 1863.

45 Carroll County Visitor Center, "Corbit's Charge."

46 OR 27, pt. 2, 695; Susan Cooke Soderberg, *A Guide to Civil War Sites in Maryland: Blue and Gray in a Border State* (Shippensburg, PA, 1986), 45.

that, though at times full of spirits, he occasionally grew abstracted and thoughtful."[47]

Stuart told the assembly that he expected the decisive battle of the war would soon occur. "General Stuart," his host inquired, "do you have any doubt about the outcome of the battle of which you spoke?" "None at all," he responded. "I have the utmost confidence in our men, and I know that if they are given a ghost of a chance they are sure to win."[48]

While Stuart counseled with his officers and enjoyed tea, others tended to the dead and wounded in the streets of Westminster. The two dead men from Delaware, Cpl. William Vandegrift and Pvt. Daniel Welsh, were buried in temporary graves at the Old Union Church, which also served as a hospital for the wounded of both sides. Late in the afternoon of June 29, local women asked Stuart for permission to bury Confederate lieutenants Murray and Gibson. The appreciative general readily agreed, and "the bodies of these young heroes were left in their charge." The ladies carefully tended to the remains and laid them to rest in the graveyard of Ascension Episcopal Church. Murray was buried under a marked tombstone, while Gibson's body was placed in an unmarked grave next to him. Two years after the war, Gibson's body was claimed and removed to Virginia. Murray's body rests in the church graveyard to this day.[49]

It was approaching midnight before Stuart and his command extricated themselves and rode north to Union Mills, a small settlement on Little Pipe Creek that featured a large grist mill. Two brothers, Andrew and William Shriver, ran the mill. William was a Confederate sympathizer while Andrew was a strong Unionist whose was in the 26th Pennsylvania Volunteer Militia in Harrisburg. The Confederate cavalrymen spread out and made themselves at home. For the second time in three days a brave but foolhardy charge by a small detachment of Union cavalry had cost Stuart both casualties and time. The visit to Westminster had set Stuart's schedule back yet another full day.

*　*　*

---

47 Hering and Pearson accounts, in Klein, *Just South of Gettysburg*, 64-65, 72; *Baltimore American*, July 2, 1863.

48 Pearson account, 72.

49 *Baltimore American*, July 3, 1863.

Stuart and his troopers were in Westminster when Brig. Gen. Beverly H. Robertson received orders from Robert E. Lee to leave one regiment of his command to picket south of the Potomac and to report to him. Robertson left Ashby's Gap that evening, finally on the move executing the orders left him by Stuart. His brigade and Grumble Jones's command would not reach the Army of Northern Virginia until the morning of July 3. Had Robertson obeyed Stuart's orders, both brigades would have rejoined the Virginia army in Chambersburg in time to lead the infantry's advance toward Gettysburg on the morning of July 1. Instead he had dillydallied for days, meaning that Lee would march out of Chambersburg on July 1 without a cavalry escort.[50]

* * *

In Richmond, meanwhile, Confederate authorities remained alarmed about the actions of Maj. Gen. John A. Dix's army on the Peninsula. "General Lee wants [Gen. P. G. T.] Beauregard to collect an army in Virginia to protect his communications," observed war department clerk Robert Kean in his diary. "It will hardly be attempted." Kean also noted, "There is some stir about the command here. [Secretary of War James A. Seddon] has directed an order assigning Hill (D. H.). [Adjutant General Samuel] Cooper brought it back and told him he had better see the President before issuing it as he thought the President had other views," he continued. "I have not heard the issue." Kean concluded by observing that Seddon knew from prior observation that Maj. Gen. Arnold Elzey, commander of the defenses of Richmond during the Stoneman Raid during the Chancellorsville campaign, was "wholly incompetent."[51]

News about the recent command change in the Army of the Potomac quickly spread throughout the North.

50 Mosby, *Stuart's Cavalry in the Gettysburg Campaign*, 200-201. Robertson would be relieved of command at the end of the Gettysburg campaign and never lead troops of the Army of Northern Virginia again. That October, he was assigned to command the Second Subdistrict of the Military District of South Carolina. Robertson spent the rest of the war in the Carolinas and surrendered with Gen. Joseph E. Johnston in late April 1865.

51 Younger, *Inside the Confederate Government*, 78-79.

"But, alas! it was Hooker's army no longer," lamented a correspondent for the *Cincinnati Gazette* stationed in the nation's capital. "Washington was all a-buzz with the removal. A few idol-worshippers hissed their exultation at the constructive disgrace; but for the most part, there was astonishment at the unprecedented act and indignation at the one cause to which all attributed it. . . . Never before, in the history of modern warfare, had there been such a case," continued the outraged reporter. "There was little regret for Hooker personally; it was only the national sense of fair play that was outraged."[52]

A *Chicago Tribune* editorial pondered whether the nation was "as well prepared as we should be for possible disasters." It was a legitimate concern. Would Meade be up to the challenge under such incredibly difficult circumstances, particularly since he neither wanted nor sought the weighty command?[53]

Major Henry Livermore Abbott of the 20th Massachusetts Infantry, a popular and competent Harvard-trained soldier, left behind an especially good description of Meade written just a few days after he assumed command of the army. "In person," began Livermore, "Meade is a tall, thin, lantern-jawed, respectable [man] wearing spectacles, looking a good sort of a family doctor. Uncle John Sedgwick, as have most other of our good officers, long ago told us that McClellan was the first choice, [Maj. Gen. William B.] Franklin the 2nd & Meade the 3rd. An extremely good officer you see, with no vanity or nonsense of any kind, knowing just exactly what he could do & what he couldn't." Abbott concluded that nearly everyone in the Army of the Potomac was "elated" by Hooker's removal.[54]

Abbott's anecdotal assumption aside, not everyone approved of Meade's appointment. A civilian from Louisville, Kentucky, reflected the opinions of many in and out of the army in a telegram to President Lincoln: "Call McClellan to the head of the armies of the Government, [Maj. Gen. Don Carlos] Buell to command of Army of the Potomac, and [Maj. Gen. William B.] Franklin to Army of the Cumberland. There will be no necessity for draft. Volunteers will enlist by thousands. Rebellion will be crushed in ninety days." Many of the Army of the Potomac's soldiers clamored for the return to command of their old hero, George B. McClellan. In fact, men cheered when rumors flew that "Little Mac" was soon to

52 "The Battles of Gettysburgh: *Cincinnati Gazette* Account," in Moore, *Rebellion Record*, 7:84-85.

53 *Chicago Tribune*, July 2, 1863.

54 Robert Garth Scott, ed., *Fallen Leaves: The Civil War Letters of Major Henry Livermore Abbott* (Kent, OH, 1991), 189.

be back in command. Confirmation that it was Meade, who was largely unknown to the rank and file of the army outside the V Corps, who now held the reins of power did little to restore their confidence in the army's high command.[55]

* * *

The men of what was now George Meade's army trudged northward on muddy roads, at times finding cheer despite the ever-changing weather. "Monday morning it rained," wrote a soldier in the 137th New York. "At an early hour we passed through Frederick city, taking the road northward for Pa. A few of the most patriotic in the city were up, and the old stars and stripes waved from their windows, proudly on the morning air. One, an old man whose head was silvered o'er with the snows of many winters, was waving the dear old flag. All honor to the brave old patriot."[56]

Two of the corps, the I and the XI, marched from Frederick to Emmitsburg. "Soon after the [I] corps came to a halt for the night," Maj. Thomas Chamberlin of the 150th Pennsylvania recounted, "some practical joker quietly spread the report that the Mother Superior of the convent in the outskirts of the town had invited all the commissioned officers to a reception, with suitable refreshments, to be held in the main building of the institution that evening." Most who heard the story "instantly recognized it as absurdity," but a few men "were foolish enough to go back into the town and prowl around the convent, which of course they found shrouded in darkness."[57]

Hancock's II Corps made the "the longest march in its history," according to the 19th Maine's John Day Smith. After tramping for almost four hours from Monocacy Junction toward Liberty and Johnsville, Brig. Gen. William Harrow's brigade encountered a knee-deep ford on a steep-banked creek. Someone had thrown a hand-hewn, flat-topped log across the creek as a "very respectable crossing for pedestrians" if they crossed single-file—a time-consuming endeavor.

---

55 *OR* 27, 3:410. All three officers named—McClellan, Buell, and Franklin—had been relieved of command after failures in the field. McClellan, of course, had been let go in the fall of 1862, Buell led the Army of the Ohio before it was merged into the Army of the Tennessee, and Franklin commanded one of Maj. Gen. Ambrose E. Burnside's Grand Divisions during the Fredericksburg campaign. All were in disfavor with the administration.

56 "Letter from the 137th," *Onondaga Standard* (Syracuse, NY), July 25, 1863.

57 Chamberlin, *History of the One Hundred and Fiftieth Regiment Pennsylvania Volunteers*, 115-116.

The officers ordered the men to wade across, and the column began bunching together as soldiers halted to remove their shoes and stockings and roll up their trousers. Others scurried to the side and ran over the log crossing. One of division commander Brig. Gen. John Gibbon's staff officers rode back and forth urging the regimental officers to compel their men to ford the creek instead of using the log. When the 1st Minnesota's Col. William Colvill took compassion on his men and allowed them to use the dry crossing, he found himself under arrest.[58]

Straggling remained a significant issue. "Long before night fell most of the troops were fagged out and kept moving only under great suffering," recalled a captain in the 1st Delaware Infantry named William P. Seville. "They were informed that it was regarded as of the utmost importance that the command should reach Uniontown that night, and the men endured their hardships with commendable fortitude." Near the end of what Seville called "this memorable march," the column halted for a brief rest and a general and his staff trotted past. One of the Delaware men yelled, "Oh, don't stop! Get fresh horses and let's go ahead. We are not tired." The announcement was greeted with laughter "loud and long, in which the general joined. After this, whenever the column halted, many voices would shout, 'Why don't you get fresh horses?'"[59]

As soldiers in every army throughout history have been wont to do, some found humor in their otherwise wearisome trek. The 5th New Hampshire's Lt. Thomas L. Livermore remarked, "The very names of the towns we passed through were reviving, such as Liberty, Uniontown, etc., and they seemed almost like New England in their neatness. I recollect a negro," continued Livermore, "who had come from Virginia with us, as he trudged along beside the ranks, and who hearing some one inquire how far it was to Liberty, said, with a broad grin, 'It's a long way to liberty, sah!'"[60]

Most of Col. George L. Willard's men were captured at Harpers Ferry in mid-September of 1862 and held as prisoners thereafter. Their reputation suffered as a result, evoking the derisive moniker "Harpers Ferry Cowards." After being paroled and transported to Camp Douglas in Chicago, the brigade eventually returned to

58 Smith, *The History of the Nineteenth Regiment of Maine Volunteer Infantry*, 61-62.

59 William P. Seville, *History of the First Regiment, Delaware Volunteers* (Dover, DE, 1884), 79.

60 Thomas L. Livermore, *Days and Events, 1860–1866* (Boston, 1920), 235. Livermore was a native of Illinois but would become perhaps the most famous historian from the state of New Hampshire, mostly because of his invaluable reference book *Numbers and Losses in the Civil War in America, 1861-1865* (New York, 1900).

Virginia. It marched out of Centreville on June 13 and had recently joined Brig. Gen. Alexander Hays's II Corps division.

"The army seldom made a longer march in a single day: from Monocacy to Liberty—to Johnsville—to Union Bridge—to Uniontown, Maryland, a distance of thirty-three miles," recalled the 125th New York's chaplain Ezra D. Simons after the war. "There was no halting for meals. No coffee was cooked that day. Ere the camp was reached men fell out on the way by hundreds. When far into the night the head of the column halted at the appointed place, only a handful lay down to rest—to sleep, regardless of the rain which fell on our uncovered faces." General Gibbon found a creative way to reward two regiments in his division and improver morale when he excused the 15th and 19th Massachusetts from picket duty and other outside details "for marching to-day in the best and most compact order, and with the least straggling from their ranks."[61]

The hard marching moved the Army of the Potomac much closer to the Rebels, and many soldiers began to think seriously about the prospects of a fight and their fates. That night, Capt. Edgar A. Burpee of the 19th Maine, part of General Harrow's command, shared a shelter tent with Capt. George D. Smith. "I think we are on the eve of a terrible battle and I feel that I shall be killed or wounded," confessed Smith. "Don't think that way," Burpee admonished. "We all feel as if we might get hit." Smith could not be moved from his heavy thoughts. "No," he replied, "but I have a presentment that something is going to happen to me and I hope I shall be prepared to die."[62]

The 141st Pennsylvania of Brig. Gen. Charles Graham's brigade, III Corps, was on the road at 7:00 a.m. The Keystone men marched north and northeast some 20 miles through Woodsboro and Middleburg before camping a mile beyond Taneytown. Chaplain David Craft mentioned that "the regiment was detailed as rear guard to the corps, whose duty was to pick up all stragglers and help them forward to their respective companies, a task both difficult and unpleasant. This was particularly the case on this day's march," he continued, "since a considerable number of the men belonging to other commands got their canteens filled with

---

61 Ezra D. Simons, *A Regimental History: The One Hundredth and Twenty-fifth New York State Volunteers* (New York, 1888), 85; Abijah P. Marvin, *History of Worcester in the War of the Rebellion* (Cleveland, 1870), 191. The 15th Massachusetts was in Brig. Gen. William Harrow's brigade, and the 19th in Col. Thomas Hall's brigade, both in the II Corps.

62 Smith, *History of the Nineteenth Regiment of Maine Volunteer Infantry*, 56-57. Three days later, Captain Smith died at Gettysburg.

whisky, became intoxicated and were left behind because they were too drunk to travel."[63]

When the 12th New Hampshire of Brig. Gen. Joseph Carr's brigade reached Taneytown at 6:00 p.m., Asa Bartlett rejoiced. "It was immediately detailed for provost duty, which gave its members the freedom of the town, while the other troops, encamped outside, were not allowed to enter," recalled the III Corps soldier. "This was rare good luck for the boys, who had long before learned by experience the great advantage of being at the head instead of in the rear of a moving column, and who quite as quickly appreciated a change of army fare for the more relishable, if not as healthy, doughnuts, cakes, and pies with which the glad citizens freely supplied them."[64]

Edwin Houghton, a lieutenant in the 17th Maine, part of Col P. Régis de Trobriand's brigade, recalled the enthusiastic reception. "Ladies and young girls distributed beautiful bouquets of flowers to the officers and soldiers; groups of fair damsels, bewitchingly posted in conspicuous places, sang patriotic airs, as the 'boys in blue' marched by, and the passage of troops being a novelty, the citizens turned out en masse. Long after tattoo," he continued, "groups of ladies and gentlemen were promenading through our camps, actuated by a curiosity to see how soldiers really lived in the 'tented field.'" The 141st Pennsylvania's Sgt. J. D. Bloodgood, from a different brigade in the same division, agreed: "That night our camp was thronged with citizens—largely ladies—and they gave us a most cordial reception. Two little girls sang 'Maryland, My Maryland,' and other patriotic songs, which greatly cheered and encouraged us."[65]

Meade's former V Corps, now in its first full day of duty under Maj. Gen. George Sykes, marched toward Frederick. A soldier in the 118th Pennsylvania, Col. William S. Tilton's brigade, thought the trek northward "a parade occasion." The

---

63 Craft, *History of the One Hundred Forty-first Regiment, Pennsylvania Volunteers,* 111-112. Sgt. J. D. Bloodgood, also of the 141st Pennsylvania, recalled the effect the whiskey had on the men that same day: "Previous to the day's march there had been little straggling, especially since crossing the Potomac, but by some means a considerable number of the boys in the corps had procured whiskey, and instead of it being a help to them on the march, it proved to be a hindrance, for they grew very tired before they had gone a half dozen miles. Some of them were too drunk to travel and had to be left behind." "Personal Reminiscences of the War, Rev. J. D. Bloodgood, Ph. B," *Northern Christian Advocate* (Syracuse, NY), July 18, 1889.

64 Bartlett, *History of the Twelfth Regiment, New Hampshire,* 118.

65 Houghton, *Campaigns of the Seventeenth Maine,* 84; Bloodgood, "Personal Reminiscences of the War."

citizens, he recalled, "lined the sidewalks and crowded the windows. The reception was generous and the people demonstrative." At 2:00 p.m., the column passed through Mount Pleasant and then halted five hours later past Liberty in Frederick County.[66]

The Pennsylvania Reserves passed noisily through Union Town, "where a pontoon train that accompanied us that day created much wonderment among the rustics, who did not believe we could do much with our 'gun boats' up in the mountains," mocked the 2nd regiment's Adjutant E. M. Woodward. The 22nd Massachusetts, also part of Tilton's brigade, bivouacked about a mile from Frederick near the cemetery and Ballenger's Creek. "Again the spires of Frederick town, in the Monocacy Valley, greeted our eyes, and in the bright sunlight of the beautiful June morning," Sgt. John W. Reed recalled. Everything looked "beautiful and refreshing . . . surrounded by smiling grain-fields, green trees, mountain background, intervening meadows and valleys, which so strikingly mark this lovely region."[67]

Sedgwick's VI Corps departed Hyattstown and paused in Frederick. According to Pvt. Leonard G. Jordan of the 10th Maine Battalion (the headquarters guard detachment), "The few hours spent in Frederick sufficed to pour out whiskey in great abundance, and the army of the Potomac was probably never more generally drunk than at that time. It is well that the disgusting scene was never repeated." The corps tramped on through Newmarket and Ridgeville before halting for the night near New Windsor.[68]

Henry Slocum's XII Corps left Frederick and tramped to Taneytown and Bruceville, while General Meade moved with his headquarters staff from Frederick to Middleburg. As the provost guard, elements of the 93rd New York marched between Woodbury and Middleburg, with "the roadway . . . bordered by tall cherry trees, hanging full of luscious fruit," recalled a soldier. "The mature trees were soon filled with as many soldiers as its limbs could bear. After eating their fill, the tree climbers kindly threw down well-laden boughs to those men waiting below. For some time," he continued,

> Brigadier General Robert O. Tyler of the Army of the Potomac's Reserve Artillery had been seated on a horse block. Seeing a heavily laden branch fall near him, he reached for it.

66 *History of the 118th Pennsylvania,* 232.

67 Woodward, *Our Campaigns,* 262; Parker and Carter, *Henry Wilson's War,* 328.

68 Jordan, "History of the Tenth Maine Battalion," 353.

He grabbed it just as a private of the 20th Indiana named Meacham was about to pick it up. The latter, unaware of the rank of his successful rival, savagely kicked the general's posterior and sent him sprawling in the mud and knocking Tyler's spectacles off. The laughing of the bystanders seemed to enrage the general more than the unexpected kick, and he ordered the offender to be placed under guard until evening. However, during the march, Meacham disappeared and no one heard any more of the incident (or him).[69]

The new commander of the Army of the Potomac handed a courier dispatches for Generals Gregg and Halleck and ordered him to ride to the telegraph station in Glen Rock, Pennsylvania, along the line of the Northern Central Railway. The messenger crossed the state line and picked his way through hilly southern York County to avoid roving Confederates. At 9:00 p.m. he paused for dinner in the hamlet of Marburg and set off alone in the darkness. The unfamiliar country roads soon confused him, and he stopped after midnight at a farmhouse near Green Ridge to ask directions. The German-speaking farmer, George Bear, mistakenly believed the rider was a Rebel and, fearing for his family's safety, shot him. When Bear searched the body and discovered the dispatches, he realized his tragic error and later surrendered to the authorities. The unlucky courier, a New Yorker, was buried in the graveyard of nearby Stone Church.[70]

The command change from Hooker to Meade dominated the conversations that night around the campfires. "The most of us were not very greatly concerned in the change," shrugged Sgt. J. D. Bloodgood of the 141st Pennsylvania, "for changes had occurred so often that we had hardly had time to become very much attached to any one of them. Besides," added the III Corps soldier, "Hooker had failed at Chancellorsville, not through any fault of his, only that he had placed an incompetent officer in charge of a most important point, and he had brought disaster upon the whole army." Bloodgood admitted that he and his comrades did not know much about Meade, "and didn't spend any time in looking up his history.

---

69 David H. King, A. Judson Gibbs, and Jay H. Northup, *History of the Ninety-third Regiment, New York Volunteer Infantry, 1861–1865* (Milwaukee, 1895), 402. The 20th Indiana belonged to Brig. Gen. Hobart Ward's brigade, David Birney's division, Sickles's III Corps. Meacham may have been a fake name, for there is no one on the roster of the 20th Indiana by that name.

70 George R. Prowell, *History of York County, Pennsylvania*, 2 vols. (York, PA, 1907), 1:954. The slain courier was likely Pvt. Jacob G. Otto of the 6th New York Cavalry. Local records indicate that his father traveled from New York and disinterred his son's remains for reburial in his hometown. A military tribunal in Frederick acquitted Bear that August and allowed him to return home. Now a broken man, Bear sold his mill and farm in 1864 and retired. Green Ridge is now known as Brodbecks.

All we wanted was a fair chance at Lee's army and we felt confident that we could demolish it."[71]

Long after the war, the 121st New York's Lt. Delevan Bates, who had been part of Joseph J. Bartlett brigade, Horatio Wright's division, VI Corps, commented with hindsight that "Gen. Hooker was relieved from command and General George G. Meade was placed at the head of the army. He apparently had a well-defined idea of what he wanted the army to do—It was to get into Pennsylvania at the earliest possible date, and fight the rebel army wherever we struck them."[72]

* * *

The opinionated and constantly fretting secretary of the navy, Gideon Welles, was worried but cautiously optimistic. A leadership change atop the country's most prominent field command in the middle of a campaign was a grave risk. "Great apprehension prevails. The change of commanders is thus far well received," he scribbled in his diary. "No regret is expressed that Hooker has been relieved. This is because of the rumor of his habits, the reputation that he is intemperate, for his military reputation is higher than that of his successor. Meade has not so much character as such a command requires. He is, however, kindly favored; will be well supported, have the best wishes of all, but does not inspire immediate confidence. A little time may improve this, and give him name and fame."[73]

While Welles was writing in his journal, Secretary of the Treasury Salmon P. Chase was penning a lengthy letter to his daughter and confidante Kate. "You must have been greatly astonished by the relieving of General Hooker; but your astonishment cannot have exceeded mine," he assured her. "He was relieved at his own request and request must have been very suddenly resolved on; for his telegram asking to be relieved was dated at eight on Saturday night; and I received one from Butterfield dated at Six or half past suggesting some military movements in Virginia in which there was not the slightest allusion to Hooker's purpose. What prompted his request," Chase confessed, "I do not know. I did not hear of it nor of

---

71 Bloodgood, "Personal Reminiscences of the War."

72 "The March to Gettysburg," *Otsego* (NY) *Republican*, Jan. 20, 1894.

73 Welles, *Diary*, 1:351.

the appointment of Gen. Meade in his place till Sunday, when at a Meeting of the Heads called for a different purpose, having no connection with Hooker's affairs, the President mentioned it to us." Chase added that Meade was preferred by a majority of officers to anyone except Hooker, and perhaps even more than Hooker. Although Meade was "taken entirely by surprise, [he] accepted it in a modest telegram and at once entered on his duties."

Secretary Chase took a moment to describe the military situation to Kate. "There has been a good deal of alarm here yesterday and today because of the enemy's cavalry coming very close to the city with supposed designs on the Washington & Baltimore & Baltimore & Ohio Railroads," he began. "I should not be surprised by the cutting of either or both of them, but I attach no great consequence to these raids." He continued:

> While the rebels are doing these things near Washington we are doing the same things near Richmond; where you have doubtless seen a detachment from Gen. Dix's command on Friday or Saturday burnt the bridge across the South [Anna] & captured Gen. W. F. Lee, other officers & privates & many mules & wagons. Still these things are pleasanter to do than to suffer. There is of course a great deal of concern about the military operations of the two great armies; a concern naturally increased by the action of Gen. Hooker. In respect to these I hope [for] the best, and trust in God. If our cause is just & right will He not bless it? Will He suffer the cause to fail because of the unworthiness of those who sustain it?[74]

*   *   *

John Buford detached the Reserve Brigade of cavalry, which was now commanded by his newly promoted protégé Wesley Merritt. Pursuant to Pleasonton's orders, Buford sent the brigade to Mechanicsville (modern-day Thurmont, Maryland) to escort the division's wagon trains, protect the rear, and bring up stragglers.

Buford's 1st and 2nd Brigades left at 9:00 a.m., riding out along the National Road. The long column of cavalry headed for Cavetown and Monterey Springs, Maryland, along the base of South Mountain, riding toward Pennsylvania via the Monterey Pass. Few knew the long day's ride would be so pleasant and beautiful. The journey, declared Maj. John Beveridge, "was the most delightful of my army

74 Nevin, *The Salmon P. Chase Papers*, 4:72-73.

Brig. Gen. Wesley Merritt commanded the Reserve Brigade of Buford's division of Union cavalry in the Army of the Potomac.

LOC

life. The day was perfect; the roads were good. We passed over the mountains twice, and had charming views."[75]

When the long column of dusty horsemen reached the Mason-Dixon line, the guidon carrier of Company G of the 17th Pennsylvania Cavalry, Devin's brigade, sat astride the line and announced to each company as it passed that it was entering the soil of their home state of Pennsylvania. The men of the 17th "raised their caps and lustily cheered, again and again, for the old Keystone State and Old Glory." "We crossed the Pennsylvania line in the afternoon, soon coming again into the mountains, beholding some wild and beautiful scenery, and receiving cordial expressions of pleasure from the inhabitants along the route," recounted a member of the 8th New York Cavalry. "We heard of the movements of the enemy all the way, they having passed through two or three days previous, seizing all the valuable horses they could find, but doing little other damage." The march north through Maryland was almost joyous. "As we came along up from the Potomac, each town we passed through had flags flying and citizens crowding the

---

75 The Reserve Brigade consisted of about 1,700 men present for duty on June 29, but its officer corps had been decimated. The brigade lost 21 of its 52 officers during this period, leaving only one officer per company. Don Caughey, the historian of the Reserve Brigade, did an analysis of the reasons why the Regulars were sent to Mechanicsville over Buford's objections. "Why was the Reserve Brigade guarding wagon trains? The answer is simply attrition, of officers even more than enlisted men," he wrote. "By the end of June 1863, the brigade was simply fought out, and needed a day or two to reorganize before returning to the fight. During the preceding two months, each of its regiments averaged losses in excess of 15% of their enlisted strength and nearly half of their officers." Don Caughey, "Reserve Brigade Attrition in the Gettysburg Campaign," http://regularcavalryincivilwar.wordpress.com/2013 /06/20/reserve-brigade-attrition-in-the-gettysburg-campaign/ last accessed Dec. 9. 2022.

streets," recalled Eli Ditzler of the 8th Illinois Cavalry. "The ladies waved their handkerchiefs and the air was rent with cheer after cheer. Made me feel homesick to see how happy free people were."[76]

As the 1st Division drew closer to Gettysburg, Buford's attention turned to his primary mission of gathering as much intelligence as possible about the disposition of the enemy. The command rode into the village of Fountaindale, situated at the eastern end of the important South Mountain route known as Monterey Pass. To their delight, Buford's troopers found the area abounding "in forage and water for our jaded horses." The tired men led their mounts up "the long ascending road, winding its way around the sides of the rocky cliffs for over two miles until we reached the summit of the pass, and here we passed an institution of health called Monterey Springs." They camped at the base of South Mountain after having ridden nearly 40 miles that day.[77]

Many troopers recorded seeing an old man standing with his hat in his hand and tears streaming down his face as they trotted past. Buford and some of his staff rode to the top of nearby Jack's Mountain, where the general took in the spectacular view of the Cumberland Valley. He gazed long and hard and did not like what he saw. Stretched out across the valley was a carpet of flickering Confederate campfires. Speaking to no one in particular, Buford announced, "Within forty-eight hours the concentration of both armies will take place on a field within view and a great battle will be fought."[78]

---

76 Beveridge, "The First Gun at Gettysburg," 88; Moyer, *History of the Seventeenth Regiment*, 48; "Genesee," "From the 8th Cavalry—List of Killed and Wounded," *Rochester Daily Union and Advertiser*, July 9, 1863; Winfield Scott Hall, *The Captain: William Cross Hazelton* (Riverside, IL, 1994), 40-41. It is worth noting that Buford did not obey Pleasonton's orders for the march into Pennsylvania. Pleasonton had directed Buford to ride from Middletown through Beallsville, Wolfsville, and then Emmitsburg. Instead, Buford traveled a route farther west through Boonsboro and Cavetown, Maryland, and then on to Monterey Springs and Fountaindale. Buford never explained why he diverged from Pleasonton's prescribed route, and Pleasonton never mentioned the lack of compliance with his orders. Pleasonton and Buford knew each other very well, having served together in the old 2nd Dragoons for more than a decade before the Civil War. In all likelihood, Pleasonton trusted Buford to carry out the spirit, if not necessarily the letter, of his orders. OR 27, pt. 3, 400-401 and pt. 1, 926.

77 Frank diary, entry for June 30, 1863; Anonymous letter by a member of the 8th Illinois Cavalry, *Aurora Beacon*, Aug. 20, 1863; Chapman diary, entry for June 29, 1863.

78 Col. George H. Sharpe to J. Watts DePuyster, Aug. 15, 1867, quoted in J. Watts DePuyster, *Decisive Conflicts of the Civil War* (New York, 1867), 30; Lt. Col. Theo. Bean, "Address at the Dedication of the 17th Pennsylvania Cavalry Monument of September 11, 1889," *Pennsylvania at Gettysburg*, 2 vols. (Harrisburg, PA, 1904), 2:858.

"By the examination of a local map obtained in the neighborhood, the remarkable convergence of broad highways at Gettysburg was first clearly disclosed to the officers in command, and indicated the approximate field of the coming conflict," recalled Lt. Col. Theodore W. Bean of the 17th Pennsylvania Cavalry. "To this point, under general instructions, Buford hastened and directed his next day's march."[79]

Once down from the mountain, Buford and his troopers camped two miles from Fairfield. Lieutenant John H. Calef, commanding the battery of horse artillery assigned to Buford, described the day's march as "very long and fatiguing . . . horses very much used up." Both men and animals welcomed the opportunity to rest. The regimental historian of the 17th Pennsylvania described the rigors of the march north as the men of his regiment prepared to bed down for the night. "The division had been marching and picketing for almost a week with no rest for man or beast. They had marched all night to reach this point. . . . The column halted before the light of day with orders to dismount and stand to horse," he wrote. "[A]n hour passed and the gray dawn . . . lighted up a picture I can never forget. The men, who were completely exhausted, had slipped the bridle rein over their arms and lay down in a bed of dust (8 inches deep) that almost obscured them from sight. Their jaded steeds seemed to know they should not move, and propping themselves with extended necks and lowering heads, stood like mute sentinels over their riders dead in sleep."[80]

Company G of the 17th Pennsylvania Cavalry had been raised in the area around Waynesboro, and its members requested that they be allowed to visit their homes on the night of June 29. Devin granted their request—with the caveat that they return in time for morning roll call. Not a man of Company G was absent the next morning.[81]

*   *   *

David M. Gregg's 2nd Cavalry Division marched from New Market and Ridgeville to New Windsor, Pennsylvania, while Judson Kilpatrick's 3rd Cavalry Division rode from Frederick to Littlestown, Pennsylvania. Kilpatrick's division was widely dispersed. Newly promoted Elon J.

---

79 Bean, "Address at the Dedication of the 17th Pennsylvania Cavalry Monument," 2:876.

80 John H. Calef, "Gettysburg Notes: The Opening Gun," in *JMSIUS*, vol. 40 (1889), 47; DePuyster, *Decisive Conflicts*, 57-58.

81 Moyer, *History of the Seventeenth Regiment*, 48-49.

Farnsworth's 1st Brigade marched with Kilpatrick to Littlestown. The 1st and 7th Michigan of Kilpatrick's 2nd Brigade, under another new brigadier, George A. Custer, were sent with orders to reach Emmitsburg, Maryland, on June 29 and then ride northeast across the Mason-Dixon line to join Kilpatrick the next day. Custer's two remaining regiments, the 5th and 6th Michigan, had been performing arduous scouting duty in and around Gettysburg. They reached Kilpatrick's camps at Littlestown that night, where the troopers got their first look at their new brigade commander.[82]

Custer may have been anticipating his promotion because he managed to quickly secure a unique custom-made uniform that looked smarter and fit better than any in the entire Cavalry Corps. Captain James H. Kidd, commander of Company E of the 6th Michigan, recalled elements of his young commander's natty garb: a suit of black velvet trimmed in gold lace, "blue navy" shirt, crimson necktie, and broad-brimmed black hat turned down rakishly on one side. To most men in the brigade Custer was nothing more than a name. "Who is [Custer], and what is he like?" mused a trooper with the 1st Michigan. "No one knows, only they say he is a young sort of fop in his looks, with long, golden, curly hair. Someone says he is a quick nervous boy, and fights the fight before his opponent is ready." Tall, brash, handsome, athletic, and a born horseman, the "Boy General with the Golden Locks," as Custer soon came to be known, was still an unknown commodity as a field commander. That would change soon enough.[83]

* * *

While the Army of the Potomac marched northward under its new leader, many of Meade's fellow Pennsylvanians lamented that they would not arrive in time to prevent the Rebels from attacking Harrisburg. A correspondent in that city interviewed a young friend who had just arrived from Carlisle, where he somehow had managed to meet with unnamed Confederate generals who had freely discussed their plans for seizing the capital. The officers showed the informant a complete map of Harrisburg's defenses and told him they knew the locations of the fords on the Susquehanna River. The generals also claimed to have intelligence as to the number and composition of the defenders.

82 James H. Kidd, *Personal Recollections of a Cavalryman with Custer's Michigan Brigade in the Civil War* (Ionia, MI, 1908), 124-125.

83 Ibid., 129; John A. Bigelow, "Draw Saber, Charge!", *National Tribune*, May 27, 1886.

They bragged that the militia would not withstand two volleys of musketry before running off.[84]

Pennsylvanian Simon Cameron, President Lincoln's first secretary of war, sent a telegram to his former boss. "We have reliable and undoubted information from three distinct sources," he began, "that Gen. Lee has nearly, if not quite, 100,000 men between Chambersburg, on the upper side of South Mountain, and Gettysburg, on the east side of the mountain and the Susquehanna River. His columns at present extend from Shippensburg to near Harrisburg, and from Gettysburg to near Columbia." Cameron believed the Rebels, with 250 pieces of artillery, would cross the Susquehanna within 48 hours unless Meade attacked Lee tomorrow. "Let me impress upon you the absolute necessity of action by Meade to-morrow, even if attended with great risk," stressed the former cabinet member, "because if Lee gets his army across the Susquehanna, and puts our armies on the defensive of that line, you will readily comprehend the disastrous results that must follow to the country."[85]

The situation was indeed dire. "My people driven over Columbia bridge. It is burned," telegraphed Department of the Susquehanna commander Darius Couch to Meade. "I hold the opposite side of the river in strength at present. I am looking for considerable destruction on all railroad lines. Twenty-five thousand men are between Baltimore and this place. I have only 15,000 men, such as they are, on my whole line, say 9,000 here."[86]

Efforts continued to raise troops, including free blacks who Couch finally accepted into the service. *The New York Times* correspondent marveled at the sight:

> Two companies of negroes were armed yesterday and marched through the streets, strange to say, without being insulted. The thought seemed to impress itself on every mind that there was bone and muscle even if the skin was black. The darkies themselves are highly delighted. They polish up their muskets and stuff their cartridge boxes full, laughing and chatting all the time as merrily as possible—tickled as a child with a new toy. These men have never been drilled much, and are officered by colored men, but I am inclined to think they will fight as well as the militia. When we consider the fearful risk they run we must acknowledge that it requires a high order of courage for a negro to enlist.[87]

---

84 *New York Times*, July 1, 1863.

85 *OR* 27, pt. 3, 409.

86 Ibid., 407.

87 *New York Times*, July 1, 1863.

The tables turned that night in Carlisle, which witnessed a rather rare event: Pennsylvanians acting as foragers. George Doles's Georgians were still in camp around Dickinson College and the local lads who routinely interacted with them (despite their "accent," which made it hard to understand them) decided the time had come to pilfer some useful items. Eight boys crept out after dark and somehow managed to steal a pair of bundled tents. "Now we had what we had long desired—a tent to eat in and a tent to sleep in, and we were all fixed to go into camp for the rest of our school vacation," gloated Edward Beetem. Boys being boys, they delighted in retelling their adventure to anyone who would listen.

What they did not know was that the small "victory" represented the first of many Confederate reversals.[88]

Farther south in Virginia, General Dix was still preparing to move on Richmond.

"While the Rebels are evidently getting themselves into 'a scrape' in Pennsylvania and Maryland, our forces are pushing on toward a flank movement on the Rebel Capital," wrote a soldier of the 139th New York under the pseudonym "Eagle." "Our scouts bring us news to the effect that the garrison in Richmond numbers from 40,000 to 50,000 men, who are ill-assorted, and many of them the poorer troops in the whole Confederacy," he continued. "The North Carolina and Louisiana troops, it is reported, cannot be depended upon at all. Quite a meeting occurred among them recently within the lines of the Rebel Capitol, and but for being overpowered by a superior number of Virginia soldiers, there must have been a complete upset of affairs, right under the nose of the conspirators." The New Yorker predicted that Dix's troops would cut the telegraph communications to Richmond and destroy the railroads leading north from the city. "[W]e expect to attack it in the direction least expected," he predicted. "We possess the key of their defenses, and shall enter at some point or other. Therefore, do not be surprised if the Stars and Stripes is floating over Capitol Square on the 4th of July, and the hated Libby Prison is in ruins."[89]

88 Beetem, *Experiences of a West Ward Boy*, 5.

89 Styple, *Writing and Fighting the Civil War*, 199.

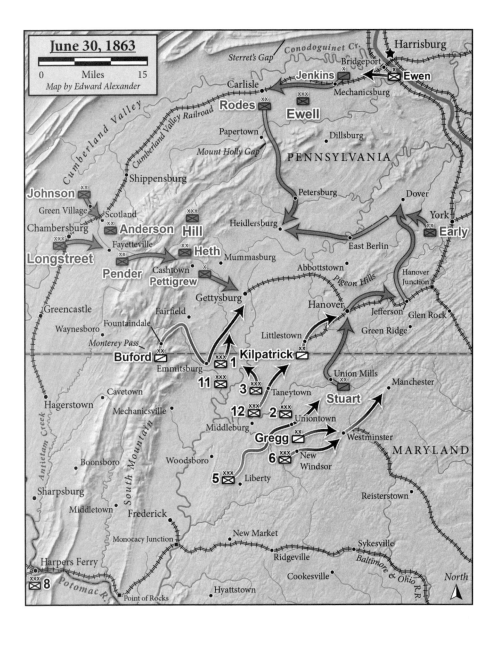

Harrisburg

Conodoguinet Cr.

Sterret's Gap

Bridgeport

Jenkins

Ewen

Carlisle

Mechanicsburg

Rodes

Ewell

Papertown

Dillsburg

Mount Holly Gap

PENNSYLVANIA

Shippensburg

Petersburg

Dover

Johnson

Green Village

Scotland

York

Chambersburg

Anderson

Hill

Heidlersburg

Early

Longstreet

Fayetteville

Heth

East Berlin

Hanover
Junction

Pender

Cashtown

Mummasburg

Abbottstown

Pigeon Hills

Pettigrew

Greencastle

Fairfield

Gettysburg

Hanover

Jefferson

Glen Rock

Waynesboro

Fountaindale

Littlestown

Green Ridge

Monterey Pass

Buford

Emmitsburg

Kilpatrick

1

Hagerstown

Cavetown

11

Union Mills

Manchester

Mechanicsville

3

Taneytown

Stuart

Middleburg

12

2

Uniontown

Westminster

Boonsboro

Woodsboro

Gregg

MARYLAND

Sharpsburg

6

New
Windsor

Middletown

Frederick

5

Liberty

Reisterstown

Monocacy Junction

New Market

Sykesville

Ridgeville

Baltimore & Ohio R.R.

North

Harpers Ferry

Cookesville

8

Potomac R.

Point of Rocks

Hyattstown

Antietam Creek

South Mountain

TUESDAY, JUNE 30, 1863

The Southern soldiers occupying the towns near the Susquehanna River rose on Tuesday morning and prepared to march toward Robert E. Lee's designated rendezvous points. In some cases, they would be retracing the same routes they had tramped just days earlier. Bitter disappointment coursed through the ranks that Harrisburg would remain in Union hands. Others expressed excitement and confident anticipation as they prepared for what was surely shaping up to be a large battle. A decisive victory on Northern soil might force Abraham Lincoln to the bargaining table, and many believed Southern independence hung in the balance. Reports coursed through several regiments that Richmond had dispatched reinforcements for the expected decisive struggle. "Various rumors viz. Beauregard on the march to join us," speculated the 57th Virginia's Dr. Charles Edward Lippitt in his diary.[1]

Richard Ewell needed to reconstitute his scattered Second Corps. He designated Heidlersburg in northern Adams County as the rendezvous point for Robert Rodes's and Jubal Early's divisions, which would march, respectively, from Carlisle and York. Edward Johnson's men, still well to the west near Green Village, would take another route.

---

1 Lippitt diary, entry for June 30, 1863. Confederate Gen. Pierre G. T. Beauregard had been relieved of command of the Army of Mississippi following the disaster at Shiloh and after sitting on the sideline for months, was assigned to command at Charleston, South Carolina. He rose to fame early in the war as the commander of Southern forces at Fort Sumter and First Manassas.

Rodes's men rose in the misty pre-dawn hours and by 3:00 a.m. began filing south out of Carlisle, a time-consuming process that took until noon. Edward Beteem and other local lads climbed the stairs of the Second Presbyterian Church to watch the martial procession of the enemy. "Although most of their regimental bands played 'Dixie,' their marching was nothing like what one sees in a parade," observed an unimpressed Beteem after the war. "They just trod along, making no attempt to keep in line nor step." Many people lined the public square and Hanover Street to observe the Confederates depart. "The rougher element of the town hurled at them all sorts of remarks—'Well, you didn't get to Harrisburg'; 'Go on home and stay home'; 'The Union boys will fix you'; 'You better keep on marching South till you get home'; 'You'll never see the Cumberland Valley again', and so forth."[2]

With the taunts ringing in their ears, the miles-long column of soldiers slowly headed toward Papertown and the long hike over South Mountain at Mount Holly Gap. "I think there are more rocks at this place than in all of North Carolina," believed Capt. James Harris of the 30th North Carolina. "The whole side of the mountain seems completely covered for 2 or 3 ft. deep altogether with small stones. In crossing this mountain our whole division could be plainly seen at once. The road was as straight as you ever saw a stretch on a R.R., the ascents and descents being gradual. If you wish to go to see a show of babies, just go to Pennsylvania," continued Harris in a letter home to a friend penned after he had passed through Petersburg. "I am glad to fight this generation for I should be afraid to risk it the next. I suggested that they should change the name of the little village which we passed to Babytown. It seemed to please a lady standing in her yard, with chuckle headed little fellow in her arms and about ½ dozen swinging around the skirt of her dress all nearly about the same size—very much."[3]

The Southern troops left the paved Baltimore Turnpike at Petersburg to take a dirt side road angling off toward Heidlersburg. It had been a miserable hike of almost 20 miles from Carlisle, with poor weather making the ascent and descent of the mountains more treacherous. "It drizzled & showered frequently & the latter

---

2 Beteem, *Experiences of a West Ward Boy*, 5. The design of the Second Presbyterian Church, located at the southeastern corner of East Pomfret and South Hanover streets, resembled a Grecian temple. It was one of just two Carlisle churches to go forward and hold worship services on Sunday, June 28, with both local congregants and visiting Confederates present in the pews.

3 Taylor, "Ramseur's Brigade in the Gettysburg Campaign," 31.

Brig. Gen. William "Extra Billy" Smith, a former governor of Virginia, led a brigade in Early's Division, Ewell's Second Corps, Army of Northern Virginia. He served as governor again from 1864–1865.

LOC

part of the road was muddy & slippery," grumbled Samuel Pickens of the 5th Alabama.[4]

* * *

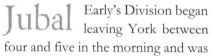

Jubal Early's Division began leaving York between four and five in the morning and was completely gone by 7:00 a.m. About noon Early, his staff, and three of his brigade commanders (Harry Hays, William "Extra Billy" Smith, and Isaac Avery) stopped for lunch at a hotel in Davidsburg along the route of march toward East Berlin. Early paid for the meal with Confederate money, stepped outside, and heard the grumbling thunder of artillery from the direction of Hanover, about 10 miles to the south. He paused to ponder the meaning of the cannonade and concluded that it was nothing more than militia skirmishing. But who were the militia skirmishing with?

Whether that thought entered Early's mind will never be known. What we do know is that instead of trying to contact the Confederates engaging what he believed to be merely militia, the Virginia general mounted his horse and rode west toward Heidlersburg. Each step of Early's horse put additional distance between his infantry division and Jeb Stuart's struggling cavalry, and made it that much harder for the cavalier to locate Second Corps troops.[5]

---

4 Hubbs, *Voices from Company D*, 181. Papertown, at the time home to several paper mills, is now known as Mount Holly Springs. Petersburg, now York Springs, was known in the 19th century for its medicinal sulfur springs.

5 James McClure, *East of Gettysburg: A Gray Shadow Crosses York County, Pa.* (York, PA, 2003), 88.

John C. Early, Jubal's youthful nephew, accompanied the column. "General Early had gone on toward York, and General Ewell, desiring to recall him, sent my father on with orders to that effect," he recalled after the war. "General Ewell himself left Carlisle shortly afterward with the soldiers under his command, marching toward Gettysburg and taking me under his especial charge. . . . The old General was very kind to me. As we rode along, we saw many fine wax cherries on the road. I enjoyed these hugely, and so did the General. I brought him so many boughs of them for his consumption," he continued, "that I began to wonder, boy-like, how so small a man could hold so many cherries."[6]

Ed Johnson's command made the short southeasterly trek through Green Village to Scotland. Green Village physician Charles McClay took note that the "rebel army began to return from down the valley. They went out the Scotland road." The doctor walked to Shirk's Hill after the Rebels left. To his surprise, "the woods and fields all around were covered with hundreds of hides cut to pieces to render them useless." Large groups of soldiers were crossing the fields in a direct line for Fayetteville, ignoring the roads in their haste. McClay climbed to the highest point on the hill. "From Monn's [Mill] down to Hargleroad's mill and over the old camp meeting ground, the rebels lay in immense numbers," he marveled. "Drums were beating and the ear-piercing fife and the shrill notes of the trumpet were all calling to arms. We gazed on the scene and silently invoked the great God of battles to protect our Army and Nation from this great force of misguided men."[7]

*   *   *

The "misguided men" from Dixie still controlled parts of Cumberland, Franklin, and York counties, with Adams County squarely in their crosshairs. Albert Jenkins's mounted brigade of infantry was still operating in the Mechanicsburg area. Jenkins did yet not know that Ewell had abandoned Carlisle, but the Union high command in Harrisburg did. "Scouts report a force of rebels having left Carlisle this morning on the Baltimore pike," wired Darius Couch to

---

6 Early, "A Southern Boy's Experience at Gettysburg," 419.

7 Hoke, *Reminiscences*, 186. Shirk's Hill is the present-day Presidential Heights on U.S. 11 about 3.5 miles north of Chambersburg, north of Salem Avenue. Monn's farm and mill were on a bend in Conococheague Creek near today's Cornerstone Road. Green Village and Scotland are about two miles apart. After passing through Scotland, the main road went through Black Gap and intersected the Chambersburg-Gettysburg Turnpike at Greenwood.

Gen. John Ewen commanded a brigade in the Department of the Susquehanna defending Harrisburg.

History of West Chester County

Secretary of War Edwin M. Stanton. Couch directed Maj. Gen. William F. "Baldy" Smith to find and cut off Jenkins's route of retreat to Carlisle.[8]

General Smith chose Brig. Gen. John Ewen's brigade of New York militia to lead the advance. Ewen was to reconnoiter out the Carlisle Pike and locate, engage, and cut off the Confederates. Ewen allowed the men of the 22nd and 37th New York State National Guard to have breakfast before they marched, and he permitted any man who felt unable to keep up to drop out and report to their regimental surgeons; none did. The inexperienced and incompetent officer ordered his men to carry only their canteens, arms, and ammunition. No haversacks were allowed. "If he had possessed any practical experience, he would have at least required his men to carry their haversacks," complained George Wingate of the 22nd New York State Nation Guard. These troops would have nothing to eat for lunch or dinner, which caused what Wingate described as "great suffering."[9]

The New Yorkers took to the road at 10:30 a.m., halting briefly at Baldy Smith's headquarters on Bridgeport Heights. The general joined the column, which continued through fields over Bridgeport Heights to its southern side, where it turned onto the Carlisle Pike and marched to Oyster's Point. The column moved another mile to a clover field and formed a line of battle there about noon. Lieutenant Frank Stanwood's cavalry detachment rode forward to search for the enemy. After about an hour Smith decided to return to Bridgeport Heights about 1:00 p.m. and ordered Ewen to follow him, with the New Yorkers thinking their day's work was over.

8 *OR* 27, pt. 3, 434.

9 Wingate, *Twenty-Second Regiment*, 192-193; *OR* 27, pt. 2, 220, 235.

Unbeknownst to the militia, Jenkins had formed his brigade about two miles from Sporting Hill around Silver Creek with every intention of leading the Confederate advance on Harrisburg later that day. The creek provided a good water source for men and horses, and a nearby bluff offered a good view of the vicinity. He sent out foraging parties, posted his picket line near the church, and awaited the arrival of the infantry on the western edge of Sporting Hill.[10]

Ewen stopped his men long enough for Capt. Henry Landis's battery to join the column and informed the Philadelphians that they were headed back to the fort. The column had just resumed its march when Lieutenant Stanwood galloped up to report that he had encountered Confederate pickets west of Sporting Hill, and they had opened fire on him. Ewen called for Smith's chief of artillery Lt. Rufus King, Jr., a young West Point-trained officer who was also the son of a Union general of the same name. King expressed the opinion that because it was only 1:00 p.m., there was plenty of daylight left to organize an attack on Jenkins. "Gen Ewen rode out along our line talking to the men," recorded one, "saying that we ought to return and try to find the enemy and that it was the opinion of [King] that we should do so." Ewen gave a short speech to inspire his troops, declaring that "the eyes of the country and the state of New York were upon us." After Ewen sent a galloper to Smith to advise him of his decision, his column about-faced and headed west on the Carlisle Pike.[11]

Jenkins quickly realized that the significant force of advancing Union infantry was aiming to cut him off while his mounted infantrymen were scattered about the countryside. He ordered Lt. Col. Vincent Witcher and his 34th Battalion of Virginia Cavalry, along with Capt. Thomas E. Jackson's battery of horse artillery, "to hold the enemy in check at all hazards." Witcher and 400 veterans moved to carry out Jenkins's orders.[12]

It was about 3:00 p.m. when Ewen's brigade began climbing the western slope of Sporting Hill. Witcher's dismounted skirmishers, hidden in Moses Eberly's sturdy bank barn, waited until they were within range and opened fire. The balance of the Virginians remained about 500 yards to the rear in Gleim's Woods. The

10 Schuricht diary, entry for June 30, 1863, *Richmond Dispatch*, April 5, 1896; "Jenkins' Brigade," *Richmond Enquirer*, July 17, 1863; Charles Leland, *Memoirs* (New York, 1893), 253, 307.

11 John Irvin Murray diary, entry for June 30, 1863, Archives, New York Historical Society, New York, NY.

12 Wingate, *Twenty-Second Regiment*, 197; Vincent A. Witcher to John W. Daniel, March 15, 1900, John W. Daniel Papers, Albert and Shirley Small Special Collections Library, UVA.

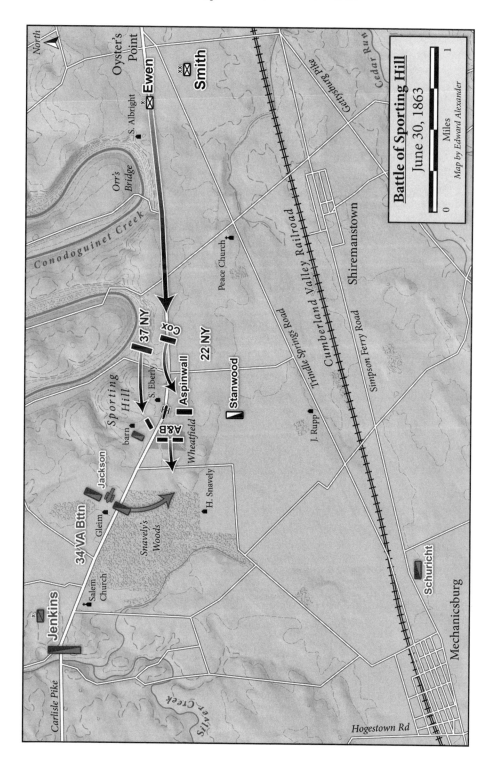

Battle of Sporting Hill
June 30, 1863

Map by Edward Alexander

Miles

Col. John Lloyd Aspinwall commanded the 22nd New York State National Guard in the defenses of Harrisburg.

LOC

green New Yorkers fell to their knees at the command of their officers. Ewen's skirmishers advanced about 200 yards, or nearly half the distance to the barn and Witcher's advance line of skirmishers.[13]

Ewen then made the first of several tactical errors. He left his column in place without orders for nearly 10 minutes, with only skirmishers facing northwest toward the barn. Witcher quickly realized that Ewen's left flank was wide open. King and Ewen were on the crest of Sporting Hill watching Confederate movements while a party of Witcher's skirmishers crossed the Carlisle Pike and deployed in a dense and extensive woodlot called Snavely's Woods. Ewen either failed to notice the enemy movement or disregarded it. King, however, recognized that the Rebels were about to flank Ewen's New Yorkers and ordered Companies A and C of the 22nd New York State National Guard to "seize and hold" the woods.[14]

By this time it was about 4:00 p.m. Ewen finally decided to form his men into line of battle. He deployed Col. Lloyd Aspinwall and four companies of the 22nd New York south of the Carlisle Pike and Maj. James Cox and the other three companies of the 22nd and the 37th New York State National Guard north of the highway. Aspinwall's battalion advanced west, its flank fully exposed to the Southern skirmishers at the barn. The colonel directed his men to lie down in a wheatfield once the fire grew heavy.[15]

13 OR 27, pt. 2, 235; Wingate, *Twenty-Second Regiment*, 194-195.

14 Wingate, *Twenty-Second Regiment*, 194-195.

15 Ibid.; OR 27, pt. 2, 220, 235; Lloyd Aspinwall, letter, *New York Times*, July 26, 1863.

Ewen next directed the men north of the Carlisle Pike to advance across a small ridge to their front, which also included a wheatfield. "As the leading files came over the brow of the hill," remembered one Empire Stater, "a severe fire was opened upon them." Several New Yorkers fell wounded, including Lt. William C. Abbe of Company F of the 37th New York. Cox's 22nd crested the ridge and took cover, but the 37th refused to advance, its members on their knees or hugging the ground. Ewen ordered the soldiers to "rise and deploy forward" about 30 yards through the wheatfield to the base of the ridge, but they still refused to move. Their inability to move under fire frustrated Ewen sent Maj. J. Henderson Grant of his staff to order Company I of the 22nd to use whatever force necessary, including bayonets, to compel the 37th to advance. When the militiamen heard this threat they hastened to obey, moving to the bottom of the ridge and using a fence there for cover.[16]

"This was the position of affairs for about half an hour," recounted one witness. Before long, a "louder explosion than had yet occurred was heard in the distance and whirr came a shell directly over our skirmishers, and over [Cox's] battalion, and exploded just beyond—a beautiful line shot, but a little too high." Although the shell hit nothing of consequence, the next two artillery rounds panicked Cox's men. Ewen had no artillery to offer counter-battery fire, so the New Yorkers were at the mercy of Jackson's guns. Untrained and overmatched, they broke and ran to the south of the Carlisle Pike before finally rallying on Aspinwall's left.[17]

Though Major Cox's New Yorkers had orders to advance, the guns had also frightened them and froze the soldiers into position. Lieutenant Stanwood's moving cavalry drew the attention of Jackson's Confederate gunners, who switched front and opened on the Union troopers. "Our cavalry wheeled their horses and galloped back from whence they came," recalled a member of the 37th New York. The sight unnerved the the Empire State troops, who "laid very quiet." A Union man watched as a mounted Confederate scout closed the distance on a daring and dangerous reconnoiter. "We saw one of the Rebels on a fine Horse with his gray uniform on ride boldly out and follow [Stanwood's horsemen] some distance when he quickly turned back again and disappeared among the trees." The

---

16 OR 27, pt. 2, 235; Wingate, *Twenty-Second Regiment*, 194-195; "Skirmish at Sporting Hill," *New York Herald*, July 1, 1863; "Harrisburgh," *New York Times*, July 3, 1863.

17 Wingate, *Twenty-Second Regiment*, 195-196.

brave enemy soldier, admitted the militiaman, "was the first rebel in arms we had seen."[18]

Jackson realized his shells were not accomplishing much by firing at that angle, so he shifted his attention to Aspinwall's seven companies in the wheatfield. "Our men behaved nobly, not flinching in the least," bragged one of the embattled New Yorkers. "A number of shots struck directly in their front, but without causing a panic or doing any great amount of injury." Most of the shells whizzed harmlessly overhead, tearing up the ground but not injuring the Guardsmen. One of Jackson's rounds, however, hurled into the massed infantry of the 37th New York, wounding two of them. All told, the noisy artillery fire wounded one officer and seven enlisted men.[19]

When General Smith heard the barking of Jackson's guns, he sent for Landis's battery, which had by this time returned to its base. The arrival of these guns about 5:00 p.m. overjoyed Major Cox, who tossed his hat in the air in celebration while others joined with shouts of glee. "It was with the utmost difficulty that the men could be kept from cheering," reported one eyewitness. The officers eventually managed to silence the jubilant New Yorkers to keep them from giving away their precise position, but only after Landis's guns had unlimbered, loaded, and fired their first rounds. Lieutenant King ordered Lt. Samuel Clarke Perkins to deploy his two-gun section in the center of Ewen's line, where it unlimbered on a small knoll in a field of corn.[20]

According to one observer, a Union shell "burst in the barn with such effect that instantly its two great doors were swung open and a swarm of Confederate skirmishers came rushing out and made for the woods." It took Ewen about two hours, but he finally managed to drive Witcher's 50 obstinate skirmishers out of the barn and surrounding area. The gunners also engaged Jackson's battery in counterbattery fire for half an hour.[21]

18 Murray diary, entry for June 30, 1863.

19 Wingate, *Twenty-Second Regiment*, 194-195; OR 27, pt. 2, 235; "Skirmish at Sporting Hill."

20 Wingate, *Twenty-Second Regiment*, 196; Woodruff Jones, *1st Philadelphia Light Artillery in the Army of the Susquehanna, 1863*, Cooper Wingert, ed. (Enola, PA, 2011), 10; OR 27, pt. 2, 235; A. J. Pleasonton, *Third Annual Report of Brigadier General A. J. Pleasonton, Commanding the Home Guard of the City of Philadelphia, to the Hon. Alexander Henry, Mayor for 1863* (Philadelphia, 1864), 82, 88.

21 Wingate, *Twenty-Second Regiment*, 196; OR 27, pt. 2, 235; Jones, *Philadelphia Light Artillery*, 10-11; "A Skirmish—Rebels Retreat," *Harrisburg Daily Patriot and Union*, July 1, 1863.

About 6:00 p.m., a shell arched farther in its flight and fell among Witcher's men, injuring several. Witcher ordered his wounded into ambulances, ordered the rest to mount up, and instructed Jackson to limber his guns and withdraw, ending the fighting. The long Sporting Hill skirmish proved surprisingly deadly for the Confederates, who lost as many as 15 killed and 20-30 wounded. The dead Rebels were initially buried in a field across the road from the Moses Eberly barn.[22]

* * *

While fighting raged at Sporting Hill, artillery fire off to the south caught Ewen's ear. "There were several discharges of artillery on our left, demonstrating the existence of a body of the enemy in that direction," he reported. In order to avoid being flanked, he refused part of Aspinwall's force to repulse any such effort. Some of Aspinwall's men reported the presence of Confederate cavalry on the left, even though some of them were Stanwood's Union troopers who had fled earlier.[23]

Lieutenant Hermann Schuricht of the 14th Virginia Cavalry had led his Company D and one of Jackson's guns toward Mechanicsburg. "Early in the morning I was ordered to report with my company at headquarters, and General Jenkins directed me to proceed at once with my company and one cannon of Jackson's Battery to Mechanicsburg, to hold this town until ordered otherwise, and to destroy the railroad track as far as possible," Schuricht recounted. "Greatly flattered to be entrusted with an expedition, properly belonging to an officer of higher rank, I started my command to Mechanicsburg, and when we came in sight of the town I dispatched a patrol to reconnoitre." The detachment spotted a small company of Federal cavalry that had just ridden into the town. The Yankees hastily retreated.

Schuricht entered Mechanicsburg and posted his pickets in the streets, which were empty because most of the inhabitants had hidden themselves away indoors.

22 Jones, *1st Philadelphia Light Artillery*, 11; "The Situation"; "Skirmish at Sporting Hill." According to researchers Jim Schmick and Cooper Wingert, workers exhumed the dead Confederates in 1895 and transported the remains to Rose Hill Cemetery near Hagerstown, Maryland. They lie in the unknown section of the Washington Confederate Cemetery within Rose Hill. The original burial site is under the ramp across today's I-81 from the preserved Eberly barn. For much of the late 20th century, this area served as the volleyball courts for the Holiday Inn before they were demolished.

23 OR 27, pt. 2, 235.

Schuricht directed most of his small command to an elevation east of the town overlooking the railroad and turnpike, and ordered them to demolish the tracks. "We were repeatedly interrupted in this work by the reappearance of Yankees, and had to keep up a lively skirmish all day," he continued. "We also observed many and demonstrative people in the woods, some distance to our right, and I ordered Lieutenant Jackson to warn them off by some shots." Schuricht could hear the guns thundering at Sporting Hill and believed he, too, was being flanked. Before long orders from Witcher arrived for Schuricht to "leave Mechanicsburg after dark and fall back to Carlisle." His men tore up a few rails of the already battered Cumberland Valley Railroad but did no other significant damage before retreating.[24]

Carlisle's jubilation at finally being free of Rebels proved short-lived. The main body of the 14th Virginia Cavalry entered the recently vacated town between 2:00 p.m. and 3:00 p.m. Albert Jenkins had sent the Virginians of the 14th regiment there to secure his line of communications once he finally got word that Ewell's infantry had departed two hours earlier. "It soon became evident that they were not under the same discipline which characterized those [of Ewell's corps] which had been here," reported Cumberland County deputy sheriff Simpson K. Donavin of the Rebel horsemen.[25]

The Virginians "wildly rode about Carlisle, no doubt to learn if all troops and cavalry had left it. Col. [James] Cochran was their commander," observed resident Charles G. Beteem. "They acted like cowboys. They yelled and flashed their sabers, and their conduct was such that the populace became greatly alarmed. They made a great stir and racket. Finally, they made for the college campus and there set up their pup-tents and tethered their horses." A citizens' committee visited Cochran in the hope that he would restrain his men, who Beteem later wrote were "yelling like Texas cattle-men." The colonel replied that he would abide by Ewell's orders and his men would remain quiet and orderly.[26]

According to a local newspaper, Cochran's assurance did not last very long. "They had not been in town half an hour until they were riding wildly through the streets," reported the *Carlisle Herald.* "Things only got worse when they found whiskey as this exciting drink appeared to madden them. They tore through the

---

24 Schuricht diary, entry for June 30, 1863, *Richmond Dispatch*, April 5, 1896.

25 "Rebel Occupancy of Carlisle," *Carlisle American*, July 15, 1863.

26 Beteem, *Experiences of a West Ward Boy*, 6.

streets, cursing and yelling, and playing the demon, as demons only can play it." Only General Jenkins's arrival calmed the exuberant Virginians.[27]

The rest of Jenkins's men reached Carlisle after midnight. The long-bearded general held a council of war in a nearby house. "It was decided that I should cover the rear with two pieces of [Capt. Wiley Griffin's] Baltimore Light Artillery, and 34th Batt. and 2 Cos. of the 36th, whilst other commands threw flankers on both sides of the road," recounted Colonel Witcher. Jenkins and the balance of his brigade rode off on the Baltimore Pike and reached Petersburg about 2:00 a.m., where they bivouacked, horses saddled and arms "ready to hand."[28]

*　　*　　*

Ewell was not the only Confederate corps leader repositioning his men that day. A. P. Hill moved Pender's Division from Fayetteville to Cashtown under a light but steady rain that fell throughout the day. The men camped in the latter place within proximity of Harry Heth's command. Johnston Pettigrew of Heth's Division advanced his large brigade east along the Chambersburg Pike into Gettysburg to collect supplies, but quickly withdrew when the men spotted Union cavalry in the town. John Brockenbrough's Virginia brigade, one of the worst disciplined and least dependable outfits in the entire army, trailed Pettigrew. "Marched from Cashtown through New Salem down the road to support Gen. Pettigrews brigade that went to drive the yankees from Gettysburg," was how the 47th Virginia's Pvt. Robert T. Douglass explained the event in his diary. "Returned to camp without firing a gun. Orders to remain in camp & keep our guns in order."[29]

Hill's remaining division under Richard Anderson remained at Fayetteville along the turnpike to Gettysburg and York. The 19th Mississippi's adjutant A. L. Peel took his time there in stride. "I don't feel very well, have spent the day lounging about camp; have furnished several guards to citizens," he penned. "A good many citizens are badly frightened, others don't care. These Dutch girls don't

---

27 "Citizens Plunder the Post" and "Tuesday and Second Arrival of Jenkins," *Carlisle Herald*, July 31, 1863.

28 Witcher to Daniel, March 1, 1900, Jan. 26, 1906, March 1, 1906, and March 22, 1906; Schuricht diary, entry for June 30, 1863.

29 Douglass diary, entry for June 30, 1863. New Salem, founded in 1845, later was renamed McKnightstown for tavern owner Thomas McKnight.

wear stockings & wear very short dresses, I think that they love to climb cherry trees."[30]

Two of James Longstreet's First Corps divisions under McLaws and Hood marched from Chambersburg east to Fayetteville. George Pickett's Division remained in camp around Chambersburg. "You never saw a country so densely populated as this. The farms are so small. One of ours would make twenty of these," observed Capt. Charles M. Blackford. Chambersburg was as quiet and orderly as on a Sunday, and the ladies and children freely walked about the town without any disrespect or unkind word from the soldiers. So could the men, "who literally swarm the streets." Blackford had not talked to any citizens since crossing the state line and did not intend to start now. "Never in my life have I seen so many ugly women as I have seen since coming to this place," he wrote in a letter home. "It may be that the pretty ones do not show themselves but the ugly ones parade around everywhere. The men are not remarkable either way. They have an awkward Dutch look and the analogy between them and horses and barns is perfect. Men, women and children are all afflicted with a Yankee twang that grates against my nerves and eardrums most terribly."[31]

Most residents would not have agreed that Chambersburg was "quiet and orderly." Bank president William Heyser chronicled the destruction he witnessed: "The troops are busy destroying the Franklin Railroad at both north and south ends of the County. Along with sills of the road, they pile on all the fence they can find to heat and twist the rails." Another force of about 500 men was sent to destroy the railroad depot and buildings, starting with the large turntable. They pulled down the engine house after an immense amount of work. "I tried to reason with a nearby officer about the wanton destruction. Their answers were always the same, 'This is in retaliation for your troops work in the South, particularly Fredericksburg.'" Heyser later climbed into the belfry of the German Reformed Church to see if his farm had suffered any damage, but the heavy foliage prevented him from doing so. He could, however, see damage inflicted on the Cumberland Valley Railroad, which he could mark "by the smoke of the burning ties."[32]

Many civilians in Virginia applauded the occasional destruction when they learned of such incidents. Harassed repeatedly by Union raids, they longed for the

---

30 Peel diary, entry for June 30, 1863. Peel would be killed the following May at Spotsylvania Court House.

31 Blackford, *Letters from Lee's Army*, 186-87.

32 Heyser diary, entry for June 30, 1863.

Army of Northern Virginia to wreak vengeance upon the Keystone State. "Many exciting rumours today about the Yankees being at Hanover Court-House, within a few miles of us," wrote angry Virginian Judith McGuire in her diary. "They can be traced everywhere by the devastation which marks their track. There are rumours that our army is in Pennsylvania. So may it be! We are harassed to death with their ruinous raids, and why should not the North feel it in their homes? Nothing but their personal suffering will shorten the war. I don't want their women and children to suffer," she continued, "nor that our men should follow their example, and break through and steal. I want our warfare carried on in a more honourable way; but I do want our men and horses to be fed on the good things of Pennsylvania; I want the fine dairies, pantries, granaries, meadows, and orchards belonging to the rich farmers of Pennsylvania, to be laid open to our army; and I want it paid for with our Confederate money, which will be good at some future day." She concluded her long entry by adding, "I want their horses taken for our cavalry and wagons, in return for the hundreds of thousands that they have taken from us; and I want their fat cattle driven into Virginia to feed our army. It amuses me to think how the Dutch farmers' wives will be concealing the golden products of their dairies, to say nothing of their apple-butter, peach-butter, and their wealth of apple-pies."[33]

The *Richmond Daily Dispatch* was also miffed when it editorialized against General Lee's "strict orders to 'respect private property.' We were greatly disappointed at this in the first instance, for we had hoped that the Yankees would be made to feel a portion, at least of the injuries they have wantonly inflicted on us. Nevertheless," continued the paper,

> we can imagine a very good apology for such an order. It is no doubt the object of the General to make war support war—that is to support his army in the enemy's country. Should he allow his soldiers to pillage and burn indiscriminately, he would defeat the end in view, for the Yankees finding there was no hope for them would retire, and burn the country as they went before them—besides nothing is so fatal to the discipline of an army as a habit of plundering. They soon to think of nothing else, become demoralized, and fall an easy prey to their enemies. Doubtless Gen Lee had this fact, attested by all history, in view when he issued the order in question. He cannot afford to let the discipline of his army be relaxed, especially at this time, when he has a powerful army of the enemy to fight and that too in that enemy's own country.

---

33 McGuire, *Diary of a Southern Refugee*, 224-225.

The general's "intended movements," of course, remained obscure:

[W]e are unable to conjecture what they are as the *New York Herald* itself or even the *Times*, or in fact any other Northern journal that has tried its hand at prophesying. Some suppose that he means to attack Washington and Baltimore, some that his object is Philadelphia, some that he merely means to make a raid into Pennsylvania, and return, and some again that be intends to carry on the war on the enemy's soil, and make it support itself. Where so many doctors disagree it were folly in us to pretend to decide. We only know that he means to do something, but what it is nobody seems to know except himself.[34]

While civilians like Judith McGuire and Southern newspapers judged events from afar, Confederates on the ground north of the Mason-Dixon line marched and camped in high spirits. "The invasion of Pennsylvania was wise and prudent from the standpoint of both arms and statesmanship. Everything promised success," James F. Crocker of the 9th Virginia, part of Lewis Armistead's Brigade, wrote many years later. "Never was the Army of Northern Virginia in better condition. The troops had unbounded confidence in themselves and in their leaders. They were full of the fervor of patriotism—had abiding faith in their cause and in the favoring will of Heaven." Crocker admitted he and his comrades were elated to invade the country of an enemy that had likewise invaded theirs. "On the contrary, the Federal army was never so dispirited, as I afterwards learned from some of its officers. And this was most natural. They marched from the bloody fields of Fredericksburg and Chancellorsville, the scenes of their humiliating and bloody defeat, to meet a foe from whom they had never won a victory."[35]

In Gettysburg, Sarah Broadhead worried that the Army of Northern Virginia indeed might again prove victorious: "It begins to look as though we will have a battle soon and we are in great fear. I see by the papers that General Hooker has been relieved, and the change of commanders I fear may give great advantage to the enemy, and our army may be repulsed."[36]

* * *

34 *Richmond Daily Dispatch*, June 30, 1863.

35 James F. Crocker, "Gettysburg—Pickett's Charge," *SHSP*, vol. 33, 121.

36 Broadhead diary, entry for June 30, 1863.

John Imboden's Confederate cavalry brigade had camped overnight in Richey's Woods, just north of Mercersburg on the road from Cove Gap. Imboden and his staff rode into town during the morning hours to requisition 5,000 pounds of bacon, 20 barrels of flour, two barrels of molasses, two barrels of sugar, two sacks of salt, and 150 pairs of shoes. "There was no alternative," lamented Dr. Thomas Creigh, because for the time being they were "under Jeff Davis' rule. We were powerless, and it had to be complied with by 11:30 a.m." If the townspeople did not furnish the goods, Imboden threatened to quarter his men with them. "Committees were appointed to go around with them when most of articles were given, rather stolen," corrected Creigh. "They did not exact anything of the ministers and so in the good providence of God we escaped."[37]

"If they go on this way for a week or two we will have nothing to eat ourselves," worried Dr. Philip Schaff. "They say as long as Yankees have something, they will have something." General Imboden, who Schaff described as "a large, commanding, and handsome officer," told him, "You have only a little taste of what you have done to our people in the South. Your army destroyed all the fences, burnt towns, turned poor women out of house and home, broke pianos, furniture, old family pictures, and committed every act of vandalism. I thank God that the hour has come when this war will be fought out on Pennsylvania soil."[38]

About 3:30 p.m., Imboden's men broke camp and marched south through Mercersburg. Schaff estimated their strength at 1,100 men, including 300 cavalrymen, 6 pieces of artillery, 50 wagons (mostly marked "U.S."), and a large number of horses stolen from the neighborhood. Late in the evening more Rebels passed through Mercersburg leading another 100 captured horses. According to Schaff, Imboden informed a citizen that if he had the power, he would burn every town and lay waste every farm in Pennsylvania. "He told Mrs. Skinner, who wanted her horses back, that his mother had been robbed of everything by Yankee soldiers, and was now begging her bread. Mrs. S. replied, 'A much more honorable occupation than the one her son is now engaged in; you are stealing it.'" The Rebels disappeared soon enough on a march southeast toward Greencastle. "They are now gone," sighed a relieved Creigh. "May we never see the like again among us."[39]

---

37 "Mercersburg in War Times," *Mercersburg Journal*, Jan. 23, 1903; Creigh diary, entry for June 30, 1863. A. Richey's farm was near the intersection of today's Buchanan Trail W and Fort Loudon Road.

38 Schaff, "The Gettysburg Week," 25.

39 Ibid.; Creigh diary, entry for June 30, 1863.

* * *

Early that morning, Jeb Stuart and his staff crowded into William Shriver's dining room in Union Mills, Maryland, for a sumptuous breakfast, after which the family moved over to the piano. "I wish you had heard General Stuart sing accompanied by all the rest, 'If you want be a bully boy, jine the cavalry,'" recalled Kate Shriver. "His eyes sparkled and he kept time with his spirit, and with it all the elegant gentleman. General [Fitz] Lee joined and Major McClellan played and sang some splendid songs. General Stuart promised to come and see us if he ever got within 25 miles."[40]

During the night Stuart had learned a large body of Union cavalry was camped just seven miles distant at Littlestown, Pennsylvania. With a dangerous enemy just across the Mason-Dixon line, Stuart knew an encounter was likely and that he would need a guide. William Shriver's 16-year-old son Herbert knew the roads intimately and offered his services. Stuart had to persuade Mrs. Shriver to allow her young son to accompany his cavalry and promised to arrange an appointment to the Virginia Military Institute for him if she allowed the teen to go. She grudgingly gave her consent and the boy set off on the greatest adventure of his life—riding alongside Jeb Stuart.[41]

The Mason-Dixon line and Pennsylvania were just five miles distant, and Littlestown another two miles beyond that. The Southerners watered their horses in a stream while Stuart dispatched scouts to reconnoiter. The riders spotted a large force of Union troops near Littletown and reported back to Stuart "with raised hands, riding with dangerous speed, reporting with lost breath, almost in panic." Stuart consulted with his officers and opted not to attack. Instead, he decided to detour toward Hanover on a dirt road—a choice that would have far-reaching consequences. He hoped to slip by any Yankee horsemen and link up with Ewell's infantry somewhere near the Susquehanna River.[42]

---

40 Kate Shriver account, in Klein, *Just South of Gettysburg*, 197. The lyrics written by Kate are not the precise words found in the song. It is possible Stuart was singing a variation or having fun with the words.

41 David Shriver Lovelace, *The Shrivers: Under Two Flags* (Westminster, MD, 2003), 28. Stuart delivered upon his promise: Herbert enrolled at VMI and was wounded during the May 1864 battle of New Market.

42 Shriver account, 201-202.

Stuart paroled his Delaware prisoners early that morning. A battle with Federal cavalry seemed inevitable, and the last thing Stuart wanted was to be hampered with captives during a fight. He called an impromptu conference with his prisoners while Union Capt. Charles Corbit and Lt. Caleb Churchman listened attentively. After commending their gallantry, Stuart added the Delawareans "ought to be fighting for the Confederacy, rather than against it." Corbit's unlikely charge nearly cost Stuart more than just a day's delay on June 29: the head of Maj. Gen. Winfield Scott Hancock's column was only three miles away from Westminster that night. The charge nearly enabled the Union infantry to catch up to Stuart's exhausted horsemen. Hancock sent a special messenger to General Meade in the hope that Brig. Gen. David M. Gregg's 2nd Cavalry Division would arrive in time to intercept Stuart's column. Luckily for Stuart, Gregg's men did not interrupt his ride. Judson Kilpatrick, however, was another matter. Kilpatrick's specific task for June 30 was locating the main body of Ewell's corps, which was believed to be moving east from Chambersburg.[43]

John Chambliss and his brigade rode in the advance of Stuart's column along the Hanover Road, with mounted patrols scattered on both sides to collect serviceable horses and supplies and to watch for the Federal cavalry they now knew to be operating in the area. Breathed's six guns as well as the 150 captured wagons were next in line, followed by Wade Hampton's command, which had the job of guarding the wagons. Fitz Lee's Brigade brought up the rear and had the important task of guarding the column's left and rear. It would soon be sent farther west to a position between the Littlestown and Hanover roads.

The long column of sleepy Confederate horsemen slowly made its way northward. "Both men and horses being worn out," remembered Lt. George W. Beale of the 9th Virginia Cavalry, "all of us regarded the prospect of a fight with no little regret and anxiety." Led by young Herbert Shriver, Stuart managed to cover a few miles on the main road before turning Chambliss's and Hampton's brigades (as well as the long train of wagons) onto a secondary parallel route running over Conewago Hill and into Hanover. The road rose and fell with each mile. The mules hauling the heavily laden wagons could barely make it up the steep inclines. Curses and shouts ran loudly up and down the train as frustrated teamsters whipped and threatened the stubborn mules to press on. Despite their best efforts, the gap

---

43 Wilson, *Captain Charles Corbit's Charge*, 18-19; Statement of Charles H. Morgan, in Ladd, *Bachelder Papers*, 3:1348.

Newly promoted Brig. Gen. George Armstrong Custer commanded the 2nd Brigade, 3rd Division of cavalry, in the Army of the Potomac.

LOC

between the head of the wagon train and the rear of Chambliss's column lengthened.[44]

Fitz Lee's men followed a parallel road to screen Stuart's vulnerable left flank, and the general dispatched small patrols to search for the enemy. Early in the march, one of these detachments spotted Kilpatrick's column riding directly into Stuart's intended path and Lee sent a dispatch to warn Stuart. Unfortunately, the courier was captured and Stuart rode along blissfully unaware that he was on a collision course with the lead elements of a division of 3,500 Union horsemen. His decision to bypass Kilpatrick by going to Hanover had instead carried him directly toward the enemy.[45]

Fortunately for the Confederates, Kilpatrick's command was scattered. All he had with him were Brig. Gen. Elon J. Farnsworth's brigade and the four regiments of Brig. Gen. George A. Custer's 1,975-strong Michigan Cavalry Brigade. The diminutive Kilpatrick rode at the head of the column, followed by his staff and headquarters escort comprised of a squadron of the 1st Ohio Cavalry.[46]

The 18th Pennsylvania, part of Farnsworth's brigade, was a green regiment, with most of its members hailing from south-central Pennsylvania. A squad of 40

---

44 Beale, *History of the Ninth Virginia Cavalry*, 81.

45 *New York Herald*, July 3, 1863.

46 Henry C. Parsons, "Gettysburg: The Campaign was a Chapter of Accidents," *National Tribune*, Aug. 7, 1890; John P. Nicholson, comp., *Pennsylvania at Gettysburg: Ceremonies at the Dedication of the Monuments Erected by the Commonwealth of Pennsylvania to Mark the Positions of the Pennsylvania Commands Engaged in the Battle*, 4 vols. (Harrisburg, PA, 1893), 2:868.

Brig. Gen. Elon J. Farnsworth, also recently promoted, led the 1st Brigade, 3rd Division of cavalry, in the Army of the Potomac.

USAHEC

troopers under Lt. Henry C. Potter served as the 18th's rearguard, trailing about a mile behind the main body to keep a sharp eye out for stragglers and Confederates in case of a surprise attack from that direction. The combination of heavy rains and thousands of horses had churned the roads into quagmires, slowing the cavalry's advance. The Northern troopers had been marching and skirmishing in mostly hot weather and without adequate food or rest. Their horses were tired, and their backs sore. Worn-out mounts dropped alongside the road, forcing dozens of cavalrymen to gather their saddles and equipment, sling them over their shoulders, and trudge along to try and keep up with the column.[47]

As his troops approached Hanover, Kilpatrick ordered the national colors unfurled—a welcome sight for loyal citizens living near the Mason-Dixon line. "At Hanover, the inhabitants came out in throngs to greet us, freely giving bread, meats, coffee, pie, cake, etc.," recalled the chaplain of the 5th New York Cavalry, also of Farnsworth's command, in his journal. Another trooper of the same regiment remembered fondly how he and his comrades "were warmly greeted by the local people—especially the ladies, who waved the starry flags and sang patriotic songs, besides distributing refreshments through the ranks. We found it quite different to the treatment we received from the fair sex in Virginia."[48]

---

47 Kidd, *Personal Recollections*, 124-125.

48 Richard E. Beaudry, ed., *War Journal of Louis N. Beaudry, Fifth New York Cavalry* (Jefferson, NC, 1996), 46; Letter from an unidentified trooper of the 5th New York Cavalry, in R. L. Murray, ed., *Letters from Gettysburg: New York Soldiers' Correspondences from the Battlefield* (New York, 2005), 142.

Kilpatrick and Farnsworth rode into Hanover, where they stopped for a short time to examine a large map of York County. Kilpatrick and his staff soon rode on, leaving Farnsworth to dismount and rest his regiments. His men lined the streets, enjoying the hospitality of the local citizenry. The lead elements of the column had already passed through Hanover and were heading north on the Abbottstown Road about three miles from the edge of town. Members of the 18th Pennsylvania Cavalry were still acting as the rear guard when they spotted scouting parties from Stuart's command moving along the same road. After the exchange of a few potshots the Keystone State men galloped off to warn Kilpatrick that the enemy had been found and was gaining on them.[49]

Kilpatrick, meanwhile, dismounted for a short halt to allow Farnsworth's regiments to close on his elevated position beyond the Pigeon Hills north of Hanover near the York Pike. It was nearly 10:30 a.m. A lone discharge from a field piece boomed from the hills south of town, its low dull blast reverberating through the air. The thunder startled men and horses alike. Kilpatrick, who had no idea what was unfolding, looked back in the direction of Hanover in an effort to understand what had just happened. "Our brigade was drawn up in a column of fours in the main street, and we were enjoying ourselves finely, when the report of a cannon and the bursting of a shell in our rear caused a great commotion," explained a trooper with the 5th New York Cavalry. "The rebels had attacked our rear. It was so unexpected as to almost create a panic."[50]

The head of Chambliss's column had run into the end of Farnsworth's column at the intersection of the Littlestown Road and the Westminster Road in Buttstown, just west of Hanover. Captain James Breathed had unlimbered his guns and opened on the vulnerable Union troopers, a barrage that was soon followed by small arms fire. When it became clear this was no accident or friendly fire, Kilpatrick sent a courier north to Abbottstown to find Custer and the 1st and 7th Michigan and order them back to Hanover with all haste. Kilpatrick leaped into the saddle of his already jaded mount and spurred it back down the pike toward the Pigeon Hills he had just crossed, followed closely by his headquarters escort.[51]

49 Regimental Publication Committee, *History of the Eighteenth Regiment of Cavalry, Pennsylvania Volunteers, 1862–1865* (New York, 1909), 87-88, 217.

50 Murray, *Letters from Gettysburg*, 142.

51 Samuel L. Gillespie, *A History of Company A, First Ohio Cavalry, 1861–1865* (Columbus, OH, 1898), 149. Buttstown or Pennville are postwar names for what was informally called Mudville during the war.

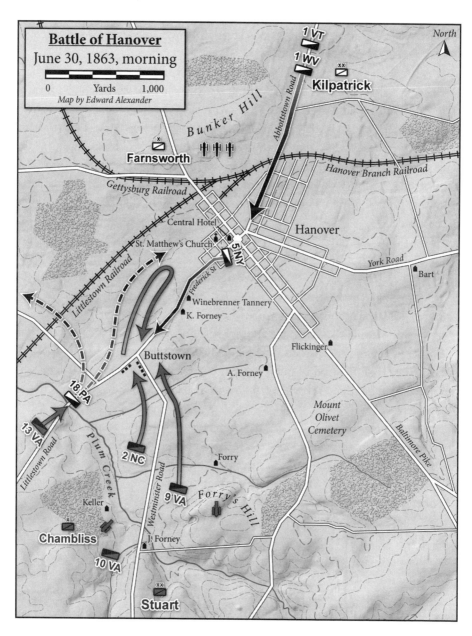

Not everyone fully realized what the firing actually signified. Some troopers from the 5th New York Cavalry and the 1st Vermont Cavalry were in the town square at the time. For a while, the mounted men believed the noise to be nothing more than a welcome salute set loose in their honor. The screaming whine of an artillery shell passing overhead and crashing in the town quickly disabused them of this mistaken notion.[52]

A detachment of Chambliss's 13th Virginia Cavalry charged into Lieutenant Potter's men along Frederick Street. "[F]or a moment, all was confusion," admitted Capt. John W. Phillips of the 18th Pennsylvania. "The impetuous charge of the enemy brought some of their troops in the midst of our men, and hand-to-hand contests were had with the sabre." As the Virginians slashed away at the inexperienced Pennsylvanians, Chambliss ordered Breathed to unlimber on a ridge overlooking Hanover on either side of the road leading to Westminster. It was from that point that Breathed had fired the shots heard by Kilpatrick and the men in the streets.[53]

The 13th Virginia Cavalry's determined charge scattered the 18th Pennsylvania's ambulances and split the regiment's hastily mounting troopers in twain. "The attack was determined and fierce, the main and side streets [of the town] swarmed with rebel cavalry. The Eighteenth Pennsylvania was routed," admitted Kilpatrick candidly in his official after-action report. Part of the 18th fled west toward McSherrystown while another section was driven, as Stuart reported, "pell-mell through the town" up Frederick Street. Captain John Esten Cooke of Stuart's staff rode forward to find out what was taking place. "Well, General," he reported when he rode back to inform Stuart, "Chambliss has driven them, and is going right in."

"Good!" declared the cavalier. "Tell him to push on and occupy the town, but not to pursue them too far." Cooke left to give Chambliss his orders and found the Virginian advancing in column of fours, preparing to charge the enemy drawn up on the outskirts of the town. The sight stunned the staff officer: instead of a small opponent, Chambliss was about to face off against a strong enemy force.[54]

A battalion of the 2nd North Carolina Cavalry, acting in support of Chambliss's Virginians, raced its mounts across fields to strike the flank of the retreating Pennsylvanians. "Here the [2nd North Carolina] behaved in a most gallant manner, charging a heavy force of Yankees where two Regts., though double the 2nd in numbers, refused to charge," recalled a Tar Heel captain. "It was here . . . the cutting and slashing was done," wrote the 18th Pennsylvania's Lieutenant Potter, "and for a few in the very front it was a hand-to-hand fight."

52 Boudrye, *Historic Records of the Fifth New York Cavalry*, 107.

53 Trout, *Galloping Thunder*, 281.

54 OR 27, pt. 1, 992, and pt. 2, 695; Cooke, *Wearing of the Gray*, 240.

Cooke agreed. "We had apparently waked up a real hornet's nest," he admitted. In minutes the hand-to-hand struggle spread toward the town square. The half of the 18th Pennsylvania still in town fled to the railroad depot. For the moment, Hanover was in Confederate possession.[55]

Farnsworth, meanwhile, was riding at the head of his brigade near the tiny hamlet of New Baltimore about a mile north of Hanover when the noise of the fight raging behind him reached his ears. The young general promptly directed the 1st West Virginia and the 1st Vermont to wheel, ride toward town, and form a line of battle to the southeast. Farnsworth wanted to see things for himself, so he spurred his horse toward the square and ended up amid the confusion on the Abbottstown Road. Responding to Farnsworth's orders, Maj. Charles Capehart of the 1st West Virginia Cavalry rallied his men for the task facing them. "Remember, boys," he admonished, "we are on the free soil of old Pennsylvania, with Stars and Stripes unfurled to cheer us on to battle. We will drive the rebels off her soil!"[56]

When the Virginians and North Carolinians thundered into the center of town, they found Maj. John Hammond's 5th New York Cavalry spread out in the square with many of its men dismounted. A local ran up to Hammond and, pointing to a vacant field a block away, recommended using it to form his regiment. "With his accustomed coolness and bravery, Maj. Hammond . . . quickly withdrew from the street to the open field near the rail road depot, [and] ordered the boys into line," recalled the 5th New York's chaplain.[57]

Once formed, Hammond ordered his New Yorkers to charge. They crashed into the Confederates gathered on Frederick Street. Two companies of the newly arrived 1st Vermont also joined Hammond's counterattack, as did a handful of the rearguard detail of the 18th Pennsylvania under Lt. Henry Potter's command. Major Joseph E. Gillette, the commander of the 13th Virginia, toppled from the saddle with a serious gunshot wound to the neck. Outnumbered, and with one regimental commander down and the momentum now swinging to the Federals, the Virginians and North Carolinians simultaneously fell and were pushed back down the street about a mile beyond the town to where some of Chambliss's men

55 Blackford, *War Years with Jeb Stuart*, 225, Graham, "From Brandy Station"; *History of the Eighteenth Pennsylvania Cavalry*, 88; Cooke, *Wearing of the Gray*, 241.

56 OR 27, pt. 1, 1011; Hanover Chamber of Commerce, *Prelude to Gettysburg: Encounter at Hanover* (Mechanicsburg, PA, 1962), 46; Anthony, *Anthony's History of the Battle of Hanover*, 15; J. P. Allum, "The Fight at Hanover," *NT*, Sept. 29, 1887.

57 Boudrye, *Historic Records of the Fifth New York Cavalry*, 64-65.

were driving Kilpatrick's ambulance wagons and stores south toward Mudtown and away from the bluecoats. "For a few moments the enemy made heroic resistance, but finally broke and fled," wrote a New Yorker. The stubborn Confederates "rallied again and again but were met with irresistible onsets, which finally compelled them to retire behind the hills under cover of their guns." As Major Hammond noted, however, the momentum of the charge broke down when "we found a large force [of the Rebels] drawn up in the road as a reserve, and received from them a severe fire, causing the men to halt for a moment."[58]

That large force was Col. Richard L. T. Beale's nearly 500-strong 9th Virginia Cavalry, and it had been waiting for the Federals near the intersection of Frederick Street and the Westminster Road. The murderous Virginia volley emptied many saddles of the 5th New York. "Our men in the road opened fire on them," reported Beale, "and as soon as the fence could be broken down, a small party charged with the sabre. The mounted Federals retreated behind a line of dismounted men, who now advanced, extending across our front as far to the right as we could see." The troopers of the 5th New York and 18th Pennsylvania retreated down Frederick Street, which was now littered with the victims of mounted charges and countercharges.[59]

A determined Elon Farnsworth rallied his troops and ordered them to form. Once they had done so he drew his saber with a flourish and told the men to do the same before bellowing orders to charge. With their blades pointed at their foes the screaming New Yorkers, Vermonters, and West Virginians dug in their spurs and surged forward, "driving the rebels in confusion along the road and through the fields."[60]

It was shortly after 11:00 a.m. when Judson Kilpatrick's hell-for-leather dash brought him to Hanover's square—just as Farnsworth's charge repulsed the Southerners. A rousing cheer by his troopers greeted the division commander, whose stirrups, recalled one witness, sported pieces of grass, corn, and wheat stalks. Kilpatrick selected the tall Central Hotel as a post from which to observe the enemy. He reined up in front of the building, leaving his exhausted, loyal horse to die of exhaustion after a determined eight-mile gallop. Kilpatrick ordered his two

---

58 Daniel T. Balfour, *13th Pennsylvania Cavalry* (Lynchburg, VA, 1986), 21; Boudrye, *Historic Records of the Fifth New York Cavalry*, 65; OR 27, pt. 1, 1008.

59 Beale, *History of the Ninth Virginia Cavalry*, 83; *Prelude to Gettysburg*, 47.

60 Stephen A. Clark, "Hanover, Pa.," *National Tribune*, Feb. 23, 1888; OR 27, pt. 1, 1008.

Lt. Col. William H. F. Payne, commander of the 2nd North Carolina Cavalry, was captured during the Battle of Hanover.

LOC

batteries deployed on nearby Bunker Hill, from which they traded a severe counterbattery fire with Breathed's and McGregor's thundering guns.[61]

Stuart tried to rally his troopers as the fighting to the south of Hanover rolled northward, filling the streets of the town with hand-to-hand combat. Lieutenant Colonel William Payne, commander of the 2nd North Carolina Cavalry, found himself in a twist near the Winebrenner Tannery on Frederick Street. Slightly wounded and unhorsed, Payne somehow landed in one of the tannery's open dye vats while trying to escape. He sank to his shoulders in the vile goop with Pvt. Abram Folger of the 5th New York towering over him demanding his surrender. Payne's "gray uniform with its velvet facing and white gauntlet gloves, his face and hair had been completely stained, so that he presented a most laughable sight," chortled Folger. Dripping with the whiskey-colored liquid, Payne was not as amused as his captor, who marched the Southern officer into Kilpatrick's presence. The general snickered in delight at Payne's plight and "congratulated him on his appearance." Folger, who had been captured by some of Payne's troopers in 1862, was happy to return the favor.[62]

Farnsworth's determined charge swept most of the Tar Heels and Virginians from Hanover. Stuart and his staff arrived just in time to watch the Confederates fleeing from the town, and the cavalry chief tried to rally his troopers. A high, ill-kept hedge with periodic gaps of lower growth lined the Westminster Road on each side. Stuart waved his saber with a laugh and called out to his engineering

---

61 Clark, "Hanover, Pa."; Cooke, *Wearing of the Gray*, 241.

62 *Prelude to Gettysburg*, 93-94; D. H. Robbins, "Stuart at Hanover," *National Tribune*, June 30, 1908; William H. Payne to Joseph R. Anderson, Dec. 13, 1903, in John Coski, ed., "Forgotten Warrior," *North & South*, vol. 2, no. 7 (Sept. 1999), 81.

officer. "Rally them, Blackford!" With that, Stuart jumped his mare "Virginia" over the hedge into the field, followed a moment later by Captain Blackford. To their surprise, the officers were only about 10 paces in front of an enemy flanking party of 25 or 30 men, all of whom called for Stuart and Blackford to halt. The Federals galloped after the two fleeing officers into a field of timothy east of the road in "hot pursuit," as Blackford remembered it, "firing as fast as they could cock their pistols."

Stuart and Blackford were galloping just a handful of strides ahead of their pursuers when an obstacle appeared before them. "We did not see, nor did our horses until close to it, a huge gully fifteen feet wide and as many deep stretched across our path," recalled Blackford. "There were only a couple of strides of distance for our horses to regulate their step and Magic [Blackford's horse] had to rise at least six feet from the brink." The officers galloped side by side and made the jump. Blackford turned to watch Stuart. "I shall never forget the glimpse I then saw of [Virginia] away up in mid-air over the chasm and Stuart's fine figure sitting erect and firm in the saddle." When their pursuers saw the two horses begin their leap, they realized there was some sort of danger ahead and barely avoided plunging headlong into the ditch. Now at a standstill, they watched in frustration as the Confederate officers escaped, little knowing they had come within a few feet of killing or capturing Jeb Stuart.[63]

Stuart formed a line of skirmishers to discourage any thoughts of an assault by the Federal cavalry while his horse artillery pounded the town. The combination of the cannon fire and the timely arrival of the rest of Chambliss's command convinced Farnsworth to break off and retire toward the town square. It was now noon. For two hours, the Federals had blocked Stuart's efforts to head north to find Early's infantry. The lull permitted local townspeople to assist Kilpatrick's troopers rescue wounded men and throw up rude barricades made of store boxes, wagons, hay ladders, fence rails, and any other available material to help keep the Confederate cavalry out of Hanover.[64]

Major Hammond, meanwhile, reformed his depleted 5th New Yorkers near the commons and posted skirmishers and a reserve line at the town limits near the Winebrenner Tannery and the Karle Forney farm along Frederick Road. Farnsworth's other regiments reorganized while the scattered remnants of companies fell back into line. Farnsworth directed Hammond to withdraw most of

---

63 Blackford, *War Years with Jeb Stuart*, 226-227.

64 *OR* 27, pt. 1, 992.

his command to Bunker Hill to support Lt. Samuel S. Elder's battery there. Before Hammond could do so, Kilpatrick countermanded those instructions. "I was ordered by General Kilpatrick to flank the enemy's position and capture [Breathed's] battery if possible, and to order an advance of the skirmishers on the right, which was done," Hammond reported. His weary New Yorkers, consisting of only eight depleted companies, rode obediently to the eastern edge of Hanover between Abbottstown and York streets. Kilpatrick ordered the 1st Vermont to support Elder's guns on Bunker Hill and directed Col. Nathaniel P. Richmond to correct the skirmish line of his 1st West Virginia Cavalry. Richmond connected his left flank with the right flank of the 1st Vermont and hunkered his men down behind the hasty barricades thrown up across Baltimore Street and nearby side streets. To Richmond's right rear were the 18th Pennsylvania's troopers, who supported his exposed flank along Frederick Street.[65]

At this time, captured Lieutenant Colonel Payne was brought before Kilpatrick for interrogation about the strength and disposition of Stuart's command. In a convincing performance intended "to prevent any further attack" by Kilpatrick, Payne lied to the brigadier by telling him that Stuart had more than 12,000 troopers with him. The ruse may have worked—Kilpatrick's command decisions for the rest of the day were tempered with a great deal of caution.[66]

In the meantime, Custer's Michigan Cavalry Brigade began arriving on the field. When they heard from a citizen that "a large force of the enemy" had been seen near Hanover, Col. George Gray and his 6th Michigan, who had been left behind at Littlestown that morning to reconnoiter, rode to Hanover to join the rest of Custer's brigade. The 6th Michigan's route fortuitously brought them squarely onto Stuart's flank, which lay between them and their destination, the town square.[67]

The Michigan men turned east off the Littlestown Road toward the unmistakable thunder of artillery directly into a sprawling field of ripening wheat. When they crested a rise to the north, they spotted the vanguard of what appeared to be Confederate cavalry riding just ahead supporting an unlimbered battery. These troopers were Col. J. Lucius Davis's 10th Virginia Cavalry of Chambliss's Brigade, supporting the guns of Capt. William M. McGregor's battery on the Keller

---

65 Ibid., 1009; George A. Rummel, III, *Cavalry on the Roads to Gettysburg: Kilpatrick at Hanover and Hunterstown* (Mechanicsburg, PA, 2000), 270-271.

66 Anthony, *Anthony's History of the Battle of Hanover*, 18.

67 Kidd, *Personal Reminiscences*, 125-127.

farm west of Westminster Road. The gunners soon spotted the Michigan horsemen moving on their flank, swung their pieces to the left, and "opened on the head of the regiment . . . with shell, wounding several me and horses." Colonel Gray was as surprised to stumble upon Rebel cavalry as Lieutenant Potter had been that morning.[68]

The 10th Virginia cavalrymen formed a line four abreast and joined McGregor's gunners. Gray decided to attack the thin line of Virginians, who numbered fewer than 300 men but stretched for nearly a mile from McGregor's position to the Littlestown Road. Gray's 600 Wolverines fanned out slightly from their column and pounded forward. The weight of their charge scattered many of the 10th Virginia's skirmishers and nearly carried to McGregor's guns. Before they punched through too deeply, the rest of the 10th, mounted and ready to countercharge, arrived. The Virginians set spurs and, despite Gray's superior numbers, drove the Michiganders back while McGregor's guns blasted away at close range.[69]

Fitz Lee's troopers also began arriving on the scene, just in time for some of them to crash into Gray's right flank and check any further advance. Lee looked through his field-glass, turned to the 1st Virginia Cavalry leading his column's advance, and yelled, "Charge them, boys, there isn't many of them!" Gray knew he was badly outnumbered, outgunned, and without any reinforcements. After deploying two companies as a covering force, he broke off and led his remaining companies west to Hanover to report to Custer.[70]

Colonel Russell A. Alger's 5th Michigan Cavalry had also been left at Littlestown. Colonel Alger moved his command toward Hanover about noon. The Wolverines arrived from the south along the Littlestown Road sometime after 3:00 p.m.—and promptly ran into some of Fitz Lee's troopers. Alger ordered a charge and his men drew their sabers and spurred their mounts into Lee's riders, driving them back down the road. Flushed with success, Alger dismounted his entire regiment and pursued the fleeing Virginians on foot, "killing and capturing quite a number" with their deadly seven-shot Spencer rifles. The Wolverines advanced through town in their first real skirmish and remained in position south of Hanover and west of Stuart, engaging in fitful exchanges of fire until the sun went down.

68 Ibid., 127; Rummel, *Cavalry on the Roads to Gettysburg*, 277.

69 Rummel, *Cavalry on the Roads to Gettysburg*, 277.

70 Haden, *Reminiscences of J.E.B. Stuart's Cavalry*, 28.

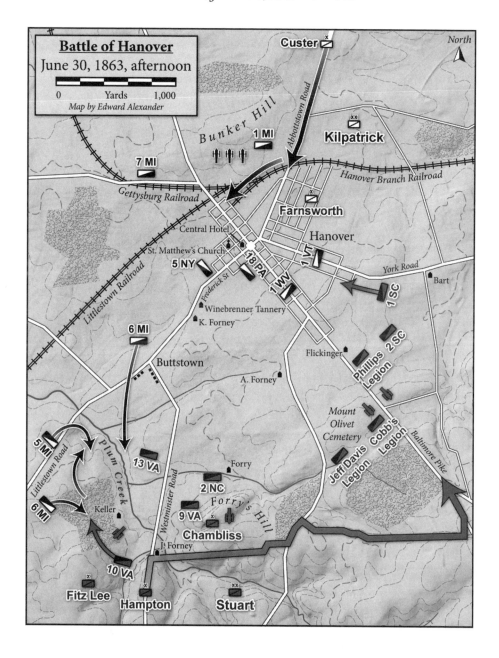

Battle of Hanover
June 30, 1863, afternoon

0   Yards   1,000
Map by Edward Alexander

North

Custer

Kilpatrick

Abbottstown Road

Bunker Hill

1 MI

7 MI

Hanover Branch Railroad

Gettysburg Railroad

Farnsworth

Central Hotel

Hanover

St. Matthew's Church

5 NY

Littlestown Railroad

18 PA

1 VT

1 WV

York Road

Bart

1 SC

Frederick St

Winebrenner Tannery

K. Forney

6 MI

Buttstown

A. Forney

Flickinger

2 SC

Phillips Legion

Mount
Olivet
Cemetery

Cobb's
Legion

Baltimore Pike

5 MI

Littlestown Road

Plum Creek

13 VA

Forry

Jeff Davis
Legion

6 MI

Keller

2 NC

9 VA

Forry's Hill

Chambliss

Westminster Road

J. Forney

10 VA

Fitz Lee

Hampton

Stuart

Like many of their comrades in the 6th Michigan Cavalry, they did not join the rest of their brigade until later that evening.[71]

Most of the balance of the Michigan Cavalry Brigade reunited in Hanover late that afternoon. After studying the Confederate line arrayed on the hills south of town, Custer directed his regiments, which were reforming near the railroad depot, to dismount. Every fourth trooper led his horse and those of three comrades to the rear—standard procedure when cavalry fought dismounted. "It was here that the brigade first saw Custer," remembered Capt. James H. Kidd of the 6th Michigan. "As the men of the Sixth . . . were deploying forward across the railroad into a wheatfield beyond, I heard a voice new to me, directly in rear of the portion of the line where I was, giving directions for movement, in clear, resonant tones, and in a calm confident manner, at once resolute and reassuring." Kidd turned to see who was speaking. "My eyes were instantly riveted upon a figure only a few feet distant, whose appearance amazed if it did not for the moment amuse me," he admitted. "It was [Custer] who was giving the orders . . . and that he was in command of the line." The fight marked Custer's maiden combat as a brigadier. As Kidd and his comrades would soon learn, the young general was determined to lead his brigade with a resolute hand.[72]

Custer and Kilpatrick climbed up the steps to the lofty steeple of St. Matthew's Church on Chestnut Street in Hanover, from which they could see what appeared to be unsupported Confederate artillery deployed at the Keller farm. (The 10th Virginia Cavalry and Fitz Lee's advancing brigade were both hidden behind a ridge.) Kilpatrick had seen enough to make a decision, and ordered Custer to dismount Colonel Gray's 6th Michigan and form a single line of battle west of town. Once Custer had done so, Gray's troopers advanced in "a line of battle one mile in length" through the Forney farm fields, crawling on their hands and knees through brambles and brush most of the way. Their movement caused some of Chambliss's and Lee's men to think that a general advance of Kilpatrick's entire command was underway.[73]

---

71 Rummel, *Cavalry on the Roads to Gettysburg*, 283; John Robertson, comp., *Michigan in the War* (Lansing, MI, 1882), 578.

72 Kidd, *Personal Recollections*, 128.

73 Gillespie, *History of Company A, First Ohio Cavalry*, 150; Robertson, *Michigan in the War*, 580; E. A. Paul, "Operations of Our Cavalry—The Michigan Cavalry Brigade," *New York Times*, Aug. 6, 1863.

About 2:00 p.m., Hampton's cavalry brigade accompanying the lumbering wagon train arrived near Stuart's position. The horses and the famished (and virtually unmanageable) mule teams had reduced Hampton's advance to a slow pace. The result, wrote Stuart after the campaign, left the burly South Carolinian's command "a long way behind." Hampton moved the wagons along the Westminster Road before circling them into a large clearing on the east side.[74]

Colonel Gray and his Michiganders, meanwhile, were moving toward the wagon train park and eventually crept and crawled to within 300 yards of Stuart's guns on the hill southwest of town. On Custer's order, the Wolverines rose and let fly a volley from the Spencer rifles and Colt revolvers. The sudden burst of hot lead shocked even the artillery crews, who began heading backward in anticipation of a large-scale enemy advance. Those not wounded in the initial volley scrambled for cover, but not before Gray's men took fifteen prisoners.[75]

Fitz Lee rushed enough troopers to the ridge to force Gray's men down the slope, but Custer rallied the 6th Michigan and sent it forward a second time. Although the troopers failed to dislodge the Southerners, the fearsome rapidity of their firepower momentarily silenced the field pieces and wreaked havoc in the ranks of the artillerists. Taking up strategic positions while shot and cannister boomed and shrieked in the warm air around them, the men of the 6th Michigan hung on, forcing Fitz Lee to rush a majority of his brigade into position to hold the ridge. After trading shots with Lee's and Chambliss's cavalrymen for about an hour, the Wolverines pulled back into town about sunset and reformed by the railroad, their participation in the fighting at an end. Mutual cessation of the artillery duel brought a second lull to the contest.[76]

Perceiving a potential threat from Hampton's newly arrived brigade to the southeast, Kilpatrick ordered his two batteries of horse artillery off Bunker Hill and into Hanover near the depot and the commons. Hampton, however, merely feigned a charge down the York Road with his 1st South Carolina Cavalry, which caused some consternation amongst the pickets of the 1st Vermont Cavalry posted there, before wheeling his gray riders around and returning to his original position on Stuart's right.[77]

74 McClellan, *Life and Campaigns of Stuart*, 329.

75 Anthony, *Anthony's History of the Battle of Hanover*, 146.

76 Rummel, *Cavalry on the Roads to Gettysburg*, 288.

77 Ibid., 289.

Everyone had had enough fighting for one day by the time the sun began to set. Except for the occasional rattle of small arms fire on the outskirts of town, the battle of Hanover was over. "Not until night had fallen did Stuart deem it prudent to withdraw from Hanover," recalled Major McClellan. Kilpatrick maintained his defensive position. The Yankees, explained McClellan, showed "no disposition as to hinder Stuart's withdrawal."[78]

Kilpatrick's dispatch to Alfred Pleasonton claimed, inaccurately, a rousing success. "After a fight of about two hours, in which the whole command at different times was engaged, I made a vigorous attack upon their center, forced them back upon the road to Littlestown, and finally succeeded in breaking their center," he claimed. "My loss is trifling. I have gone into camp at Hanover. . . . We have plenty of forage, the men are in good spirits, and we don't fear Stuart's whole cavalry." Kilpatrick claimed his losses were 19 killed, 41 wounded, and 123 missing. "For a moment, and a moment only, victory hung uncertain," continued his drama-filled prose. "For the first time our troops had met the foe in close contact, but they were on their own free soil. . . . The foe turned and fled. He had for the first and last time polluted with his presence the loyal town of Hanover."[79]

The fighting at Hanover cost Stuart more than 150 casualties and added another full day's delay to his schedule. Stuart stubbornly hung on to the captured wagons, which further hindered his ability to move quickly. As darkness fell, Stuart withdrew from the ridges and fields south of Hanover. After consulting with his brigade commanders, he decided to ride nine miles east to Jefferson and then turn north for York, a route he hoped would help him avoid any more contact with the enemy while he continued his search for Ewell's infantry. Stuart ordered the wagon train back onto the road and sent the rolling stock ahead of the main column, with Fitz Lee's cavalry in charge of it and the 400 new prisoners captured since the mass paroles at Cooksville. Finally relieved of overseeing the lumbering wagon train, Hampton's troopers brought up the rear while Chambliss's Brigade and the horse artillery rolled along sandwiched in the middle. The last horse soldiers were on the road to Jefferson by 10:00 p.m. The weary Confederate cavalrymen knew that they were not going to get any rest any time soon.[80]

---

78 McClellan, *Life and Campaigns of Stuart*, 329.

79 *OR* 27, pt. 1, 986-987, 992.

80 Lida Bowman Meckley Reminiscences of the Civil War, Rudisill Family Papers, YCHC; John Krepps, "Before and After Hanover: Tracing Stuart's Cavalry Movements of June 30,

"Being broken down & in no condition to fight, we turned off towards Jefferson, Pa.," noted one of Fitz Lee's officers in his diary that night. Stuart soon picked up news that Early's Division of Ewell's Second Corps was at York. The road there was a meandering one that added still more miles and hours to what had already been a grueling and slow-moving expedition. What Stuart had no way of knowing was that the intelligence was six days old. By the time Stuart moved toward York, the bulk of Ewell's command had already moved to the area around Carlisle 20 miles north and west of York. Early's infantry was already on its way to Cashtown and had stopped at Heidlersburg for the night 15 miles northwest of Hanover by the time Stuart had arrived there.[81]

Still Stuart's column trudged and rolled on through the night, destined to arrive at Dover (eight miles northwest of York) in the morning only to find no Confederates in sight. In fact, Stuart was riding away from Ewell's Corps. The weary troopers would not reach Gettysburg until the evening of July 2—eight days and many miles after starting their exhausting ride from Rector's Crossroads.

While Stuart and Kilpatrick dueled at Hanover, Federal officials pondered reports that the Rebels were backtracking and appeared to be concentrating their troops.

"As telegraphed previously, part of the rebel forces, if not all, have fallen back toward Chambersburg, passing Shippensburg last night in great haste," tapped out Maj. Gen. Darius Couch from his headquarters in Harrisburg to Henry Halleck in Washington. "I expect to hear every minute that my cavalry, under Gen. Smith, has re-occupied Carlisle," continued Couch. "My latest information is that Early, with his 8,000 men, went toward Gettysburg or Hanover, saying they expected to fight a great battle there. At Carlisle they said that they were not going to be outflanked by Hooker." Couch sent another telegram, this one to Secretary of War Stanton: "Scouts report a force of rebels having left Carlisle this morning by the Baltimore

1863," *Blue & Gray*, vol. 21, no. 1 (2003), 54-55; OR 27, pt. 2, 696; McClellan, *Life and Campaigns of Stuart*, 329.

81 Swank, *Sabres, Saddles, and Spurs*, 73.

pike, and that Ewell, from York, went northwesterly, which would unite their two forces."[82]

With much of the Army of the Potomac still down on Maryland, George Meade hustled his troops northward to intercept Lee's scattered army. "We have been marching quite rapidly all day and sometimes at a double quick," wrote the 20th Connecticut's Cpl. Horatio D. Chapman in his diary. "It is again reported that Lee's army is north of us and has entered the state of Pennsylvania and that the advance of our army is very near the confederate army, and that before long the two armies will meet and in all probability a terrible battle will ensue, and I am willing with thousands and tens of thousands of others of my fellow soldiers to do, to dare, sacrifice and suffer, if by any means this war will be brought to a termination. We hope," Chapman added, "to capture or so cripple the confederate army here on northern soil that the south will give up the contest and an honorable peace be restored. But time will determine."[83]

The thought of death was not on the mind of 22-year-old Sgt. Matthew Marvin, a prewar leather store clerk who had been serving with the 1st Minnesota since the beginning of the conflict. "There is some fun in Soldiering in a country like this whare the citizens are at least half humane," he told his diary. "The country is thickly settled is well watered & plenty of timber."[84]

The 15th New Jersey's Lucien A. Vorhees took a few minutes to write to his hometown newspaper about "the sore feet, aching shoulders, lame limbs and stiff joints," all of which could be left "to the imagination of your readers. Suffice to say," added,

we have traveled 85 miles, in the least calculation, in five consecutive days, over a rough, hilly route, with stormy weather to increase our sufferings and add to the horrors of a forced march. As drops of perspiration rolled down the sunburnt cheek of the burdened soldier, we thought no man or woman could hesitate to use every effort to end this unholy

---

82 Wingate, *History of the Twenty-Second Regiment*, 199-200.

83 Horatio D. Chapman diary, entry for June 30, 1863, in *Civil War Diary of a Forty-niner*, 20.

84 Matthew Marvin diary, entry for June 30, 1863, in "Memorandum and diary notes," Marvin Papers, Minnesota Historical Society, St. Paul, as cited in Hage, "The Battle of Gettysburg as Seen by Minnesota Soldiers," 249. Marvin volunteered early in the war and paid a price for his long service. His first injury was a wound in the foot at Bull Run, and he was later struck in the thigh when a gun accidentally discharged while his regiment was encamped. Given the horror that awaited the 1st Minnesota on July 2, Marvin was one of the lucky ones. A second foot wound ended his service and he was mustered out.

war by the prompt crushing out of all traitors and their abettors; but alas the hardships endured are not realized by all. God forbid that it should continue so long. Our destination is unknown . . . the men are doing well, and their spirits are still buoyant.[85]

An afternoon shower that drenched the troops and rendered the roads muddy and difficult to traverse did nothing to dampen the enthusiasm of the men of the 141st Pennsylvania as they tramped closer to their native soil with each step. "Our men are in fine spirits and the long marches have only made them more hardy and strong than ever—very few have fallen behind since we left Aquia Creek," declared Maj. Israel P. Spaulding. "The citizens here are highly pleased with our approach. Crowds are gathered at every corner to see and cheer us on. Our camp this morning is full of citizens with their families walking around. A carriage is now before our tent with some little girls singing a patriotic song. Everything seems to be like civilization again."[86]

"When we reached the line," remembered Charles Sprague of the 44th New York, V Corps, "something unusual occurred. We were brought to attention; the colors, which always were covered with cases, were taken out, the drummers and fifers played, 'Ain't You Glad to Get Out of the Wilderness?' while we marched steadily in the 'cadenced step' across the border into a free state." A member of the 137th New York, part of the XII Corps, recorded, "Tuesday we marched 12 miles to Littlestown, Pa. The advance of the twelfth corps had a slight skirmish with a few rebel scouts. The inhabitants of Littlestown were overjoyed at our presence, not knowing that we were coming. The ladies came out with water and eatables for the tired and careworn soldiers. They have their reward."[87]

The I Corps' Iron Brigade passed over the Mason-Dixon line about mid-morning. "This is the first time since the war began that we have been obliged to go into a free state," Capt. Nathaniel Rollins of the 2nd Wisconsin scrawled in his diary. "The people are loyal and seriously in earnest."[88]

85 "Army Correspondence," *Flemington* (NJ) *Republican*, July 10, 1863.

86 Craft, *History of the One Hundred Forty-first Regiment, Pennsylvania*, 112. Spalding was a wealthy and influential farmer from Wysox, PA, the sheriff of Bradford County, and was instrumental in raising the regiment. He would be mortally wounded on July 2 and linger until July 28.

87 "Fourth of July, '63, As It Dawned for a Soldier at Gettysburg," *Canton* (OH) *Repository*, July 3, 1886; "Letter from the 137th," *Onondaga Standard* (Syracuse, NY), July 25, 1863.

88 Nathaniel Rollins, Diary Excerpts from Gettysburg Battlefield, June 30–July 6, 1863, unpublished manuscript in the Wisconsin Historical Society Archives, Madison, WI. Rollins

Unlike much of the rest of the army, Winfield Hancock's II Corps enjoyed a much-needed break in the vicinity of Frederick. Irish-born Maj. St. Clair Mulholland of the 116th Pennsylvania relished "[t]wo days of delightful rest with fresh bread, and many city luxuries from the stores of Frederick." According to Mulholland, "Candy was in great demand, and a bronzed veteran with a stick of candy in one hand and a doughnut in the other was not an unusual sight. The farmers flocked into camp with produce, and a grateful sense of gratified hunger prevailed in the ranks. In the evening songs were heard from all the camps, and fires blazed all over the country. Everyone's spirits rose and one of the happiest nights of the march passed away." Resting at Uniontown, Theodore Reichardt bemoaned the fact that his Battery A, 1st Rhode Island Light Artillery had rumbled 139 miles since June 14. Whiskey, he complained to his diary, "is very abundant around here."[89]

II Corps division commander John Gibbon penned a letter to his wife. "Our cavalry reached . . . [Westminster] this morning and we hear, today, came up with the enemy's rear guard and had a fight with it. We have remained quiet today," he continued, "having had a very long march of 30 miles yesterday, but the rest of this army is in motion and I presume we also shall be early tomorrow morning We are now rapidly approaching the enemy and under our new commander, I believe, can whip him." Gibbon assured her that the army's spirits had "improved by the change and we all now congratulate ourselves that we shall, at least, have an honest administration of affairs at Headquarters." The day, he added, was one of awaiting "the developments which the next days were to bring forth."[90]

Writing from his brigade's bivouac near Taneytown, Col. Robert P. McAllister of the 11th New Jersey, Andrew A. Humphreys's III Corps division, was pleased to see the numerous demonstrations of loyalty by the local citizenry. "They seemed to be more loyal than the people in some parts of the North," he observed. "I don't know what is before us. But we suppose we will have some fighting to do. If we get a little rest, we will be ready for it. We have now travelled about 150 miles or more, and have performed the longest and hardest marches of the war. As a general thing, the troops are in good spirits and in good health. This country is healthy—good

---

would be taken prisoner the following day at Gettysburg and refuse a parole. He would spend the rest of the war in captivity.

89 Mulholland, *The Story of the 116th Regiment*, 129; Reichardt, *Diary of Battery A, 1st Rhode Island*, 68.

90 Gibbon, *Recollections*, 131.

water, pure air, very different from Virginia. We seem to breathe another atmosphere, and the men seem to be perfectly delighted."[91]

While George Sykes's V Corps marched from Frederick to Union Mills, a local woman labored through the day at her kitchen table making "the celebrated Maryland biscuits." As soon as each batch was baked and the pans cool enough to handle, she sent them outside with her children, who stood by the gateway handing out two or three biscuits to each soldier.[92]

Whitelaw Reid, a special field correspondent for the *Cincinnati Gazette*, paused at Frederick en route to rendezvousing with the army. "An hour after breakfast sufficed for buying a horse and getting him equipped for the campaign," he penned. "Drunken soldiers were still staggering about the streets, looking for a last drink, or a horse to steal." The provost guards finally corralled the miscreants and restored order. The arrival of the V Corps at Union Mills greatly pleased William Shriver, who had seen Stuart's cavalry leave his farm that morning.[93]

Corporal Charles Smedley of the 90th Pennsylvania arose at 5:00 a.m. Shortly thereafter "an old gentleman and lady came into camp, bringing bread, butter, biscuits and doughnuts, and gave them to us, saying, 'poor fellows, we'll give you all we have, if you will drive the rebels off, and hope you'll not get killed.'" After a hearty breakfast Smedley and his comrades departed at 8:00 a.m. Near Emmitsburg they encountered the XI Corps, also headed for Pennsylvania. "As soon as we crossed the line, we gave nine cheers," recalled a happy Smedley. "After stopping, we were told to put up our tents. My feet are very sore and blistered."[94]

Even with high spirits the forced marching took its toll on the road-weary Union army. Corporal Newton T. Hartshorn of the U.S. Engineer Battalion camped in a small grove near Taneytown. Long columns of abandoned shoes lined the road. "Several regiments on their way to Gettysburg had received new footwear," he explained. "The men had been in column and discarded the old shoes as they sat in line. The change was quickly made, as the undisturbed lines of shoes indicated."[95]

91 Robertson, *The Civil War Letters of General Robert McAllister*, 330.

92 William H. Powell, *The Fifth Army Corps (Army of the Potomac): A Record of Operations During the Civil War* (New York, 1896), 509.

93 Ibid.; Moore, ed., *Rebellion Record*, 7:86.

94 Charles Smedley, *Life in Southern Prisons; From the Diary of Corporal Charles Smedley of Company G, 90th Regiment, Penn'a Volunteers* (Lancaster, PA, 1865), 54.

95 *Springfield* (MA) *Republican*, June 29, 1913.

Brig. Gen. John W. Geary commanded the 2nd Division of the XII Corps of the Army of the Potomac.

LOC

General Meade knew a large battle was brewing, and very soon, thus he issued a circular urging his men to be faithful to the large task before them. "The commanding general requests that previous to the engagement soon expected with the enemy, corps and all other commanding officers address their troops, explaining to them briefly the immense issues involved in the struggle," it began:

> The enemy are now on our soil. The whole country now looks anxiously to this army to deliver it from the presence of the foe. Our failure to do so will leave us no such welcome as the swelling of millions of hearts with pride and joy at our success would give to every soldier of this army. Homes, firesides and domestic altars are involved. The army has fought well heretofore; it is believed that it will fight more desperately and bravely if it is addressed in fitting terms. Corps and other commanders are authorized to order the instant death of any soldier who fails in his duty at this hour.[96]

Brigadier General John W. Geary's division of Slocum's XII Corps arrived in Littlestown early that afternoon. The citizens there could speak of little but the cavalry battle at Hanover. After he heard reports of the shooting between the opposing cavalry ahead, Geary prepared to fight. "At 5 o'clock on the morning of the 30th, the division . . . marched through Taneytown and Littlestown, encamping near the latter place at noon," recounted Geary. "A half hour before reaching this place our cavalry had there [Hanover] a skirmish with that of the rebels. The command was hastened forward and dispositions made to receive the enemy, who, however, retired in the direction of Hanover."[97]

Colonel Charles Candy, who was in command of one of Geary's three infantry brigades, went into more detail in his official report. "On the arrival of this division [Second] at Littlestown," he later explained, "this brigade was ordered to take a position in the woods on the right of the town [Littlestown], in the direction of Hanover, and on the right of the road, and hold it at all hazards. The cavalry skirmishing with the enemy in the front, formed in column by two battalions front, threw forward skirmishers, and picketed to my front and right." None of Geary's men were engaged in the fighting, but their position threatened Stuart's left at Hanover.[98]

*   *   *

The question on the minds of those in Washington was whether the Army of the Potomac would arrive in Pennsylvania in time to stop Lee's Virginia army from capturing the state capital or inflicting other substantial damage. Shortly after noon General Halleck instructed Couch in Harrisburg, "Every possible effort should be made to hold the enemy in check on the Susquehanna till Gen. Meade can give him battle. I have no direct communication with Gen. Meade, but he wishes you to be in readiness to act in concert with him. You will probably be able to learn his movements from the country people. He will be close on the enemy's right and rear."

With a major battle brewing, a few officers took time to adjust their command structure. Some of the shakeups did not meet with approval from the rank and file. The popular Col. James A. Beaver of the II Corps's 148th Pennsylvania was still recuperating from a wound inflicted at Chancellorsville, so Lt. Col. Robert McFarlane was in charge. Brigade commander Edward E. Cross wanted a more experienced officer, so he reassigned Col. H. Boyd McKeen from the 81st Pennsylvania to the 148th Regiment. "This act of Colonel Cross was wholly unjustifiable," declared outraged adjutant Joseph W. Muffly, "the culmination of a series of insults and indignities, which, taking advantage of Beaver's absence, he had inflicted on the regiment. It was bitterly resented by the men and as I passed

97 Ibid., pt. 1, 825.

98 Ibid., pt. 1, 835-836.

through the camp late at night I found men gathered in groups discussing the act and expressing their indignation in very strong language."[99]

* * *

Angst continued to mount in the nation's capital. Reporter Whitelaw Reid, who departed the city early that morning for Frederick, wrote about what was transpiring in the capital. "Washington was again like a city besieged, as after Bull Run. All night long, troops were marching; orderlies with clanking sabres clattering along the streets; trains of wagons grinding over the bouldered avenue; commissaries were hurrying up their supplies; the quartermaster's department was like a bee-hive; every thing was motion and hurry." He continued:

> From the War Department came all manner of exciting statements; men were everywhere asking what the President thought of the emergency. Trains had again come through regularly from Baltimore, but how long could it continue? Had not Stuart's cavalry been as near as the old Blair place at Silver Springs, and might they not cut the track any moment they chose? Might they not, indeed, asked the startled bankers, might they not indeed charge past the forts on the Maryland side, pay a hurried visit to the President and Cabinet, and replenish their army chests from our well-stored vaults?[100]

Secretary of the Treasury Salmon P. Chase admitted he was anxious, but he also realized Lee's gamble was a big one that offered decisive opportunities. "If I could explain the movements in Pennsylvania and Maryland I should be glad; but no thicker darkness envelopes any one than myself," he complained to a friend. "It seems to me now as it has seemed from the first that there need be nothing alarming in this invasion; that on the contrary it offers a capital opportunity to strike the most fatal blows the rebellion has yet received. A raid of rebel cavalry near Washington is not agreeable; but it has not much practical significance, unless followed up [by] any attack, which Lee will hardly undertake. The same thing can be said of the raid of Spear from Dix's army to Hanover Junction last week—useless unless a prelude to an attack on Richmond." He continued venting his frustration.

---

99 Muffly, *The Story of Our Regiment*, 244.

100 "The Battles of Gettysburgh: 'Cincinnati Gazette' Account," in Moore, ed., *Rebellion Record*, 7:85.

John G. Nicolay was a personal secretary and confidant of President Lincoln.

LOC

"But how idle it seems to me to speculate on Military affairs! The President consults only Stanton & Halleck in the management of the War. I look on from the outside and, as well as I can, furnish the means." Chase noted that he could only control events in his department and that he did the best he could at that.[101]

"Stirring times seem to be upon us again," Lincoln's secretary John G. Nicolay told his friend Therena Bates. "It appears pretty evident that Lee has taken most of his army into Maryland and Pennsylvania, with perhaps the design of taking Baltimore or Washington—his object not being as yet sufficiently developed to say with any certainty what it is. At present the rebel army is scattered about over Pennsylvania gathering up forage and stealing supplies. That State is almost completely paralyzed by fear or entirely apathetic and is moving in a very feeble way to help herself. Whether as danger presses her she will arouse herself to more vigorous action is yet a danger."

Nicolay went on to tell Bates about the Army of the Potomac's change of command and its new commander: "He is a good officer so far as he has been tried; but as we have had six different commanders fail in the task he [Lincoln] assumes it is idle to say in advance whether or not he will make the seventh."[102]

101 Niven, *The Salmon P. Chase Papers*, 4:74.

102 Burlingame, *With Lincoln in the White House*, 117-118.

One of the most threatened towns, although not necessarily one with "well-stored vaults," was Gettysburg. "There were daily, almost hourly, reports of raids into Penn'a, and once or twice some Cavalry came as far as Cashtown and retreated," penned Fannie J. Buehler, the wife of the town's postmaster. "At first we were very much frightened by the thought of Rebel soldiers invading our town, taking possession of our new court house and other buildings, and doing all kinds of bad things, such as we read of in the papers. As day by day passed, and they did not come, we lost faith in their coming, and it grew to be an old story. We tried to make ourselves believe they would never come, and we made merry over the reports which continued to be circulated until they really came. When we saw them, we believed." She added, "We [had] even laughed and joked among ourselves, little dreaming they were so near."[103]

Some soldiers also found humor on the eve of what many believed would be a grim and deadly encounter in the Keystone State. On the night of June 30, Lt. J. Clyde Miller of the 153rd Pennsylvania led a detail on the advanced picket line. "Orders were to fire on any one," he recalled, "or force appearing in front, and not to demand the giving of the countersign. It was a murky, misty night, and not liking the looks of what I thought was suspicious in front of my line, I told the boys I would scout out in front to see if there were any Johnnies there, and that on my return I would be whistling 'Yankee Doodle' softly so they would know who it was; but when half way back, the firing commenced on the left of the line, and hearing the rush coming through the cornfield, and thinking it was cavalry, and knowing my men would also commence firing to prevent a break through, I admit, candidly, that I forgot all about my whistling 'Yankee Doodle,' and got back into line far quicker than when I went out. The laugh was on us when day light came, as the numerous dead in our front was seen to be not rebels, but innocent sheep, which would not even bite a Union soldier."[104]

"The sky was clear of clouds and filled with bright glittering stars. The moon threw a calm, mellow light over our camp, and the surrounding hills," remembered J. Montgomery Bailey of the 17th Connecticut from camp at Emmitsburg. "We felt that our marching was about done for the present, and that we were on the eve of a heavy struggle. The solemnity which always foreruns a battle, pervaded our minds, intensifying our thoughts of home, and weaving shadows of anxiety across our future." He reflected on the prevailing rumors. "Lee had destroyed Harrisburg,

103 Buehler, *Recollections of the Rebel Raid*, GNMP.

104 Keifer and Mack, *History of the 153rd Pennsylvania*, 139.

routed the militia, and was rapidly advancing on us by way of Gettysburg. I stood leaning against a camp stake, gazing dreamily across the hill, with mind reverting to Chancellorsville and filled with anticipations of a second edition so soon to be issued. In imagination I was amid the carnage, surrounded by gleaming bayonets and staggering wounded, while the air resounded with the unearthly hiss and whiz of shot and shell, and piercing cries of the mangled combatants."[105]

*   *   *

Brigadier General David M. Gregg's 2nd Cavalry Division rode from New Windsor to Westminster, and then on to Manchester, Maryland. The troopers camped there for the night, holding the eastern end of the defensive line along Pipe Creek laid out by the Army of the Potomac's engineers.[106]

*   *   *

John Buford roused his men at 2:00 a.m. on June 30. "Soon after 3 we got the men in the saddle and moved out," recalled Col. George H. Chapman of the 3rd Indiana Cavalry.

The Yankee troopers struggled through the dense fog toward Fairfield via the Jack's Mountain Road (which parallels the south side of mountain) with the 8th Illinois Cavalry in the lead. A small portion of Buford's command, comprised of a detachment of the 6th New York Cavalry, took the parallel Iron Springs Road on the north side of Jack's Mountain to cover Buford's flank. After half an hour's ride, and having reached the foot of Jack's Mountain, the Illinois troopers encountered enemy infantry from Brig. Gen. Joseph Davis's Mississippi brigade (Company B, 52nd North Carolina) and Brig. Gen. James J. Pettigrew's North Carolina brigade, both belonging to Henry Heth's Third Corps division. One Unionist described the location as "a strong outpost of the enemy" on the Peter Musselman farm near a bridge over the swift-moving Tom's Creek. Captain Benjamin Little of the 52nd North Carolina claimed the rest of his regiment came up to support Company B, which skirmished with the Union troopers and swept them away. At the same time,

105 J. Montgomery Bailey, "Under Guard, or, Sunny South in Slices," *Danbury* (CT) *Times*, Oct. 8, 1863.

106 *OR* 27, pt. 3, 400.

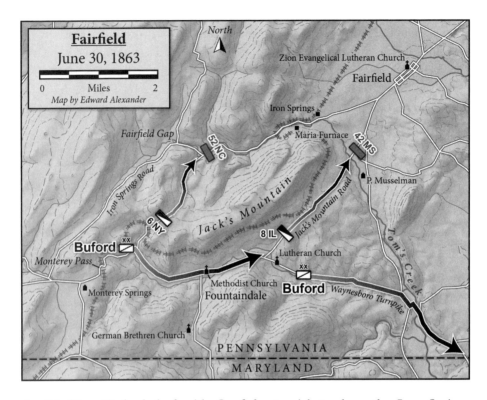

the 6th New York clashed with Confederate pickets along the Iron Springs Road.[107]

This unexpected and chance encounter could have been avoided if the local citizenry had been more forthcoming with information. The Confederates were there to guard the mouth of the Fairfield Gap, which provided the direct route to Fountaindale and the Monterey Pass, and to protect Tom's Creek, a fast-moving stream that provided an excellent water source. The picket post manned by the Tar Heels under Lt. W. E. Kyle was about five miles from the rest of the regiment and thus the rest of their brigade, which was camped at Cashtown. The North Carolinians believed Buford's horse soldiers were part of a Union picket post

---

107 Chapman diary, entry for June 30, 1863; Cheney, *History of the Ninth New York Cavalry*, 101-102. See *History of Cumberland and Adams Counties* (Chicago, 1886), 445, for the identification of Peter Musselman as the owner of the farm where this encounter occurred. Walter Clark, ed., *Histories of the Several Regiments and Battalions from North Carolina in the Great War, 1861–65* (Goldsboro, NC, 1901), 3:236; David G. Martin, *Gettysburg, July 1* (New York, 1995), 40; Sarah Sites Thomas, Tim Smith, Gary Kross, and Dean S. Thomas, *Fairfield in the Civil War* (Gettysburg, PA, 2011), 42; Account of Capt. Benjamin F. Little, Co. F, 52nd North Carolina Infantry, copy in files, GNMP.

rather than a large force of cavalry patrolling south-central Pennsylvania gathering intelligence about the disposition of the Army of Northern Virginia.[108]

An officer of Buford's experience realized immediately that an isolated force of Confederate infantry without a cavalry screen so far north of the Mason-Dixon line was part of a much larger infantry command operating nearby. "I determined to feel it and drive it, if possible," he later explained. Buford briefly considered unlimbering Calef's guns and having them open on the Southerners, but he was worried the artillery fire might be heard at Lee's headquarters and trigger a larger engagement. "[W]e encountered the Rebels the next morning; as they were in force here we were about to open against infantry," recalled one of Buford's troopers, "but as we were dismounting orders came which were to the effect that we should tumble back and take the branch road to Emmitsburg." The Tar Heels would also withdraw from their exposed position that night. Thus, explained one Unionist, the opposing forces "mutually recoiled from each other."[109]

During those brief minutes of skirmishing, however, a ricocheting Confederate ball struck Pvt. Thomas Withrow of the 8th Illinois in the abdomen and knocked him from his saddle. The ball did not break his skin or the wound may have been fatal. Infuriated at being unhorsed, Withrow swore revenge. The bruised trooper took cover behind a barn and began popping away at the Confederates with his carbine. He was close enough to overhear an enemy officer direct his men to search the barn, so he hid in a hay pile. The Southern infantrymen thrust their bayonets into the stack looking to make sure nobody was hiding there, and the steel points narrowly missed Withrow. One Confederate passed so close that Withrow could have killed him easily, but he valued his own life "more than that of a rebel colonel." The Southerners left when they failed to find the Union trooper. The farmer upon whose land the brief exchange occurred got quite a surprise when he came out to make sure nothing had been stolen and found Withrow occupying his barn. Relieved that the trespasser was a Yankee, the farmer invited the Illinois native into his home for dinner. Withrow gratefully accepted before setting off toward Gettysburg on foot.[110]

Buford had made a prudent choice. He did not know the strength of the force opposing him or the number of artillery pieces supporting it. In addition, he was under orders to observe, not engage, enemy infantry. Withrow's light wound aside,

108 Clark, ed., *Histories of the Several Regiments*, 3:236.

109 *Aurora* (IL) *Beacon*, Aug. 20, 1863; DePuyster, *Decisive Conflicts*, 52.

110 Hard, *History of the Eighth Cavalry Regiment*, 256.

Maj. Gen. John F. Reynolds commanded the I Corps and then a wing of the Army of the Potomac. He died on July 1 at Gettysburg, the highest-ranking officer to perish in the battle.

LOC

Buford did not report any casualties. The Rebels lost one Mississippian killed and three wounded.[111]

The encounter with Heth's Rebel infantry at Fairfield triggered Buford to jot a quick report to his wing commander, Maj. Gen. John F. Reynolds, whose headquarters were at Emmitsburg. "The enemy has increased his forces considerably," Buford reported via mounted courier. "His strong position is just behind Cashtown. My party toward Mummasburg met a superior force, strongly posted. Another party [the detachment of the 6th New York Cavalry] that went up the road due north, 3 miles out, met a strong picket; had a skirmish, and captured a prisoner of Rodes' division. Another party that went toward Littlestown heard that Gregg or Kilpatrick had a fight with Stuart, and drove him to Hanover." This concise yet detailed report accurately described the whereabouts of the Confederate forces around Fairfield and Cashtown while reporting the proximity of Jeb Stuart's troopers.[112]

Buford pushed his column seven miles through a light drizzle and arrived at Emmitsburg about 10:00 a.m., where he consulted with Reynolds in person. The cavalryman recounted the Fairfield skirmish to a general now in command of about one-half of the Army of the Potomac. Knowing it was imperative that he fully understand all that Buford had discovered, and now aware that a large force of

111 Ibid., 255-256.

112 OR 27, pt. 1, 922. Here, Buford refers to the beginning phases of the June 30, 1863, battle of Hanover, which evolved into a day-long slug match with Brig. Gen. Judson Kilpatrick's 3rd Cavalry Division. For a detailed discussion of these events, see Eric J. Wittenberg and J. David Petruzzi, *Plenty of Blame to Go Around: Jeb Stuart's Controversial Ride to Gettysburg* (El Dorado Hills, CA, 2006).

enemy infantry was close to his headquarters, Reynolds sent a staff officer along with Buford, who would ensure that the most current intelligence was relayed back to the wing commander. Once the brief meeting ended, Buford turned his brigades north and rode the eight miles to Gettysburg along the Emmitsburg Road, passing Federal infantry tramping in the same direction.[113]

Given his later reporting on the subject, there is little doubt Buford stewed over his Fairfield experience during his ride toward Gettysburg. "The inhabitants knew of my arrival and the position of the enemy's camp, yet no one gave me a particle of information, nor even mentioned the fact of the enemy's presence," he complained. "The whole community seemed stampeded, and afraid to speak or act, often offering as excuses for not showing some little enterprise, 'The rebels will destroy our houses if we tell anything.' Had any one given me timely information, and acted as a guide that night," he concluded, "I could have surprised and captured this force, which proved the next day to be two Mississippi regiments of infantry and two guns." Buford's frustration is understandable, but some of this criticism seems unfair. Whether the local citizenry even knew of the presence of Buford's troopers, for example, has never been determined. Fair or not, the silence of these Pennsylvania farmers drew the ire of a Kentuckian who had little enough tolerance for civilians as it was.[114]

Buford's troopers crossed the Mason-Dixon line and approached Marsh Creek, passing the camps of the I Corps. "They had plenty of news for us, and it was of an exciting character," recalled one of the corps' artillerists. "They would sing out as they rode by, 'We have found the Johnnies; they are just above and to the left of us, and the woods are full of 'em.'" The men of the 6th New York Cavalry reported that they had tried to go to Gettysburg by the shorter route that morning but had encountered Confederate infantry in sufficient numbers to compel them to turn back and approach by the Emmitsburg route. The same artillerist also overheard Maj. William E. Beardsley of the 6th New York tell his

---

113 The Marcellus E. Jones Journal, entry for June 30, 1863, Perrin-Wheaton Chapter, National Society of the Daughters of the American Revolution, Wheaton, IL; Harry W. Pfanz, *Gettysburg: The First Day* (Chapel Hill, NC, 2001), 39.

114 *OR 27*, pt. 1, 926. According to Thomas, Smith, Kross, and Thomas, in *Fairfield in the Civil War*, 43, the local citizenry does not deserve blame on this issue. "Over the years, many historians have given credence to Buford's comments, but in reality, the citizens of Fairfield had no knowledge of Buford's arrival at Fountaindale and Monterey that night. And the idea that Buford's cavalry could have, or would have even attempted, to capture or destroy a force of Confederate infantry is highly questionable."

battery commander that Lee's entire army was in front of them and that the cavalry was advancing to bring on an engagement.[115]

The lead elements of Buford's column clattered into Gettysburg at 11:00 a.m. on June 30. The first to arrive were scouts from the 3rd Indiana and 8th Illinois of Gamble's brigade. Their dash into town netted several surprised Confederate soldiers who "seemed to be straggling through the streets and mingling with the citizens."[116]

Lieutenant A. H. Moore of the 7th Tennessee, part of Brig. Gen. James J. Archer's Brigade of Heth's Division (Hill's Third Corps), had orders to take 40 men east toward Gettysburg to picket the road from Cashtown. Cavalry normally performed this sort of critical duty, but there were no horse soldiers available to screen the advance that morning. As a result, infantry—which was not well suited to this sort of duty—had no choice but to perform this important task. "Here, about mid-day, I observed some Federal cavalry ride to the top of an eminence, and after reconnoitering they retired," Moore remembered. "This was the first appearance of the enemy yet seen by any of Hill's Corps. These appeared to be scouts, and not of any regular command—at least they did not come in any force. As they retired, I sent a man back to report to General Archer; I remained with my command for the rest of the day and night." These cavalry "scouts" were probably troopers from Captain Harry Sparks's command.[117]

The Federals received a hero's welcome from the townspeople, who flooded them with food, drinks, and rumors about the Confederates. The column halted in the streets for half an hour while Buford and his brigade commanders reconnoitered. A citizen rode along with the advancing Federals, telling all who would listen that 6,000 Rebel cavalry was waiting for them on the other side of town. A local couple invited Capt. William C. Hazelton of the 8th Illinois Cavalry into their home for a meal. When they asked, "Can't we do something for you?" Hazelton replied, "You will have the opportunity to do something for us tomorrow." "Why?" asked the startled citizens. "Will there be a battle?"[118]

115 Augustus C. Buell, "Story of a Cannoneer," part 3, *National Tribune*, Oct. 24, 1889.

116 Martin, *Gettysburg, July 1*, 42.

117 A. H. Moore, "Heth's Division at Gettysburg," *Southern Bivouac*, vol. 3, no. 9 (May 1885), 384.

118 *Aurora* (IL) *Beacon*, August 20, 1863; W. C. Hazelton, "An Address Made at a Regimental Reunion," *Gettysburg Star and Sentinel*, Sept. 1, 1891.

"As we advanced on Gettysburg, the Rebels fell back and, oh, how glad the people were!" declared Eli Ditzler of the 8th Illinois. "On street corners fair misses collected and sang 'Star Spangled Banner' for us as we passed, and there were roaring cheers." Later, after the regiment established its camp, Ditzler rode back into town to buy some small articles. "Ladies on the streets with baskets filled would give us all the pies, cakes, and goodies we wanted . . . I stopped at a house where seminary girls boarded. They gave me a bouquet and sang songs to the accompaniment of the piano—all for my benefit, dirty and rough as I was. How sweet it sounded!" Private Thomas B. Kelley of the 8th Illinois had similar fond recollections of that day when he wrote, "The women brought out bread, coffee, milk and cake for us, and I can tell you that nothing ever tasted better. It was the first time in 18 months that soft bread had passed my lips."[119]

"That reception was a good deal of a surprise to us," recalled an officer in the 6th New York Cavalry of Devin's brigade. Captain William H. Redman of the 12th Illinois Cavalry watched as "young Ladies came out in the streets by the hundreds—handing us bouquets and singing to us as we passed along, 'My Lover has Gone to War'—a very beautiful song which made us all feel good." Redman liked the town, noting, "the people are truly loyal and look upon us . . . as . . . rescuers." After days on the march the horse soldiers were filthy and smelled even worse than they looked, but they were a sight for sore eyes after Early's Rebels had swept through the place four days earlier.[120]

After establishing his headquarters at Tate's Eagle Hotel, west of the town square about one mile from a prominent Lutheran seminary atop a commanding ridge just west of Gettysburg. Buford scrawled another update to Reynolds. "The main force—[Richard] Anderson's Division—encamped last night 9 miles NW of Gettysburg on Chambersburg Pike—at base of South Mountain 1 mile beyond Cashtown," he reported at 11:30 a.m. "One Regt of Infty came near Gettysburg at 11 a.m. and retired as I advanced. The main force is believed to be marching north of Gettysburg through Mummasburg, Hunterstown, Hampton & towards Berlin & York. I will send parties out on roads towards the supposed position of the enemy." He signed the note with a simple "Buford." The cavalryman sent a galloper with this important intelligence to Reynolds, who was less than 10 miles distant. For reasons that remain unexplained, the report did not reach Reynolds's

119 Hall, *The Captain*, 41; "Opened the Fight at Gettysburg," *Boston Sunday Globe*, Dec. 5, 1909.

120 "Gettysburg Honor to Girls of '63," *New York Times*, July 1, 1913; William H. Redman to his mother, July 1, 1863, Redman Papers.

headquarters until nearly three that afternoon. Before he received this information, Reynolds contemplated taking a position on Marsh Creek between Gettysburg and Emmitsburg as the spot for the army to make its stand. Buford's reports persuaded Reynolds to shift instead farther north to Gettysburg. Buford also scribbled a quick note to General Pleasonton at 12:20 p.m.: "My extreme left reports a large force coming toward Fairfield, in a direction to strike the Emmitsburg road this side of Marsh Creek. Reliable."[121]

While Buford was passing along intelligence to his superiors, he was also declaring martial law in Gettysburg. The hard-nosed general jailed a suspected spy, issued strict orders prohibiting local tavern owners from selling alcohol to his troops, and had leaflets printed to that effect. In addition to everything else he had learned, Buford discovered a citizen for whom Robert E. Lee had signed a pass that morning in Chambersburg—solid evidence of the whereabouts of the Confederate commander's headquarters. The armies were now in proximity, and major fighting could break out at any time. The last thing he needed was for his troopers to be impaired by alcohol. Buford directed Gamble and Devin to establish their camps near the Lutheran Seminary, and then set about planning his defense of the town.[122]

* * *

Gettysburg, home to about 2,000 residents, was the seat of Adams County. It rests in a basin surrounded by mountains between 10 to 20 miles from the town square. A series of ridges and hills extend to the north and west. About a mile west of the square is Seminary Ridge, which extends on a north-south axis with the Lutheran Seminary the most prominent point on the eponymous ridge. The long ridge was heavily wooded south of the seminary complex. About half a mile farther west was the more open McPherson's Ridge with its twin crests. A wealthy local businessman named Edward McPherson

---

121 John Blosher to John B. Bachelder, Dec. 8, 1890, copy in files, GNMP; John Buford to John F. Reynolds, June 30, 1863, Army of the Potomac Bureau of Military Information, RG 393I, Entry 3980, Box 11, NARA (this dispatch does not appear in the *Official Records*); OR 27, pt. 3, 417-418 and pt. 1, 922. Reynolds told Meade that "it might be necessary to dispute the enemy across (Marsh) Creek, in order to take up position behind Middle Creek."

122 Gerald R. Bennett, *Days of Uncertainty and Dread* (Littlestown, PA, 1994), 18; Edwin C. Fishel, *The Secret War for the Union: The Untold Story of Military Intelligence in the Civil War* (Boston, 1996), 506.

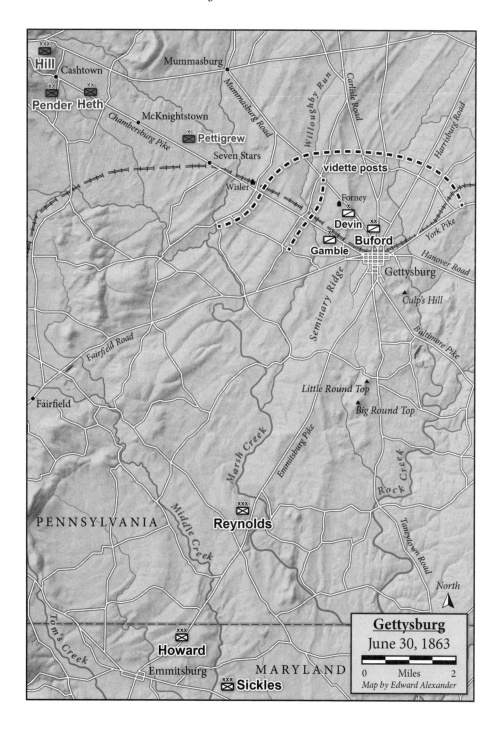

Gettysburg
June 30, 1863

0   Miles   2
Map by Edward Alexander

owned the farm and most of the ridge that bore his name. Two barns and a large farmhouse sat between the crests of the ridge south of the Chambersburg Pike.[123]

The small creek named Willoughby Run flows south along the western base of McPherson's Ridge. Beyond it, roughly two miles from the town square, are the highest elevations of Herr's Ridge and Belmont Schoolhouse Ridge, that latter of which merges into the former on a northwesterly diagonal angle just below the Chambersburg Pike. Herr's Tavern provided accommodations and food for travelers at that point. Another valley lay to the west of Herr's Ridge, with Knoxlyn Ridge rising another mile or so farther west. Ephraim Wisler's blacksmith shop sat atop the crest of Knoxlyn Ridge overlooking March Creek, a wide, swift brook running through the valley beyond. These terrain features would play a critical role in a drama John Buford was about to script.

Like any good soldier, Buford took note of the terrain to the south and east of Gettysburg as he approached the town. With large hills at both ends (Cemetery Hill in the north and the Round Tops in the south) and a prominent ridge connecting those hills, Buford understood that the ground offered an excellent defensive position for the army. Armed with the knowledge that a large force of the enemy situated near Cashtown might advance on Gettysburg from the west, Buford settled upon a delaying action north and west of the town—a covering force action in modern military parlance—wherein his troopers would hold successive defensive positions until Reynolds's infantry, six miles distant at Emmitsburg, could arrive and occupy the strategic high ground.

About 4:00 p.m. on June 30, Gettysburg resident Daniel Skelly beheld a sight he would recall clearly decades later: a mounted Buford at the corner of the Chambersburg Pike and Washington Street in front of the Eagle Hotel. The cavalryman "sat on his horse in the street in front of me, entirely alone, facing to the west, and in profound thought. It was the only time that I ever saw the General and his calm demeanor and soldierly appearance, as well as the fact that his uniform was different from any general's I had ever seen, struck me forcibly," recalled Skelly. "He wore a sort of hunting coat of blouse effect. It is possible that from that position he was directing through his aides the placing of his two brigades of cavalry . . . to the west and northwest of town.[124]

---

123 Edward McPherson did not live on or work the farm that bore his name. He leased the farm to John Slentz, who resided there when the war arrived in his yard on June 30, 1863.

124 Daniel A. Skelly, *A Boy's Experiences During the Battles of Gettysburg* (Gettysburg, PA, 1932), 10.

Brig. Gen. J. Johnston Pettigrew led a
brigade in Heth's Division in Hill's Third
Corps of the Army of Northern Virginia.

USAHEC

Once he had carefully chosen the ground, Buford saw to it that "arrangements were made for entertaining" the Confederates. He ordered Gamble to proceed west with his brigade past the seminary and select the best lines of defense along the Chambersburg Pike. Buford and Devin, meanwhile, climbed to the top of a nearby belfry—perhaps the cupola of the Lutheran Seminary—to reconnoiter the ground from a different perspective.[125]

It was at this time that Buford's lead elements encountered Confederate infantry advancing east along the Chambersburg Pike. Third Corps leader A. P. Hill had approved the move, using Pettigrew's large brigade of North Carolina infantry (Heth's Division) and 15 wagons to forage for supplies in Gettysburg. Heth gave Pettigrew specific verbal instructions for this expedition, which Lt. Louis G. Young of Pettigrew's staff would later recall. "General Early had levied on Carlisle, Chambersburg, and Shippensburg, and had found no difficulty in having his requisitions filled," remembered Young. "It was supposed that it would be the same in Gettysburg. It was told to General Pettigrew that he might find the town in possession of a home-guard, which he would have no difficulty in driving away; but, if, contrary to expectations, he should find any organized troops capable of making resistance, or any portion of the Army of the Potomac, he should not attack it. The orders to him were peremptory, not to precipitate a fight," Young insisted. "General Lee with his columns scattered, and lacking the information of his

125 *OR* 27, pt. 1, 923-927; William Gamble to William L. Church, March 10, 1864, copy in files, GNMP; Hall, *History of the Sixth New York Cavalry*, 377.

adversary, which he should have had from his cavalry, was not ready for battle—hence the orders."[126]

Pettigrew had with him approximately 2,000 men from three of his four North Carolina regiments (the 11th, 26th, and 47th), as well as the Donaldsonville Artillery of Louisiana for "intimidating" purposes. About 9:30 a.m., a line of Pettigrew's soldiers "at least a mile and a half in length" moved along the Chambersburg Pike toward Gettysburg. A local physician on his way to visit a patient informed Pettigrew that four or five thousand Union soldiers were in the area—news that naturally made the inexperienced brigadier more cautious. The Confederates stopped short of Willoughby Run to await word from the skirmishers that there was a clear line of march into the town. The approach of a large body of the enemy worried many of Gettysburg's residents. "We had a good view of them from our house," recalled Sarah Broadhead, "and every moment expected to hear the booming of cannon, and thought they might shell the town."[127]

The Confederate pickets interrogated other residents and continued advancing as far east as Seminary Ridge. Once there, Pettigrew and many of his men spent about an hour on the ridge and vicinity reconnoitering and interviewing citizens. Around that time the pickets saw something in the distance that brought them up short: a column of enemy troopers entering town from the south. What the Rebels did not yet know was that the riders were part of Buford's cavalry column. The news was reported to Pettigrew: "a large force of cavalry near the town, supported by an infantry force."[128]

Pettigrew was more than willing to fight Union cavalry, but he was unsure of the strength of the force opposing him and only his brigade was up. The North Carolinian prudently withdrew west to the banks of Marsh Creek. Under strict orders not to bring on a general engagement, explained Lieutenant Young, they "did not enter the town . . . but examined it with their field glasses." Pettigrew left behind "pickets about four miles from Gettysburg" and deployed one regiment on each side of the Chambersburg Pike and the third straddling the road in front, or

---

126 Louis G. Young, "Pettigrew's Brigade at Gettysburg, 1-3 July 1863," Clark, ed., *Histories of the Several Regiments*, 5:115.

127 Professor Michael Jacobs, *Notes on the Rebel Invasion of Maryland and Pennsylvania and the Battle of Gettysburg, July 1st, 2nd, and 3rd, 1863* (Gettysburg, PA, 1864), 21-22; Sarah M. Broadhead diary, entry for June 30, 1863. Pettigrew left his fourth regiment, the 52nd North Carolina, at Cashtown, perhaps because of the detachment of troops that had skirmished with Buford at Fairfield that morning.

128 OR 27, pt. 2, 627.

east, of the other two. One eyewitness described the deployment as "two regiments defiled under cover of a hill, one to the right of the road, the other to the left, whilst a third was sent a short distance forward to induce a pursuit." Given this arrangement, Pettigrew may have been trying to lure Buford into something approximating a trap.[129]

If the Rebels could see the Union cavalrymen, the reverse was also true. As they rode through Gettysburg, Gamble's men spotted Pettigrew's troops. Companies D and E, commanded by Capt. Henry J. Hotopp of the 8th Illinois, dashed forward to determine the intentions of the hostile infantry. "Buford's cavalry followed us at some distance, and Lieutenant Walter H. Robertson and I, of Pettigrew's staff, remained in the rear to watch it," recalled Lieutenant Young years later. "This we easily did, for the country is rolling, and from behind the ridges we could see without being seen and we had a perfect view of the movements of the approaching column. Whenever it would come within three or four hundred yards of us we would make our appearance, mounted, when the column would halt until we retired. This was repeated several times. It was purely an affair of observation on both sides," concluded the staff officer, "and the cavalry made no effort to molest us."[130]

Despite waiting for about two hours, Buford's troopers refused to advance into what would surely have been a one-sided killing zone. Pettigrew moved farther west, pulling the 11th and 47th regiments back to a spot between the hamlets of McKnightstown and Seven Stars, but still within supporting distance of the 26th North Carolina, which picketed Marsh Creek. He sent his fourth regiment, the

---

129 "The Journal of Marcellus E. Jones," entry for June 30, 1863; Jacobs, *Notes on the Rebel Invasion*, 22. While Pettigrew's men were on Seminary Ridge, Jaquelin Marshall Meredith, the chaplain of Heth's Division, together with the division's surgeon, Dr. E. B. Spence, rode into Gettysburg to procure medical supplies. The two men rode about five miles east without seeing any enemy troops. The Southerners reached the town, dismounted, tied their horses at the first apothecary they found, and went into the store. A few minutes later they spotted one of Pettigrew's regiments coming from the direction of the town at a quick march. The two non-combatants hastily mounted and joined the regimental colonel at the head of the column, riding with him back to Cashtown. "The Doctor and I were told that a superior force of the enemy were moving on Gettysburg," recalled Meredith. "We were not followed nor did any Federal cavalry attack, or even show itself in rear or flank during the one hour and a half, to two hours that this regiment took to proceed in orderly march back to Cashtown." Jaquelin Marshall Meredith, "The First Day at Gettysburg: Tribute to Brave General Harry Heth, Who Opened the Great Battle," *SHSP*, vol. 24 (1896), 182-183.

130 Young, "Pettigrew's Brigade at Gettysburg," 5:116.

52nd North Carolina, the Donaldsonville battery, and his wagons on to Cashtown.[131]

Captain William W. Chamberlaine was a staff officer for Maj. William J. Pegram, the commander of the artillery battalion attached to A. P. Hill's Third Corps. Pegram's battalion rumbled through Cashtown Pass and was descending South Mountain when the trudging column of Third Corps infantry in front suddenly halted. Such situations, explained Chamberlaine, usually indicated "that the enemy has been seen." Though this was indeed the case, they were much farther east around Gettysburg. The column had stopped short because Pettigrew's Brigade was returning along the same road after its near encounter with Buford's troopers. News of the presence of Union soldiers in Gettysburg spread quickly through the ranks.[132]

On the other side of the lines, Buford reported the presence of Confederate infantry to General Pleasonton. "I entered this place to-day at 11 a.m. Found everyone in a terrible state of excitement on account of the enemies' advance on the place. He had approached to within half a mile of the town when the head of my column entered," Buford noted. He continued:

> His force was terribly exaggerated by reasonable and truthful but inexperienced men. On pushing him back to Cashtown, I learned from reliable men that Anderson's division was marching from Chambersburg by Mummasburg, Hunterstown, Abbottstown, on toward York. I have sent parties to the two first-named places, Cashtown, and a strong force toward Littlestown. . . . My men and horses are fagged out, I have not been able to get any grain yet. It is all in the country and the people talk instead of working. Facilities for shoeing are nothing. Early's people seized every shoe and nail they could find . . . no reliable information could be obtained from the inhabitants. . . . P.S. The troops that are coming here were the same I found early this morning at Millersburg or Fairfield. General Reynolds has been advised of all that I know.[133]

Buford also sent a dispatch to Reynolds: "I have pushed the pickets, or rather the rear guard of the Rebs, six miles toward Cashtown. I am satisfied that the force

---

131 Earl J. Hess, *Lee's Tar Heels: The Pettigrew-Kirkland-MacRae Brigade* (Chapel Hill, NC, 2002), 116.

132 William W. Chamberlaine, *Memoirs of the Civil War Between the Northern and Southern Sections of the United States of America, 1861–1865* (Washington, D.C., 1912), 64.

133 OR 27, pt. 1, 923.

that came here this morning was the same that I found at Fairfield." Buford was right.[134]

Pettigrew also kicked the news of what he had found up the command chain by relaying the information to General Heth. The new division leader, who had only been with the army since Chancellorsville, refused to believe a large force of enemy cavalry was in the town. The two officers were discussing this intelligence when General Hill rode up and asked Pettigrew to repeat his report. Pettigrew, who by this time was almost certainly frustrated by the failure of his division commander to believe him, called up staff officer Lieutenant Young to confirm the story. Young's account tracked Pettigrew's report. Both officers made it abundantly clear they had seen disciplined enemy troops and not members of a home guard.[135]

To the surprise of both officers, Hill dismissed the report out of hand. The corps leader was confident that Buford's command was still in the Loudoun Valley of Virginia and refused to accept the possibility that his division could be in his front. "I still cannot believe that any portion of the Army of the Potomac is up," Hill stated; he paused a moment before adding, "I hope that it is, for this is the place I want it to be."[136]

Off to the east, meanwhile, Buford established vidette posts along a seven-mile front stretching from the Fairfield Road on the southern end of this line north and east to the Harrisburg Road on the northeastern end of the line. Well aware that the Confederates had a large camp along the Chambersburg Pike near Cashtown, Buford also posted videttes along the pike about four miles from the center of town so he would have advance warning of any enemy approach. He intended for his videttes to make their stand as far away from the defensible high ground to the south and east of Gettysburg as possible. Hopefully, John Reynolds's infantry would arrive before his troopers were driven through the town and away from that good defensible ground.

Troopers of the 8th New York Cavalry peeled off to the left and advanced through McPherson's Woods southwest of the Chambersburg Pike while a squadron of the 8th Illinois advanced about three miles out the pike, establishing one vidette post on the road, three posts south of it, two posts north of the road, and one at the Wistler blacksmith shop on Knoxlyn Ridge overlooking Marsh

---

134 John Buford to John F. Reynolds, June 30, 1863, 4 p.m., RG 393, Entry 3980, Army of the Potomac, 1861–1865, Miscellaneous Letters, Reports, and Lists Received, NARA.

135 Hess, *Lee's Tar Heels*, 116.

136 W. H. Swallow, "The First Day at Gettysburg," *Southern Bivouac*, N.S. 1 (Dec. 1885), 441.

Creek. This last vidette post consisted of Pvts. Thomas Benton Kelley and James Hall, Sgts. Levi Shaffer and George Heim, and Lt. Alex Riddler of Company E, 8th Illinois. The 12th Illinois and the 3rd Indiana fell into line north of the 8th Illinois. Devin's troopers deployed their videttes north and east of Gamble's thin line.

The videttes posted themselves at intervals of 30 feet, using fence posts and rail fences as shelter. A typical vidette post consisted of four or five enlisted men with an officer or non-commissioned officer in charge, with a vidette reserve waiting close behind. "The order was for double posts, and two men were placed on each post with a corporal or sergeant," recalled Pvt. Thomas B. Kelley of the 8th Illinois. "We had several posts on or near the road, and others spread out on either side, along the creek."[137]

Half of the command's horses were kept bridled and the men slept in shifts, prepared to go into action at any moment. Each spent two hours on duty and four hours off. No more than 200 of Gamble's troopers manned the vidette posts; the rest stayed with the main line of battle atop McPherson's Ridge. Devin made similar dispositions north and east of town. His farthest left vidette post was stationed on the Chambersburg Pike and was commanded by Cpl. Alphonse Hodges of Company F, 9th New York. These videttes were ordered "not to fire on anyone approaching from the front, but to notify the pickets in each direction and the reserve." Devin stationed other vidette posts among and around the Forney farm buildings on the Mummasburg Road.[138]

H. O. Dodge of the 8th Illinois was on the picket line on the evening of June 30. "We remained there all night, and nothing occurred to break the monotony of the watching," he recalled. "We felt sure that a great battle was impending, for on the hillsides away down on the Chambersburg road we could plainly see the glowing campfires of the enemy, while now and then we could distinguish a soldier who walked between us and the fire."[139]

Morgan Hughes served in Company E of the 8th Illinois. "I remember that night of having charge of a reserve picket-post out on a turnpike near a farmer's house, and how he invited us all in to supper, and wanted the man out on post to come in, too," he recalled years after the war. "And when I explained that he was on

137 Coddington, *The Gettysburg Campaign*, 266; "Opened the Fight at Gettysburg."

138 Ibid.; Gary M. Kross, "Fight Like the Devil to Hold Your Own," *Blue & Gray*, vol. 12, no. 3 (Feb. 1995), 12; Cheney, *History of the Ninth Regiment*, 103.

139 H. O. Dodge, "Opening the Battle. Lieut. Jones, the 8th Ill. Cavalryman, Fired the First Shot at Gettysburg," *NT*, Sept. 24, 1891.

Lt. John H. Calef, commander, Battery A, 2nd U.S. Artillery, served with John Buford's First Cavalry Division.

USAHEC

duty, the kind soul offered to take his place while he came and ate supper; and how the same old farmer came out and chatted with us till late at night." The men on the picket lines spent a long night alternating between stress and boredom as they kept a sharp eye out for the inevitable advance of the enemy.[140]

John Slentz, the tenant who farmed Edward McPherson's land along the Chambersburg Road, watched helplessly while Buford's troopers tore down his fences to remove impediments to battle and hungrily eyed his livestock. They also used the fence rails for firewood. Concerned for his few worldly possessions, Slentz and his family hid what they could and took cover.[141]

With nothing left to do, Devin's and Gamble's brigades, supported by Lt. John Calef's battery with its six three-inch rifles, waited for whatever was coming next. "[W]e of the artillery were not imbued with the idea that a great battle was pending," Calef admitted. Buford firmly believed otherwise. Trooper A. R. Mix of the 9th New York needed new boots, for his were "just about gone." He got permission to ride into town to look for new ones, found a decent pair that fit, but could not pick them up until the next morning. When Mix approached Buford for permission to leave the ranks on July 1 to get the boots, Buford instructed one of his staff officers to give the trooper a pass. "Mix," he added, "you take all of your belongings with you, for we'll be in line when you come back." Buford harbored no illusions about what awaited his command.[142]

140 Morgan Hughes, "People of Gettysburg. How They Inspired the Cavalry to Do Their Effective Work," *NT*, March 24, 1892.

141 John Slentz Claims Reparation Files, copy in files, GNMP.

142 Calef, "Gettysburg Notes," 47; A. R. Mix, "Experiences at Gettysburg," *NT*, Feb. 22, 1904.

Buford ordered scouting parties to scatter to the four points of the compass to locate the precise dispositions of the enemy. Gamble sent out groups west toward Cashtown while Devin's scouts headed north and east, reconnoitering the country and capturing Rebel stragglers who provided critical information under interrogation. This was intelligence gathering at its best, and it quickly bore fruit because the reports sent back to Buford convinced him the entire Army of Northern Virginia was converging quickly on Gettysburg.[143]

Buford sent a detailed intelligence report to Reynolds at 10:30 p.m. "The Reserve Brigade, under General Merritt, is at Mechanicstown with my trains. General Pleasonton wrote he would inform me when he relieved it. To-day I received instructions saying it would picket toward Hagerstown and south," he began before getting to the real meat of the communication:

> I am satisfied that A.P. Hill's corps is massed just back of Cashtown, about 9 miles from this place. Pender's division of this (Hill's) corps came up to-day—of which I advised you, saying, "The enemy in my front is increased." The enemy's pickets (infantry and artillery) are within 4 miles of this place, on the Cashtown [Chambersburg] road. My parties have returned from Cashtown to Oxford in several places. They heard nothing of any force having passed over it lately. The road, however, is terribly infested with prowling cavalry parties. Near Heidlersburg to-day, one of my parties captured a courier of Lee's. Nothing was found on him. He says Ewell's corps is crossing the mountains from Carlisle, Rodes' division being at Petersburg in advance. Longstreet, from all I can learn, is still behind Hill. I have many rumors of the enemy advancing upon me from toward York. I have to pay attention to some of them, which causes me to overwork my horses and men. I can get no forage nor rations; am out of both. The people give and sell the men something to eat, but I can't stand that way of subsisting; it causes dreadful straggling. Should I have to fall back, advise me by what route.[144]

This remarkably accurate intelligence report provided Reynolds with a rich and full picture of the disposition of Lee's army and enabled the wing commander to plan accordingly for July 1.

Once the message to Reynolds was in the hands of a rider, Buford penned a similar dispatch to General Pleasonton before asking, "When will the reserve be relieved, and where are my wagons? I have no need of them, as I can find no forage. I have kept General Reynolds informed of all that has transpired." Buford, whose

---

143 Bates, *The Battle of Gettysburg*, 55.

144 *OR* 27, pt. 1, 923-924.

Lt. Col. Joseph Dickinson served on the staff of General Buford in the 1st Division of cavalry.

LOC

concern about the absence of his Regulars and state of his horses is evident, knew his dispositions were good and that his veterans could delay the advancing Confederates for a time. The question was for how long.[145]

That same afternoon, General Meade summoned one of his staff officers, Lt. Col. Joseph Dickinson, to his tent. The staffer was to ride to Emmitsburg to meet with Reynolds and share Meade's intentions with him, then go on to Gettysburg to meet with Buford, and finally return to Reynolds to ensure that the latter had the benefit of Buford's observations and plans. Dickinson found Reynolds near Emmitsburg and they talked for about 20 minutes before the staff officer rode on to Gettysburg. He located Buford at his headquarters at the Eagle Hotel. Dickinson left a detailed account of the meeting that is worth presenting at length:

> The General had been engaged in thoroughly informing himself of the movements of the hostile forces, through the instrumentality of his own scouts and that of a number of patriotic citizens of Gettysburg, who were engaged voluntarily in scouring the country in every direction if possible . . . there sat General Buford, cool, calm, and serenely receiving the reports, quietly weighing in his military mind their value, but saying nothing. . . . This was indeed a trying time and position for a commander of two small brigades of cavalry to be placed in, and yet there was not wisdom enough existing to have made a better choice. The modest yet brave, retiring yet efficient, quiet yet vigilant, unostentatious but prompt and persevering, gallant General John Buford was, at least for once, the right man in the right place . . . for I doubt, if ever the skill and courage of any officer were put to a sterner or

145 Ibid., 924.

more decisive test than upon that night of June 30, 1863, at Gettysburg, and yet show himself so fully equal to the emergency as did General John Buford.[146]

Dickinson departed on his long ride back to headquarters after midnight. Both Buford and Dickinson wanted to make sure Meade had the benefit of what the staff officer had learned consulting face-to-face with Reynolds and Buford. The primary conclusion was this: "that it was extremely essential, in order to secure and hold a choice of positions, that General Reynolds should be notified to proceed to Gettysburg, both agreeing that a battle has to be fought nearby." Dickinson sent a staff officer to Reynolds to brief him on the meeting with Buford and to instruct him to move his command to Gettysburg the next morning before riding off to brief Meade. The die was cast: the Army of the Potomac would make its stand at Gettysburg.[147]

John Buford was not as calm as he appeared to Dickinson. In fact, he was quite concerned. The cavalryman recognized that his small force faced potentially overwhelming odds—especially if the Confederate infantry advanced from more than one direction. Although his dispatches to Reynolds and Pleasonton requested that the Reserve Brigade be returned to him, his requests fell upon deaf ears: the Reserve Brigade did not receive orders to ride to Gettysburg until the morning of July 3. When Dickinson set eyes upon Buford, he knew it was more likely than not that Buford would face the Confederate infantry with only two of his three brigades, with his favorite one detached for less vital duty.[148]

Buford's anxiety was more visible during a meeting with his brigade commanders that night when he voiced concern that the upcoming fight might begin "in the morning before the infantry can come up." Tom Devin, who was always spoiling for a fight, announced that he would hold his position the next day. "No, you won't," shot back the pragmatic Buford. "They will attack you in the morning and they will come booming—skirmishers three deep. You will have to fight like the devil to hold your own until supports arrive. The enemy must know the importance of this position and will strain every nerve to secure it, and if we are able to hold it we will do well."[149]

---

146   Bvt. Brig. Gen. Joseph Dickinson, "A Gettysburg Incident," in *The Proceedings of the Buford Memorial Association*, 23-25.

147   Ibid., 25.

148   *OR* 27, pt. 1, 923-924.

149   Aaron B. Jerome, "Buford on Oak Hill," in DePuyster, *Decisive Conflicts*, 151-152.

Buford ordered his signal officer, Lt. Aaron B. Jerome, to "seek out the most prominent points and watch everything; to be careful to look out for camp-fires, and in the morning, for dust." Jerome observed that "Buford seemed anxious, more so than I ever saw him," as he fretted about his "arrangements for entertaining" the Confederates the next morning. The worried cavalryman slept fitfully before rising about 3:00 a.m. He woke Dr. Elias Beck, the regimental surgeon of the 3rd Indiana Cavalry, "and when the gray of the morning began to make its first appearance he was in the saddle, and watching for the approaching enemy."[150]

Buford's two brigades bivouacked in a large field near the Lutheran Seminary, where the men unsaddled their hungry horses and turned them out to graze. Companies C and M of the 9th New York Cavalry were directed to set up their bivouac on the grounds of Pennsylvania (now Gettysburg) College, securing the campus and its prominent cupola for Union use.

The mounts were exhausted after days of rapid marching and insufficient food, so the chance to graze and rest was a welcome one. We "fared luxuriously among the substantial farmers," boasted one of the cavalrymen, "procuring loaves of bread of fabulous size, milk, butter and eggs in abundance, so that we felt compensated for our extra march." Trooper James Bell of the 8th Illinois rode into town on the evening before the battle and found that "every one wanted to talk and at every house they would ask me in to eat supper. It done me lots of good to go there." Thomas G. Day of the 3rd Indiana also was invited to dinner. He cleaned his horse and himself up as best he could and rode into Gettysburg for a delightful meal. The same family asked him back for breakfast, an invitation he readily accepted. Intervening circumstances would make that impossible.[151]

By the time the 2,700 officers and enlisted men of the 1st Division hunkered down for the night, Confederate campfires were visible flickering in the distance. To a man, they knew battle awaited them the next morning. They made the most of that lovely early summer evening. "Thus picketed, thus bivouacked, beneath our own skies, on our own soil, with a sense of security and a feeling of homeness, thinking of the loved ones, and breathing prayers to Him who had blessed us and

150 DePuyster, *Decisive Conflicts*, 152; "J. H. S.," "Washington Letter," *Fort Wayne Journal-Gazette*, Nov. 29, 1885.

151 "Genesee," "From the 8th Cavalry"; James A. Bell to Gusta Ann Hallock, July 11, 1863, Bell Papers, HL; Thomas G. Day, "Opening the Battle. A Cavalryman's Recollections of the First Day's Fight at Gettysburg," *National Tribune*, July 30, 1903.

our arms, we lay down upon the greensward, pillowing our heads on our saddles, to rest and to sleep, little dreaming the morrow would usher in a battle so sanguinary which would determine the destiny of the Republic, and fix the fate of human liberty on the earth," declared an officer in the 8th Illinois Cavalry.[152]

An early historian of the town of Gettysburg waxed poetic about the night of June 30, 1863. "The vast details of the coming slaughter were complete, and the hills and valleys about Gettysburg were lit up by the extended camp-fires of two mighty armies, and night and quiet reigned over all," he wrote. "Many a poor, brave fellow, for the last time as he lay down to quiet sleep, looked upon the twinkling stars and thought and dreamed of his far-away home and the loved ones there, and wondered if he would ever be there with them again."[153]

152 OR 27, pt. 1, 924; John W. Busey and David G. Martin, *Regimental Strengths and Losses at Gettysburg* (Hightstown, NJ, 1994), 101-102; Edward C. Reid, Diary, entry for June 30, 1863, Edward C. Reid Papers, Illinois State Historical Society, Springfield, IL; Beveridge, "Address," 17.

153 *History of Cumberland and Adams Counties, Containing History of the Counties, Their Townships, Towns, Villages, Schools, Churches, Industries, Etc., Portraits of Early Settlers and Prominent Men; Biographies* (Chicago, 1886), 156.

EPILOGUE

July 1, 1863, proved to be a day of destiny for many of the soldiers of both armies. The Rebels' "picnic in Pennsylvania" gave way to musketry and artillery fire when Henry Heth's Division advanced east from its overnight camps near Cashtown and collided with Brig. Gen. John Buford's cavalry west of Gettysburg near Marsh Creek. Buford's troopers stubbornly held off the Southerners long enough for John Reynolds to arrive with his I Corps infantry. Reynolds was killed shortly after deploying the lead elements along McPherson's Ridge, and command of the field devolved onto Maj. Gen. Abner Doubleday. Terrified citizens huddled in their cellars as the long-anticipated major battle in Pennsylvania began in earnest.[1]

The I Corps's Iron Brigade launched a counterattack against Heth's southernmost Confederates comprised of Brig. Gen. James J. Archer's veteran but small brigade. The Western troops drove the Rebels back through the woods and captured Archer, who would spend months in a Northern prison, lose his good health, never fully recover, and die before the war ended. A similar northward thrust by other Union troops including the Iron Brigade's 6th Wisconsin snatched up hundreds of Joe Davis's Mississippians and North Carolinians who had gathered in and along an unfinished railroad cut north of the Chambersburg Pike.

---

1 For detailed accounts of the fighting on the first day of the battle, see Martin, *Gettysburg, July 1* or Harry W. Pfanz, *Gettysburg: The First Day*. The best dedicated account of the opening cavalry action is Eric J. Wittenberg, *"The Devil's to Pay": John Buford at Gettysburg: A History and Walking Tour* (El Dorado Hills, CA, 2014).

Brig Gen. James J. Archer led a brigade in Heth's Division, Hill's Corps, Army of Northern Virginia. He was the first general captured since Robert E. Lee took command of the army.

LOC

Major General Oliver O. Howard of the XI Corps rode into the town and took command of the hard-pressed Union forces, relieving Doubleday.[2]

As the day wore on, tens of thousands of troops from both armies arrived at or near the battlefield. By 2:00 p.m. Rodes's and Early's infantry divisions arrived from the north. They pushed back elements of the XI Corps north of Gettysburg and added pressure to the beleaguered I Corps. Later that afternoon Pender's fresh division shattered the Union lines west of town and sent the Federals tumbling back through town to Cemetery Hill and beyond. The Northerners rallied on Cemetery Hill and began digging

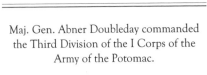

Maj. Gen. Abner Doubleday commanded the Third Division of the I Corps of the Army of the Potomac.

LOC

2 Lance J. Herdegen, *The Iron Brigade in the Civil War and Memory: The Black Hats from Bull Run to Appomattox and Thereafter* (El Dorado Hills, CA, 2012).

in while desperately awaiting reinforcements. Generals Hill and Ewell decided against pressing their advantage by attacking the high ground.

General Meade, who was still in Maryland when the battle began, sent Maj. Gen. Winfield S. Hancock to take charge at Gettysburg. Hancock worked with Howard to restore order as several additional Union infantry corps marched toward Gettysburg. Meade arrived late that night and after being briefed on the situation decided to stay and fight. More than 15,500 men combined fell on July 1.

* * *

Jeb Stuart's sleep-deprived troopers began filing out of their camps surrounding Dover, Pennsylvania, early on July 1. They departed several hours, each of the three brigades taking a different route through hilly northwestern York County to Dillsburg, a village near the border with Cumberland County. Stuart reported, "I still believed that most of our army was before Harrisburg, and justly regarded a march to Carlisle as the most likely to place me in communication with the main army." He also thought he could find rations there.[3]

Colonel Richard L. T. Beale of the 9th Virginia wrote that on the march from Dover, "a good many prisoners were taken, being chiefly men going to rejoin their regiments. Among them was a young surgeon, traveling with a span of line horses, handsome buggy, and colored servant. His surprise at being halted by our picket was manifest. His handsome buggy was brought to Virginia."[4]

"You should have seen the Dutch people in York Co. turning out with water and milk and bread and butter and 'apple butter' for the 'ragged rebels.' I was quite surprised at the tone of feeling in that part of the State," wrote 18-year-old Lt. F. Halsey Wigfall of Breathed's horse artillery to his sister. He continued:

> In two or three instances I found people who seemed really glad to see us and at scores of houses they had refreshments at the door for the soldiers. The people generally seemed not to know exactly what to expect and I don't think would have been at all astonished if every building had been set on fire by us as we reached it, nor would a great many have been surprised if we had concluded the business by massacring the women and children![5]

3 OR 27, pt. 2, 709.

4 Beale, History of the Ninth Virginia Cavalry, 83-84.

5 D. Giraud Wright, A Southern Girl in '61: The War-Time Memories of a Confederate Senator's Daughter (New York, 1905).

Stuart continued on to Carlisle that evening with Fitz Lee's Brigade while Hampton camped his brigade just northwest of Dillsburg, and Chambliss rested near Churchtown. When he encountered some of Baldy Smith's militia guarding Carlisle, Stuart sent a flag of truce asking them to surrender. Smith refused. Stuart's horse artillery shelled the town and his men torched the Carlisle Barracks and the nearby gasworks. After midnight, a messenger located Stuart and informed him of Lee's orders to march to Gettysburg, where a battle was taking place.[6]

*   *   *

That same day, John D. Imboden's Northwestern Brigade marched for 16 miles from its campsites west of Greencastle through the lower Cumberland Valley to Chambersburg. The Virginia horsemen and McClanahan's Battery arrived about 4:00 p.m. to relieve Pickett's Division and raid the local grist mills for flour in accordance with Lee's most recent instructions. They were also to protect the army's wagon trains and patrol the roads leading toward Gettysburg. If Imboden could not obtain flour in Chambersburg, he was to send wagons north to Shippensburg, which Lee believed contained 700 to 800 barrels.[7]

"Imboden's cutthroats entered our town—an order was issued by the General for a large amount of provisions," complained Chambersburg merchant Jacob Hoke. "Among the articles demanded were 5,000 pounds of bacon." When no one responded to the requisitions, Imboden dispatched Col. George H. Smith and Maj. David B. Lang of the 62nd Virginia to enforce his demands. A town official, former judge Francis M. Kimmel, informed the officers that previous Confederate visits had cleaned out all of the provisions. When Kimmel produced a copy of Lee's orders against plundering the homes of private citizens, the Southerners backed down. The townspeople remained uneasy, worried the Rebels might start mischief. "No troops that entered our town created greater consternation among our people than these free-booters of Imboden," Hoke groused. "It had gotten out that they were going to search our houses for provisions, and all were in consternation and

---

6 For much more on Stuart's activities on June 30 and July 1, see Scott Mingus, *Confederate Calamity: Jeb Stuart's Confederate Cavalry Ride Through York County, Pa.* (Scotts Valley, CA, 2015) and Wittenberg and Petruzzi, *Plenty of Blame to Go Around.*

7 OR 27, pt. 3, 948.

fear, when suddenly, and to our great relief, they at once withdrew and went off towards Gettysburg."[8]

Imboden's men rode east to Greenwood, where that night they relieved Pickett as instructed.

* * *

Stuart and Imboden were not the only Confederate cavalry officers to have their commands on the road on July 1. Brigadier General William "Grumble" Jones's Brigade splashed across the Potomac River at Williamsport, Maryland, and headed north to guard the wagon trains and keep an eye on the Union forces still at Harpers Ferry. Part of Beverly H. Robertson's Brigade—the 4th and 5th North Carolina cavalry—also forded the Potomac and rode north to Greencastle, Pennsylvania. Albert Jenkins's Brigade accompanied Rodes's Division to Gettysburg, where in the fighting on July 1 General Jenkins suffered a wound that incapacitated him for the rest of the battle.[9]

Captain John H. "Hanse" McNeill and about 60 of his partisan rangers rode into Mercersburg at 1:00 p.m. They were the last of the many Confederates to visit that western Franklin County town. Though brief, their stay "was the most terrific of any we have had," a resident recalled. They headed for the stores, which had either already sent off their inventory to safety across the mountains or lost it to previous raiders. A young local man offered his services to McNeil and guided four Rebels north to various locations in the Little Cove where merchants Shirts, McKinstry, and Fitzgerald had hidden their merchandise. While they were gone, Constable Wolfe rounded up an armed posse to capture them as they left the Cove. When they heard other Rebels were nearby, most of the men deserted. Wolfe and McKinstry pressed on to the Fritz farm and other locations only to discover the hidden merchandise was gone. So were six or seven free black residents, including Amos Barnes, who the Rebels reportedly had taken.[10]

8 Hoke, *Reminiscences*, 74.

9 Vertical files on Robertson's, Jones's, and Jenkins's brigades, GNMP.

10 "Mercersburg in War Times," *Mercersburg* (PA) *Journal*, Jan. 23, 1903.

On Virginia's Peninsula, Union General Dix, head of the Department of Virginia, began to move parts of his command north toward Richmond to threaten the capital.

Dix sent Brig. Gen. George W. Getty and 10,000 men of the VII Corps to destroy the Richmond & Fredericksburg Railroad's wooden bridge over the South Anna River. As a diversion, another 6,000 soldiers from the IV Corps under Maj. Gen. Erasmus D. Keyes moved from Yorktown and Williamsburg toward Bottom's Bridge on the Chickahominy River. When his lead brigade encountered a strong line of Confederate skirmishers near Baltimore Cross Roads about 7:00 p.m., Keyes halted well short of the bridge and sent a message to Dix asking if he should withdraw. Keyes eventually pulled back to White House Landing along the Pamunkey River on July 2 and refused Dix's entreaties to advance. His refusal to move ended any hope of opening a second front in Virginia.[11]

* * *

President Lincoln and his cabinet keenly tracked incoming news. "We have reports that the Rebels have fallen back from York," Secretary of the Navy Gideon Welles penned in his diary, "and I shall not be surprised if they escape capture, or even a second fight, though we have rumors of hard fighting to-day." "This is an anxious day," Secretary of the Treasury Salmon P. Chase scribed in his journal. "Meade's army seems to be drawing right to the rebel positions. Is he not too far to the right? May not Lee turn his left and so get between him and Washington? These are questions much discussed. Gen. Halleck and the President both seem uneasy. Everything in Meade's despatches—neither frequent or long however—indicate prudence, courage & activity—I trust all will go well."[12]

* * *

All was not going well with Meade's army that night. John Reynolds was dead and several brigade and regimental commanders were also casualties or were missing. Thousands of wounded men dotted the fields north and west of

---

11 For a detailed discussion of these events, see Noah Andre Trudeau, "Gettysburg's Second Front: The 'Blackberry Raid'," *Gettysburg Magazine*, No. 11 (July 1994), 6-18. Bottom's Bridge connected New Kent County with Henrico County.

12 Welles, *Diary*, 1:354; Niven, *The Salmon P. Chase Papers*, 1:426.

Gettysburg, behind enemy lines and out of reach of their comrades. The survivors of the shattered I and XI corps feverishly constructed works and earthen artillery lunettes on Cemetery and Culp's hills, even as Maj. Gen. Daniel Sickles's III Corps arrived and took position south of town. General Meade rode into the Union lines during the night to take command personally. His other five corps closed on Gettysburg within supporting distance; all would be on the field on July 2.

Longstreet's Corps, minus Pickett's Division and Brig. Gen. Evander Law's brigade, marched across South Mountain and reached Gettysburg well after dark. Lee wanted Ewell to withdraw from the town and join his line on Seminary Ridge but Ewell sent word that such a retrograde, giving up hard-won territory, would have a negative effect on morale. Hence, the opposing armies settled into what has traditionally been described as "fishhook-shaped" lines.

* * *

July 2 saw a second day of intense fighting at Gettysburg, as heretofore obscure locations—Little Round Top, Devil's Den, Rose Farm, the Peach Orchard, the Wheatfield, and Cemetery Hill—became legendary by nightfall. Winfield Hancock proved to be a charismatic, skillful replacement for Darius Couch in command of the II Corps. A. P. Hill and Richard Ewell struggled in their roles as corps commanders, and the Army of Northern Virginia, despite widespread attacks and some territorial gains, failed to drive off the Army of the Potomac in Meade's first test as an army commander in the field.[13]

General Lee waited impatiently for Longstreet to get into position after a lengthy countermarch to avoid Union observation and attack the Union left flank. As Longstreet soon discovered, Union III Corps commander Dan Sickles had moved his corps forward to assume a crooked salient-style front far too long for his corps to adequately man. The Rebel attack began late that afternoon with Hood's Division, but Hood suffered a gruesome wound in the arm and his assault lost cohesion and direction. To his left, McLaws' Division, particularly Brig. Gen. William Barksdale's Mississippi brigade, made some headway between the Rose Farm and Peach Orchard, cracking open the III Corps front. Sickles lost a leg when a shell fragment slammed into it, necessitating amputation. Timely reinforcements from George Sykes's V Corps helped halt the persistent enemy thrusts, as did the arrival of troops sent by Hancock from Cemetery Ridge. Determined Confederate

---

13 For details, see Harry W. Pfanz, *Gettysburg: The Second Day* (Chapel Hill, NC, 1998).

attacks farther up the line, most notably from elements of Richard Anderson's Division of Hill's Corps, failed to break open the center of Meade's front.

Night was falling when part of Jubal Early's Division attacked East Cemetery Hill and "Allegheny" Johnson sent his men up the steep wooded slopes of Culp's Hill. Both assaults ultimately failed, although Johnson's soldiers did gain a foothold on the high rocky wooded terrain. Once again timely Federal reinforcements, coupled with Confederate command failures, proved critical to holding the Union lines. On Cemetery Hill, Harry Hays's Louisiana Tigers and Col. I. E. Avery's North Carolinians briefly reached the Union artillery lunettes near the summit but were beaten back by determined resistance.[14]

More than 20,000 men were killed, wounded, or captured on July 2—more than at Fredericksburg the previous winter. General Meade held a nighttime council of war in the Leister house along the Taneytown Road and decided, again, to stay put. He correctly discerned that Lee would focus his attention on the Union center next, and dispatched reinforcements accordingly.

*   *   *

Once he learned Lee was at Gettysburg, Stuart hustled his three brigades southwest through York and Cumberland counties toward Adams County. More than 1,000 of his men had fresh mounts, courtesy of the unwilling farmers along his routes of march. Most of these domestic animals, many of them plow horses or carriage horses, had never experienced combat. Wade Hampton's command, acting as Stuart's rear guard, clashed with Brig. Gen. George Armstrong Custer's Wolverines at Hunterstown in the late afternoon of July 2. The Confederates came close to capturing Custer but the dismounted general's orderly snatched him to safety. Stuart finally arrived at Lee's headquarters late in the day, and delivered the captured Union supply wagons to the quartermaster.[15]

Robertson's North Carolina cavalry brigade moved from Greencastle north to Chambersburg. Grumble Jones detached the 12th Virginia Cavalry to guard the ford at Williamsport, Maryland, and then moved with the rest of his depleted

---

14 For more information, see Harry W. Pfanz, *Gettysburg: Culp's Hill and Cemetery Hill* (Chapel Hill, NC, 1993) and Scott L. Mingus, Sr., *The Louisiana Tigers in the Gettysburg Campaign, June–July 1863* (Baton Rouge, LA, 2009).

15 Eric J. Wittenberg, *Protecting the Flank at Gettysburg: The Battles for Brinkerhoff's Ridge and East Cavalry Field, July 2–3, 1863* (El Dorado Hills, CA, 2013), 19-20.

brigade—the 6th, 7th, and 11th Virginia, together with Capt. R. Preston Chew's battery, toward Chambersburg.

* * *

With telegraphic communication established with the Army of the Potomac at Gettysburg, news of the fighting reached Washington.

"Met [Radical Republican Senator Charles] Sumner and went with him to the War Department," Secretary Welles wrote in his diary. "The President was there, and we read dispatches received from General Meade. There was a smart fight, but without results, near Gettysburg yesterday. A rumor is here that we have captured six thousand prisoners, and on calling again this evening at the War Department I saw a telegram which confirms it. General Reynolds is reported killed. The tone of Meade's dispatch is good."[16]

* * *

The fighting resumed at Gettysburg well before dawn on July 3 when troops from the Union XII Corps on Culp's Hill launched a spoiling attack against Ewell's infantry. The vicious fighting that followed for several hours resulted in heavy casualties and failed to dislodge the Federals from their extensive breastworks. A limited Union counterattack across Spangler's Meadow, one of the few Northern attacks at Gettysburg, failed miserably.

Early in the afternoon, a massive Confederate artillery bombardment intended to soften Meade's center to open the way for a large infantry assault got underway. The noise carried eastward well into Lancaster County and reportedly as far south as Baltimore. Union soldiers huddled behind stone walls or hugged the earth to avoid incoming shells, many of which passed harmlessly overhead to explode behind the main line. At one point, Meade had to move his headquarters from the Leister house when enemy shells peppered the area and killed some orderlies and horses. "Every size and form of shell known to British or American gunnery shrieked, whirled, moaned, and whistled, and wrathfully fluttered over our ground," wrote *New York Times* correspondent Samuel Wilkeson, whose 19-year-old son Bayard, a battery commander, had been mortally wounded on July 1. "As many as six in a second, constantly two in a second, bursting and screaming

16 Welles, *Diary*, 1:354.

over and around the head-quarters. They burst in the yard—burst next to the fence on both sides, garnished, as usual, with the hitched horses of aides and orderlies. . . . Soldiers in Federal blue were torn to pieces in the road and died with the peculiar yell that blends the extorted cry of pain with horror and despair."[17]

When the cannonade concluded, brigades from three different divisions under George Pickett, Harry Heth's (now under Brig. Gen. J. Johnston Pettigrew), and Dorsey Pender's (under Maj. Gen. Isaac Trimble) stepped forward in a grand assault that became known to history as "Pickett's Charge." Under James Longstreet's overall direction, the three assault columns, with brigades under Cadmus Wilcox and David Lang of Anderson's Division in support, targeted the Union center. Union firepower, much of it disgorged from well-placed artillery tubes under Brig. Gen. Henry Hunt, coupled with strong reserves, blunted the assault and left thousands of Confederates killed, wounded, or captured. "It's all my fault," Lee informed his shaken survivors as they returned to Seminary Ridge.[18]

·   *   *   *

On the southern edge of the battlefield, Brig. Gen. Elon Farnsworth died leading his cavalry brigade on a fruitless attack against infantry belonging to Hood's Division near Big Round Top. Farnsworth sported his general's star for just five days before meeting his untimely death. Dismounted Northern skirmishers to the west across the Emmitsburg Road, from Brig. Gen. Wesley Merritt's Reserve Brigade, sniped at long range with elements of Brig. Gen. George T. Anderson's Brigade and Hart's South Carolina battery. Major Samuel H. Starr's 6th U.S. Cavalry was chopped to bits by Grumble Jones's regiments at Fairfield late that afternoon, squandering an opportunity to block Lee's primary retreat route.[19]

About the same time as the Pickett-Pettigrew-Trimble assault, Stuart's exhausted cavalry clashed with elements of Pleasonton's Cavalry Corps in farm fields east of Gettysburg. The fighting featured full-thunder mounted cavalry

---

17 John S. C. Abbott, *The History of the Civil War in America* (New York, 1873), 411.

18 James A. Hessler and Wayne E. Motts, *Pickett's Charge at Gettysburg: A Guide to the Most Famous Attack in American History* (El Dorado Hills, CA, 2015).

19 For a detailed discussion, see Eric J. Wittenberg, *Gettysburg's Forgotten Cavalry Actions: Farnsworth's Charge, South Cavalry Field, and the Battle of Fairfield, July 3, 1863* (El Dorado Hills, CA, 2011).

Brig. Gen. Henry Hunt commanded the artillery of the Army of the Potomac. He feuded with General Hancock over the placement and operation of batteries at Gettysburg.

LOC

charges and savage hand-to-hand mêlée combat, as well as longer-range small arms firefights and dueling horse artillery.[20]

* * *

The opposing armies faced one another on July 4. Any fighting consisted of limited Union probes and light skirmishing between the lines. Lee began withdrawing his beaten army from Gettysburg as a massive rainstorm roared through Adams County during the night. His rear guard engaged in spirited combat near Monterey Pass on South Mountain, fighting that allowed the Army of Northern Virginia, with Imboden's cavalry protecting the miles-long wagon train of wounded, to head south to the rain-swollen Potomac River.

In Washington, Secretary Welles penned in his diary, "Lee and the Rebels may escape in consequence. If they are driven back, Halleck will be satisfied. That has been his great anxiety, and too many of our officers think it sufficient if the Rebels quit and go off, that it is unnecessary to capture, disperse, and annihilate them."[21]

* * *

The butcher's bill for the three days of fighting at Gettysburg was staggering. The Army of the Potomac went into battle with 93,534

20 For details, see Wittenberg, *Protecting the Flank at Gettysburg*, 33-116.

21 Welles, *Diary*, 1:358.

officers and men present for duty and suffered 22,813 casualties, or 24.3% of its total while fighting on the defensive. Losses among the officer corps were especially heavy: John Reynolds of the I Corps was killed, while Dan Sickles (III Corps) and Winfield Scott Hancock (II Corps) were severely wounded. Brigade and regimental commanders were also hard-hit, meaning the army's leadership was largely decimated.[22]

The Army of Northern Virginia went into battle with 70,226 officers and men present for duty and suffered 22,874 casualties, or 32.6% of its total, largely because Lee was on the offensive for the entire battle. Fortunately for the Rebels, none of the corps commanders were injured, but Lee's division and brigade losses were extensive. Two of his best division leaders, Hood and Pender, were both wounded, the latter mortally. Lee's army was incapable of replacing these severe losses and was never again able to press the offensive for any extended period of time.[23]

* * *

On July 11, Lee's engineers constructed earthworks to protect the river crossing at Williamsport; Meade, his army battered and bruised, was unable launch an attack until Lee had withdrawn across the river three days later. Rearguard action at Falling Waters, south of Williamsport, resulted in the mortal wounding of Confederate General Pettigrew. Lee's army slipped back into Virginia and, after two more weeks of minor skirmishes and engagements, finally reached safety in early August, ending the Gettysburg Campaign.[24]

* * *

An incensed Abraham Lincoln composed, but wisely did not send, a scathing letter to Meade:

I have just seen your despatch to Gen. Halleck, asking to be relieved of your command, because of a supposed censure of mine. I am very—very—grateful to you for the

---

22 Busey and Martin, *Regimental Strengths and Losses*, 239.

23 Ibid., 281.

24 See Eric J. Wittenberg, J. David Petruzzi, and Michael F. Nugent, *One Continuous Fight: The Retreat From Gettysburg and the Pursuit of Lee's Army of Northern Virginia, July 4-14, 1863* (El Dorado Hills, CA, 2008).

magnificent success you gave the cause of the country at Gettysburg; and I am sorry now to be the author of the slightest pain to you. But I was in such deep distress myself that I could not restrain some expression of it. I had been oppressed nearly ever since the battles at Gettysburg, by what appeared to be evidences that yourself, and Gen. Couch, and Gen. Smith, were not seeking a collision with the enemy, but were trying to get him across the river without another battle. What these evidences were, if you please, I hope to tell you at some time, when we shall both feel better. The case, summarily stated is this. You fought and beat the enemy at Gettysburg; and, of course, to say the least, his loss was as great as yours. He retreated; and you did not, as it seemed to me, pressingly pursue him; but a flood in the river detained him, till, by slow degrees, you were again upon him. You had at least twenty thousand veteran troops directly with you, and as many more raw ones within supporting distance, all in addition to those who fought with you at Gettysburg; while it was not possible that he had received a single recruit; and yet you stood and let the flood run down, bridges be built, and the enemy move away at his leisure, without attacking him. And Couch and Smith! The latter left Carlisle in time, upon all ordinary calculation, to have aided you in the last battle at Gettysburg; but he did not arrive. At the end of more than ten days, I believe twelve, under constant urging, he reached Hagerstown from Carlisle, which is not an inch over fifty-five miles, if so much. And Couch's movement was very little different.

Again, my dear general, I do not believe you appreciate the magnitude of the misfortune involved in Lee's escape. He was within your easy grasp, and to have closed upon him would, in connection with our other late successes, have ended the war. As it is, the war will be prolonged indefinitely. If you could not safely attack Lee last Monday, how can you possibly do so South of the river, when you can take with you very few more than two thirds of the force you then had in hand? It would be unreasonable to expect, and I do not expect you can now effect much. Your golden opportunity is gone, and I am distressed immeasurably because of it.

I beg you will not consider this a prosecution, or persecution of yourself. As you had learned that I was dissatisfied, I have thought it best to kindly tell you why.[25]

Meade tried to resign as commander of the army, but his resignation was refused. He remained in command of the Army of the Potomac for the balance of the Civil War.

The failure to bring Lee to a decisive battle while his army was trapped on the banks of the flooded Potomac River triggered a controversy that rages to this day.

25 Basler, Pratt, and Dunlap, *Collected Works*, 6:327-328.

* * *

As the residents of Gettysburg and its environs began returning to their homes and farms, many discovered that the fighting had left their properties in shambles. "There was not a board or a rail of fencing left on the place," Nathaniel Lightner recalled as he surveyed his war-torn farm along the Baltimore Pike. "Not a chicken, pig, cow, or dog could be found. The [army] mules had eaten up the orchard of four-year-old trees down to the stalks. The garden was full of bottles and camp litter; the meadow of hides and offal of beeves, which had been shot down in their tracks and dressed on the spot, as meat was needed."[26]

Lincoln arrived in Gettysburg on November 18, 1863, where on the following day he delivered a two-minute speech that has come to be known in history as the Gettysburg Address. "We are met on a great battle-field of that war," the president remarked. "We have come to dedicate a portion of that field, as a final resting place for those who here gave their lives that that nation might live. It is altogether fitting and proper that we should do this. But, in a larger sense, we can not dedicate—we can not consecrate—we can not hallow—this ground. The brave men, living and dead, who struggled here, have consecrated it, far above our poor power to add or detract. The world will little note, nor long remember what we say here, but it can never forget what they did here."[27]

* * *

The war in the Eastern Theater would continue for more than 18 months before ending in Lee's surrender at Appomattox Court House in Virginia on April 9, 1865. By that time Jeb Stuart, John Buford, A. P. Hill, Robert Rodes, Albert Jenkins, Dorsey Pender, John Sedgwick, and several other leading officers who participated in the Gettysburg Campaign were in their graves. Less than a week later Abraham Lincoln would join them after being assassinated in Ford's Theater.

26 Nathaniel Lightner account, ACHS.

27 See Garry Wills, *Lincoln at Gettysburg: The Words That Remade America* (New York, 2006).

APPENDIX 1

ORDER OF BATTLE, TUESDAY, JUNE, 30, 1863

DEPARTMENT OF THE SUSQUEHANNA
Maj. Gen. Darius Nash Couch,
GHQ in Harrisburg, PA

Fort Washington (near Bridgeport, PA)
Brig. Gen. William Hall, NY State NG

1st Division
BG William Farrar "Baldy" Smith

1st Brigade (at Fort Washington):
BG Joseph Farmer Knipe
8th NY State NG: Col. Joshua M. Varian
71st NY State NG:
Col. Benjamin Lamb Trafford

2nd Brigade (at Marysville, PA)
BG Philip Schuyler Crooke
13th NY State NG:
Col. John Blackburne Woodward
28th NY State NG: Col. Michael Bennett
68th NY State NG (at High Spire, PA):
Col. David S. Forbes
28th PA Volunteer Militia [3 cos.]:
Maj. William Huntting Jessup

3rd Brigade (at Fort Washington)
BG Jesse C. Smith
23d NY State NG: Col. William Everdell, Jr.
52d NY State NG: Col. Matthias W. Cole
56th NY State NG: Col. John Quincy Adams
67th NY State NG: Col. Chauncey Abbott

4th Brigade: BG John Ewen
11th NY State NG (near New Cumberland, PA):
Col. Joachim Maidhof
22d NY State NG (near Oyster's Point):
Col. John Lloyd Aspinwall
37th NY State NG (near Oyster's Point):
Col. Charles Roome

5th Brigade at Oyster's Point near White Hill
(modern Camp Hill, PA): Col. William Brisbane
28th PA Volunteer Militia: Col. James Chamberlin
(3 companies at Marysville)
30th PA Volunteer Militia: Col. William N. Monies
32nd PA Volunteer Militia ("Gray Reserves"):
Col. Charles Somers Smith
33rd PA Volunteer Militia ("Blue Reserves"):
Col. William W. Taylor

1st Division Chief of Cavalry:
Maj. John Estill Wynkoop, 7th PA Cavalry

1st NY Cavalry [Co. C] (at Churchtown, PA, in the
evening): Capt. William Henry Boyd
Regular Army recruits: Capt. Frank Stanwood,
3rd US Cavalry (from Carlisle Barracks)
Curtin Guards: Capt. Frank Murray (entered
Mechanicsburg, PA, on June 30)
Miscellaneous cavalry recruits assembling near
modern-day Penbrook, PA

Art. Battery: Lt. Comdr. Pendleton G. Watmough,
US Navy (had been at Shippensburg, PA)

1st Division Chief of Artillery:
Lt. Edward P. Muhlenberg, 5th US Artillery

1st Philadelphia Battery:
Capt. Henry David Landis (at Oyster's Point)

Independent Philadelphia battery:
Capt. Elihu Spencer Miller (at Oyster's Point)

Independent Philadelphia battery [L]: 4 guns from
Capt. Benoni Frishmuth (at Bridgeport, PA)

Harrisburg (Camp Curtin)
Col. James Addams Beaver

The following commands were also in the field:

Bainbridge, PA: Maj. Granville Owen Haller
(ADC to Major General Couch)

20th PA Volunteer Militia: Col. William B. Thomas

Chambersburg, PA (Confederate-occupied):

McClure's Independent Company, PA Militia:
Col. Alexander Kelly McClure (disbanded)

Columbia, PA: Col. Jacob Gellert Frick, 27th PVM

26th PA Volunteer Militia [commissary guard
detachment]: Capt. Christopher Wilson Walker

27th PA Volunteer Militia (6th Brigade, 1st Division):
Lt. Col. David B. Green

Case's Columbia Company [Black non-mustered
volunteer home guards]: Capt. William Gardner Case

Three companies of white non-mustered volunteer
home guards from western Lancaster County.

Columbia Artillery: Lt. Delaplaine J. Ridgway

Patapsco (MD) Guards: Capt. Thomas S. McGowan
(from the York US Army General Hospital)

York US Army General Hospital "Invalid Battalion":
Capt. John M. Johnsten

87th PA: 50 men who had retreated from Winchester
to York, and then to Columbia.

Cavalry: Maj. Charles McLean Knox, Jr.

9th NY Cavalry, ADC to Major Haller

1st Troop, Philadelphia City Cavalry:
Capt. Samuel Jackson Randall

Adams County Home Guard Cavalry:
Capt. Robert Bell

Lancaster County Scouts: Capt. Matthew M. Strickler

Fenwick, PA: BG Charles Yates

5th NY State NG: Col. Louis Burger

12th NY State NG: Col. William Greene Ward

Two companies were at Sterrett's Gap and one at
Marysville, PA, guarding the railroad bridge.

Fort Washington (Unassigned):

26th PA Volunteer Militia: Col. William W. Jennings
(retreated from Gettysburg on June 26-28; slowly
regrouped in the fort through June 30)

Carlisle Barracks garrison:
Capt. David H. Hastings (250 men and 4 guns)

Huntingdon, PA: Col. Nelson Appleton Miles
(organizing a brigade of local troops)

Wallace's Company, Home Guard:
Capt. William W. Wallace

Co. F, 2nd Potomac (MD) Home Brigade Cavalry:
Capt. George Denton "Dent" Summers

McConnellsburg, PA

Independent Battalion, PA Militia: Col. Jacob Szink

12th PA Cavalry: Lt. Col. Joseph L. Moss
(from Milroy's 2nd Division, VIII Corps)

Mount Union, PA: Col. Joseph Williamson Hawley

65th NY State NG:

Lt. Col. William F. Berens (five companies at Bell's
Mills and two at Mapleton guarding the canal
and Juniata River bridges)

74th NY State NG: Col. Watson A. Fox
(commanding both the 65th and 74th)

29th PA Volunteer Militia (partial):
Col. Joseph Williamson Hawley

Mustered-out former members of the 125th PA:
Maj. John Jacob Lawrence

Cavalry company: Capt. B. Mortimer Morrow
(most enrolled in the 22nd PA Cavalry in mid-July)

Artillery section [2: 12#]:
Pvt. Edward M. Allen, 65th NYSNG

Orbisonia, PA
29th PA Volunteer Militia [5 cos.] assigned there
on June 27: Lt. Col. Norris Levis Yarnall

MIDDLE DEPARTMENT (VIII CORPS)
Maj. Gen. Robert Cumming Schenck,
GHQ in Baltimore, MD

Baltimore, MD: BG Erasmus Barnard Tyler

47th NY State NG: Col. Jeremiah V. Meserole
84th NY State NG: Col. Frederick Augustus Conkling
1st DE Cavalry: Maj. Napoleon Bonaparte Knight
Purnell (MD) Cavalry [B]: Capt. Thomas H. Watkins
5th NY Heavy Artillery [B & C]: Maj. Caspar Urban
Maryland Jr. Battery [A & B]: Capt. John M. Bruce

Annapolis, MD: Col. Carlos Adolphus Waite
Purnell (MD) Cavalry [B]:
3rd Potomac Home Brigade: Lt. Col. Charles Gilpin
2nd MD Cavalry [5 cos.]: Capt. William F. Bragg

District of Delaware:
3rd PA Heavy Artillery [M]:
Fort Delaware: BG Albin Francisco Schoepf
5th DE: Col. Henry S. McComb
Independent Battery A, PA Heavy Artillery:
Capt. Stanislaus Mlotkowski
Hamilton's Independent Battery G, Pittsburgh Heavy
Artillery: Capt. John Jay Young

2nd Division, VIII Corps
(nominally under Maj. Gen. Robert Houston Milroy)

Bloody Run (now Everett), PA: Col. Lewis Burton
Pierce (marched to Bedford, PA, on June 30)
18th CT (partial):
110th OH (partial):
116th OH (partial): Col. James Washburn
122nd OH (partial): Capt. Benjamin T. Sells
123rd OH (partial): Capt. Frederick K. Shawhan
87th PA (partial): Maj. Noah G. Ruhl
12th WV: Col. John Benedict Klunk (in charge of the
infantry at Bloody Run/Bedford)

13th PA Cavalry (partial): Col. James A. Galligher
1st NY Cavalry (partial): Maj. Alonzo Adams
(in charge of the cavalry at Bloody Run/Bedford)
1st WV Artillery [D]: Capt. John Carlin
(two sections arrived in Wheeling on June 30)
About 2,500 local home guard and emergency troops
in Bedford Co.: Col. Jacob C. Higgins

Harpers Ferry, WV:
BG Washington Lafayette Elliott

18th CT (partial): Maj. Henry Peale
(moving toward Frederick, MD, on June 30)
6th MD: Col. John Watt Horn
1st NY Cavalry (partial):
Col. Andrew Thomas McReynolds
110th OH (partial): Col. Joseph Warren Keifer
116th OH (partial): Lt. Col. Thomas Francis Wildes
122nd OH (partial): Col. William Henry Ball
123rd OH (partial): All three field officers and most
line officers had been captured.
13th PA Cavalry (partial): Maj. Michael Kerwin
67th PA: Lt. Col. Horace Blois Burnham
87th PA (partial): Col. John William Schall (50 men
were with Frick's command at Columbia, PA)
1st WV Artillery [D, one section]: Lt. Charles Theaker
1st WV Cavalry [K], Capt. Thomas Weston Rowand
3rd WV Cavalry [D&E]: Capt. James R. Utt
5th US Artillery [L]: Lt. Edmund Dana Spooner

1st Division, VIII Corps: BG Benjamin F. Kelley
(Harpers Ferry, WV)

2nd Brigade: BG William Hopkins Morris
5th MD: Maj. Salome Marsh
(from Milroy's 2nd Division)
50th NY Engineers [G]: Col. William Henry Pettes
Gaskill's Engineering Co. (PA):
Lt. William Penn Gaskill

3rd Brigade: Col. Benjamin Franklin Smith
126th OH: Col. Benjamin Franklin Smith
(at Harpers Ferry with Elliott's command)
106th NY: Col. Edward Christopher James
(at Harpers Ferry with Elliott's command)

138th PA: Col. Matthew Robert McClennan
(at Harper's Ferry with Elliott's command)
15th WV: Col. Maxwell McCaslin
(at Martinsburg, WV)

1st Potomac (MD) Home Brigade
Cavalry Battalion: (at Martinsburg)

2nd Potomac (MD) Home Brigade
Cavalry Battalion: (at Martinsburg)

4th Brigade: Col. Jacob Miller Campbell
54th PA: Lt. Col. John Park Linton
1st WV: Col. Joseph Thoburn
Lafayette (PA) Cavalry: Capt. Alexander V. Smith
(company joined 22nd PA Cavalry in July)
Washington County (PA) Cavalry: Capt. Andrew J.
Greenfield (joined 22nd PA Cavalry in July)
Ringgold (PA) Cavalry: Capt. John Keys, at New
Creek, WV (joined 22nd PA Cavalry in July)
1st WV Artillery [E]: Capt. Alexander C. Moore
5th Brigade: Col. James Adelbert Mulligan

2nd (MD) Potomac Home Brigade: Col. Robert Bruce
23rd IL: Col. James Adelbert Mulligan
14th WV: Maj. Daniel D. Johnson
1st IL Artillery [L]: Capt. John Rourke

6th Brigade: Col. Nathan Wilkinson
6th WV: Col. Nathan Wilkinson
11th WV: Maj. Van H. Bukey

3rd Division, VIII Corps: BG Eliakim Parker
Scammon, GHQ at Charleston, WV
1st Brigade: Col. Rutherford Birchard Hayes
23rd OH: Col. Rutherford Birchard Hayes
5th WV: Lt. Col. Abais Allen Tomlinson
13th WV: Col. William Rufus Brown
1st WV Cavalry [2 cos.]:
3rd WV Cavalry [G]: Capt. John Seashoal Witcher
Simmonds' (KY) Battery [A]: Capt. Seth J. Simmonds

2nd Brigade: Col. Carr Bailey White
12th OH: Lt. Col. Jonathan D. Hines

34th OH: Maj. John W. Shaw
91st OH: Col. John Alexander Turley
2nd WV Cavalry [G & K]: Capt. Edward S. Morgan
1st OH Independent Battery:
Capt. James R. McMullin

1st Separate Brigade: BG Henry Hayes Lockwood
(not present, with Army of the Potomac)
1st (MD) Eastern Shore: Col. James Wallace (with
Army of the Potomac)
2nd (MD) Eastern Shore: Col. Robert S. Rogers
1st (MD) Potomac Home Guard Battalion: Col.
William Pinckney Maulsby (with AOP)
1st DE Cavalry [4 cos.]: Maj. Napoleon Bonaparte
Knight
Smith's (MD) Cavalry: Capt. George W. P. Smith
Purnell Legion (MD) Cavalry [A & C]:
11th NY Cavalry [3 cos.]: Lt. Henry C. Bates

2nd Separate Brigade: Bvt. BG William Hopkins
Morris, at Baltimore and Cockeysville, MD
5th DE (at Fort Delaware as prison guards)
7th NY State NG: Col. Marshall Lefferts
17th NY State NG: Lt. Col. John P. Jenkins
18th NY State NG: Col. James Rider
55th NY State NG: Lt. Col. Samuel Graham
69th NY State NG: Col. Mathew Murphy
1st CT Cavalry Battalion:

2nd US Artillery [I]: Lt. James E. Wilson
5th NY Heavy Art.: Col. Samuel Graham
8th NY Heavy Art.: Col. Peter Augustus Porter

3rd Separate Brigade: BG Henry Shaw Briggs, at
Baltimore, Frederick, Frederick Junction,
and Relay House, MD
3rd DE: Col. Samuel Howell Jenkins
Purnell (MD) Legion: Maj. Robert G. King
14th NJ: Col. William Snyder Truex
150th NY: Col. John Henry Ketcham
151st NY: Col. William Emerson
138th PA: Maj. Lewis A. May

4th Separate Brigade: BG William Woods Averell, at
Beverly, Buckhannon, Bulltown, Clarksburg,
Parkersburg, and Weston, WV

28th OH: Maj. Ernest Schache

2nd WV: Col. George Robert Latham

3rd WV: Lt. Col. Francis W. Thompson

8th WV: Col. John Hunt Oley

10th WV: Col. Thomas Maley Harris

16th IL Cavalry [C]: Lt. Julius Jeahne

3rd Independent Company OH Cavalry:
Capt. Frank Smith

14th PA Cavalry: Col. James Martinus Schoonmaker

1st WV Cavalry [A]: Capt. Harrison H. Hagan

3rd WV Cavalry [E]: Capt. Lot Bowen

3rd WV Cavalry [H]: Capt. William H. Flesher

3rd WV Cavalry [I]: Lt. George A. Sexton

WV Artillery, Battery B: Capt. John V. Keeper

WV Artillery, Battery G: Capt. Chatham T. Ewing

French's Command: (most departed Harpers Ferry
on June 29/30 for Frederick, MD):
Maj. Gen. William Henry French

1st MD: Col. Nathan T. Dushane

4th MD: Col. Richard Bowerman

7th MD: Lt. Col. Charles E. Phelps

8th MD: Col. Andrew W. Denison

14th NJ: Col. William Snyder Truex

151st NY: Col. William Emerson

17th Independent Artillery Battery:
Capt. Milton L. Milner

4th Battery, 1st ME Light Art:
Capt. O'Neil Watson Robinson, Jr.

6th NY Heavy Art.: Col. John Howard Kitching

1st WV Art. [F]: Capt. Thomas Augustus Maulsby

Baltimore (MD) Battery: Capt. Frederick William
Alexander (from Milroy's 2nd Division)

1st MA Heavy Art. [B, C, H, & I]: Lt. Jonathan B.
Hanson (from Milroy's 2nd Division)

**DEPARTMENT OF WASHINGTON
(XXII CORPS)**

Maj. Gen. Samuel Peter Heintzelman, GHQ
at Fort Lyon in Alexandria, VA

District of Washington: BG John Henry Martindale

2nd DC: Col. Charles Madison Alexander

34th MA: Col. George Duncan Wells

39th MA: Col. Phineas Stearns Davis

14th NH: Col. Robert Wilson

11th NY Cavalry [6 cos.]: Col. James Barrett Swain

27th PA [F]: Capt. John Miller Carson (mustered out)

150th PA [K]: Lt. Thomas Getchell

157th PA [3 cos.]: Maj. Thomas H. Addicks

US Ordnance Detachment:
Lt. Col. George Douglas Ramsay

Fort Washington, MD:
Col. Charles Spencer Merchant

16th IN Battery: Capt. Charles R. Deming

3rd PA Reserves: Maj. William Briner

4th PA Reserves: Lt. Col. Richard H. Woolworth

Cavalry: Col. Sir Percy Wyndham

Detachment 1: Lt. Col. David Ramsay Clendenin

Detachment 2: Lt. Col. John Leverett Thompson

Detachment 3: Lt. Col. Robert Johnstone

2nd MA Cavalry (battalion):
Col. Charles Russell Lowell, Jr.

Defenses North of the Potomac

1st Brigade: Col. James Meech Warner

1st ME Heavy Art. [M]: Capt. James G. Swett

2nd PA Heavy Art.: Col. Augustus Abel Gibson

1st VT Heavy Art: Col. James Meech Warner

2nd Brigade: Col. Lewis O. Morris

1st ME Heavy Art: Col. Daniel Chaplin

7th NY Heavy Art.: Col. Lewis O. Morris

9th NY Heavy Art: Col. Joseph Welling

9th NY Battery: Capt. Emil Schubert

3rd Brigade: Col. Alexander Moore Piper
2nd MA Cavalry [6 cos.]:
Col. Charles Russell Lowell, Jr.
10th NY Heavy Art.: Col. Alexander Moore Piper

District of Alexandria:
Brig Gen. John Potts Slough

1st DC: Lt. Col. Lemuel Towers
23rd ME: Col. William Wirt Virgin (departed
Harper's Ferry on June 24 for Portland, ME)
153rd NY: Col. Edwin Page Davis
PA Independent Artillery [H]:
Capt. William Borrowe

Defenses South of the Potomac:
BG Gustavus Adolphus De Russy

1st Brigade: Col. Thomas Redding Tannatt
1st MA Heavy Art.: Col. Thomas Redding Tannatt
2nd NY Heavy Art.:
Col. Joseph Nelson Garland Whistler
5th NY Heavy Art. [I, K, L & M]: Maj. Gustavus
French Merriam
47th NY NG: Col. Jeremiah Vanderbilt Meserole
(from Smith's NYSNG 2nd Brigade)
10th MI Battery: Capt. John C. Schuetz (transferred to
artillery Camp Berry)

2nd Brigade: Col. Leverette Ward Wessells
19th CT Heavy Art. [Battalion 2]:
Col. Elisha Strong Kellogg
3rd NY Artillery Battalion:
Capt. Leander Schamberger
16th WV: Lt. Col. Samuel W. Snider (mustered out)

3rd Brigade: Col. Henry Larcom Abbot
1st CT Heavy Art: Col. Henry Larcom Abbot
178th NY Inf.: Lt. Col. Charles F. Smith
1st RI Art. [H]: Capt. Jeffrey Hazard
1st WI Heavy Art. [A]: Capt. Charles C. Meservey

Railway Guard:
109th NY: Col. Benjamin Franklin Tracy

Artillery Camp of Instruction (Camp Berry):
BG Albion Parris Howe

1st MD Art. [B]: Capt. Alonzo Snow
1st MI Art. [K]: Capt. John C. Schuetz
1st NY Art. [A]: Capt. Thomas H. Bates
12th NY Battery: Capt. George F. McKnight
17th NY Battery: Capt. George T. Anthony
27th NY Battery: Capt. John B. Eaton
30th NY Battery: Capt. Adolph Voegele
32nd NY Battery: Capt. Charles von Kusserow
12th OH Battery: Capt. Aaron C. Johnson
1st PA Art. [C]: Capt. Jeremiah McCarthy
Hastings' Keystone (PA) Battery:
Capt. Matthew Hastings
1st WV Art. [A]: Capt. George Furst

Abercrombie's Division:
BG John Joseph Abercrombie

1st Brigade: Col. Francis Fessenden
25th ME: Col. Francis Fessenden
(mustered out on June 30)
27th ME: Col. Mark Fernald Wentworth
Jewett's Independent Brigade:
Col. Albert Burton Jewett
6th MI Cavalry [2 cos.]: Capt. Charles W. Deane
10th MA Independent Battery: Capt. Jacob H. Sleeper
11th NY Cavalry [E, F & I]: Maj. Joseph C. Kenyon
10th VT: Lt. Col. William W. Henry

DEPARTMENT OF VIRGINIA (VII CORPS)
Maj. Gen. John Adams Dix

Fort Monroe (Hampton, VA)
3rd PA Heavy Artillery: Col. Joseph Roberts

Norfolk, VA: BG Egbert Lodovicus Viele
7th NY Independent Battery:
148th NY: Lt. Col. George Murray Guion
173rd PA: Col. Daniel Nagle
177th PA: Col. George Berryhill Wiestling

1st Division: BG Michael Corcoran

1st Brigade: BG Henry Dwight Terry
1st Battalion NY Sharpshooters:
Capt. Thomas S. Bradley
130th NY: Col. Alfred Gibbs
152nd NY: Col. Alonzo Ferguson
167th PA: Lt. Col. Joseph DePuy Davis
26th MI: Col. Judson Smith Farrar

2nd Brigade: Col. Robert Sanford Foster
13th IN: Lt. Col. Cyrus Johnson Dobbs
6th MA: Col. Albert Skinner Follansbee
7th MA Independent Battery:
112th NY "Chautauqua Regt.":
Col. Jeremiah Clinton Drake
169th NY "Troy Regiment": Col. Clarence Buell
(wounded at Suffolk); Lt. Col. John McConihe
165th PA: Col. Charles Henry Buehler
166th PA Drafted Militia: Col. Andrew Jackson
Fulton

3rd Brigade "Irish Legion": Col. Matthew Murphy
10th NJ: Col. Henry Ogden Ryerson
155th NY: Col. William McEvily
164th NY "Buffalo Irish Regiment": Col. James
Power McMahon
170th NY: Col. James Patrick McIvor
182nd NY "69th NY NG Artillery":
Lt. Col. Thomas M. Reid

Divisional Artillery: Capt. Frederick M. Follett
1st DE Battery: Capt. Benjamin Nields
19th NY Independent Battery: Capt. William H. Stahl
4th US. Art. [D]: Capt. Frederick Maximus Follett
4th US Art. [L]: Capt. Robert V. W. Howard

2nd Division: BG George Washington Getty
(Hanover Court House, VA)

1st Brigade: Col. Samuel M. Alford
10th NH: Col. Michael Thomas Donohoe
3rd NY "Albany Regiment":
Lt. Col. Eldridge G. Floyd

89th NY: Lt. Col. Theophilus L. England
103rd NY "Seward Infantry": Maj. Benjamin Ringold
117th NY "Fourth Oneida Regt.":
Col. William Russell Pease
2nd Brigade: Col. Edward Harland
8th CT: Col. John E. Ward
11th CT: Col. Griffin Alexander Stedman
15th CT: Col. Charles Leslie Upham
16th CT: Col. Francis Beach

3rd Brigade: Col. Arthur Henry Dutton
21st CT: Col. Arthur Henry Dutton
13th NH: Col. Aaron Fletcher Stevens
25th NJ: Col. Andrew Derrom
4th RI: Col. William Henry Peck Steere

Divisional Artillery:
1st PA Art. [A]: Capt. John G. Simpson
5th US Art.: [A]: Capt. Charles Philip Muhlenberg
Cavalry: Col. Samuel Perkins Spear
1st NY Mounted Rifles:
Lt. Col. Benjamin Franklin Onderdonk
11th PA Cavalry: Col. Samuel Perkins Spear

Spinola's Independent Brigade:
BG Francis Barretto Spinola
158th PA: Col. David Bell McKibben
169th PA: Col. Lewis W. Smith
171st PA: Col. Everard Bierer

Wardrop's Independent Brigade:
Col. David W. Wardrop
99th NY: Col. David W. Wardrop
118th NY "Adirondack Regt.":
Lt. Col. Oliver Keese II

Wistar's Independent Brigade: BG Isaac Jones Wistar
16th NY Independent Battery: Capt. Milo W. Locke
19th WI: Col. Horace Turner Sanders
9th VT: Col. Dudley Kimball Andross

IV Corps: BG Erasmus D. Keyes
(Bottom's Bridge on the Chickahominy River)

1st Division: BG Rufus King

1st Brigade: BG Hector Tyndale
2nd MA Cavalry [A, B, C, D, K]:
2nd NY Cavalry Battalion:
8th NY Independent Battery:

2nd Brigade: Col. George Earl Church
5th PA Cavalry Detachment
11th RI: Col. George Earl Church
1st PA Artillery [I]: Capt. Theodore Miller
2nd WI Independent Battery: Capt. Charles Berger

3rd Brigade: Col. Charles Klecker
168th NY: Col. William R. Brown
172nd PA: Lt. Col. James A. Johnson

2nd Division: BG George Henry Gordon

1st Brigade: Col. William Gurney
127th NY: Lt. Col. Stewart Woodward
142nd NY: Col. Newton M. Curtiss
143rd NY: Col. Horace Boughton
144th NY: Col. David E. Gregory

2nd Brigade: Col. Burr Porter
22nd CT: Col. George S. Burnham
40th MA: Col. Burr Porter
141st NY: Col. William Kenneth Logie
4th WI Battery: Capt. John F. Vallee

West's Advanced Brigade: Col. Robert M. West
139th NY: Col. Anthony Conk
178th PA: Col. James Johnson
5th PA Cavalry: Col. Robert M. West

ARMY OF THE POTOMAC
Maj. Gen. George Gordon Meade
(moved GHQ from Middleburg to Taneytown, MD)

I CORPS
Maj. Gen. John F. Reynolds (commanding left wing,
including I, III, and XI Corps, marched from

Emmitsburg to Marsh Creek and
Moritz Tavern in Adams County, PA)

1st Division: BG James Samuel Wadsworth

1st Brigade "Iron Brigade": BG Solomon Meredith
19th IN: Col. Samuel J. Williams
24th MI: Col. Henry Andrew Morrow
2nd WI: Col. Lucius Fairchild
6th WI: Lt. Col. Rufus R. Dawes
7th WI: Col. William Wallace Robinson
2nd Brigade: BG Lysander Cutler
7th IN: Col. Ira Glanton Grover
76th NY: Maj. Andrew J. Grover
84th NY (14th NYSNG): Col. Edward Brush Fowler
95th NY: Col. George Hogg Biddle
147th NY: Lt. Col. Francis Charles Miller
56th PA [cos. A, B, C, D, F, G, H, I, and K]: Col.
John William Hoffman

2nd Division: BG John Cleveland Robinson

1st Brigade: BG Gabriel Rene Paul
16th ME: Col. Charles William Tilden
13th MA: Col. Samuel Haven Leonard
94th NY: Col. Adrian Rowe Root
104th NY: Col. Gilbert G. Prey
11th PA: Col. Richard Coulter
107th PA: Lt. Col. James McThomson

2nd Brigade: BG Henry Baxter
12th MA: Col. James Lawrence Bates
83rd NY (9th NYSNG):
Lt. Col. Joseph Anton Moesch
97th NY: Col. Charles Wheelock
88th PA: Maj. Benezet Forst Foust
90th PA: Col. Peter Lyle

3rd Division: Maj. Gen. Abner Doubleday

1st Brigade: BG Thomas Algeo Rowley
80th NY (20th NYSNG): Col. Theodore Burr Gates
121st PA: Col. Chapman Biddle

142nd PA: Col. Robert Parson Cummins

151st PA: Lt. Col. George Fisher McFarland

2nd Brigade: Col. Roy Stone

143rd PA: Col. Edmund Lovell Dana

149th PA: Lt. Col. Walton Dwight

150th PA: Col. Langhorne Wister

3rd Brigade: BG George Jefferson Stannard

12th VT: Capt. Norman E. Perkins

13th VT: Col. Francis Voltaire Randall

14th VT: Col. William Thomas Nichols

15th VT: Lt. Col. William Wallace Grout (Col. Redfield Proctor was ill and in reserve)

16th VT: Col. Wheelock Graves Veazey

Artillery Brigade: Col. Charles Shiels Wainwright

2nd ME Art. [B] [6: 3"]: Capt. James Abram Hall

5th ME Art. [E] [6: 12#]: Capt. Greenleaf T. Stevens

1st NY Art [E] (attached to Battery L)

1st NY Art [L] [6: 3"]: Capt. Gilbert Henry Reynolds

1st PA Art. [B] [4: 3"]: Capt. James H. Cooper

4th US Art. [B] [6: 12#]: 1st Lt. James Stewart

II CORPS

Maj. Gen. Winfield Scott Hancock,
(rested in camp at Unionville, MD)

1st Division: BG John Curtis Caldwell

1st Brigade: Col. Edward E. Cross

5th NH: Lt. Col. Charles E. Hapgood

61st NY: Lt. Col. Knut Oscar Broady

81st PA: Lt. Col. Amos Stroh

148th PA: Lt. Col. Robert McFarlane

2nd Brigade: Col. Patrick Kelly

28th MA: Col. Richard Byrnes

63rd NY [A and B]: Lt. Col. Richard Charles Bentley

69th NY [2 cos.]: Capt. Richard Moroney

88th NY [2 cos.]: Capt. Denis Francis Burke

116th PA: Maj. St. Clair Augustin Mulholland

3rd Brigade: BG Samuel Kosciusko Zook

52nd NY: Lt. Col. Charles Godfrey Freudenberg

57th NY: Lt. Col. Alfred B. Chapman

66th NY: Col. Orlando Harriman Morris

140th PA: Col. Richard Pettit Roberts

4th Brigade: Col. John Rutter Brooke

27th CT [D & F]: Lt. Col. Henry Czar Merwin

2nd DE: Col. William Pritchard Baily

64th NY: Col. Daniel Galusha Bingham

53rd PA: [cos. A, B, & K detached as provost guard]: Lt. Col. Richards McMichael

145th PA: Col. Hiram Loomis Brown

2nd Division: BG John Gibbon

1st Brigade: BG William Harrow

19th ME: Col. Francis Edward Heath

15th MA: Col. George Hull Ward

1st MN (Co. 2, Minn. Sharpshooters attached): Col. William J. Colvill, Jr.

82nd NY: Lt. Col. James Huston

2nd Brigade: BG Alexander Stewart Webb

69th PA: Col. Dennis O'Kane

71st PA: "1st California Regiment": Col. Richard Penn Smith

72nd PA "Philadelphia Fire Zouaves": Col. Dewitt Clinton Baxter

106th PA: Lt. Col. William Lovering Curry

3rd Brigade: Col. Norman Jonathan Hall

19th MA: Col. Arthur Forrester Devereux

20th MA: Col. Paul Joseph Revere

7th MI: Lt. Col. Amos E. Steele, Jr.

42nd NY "Tammany Regiment": Col. James E. Mallon

59th NY [A, B, C, D]: Lt. Col. Max A. Thoman

1st MA Sharpshooters (attached): Capt. William Plummer

3rd Division: BG Alexander Hays

1st Brigade "Gibraltar Brigade":
Col. Samuel Sprigg Carroll
14th IN: Col. John Coons
4th OH: Lt. Col. Leonard Willard Carpenter
8th OH: Lt. Col. Franklin Sawyer
7th WV: Lt. Col. Jonathan Hopkins Lockwood

2nd Brigade: Col. Thomas Alfred Smyth
14th CT "Nutmegs": Maj. Theodore Grenville Ellis
1st DE.: Lt. Col. Edward Paul Harris
12th NJ: Maj. John T. Hill
10th NY (battalion) "National Zouaves":
Maj. George Faulkner Hopper
108th NY: Lt. Col. Francis Edwin Pierce
3rd Brigade: Col. George Lamb Willard
39th NY [A, B, C, & D]: "Garibaldi Guards":
Maj. Hugo Hildebrandt
111th NY: Col. Clinton Dugald MacDougall
125th NY: Lt. Col. Levin Crandell
126th NY: Col. Eliakim Sherrill

Artillery Brigade: Capt. John Gardner Hazard
1st NY Art. [B] and 14th NY "Brooklyn Battery"
[4: 10#]: Lt. Albert Sheldon
1st RI Art. [A] [6: 3"]: Capt. William Albert Arnold
1st RI Art. [B] [6: 12#]: Lt. Thomas Frederick Brown
1st US Art. [I] [6: 12#]:
1st Lt. George Augustus Woodruff
4th US [A] [6: 3"]: 1st Lt. Alonzo Hereford Cushing

III CORPS
Maj. Gen. Daniel Edgar Sickles
(marched from Taneytown to Bridgeport, MD)

1st Division: Maj. Gen. David Bell Birney

1st Brigade: BG Charles Kinnaird Graham
57th PA [A, B, C, E, F, H, I & K] Col. Peter Sides
63rd PA: Maj. John Anderson Danks
68th PA: Col. Andrew Hart Tippin
105th PA "Wildcats": Col. Calvin Augustus Craig

114th PA: "Collis's Zouaves":
Lt. Col. Frederick Fernandez Cavada
141st PA: Col. Henry John Madill

2nd Brigade: BG John Henry Hobart Ward
20th IN: Col. John Wheeler
3rd ME: Col. Moses B. Lakeman
4th ME: Col. Elijah Walker
86th NY: Lt. Col. Benjamin Lucius Higgins
124th NY: "Orange Blossoms":
Col. Augustus Van Horne Ellis
99th PA: Maj. John W. Moore
1st US Sharpshooters: Col. Hiram Berdan
2nd US Sharpshooters (8 cos.):
Maj. Homer Richard Stoughton

3rd Brigade: Col. Philippe Régis Dénis
de Keredern de Trobriand
17th ME: Lt. Col. Charles Benjamin Merrill
3rd MI: Col. Byron Root Pierce
5th MI: Lt. Col. John Pulford
40th NY "Mozart Regiment":
Col. Thomas Washington Egan
110th PA [A, B, C, E, H & I]:
Lt. Col. David Mattern Jones

2nd Division: BG Andrew Atkinson Humphreys

1st Brigade: BG Joseph Bradford Carr
1st MA: Lt. Col. Clark B. Baldwin
11th MA: Lt. Col. Porter D. Tripp
16th MA: Lt. Col. Waldo Merriam
12th NH: Capt. John F. Langley
11th NJ: Col. Robert McAllister
26th PA: Maj. Robert Lewis Bodine

2nd Brigade "Excelsior Brigade": Col. W. R. Brewster
70th NY: Col. John Egbert Farnum
71st NY: Col. Henry Langdon Potter
72nd NY: Col. John S. Austin
73rd NY "2nd Fire Zouaves":
Maj. Michael William Burns
74th NY: Lt. Col. Thomas Holt
120th NY: Lt. Col. Cornelius Depuy Westbrook

3rd Brigade: Col. George Childs Burling
2nd NH: Col. Edward Lyon Bailey
5th NJ: Col. William Joyce Sewell
6th NJ: Lt. Col. Stephen Rose Gilkyson
7th NJ: Col. Louis Raymond Francine
8th NJ: Col. John Ramsey
115th PA: Maj. John Peter Dunne

Artillery Brigade: Capt. George E. Randolph
1st NJ Art. [B] [6: 10#]: Capt. Adoniram Judson Clark
1st NY Art. [D] [6: 12#]: Capt. George B. Winslow
4th NY Independent Battery [6: 10#]:
    Capt. James E. Smith
1st RI Art. [E] [6: 12#]: Lt. John Knight Bucklyn
4th US Art. [K] [6: 12#]: 1st Lt. Francis Webb Seeley

V CORPS
Maj. Gen. George Sykes,
(marched from Liberty to Union Mills, MD)

1st Division: BG James Barnes

1st Brigade: Col. William Stowell Tilton
18th MA: Col. Joseph Hayes
22nd MA: Lt. Col. Thomas Sherwin, Jr.
1st MI: Col. Ira Corey Abbott
118th PA "Corn Exchange Regiment":
    Lt. Col. James Gwyn

2nd Brigade: Col. Jacob Bowman Sweitzer
9th MA: Col. Patrick Robert Guiney
32nd MA: Col. George Lincoln Prescott
4th MI: Col. Harrison H. Jeffords
62nd PA: Lt. Col. James C. Hull

3rd Brigade: Col. Strong Vincent
20th ME: Col. Joshua Lawrence Chamberlain
16th MI: Lt. Col. Norval E. Welch
44th NY: Col. James Clay Rice
83rd PA: Capt. Orpheus Saeger Woodward

2nd Division: BG Romeyn Beck Ayres

1st Brigade: Col. Hannibal Day
3rd US [B, C, E, G, I & K]: Capt. Richard G. Lay
4th US [C, F, H & K]: Capt. Julius Walker Adams, Jr.
6th US [D, F, G, H & I]: Capt. Levi Clark Bootes
12th US [1–Batn.: A, B, C, D & G; 2–Batn.: A, C &
    D]: Capt. Thomas Searle Dunn
14th US [1–Batn.: A, B, D, E, F & G: 2–Batn.: F &
    G]: Maj. Grotius Reed Giddings

2nd Brigade: Col. Sidney Burbank
2nd US [B, C, F, H, I & K]: Maj. Arthur Tracy Lee
7th US [A, B, E & I]: Capt. David Porter Hancock
10th US [D, G & H]: Capt. William Clinton
11th US [B, C, D, E, F & G]:
    Maj. DeLancey Floyd-Jones
17th US [1–Batn.]: A, C, D, G & H; 2–Batn.: A & B]:
    Lt. Col. James Durell Greene

3rd Brigade: BG Stephen Hinsdale Weed
140th NY: Col. Patrick Henry O'Rorke
146th NY: Col. Kenner Garrard
91st PA: Lt. Col. Joseph Hill Sinex
155th PA: Lt. Col. John Herron Cain

3rd Division: BG Samuel Wylie Crawford

1st Brigade: Col. William McCandless
1st PA Res. (9 cos.): Col. William Cooper Talley
2nd PA Res.: Lt. Col. George Abisha Woodward
6th PA Res.: Lt. Col. Wellington Henry Ent
13th PA Res. "Bucktails": Col. Charles F. Taylor

3rd Brigade: Col. Joseph Washington Fisher
5th PA Res: Lt. Col. George Dare
9th PA Res: Lt. Col. James M. Snodgrass
10th PA Res: Col. Adoniram Judson Warner
11th PA Res: Col. Samuel McCartney Jackson
12th PA Res [A, B, C, D, E, F, G, H & I]:
    Col. Martin Davis Hardin II

Artillery Brigade: Capt. Augustus Pearl Martin
MA Art. (Battery C) [6: 12#]: Lt. Aaron F. Walcott
1st NY Art. (Battery C) [4: 3"]: Capt. Almont Barnes

1st OH Art. (Battery L) [6: 12#]:
Capt. Frank C. Gibbs
5th US Art. (Battery D) [6: 10#]:
Capt. Charles Edward Hazlett
5th US Art. (Battery I) [4: 3"]:
1st Lt. Malbone Francis Watson

VI CORPS
Maj. Gen. John Sedgwick
(marched from New Windsor to Manchester, MD)

1st Division: BG Horatio Gouverneur Wright

1st Brigade: BG Alfred Thomas Archimedes Torbert
1st NJ: Lt. Col. William Henry, Jr.
2nd NJ: Lt. Col. Charles Wiebecke
3rd NJ: Col. Henry Willis Brown
15th NJ: Col. William Henry Penrose

2nd Brigade: BG Joseph Jackson Bartlett
5th ME: Col. Clark Swett Edwards
121st NY: Col. Emory Upton
95th PA: Lt. Col. Edward Carroll
96th PA: Maj. William Henry Lessig

3rd Brigade: BG David Allen Russell
6th ME: Col. Hiram Burnham
49th PA [A, B, C, & D]: Lt. Col. Thomas M. Hulings
119th PA: Col. Peter Clarkson Ellmaker
5th WI: Col. Thomas Scott Allen

2nd Division: BG Albion Parris Howe

1st Brigade: Col. Lewis Addison Grant
2nd VT: Col. James Hicks Walbridge
3rd VT: Col. Thomas Orville Seaver
4th VT: Col. Charles Bradley Stoughton
5th VT: Lt. Col. John Randolph Lewis
6th VT: Col. Elisha Leonard Barney

3rd Brigade: BG Thomas Hewson Neill
7th ME [B, C, D, F, I, & K]: Lt. Col. Selden Connor
33rd NY (detachment): Capt. Henry J. Gifford

43rd NY: Lt. Col. John Wilson
49th NY: Col. Daniel Davidson Bidwell
77th NY: Lt. Col. Winsor Brown French
61st PA: Lt. Col. George Fairlamb Smith

3rd Division: BG John Newton

1st Brigade: BG Alexander Shaler
65th NY: Col. Joseph Eldridge Hamblin
67th NY: Col. Nelson Cross
122nd NY: Col. Silas Titus
23rd PA: Lt. Col. John Francis Glenn
82nd PA: Col. Isaac Charles Mifflin Bassett

2nd Brigade: Col. Henry Lawrence Eustis
7th MA: Lt. Col. Franklin Powers Harlow
10th MA: Lt. Col. Joseph B. Parsons
37th MA: Col. Oliver Edwards
2nd RI: Col. Horatio Rogers, Jr.

3rd Brigade: BG Frank Wheaton
62nd NY: Col. David John Nevin
93rd PA: Maj. John Irwin Nevin
98th PA: Maj. John Benedict Kohler
139th PA: Col. Frederick Hill Collier

Artillery Brigade: Col. Charles Henry Tompkins
MA Art. [Battery 1]: [6: 12#]:
Capt. William H. McCartney
NY Art. [Battery 1] [6: 3"]: Capt. Andrew Cowan
NY Art. [Battery 3]: [6: 10#]: Capt. William A. Harn
1st RI Art. [C]: [6: 3"]: Capt. Richard Waterman
1st RI Art. [G]: 6: 10#]: Capt. George W. Adams
2nd US Art. [D]: [6: 10#]: 1st Lt. Edward B. Williston
2nd US Art. [G: [6: 12#]: 1st Lt. John Hartwell Butler
5th US Art. [F] [6: 10#]: 1st Lt. Leonard Martin

XI CORPS
Maj. Gen. Oliver Otis Howard (marched through
Emmitsburg, MD, to St. Joseph's Academy)

1st Division: BG Francis Channing Barlow

1st Brigade: Col. Leopold von Gilsa
41st NY [A, B, C, D, E, G, H, I & K]:
Lt. Col. Detleo von Einsiedel
54th NY: Maj. Stephen Kovacs
68th NY: Col. Gotthilf Bourry
153rd PA: Maj. John Frederick Frueauff

2nd Brigade: BG Adelbert Ames
17th CT: Lt. Col. Douglas Fowler
25th OH: Lt. Col. Jeremiah Williams
75th OH: Col. Andrew Lintner Harris
107th OH: Col. Seraphim Meyer

2nd Division: BG Adolf von Steinwehr

1st Brigade: Col. Charles L. Coster
134th NY: Lt. Col. Allan Hyer Jackson
154th NY: "Hardtack Regiment":
Lt. Col. Daniel B. Allen
27th PA: Lt. Col. Lorenz Cantador
73rd PA: Capt. Daniel F. Kelley

2nd Brigade: Col. Orland Smith
33rd MA: Col. Adin Ballou Underwood
136th NY: Col. James Wood, Jr.
55th OH: Col. Charles B. Gambee
73rd OH: Lt. Col. Richard Long

3rd Division: Maj. Gen. Carl Schurz

1st Brigade: BG Alexander Schimmelfennig
82nd IL: Col. Frederick Hecker
45th NY: Col. George von Amsberg
157th NY: Col. Philip Perry Brown, Jr.
61st OH: Col. Stephen Joseph McGroarty
74th PA: Col. Adolph von Hartung

2nd Brigade: Col. Waldimir B. Krzyzanowski
58th NY: Lt. Col. August Otto
119th NY: Col. John Thomas Lockman
82nd OH: Col. James Sidney Robinson
75th PA: Col. Francis Mahler

Artillery Brigade: Maj. Thomas W. Osborn
1st NY Art. [I] [6: 3"]:
Capt. Michael Nicolaus Wiedrich
NY Art. [Battery 13] [4: 3"]: 1st Lt. William Wheeler
1st OH Art. [I] [6: 12#]: Capt. Hubert A. C. Dilger
1st OH Art. [K] [4: 12#]: Capt. Lewis Heckman
4th US Art. [G] [6: 12#]: 1st Lt. Bayard Wilkeson

XII CORPS
Maj. Gen. Henry Warner Slocum (commanding right
wing: 12th Corps and for a time 5th & 6th Corps;
marched from Taneytown and Bruceville, MD,
to Littlestown, PA)

1st Division: BG Alpheus Starkey Williams

1st Brigade: Col. Archibald L. McDougall
5th CT: Col. Warren Wightman Packer
20th CT: Lt. Col. William Burr Wooster
3rd MD: Col. Joseph Martin Sudsburg
123rd NY: Lt. Col. James Clarence Rogers
145th NY: Col. Edward Livingston Price
46th PA: Col. James Levan Selfridge

2nd Brigade: BG Henry Hayes Lockwood
1st (MD) Eastern Shore Inf.: Col. James Wallace
1st (MD) Potomac Home Brigade:
Col. William Pinckney Maulsby
150th NY: Col. John Henry Ketcham

3rd Brigade: BG Thomas Howard Ruger
27th IN: Col. Silas Colgrove
2nd MA: Lt. Col. Charles Redington Mudge
13th NJ: Col. Ezra Carman
107th NY: Col. Nirom Marium Crane
3rd WI: Col. William Hawley

2nd Division: BG John White Geary
(marched to Hanover, PA)
1st Brigade: Col. Charles Candy
5th OH: Col. John Halliday Patrick
7th OH: Col. William R. Creighton
29th OH: Capt. Wilbur F. Stevens
66th OH: Col. Eugene Powell

28th PA: Capt. John Flynn

147th PA [A, B, C, D, E, F, G, & H]:
Lt. Col. Ario Pardee, Jr.

2nd Brigade: Col. George Ashworth Cobham, Jr.

29th PA: Col. William Rickards, Jr.

109th PA: Capt. Frederic Louis Gimber

111th PA: Lt. Col. Thomas McCormick Walker

3rd Brigade: BG George Sears Greene

60th NY: Col. Abel Godard

8th NY: Lt. Col. Herbert von Hammerstein

102nd NY: Col. James Crandall Lane

137th NY: Col. David Ireland

149th NY: Col. Henry Alanson Barnum

Artillery Brigade: 1st Lt. Edward D. Muhlenberg

1st NY Art. [M] [4: 10#]: Lt. Charles E. Winegar

PA Art. [E] [6: 10#]: Lt. Charles A. Atwell

4th US Art. [F] [6: 12#]: 2nd Lt. Sylvanus T. Rugg

5th US Art. [K] [4: 12#]: 1st Lt. David Hunter Kinzie

CAVALRY CORPS
BG Alfred Pleasonton

1st Division: BG John Buford

1st Brigade: Col. William Gamble, moved from near Fairfield via Emmitsburg to Gettysburg, PA

8th IL Cavalry: Maj. John Lourie Beveridge

12th IL Cavalry [E, F, H, & I]:
Capt. George W. Shears

3rd IN Cavalry [A, B, C, D, E, & F] (attached to 12th IL Cavalry): Col. George Henry Chapman

8th NY Cavalry: Lt. Col. William L. Markell

2nd Brigade: Col. Thomas Casimer Devin (moved from near Fairfield via Emmitsburg to Gettysburg, PA)

6th NY Cavalry [B, C, E, G, H, & I]:
Maj. William Elliot Beardsley

9th NY Cavalry: Col. William Sackett

17th PA Cavalry: Col. Josiah Holcomb Kellogg

3rd WV Cavalry [A & C]: Capt. Seymour B. Conger

Reserve Brigade: BG Wesley Merritt

6th PA Cavalry: Maj. James H. Haseltine

1st US Cavalry: Capt. Richard S. C. Lord

2nd US Cavalry: Capt. Theophilus F. Rodenbaugh

5th US Cavalry: Capt. Julius Wilmot Mason

6th US Cavalry: Maj. Samuel Henry Starr

2nd Division: BG David McMurtrie Gregg (moved from New Windsor to Westminster and then to Manchester, MD)

1st Brigade: Col. John Baillie McIntosh

1st MD Cavalry [A, B, C, D, E, F, G, H, I, K, & L]: Lt. Col. James Monroe Deems

Purnell Legion Cavalry (MD) [A]:
Capt. Robert E. Duvall

1st NJ Cavalry: Maj. Myron Holley Beaumont

1st PA Cavalry: Col. John P. Taylor

3rd PA Cavalry: Lt. Col. Edward S. Jones

3rd Brigade: Col. John Irvin Gregg

1st ME Cavalry [A, B, C, D, E, F, G, H, I, K, & M]: Lt. Col. Charles Henry Smith

10th NY Cavalry: Maj. Matthew Henry Avery

4th PA Cavalry: Lt. Col. William Emil Doster

16th PA Cavalry: Lt. Col. John Kincaid Robison

3rd Division: BG Hugh Judson Kilpatrick (moved from Littlestown, PA, to Hanover)

1st Brigade: BG Elon John Farnsworth

5th NY Cavalry: Maj. John Hammond

18th PA Cavalry: Lt. Col. William Penn Brinton

1st VT Cavalry: Lt. Col. Addison Webster Preston

1st WV Cavalry [B, C, D, E, F, G, H, L, M, & N]:
Col. Nathaniel P. Richmond

2nd Brigade "Wolverines":
BG George Armstrong Custer

1st MI Cavalry: Col. Charles H. Town

5th MI Cavalry: Col. Russell Alexander Alger

6th MI Cavalry: Col. George Gray

7th MI Cavalry (10 cos.): Col. William d'Alton Mann

1st Brigade of Horse Artillery:
Capt. James Madison Robertson
9th MI Art. Battery: [6: 3"]: Capt. Jabez James Daniels
6th NY Independent Art. Battery: [6: 3"]:
Capt. Joseph W. Martin
2nd US Art. [B & L] [6: 3"]: 1st Lt. Edward Heaton
2nd US Art. [M]: [6: 3"]: 1st Lt. Alexander
Cummings McWhorter Pennington, Jr.
4th US Art. [E]: [4: 3" Rodmans]:
1st Lt. Samuel Sherer Elder

2nd Brigade of Horse Artillery: Capt. John C. Tidball
1st US Art. [C & G]: [4: 3"]: Capt. Alanson M. Randol
1st US Art. [K]: [6: 3"]: Capt. William M. Graham, Jr.
2nd US Art. [A] [6: 3"]: 2nd Lt. John Haskell Calef
3rd PA Heavy Art. [H, serving as light art.] [2: 3"]:
Capt. William D. Rank

Army Artillery Reserve
BG Robert Ogden Tyler
(moved from Bruceville to Taneytown, MD)

1st Regular Artillery Brigade:
Capt. Dunbar Richard Ransom
1st US Art. [H] [6– 12#]: 1st Lt. Chandler Price Eakin
3rd US Art. [F & K]: [6–12#]:
1st Lt. John Graham Turnbull
4th US Art. [C] [6: 12#]:1st Lt. Evan Thomas
5th US Art. [C] [6: 12#]:
1st Lt. Gulian Verplanck Weir

1st Volunteer Artillery Brigade:
Lt. Col. Freeman McGilvery
MA Art. [Battery 5] [6: 3"] [NY Art. (Battery 10)
attached]: Capt. Charles A. Phillips
MA Art. [Battery 9] [4: 12#]: Capt. John Bigelow
NY Art. [Battery 15] [4: 12#]: Capt. Patrick Hart
PA Art. [C & F] [6: 3"]: Capt. James Thompson

2nd Volunteer Artillery Brigade: Capt. Elijah D. Taft
CT Art. [Battery 2] [4: James & 2: 12# howitzers]:
Capt. John W. Sterling
NY Art. [Battery 5] [6: 20#]: Capt. Elijah D. Taft

3rd Volunteer Artillery Brigade:
Capt. James F. Huntington
NH Art. [Battery 1] [6: 3"]: Capt. Frederick M. Edgell
1st OH [H] [6: 3"]: Capt. James F. Huntington
1st PA [F & G] [6: 3"]: Capt. Robert Bruce Ricketts
WV [C] [4: 10#]: Capt. Wallace Hill

4th Volunteer Artillery Brigade:
Capt. Robert H. Fitzhugh
6th ME Art. [Battery 8] [4: 12#]:
1st Lt. Edwin Barlow Dow
MD Art. [Battery A] [6: 3"]: Capt. James H. Rigby
1st NJ Art. [Battery 1] [6: 10#]:
Lt. Augustin N. Parsons
1st NY Art. [G] [6: 12#]: Capt. Nelson Ames
1st NY Art. [K] [6: 3"] [NY Art. (Battery 11)
attached]: Capt. Robert Hughes Fitzhugh

* * *

ARMY OF NORTHERN VIRGINIA
Gen. Robert Edward Lee
(GHQ at Chambersburg, PA)

FIRST CORPS
Lt. Gen. James Longstreet

McLaws's Division: Maj. Gen. Lafayette McLaws
(marched from Chambersburg to Fayetteville, PA)

Kershaw's Brigade: BG Joseph Brevard Kershaw
2nd SC: Col. John Doby Kennedy
3rd SC: Lt. Col. David Langston
7th SC: Col. David Wyatt Aiken
8th SC: Col. John Williford Henagan
15th SC: Col. William Davie de Saussure
3rd SC Battalion: Lt. Col. William George Rice

Semmes's Brigade: BG Paul Jones Semmes
10th GA: Col. John B. Weems
50th GA: Col. William R. Manning
51st GA: Col. Edward Ball
53rd GA: Col. James Phillip Simms
Barksdale's Brigade: BG William Barksdale

13th MS: Col. James W. Carter

17th MS: Col. William Dunbar Holder

18th MS: Col. Thomas M. Griffin

21st MS: Col. Benjamin Grubb Humphreys

Wofford's Brigade: BG William Tatum Wofford

16th GA: Col. Goode Bryan

18th GA: Lt. Col. Solon Zachery Ruff

24th GA: Col. Robert McMillan

Cobb's (GA) Legion: Lt. Col. Luther Johnson Glenn

Phillips's (GA) Legion: Lt. Col. Elihu Sandy Barclay

3rd GA Sharpshooter Battalion: Lt. Col. Nathan
Hutchins, Maj. William D. Bringle

McLaws's Division Artillery:
Col. Henry Coalter Cabell

1 NC Art. [A]: [2: 12# & 2: 3"]: Capt. Basil C. Manly

Pulaski (GA) Art.: [2: 10# & 2: 3"]:
Capt. John C. Fraser

1st Richmond (VA) Howitzers: [2: 12# & 2: 3"]:
Capt. Edward Stephens McCarthy

Troup (VA) Art.: [2: 12# howitzers & 2: 10#]:
Capt. Henry H. Carleton

Pickett's Division: Maj. Gen. George E. Pickett
(at Chambersburg, PA)

Garnett's Brigade: BG Richard Brooke Garnett

8th VA: Col. Eppa Hunton

18th VA: Lt. Col. Henry Alexander Carrington

19th VA: Col. Henry Gantt

28th VA: Col. Robert Clotworthy Allen

56th VA: Col. William Dabney Stuart

Armistead's Brigade: BG Lewis Addison Armistead

9th VA: Maj. John Crowder Owens

14th VA: Col. James Gregory Hodges

38th VA: Col. Edward Claxton Edmonds

53rd VA: Col. William Roane Aylett

57th VA: Col. John Bowie Magruder

Kemper's Brigade: BG James Lawson Kemper

1st VA: Col. Lewis Burwell Williams, Jr.

3rd VA: Col. Joseph Mayo, Jr.

7th VA: Col. Waller Tazewell Patton

11th VA: Lt. Col. Kirkwood Otey

24th VA: Col. William Richard Terry

Pickett's Division Artillery
(38th Battalion, VA Light Art.): Maj. James Dearing

Fauquier (VA) Art.: [4: 12# and 2: 20#]:
Capt. Robert Mackey Stribling

Hampden (VA) Art.: [2: 12#, 1: 3" and 1: 10#]:
Capt. William Henderson Caskie

Richmond (VA) Fayette Art.: [2: 12# and 2: 10#]:
Capt. Miles Cary Macon

Virginia Battery: [4: 12#] Capt. Joseph Gray Blount

Hood's Division: Maj. Gen. John Bell Hood
(marched from Chambersburg to Fayetteville, PA)

Anderson's Brigade: BG George Thomas Anderson

7th GA: Col. William Wilkinson White

8th GA: Col. John R. Towers

9th GA [B, C, D, E, F, G, H, I, & K]: |
Lt. Col. John Clarke Mounger

11th GA: Col. Francis H. Little

59th GA: Col. William A. Jackson Brown

Law's Brigade: BG Evander McIvor Law
(sent to New Guilford, PA)

4th AL: Lt. Col. Laurance Houston Scruggs

15th AL: Col. William Calvin Oates

44th AL: Col. William Flake Perry

47th AL: Lt. Col. Michael Jefferson Bulger

48th AL: Col. James Lawrence Sheffield

Robertson's Brigade "Hood's Texas
Brigade": BG Jerome Bonaparte Robertson

3rd AR: Col. Vannoy Hartrog Manning

1st TX: Lt. Col. Philip Alexander Work

4th TX: Col. John Cutlett G. Key

5th TX: Col. Robert Michael Powell

Benning's Brigade: BG Henry Lewis Benning

2nd GA: Lt. Col. William Terrell Harris

15th GA: Col. Dudley McIver DuBose

17th GA: Col. Wesley C. Hodges

20th GA: Col. John Augustus Jones

Hood's Division Artillery: Maj. Mathias W. Henry
Branch (NC) Art.: [3: 12# and 2: 10#]:
Capt. Alexander C. Latham
German (SC) Art.: [4: 12#]:
Capt. William Kunhardt Bachman
Palmetto (SC) Art.: [2: 12# & 2: 10#]:
Capt. Hugh Richardson Garden
Rowan (NC) Art.: [2: 12#, 2: 3" & 2: 10#]:
Capt. James Reilly

Reserve Artillery: Col. James Burdee Walton
Alexander's Battery: Col. Edward Porter Alexander
Ashland (VA) Art.: [2: 20# & 2: 12#]:
Capt. Pichegru Woolfolk, Jr.
Bedford (VA) Art.: [4: 3"]: Capt. Tyler C. Jordan
Brooks (SC) Art.: [4: 12# howitzers]:
Capt. William W. Fickling
Madison (LA) Art.: [4: 24# howitzers]:
Capt. George V. Moody
Richmond (VA) Battery: [3: 3" & 1: 10#]:
Capt. William Watts Parker
Bath (VA) Battery: [4: 12#]: Capt. Osmond B. Taylor
Washington (LA) Art.: Maj. Benjamin F. Eshleman
Co.1: [1: 12#]: Capt. Charles Winder Squires
Co.2: [2: 12# & 1: 12# howitzer]:
Capt. John B. Richardson
Co.3: [3: 12#]: Capt. Merritt B. Miller
Co.4: [2: 12# & 1: 12# howitzer]:
Capt. Joseph Norcom

SECOND CORPS
Lt. Gen. Richard Stoddert Ewell
Maj. Gen. Isaac Ridgeway Trimble, ADC

Early's Division: Maj. Gen. Jubal Anderson Early,
(marched from York toward Heidlersburg, PA)

Hays's Brigade "Louisiana Tigers"/
First Louisiana Brigade: BG Harry Thompson Hays
5th LA: Maj. Alexander Hart
6th LA: Lt. Col. Joseph Hanlon
7th LA: Col. David Bradfute Penn
8th LA: Col. Trevanion Dudley Lewis

Smith's Brigade: BG William "Extra Billy" Smith
13th VA: Col. James Barbour Terrill (left in
Winchester when Early marched north to PA)
31st VA: Col. John Stringer Hoffman
49th VA: Lt. Col. Jonathan Catlett Gibson
52nd VA: Lt. Col. James Henry Skinner
58th VA: Col. Francis Howard Board (left in
Winchester when Early marched north to PA)

Hoke's Brigade: Col. Isaac Erwin Avery
(substituting for BG Robert Frederick Hoke,
wounded at Chancellorsville)
6th NC: Col. Isaac Erwin Avery
21st NC: Col. William Whedbee Kirkland
54th NC: Col. Kenneth McKenzie Murchison (left in
Winchester when Early marched north to PA)
57th NC: Col. Archibald Campbell Godwin

Gordon's Brigade: BG John Brown Gordon
13th GA: Col. Thomas Milton Smith
26th GA: Col. Edmund Nathan Atkinson
31st GA: Col. Clement Anselm Evans
8th GA: Lt. Col. William L. McLeod
60th GA: Capt. Walters Burras Jones
61st GA: Col. John Hill Lamar

Early's Division Artillery: Lt. Col. Hilary Pollard Jones
Charlottesville (VA) Art.: [4: 12#]:
Capt. James McDowell Carrington
Courtney (VA) Art.: [4: 3"]: Capt. William A. Tanner
Louisiana Guard Art.: [2: 10# & 2: 3"]:
Capt. Charles A. Green
Staunton (VA) Art.: [4: 12#]:
Capt. Asher Waterman Garber

Johnson's Division: Maj. Gen. Edward Johnson,
(marched from Greenville to Scotland, PA)

Steuart's Brigade:
BG George Hume "Maryland" Steuart
1st [2nd] MD Battalion: Lt. Col. James R. Herbert
1st NC: Lt. Col. Hamilton Allen Brown
3rd NC: Maj. William Murdoch Parsley
10th VA: Col. Edward Tiffin Harrison Warren

23rd VA: Lt. Col. Simeon Taylor Walton

37th VA: Maj. Henry Clinton Wood

"Stonewall Brigade": BG James Alexander Walker

2nd VA: Col. John Quincy Adams Nadenbousch

4th VA: Maj. William Terry

5th VA: Col. John Henry Stover Funk

27th VA: Lt. Col. Daniel McKeloran Shriver

33rd VA: Capt. Jacob Burner Golladay

Jones's Brigade: BG John Marshall Jones

21st VA: Capt. William Perkins Moseley

25th VA: Col. John Carleton Higginbotham

42nd VA: Lt. Col. Robert Woodson Withers

44th VA: Maj. Norval Cobb

48th VA: Lt. Col. Robert Henry Dungan

50th VA: Lt. Col. Logan Henry Neal Salyer

Nicholls's Brigade "Second Louisiana Brigade":
Col. Jesse Milton Williams

1st LA: Lt. Col. Michael Nolan

2nd LA: Lt. Col. Ross E. Burke

10th LA: Maj. Thomas N. Powell

14th LA: Lt. Col. David Zable

15th LA: Maj. Andrew Brady

Johnson's Division Artillery: Maj. Joseph W. Latimer

1st MD Art. Battery: [4: 12#]:
Capt. William F. Dement

Alleghany (VA) Art.: [2: 12# & 2: 3"]:
Capt. John Cadwalader Carpenter

Chesapeake (MD) Art.: [4: 10#]:
Capt. William D. Brown

Lee (VA) Art.: [1: 10#, 1: 3" & 2: 20#]:
Capt. Charles James Raine

Rodes's Division: Maj. Gen. Robert Emmett Rodes,
(marched from Carlisle via Petersburg
to Heidlersburg, PA)

Daniel's Brigade: BG Junius Daniel

32nd NC: Col. Edmund Crey Brabble

43rd NC: Col. Thomas Stephens Kenan

45th NC: Lt. Col. Samuel Hill Boyd

53rd NC: Col. William Allison Owens

2nd NC Battalion: Lt. Col. Hezekiah L. Andrews

Doles's Brigade: BG George Pierce Doles

4th GA: Lt. Col. David Read Evans Winn

12th GA: Col. Edward S. Willis

21st GA: Col. John Thomas Mercer

44th GA: Col. Samuel Prophet Lumpkin

Iverson's Brigade: BG Alfred Iverson, Jr.

5th NC: Capt. Speight Brock West

12th NC: Lt. Col. William Smith Davis

20th NC: Lt. Col. Nelson Slough

23rd NC: Col. Daniel Harvey Christie

Ramseur's Brigade:
BG Stephen Dodson Ramseur

2nd NC: Maj. Daniel Washington Hurtt

4th NC: Col. Bryan Grimes

14th NC: Col. Risden Tyler Bennett

30th NC: Col. Francis Marion Parker

O'Neal's Brigade: Col. Edward Asbury O'Neal

3rd AL: Col. Cullen Andrews Battle

5th AL: Col. Josephus Marion Hall

6th AL: Col. James Newell Lightfoot

12th AL: Col. Samuel Bonneau Pickens

26th AL: Lt. Col. John Chapman Goodgame

Rodes's Division Artillery: Lt. Col. Thomas H. Carter

Jeff Davis (AL) Art.: [4: 3"]: Capt. William J. Reese

King William (VA) Art.: [2: 10# & 2: 12#]:
Capt. William Pleasants Page Carter

Morris (VA) Art.: [4: 12#]:
Capt. Richard Channing Moore Page

Orange (VA) Art.: [2: 10# & 2: 3"]:
Capt. Charles William Fry

Artillery Reserve: Col. John Thompson Brown

1st Virginia Art. Battalion: Capt. Willis J. Dance

2nd Richmond Howitzers: [4: 10#]:
Capt. David Watson

3rd Richmond Howitzers: [4: 3"]:
Capt. Benjamin Hodges Smith, Jr.
Powhatan Art.: [4: 3"]: Lt. John M. Cunningham
Rockbridge Art.: [4: 20#]: Capt. Archibald Graham
Salem Art.: [2: 3"]: Lt. Charles Beale Griffin

Nelson's Art. Battalion: Lt. Col. William Nelson
Amherst (VA) Art.: [3: 12# & 1: 3"]:
Capt. Thomas Jellis Kirkpatrick
Fluvanna (VA) Art.: [3: 12# & 1: 3"]:
Capt. John Livingston Massie
Georgia Battery: [1: 10# & 2: 3"]:
Capt. John Milledge, Jr.

THIRD CORPS
Lt. Gen. Ambrose Powell Hill

Anderson's Division:
Maj. Gen. Richard H. Anderson (at Fayetteville, PA)

Wilcox's Brigade: BG Cadmus Marcellus Wilcox
8th AL: Lt. Col. Hilary Abner Herbert
9th AL: Capt. Joseph Horace King
10th AL: Col. William Henry Forney
11th AL: Col. John Caldwell Calhoun Sanders
14th AL: Col. Lucius Pinckard

Mahone's Brigade: BG William Mahone
6th VA: Col. George Thomas Rogers
12th VA: Col. David Addison Weisiger
16th VA: Col. Joseph Hutchinson Ham
41st VA: Col. William Allen Parham
61st VA: Col. Virginius Despeaux Groner

Wright's Brigade: BG Ambrose Ransom Wright
3rd GA: Col. Edward J. Walker
22nd GA: Col. Joseph Wasden
48th GA: Col. William Gibson
2nd Ga. Battalion: Maj. George W. Ross

Posey's Brigade: BG Carnot Posey
12th MS: Col. William H. Taylor
16th MS: Col. Samuel E. Baker
19th MS: Col. Nathaniel Harrison Harris

48th MS: Col. Joseph McAfee Jayne

Perry's Brigade: Col. David Lang
(substituting for ill BG Edward Aylesworth Perry)
2nd FL: Maj. Walter Raleigh Moore
5th FL: Capt. Richmond N. Gardner
8th FL: Lt. Col. William Peter Baya

Anderson's Division Artillery:
Sumter (GA) Battalion: Maj. John Lane
Co. A: [3: 10#, 1: 12# & 1: 3"]:
Capt. Hugh Madison Ross
Co. B: [2: 12# & 4: 12# howitzers]:
Capt. George M. Patterson
Co. C: [2: 20# & 3: 3"]: Capt. John T. Wingfield

Heth's Division: Maj. Gen. Henry Heth
(at Cashtown, PA)

Pettigrew's Brigade: BG James Johnston Pettigrew,
(marched nearly to Gettysburg but was
recalled to Cashtown, PA)
11th NC: Col. Collett Leventhorpe
26th NC: Col. Henry King Burgwyn, Jr.
47th NC: Col. George H. Faribault
52nd NC: Col. James Keith Marshall

Archer's Brigade: BG James Jay Archer
5th AL Battalion:
Maj. Albert Sebastian Van de Graaff
13th AL: Col. Birkett Davenport Fry
1st TN: Lt. Col. Newton J. George
7th TN: Col. John Amenas Fite
14th TN: Capt. Bruce L. Phillips

Davis's Brigade: BG Joseph Robert Davis
2nd MS: Col. John Marshall Stone
11th MS: Acting Col. Francis M. Green
42nd MS: Col. Hugh Reid Miller
55th NC: Col. John Hugh Kerr Connally

Brockenbrough's Brigade:
Col. John Mercer Brockenbrough
22nd VA Battalion: Maj. John Samuel Bowles

40th VA: Capt. Thomas Edwin Betts

47th VA: Col. Robert Murphy Mayo

55th VA: Col. William Steptoe Christian

Heth's Division Artillery: Lt. Col. John J. Garnett

Donaldsonville (LA) Art.: [2: 3" & 1: 10#]:
Capt. Victor Maurin

Huger (VA) Art.: [2: 12#, 1: 3" & 1: 10#]:
Capt. Joseph D. Moore

Lewis (VA) Art.: [2: 12# & 2: 3"]:
Capt. John W. Lewis

Norfolk (VA) Blues Art.: [2: 12# & 2: 3"]:
Capt. Charles R. Grandy

Pender's Division: Maj. Gen. William Dorsey Pender
(marched from Fayetteville to Cashtown, PA)

Lane's Brigade: BG James Henry Lane

7th NC: Capt. John Mcleod Turner

18th NC: Col. John Decatur Barry

28th NC: Col. Samuel D. Lowe

33rd NC: Col. Clarke Moulton Avery

37th NC: Col. William M. Barbour

Thomas's Brigade: BG Edward Lloyd Thomas

14th GA: Col. Robert Warren Folsom

35th GA: Col. Bolling Hall Holt

45th GA: Col. Thomas Jefferson Simmons

49th GA: Col. Samuel Thomas Player

Scales's Brigade: BG Alfred Moore Scales

13th NC: Col. Joseph Henry Hyman

16th NC: Capt. Leroy W. Stowe

22nd NC: Col. James Conner

34th NC: Col. William Lee Joshua Lowrance

38th NC: Col. William J. Hoke

McGowan's Brigade: Col. Abner Monroe Perrin

1st SC: Maj. Comillus Wycliffe McCreary

1st SC Rifles: Capt. William M. Hadden

12th SC: Col. John Lucas Miller

13th SC: Col. Benjamin Thomas Brockman

14th SC: Lt. Col. Joseph Newton Brown

Pender's Division Artillery: Maj. William T. Poague

Albemarle (VA) Art.: [1: 12# howitzer, 1: 10#
& 2: 3"]: Capt. James Walter Wyatt

Charlotte (NC) Art.: [2: 12# & 2: 12# howitzers]:
Capt. Joseph Graham

Madison (MS) Art.: [3: 12# & 1: 12# howitzer]:
Capt. George Ward

Warrington (VA) Battery: [2: 12# & 2: 12#
howitzers]: Capt. James Vass Brooke

Third Corps Artillery: Col. Reuben Lindsay Walker

McIntosh's Art. Battalion:
Maj. David George McIntosh

Danville (VA) Art.: [4: 12#]: Capt. Robert Sidney Rice

Hardaway (AL) Art.: [2: Whitworths & 2: 3"]:
Capt. William B. Hurt

2nd Rockbridge (VA) Art.: [2: 12# & 2 or 4: 3"]:
Lt. Samuel Wallace

Richmond (VA) Battery: [4: 3" or 2: 12# & 2: 3"]:
Capt. Marmaduke Johnson

Pegram's Art. Battalion: Maj. William R. J. Pegram

Crenshaw (VA) Art.: [2: 12# & 2: 12# howitzers]:
Capt. William Crenshaw

Fredericksburg (VA) Art.: [2: 12# & 2: 3"]:
Capt. Edward Avenmore Marye

Letcher (VA) Art.: [2: 12# & 2: 3"]:
Capt. Thomas Alexander Brander

Pee Dee (SC) Art.: [4: 3"]: Lt. William E. Zimmerman

Purcell (VA) Art.: [4" 12#]: Capt. Joseph McGraw

Stuart's Cavalry Division: Maj. Gen. James Ewell
Brown Stuart (fought the battle of Hanover and then
rode through Jefferson and New Salem to Dover, PA)

Hampton's Cavalry Brigade: BG Wade Hampton III

1st NC Cavalry: Col. Laurence Simmons Baker

1st SC Cavalry: Col. John Logan Black

2nd SC Cavalry: Maj. Thomas Jefferson Lipscomb

Cobb's (GA) Legion Cavalry:
Lt. Col. William Gaston Delony

Jeff Davis's (MS) Legion Cavalry:
Lt. Col. Joseph Frederick Waring

Phillips's (GA) Legion Cavalry:
Lt. Col. Jefferson C. Phillips

Fitz Lee's Cavalry Brigade: BG Fitzhugh Lee
1st MD Cavalry Battalion: Maj. Harry Ward Gilmor
1st VA Cavalry: Col. James Henry Drake
2nd VA Cavalry: Col. Thomas Taylor Munford
3rd VA Cavalry: Col. Thomas Howerton Owen
4th VA Cavalry: Col. Williams Carter Wickham
5th VA Cavalry: Col. Thomas Lafayette Rosser

W.H.F. "Rooney" Lee's Cavalry Brigade:
Col. John Randolph Chambliss, Jr.
2nd NC Cavalry: Capt. William A. Graham, Jr.
9th VA Cavalry: Col. Richard Lee Turberville Beale
10th VA Cavalry: Col. James Lucius Davis
13th VA Cavalry: Capt. Benjamin F. Winfield

Jones's Cavalry Brigade: BG William Edmondson
"Grumble" Jones (moved toward Williamsport, MD)
6th VA Cavalry: Maj. Cabell Edward Flournoy
7th VA Cavalry: Lt. Col. Thomas C. A. Marshall, Jr.
11th VA Cavalry: Col. Lunford Lindsay Lomax
35th Battalion, VA Cavalry: Lt. Col. Elijah Viers
White (with Early's division near Heidlersburg, PA)

Robertson's Cavalry Brigade:
BG Beverly Holcombe Robertson
4th NC Cavalry: Col. Dennis Dozier Ferebee
5th NC Cavalry (63rd NC): Maj. James H. McNeill

Jenkins's Cavalry Brigade: BG Albert Gallatin Jenkins
(moved from near Harrisburg to Cashtown, PA)
14th VA Cavalry: Col. James Addison Cochran
16th VA Cavalry: Col. Milton Jameson Ferguson
17th VA Cavalry: Col. William Henderson French
(with Early's division; near Heidlersburg, PA)
34th Battalion, VA Cavalry:
Lt. Col. Vincent Addison Witcher
36th Battalion, VA Cavalry: Capt. Cornelius T. Smith
Jackson's (VA) Battery (attached):
Capt. Thomas E. Jackson

Horse Artillery Battalion: Maj. Robert F. Beckham

Breathed's (VA) Battery: [4: 3"]:
Capt. James Breathed
Chew's (VA) Battery: [5 guns]: Capt. Robert P. Chew
Griffin's (MD) Battery: [4: 10#]: Capt. Wiley Hunter
Griffin (with Jenkins's brigade)
Hart's (SC) Battery: [3: Blakelys]:
Capt. James Franklin Hart
McGregor's (VA) Battery: [2: 12# & 2: 3"]:
Capt. William Morrell McGregor

Independent command
Imboden's Northwestern Cavalry Brigade:
BG John Daniel Imboden (moved from Hancock,
MD, to McConnellsburg, PA)
18th VA Cavalry: Col. George William Imboden
62nd VA Mounted Infantry: Col. George Hugh Smith
Virginia Partisan Rangers: Capt. John Hanson McNeill
Staunton (VA) Artillery: [6 guns]:
Capt. John H. McClanahan

DEPARTMENT OF RICHMOND
Maj. Gen. Arnold Elzey;
Maj. Gen. Daniel Harvey Hill (beginning July 1)
GHQ in Richmond, VA

Richmond Defenses: Col. Thomas Smith Rhett
4th Infantry Battalion, Local Defense Troops
(organized in June 1863)

First Division, Inner Line: Lt. Col. John Wilder
Atkinson
10th VA Heavy Artillery [5 companies]:
Maj. James O. Hensley
19th VA Heavy Artillery [5 companies]:
Maj. Nathaniel R. Cary

Second Division, Inner Line: Lt. Col. James Howard
18th VA Heavy Artillery:
Maj. Mark Bernard "Bunny" Hardin
20th VA Heavy Artillery: Maj. James E. Robertson

Artillery Battalion: Lt. Col. Charles Edward
Lightfoot (available to Rhett, but independent)
Alexandria (VA) Artillery: Capt. David Lowe Smoot

Carolina (VA) Light Artillery:
Capt. Thomas Rowe Thornton
Nelson Light Artillery [2]: Capt. James Henry Rives
Surry (VA) Light Artillery:
Capt. James DeWitt Hankins

Cooke's Brigade: BG John Rogers Cooke
(defending New Bridge Road)
15th NC: Col. William McRae
27th NC: Col. John Alexander Gilmer, Jr.
46th NC: Col. Edward Dudley Hall
48th NC: Col. Robert Clinton Hill
Cooper's Battery: Capt. Raleigh L. Cooper

Wise's Brigade: BG Henry Wise
(elements in New Kent County, VA)
26th VA: Col. Powhatan Robertson Page
46th VA: Col. Richard Thomas Walker Duke
59th VA: Col. William Barksdale Tabb
Holcombe Legion [Cavalry]:
Col. William Pinckney Shingler
10th VA Cavalry [D]: Capt. Louis J. Hawley
15th VA Cavalry [C]: Capt. Edward W. Capps
32nd Battalion, VA Cavalry: Maj. John R. Robertson
4th VA Heavy Artillery: Col. John Thomas Goode
Artillery: Maj. Alexander W. Stark
BGMatthews Light Artillery:
Capt. Andrew Dewees Armistead
BGMcComas Light Artillery: Capt. David A. French

Godwin's Cavalry
42nd Battalion, VA Cavalry:
Lt. Col. William Todd Robins

Maury's Command:
Lt. Col. John Minor Maury
(at Chapin's Bluff, VA)
Gloucester (VA) Artillery:
Capt. Thomas Ball Montague
King and Queen (VA) Art:
Capt. Alexander Fleet Bagby
Lunenburg (VA) Artillery:
Capt. Cornelius Tacitus Allen
Pamunkey (VA) Artillery:
Capt. Andrew Judson Jones

Smith's Command: Maj. Francis W. Smith
(at Drewry's Bluff, VA)
Johnston (VA) Artillery: Capt. Branch Jones Epes
Neblett (VA) Heavy Artillery:
Capt. Wiley G. Coleman
Southside (VA) Artillery: Capt. John William Drewry
United (VA) Artillery: Capt. Thomas Kevill

In July, Maj. Gen. Robert Ransom's brigade was
temporarily assigned to the Department of Richmond.

APPENDIX 2

THE ITINERARIES OF THE ARMIES
June 22–30, 1863

The Army of the Potomac and Cooperating Forces in the Gettysburg Campaign[1]

June 22: The Cavalry Corps and Barnes's division of the V Corps returned from Upperville to Aldie. Stahel's cavalry division moved from Buckland Mills via New Baltimore to Warrenton. Skirmishes near Dover and Aldie, VA, and at Greencastle, PA.

June 23: Stahel's cavalry division moved from Warrenton via Gainesville to Fairfax Court House.

June 24: Newton's division, VI Corps, moved from Germantown to Centreville; XI Corps from Cow-Horn Ford, or Trappe Rock, on Goose Creek to the south bank of the Potomac at Edwards Ferry, VA. Stahel's division moved from Fairfax Court House to near Dranesville. Skirmish at Sharpsburg, MD.

June 25: I Corps marched from Guilford Station, VA, to Barnesville, MD; III Corps, from Gum Springs, VA, to the north side of the Potomac at Edwards Ferry and the mouth of the Monocacy; the XI Corps, from Edwards Ferry, VA, to Jefferson, MD; and the artillery reserve from Fairfax Court House, VA, to near Poolesville, MD. These commands crossed the Potomac at Edwards Ferry. II Corps marched from Thoroughfare Gap and Gainesville to Gum Springs. Howe's division (VI Corps) moved from Bristoe Station to Centreville. Two brigades of Crawford's division of Pennsylvania Reserves, from the Washington defenses, marched from Fairfax Station and Upton's

1 Based upon *The Battle of Gettysburg: from the History of the Civil War in America*, by Louis Philippe Albert d'Orléans, Comte de Paris (Philadelphia: The J. C. Winston Co., 1907); Richard C. Drum, *Itinerary of the Army of the Potomac, and Co-operating Forces in the Gettysburg Campaign, June 5-July 31, 1863*; *Organization of the Army of the Potomac and Army of Northern Virginia at the Battle of Gettysburg*; and *Return of Casualties in the Union and Confederate Forces* (Washington, D.C.: U.S. Government Printing Office, 1888).

Hill to Vienna. Stannard's Vermont brigade, also from the defenses of Washington, left the mouth of the Occoquan en route to join the Army of the Potomac. Stahel's division rode from near Dranesville, VA, via Young's Island Ford on the Potomac en route to Frederick, MD. Skirmishes at Thoroughfare Gap and Haymarket, VA, and near McConnellsburg, PA.

June 26: Headquarters, Army of the Potomac moved from Fairfax Court House, VA, via Dranesville and Edwards Ferry to Poolesville, MD; the I Corps from Barnesville to Jefferson, MD; the II Corps from Gum Springs, VA, to the north side of the Potomac at Edwards Ferry; the III Corps from the mouth of the Monocacy to Point of Rocks, MD; the V Corps from Aldie, VA, via Carter's Mills, Leesburg, and Edwards Ferry to within four miles of the mouth of the Monocacy River; the VI Corps from Germantown and Centreville to Dranesville; the XI Corps from Jefferson to Middletown, MD; the XII Corps from Leesburg, VA, via Edwards Ferry, to the mouth of the Monocacy; and the Cavalry Corps (Buford's and Gregg's divisions), from Aldie to Leesburg. Stahel's division was en route between the Potomac and Frederick. Crawford's Pennsylvania Reserves moved from Vienna to Goose Creek. Skirmish near Gettysburg, PA.

June 27: Headquarters, Army of the Potomac moved from Poolesville to Frederick; I Corps from Jefferson to Middletown, MD; II Corps from near Edwards Ferry via Poolesville to Barnesville; the III Corps from Point of Rocks via Jefferson to Middletown, MD; the V Corps from a point between Edwards Ferry and the mouth of the Monocacy to Ballinger's Creek, near Frederick; VI Corps from Dranesville via Edwards Ferry to near Poolesville; XII Corps from near the mouth of the Monocacy via Point of Rocks to Knoxville, MD; Buford's cavalry division rode from Leesburg via Edwards Ferry to near Jefferson; Gregg's cavalry division went from Leesburg via Edwards Ferry toward Frederick; and the artillery reserve from Poolesville to Frederick. Stahel's cavalry division reached Frederick. Crawford's Pennsylvania Reserves moved from Goose Creek via Edwards Ferry to the mouth of the Monocacy. Skirmishes near Fairfax Court House, VA, and Hanover Junction, PA.

June 28: I Corps marched from Middletown to Frederick; II Corps from Barnesville to Monocacy Junction; III Corps from Middletown to near Woodsboro; VI Corps from near Poolesville to Hyattstown; XI Corps from Middletown to near Frederick; and XII Corps from Knoxville to Frederick. Buford's cavalry division moved from near Jefferson to Middletown; Gregg's cavalry division reached Frederick, then rode to Newmarket and Ridgeville. Crawford's Pennsylvania Reserves marched from the mouth of the Monocacy and joined the V Corps at Ballinger's Creek. Stahel's cavalry division was assigned to the Cavalry Corps as the 3rd Division under Brig. Gen. Judson Kilpatrick, with Brig. Gen. Elon J. Farnsworth commanding the 1st Brigade and Brig. Gen. George A. Custer the 2nd Brigade. Maj. Gen. D. E. Sickles resumed command of the III Corps, relieving Maj. Gen. D. B. Birney, who had been temporarily in command. Major General George G. Meade relinquished command of the V Corps to Maj. Gen. George Sykes and assumed command of the Army of the Potomac, relieving Major General Hooker. Skirmishes between Offutt's Crossroads and Seneca, and near Rockville, MD, and at Fountain Dale, Wrightsville, and Oyster's Point, PA.

June 29: Headquarters, Army of the Potomac moved from Frederick to Middleburg; I and XI Corps marched from Frederick to Emmitsburg; II Corps from Monocacy Junction via Liberty and Johnsville to Uniontown; III Corps from near Woodsboro to Taneytown; V Corps from Ballinger's Creek via Frederick and Mount Pleasant to Liberty; VI Corps from Hyattstown via Newmarket and Ridgeville to New Windsor; XII Corps from Frederick to Taneytown and Bruceville; Gamble's and Devin's brigades, of Buford's cavalry division, from Middletown via Boonsboro, Cavetown, and Monterey Springs to near Fairfield; Merritt's reserve cavalry brigade, of the same division, from

Middletown to Mechanicstown; Gregg's cavalry division from New Market and Ridgeville to New Windsor; Kilpatrick's cavalry division from Frederick to Littlestown; and the artillery reserve from Frederick to Bruceville. Skirmishes at Muddy Branch and Westminster, MD, and at McConnellsburg and near Oyster's Point, PA.

June 30: Headquarters, Army of the Potomac moved from Middleburg to Taneytown; I Corps from Emmitsburg to Marsh Run; III Corps from Taneytown to Bridgeport; V Corps from Liberty via Johnsville, Union Bridge, and Union to Union Mills; VI Corps from New Windsor to Manchester; XII Corps from Taneytown and Bruceville to Littlestown; Gamble's and Devin's brigades from near Fairfield via Emmitsburg to Gettysburg; Gregg's cavalry division from New Windsor to Westminster and then to Manchester; Kilpatrick's cavalry division from Littlestown, PA, to Hanover; and the artillery reserve from Bruceville to Taneytown. Kenly's and Morris's brigades of French's division left Maryland Heights for Frederick, and Elliott's and Smith's brigades of the same division moved from the Heights by way of the Chesapeake and Ohio Canal, for Washington, D.C. Battle of Hanover and skirmishes at Westminster, MD, and Fairfield and Sporting Hill, near Harrisburg.

The Army of Northern Virginia in the Gettysburg Campaign, June 1863[2]

June 22: Rodes's and Johnson's divisions and Jenkins's Brigade moved from Hagerstown to Chambersburg, PA, with Rodes halting near Greencastle. Early's Division crossed the Potomac at Shepherdstown, marched through Sharpsburg, and camped on the Hagerstown Road three miles from Boonsboro. Anderson's Division marched from Berryville to Roper's Farm on the road to Charles Town. Hood's Division moved to Millwood. Stuart's cavalry concentrated near Upperville.

June 23: Rodes's Division was at Greencastle. Early's Division moved from Boonsboro via Cavetown, Smithsburg, and Ridgeville to Waynesboro, PA. Anderson's Division arrived at Shepherdstown. Hood's Division camped at Millwood. Stuart's men were near Rector's Cross Roads.

June 24: Rodes's Division marched from Greencastle through Chambersburg to the Conococheague River; Early's Division marched from Waynesboro through Quincy and Altodale to Greenwood, PA. McLaws's Division arrived at Summit Point and Hood's Division reached Bunker Hill. Pickett's Division marched from Berryville to Darkesville. Anderson's Division crossed the Potomac and marched to Boonsboro. Pender's Division arrived at Shepherdstown. Hampton's, Fitzhugh Lee's, and W. H. F. Lee's cavalry brigades moved to Salem Depot. Robertson's and Jones's cavalry brigades remained near Upperville.

June 25: Rodes's and Johnson's divisions moved from Chambersburg toward Carlisle. Early's Division rested at Greenwood. Anderson's Division marched from Boonsboro to Hagerstown. Pender's Division crossed the Potomac at Shepherdstown and marched to Fayetteville, PA. McLaws's Division moved from Summit Point to Martinsburg. Hood's Division arrived at Falling

2 Based upon *Final Report on the Battlefield of Gettysburg*, 2 vols. (Albany, NY: J. B. Lyon, 1900), 1:159-163.

Waters on the Potomac. Pickett's Division and the reserve artillery crossed the Potomac at Williamsport. Hampton's, Fitzhugh Lee's, and W. H. F. Lee's cavalry brigades moved from Salem Depot to Hay Market, VA. Jenkins's Brigade moved with Rodes's Division toward Carlisle.

June 26: Rodes's and Johnson's divisions and Jenkins's Brigade were on the road between Chambersburg and Carlisle. Early's Division moved from Greenwood across South Mountain via Cashtown to Mummasburg. His advance cavalry skirmished with Pennsylvania militia at Gettysburg. Gordon's Brigade marched through Gettysburg and camped east of the town. McLaws's Division crossed the Potomac and camped near Williamsport. Hood's Division crossed at Williamsport and marched to Greencastle, PA. Pickett's Division passed through Hagerstown to Greencastle. Anderson's Division marched from Hagerstown to a point two miles beyond Greencastle. Stuart's three cavalry brigades moved from Buckland through Brentsville to near Wolf Run Shoals.

June 27: Rodes's and Johnson's divisions arrived at Carlisle. Early's Division moved from Mummasburg via Hunterstown, New Chester, Hampton, and East Berlin to Big Mount. McLaws's Division marched from Williamsport via Hagerstown, Middleburg, and Greencastle, camping within five miles of Chambersburg. Hood's Division arrived at Chambersburg. Pickett's Division passed through Chambersburg and camped three miles north of town. Anderson's Division marched through Chambersburg to Fayetteville. Stuart's cavalry moved from Wolf Run Shoals, on the Occoquan River, via Fairfax Station and Dranesville and crossed the Potomac into Maryland at a point below the mouth of Seneca Creek.

June 28: Rodes's and Johnson's divisions were at Carlisle. Early's Division moved from Big Mount via Weigelstown to York, with Gordon's Brigade proceeding to Wrightsville on the Susquehanna River. Hill's Corps halted at Fayetteville. Longstreet's Corps camped near Chambersburg. Stuart's cavalry moved via Darnestown and Rockville, MD, to Brookeville.

June 29: Heth's Division moved from Fayetteville to Cashtown. Pender's and Anderson's divisions remained at Fayetteville, on the Chambersburg and Gettysburg Road. Johnson's Division countermarched from Carlisle to Greenville. Rodes's Division remained at Carlisle and Early's Division stayed at York and Wrightsville. Longstreet's Corps remained in position at or near Chambersburg. Stuart's cavalry moved through Cooksville, Sykesville, and Westminster to Union Mills.

June 30: Pender's Division moved from Fayetteville to Cashtown; Heth's Division was at Cashtown; and Anderson's was at Fayetteville. Rodes's Division moved from Carlisle via Petersburg to Heidlersburg; Early's Division moved from York through East Berlin and encamped three miles from Heidlersburg. Johnson's Division marched from Greenville to Scotland. Hood's and McLaws's divisions moved from Chambersburg to Fayetteville; Pickett's Division remained at Chambersburg. Stuart's cavalry moved from Union Mills through Hanover to Jefferson. Cavalry battle at Hanover.

July 1: Heth's and Pender's divisions marched from Cashtown to Gettysburg. Anderson's Division moved from Fayetteville via Cashtown to Gettysburg. Rodes's Division marched from Heidlersburg via Middletown to Gettysburg. Early's Division passed through Heidlersburg and marched on the direct road to Gettysburg. Johnson's Division marched from Scotland to Gettysburg. McLaws's and Hood's divisions marched from Fayetteville to Marsh Creek, within four miles of Gettysburg. Pickett's Division remained with the wagon trains at Chambersburg while detachments destroyed the buildings of the Cumberland Valley Railroad. Stuart's cavalry moved from Dover through Dillsburg to Carlisle. Jones's Brigade of cavalry crossed the Potomac at Williamsport and moved to Greencastle. First day of the three-day battle of Gettysburg.

BIBLIOGRAPHY

Primary Sources

Newspapers

Adams Sentinel
Alexandria Gazette
Alta California (San Francisco)
Augusta (GA) *Chronicle & Sentinel*
Aurora (IL) *Beacon*
Baltimore American
Boston Sunday Globe
Brooklyn Daily Eagle
Canton (OH) *Repository*
Carlisle (PA) *American*
Carlisle (PA) *Herald*
Chambersburg (PA) *Repository*
Chambersburg (PA) *Valley Spirit*
Charleston (SC) *Mercury*
Charlotte Observer
Chicago Tribune
Culpeper Star Exponent
Columbia (PA) *Spy*
Columbus (GA) *Daily Enquirer*
Daily Constitutional Union (Washington, D.C.)
Daily National Intelligencer (Washington, D.C.)
Dublin (Ireland) *Freeman's Journal*
Flemington (NJ) *The Republican*
The Fort Wayne Journal-Gazette
Franklin (County, PA) *Repository and Transcript*

Fulton (County, PA) *Democrat*

Gettysburg Compiler

Greencastle (PA) *Pilot*

Harrisburg Daily Patriot and Union

Harrisburg Evening Telegraph

Hartford (CT) *Daily Courant*

Lancaster (PA) *Daily Evening News*

Lancaster (PA) *Daily Express*

Lowell (MA) *Daily Citizen and News*

Macon (GA) *Telegraph*

Madison (WI) *Daily Patriot*

The Manchester Guardian (Manchester, England)

Memphis Commercial Appeal

Mercersburg (PA) *Journal*

The Mount Carmel Mirror

The National Tribune

New Hampshire Patriot & State Gazette (Concord, NH)

New York Herald

New York Times

New York Tribune

The News and Observer (Raleigh, NC)

Norwalk (OH) *Reflector*

The Observer (London, England)

Otsego (NY) *Republican*

Philadelphia Inquirer

Philadelphia Weekly Times

Randolph Enterprise

The Rochester (NY) *Daily Union & Advertiser*

Richmond Daily Dispatch

Richmond Daily Examiner

Richmond Enquirer

Richmond Whig

San Francisco County Call

Savannah (GA) *Republican*

St. Mary's Beacon (Leonardtown, Maryland)

The Standard (London, England)

The Tennessean (Nashville)

The Times (London, England)

Vermont Chronicle

Washington Evening Star

Watertown (NY) *Daily Reformer*

The Weekly British Whig (Kingston, Ontario)

Wheeling (WV) *Daily Intelligencer*

Wheeling (WV) *Register*
York (PA) *Gazette*

Manuscripts, Letters, Diaries, and Related Materials

Archives, Adams County Historical Society, Gettysburg, Pennsylvania:
Nathaniel Lightner Account

Special Collections, Bowdoin College, Brunswick, Maine:
Oliver Otis Howard Papers

Manuscripts Collection, Brandy Station Foundation, Brandy Station, Virginia:
Thomas Marshall letter of June 4, 1863

Special Collections, Brown University Library, Providence, Rhode Island:
John B. McIntosh Letters

Special Collections, Connecticut Historical Society, Hartford, Connecticut:
Norman Ball Diary

Special Collections, Cornell University, Ithaca, New York:
John Scott Diary

Archives, Cumberland County Historical Society, Carlisle, Pennsylvania:
Reminiscences of Nettie Jane Blair
Young Girl's Pocket Diary, entry for June 26, 1863, transb. by Frank Kline

Public Archives of Delaware, Dover, Delaware:
RG 1801, Box 55510, Governor's Correspondence
A. H. Huber, "Account of the 1st Del. Cavalry at Westminster, MD, 1863"
RG 1810.035, Box 390195
A. H. Huber, "The Real Facts About the Fight at Westminster, MD, June 29, 1863"

Philip Dodson Collection, York, Pennsylvania:
George K. Bratton Gettysburg Campaign Letters

Special Collections, Perkins Library, Duke University, Durham, North Carolina:
Freedley Letters
John R. Porter Diary

Special Collections, Emory University, Atlanta, Georgia:
Theodore Fogel Papers

Archives, First Troop, Philadelphia City Cavalry, Philadelphia, Pennsylvania:
Gettysburg Telegrams

Archives, Franklin County Historical Society, Chambersburg, Pennsylvania:
Andrew K. McClure Letters 1861-1865

Archives, Fredericksburg and Spotsylvania National Military Park, Fredericksburg, Virginia:

Jesse R. Sparkman Diary

Special Collections, Musselman Library, Gettysburg College, Gettysburg, Pennsylvania:
   Civil War Collection
      Joseph Hooker letter to Maj. Gen. E. D. Townsend, September 28, 1875

Archives, Gettysburg National Military Park, Gettysburg, Pennsylvania:
   John Blosher to John B. Bachelder letter of December 8, 1890
   Sarah M. Broadhead Diary
   William Gamble letter to William L. Church, March 10, 1864
   J. B. Johnson, "A Limited Review of What One Man Saw at the Battle of Gettysburg"
   Account of Capt. Benjamin F. Little, Co. F, 52nd North Carolina Infantry
   Edwin Loving Diary
   Phillips Legion File
      T. M. Mitchell diary
   John Slentz Claims Reparation Files
   Ben Thaxter Diary

Blair Graybill Collection, Charlottesville, Virginia:
   Virgil Brodrick Papers

Archives, Hancock County Museum, Findlay, Ohio:
   Anonymous diary of a Civil War Soldier in Company F, 126th Ohio Volunteer
      Infantry, August 23, 1862 through August 3, 1863

Margaret Tucker Scott and James C. Branham, Jr. Collection, Fredericksburg, Virginia:
   Civil War Letters of Pvt. Joseph F. Shaner, CSA

Archives, Historical Society of Pennsylvania, Philadelphia, Pennsylvania:
   Louis Henry Carpenter Letters from the Field, 1861-1865
   James Cornell Biddle Papers
   Fahnestock Family Papers
   Meade Family Papers

Archives, Historical Society of Schuylkill County, Pottsville, Pennsylvania:
   Diary of Capt. Jacob Haas, Co. G, 96th Pennsylvania

Archives, Albert Huntington Library, San Marino, California:
   James A. Bell Papers
   Joseph Hooker Papers

Archives, Illinois State Library, Springfield, Illinois:
   Edward F. Reid Diary

Archives, Indiana Historical Society Library, Indianapolis, Indiana:
   George H. Chapman Diary

Special Collections, Jackson County Public Library, Ripley, West Virginia:

Addison A. Smith, "A Story of the Life and Trials of a Confederate Soldier and the Great Loop He Made in Three Years"

George Hay Kain III Collection, York, Pennsylvania:
  J. Jerome Miller Diary

Archives, Kittochtinny Historical Society, Chambersburg, Pennsylvania:
  Thomas Creigh Diary

Manuscripts Division, Library of Congress, Washington, D.C.:
  Jefferson Davis Papers
  Gilpin Family Papers
    Samuel J.B.V. Gilpin Diary
  David M. Gregg Papers
  Jedediah Hotchkiss Papers
  Abraham Lincoln Papers
  Alfred Pleasonton Papers
  Gideon Welles Papers
    Diary for November 1862-July 22, 1864
  Wigfall Family Papers

Archives, Mennonite Historical Society, Chambersburg, Pennsylvania:
  Henry B. Hege Letters

Michigan State Archives, Lansing, Michigan:
  Eugene Stocking Papers

Archives, Minnesota Historical Society, St. Paul, Minnesota:
  Orrin F. Smith and Family Papers
    Charles E. Goddard Civil War Papers
  Marvin Papers
    Matthew Marvin Diary 1863
  James A. Wright, "The Story of Company F, the First Regiment"

Mississippi Department of Archives and History, Jackson, Mississippi:
  Civil War Diary of William H. Hill
  Augustus L. P. Vairin Civil War Diary

Monroe County Library System, Monroe, Michigan:
  Lawrence Frost Collection of Custeriana

Special Collections, Morrisville State College, Morrisville, New York:
  Robert T. Douglass Diary

Perrin-Wheaton Chapter, National Society of the Daughters of the American Revolution, Wheaton, Illinois:
  The Marcellus E. Jones Journal

Pouge Special Collections and Archives Library, Murray State University Libraries, Murray, Kentucky:

John Frank Locke, Diary of the Civil War: July 16, 1861 – February 18, 1864

National Archives and Records Administration, Washington, DC:

RG 393, Letters Received, Telegrams, Reports, and Lists Received by Cavalry Corps, 1861-1865

RG 393, Entry 3980, Army of the Potomac, 1861-1865, Miscellaneous Letters, Reports, and Lists Received

RG 393, Part 1, Entry 3986, "Two or More Name File," 1861-1865

RG 393I, Entry 3980, Box 11, Army of the Potomac Bureau of Military Information

Archives, Navarro College, Corsicana, Texas:

Pearce Civil War Collection
Abraham Lincoln letter of June 22, 1863

Archives, Newville Historical Society, Newville, Pennsylvania:

William McCandlish Diary

Archives, New York Historical Society, New York, New York:

John Irvin Murray Diary

North Carolina Department of History and Archives, Raleigh, North Carolina:

John C. Gorman to Friend Holden, June 22, 1863, "Our Army Correspondence"
Thomas Perrett Papers, "A Trip that Didn't Pay"

Special Collections, North Carolina Historical Commission, Raleigh, North Carolina:

Diary of James Beverly Clifton

Archives, Old Colony Historical Society, Taunton, Massachusetts:

Darius N. Couch Post-war Journal

Archives, Old Court House Museum, Winchester, Virginia:

To Gettysburg & Back: The 1863 Diary of Robert Sherrard Bell
James Poe Collection
William E. Vanauken Letters
Eseck S. Wilber Letters

Archives, State Library of Virginia, Richmond, Virginia:

Fluvanna County Confederate Soldiers Letters
Ross Family Correspondence

Tom K. Savage Collection, Atlanta, Georgia:

Alonzo West Papers

Friends Historical Library, Swarthmore College, Swarthmore, Pennsylvania:

Kimber L. Johns diary, entry for June 5, 1863

South Caroliniana Library, University of South Carolina, Columbia, South Carolina:

David Wyatt Aiken Papers

Archives, Susquehanna County Historical Society, Montrose, Pennsylvania:
  Charles N. Warner Diaries, 1862-1865

Special Collections, Howard-Tilton Memorial Library, Tulane University, New Orleans:
  Louisiana Historical Association Collection
      George P. Ring Diary

Archives, United States Army Heritage and Education Center, Carlisle, Pennsylvania:
  Robert L. Brake Collection
          J. C. Atticks Diary, June and July 1863
          Blackwood K. Benson letter of July 29, 1863
          Francis P. Fleming Letters
          William Brock Judson Memoirs
          William Perry Diary
          Samuel Pickens Diary
  Civil War Documents Collection
          Thomas Crowl Correspondence
  Civil War Times Illustrated Collection
          George Greer Diary
  John C. Keses Papers
  Civil War Miscellaneous Collection
  Charles Chapin Letter of June 24, 1863
  Jasper Cheney Diary
  Thomas Covert Letters
  Calvin S. Heller Diary
  Order Book of the Chief of Cavalry

Harrisburg Civil War Roundtable Collection
  James A. Stahle Papers
  John Stumbaugh Letter of July 9, 1863
  Keith R. Keller Collection
          Memoranda & Extracts made by L T Hyde from his letters
  Norwich Civil War Roundtable Collection
      J. S. Hyde Diary, June 25-July 5, 1863

  Michael Winey Collection
      Isaac Dunkelberger Diary

Special Collections, United States Military Academy Library, West Point, New York:
  James E. Harrison Papers

Special Collections, Hargrett Library, University of Georgia, Athens, Georgia:
  William G. Delony letters

Special Collections, Main Library, University of Iowa, Iowa City, Iowa:

Joseph Franklin Culver Papers

Archives, Michigan Historical Collections, Bentley Historical Library, U. of MI, Ann Arbor, MI:
  Victor E. Comte Papers
  Nathan Webb Diaries

Southern Historical Collection, Wilson Library, University of North Carolina, Chapel Hill, NC:
  Henry K. Burgwyn, Jr. Civil War Papers
  J. F. Coghill Letters
  Samuel Eaton Papers
  James E. Green Papers
  Polk-Brown-Ewell Papers
  Charles S. Venable Papers
  Thomas Ware Journal

Albert and Shirley Small Special Collections Library, University of Virginia, Charlottesville, VA:
  Blackford Family Letters, Accession #6403
  John W. Daniel Papers
  Francis Vinton Greene Diary, June 13-August 18, 1863
  Jonathan Hager Diary
  W. H. Redman Letters
  Joseph Addison Waddell Diary

Elizabeth Valent Collection, Washington Township, York County, Pennsylvania:
  Phoebe Angeline Smith Civil War Letters

Archives, Virginia Historical Society, Richmond, Virginia:
  Robert E. Lee Headquarters Papers
  Francis Smith Robertson, "Reminiscences, 1861-1865"

Archives, Virginia Military Institute, Lexington, Virginia:
  John Garibaldi Civil War Papers, Manuscript #284

Special Collections, Virginia Polytechnical Institute, Blacksburg, Virginia:
  Civil War Letters of Joseph Perrin Burrage and William Allen Burrage
  N. Claiborne Wilson and Related Papers
    Civil War Diary

Virginia State Library and Archives, Richmond, Virginia:
  John C. Donohoe Diary

West Virginia State Archives, Charleston, West Virginia:
  Francis M. Imboden diary

Archives, Western Reserve Historical Society, Cleveland, Ohio:
  Carlos P. Lyman Papers

Cooper H. Wingert Collection, Enola, Pennsylvania:

A. R. Tomlinson, "War Experiences of Major A. R. Tomlinson"

Archives, Wisconsin Historical Society, Madison, Wisconsin:
Nathaniel Rollins, Diary Excerpts from Gettysburg Battlefield, June 30–July 6, 1863

Special Collections, Yale University, New Haven, Connecticut:
Alexander S. Webb Papers

Archives, York County History Center, York, Pennsylvania:
Sam and George Blotcher Papers
James Latimer Papers

Archives, York Historical Society, York, Pennsylvania:
Rudisill Family Papers
Lida Bowman Meckley Reminiscences of the Civil War

Magazines and Periodicals

"A Skirmish—Rebels Retreat." *Harrisburg Daily Patriot and Union*, July 1, 1863.

Allum, J. P. "The Fight at Hanover." *National Tribune*, September 29, 1887.

"America. Invasion of the Northern States." *The Times*, June 29, 1863.

Beale, George W. "A Soldier's Account of the Gettysburg Campaign." *Southern Historical Society Papers*, 11 (July 1883): 320-7.

Bean, Lt. Col. Theodore W. "Address at the Dedication of the 17th Pennsylvania Cavalry Monument of September 11, 1889." *Pennsylvania at Gettysburg*. 2 vols. Harrisburg: William Stanley Ray Printers, 1904, 2:874-884.

Bender, Lida Welsh. "Civil War Memories." *The Outlook*, June 24, 1925.

Benjamin, Charles F. "Hooker's Appointment and Removal," included in Robert U. Johnson and C. Buel, eds. *Battles and Leaders of the Civil War*. 4 vols. New York: Century Publishing Co., 1884-1889, 3:239-243.

Beveridge, John L. "The First Gun at Gettysburg." *War Papers*. Military Order of the Loyal Legion of the United States, Illinois Commandery. Vol. 2. Chicago: McClurg, 1894: 79-98.

Bigelow, John A. "Draw Saber, Charge!" *National Tribune*, May 27, 1886.

Black, John H. "'Powder, Lead and Cold Steel': Campaigning in the Lower Shenandoah Valley with the Twelfth Pennsylvania Cavalry—The Civil War Letters of John H. Black." *Magazine of the Jefferson County Historical Society* 23 (1959).

Bowers, William S., ed. "William Heyser's Diary." *The Kittochtinny Historical Society Papers*, Vol. 16, 1970.

Bradwell, Isaac G. "The Burning of Wrightsville, Pennsylvania." *Confederate Veteran*, Vol. 27, 1919.

———. "Capture of Winchester, VA., and Milroy's Army in June, 1863." *Confederate Veteran*, Vol. 30, No. 9, September 1922.

Buell, Augustus C. "Story of a Cannoneer," part 3. *The National Tribune*, October 24, 1889.

Calef, John H. "Gettysburg Notes: The Opening Gun." *Journal of the Military Service Institute of the United States*, Vol. 40 (1889), 40-58.

Campbell, William J. "Stuart's Great Ride Around the Enemy." *Confederate Veteran* 9 (1901): 222.

Chase, George H. "A Scrap of History." *The National Tribune*, September 2, 1882.

Clark, Joseph L. "Extracts from the Diary of Lieutenant Joseph L. Clark." *The Maine Bugle.* Rockland, Me.: The Maine Association, Campaign 2, Call #4, October 1895.

Clark, Stephen A. "Hanover, Pa." *National Tribune,* February 23, 1888.

Clemens, Thomas G., ed. "The 'Diary' of John H. Stone, First Lieutenant, Company B, 2d Maryland Infantry, C.S.A.", *Maryland Historical Magazine,* Vol. 85 (Summer 1990).

Cooke, John Esten. "The Hampton Legion." *Philadelphia Weekly Times,* February 21, 1880.

Copeland, J. E. "The Fighting at Brandy Station." *Confederate Veteran* 30 (1922): 451.

Coski, John, ed. "Forgotten Warrior." *North & South* 2, No. 7 (September 1999): 76-89.

Crocker, James F. "Gettysburg—Pickett's Charge." *Southern Historical Society Papers,* Vol. 33, 1905.

Day, Thomas G. "Opening the Battle. A Cavalryman's Recollections of the First Day's Fight at Gettysburg." *The National Tribune,* July 30, 1903.

"The Defence and Evacuation of Winchester." *The Continental Monthly,* Vol. 4, No. 5. New York: John F. Trow, November 1863.

Dickinson, Bvt. Brig. Gen. Joseph. "A Gettysburg Incident." Included in *The Proceedings of the Buford Memorial Association.* New York: privately published, 1895, 23-25.

Dodge, H. O. "Opening the Battle. Lieut. Jones, the 8th Ill. Cavalryman, Fired the First Shot at Gettysburg." *The National Tribune,* September 24, 1891.

Early, John Cabell. "A Southern Boy's Experience at Gettysburg." *Journal of the Military Service Institution,* Vol. 43, Jan.-Feb. 1911.

Early, Jubal A. "The Invasion of Pennsylvania, by the Confederate States Army, in June 1863." *The Historical Magazine and Notes and Queries,* Vol. 1, Series 3. Morrisania, N.Y.: Henry B. Dawson, 1872-73.

Estill, Mary S. and F. B. Sexton, eds. "Diary of a Confederate Congressman, 1862-1863, II." *The Southwestern Historical Quarterly* 39, no. 1 (July 1935): 33-65.

"Exploit in McConnellsburg." Included in Frank Moore, ed., *The Rebellion Record.* 11 vols. New York: D. Van Nostrand, 1864, 7:327-8.

Ford, Charles W. "Charge of the First Maine Cavalry at Brandy Station." *War Papers Read Before the Commandery of the State of Maine, Military Order of the Loyal Legion of the United States* 2. Portland: LeFavor-Tower Co., 1902: 268-289.

Frazer, Persifor, Jr. "Philadelphia City Cavalry, Service of the First Troop Philadelphia City Cavalry during June and July, 1863." *Journal of the Military Service Institution of the United States,* Vol. 43, 1908.

Gardner, William. "Cavalry at Middleburg." *Philadelphia Weekly Times,* July 19, 1884.

"Genesee." "From the 8th Cavalry—List of Killed and Wounded." *Rochester Daily Union and Advertiser,* July 9, 1863.

"Gettysburg Honor to Girls of '63." *New York Times,* July 1, 1913.

Graham, William A. "From Brandy Station to the Heights of Gettysburg." *The News and Explorer,* February 7, 1904.

Gregg, David M. "The Union Cavalry at Gettysburg," included in *The Annals of the War, Written by Leading Participants North and South.* Philadelphia: Times Publishing Co., 1879: 372-379.

Haden, Benjamin J. *Reminiscences of J.E.B. Stuart's Cavalry.* Charlottesville, VA: Progress Publishing Co., 1912.

Harris, J. C. "Sickles at Gettysburg. His Claim Sharply Controverted by a Pennsylvania Comrade." *National Tribune,* November 4, 1886.

"Harrisburgh." *New York Times,* July 3, 1863.

Hazelton, W. C. "An Address Made at a Regimental Reunion." *Gettysburg Star and Sentinel,* September 1, 1891.

Heth, Henry. "Letter from Major-General Henry Heth, of A. P. Hill's Corps, A.N.V.," *Southern Historical Society Papers* 4 (1877): 151-160.

Hodam, James H. "From Potomac to Susquehanna." *Blue and Gray: The Patriotic American Magazine,* Vol. 2, No. 1. Philadelphia: The Patriotic American Co., July 1893.

Hudgins, F. L. "With the 38th Georgia." *Confederate Veteran,* Vol. 26, 1918.

Hughes, Morgan. "People of Gettysburg. How They Inspired the Cavalry to Do Their Effective Work." *The National Tribune,* March 24, 1892.

Hunter, Alexander. "Thirteenth Virginia Infantry Humor." *Confederate Veteran,* Vol. 16, No. 7, July 1908.

J. H. S. "Washington Letter." *The Fort Wayne Journal-Gazette,* November 29, 1885.

Jackson, J. Warren. "Diary of J. Warren Jackson." *Pennsylvania Magazine of History and Biography.* Harrisburg: Pennsylvania Historical Association, April 1963.

"Jenkins' Brigade." *Richmond Enquirer,* July 17, 1863.

Jewell, James Robbins, ed. "Theodore S. Garnett Recalls Cavalry Service with General Stuart, June 16-28, 1863." *The Gettysburg Magazine* 20 (June 1999): 44-50.

Jones, Terry L., ed. "Going Back in the Union at Last: A Louisiana Tiger's Account of the Gettysburg Campaign." *Civil War Times Illustrated,* Vol. 29, No. 6, January/February 1991.

Jordan, Brian Matthew, ed. "'Remembrance Will Cling to Us Through Life': Kate Bushman's Memoir of the Battle of Gettysburg." *Adams County History,* vol. 20, article 3 (2014): 4-21.

Kelly, John. "The Spy at Frederick, Maryland." *The National Tribune,* February 9, 1888.

Kempster, Walter, M.D. "The Cavalry at Gettysburg", Military Order of the Loyal Legion of the United States, Wisconsin Commandery. Vol. 4. Milwaukee, WI: Burdick, Armitage & Allen, 1905: 397-429.

Libby, Horatio S. "Middleburg and Upperville." *First Maine Bugle* Vol. 2, No. 6 (October 1891): 25-27.

Lochren, William. "Narrative of the First Minnesota." *Minnesota in the Civil and Indian Wars, 1861-1865.* Minneapolis: State of Minnesota, Board of Commissioners on Publication of History of Minnesota in Civil and Indian Wars, Pioneer Press, 1890.

————. "The First Minnesota at Gettysburg: Glimpses of the Nation's Struggle." *Minnesota MOLLUS,* Vol. 3, January 1890.

Malone, Bartlett Y. "The Diary of Bartlett Y. Malone." *The James Sprunt Historical Publications,* vol. 16, no. 2. Chapel Hill: The University of North Carolina Press, 1919.

Matthews, Henry H. "The Great Cavalry Fights of the War, Fleetwood Hill or Brandy Plains, June 9, 1863." *St. Mary's Beacon,* March 9, 1905.

McClellan, Henry B. "The Invasion of Pennsylvania in '63." *Philadelphia Weekly Times,* July 20, 1878.

"McConnellsburg Taken." *Fulton Democrat,* July 10, 1863.

McCreary, Albertus. "Gettysburg: A Boy's Experience of the Battle." *McClure's Magazine,* July 1909.

McLaws, Lafayette. "Gettysburg." *SHSP,* Vol. 7, 1879.

"Mercersburg in War Times," *Mercersburg (PA) Journal,* Jan. 23, 1903.

Meredith, Jaquelin Marshall. "The First Day at Gettysburg: Tribute to Brave General Harry Heth, Who Opened the Great Battle," *Southern Historical Society Papers* 24 (1896): 182-187.

Merritt, Wesley. "Personal Recollections—Beverly's Ford to Mitchell's Station, 1863." In Theophilus F. Rodenbough, ed. *From Everglade to Canon with the Second Dragoons.* New York: D. Van Nostrand, 1875: 283-303.

Milgram, James W., ed. "The Libby Prison Correspondence of Tattnall Paulding." *The American Philatelist*, December 1975, Vol. 89, No. 12.

Mix, A. R. "Experiences at Gettysburg." *The National Tribune*, February 22, 1904.

Moffat, George H. "The Battle of Brandy Station." *Confederate Veteran* 14 (February 1906): 74-75.

Monie, J. M. "Cavalry Operations Relating to the Campaign of Gettysburg, Brandy Station or Fleetwood, and Stevensburg." *The News and Observer*, August 29, 1894.

Moore, A. H. "Heth's Division at Gettysburg." *Southern Bivouac*, vol. 3, No. 9 (May, 1885): 383-395.

Mosby, John S. "General Stuart at Gettysburg." *Philadelphia Weekly Times*, December 15, 1877.

———. "Mosby's Ways." *Philadelphia Weekly Times*, April 13, 1878.

Moyer, William F. "Brandy Station: A Stirring Account of the Famous Cavalry Engagement." *The National Tribune*, March 28, 1884.

Myers, Elizabeth Salome. "How a Gettysburg Schoolteacher Spent Her Vacation in the Summer of 1863." *San Francisco Sunday Call*, August 16, 1903.

Newhall, Frederic C. "The Battle of Beverly Ford." In *The Annals of the War as Told by the Leading Participants*. Philadelphia: Times Publishing Co., 1879: 134-146.

"The North Carolina Cavalry: Its First Fight—War Records—Curious Reports—A Great Cavalry Battle—Virginia and North Carolina Exultant." *The News and Observer*, May 11, 1883.

"Opened the Fight at Gettysburg." *Boston Sunday Globe*, December 5, 1909.

Paul, E. A. "Operations of Our Cavalry—The Michigan Cavalry Brigade." *New York Times*, August 6, 1863.

Peake, John W. "Recollections of a Boy Cavalryman." *Confederate Veteran* 34 (1926): 260-262.

Potts, Lantz G. "Recollections of the Civil War." *Randolph Enterprise*, December 15, 1921 and January 5, 1922.

"Rebel Occupancy of Carlisle." *Carlisle American*, July 15, 1863.

Park, Robert E. "The Twelfth Alabama Infantry, Confederate States Army." *SHSP*, Vol. 33, 1905.

Parsons, Henry C. "Gettysburg: The Campaign was a Chapter of Accidents." *National Tribune*, August 7, 1890.

Piston, William Garrett, ed. "The Rebs Are Yet Thick About Us: The Civil War Diary of Amos Stouffer of Chambersburg." *Civil War History: A Journal of the Middle Period*, Vol. 38, No. 3, September 1992.

Purifoy, John. "With Jackson in the Valley." *Confederate Veteran*, Vol. 30, No. 10, October 1922.

Reed, Thomas B., ed. "The Last Days of the Confederacy: Lecture of Gen. J. B. Gordon, given in various parts of the country, this, at Brooklyn, NY, Feb., 1901." Included in *Modern Eloquence*. Philadelphia: John D. Davis Co., 1901.

Reunion of the First Maine Cavalry 1879-1880. n.p., 1881.

Robbins, D. H. "Stuart at Hanover." *National Tribune*, June 30, 1908.

Saussy, G. N. "Anniversary of Brandy's Battle: Fought 46 Years Ago Today." *Memphis Commercial Appeal*, June 9, 1909.

Schaff, Philip. "The Gettysburg Week." *Scribner's Magazine*, Vol. 16, No. 1, July 1894.

Shoaf, Dana B., ed. "On the March Again at Daybreak: Major John Nevin and the 93rd Pennsylvania Infantry." *Civil War Regiments*, Vol. 6, No. 3, 1999.

"Skirmish at Sporting Hill." *New York Herald*, July 1, 1863.

Smith, Thomas J. "Two Spies Instead of One." *The National Tribune*, May 1, 1884.

Stiles, A. W. "Reminiscences of the Charge of Company A, Sixth Ohio Volunteer Cavalry at Upperville, Va., June 21, 1863." *Report of the Thirty-Fifth Annual Reunion Sixth Ohio Volunteer Cavalry Association*, October 2, 1900. Garrettsville, OH: Journal Printing Co., 1900.

Swallow, W. H. "The First Day at Gettysburg," *Southern Bivouac* N.S. 1 (December 1885): 441-442.

T. H. M. "Letter from the Californians in the Massachusetts Contingent." *Alta California*, August 2, 1863.

"The Beau Sabreur Of Georgia." *Southern Historical Society Papers* 25 (1897), 149.

"The Georgia Cavalry in the Brandy Station Fight." *Savannah Republican*, June 26, 1863.

"The Latest from America: Reuter's Telegrams." *The Observer*, June 28, 1863.

"The Movements of Lee's Army." *New York Herald*, June 18, 1863.

"The North Carolina Cavalry: Its First Fight—War Records—Curious Reports—A Great Cavalry Battle—Virginia and North Carolina Exultant." *The News and Observer*, May 11, 1883.

"The Thirteenth Regiment of Virginia Cavalry in Gen. J.E.B. Stuart's Raid into Pennsylvania." *The Southern Bivouac* 1 (1883): 203-7.

Wolf, Hazel C., ed. "Campaigning with the First Minnesota: A Civil War Diary." *Minnesota History*, Vol. 25. Minnesota Historical Society, September 1944.

Taylor, Michael, ed., "Ramseur's Brigade in the Gettysburg Campaign: A Newly Discovered Account by Capt. James I. Harris, Co. I, 30th Regt. N.C.T." *Gettysburg Magazine* 17, January 1997.

Trimble, Isaac R. "The Battle and Campaign of Gettysburg." *SHSP*, Vol. 26, 1898.

Walter, Thomas F. "The Personal Recollections and Experiences of an Obscure Soldier." *Grand Army Scout and Soldiers' Mail*. Philadelphia. Vol. 3, No. 39, September 6, 1884, and No. 40, September 13, 1884.

Williamson, Edward C., ed. "Francis P. Fleming in the War for Southern Independence: Letters from the Front." *Florida Historical Quarterly*, vol. 28 (October 1949): 143-155.

Young, Louis G. "Pettigrew's Brigade at Gettysburg, 1-3 July 1863," included in Walter Clark, ed. *Histories of the Several Regiments and Battalions from North Carolina in the Great War, 1861-65*. 5 vols. Goldsboro, NC: 1901, 5:113-135.

Youngblood, William. "Unwritten History of the Gettysburg Campaign." in *SHSP*, Vol. 38, 1910.

Books and Pamphlets

Abbott, John S. C. *The History of the Civil War in America*. Springfield, MA: Henry Bill Publishing Co., 1873.

Acken, Gregory J. ed. *Inside the Army of the Potomac: The Civil War Experience of Captain Francis Adams Donaldson*. Mechanicsburg, PA: Stackpole Books, 1998.

Adams, M. K., ed. *Salt Horse and Sabers: Whitaker's War-Bull Run to Appomattox, 4 Years—82 Battles*. Privately published, 2003.

Aldrich, Thomas M. *The History of Battery A, First Regiment Rhode Island Light Artillery in the War to Preserve the Union 1861-1865*. Providence: Snow & Farnham, 1904.

Alleman, Tillie Pierce. *At Gettysburg, or What a Girl Saw and Heard of the Battle of Gettysburg*. New York: W. Lake Borland, 1889.

Avary, Myrta Lockett. *A Virginia Girl in the Civil War*. New York: D. Appleton & Co., 1903.

Baer, Elizabeth R., ed. *Shadows on My Heart: The Civil War Diary of Lucy Rebecca Buck of Virginia*. Athens, Ga.: University of Georgia Press, 1997.

Baker, George E., ed. *The Works of William H. Seward.* 5 vols. Houghton, Mifflin & Co., 1884.

Baker, Levi W. *History of the Ninth Massachusetts Battery.* South Framingham, Mass.: Lakeview Press, 1888.

Baquet, Camille. *History of the First Brigade, New Jersey Volunteers from 1861 to 1865.* Trenton, NJ: MacCrellish & Quigley, 1910.

Bardeen, Charles W. *A Little Fifer's War Diary.* Syracuse, N.Y.: s.n., 1910.

Barrett, John G., ed. *Yankee Rebel: The Civil War Journal of Edmund DeWitt Patterson.* Chapel Hill: The University of North Carolina Press, 1966.

Bartlett, Asa W. *History of the Twelfth Regiment, New Hampshire Volunteers in the War of the Rebellion.* Concord, N.H.: Ira C. Evans, 1897.

Basler, Roy P., Marion Dolores Pratt, and Lloyd A. Dunlap, eds. *The Collected Works of Abraham Lincoln,* 9 vols. Springfield, Ill.: Abraham Lincoln Association; New Brunswick, N.J.: Rutgers University Press, 1953.

Bates, Samuel P. and Richard J. Fraise. *History of Franklin County, Pennsylvania.* Chicago: Warner, Beers and Co., 1887.

Beach, William H. *The First New York (Lincoln) Cavalry from April 19, 1861 to July 7, 1865.* New York: The Lincoln Cavalry Association, 1902.

Beale, George W. *A Lieutenant of Cavalry in Lee's Army.* Boston: Gorham, 1888.

Beale, Howard K., ed. *The Diary of Edward Bates, 1859-1866.* Washington, DC: U. S. Government Printing Office, 1933.

Beale, Richard L. T. *History of the Ninth Virginia Cavalry in the War Between the States.* Richmond, Va.: B. F. Johnson Publishing Co., 1899.

Beaudry, Richard E., ed. *War Journal of Louis N. Beaudry, Fifth New York Cavalry.* Jefferson, NC: McFarland, 1996.

Beetem, Charles Gilbert. *Experiences of a West Ward Boy.* Carlisle, Pa.: Hamilton Library Association, 1963.

Benedict, George Grenville, ed. *Vermont in the Civil War. A History of the Part Taken by the Vermont Soldiers and Sailors in the War for the Union 1861-1865.* 2 vols. Burlington, Vt.: Free Press Association, 1888.

Best, Isaac O. *History of the 121st New York State Infantry.* Chicago: Lieut. Jas. A. Smith, 1921.

Betts, Rev. A. D. *Experience of a Confederate Chaplain 1861-1864.* Greenville, S.C.: privately printed, 1904.

Billings, John D. *Hardtack and Coffee; or, the Unwritten Story of Army Life.* Boston: George M. Smith & Co., 1887.

Blair, Cassandra Morris. *Letters of '63.* Detroit: Stair-Jordan-Baker, 1988.

Blackford, Susan Leigh, ed. *Letters from Lee's Army: or Memoirs of Life In and Out of the Army in Virginia During the War Between the States.* New York: A. S. Barnes, 1962.

Blackford, William W. *War Years With Jeb Stuart.* New York: Charles Scribner's Sons, 1945.

Blight, David W., ed. *When This Cruel War is Over: The Civil War Letters of Charles Harvey Brewster.* Amherst: University of Massachusetts Press, 1992.

Bliss, George. *The First Rhode Island Cavalry at Middleburg.* Providence, R. I.: privately published, 1889.

Boies, Andrew J. *Record of the Thirty-third Massachusetts Volunteer Infantry: from Aug. 1862 to Aug. 1865.* Fitchburg, Mass.: Sentinel Printing Co., 1880.

Borcke, Augustus Heros von. *Memoirs of the Confederate War for Independence.* 2 vols. Philadelphia: J. B. Lippincott, 1867.

Borcke, Augustus Heros von and Justus Scheibert. *The Great Cavalry Battle of Brandy Station.* Trans. Stuart T. Wright and F.D. Bridgewater. 1893; reprint, Gaithersburg, MD: Olde Soldier Books, 1976.

Botts, John Minor. *The Great Rebellion: The Political Life of the Author Vindicated.* New York: Harper & Bros., 1866.

Boudrye, Louis N. *Historic Records of the 5th New York Cavalry.* Albany, New York: S. R. Gray, 1865.

Bradshaw, Ada Bruce D., ed. *Civil War Diary of Charles William McVicar.* Washington, D.C.: privately published, 1977.

Broadhead, Sarah M. *The Diary of a Lady of Gettysburg, Pennsylvania from June 15 to July 15, 1863.* Hershey, Pa.: Gary T. Hawbaker, 1990.

Brooke-Rawle, William, ed. *History of the Third Pennsylvania Cavalry, Sixtieth Regiment Pennsylvania Volunteers, in the American Civil War 1861-1865.* Philadelphia: Franklin Printing Co., 1905.

Bryant, Edwin E. *History of the Third Regiment of Wisconsin Veteran Volunteer Infantry 1861-1865.* Madison, WI: Published by the Veteran Association of the Regiment, 1891.

Buehler, Fannie J. *Recollections of the Rebel Invasion and One Woman's Experience during the Battle of Gettysburg.* Gettysburg, Pa.: Star and Sentinel Print, 1900.

Burlingame, Michael, ed. *Lincoln Observed: Civil War Dispatches of Noah Brooks.* Baltimore: Johns Hopkins University Press, 1998.

————. *With Lincoln in the White House: Letters, Memoranda, and Other Writings of John G. Nicolay, 1860-1865.* Carbondale: Southern Illinois University Press, 2000.

Burlingame, Michael and John R. Turner Ettlinger, eds. *Inside Lincoln's White House: The Complete Civil War Diary of John Hay.* Carbondale: Southern Illinois University Press, 1997.

Byrne, Frank L. and Andrew T. Weaver, eds. *Haskell of Gettysburg: His Life and Civil War Papers.* Kent, OH: Kent State University Press, 1989.

Caldwell, J. F. J. *The History of the Brigade of South Carolinians Known First as "Gregg's" and Subsequently as "McGowan's Brigade".* Philadelphia: King & Baird, 1866.

Carter, William Harding. *From Yorktown to Santiago with the Sixth U.S. Cavalry.* Baltimore: The Friedenwald Co., 1900.

Casler, John O. *Four Years in the Stonewall Brigade.* Girard, Kan.: Appeal Publishing Co., 1906.

Cassedy, Edward K., ed. *Dear Friends at Home: The Civil War Letters and Diaries of Sergeant Charles T. Bowen, Twelfth United States Infantry First Battalion 1861-1864.* Baltimore: Butternut & Blue, 2001.

Chamberlaine, William W. *Memoirs of the Civil War Between the Northern and Southern Sections of the United States of America 1861-1865.* Washington, DC: Press of Byron S. Adams, 1912.

Chamberlayne, John Hampden. *Ham Chamberlayne, Virginian: Letters and Papers of an Artillery Officer in the War for Southern Independence, 1861-1865.* Richmond: Dietz, 1932.

Chamberlin, Thomas. *History of the One Hundred and Fiftieth Regiment Pennsylvania Volunteers, Second Regiment, Bucktail Brigade.* Philadelphia: F. McManus, Jr. & Co., 1905.

Chapman, Horatio D. *War Diary of a Forty-niner.* Hartford, Conn., s. n., 1929.

Cheney, Newel. *History of the Ninth Regiment, New York Volunteer Cavalry, War of 1861 to 1865.* Poland Center, NY: Martin Mere & Son, 1901.

Clark, Walter, ed. *Histories of the Several Regiments and Battalions from North Carolina in the Great War 1861-'65: Written by Members of the Respective Commands,* 5 vols. Goldsboro, N.C.: Nash Brothers, 1901.

Cockrell, Monroe F., ed. *Gunner with Stonewall: Reminiscences of William Thomas Poague.* Jackson, TN: McCowat-Mercer Press, 1957.

Coffin, Charles Carleton. *The Boys of '61 or Four Years of Fighting.* Boston: The Page Co., 1896.

Collier, John S. and Bonnie B. Collier, eds. *Yours for the Union: The Civil War Letters of John W. Chase, First Massachusetts Light Artillery.* New York: Fordham University Press, 2004.

Confederate Reminiscences and Letters, 1861-1865, 22 vols. Atlanta: Georgia Division of the United Daughters of the Confederacy, 1995-2011.

Cooke, John Esten. *Wearing of the Gray, Being Personal Portraits, Scenes & Adventures of the War.* New York: E. B. Treat & Co., 1867.

Cooney, Charles F., ed. *Common Soldier, Uncommon War: Life as a Cavalryman in the Civil War.* Bethesda, Maryland, SMD Group, 1994.

Cooper, David M. *Obituary Discourse on Occasion of the Death of Noah Henry Ferry, Major of the Fifth Michigan Cavalry, Killed at Gettysburg, July 3, 1863.* New York: John F. Trow, 1863.

Craft, David. *History of the One Hundred Forty-first Regiment, Pennsylvania Volunteers 1862-65.* Towanda, Pa.: Reporter-Journal Printing Company, 1885.

Cunningham, John L. *Three Years with the Adirondack Regiment 118th Volunteer Infantry.* Norwood, MA: The Plimpton Press, 1920.

Curtis, Orson B. *History of the Twenty-fourth Michigan of the Iron Brigade, known as the Detroit and Wayne County Regiment.* Detroit: Winn & Hammond, 1891.

Davis, Jefferson. *Rise and Fall of the Confederate Government.* 2 vols. New York: D. Appleton & Co., 1881.

Davis, Oliver Wilson. *Life of David Bell Birney, Major-General, United States Volunteers.* Philadelphia: King & Baird, 1867.

Dawes, Rufus R. *Service with the Sixth Wisconsin Volunteers.* Marietta, Ohio: E. R. Alderman & Sons, 1890.

Dayton, Ruth Woods, ed. *The Diary of a Confederate Soldier: James E. Hall, the Barbour Grays, Company H, 31st Virginia Volunteer Infantry Regiment.* Lewisburg, WV: privately published, 1961.

DePuyster, J. Watts. *Decisive Conflicts of the Civil War.* New York: McDonald & Co., 1867.

Dennison, Frederic. *Sabres and Spurs: The First Rhode Island Cavalry in the Civil War, 1861-1865.* Central Falls, RI: Press of E. L. Freeman & Co., 1876.

Dickert, D. Augustus. *History of Kershaw's Brigade.* Newberry, S. C.: Elbert H. Aull, 1899.

Donald, David Herbert, ed. *Inside Lincoln's Cabinet: The Civil War Diaries of Salmon P. Chase.* New York: Longmans, Green & Co., 1954.

Dooley, John Edward. *John Dooley, Confederate Soldier. His War Journal.* Washington, DC: Georgetown University Press, 1945.

Doster, William E. *Lincoln and Episodes of the Civil War.* New York and London: G. P. Putnam's Sons, 1915.

Doubleday, Abner. *Chancellorsville and Gettysburg.* New York: Charles Scribner's Sons, 1882.

Douglas, Henry Kyd. *I Rode with Stonewall: The War Experiences of the Youngest Member of Jackson's Staff.* Chapel Hill: The University of North Carolina Press, 1940.

Douglas, J. H. "Report of the Operations of the Sanitary Commission during and after the Battles at Gettysburg," *Documents of the U. S. Sanitary Commission.* 2 vols. New York: 1866.

Dowdey, Clifford, ed. *The War Time Papers of R. E. Lee.* Boston: Little, Brown & Co., 1961.

Dozier, Graham T., ed. *A Gunner in Lee's Army: The Civil War Letters of Thomas Henry Carter.* Chapel Hill: University of North Carolina Press, 2014.

Duganne, A. J. H. *The Fighting Quakers: A True Story of the War for Our Union.* New York: J. P. Robens, 1866.

Dunaway, Wayland Fuller. *Reminiscences of a Rebel.* New York: Neale, 1913.

Early, Jubal Anderson. *War Memoirs: Autobiographical Sketch and Narrative of the War Between the States.* Philadelphia: J. B. Lippincott, 1912.

Edgar, Alfred M. *My Reminiscences of the Civil War with the Stonewall Brigade and the Immortal 600*. Charleston, WV: 35th Star Publishing, 2011.

Elmore, Fletcher L., Jr., ed. *Diary of J. E. Whitehorn, 1st Sergt. Co. F, 12th Va., A. P. Hill's 3rd Corps, A. N. Va*. Utica, KY: McDowell Publications, 1995.

Everson, Guy R. and Edward H. Simpson, Jr., eds. *Far, Far from Home: The Wartime Letters of Dick and Tally Simpson, 3rd South Carolina Volunteers*. Oxford: Oxford University Press, 1994.

Ford, Andrew E. *The Story of the Fifteenth Regiment Massachusetts Volunteer Infantry in the Civil War 1861-1864*. Clinton, Mass.: W. J. Coulter, 1898.

Ford, Worthington C., ed. *A Cycle of Adams Letters, 1861-1865*. 2 vols. Boston, Houghton-Mifflin, 1920.

Gaff, Alan D. and Donald H. Gaff, eds. *A Corporal's Story: Civil War Recollections of the Twelfth Massachusetts*. Norman: Oklahoma University Press, 2014.

Gale, Andrew H. *Civil War Letters and Diary of Andrew H. Gale of the 137th Regiment, New York State Volunteers*. Westminster, Md.: Heritage Books, 2005.

Galwey, Thomas Francis. *The Valiant Hours: The Narrative of "Captain Brevet," an Irish-American in the Army of the Potomac*. Harrisburg, PA: Stackpole Books, 1961.

Gardner, Leonard Marsden. *Sunset Memories, 1861-1865*. Gettysburg, Pa.: Times and News, 1941.

Garnett, John J. *A Sunday Souvenir: Story of the Battle of Gettysburg*. Brooklyn, N.Y.: Eagle Book, 1888.

Garnett, Theodore S. *J.E.B. Stuart (Major General) Commander of the Cavalry Corps, Army of Northern Virginia, C.S.A.: An Address Delivered at the Unveiling of the Equestrian Statue of General Stuart, at Richmond, Virginia, May 30, 1907*. New York: The Neale Publishing Co., 1907.

Garrison, Fielding H., ed. *John Shaw Billings: A Memoir*. New York: G. P. Putnam, 1915.

Gibbon, John. *Personal Recollections of the Civil War by John Gibbon*. Dayton, OH: Morningside, 1988.

Gillespie, Samuel L. *A History of Company A, First Ohio Cavalry, 1861-1865*. Washington Court House, OH: Press of Ohio State Register, 1898.

Gilmor, Harry. *Four Years in the Saddle*. New York: Harper and Brothers, 1866.

Glazier, Willard. *Three Years in the Federal Cavalry*. New York, R.H. Ferguson & Co., 1873.

Goldsborough, W. W. *The Maryland Line in the Confederate Army, 1861-1865*. Baltimore: Guggenheimer, Weil, and Co., 1900.

Gordon, John B. *Reminiscences of the Civil War*. New York: Charles Scribner's Sons, 1903.

Gracey, Samuel L. *Annals of the Sixth Pennsylvania Cavalry*. Philadelphia: E. H. Butler & Co., 1868.

Green, Helen Binkley, ed. *Pages from a Diary, 1843-1880: Excerpts from the Diaries of Jacob Stouffer and Eliza Rider Stouffer*. Hagerstown, Md.: s. n., 1966.

Green, Wharton J. *Recollections and Reflections: An Auto of Half a Century and More*. Raleigh, N.C.: Edwards and Broughton Printing Co., 1906.

Grimsley, Daniel A. *Battles in Culpeper County, Virginia, 1861-1865*. Culpeper, Va.: Raleigh Travers Green, 1900.

Guernsey, Alfred H. and Henry M. Alden, eds. *Harper's Pictorial History of the Civil War*. 2 vols. Chicago: McDonnell Brothers, 1894.

Gurowski, Adam. *Diary from November 12, 1862, to October 18, 1863*. New York: Carleton, 1864.

Hall, Hillman A., ed. *History of the Sixth New York Cavalry (Second Ira Harris Guards), Second Brigade-First Division-Cavalry Corps, Army of the Potomac 1861-1865*. Worcester Mass.: Blanchard Press, 1908.

Haller, Granville O. *The Dismissal of Major Granville O. Haller of the Regular Army of the United States by Order of the Secretary of War in Special Orders, 331, of July 25, 1863.* Paterson, N.J.: Daily Guardian, 1863.

Hamilton, D. H. *History of Company M: First Texas Volunteer Infantry, Hood's Brigade, Longstreet's Corps, Army of the Confederate States of America.* Waco, Texas: W. M. Morrison, 1962.

Hamilton, J. G. de Roulhac, ed. *The Papers of Randolph Abbott Shotwell.* 2 vols. Raleigh: North Carolina Historical Commission, 1929.

Hankins, Samuel W. *Simple Story of a Soldier: Life and Service in the 2d Mississippi Infantry.* The University of Alabama Press, 2004.

Hard, Abner N. *History of the Eighth Cavalry Regiment Illinois Volunteers.* Aurora, Ill.: privately published, 1868.

Hartley, William R., ed. The Fighting 57th North Carolina: The Life and Letters of James Calvin Zimmerman. North Carolina: s.n., lulu.com, 2006.

Hassler, William W., ed. *The General to His Lady: The Civil War Letters of William Dorsey Pender to Fanny Pender.* Chapel Hill: The University of North Carolina Press, 1965.

Hays, Gilbert A. *Under the Red Patch; Story of the Sixty-Third Regiment, Pennsylvania Volunteers, 1861-1864.* Pittsburgh: Sixty-third Pennsylvania Volunteers Regimental Association, 1908.

Haynes, Martin A. *A History of the Second Regiment, New Hampshire Volunteer Infantry, in the War of the Rebellion.* Lakeport, N.H.: Regimental Association, 1896.

Hewitt, William. *The History of the Twelfth West Virginia Infantry: The Part It Took in the War of the Rebellion.* W.V.: Twelfth West Virginia Infantry Association, 1892.

History of the Eleventh Pennsylvania Volunteer Cavalry, Together with a Complete Roster of the Regiment and Regimental Officers. Philadelphia: Franklin Printing Co., 1902.

History of the First Regiment Minnesota Volunteer Infantry, 1861-1864. Stillwater, Minn.: Easton & Masterman, 1916.

History of the Twenty-third Pennsylvania Volunteer Infantry, Birney's Zouaves. Philadelphia: Survivors Association, 1904.

History of the 118th Pennsylvania Volunteers, Corn Exchange Regiment. Philadelphia: J. L. Smith, 1905.

History of the 121st Regiment Pennsylvania Volunteers: An Account from the Ranks. Philadelphia: Catholic Standard and Times, 1906.

History of the Nineteenth Regiment, Massachusetts Volunteer Infantry, 1861-1865. Salem, Mass.: Salem Press, 1906.

Hoke, Jacob. *The Great Invasion.* Dayton, Ohio: W. J. Shuey, 1887.

———. *Historical Reminiscences of the War: or incidents which transpired in and around Chambersburg during the War of the Rebellion.* Chambersburg, Pa.: M. A. Foltz, 1884.

Houghton, Edwin B. *The Campaigns of the Seventeenth Maine.* Portland, Me: Short & Loring, 1866.

Houghton, William R. *Two Boys in the Civil War and After.* Montgomery, Al.: The Paragon Press, 1912.

Howard, Oliver O. *Autobiography of Oliver Otis Howard, Major General United States Army.* New York: Baker and Taylor, 1907.

Howard, Wiley C. *Sketch of Cobb Legion Cavalry and Some Scenes and Incidents Remembered.* Atlanta: Atlanta Camp 159, S.C.V., 1901.

Hubbs, G. Ward, ed. *Voices from Company D: Diaries by the Greensboro Guards, Fifth Alabama Infantry Regiment, Army of Northern Virginia.* Athens: University of Georgia Press, 2003.

Husby, Karla Jean, comp. and Eric J. Wittenberg, ed. *Under Custer's Command: The Civil War Diary of James Henry Avery.* Washington, D.C.: Brassey's, 2001.

Humphreys, Henry. *Andrew Atkinson Humphreys: A Biography.* Philadelphia: The John C. Winston Co., 1924.

Jacobs, Michael. *Notes on the Rebel Invasion of Maryland and Pennsylvania and the Battle of Gettysburg.* Philadelphia: J. B. Lippincott, 1864.

Johnson, Pharris Deloach, ed. *Under the Southern Cross: Soldier Life with Gordon Bradwell and the Army of Northern Virginia.* Macon, Ga.: Mercer University Press, 2002.

Johnston, David E. *The Story of a Confederate Boy in the Civil War.* Portland, Ore.: Glass and Prudhomme Co., 1914.

Jones, John B. *A Rebel War Clerk's Diary at the Confederate States Capital.* 2 vols. Philadelphia: J. B. Lippincott, 1866.

Jones, Terry L., ed. *Campbell Brown's Civil War: With Ewell and the Army of Northern Virginia.* Baton Rouge: Louisiana State University Press,

———. *The Civil War Memoirs of Captain William J. Seymour: Reminiscences of a Louisiana Tiger.* Baton Rouge: Louisiana State University Press, 1997.

Jones, Woodruff. *1st Philadelphia Light Artillery in the Army of the Susquehanna, 1863.* Edited by Cooper Wingert. Camp Hill, PA: published by the author, 2011.

Jordan, Leonard G. "History of the Tenth Me. Battalion," in John M. Gould, ed. *History of the First-Tenth-Twenty-ninth Main Regiment, in Service of the United States Army from May 3, 1861, to June 21, 1866.* Portland, Maine: Stephen Berry, 1871.

Joslyn, Mauriel Phillips, ed. *Charlotte's Boys: Civil War Letters of the Branch Family of Savannah.* Berryville, Va.: Rockbridge Publishing Co., 1996.

Keifer, William R. and Newton H. Mack. *History of the One Hundred Fifty-third Regiment, Pennsylvania Volunteers.* Easton, Pa.: Chemical Publishing Co., 1909.

Kidd, James H. *Personal Recollections of a Cavalryman in Custer's Michigan Brigade.* Ionia, MI: Sentinel Printing Co., 1908.

King, David H., A. Judson Gibbs, and Jay H. Northup. *History of the Ninety-third Regiment, New York Volunteer Infantry, 1861-1865.* Milwaukee: Swain & Tate, 1895.

Ladd, David L. and Audrey J. Ladd, eds. *The Bachelder Papers: Gettysburg in Their Own Words.* 3 vols. Dayton, OH: Morningside, 1994-1995.

Leland, Charles. *Memoirs.* New York: D. Appleton, 1893.

Landers, Eli Pinson and Elizabeth Whitley Roberson. *Weep Not for Me, Dear Mother.* Gretna, La.: Pelican Publishing, 1998.

Lasswell, Mary, ed. *Rags and Hope: The Recollections of Val C. Giles, Four Years with Hood's Brigade, Fourth Texas Infantry, 1861-1865.* New York: Coward-McCann, 1961.

Lee, Capt. Robert E. *Recollections and Letters of Robert E. Lee.* Garden City, N.Y.: Garden City, 1924.

Lee, Susan P., ed. *Memoirs of William Nelson Pendleton, D.D., Rector of Latimer Parish, Lexington, Virginia, Brigadier-General C.S.A.; Chief of Artillery, Army of Northern Virginia.* Philadelphia: J. B. Lippincott, 1893.

Leon, Louis. *Diary of a Tar Heel Confederate Soldier.* Charlotte, N.C.: Stone Publishing, 1911.

Lewis, George. *The History of Battery E, First Regiment Rhode Island Light Artillery in the War of 1861 and 1865, to Preserve the Union.* Providence: Snow & Farnham, 1892.

Lewis, John H. *Recollections from 1860 to 1865.* Washington, D. C.: Peake & Company, Publishers, 1895.

Livermore, Thomas L. *Days and Events 1860-1866.* Boston and New York: Houghton Mifflin, 1920.

Loehr, Charles T. *War History of the Old First Virginia Regiment, Army of Northern Virginia.* Richmond: Wm. Ellis Jones, 1884.

Long, Armistead L. *Memoirs of Robert E. Lee.* New York: J. M. Stoddart & Co., 1886.

Longstreet, James. *From Manassas to Appomattox*. Philadelphia: J. B. Lippincott, 1896.

Lord, Walter, ed. *The Fremantle Diary: Being the Journal of Lieutenant Colonel James Arthur Lyon Fremantle, Coldstream Guards, on his Three Months in the Southern States*. Boston: Little, Brown, & Co., 1954.

Lynch, Charles H. *The Civil War Diary, 1862–1865, of Charles H. Lynch, 18th Conn. Vol's.* Hartford, Conn.: The Case, Lockwood and Brainard Co., 1915.

MacNamara, Daniel G. *The History of the Ninth Regiment, Massachusetts Volunteer Infantry, Second Brigade, First Division, Fifth Army Corps, Army of the Potomac, June, 1861-June, 1864*. Boston: E. B. Stillings & Co., 1899.

Mahon, Michael G., ed. *Winchester Divided: The Civil War Diaries of Julia Chase and Laura Lee*. Mechanicsburg, Pa.: Stackpole Books, 2002.

Maine at Gettysburg: Report of Maine Commissioners. Portland, Maine: The Lakeside Press, 1898.

Matteson, Ron, ed. *Civil War Campaigns of the 10th New York Cavalry With One Soldier's Personal Correspondence*. Morrisville, N.C.: Lulu.com, 2007.

Maurice, Sir Frederick, ed. *An Aide-de-Camp of Lee, Being the Papers of Colonel Charles Marshall, Sometime Aide-de-Camp, Military Secretary, and Assistant Adjutant General on the Staff of Robert E. Lee, 1862-1865*. Boston: Little, Brown & Co., 1927.

Maury, Dabney Herndon. *Recollections of a Virginian in the Mexican, Indian, and Civil Wars*. New York: Charles Scribner's Sons, 1894.

McClellan, Henry B. *The Life and Campaigns of Major General J. E. B. Stuart*. Boston: Houghton-Mifflin, 1895.

McClure, Alexander K. *Old Time Notes of Pennsylvania*. 2 vols. Philadelphia: John C. Winston Co., 1905.

McDonald, Archie, ed. *Make Me a Map of the Valley: The Civil War Journal of Stonewall Jackson's Topographer*. Dallas: Southern Methodist University Press, 1973.

McDonald, William N. *A History of the Laurel Brigade*. Baltimore, Md.: Sun Job Printing Office, 1907.

McGrath, Franklin. *History of the 127th New York Volunteers*. n.p., 1898.

McGuire, Judith White. *Diary of a Southern Refugee, During the War*. New York: E. J. Hale & Son, 1868.

McKim, Randolph H. *A Soldier's Recollections: Leaves from the Diary of a Young Confederate*. New York: Longmans, Green, and Co., 1910.

McSwain, Eleanor D., ed. *Crumbling Defenses; Or Memoirs and Reminiscences of John Logan Black, C.S.A.* Macon, Ga.: privately published, 1960.

Meade, George G., ed. *The Life and Letters of George Gordon Meade*. 2 vols. New York: Charles Scribner's Sons, 1913.

Merrill, Samuel H. *The Campaigns of the First Maine and First District of Columbia Cavalry*. Portland: Bailey & Noyes, 1866.

Messent, Peter and Steve Courtney, eds. *The Civil War Letters of Joseph Hopkins Twichell: A Chaplain's Story*. Athens: University of Georgia Press, 2006.

Meyer, Henry C. *Civil War Experiences Under Bayard, Gregg, Kilpatrick, Custer, Raulston, and Newberry, 1862, 1863, 1864*. New York: Knickerbocker Press, 1911.

Mitchell, Adele H., ed. *The Letters of Major General James E. B. Stuart*. Fairfax, VA: Stuart-Mosby Historical Society, 1990.

Mohr, James C., ed. *The Cormany Diaries: A Northern Family in the Civil War*. Pittsburgh: University of Pittsburgh Press, 1982.

Moore, Edward A. *The Story of a Cannoneer under Stonewall Jackson.* New York and Washington: The Neale Publishing Co., 1907.

Moore, Frank, ed. *Anecdotes, Poetry, and Incidents of the War: North and South 1860-1865.* New York: J. Porteus, 1867.

———. *The Rebellion Record: A Diary of American Events.* 7 vols. New York: G. P. Putnam, 1861-68.

Moore, James, M. D. *Kilpatrick and Our Cavalry.* New York: W. J. Widdleton, 1865.

Morhous, Henry C. *Reminiscences of the 123rd Regiment, N.Y.S.V.* Greenwich, N.Y.: People's Journal Book and Job Office, 1879.

Morse, John T., ed. *Diary of Gideon Welles: Secretary of the Navy under Lincoln and Johnson,* 3 vols. Boston and New York: Houghton and Mifflin, 1911.

Mosby, John S. *Stuart's Cavalry in the Gettysburg Campaign.* New York: Moffatt, Yard & Co., 1908.

Moseley, Ronald H., ed. *The Stillwell Letters: A Georgian in Longstreet's Corps, Army of Northern Virginia.* Macon, Ga.: Mercer University Press, 2002.

Moyer, Henry P. *History of the Seventeenth Regiment, Pennsylvania Volunteer Cavalry.* Lebanon, Pa.: privately published, 1911.

Muffly, Joseph W. *The Story of Our Regiment: A History of the 148th Pennsylvania Volunteers.* Des Moines, Iowa: Kenyon Printing, 1904.

Mulholland, St. Clair A. *The Story of the 116th Regiment, Pennsylvania Infantry.* Philadelphia: F. McManus, Jr. & Co., 1869.

Murray, R. L., ed. *Letters from Gettysburg: New York Soldiers' Correspondences from the Battlefield.* Wolcott, NY: Benedum Books, 2005.

Myers, Frank M. *The Comanches: A History of White's Battalion, Virginia Cavalry.* Baltimore: Kelly, Piet & Co. 1871.

Nash, Eugene Arus. *A History of the Forty-fourth Regiment, New York Volunteer Infantry in the Civil War 1861-1865.* Chicago: R. R. Donnelly & Sons, 1911.

Neese, George M. *Three Years in the Confederate Horse Artillery.* New York: Neale Publishing Co., 1911.

Nesbit, John W. *General History of Company D, 149th Pennsylvania Volunteers and Personal Sketches of the Volunteers.* Oakdale, Pa.: Oakdale Printing & Publishing Co., 1908.

Nesbitt, Mark, ed. *35 Days to Gettysburg: The Campaign Diaries of Two American Enemies.* Harrisburg: Stackpole Books, 1992.

Nevins, Allen, ed. *A Diary of Battle: The Personal Journals of Charles S. Wainwright, 1861–1865.* New York: Da Capo Press, 1998.

Newcomer, C. Armour. *Cole's Cavalry, or, Three Years in the Saddle in the Shenandoah Valley.* Baltimore: Cushing & Co., 1895.

Newell, Joseph. *"Ours," Annals of the Tenth Regiment Massachusetts Volunteers.* Springfield, MA: C. A Nichols & Co., 1875.

Nichols, G. W. *A Soldier's Story of His Regiment (61st Georgia) and Incidentally of the Lawton-Gordon-Evans Brigade, Army of Northern Virginia.* Jesup, GA: privately published, 1898.

Nicholson, John P. Nicholson, comp. *Pennsylvania at Gettysburg: Ceremonies at the Dedication of the Monuments Erected by the Commonwealth of Pennsylvania to Mark the Positions of the Pennsylvania Commands Engaged in the Battle.* 4 vols. Harrisburg: B. Slingerly, 1893.

Niven, John, ed. *The Salmon P. Chase Papers.* 5 vols. Kent, Ohio: Kent State University Press, 1994-1998.

Norton, Henry. *Deeds of Daring: or History of the Eighth New York Volunteer Cavalry.* Norwich, NY: Chenango Telegraph Printing House, 1889.

Oakey, Daniel. *History of the Second Massachusetts Regiment of Infantry. Beverly Ford. A Paper Read at the Officers' Reunion in Boston, May 12, 1884*. Boston: Geo. H. Ellis, Printer, 1884.

Oates, Dan, ed. *Hanging Rock Rebel: Lt. John Blue's War in West Virginia and the Shenandoah Valley*. Shippensburg, Pa.: Burd Street Press, 1994.

Oeffinger, John C., ed. *A Soldier's General: The Civil War Letters of Major General Lafayette McLaws*. Chapel Hill: The University of North Carolina Press, 2002.

O'Ferrall, Charles T. *Forty Years of Active Service*. New York: The Neale Publishing Co., 1904.

Opie, John N. *A Rebel Cavalryman with Lee, Stuart, and Jackson*. Chicago: Charles B. Conkey, 1899.

Page, Charles D. *History of the Fourteenth Regiment, Connecticut Vol. Infantry*. Meriden, Conn.: Horton Printing Co., 1906.

Parker, Francis J. *The Story of the Thirty-Second Regiment Massachusetts Infantry*. Boston: C. W. Calkins & Co., 1880.

Parker, John L. and Robert G. Carter. *Henry Wilson's Regiment: History of the Twenty-second Massachusetts Infantry, the Second Company Sharpshooters, and the Third Light Battery in the War of the Rebellion*. Boston: Rand Avery, 1887.

Pearson, Johnnie Perry, ed. *Lee and Jackson's Bloody Twelfth: The Letters of Irby Goodwin Scott, First Lieutenant, Company G, Putnam Light Infantry, Twelfth Georgia Volunteer Infantry*. Knoxville: University of Tennessee Press, 2010.

Peck, Rufus H. *Reminiscences of a Confederate Soldier of Co. C, 2nd Va. Cavalry*. Fincastle, VA: privately published, 1913.

Pennsylvania Gettysburg Battlefield Commission. *Pennsylvania at Gettysburg: Ceremonies of the Dedication of the Monuments Erected by the Commonwealth of Pennsylvania*. 2 vols. Harrisburg: Wm. Stanley Ray, 1904.

Pennypacker, Samuel W. *The Autobiography of a Pennsylvanian*. Philadelphia: The John C. Winston Co., 1918.

Perry, Bliss, ed. *The Life and Letters of Henry Lee Higginson*. 2 vols. Boston: Atlantic Monthly Press, 1921.

Pleasonton, A. J. *Third Annual Report of Brigadier General A. J. Pleasonton, Commanding the Home Guard of the City of Philadelphia, to the Hon. Alexander Henry, Mayor for 1863*. Philadelphia: King & Baird, 1864.

Polley, Joseph B. *A Soldier's Letters to Charming Nellie*. New York: Neale Publishing Co., 1908.

———. *Hood's Texas Brigade*. New York: Neale Publishing Co., 1910.

Porter, Burton B. *One of the People: His Own Story*. Privately published, 1907.

Powell, William H. *The Fifth Corps (Army of the Potomac): A Record of Operations During the Civil War in the United States of America, 1861-1865*. New York: G. P. Putnam's Sons, 1896.

———, ed. *Officers of the Army and Navy (Volunteer) Who Served in the Civil War*. Philadelphia: L. R. Hamersly & Co., 1893.

Preston, Noble D. *History of the Tenth Regiment of Cavalry, New York State Volunteers, August, 1861 to August, 1865*. New York: D. Appleton & Co., 1892.

Price, George F. *Across the Continent with the Fifth Cavalry*. New York: Noble Offset Printers, 1883.

Priest, John M., ed. *John T. McMahon's Diary of the 136th New York*. Shippensburg, PA: White Mane, 1993.

Prowell, George R. *History of the Eighty-seventh Regiment, Pennsylvania Volunteers*. York, Pa.: York Daily Record, 1901.

———. *History of York County, Pennsylvania,* 2 vols. Chicago: J. H. Beers, 1907.

Putnam, Sallie B. *Richmond During the War*. New York: G. Carleton & Co., 1867.

Pyne, Henry R. *The History of First New Jersey Cavalry*. Trenton, N.J.: J. A. Beecher, 1871.

Quaife, Milo M., ed. *From the Cannon's Mouth: The Civil War Letters of General Alpheus S. Williams.* Detroit: Wayne State University Press, 1959.

Quint, Alonzo H. *The Potomac and the Rapidan: Army Notes, from the Failure at Winchester to the Reinforcement of Rosecrans, 1861-1863.* Boston: Crosby and Nichols, 1864.

Rauscher, Frank. *Music on the March, 1862-'65, with the Army of the Potomac, 114th Regt. P. V., Collis' Zouaves.* Philadelphia: Wm. F. Fell & Co., 1892.

Rea, D. B. *Sketches of Hampton's Cavalry, Embracing the Principal Exploits of the Cavalry in the Campaigns of 1862 and 1863.* Columbia, SC: Steam Press, 1864.

Reagan, John H. *Memoirs with Special Reference to Secession and the Civil War.* New York: Neale Publishing Co., 1906.

Reed, Thomas Benton. *A Private in Gray.* Camden, Ark.: self-published, 1902.

Regimental Publication Committee. *History of the Eighteenth Regiment of Cavalry, Pennsylvania Volunteers, 1862-1865.* New York: Published by the Committee, 1909.

Reichardt, Theodore. *Diary of Battery A, First Regiment Rhode Island Light Artillery: Written in the Field.* Providence: N. Bangs Williams, 1865.

Report of the Joint Committee on the Conduct of the War, at the Second Session, Thirty-Eighth Congress. 3 vols. Washington, D.C.: Government Printing Office, 1865.

Rhodes, John H. *The History of Battery B, First Regiment Rhode Island Light Artillery, in the War to Preserve the Union 1861-1865.* Providence: Snow & Farnham, 1894.

Richards, H. M. M. *Pennsylvania's Emergency Men at Gettysburg.* Reading, Pa.: s. n., 1895.

Robertson, James I., Jr., ed. *The Civil War Letters of General Robert McAllister.* New Brunswick, NJ: Rutgers University Press, 1965.

Robertson, John, comp. *Michigan in the War.* Lansing, MI: W. S. George & Co., 1882.

Robson, John S. *How a One-Legged Rebel Lives: Reminiscences of the Civil War: The Story of the Campaigns of Stonewall Jackson, as Told by a High Private in the "Foot Cavalry".* Durham, N.C.: The Educator Co., 1898.

Rodgers, Sarah Sites, ed. *The Ties of the Past: The Gettysburg Diaries of Salome Myers Stewart, 1854-1922.* Gettysburg, Pa.: Thomas Publications, 1996.

Roper, John Herbert, ed. *Repairing the "March of Mars": The Civil War Diaries of John Samuel Apperson.* Macon, Ga.: Mercer University Press, 2001.

Rosenblatt, Emil and Ruth, eds. *Hard Marching Every Day: The Civil War Letters of Private Wilbur Fisk, 1861-1865.* Lawrence: University Press of Kansas, 1992.

Runge, William H., ed. *Four Years in the Confederate Artillery: The Diary of Private Henry Robinson Berkeley.* Chapel Hill: The University of North Carolina Press, 1961.

Ryan, David D., ed. *A Yankee Spy in Richmond: The Civil War Diary of "Crazy Bet" Van Lew.* Mechanicsburg, PA: Stackpole Books, 1996.

Sawyer, Franklin. *A Military History of the 8th Regiment Ohio Vol. Inf'y: Its Battles, Marches and Army Movements.* Cleveland: Fairbanks & Co., 1881.

Schiebert, Justus. *Seven Months in Rebel States During the North American War, 1863.* Trans. by Joseph C. Hayes. Tuscaloosa, Ala.: Confederate Publishing Co., 1958.

Schiller, Herbert M., ed. *Autobiography of Major General William F. Smith 1861-1864.* Dayton, OH: Morningside, 1990.

Scott, Kate M. *History of the One Hundred and Fifth Regiment of Pennsylvania Volunteers.* Philadelphia: New World Publishing Co., 1877.

Seville, William P. *History of the First Regiment, Delaware Volunteers.* Wilmington: The Historical Society of Delaware, 1884.

Silver, James, ed. *A Life for the Confederacy as Recorded in the Pocket Diaries of Private Robert A. Moore, Company "G", Seventeenth Mississippi Regiment, Confederate Guards, Holly Springs, Mississippi.* Jackson, Tenn.: McCowat-Mercer Press, 1959.

Simons, Ezra D. *A Regimental History: The One Hundred and Twenty-fifth New York State Volunteers.* New York: self-published, 1888.

Skelly, Daniel A. *A Boy's Experiences in the Battle of Gettysburg.* Gettysburg, Pa.: Privately published, 1932.

Smedley, Charles. *Life in Southern Prisons; From the Diary of Corporal Charles Smedley of Company G, 90th Regiment, Penn'a Volunteers.* Lancaster, Pa.: The Ladies and Gentlemen's Fulton Aid Society, Pearsol and Geist, 1865.

Smith, John Day. *The History of the Nineteenth Regiment of Maine Volunteer Infantry, 1862-1865.* Minneapolis, Minn.: The Great Western Printing Co., 1909.

Smith, Thomas West. *The Story of a Cavalry Regiment: "Scott's 900," Eleventh New York Cavalry from the St. Lawrence River to the Gulf of Mexico, 1861-1865.* Chicago: Veteran Assoc. of the Regiment, 1897.

Smith, William Alexander. *The Anson Guards: Company C, Fourteenth Regiment North Carolina Volunteers 1861-1865.* Charlotte: Stone Publishing Co., 1914.

Sorrel, G. Moxley. *Recollections of a Confederate Staff Officer.* New York: The Neale Publishing Co., 1905.

Sparks, David S. *Inside Lincoln's Army: The Diary of General Marsena Rudoph Patrick, Provost Marshal General, Army of the Potomac.* New York: Thomas Yoseloff, 1964.

Stephens, Robert Grier, Jr., ed. *Intrepid Warrior: Clement Anselm Evans.* Dayton, Ohio: Morningside Press, 1992.

Stewart, Robert L. *History of the One Hundred and Fortieth Regiment Pennsylvania Volunteers.* Philadelphia: Regimental Association, 1912.

Stiles, Robert. *Four Years under Marse Robert.* New York/Washington: The Neale Publishing Co., 1904.

Stocker, Jeffrey D., ed. *From Huntsville to Appomattox: R.T. Coles' History of 4th Regiment, Alabama Volunteer Infantry, C.S.A., Army of Northern Virginia.* Knoxville: The University of Tennessee Press, 1996.

Stoeckel, Carl and Ellen Battelle Stoeckel, eds. *Correspondence of John Sedgwick, Major General.* 2 vols. Privately published, 1903.

Strong, J. G. *Directory of the Borough of Carlisle… Also, an Account of the Occupation of the Place by the Rebel Army in the Year 1863.* Carlisle: s. n., 1867.

Styple, William B., ed. *Generals in Bronze: Interviewing the Commanders of the Civil War.* Kearny, NJ: Belle Grove Publishing, 2005.

———. *Our Noble Blood: The Civil War Letters of Major-General Regis de Trobriand.* Trans. By Nathalie Chartrain. Kearny, NJ: Belle Grove Publishing Co., 1997.

———. *Writing and Fighting the Civil War: Soldier Correspondence to the New York Sunday Mercury.* Kearny, N.J.: Belle Grove Publishing Co., 2000.

———. *Writing & Fighting from the Army of Northern Virginia: A Collection of Confederate Soldier Correspondence.* Kearny, N. J.: Belle Grove Publishing Co., 2003.

———. *Writing & Fighting the Confederate War: The Letters of Peter Wellington Alexander, Confederate War Correspondent.* Kearny, N. J.: Belle Grove Publishing Co., 2002.

Sullivan, James W. *Boyhood Memories of the Civil War, 1861-'65.* Carlisle, Pa.: Hamilton Library Association, 1933.

Summers, Festus P. ed. *A Borderland Confederate.* Pittsburgh: University of Pittsburgh Press, 1962.

Supplement to the Official Records of the Union and Confederate Armies. 100 vols. Wilmington, N. C.: Broadfoot, 1995.

Swank, Walbrook D., ed. *Sabres, Saddles and Spurs.* Shippensburg, Pa.: Burd Street Press, 1998.

Swinton, William. *Campaigns of the Army of the Potomac: A Critical History of Operations in Virginia, Maryland, and Pennsylvania from the Commencement to the Close of the War 1861-5.* New York: Charles B. Richardson, 1866.

Taylor, Emerson Gifford, ed. *Gouverneur Kemble Warren: The Life and Letters of an American Soldier.* Boston: Houghton-Mifflin, 1932.

Taylor, Michael W., ed. *The Cry is War, War, War: The Civil War Correspondence of Lts. Burwell Thomas Cotton and George Job Huntley, 34th Regiment North Carolina Troops.* Dayton, OH: Morningside, 1994.

The War of the Rebellion: A Compilation of the Official Records of the Union and Confederate Armies, 70 volumes in 4 series. Washington, D.C.: United States Government Printing Office, 1880-1901.

Thomas, Hampton S. *Some Personal Reminiscences of Service in the Cavalry of the Army of the Potomac.* Philadelphia: L. R. Hamersly & Co., 1889.

Thomas, Henry W. *History of the Doles-Cook Brigade, Army of Northern Virginia, C.S.A.* Atlanta: Franklin Printing, 1903.

Tobie, Edward P. *History of the First Maine Cavalry.* Boston: Press of Emery & Hughes, 1887.

———. *Service of the Cavalry in the Army of the Potomac.* Providence: N. B. Williams, 1882.

Toombs, Samuel. *New Jersey Troops in the Gettysburg Campaign from June 5 to July 31, 1863.* Orange, N. J.: The Evening Mail Publishing House, 1888.

Tower, R. Lockwood, ed. *Lee's Adjutant: The Wartime Letters of Colonel Walter Herron Taylor, 1862-1865.* Columbia: University of South Carolina Press, 1995.

Trobriand, Phillippe Regis de. *Four Years with the Army of the Potomac.* Trans. By George K. Dauchy. Boston: Ticknor & Fields, 1889.

Trout, Robert J., ed. *In the Saddle with Stuart: The Story of Frank Smith Robertson of Jeb Stuart's Staff.* Gettysburg, Pa.: Thomas Publications, 1998.

———. *Memoirs of the Stuart Horse Artillery: Moorman's and Hart's Batteries.* Knoxville: University of Tennessee Press, 2008.

———. *With Pen and Saber: The Letters and Diaries of J.E.B. Stuart's Staff Officers.* Mechanicsburg, Pa.: Stackpole Books, 1995.

Uhler, George H. *Camps and Campaigns of the 93d Regiment, Penna. Volunteers.* Harrisburg, Pa.: s.n., 1898.

Under the Maltese Cross: Antietam to Appomattox. The Loyal Uprising in Western Pennsylvania 1861-1865. Pittsburgh: The 155th Regimental Association, 1910.

Underwood, Adin B. *The Three-Years' Service of the Thirty-third Mass. Infantry Regiment, 1862–1865.* Boston: A. Williams & Co., 1881.

Vautier, John D. *History of the Eighty-eighth Pennsylvania Volunteers in the War for the Union, 1861–1865.* Philadelphia: J. B. Lippincott, 1894.

Walker, William C. *History of the Eighteenth Regiment.* Norwich, Conn.: Veterans Committee, 1885.

Ward, Joseph R. C. *History of the One Hundred and Sixth Regiment Pennsylvania Volunteers, 2d Brigade, 2d Division, 2d Corps, 1861-1865.* Philadelphia: F. McManus, Jr. & Co., 1906.

Warren, William H. *History of the Seventeenth Connecticut: The Record of a Yankee Regiment in the War for the Union.* Bridgeport, Conn.: The Danbury Times, 1886.

Welch, Spencer Glasgow. *A Confederate Surgeon's Letters to His Wife.* New York: The Neale Publishing Co., 1911.

Weld, Stephen Minot. *War Diary of Stephen Minot Weld 1861-1865*. Cambridge, MA: Riverside Press, 1912.

West, John C. *A Texan in Search of a Fight*. Waco: J. S. Hill & Co., 1901.

Weygant, Charles H. *History of the One Hundred and Twenty-Fourth Regiment, New York State Volunteers*. Newburgh, N.Y.: Journal Printing House, 1877.

White, A. G. *History of Co. F. 140th Regiment Pa. V.* Greenville, Pa.: The Beaver Printery, 1908.

Wiley, Bell Irvin, ed. *Letters of Warren Akin, Confederate Congressman*. Athens: University of Georgia Press, 1959.

Wiley, Kenneth, ed. *Norfolk Blues: The Civil War Diary of the Norfolk Artillery Blues*. Shippensburg, Pa.: Burd Street Press, 1997.

Williams, John C. *Life in Camp: A History of the Nine-Months' Service of the Fourteenth Vermont Regiment*. Claremont, N.H.: Claremont Manufacturing Company, 1864.

Williamson, James J. *Mosby's Rangers: A Record of the Operations of the Forty-Third Battalion Virginia Cavalry*. New York: R. B. Kenyon, 1896.

Wilson, James H. *Captain Charles Corbit's Charge at Westminster with a Squadron of the First Delaware Cavalry, June 29, 1863*. Wilmington: The Historical Society of Delaware, 1913.

Wilson, Lawrence. *Itinerary of the Seventh Ohio Volunteer Infantry, 1861-1864*. New York and Washington: The Neale Publishing Co., 1907.

Wingate, George W. *History of the Twenty-Second Regiment of the National Guard of the State of New York*. New York: Edwin W. Dayton, 1896.

Wise, George. *History of the Seventeenth Virginia Infantry, C.S.A.* Baltimore: Kelly, Piet, & Co., 1870.

Wise, Jennings Cropper. *The Long Arm of Lee, or the History of the Artillery of the Army of Northern Virginia*. 2 vols. Lynchburg, Va.: J. P. Bell Co., Inc., 1915.

Wittenberg, Eric J., ed. *One of Custer's Wolverines: The Civil War Letters of Brevet Brigadier General James H. Kidd, Sixth Michigan Cavalry*. Kent, OH: Kent State University Press, 2000.

Wood, James H. *The War: "Stonewall" Jackson: His Campaigns and Battles, the Regiment as I Saw Them*. Cumberland, Md.: Eddy Press, 1910.

Woodward, Evan M. *Our Campaigns; or, the Marches, Bivouacs, Battles, Incidents of Camp Life and History of Our Regiment during Its Three Years Term of Service*. Philadelphia: John E. Potter, 1865.

Worsham, John H. *One of Jackson's Foot Cavalry: His Experience and What He Saw during the War*. New York: The Neale Publishing Co., 1912.

Wright, D. Giraud. *A Southern Girl in '61: The War-Time Memories of a Confederate Senator's Daughter*. New York: Doubleday, Page & Company, 1905.

Wright, Stuart, ed. *Memoirs of Alfred H. Belo: Reminiscences of a North Carolina Volunteer*. Gaithersburg, MD: Olde Soldier Books, n.d.

Young, Jesse Bowman. *The Battle of Gettysburg: A Comprehensive Narrative*. New York: Harper & Brothers, 1913.

Younger, Edward, ed. *Inside the Confederate Government: The Diary of Robert Garlick Hill Keen, Head of the Bureau of War*. New York: Oxford University Press, 1957.

Secondary Sources

Magazines and Periodicals

Alexander, Ted. "Gettysburg's Cavalry Operations: June 27-July 3, 1863." *Blue & Gray*, Vol. 6, No. 1, October 1988.

———. "A Regular Slave Hunt: The Army of Northern Virginia and Black Civilians in the Gettysburg Campaign." *North & South*, Vol. 4, No. 7, September 2001.

Bloom, Robert L. "We Never Expected a Battle: The Civilians of Gettysburg, 1863." *Pennsylvania History,* Vol. 55.

Brennan, Patrick. "Thunder of the Plains of Brandy", Part 1. *North & South* 5 (April 2002): 14-34.

———. "Thunder on the Plains of Brandy", Part 2. *North & South* 5 (June 2002): 32-51.

Chance, Mark A. "Prelude to Invasion: Lee's Preparations and the Second Battle of Winchester," *Gettysburg Magazine*, No. 19, January 1999.

Crist, Robert G. "Highwater 1863: The Confederate Approach to Harrisburg." *Pennsylvania History*, Vol. 30, 1963.

Ent, Uzal. "Rebels in Pennsylvania." *Civil War Times Illustrated*, Vol. 37, No. 4, August 1998.

Frantz Jr., Ivan. "The Pennsylvania Railroad and the Civil War." *The Keystone*, Vol. 38, No. 3, Autumn 2005.

Gallagher, Gary W. "Brandy Station: The Civil War's Bloodiest Arena of Mounted Combat," *Blue & Gray* 9 (October 1990): 8-22, 44-53.

Greathead, J. H. "The Skirmish at McConnellsburg—A Reminiscence of the War." *Fulton Democrat*, September 21, 1894.

Hage, Anne A. "The Battle of Gettysburg as Seen by Minnesota Soldiers," *Minnesota History*, June 1963.

Hall, Clark B. "Auburn: Culpeper's Architectural and Historical Gem," *Culpeper Star Exponent*, May 1, 2008.

———. "Robert F. Beckham: The Man Who Commanded Stuart's Horse Artillery After Pelham Fell," *Blue & Gray* 10 (December 1991): 34-37.

———. "'The Army is Moving.' Lee's March to the Potomac, 1863: Rodes Spearheads the Way." *Civil War Times Illustrated*, Vol. 21, No. 3, Spring 2004.

Krepps, John. "Before and After Hanover: Tracing Stuart's Cavalry Movements of June 30, 1863." *Blue & Gray* 21, no. 1 (2003): 47-51.

Kross, Gary M. "Fight Like the Devil to Hold Your Own", *Blue & Gray*, Vol. 12, Issue 3 (February 1995), 9-24, 48-58.

Lash, Gary. "The March of the 124th New York to Gettysburg." *Gettysburg Magazine*, No. 9, July 1993.

Love, William A. "Mississippi at Gettysburg." *Publications of the Mississippi Historical Society*, Vol. 9, 1906.

Miner, Mark A. "First Fight, First Blood: The 12th West Virginia Infantry at the Second Battle of Winchester and the Battle's Legacy on One Wes Virginia Family." *Journal of the Winchester-Frederick County Historical Society,* Vol. 4, 1989.

Scott L. Mingus, Sr., "Jenkins' Cavalry Raid Through Northwestern York County." *Gettysburg Magazine* 44, (Jan. 2010): 41-52.

Nye, Wilbur S. "Prelude to the Battle: The Invasion of Pennsylvania," *Civil War Times Illustrated*, Vol. 2, No. 4, July 1963.

Omwake, Stanley. "Franklin County Through Confederate Eyes." *Papers Read Before the Kittochtinny Historical Society*, Vol. 14, June 1962.

O'Neill Jr., Robert F. "Aldie, Middleburg, and Upperville." *Gettysburg Magazine* 43 (July 2010): 7-48.

———. "The Fight for the Loudoun Valley—Aldie, Middleburg, and Upperville, Va.: Opening Battles of the Gettysburg Campaign." *Blue & Gray*, Vol. 11, No. 1, October 1993.

Scott, Joseph C. "The Infernal Balloon: Union Aeronautics in the American Civil War." *Army History*, no. 93 (Fall 2014): 6-27.

Seitter, John Reid. "Union City: Philadelphia and the Battle of Gettysburg." *Gettysburg Magazine*, No. 21 (1999).

Smith, Timothy H. "Northern Town Lot Histories of Fairfield, Pennsylvania," *Adams County History*, No. 19 (2013): 36-37.

―――. "Skirmish at Fountaindale: Sunday, June 28, 1863." *Blue & Gray*, Vol. 23, No. 1, Spring 2006.

Snyder, Harry W. "Civil War History of Carlisle." *Lamberton and Hamilton Library Association Prize Essays*, Vol. 4, 1961.

"Tablet Unveiled at Spot Where Rebels Turned." *Carlisle Sentinel*, October 26, 1929.

Tucker, Glenn. "The Cavalry Invasion of the North." *Civil War Times Illustrated*, Vol. 2, No. 4, July 1963.

Trudeau, Noah Andre. "Gettysburg's Second Front: The 'Blackberry Raid.'" *The Gettysburg Magazine* 11 (July 1994), 6-18.

Wert, Jeffry. "Gettysburg: The Special Issue." *Civil War Times Illustrated*, Vol. 27, No. 4, Summer 1988.

Wittenberg, Eric J. "And Everything is Lovely and the Goose Hangs High: John Buford and the Hanging of Confederate Spies during the Gettysburg Campaign." *The Gettysburg Magazine: Articles of Lasting Historical Interest*, No. 18 (January 1998): 5-14.

―――. "The Shelling of Carlisle." *Blue & Gray*, Vol. 24, No. 2, Summer 2007.

Books

Allardice, Bruce S. *More Generals in Gray*. Baton Rouge: Louisiana State University Press, 1995.

Andrew, Rod, Jr. *Wade Hampton: Confederate Warrior to Southern Redeemer*. Chapel Hill: University of North Carolina Press, 2008.

Anthony, William. *Anthony's History of the Battle of Hanover*. Hanover, Pa.: self-published, 1945.

Armstrong, Richard L. *25th Virginia Infantry and 9th Battalion Virginia Infantry*. Lynchburg, Va.: H. E. Howard Co., 1990.

―――. *7th Virginia Cavalry*. Lynchburg, Virginia: H. E. Howard Co., 1992.

Ashcraft, John M. *31st Virginia Infantry*. Lynchburg, Va.: H. E. Howard Co., 1988.

Bache, Richard Meade. *The Life of George Gordon Meade, Commander of the Army of the Potomac*. Philadelphia: Henry T. Coates & Co., 1897.

Bates, Samuel P. *The Battle of Gettysburg*. Philadelphia: T. H. Davis & Co., 1875.

―――. *History of Pennsylvania Volunteers, 1861-5*. Harrisburg: B. Singerly, State Printer, 1869-1871.

―――. *Martial Deeds of Pennsylvania*. Philadelphia: T. H. Davis & Co., 1876.

―――. *History of Franklin County, Pennsylvania*. Chicago: Warner, Beers & Co., 1887.

Bennett, Gerald R. *Days of Uncertainty and Dread*. Camp Hill, PA: Planks Suburban Press, 1994.

Bowden, Scott and Bill Ward. *Last Chance for Victory: Robert E. Lee and the Gettysburg Campaign*. New York: Da Capo Press, 2003.

Busey, John W., and David G. Martin. *Regimental Strengths and Losses at Gettysburg*. Hightstown, N.J.: Longstreet House, 1982.

Casdorph, Paul D. *Confederate General R. S. Ewell: Robert E. Lee's Hesitant Commander*. Lexington: The University Press of Kentucky, 2004.

Coddington, Edwin B. *The Gettysburg Campaign: A Study in Command.* New York: Charles Scribner's Sons, 1968.

Cole, Philip. *Civil War Artillery at Gettysburg: Organization, Equipment, Ammunition, and Tactics.* New York: Da Capo Press, 2002.

Chapla, John D. *50th Virginia Infantry.* Lynchburg, VA: H. E. Howard Co., 1997.

Chapman, Craig S. *More Terrible Than Victory: North Carolina's Bloody Bethel Regiment 1861-65.* Herndon, Va.: Brassey's, 1998.

Coffman, Richard M. and Kurt D. Graham. *To Honor These Men: History of the Phillips Georgia Legion Infantry Battalion.* Macon, Ga.: Mercer University Press, 2007.

Collier, Calvin L. *They'll Do To Tie To! The Story of the Third Regiment, Arkansas Infantry, C. S. A.* Little Rock, Ark.: Pioneer Press, 1959.

Collier, Kenneth C. *The 13th Georgia Regiment: A Part of the Lawton-Gordon-Evans Brigade.* Atlanta: self-published. 1997.

Collins, Darrell L. *Major General Robert E. Rodes of the Army of Northern Virginia: A Biography.* New York: Savas Beatie, 2008.

Colwell, David G. *The Bitter Fruits: The Civil War Comes to a Small Town in Pennsylvania.* Carlisle, Pa.: Cumberland County Historical Society, 1998.

Conrad, W. P. and Ted Alexander. *When War Passed This Way.* Shippensburg, Pa.: White Mane, 1987.

Cordell, Glenn R. *Civil War Damage Claims from Fulton County, Pennsylvania.* McConnellsburg, Pa.: Fulton County Historical Society, Inc., 2001.

Creighton, Margaret S. *The Colors of Courage: Gettysburg's Forgotten History, Immigrants, Women, and African Americans in the Civil War's Defining Battle.* New York: Basic Books, 2005.

Crist, Robert Grant. *Confederate Invasion of the West Shore 1863.* Carlisle, Pa.: Cumberland County Historical Society, 1963.

Currier, John M., ed. *Memorial Exercises Held in Castleton, Vermont, in the Year 1885.* Albany, N.Y.: Joel Munsell's Sons, 1885.

Davis, Burke. *Jeb Stuart: The Last Cavalier.* New York: Rinehart, 1957.

Dawson, John Harper. *Wildcat Cavalry: A Synoptic History of the Seventeenth Virginia Cavalry Regiment.* Dayton, Ohio: Morningside Press, 1982.

Delauter Jr., Roger U. *Winchester in the Civil War.* Lynchburg, Va.: H. E. Howard Co., 1992.

Divine, John E. *35th Battalion, Virginia Cavalry.* Lynchburg, Va.: H. E. Howard Co., 1985.

Douglas, Stacy C. *The Fighting Boys of Wiregrass: A Short History of the Ben Hill Guards, 38th Georgia.* Athens, Ga.: Southern Regional Publications. 1996.

Drum, Richard C. *Itinerary of the Army of the Potomac, and Co-operating Forces in the Gettysburg Campaign, June 5 – July 31, 1863; organization of the Army of the Potomac and Army of Northern Virginia at the battle of Gettysburg; and return of casualties in the Union and Confederate forces.* Washington, D.C.: Government Printing Office, 1888.

Driver Jr., Robert J. *First and Second Maryland Cavalry, C.S.A.* Charlottesville, VA: Rockbridge Publishing, 1999.

———. *1st Virginia Cavalry.* Lynchburg, VA: H. E. Howard Co., 1991.

———. *10th Virginia Cavalry.* Lynchburg, VA: H. E. Howard, 1992.

———. *5th Virginia Cavalry.* Lynchburg, VA: H. E. Howard Co., 1997.

———. *52nd Virginia Infantry.* Lynchburg, Va.: H. E. Howard Co., 1986.

———. *58th Virginia Infantry.* Lynchburg, Va.: H. E. Howard Co., 1990.

———. *14th Virginia Cavalry.* Lynchburg, Va. H. E. Howard Co., 1988.

Robert J. Driver, Jr. and Harold E. Howard. *2nd Virginia Cavalry*. Lynchburg, VA: H. E. Howard Co., 1995.

Eckert, Ralph Lowell. *John Brown Gordon: Soldier, Southerner, American*. Baton Rouge: Louisiana State University Press, 1989.

Eicher, John H. and David J. Eicher. *Civil War High Commands*. Stanford, CA: Stanford University Press, 2001.

Encounter at Hanover: Prelude to Gettysburg. Gettysburg, Pa.: Historical Publication Committee of the Hanover Chamber of Commerce, Times and News Publishing Company, 1962.

Fishel, Edwin C. *The Secret War for the Union: The Untold Story of Military Intelligence in the Civil War*. Boston: Houghton-Mifflin, 1996.

Freeman, Douglas Southall. *Lee's Lieutenants: A Study in Command*. 3 vols. New York: Scribner, 1946.

———. *R. E. Lee*. 4 vols. New York: Charles Scribner's Sons, 1935.

French, Steve. *Imboden's Brigade in the Gettysburg Campaign*. Berkeley Springs, WV: Morgan Messenger, 2008.

Frye, Dennis E. *12th Virginia Cavalry*. Lynchburg, Va.: H.E. Howard Co., 1988.

Gambone, A. M. *Major-General Darius Nash Couch: Enigmatic Valor*, Baltimore, MD: Butternut and Blue, 2000.

Gottfried, Bradley M. *Roads to Gettysburg: Lee's Invasion of the North, 1863*. Shippensburg, PA: White Mane, 2001.

———. *The Brigades of Gettysburg: The Union and Confederate Brigades at the Battle of Gettysburg*. New York: Da Capo, 2002.

Gragg, Rod. *Covered with Glory: The 26th North Carolina Infantry at the Battle of Gettysburg*. New York: Perennial, 2001.

Grunder, Charles S. and Brandon H. Beck. *The Second Battle of Winchester, June 12-15, 1863*. Lynchburg, Va.: H. E. Howard, 1989.

Hackley, Woodford B. *The Little Fork Rangers: A Sketch of Company D Fourth Virginia Cavalry*. Richmond, VA: Press of the Dietz Printing Co., 1927.

Hale, Laura V. and Stanley S. Phillips. *History of the Forty-Ninth Virginia Infantry CSA: Extra Billy Smith's Boys*. Lanham, Md.: S. S. Phillips, 1981.

Hall, Winfield Scott. *The Captain: William Cross Hazelton*. Riverside, IL: privately published, 1994.

Hefelbower, Samuel Gring. *The History of Gettysburg College, 1832-1932*. Gettysburg, Pa.: Gettysburg College, 1932.

Herdegen, Lance J. *The Iron Brigade in the Civil War and Memory: The Black Hats from Bull Run to Appomattox and Thereafter*. El Dorado Hills, CA: Savas Beatie, 2012.

Hess, Earl J. *Lee's Tar Heels; The Pettigrew-Kirkland-McRae Brigade*. Chapel Hill: The University of North Carolina Press, 2002.

Hessler, James A. *Sickles at Gettysburg: The Controversial Civil War General Who Committed Murder, Abandoned Little Round Top, and Declared Himself the Hero of Gettysburg*. El Dorado Hills, CA: Savas Beatie, 2009.

Hessler, James A. and Wayne E. Motts. *Pickett's Charge at Gettysburg: A Guide to the Most Famous Attack in American History*. El Dorado Hills, CA: Savas Beatie, 2015.

Historic Huntingdon, 1767-1909: Huntingdon Old Home Week, September 5-11, 1909. Huntingdon, Pa.: Historical Committee of the Old Home Week Association, 1909.

History of Cumberland and Adams Counties, Containing History of the Counties, Their Townships, Towns, Villages, Schools, Churches, Industries, Etc., Portraits of Early Settlers and Prominent Men; Biographies. Chicago: Warner, Beers & Co., 1886.

Hopkins, Donald A. *The Little Jeff: The Jeff Davis Legion Cavalry, Army of Northern Virginia.* Shippensburg, PA: Burd Street Press, 1999.

Huntington, Tom. *Searching for George Gordon Meade the Forgotten Victor of Gettysburg.* Mechanicsburg, PA: Stackpole Books, 2013.

Johnson, Crisfield. *History of Oswego County, NY, With Illustrations and Biographical Sketches of Some of its Prominent Men and Pioneers.* Philadelphia: L. H. Everts, 1877.

Jones, Virgil Carrington. *Ranger Mosby.* Chapel Hill: University of North Carolina Press, 1944.

Keen, Hugh C. and Horace Mewborn. *43rd Battalion Virginia Cavalry, Mosby's Command.* Lynchburg, VA; H. E. Howard Co., 1993.

Keener-Farley, Lawrence E. and James E. Schmick. *Civil War Harrisburg: A Guide to Capital Area Sites, Incidents and Personalities.* Harrisburg: Camp Curtin Historical Society, 2011.

Kesterson, Brian S. *Campaigning with the 17th Virginia Cavalry: Night Hawks at Monocacy.* Washington, W.V.: Night Hawk Press, 2005.

Kleese, Richard B. *49th Virginia Infantry.* Lynchburg, Va.: H. E. Howard Co., 2002.

Klein, Frederic Shriver. *Just South of Gettysburg: Carroll County, Maryland in the Civil War.* Westminster, MD: The Newman Press, 1963.

Knight, Charles R. *From Arlington to Appomattox: Robert E. Lee's Civil War, Day by Day, 1861-1865.* El Dorado Hills, CA: Savas Beatie, 2021.

Krepps, John T. *A Strong and Sudden Onslaught: The Cavalry Action at Hanover, Pennsylvania.* Orrtana, PA: Colecraft Industries, 2008.

Krick, Robert K. *Civil War Weather in Virginia.* Tuscaloosa: University of Alabama Press, 2007.

———. *Lee's Colonels: A Biographical Register of the Field Officers of the Army of Northern Virginia.* Dayton, OH: Morningside, 1984.

———. *9th Virginia Cavalry.* Lynchburg, VA: H. E. Howard Co., 1982.

Krumwiede, John F. *Disgrace at Gettysburg: The Arrest and Court Martial of Brigadier General Thomas A. Rowley, USA.* Jefferson, N. C.: McFarland, 2006.

Ladd, David L. and Audrey J. Ladd, eds. *John Bachelder's History of the Battle of Gettysburg.* Dayton, OH: Morningside, 1997.

Lehman, James O. and Steven M. Nolt. *Mennonites, Amish, and the American Civil War.* Baltimore: The Johns Hopkins University Press, 2007.

Longacre, Edward G. *Custer and His Wolverines: The Michigan Cavalry Brigade 1861–1865.* Conshohocken, PA: Combined Books, 1997.

———. *Fitz Lee: A Military Biography of Major General Fitzhugh Lee, C.S.A.* New York: Da Capo Press, 2004.

———. *Jersey Cavaliers: A History of the First New Jersey Volunteer Cavalry.* Hightstown, N.J.: Longstreet House, 1992.

———. *The Cavalry at Gettysburg: A Tactical Study of Mounted Operations During the Civil War's Pivotal Campaign, 9 June-14 July 1863.* Rutherford, N. J.: Fairleigh-Dickinson University Press, 1986.

Lovelace, David Shriver. *The Shrivers: Under Two Flags.* Westminster, MD: Willow Bend Books, 2003.

Martin, David G. *Gettysburg, July 1.* Conshohocken, PA: Combined Books, 1995.

Marvin, Abijah P. *History of Worcester in the War of the Rebellion.* Worcester, Mass.: s.n., 1870.

McClure, James. *East of Gettysburg: A Gray Shadow Crosses York County, Pa.* York, PA: York Daily Record, 2003.

McFadden, Elizabeth. *The Glitter and the Glory: A Spirited Account of the Metropolitan Museum of Art's First Director, the Audacious and High-Handed Luigi Palma di Cesnola.* New York: Dial Press, 1971.

McKinney, Joseph W. *Brandy Station, Virginia, June 9, 1863: The Largest Cavalry Battle of the Civil War.* Jefferson, N.C.: McFarland, 2006.

Miller, William E. *Local History: Troops Occupying Carlisle, July, 1863.* Carlisle, PA: Hamilton Library Association, 1902.

Mingus, Scott L., Sr. *Confederate Calamity: Jeb Stuart's Confederate Cavalry Ride Through York County, Pa.* Scotts Valley, CA: CreateSpace, 2015.

———. *Flames Beyond Gettysburg: The Confederate Expedition to the Susquehanna River, June 1863.* El Dorado Hills, Cal.: Savas Beatie, 2011.

———. *The Louisiana Tigers in the Gettysburg Campaign, June-July 1863.* Baton Rouge: Louisiana State University Press, 2009.

Moore, Robert H., Jr. *Chew's Ashby, Shoemaker's Lynchburg and the Newtown Artillery.* Lynchburg, VA: H. E. Howard Co., 1995.

———. *The 1st and 2nd Stuart Horse Artillery.* Lynchburg, VA: H. E. Howard Co., 1985.

Murray, Alton J. *South Georgia Rebels: The True Wartime Experiences of the 26th Regiment, Georgia Volunteer Infantry.* St. Mary's, Ga.: Self-published, 1976.

Nanzig, Thomas P. *3rd Virginia Cavalry.* Lynchburg, VA: H. E. Howard Co., 1989.

Nead, Benjamin Mathias. *Waynesboro: The History of a Settlement.* Harrisburg, Pa.: Harrisburg Publishing Company, 1900.

Nelson, John H. *Confusion and Courage: The Civil War in Fulton County, Pa., June, 1863.* McConnellsburg, Pa.: Fulton County Civil War Reenactment Advisory Committee, 1996.

Noe, Kenneth W. *The Howling Storm: Climate, Weather and the American Civil War.* Baton Rouge: Louisiana State University Press, 2020.

Nofi, Albert A. *The Gettysburg Campaign, June and July 1863.* New York: Gallery, 1986.

Nolan, Allen T. *The Iron Brigade: A Military History.* New York: McMillan & Co., 1961.

Noyalas, Jonathan A. *"My Will is Absolute Law": A Biography of Union General Robert H. Milroy.* Jefferson, NC: McFarland, 2006.

Nye, Wilbur S. *Here Come the Rebels!* Baton Rouge: Louisiana State University Press, 1965.

O'Neill, Robert F. *Chasing Jeb Stuart and John Mosby: The Union Cavalry in Northern Virginia from Second Manassas to Gettysburg.* Jefferson, NC: McFarland, 2012.

———. *The Cavalry Battles of Aldie, Middleburg, and Upperville: Small But Important Riots, June 10-27, 1863.* Lynchburg, Va.: H. E. Howard Co., 1993.

Osborne, Charles C. *The Life and Times of General Jubal A. Early, CSA: Defender of the Lost Cause.* Chapel Hill, N.C.: Algonquin, 1992.

Paradis, James M. *African-Americans and the Gettysburg Campaign.* Lanham, Md.: The Scarecrow Press, 2005.

Pfanz, Donald C. *Richard S. Ewell: A Soldier's Life.* Chapel Hill: University of North Carolina Press, 1998.

Pfanz, Harry W. *Gettysburg: Culp's Hill and Cemetery Hill.* Chapel Hill: University of North Carolina Press, 1993.

———. *Gettysburg: The First Day.* Chapel Hill: University of North Carolina Press, 2001.

———. *Gettysburg: The Second Day.* Chapel Hill: University of North Carolina Press, 1987.

Reese, Timothy J. *Sykes' Regular Infantry Division, 1861-1864: A History of Regular United States Infantry Operations in the Civil War's Eastern Theater.* Jefferson, NC: McFarland, 1990.

Riggs, David F. *13th Virginia Infantry.* Lynchburg, Va.: H. E. Howard Co., 1988.

Rummel, George A., III. *Cavalry on the Roads to Gettysburg: Kilpatrick at Hanover and Hunterstown.* Shippensburg, PA: White Mane, 2000.

Ryan, Thomas J. *Spies, Scouts, and Secrets in the Gettysburg Campaign: How the Critical Role of Intelligence Impacted the Outcome of Lee's Invasion of the North, June-July 1863*. El Dorado Hills, CA: Savas Beatie, 2015.

Scaife, William R. *The Georgia Brigade*. Atlanta: William R. Scaife, 2d Edition, 2002.

Scharf, J. Thomas. *History of West Chester County, New York, Including Morrisania, Kings Bridge, and West Farms, Which Have Been Annexed to New York City*. 2 vols. Philadelphia: L. E. Preston & Co., 1886.

———. *History of Western Maryland*, 2 vols. Philadelphia: Louis H. Everts, 1882.

Schildt, John W. *Roads to Gettysburg*. Parsons, WV: McClain Printing Co., 1978.

Sears, Stephen W. *Chancellorsville*. Boston: Houghton-Mifflin, 1996.

———. *Gettysburg*. New York: Mariner Books, 2004.

———. *Lincoln's Lieutenants: The High Command of the Army of the Potomac*. Boston: Houghton-Mifflin, 2017.

Sellers, Charles Coleman. *Dickinson College: A History*. Middletown, CT: Wesleyan University Press, 1973.

Shippensburg Historical Society. *Shippensburg, Pennsylvania in the Civil War*. Shippensburg, PA: Burd Street Press, 2003.

Slade, Jim and John Alexander. *Firestorm at Gettysburg: Civilian Voices June-November 1863*. Atglen, Pa.: Schiffer, 1998.

Soderberg, Susan Cooke. *A Guide to Civil War Sites in Maryland: Blue and Gray in a Border State*. Shippensburg, PA: White Mane, 1986.

Soper, Steve. *The Glorious Old 3rd: A History of the 3rd Michigan Infantry 1855-1865*. Portage, Mich.: Old Third Publishing, 2011.

Staats, Richard J. *The History of the Sixth Ohio Volunteer Cavalry 1861–1865*. 2 vols. Westminster, MD: Heritage Books, 2006.

Stiles, Kenneth L. *4th Virginia Cavalry*. Lynchburg, VA: H. E. Howard Co., 1985.

Stoner, Jacob H. *Historical Papers: Franklin County and the Cumberland Valley, Pennsylvania*. Chambersburg, Pa.: The Craft Press, 1947.

Sutherland, Daniel E. *Seasons of War: The Ordeal of a Confederate Community, 1861-1865*. New York: Free Press, 1995.

Tagg, Larry. *The Generals of Gettysburg: The Leaders of America's Greatest Battle*. Campbell, Cal.: Savas Publishing, 1998.

Taylor, Frank H. *Philadelphia in the Civil War: 1861-65*. Philadelphia: Dunlap Printing Company, 1913.

The Historical Publication Committee of the Hanover Chamber of Commerce. *Prelude to Gettysburg: Encounter at Hanover*. Shippensburg, PA: Burd Street Press, 1962.

Thomas, Sarah Sites, Tim Smith, Gary Kross and Dean S. Thomas. *Fairfield in the Civil War*. Gettysburg, PA: Thomas Publications, 2011.

Thomason, John W., Jr. *Jeb Stuart*. New York: Charles Scribner's Sons, 1934.

Trout, Robert J. *Galloping Thunder: The Stuart Horse Artillery Battalion*. Mechanicsburg, Pa.: Stackpole Books, 2002.

Trudeau, Noah Andre. *Gettysburg: A Testing of Courage*. New York: Harper Collins, 2002.

Valuska, David L. and Christian B. Keller. *Damn Dutch: Pennsylvania Germans at Gettysburg*. Mechanicsburg, Pa.: Stackpole Books, 2004.

Warner, Ezra J. *Generals in Blue: Lives of the Union Commanders*. Baton Rouge: Louisiana State University Press, 1964.

———. *Generals in Gray: Lives of the Confederate Commanders*. Baton Rouge: Louisiana State University Press, 1959.

Weaver, Michael. *Jenkins in Mechanicsburg: The Confederate Attempt on Pennsylvania's Capital.* Camp Hill, PA: privately published, 2001.

Welsh, Jack D., M.D. *Medical Histories of Confederate Generals.* Kent, Ohio: Kent State University Press, 1995.

————. *Medical Histories of Union Generals.* Kent, Ohio: Kent State University Press, 1996.

Wert, Jeffry D. *Cavalryman of the Lost Cause: A Biography of J.E.B. Stuart.* New York: Simon & Schuster, 2008.

White, Gregory C. *This Most Bloody & Cruel Drama: A History of the 31 Georgia Volunteer Infantry, Lawton-Gordon-Evans Brigade, Army of Northern Virginia, Confederate States of America, 1861-1865.* Baltimore: Butternut and Blue, 1997.

Wills, Garry. *Lincoln at Gettysburg: The Words That Remade America.* NY: Simon & Shuster, 2006.

Wingert, Cooper. *The Confederate Approach on Harrisburg: The Gettysburg Campaign's Northernmost Reaches.* Charleston, SC: The History Press, 2012.

Wittenberg, Eric J. *Gettysburg's Forgotten Cavalry Actions: Farnsworth's Charge, South Cavalry Field, and the Battle of Fairfield, July 3, 1863.* El Dorado Hills, CA: Savas Beatie, 2011.

————. *Protecting the Flank at Gettysburg: The Battles for Brinkerhoff's Ridge and East Cavalry Field, July 2–3, 1863.* El Dorado Hills, CA: Savas Beatie, 2013.

————. *Rush's Lancers: The Sixth Pennsylvania Cavalry in the Civil War.* Yardley, PA: Westholme Publishing, 2007.

————. *The Battle of Brandy Station: North America's Largest Cavalry Battle.* Charleston, SC: The History Press, 2010.

————. *"The Devil's to Pay": John Buford at Gettysburg. A History and Walking Tour.* El Dorado Hills, CA: Savas Beatie, 2014.

————. *The Union Cavalry Comes of Age: Hartwood Church to Brandy Station, 1863.* Washington, DC: Brassey's, 2004.

Wittenberg, Eric J. and Daniel T. Davis. *Out Flew the Sabers: The Battle of Brandy Station, June 9, 1863.* El Dorado Hills, CA: Savas Beatie, 2016.

Wittenberg, Eric J. and Scott L. Mingus, Sr. *The Second Battle of Winchester: The Confederate Victory that Opened the Door to Gettysburg.* El Dorado Hills, CA: Savas Beatie, 2016.

Wittenberg, Eric J. and J. David Petruzzi. *Plenty of Blame to Go Around: Jeb Stuart's Controversial Ride to Gettysburg.* El Dorado Hills, CA: Savas Beatie, 2006.

Wittenberg, Eric J., J. David Petruzzi, and Michael F. Nugent. *One Continuous Fight: The Retreat from Gettysburg and the Pursuit of Lee's Army of Northern Virginia, July 4-14, 1863.* El Dorado Hills, CA: Savas Beatie, 2008.

Wittenberg, Eric J., Edmund A. Sargus, Jr., and Penny L. Barrick. *Seceding from Secession: The Civil War, Politics, and the Creation of West Virginia.* El Dorado Hills, CA: Savas Beatie, 2020.

Websites

Caughey, Don. "Reserve Brigade Attrition in the Gettysburg Campaign." http://regularcavalryincivilwar.wordpress.com/2013/06/20/reserve-brigade-attrition-in-the-gettysburg-campaign/

Diary of Henry S. Seage, http://home.midsouth.rr.com/devinney/diary2.html

Valley of the Shadow Project, https://valley.lib.virginia.edu

Full Text Civil War Medal of Honor Citations, A-L, www.army.mil/medalofhonor/citations1.html

Index